FINANCIAL MANAGEMENT FOR DECISION MAKERS

SECOND CANADIAN EDITION

PETER ATRILL   PAUL HURLEY
DURHAM COLLEGE

FINANCIAL MANAGEMENT
FOR DECISION MAKERS

Pearson Canada
Toronto

Library and Archives Canada Cataloguing in Publication

Atrill, Peter
    Financial management for decision makers / Peter Atrill, Paul Hurley.—2nd Canadian ed.

Includes index.
ISBN 978-0-13-801160-4

    1. Business enterprises—Finance. 2. Decision making. 3. Accounting. I. Hurley, Paul II. Title.

| HG4026.A87 2011 | 658.15 | C2010-906063-6 |

ISBN: 978-0-13-801160-4

Vice-President, Editorial Director: Gary Bennett
Editor-in-Chief: Nicole Lukach
Acquisitions Editor: Claudine O'Donnell
Senior Marketing Manager: Leigh-Anne Graham
Senior Developmental Editor: Paul Donnelly
Project Manager: Sarah Lukaweski
Production Editor: Rachel Stuckey
Copy Editor: Jennifer McIntyre
Proofreader: Aspasia Bissas, Strong Finish
Compositor: MPS Limited, a Macmillan Company
Permissions Researcher: Joanne Tang
Art Director: Julia Hall
Cover Designer: Julia Hall
Interior Designer: Anthony Leung
Cover Image: Getty Images/Brand New Images

13 17

Printed and bound in the United States of America

For Simon and Helen
—P. A.

To my family
To Samantha Scully, taken far too young
—P. H.

Brief Contents

Contents

Chapter 4   Analyzing and Interpreting Financial Statements   104

LEARNING OUTCOMES   104

INTRODUCTION   104

Preface

We have written this book for undergraduates, postgraduates, or graduates with professional experience who wish to obtain a broad understanding of financial management. The book is aimed primarily at students who are not majoring in finance but need to understand it as part of their program in business, management, economics, engineering, or some other area. Students who are majoring in finance should find the book useful as an introduction to the main principles that can serve as a foundation for further study. Those who are not following a full-time program of study but nevertheless need an understanding of financial management to help them manage their business will find it here as well.

This book assumes no previous knowledge of finance or accounting. We introduce each topic carefully to enable the user to build their knowledge gradually. Many other finance books are too long, detailed, and mathematically demanding for the non-finance major. In contrast, this book is written in an accessible style and its use of mathematical formulas has been kept to a minimum. It rests on a solid theoretical foundation, but the main focus throughout is its practical value to readers who are primarily interested in learning financial management in order to make better decisions.

Because we recognize that many students will not have studied finance before, we have tried to minimize the use of technical jargon. Where technical terms are appropriate, we have tried to provide clear explanations.

New to This Edition

The book was originally adapted from the fourth edition of a highly successful text published in the United Kingdom. All financial statements throughout the text have been changed to conform to Canadian standards, and most real-world illustrations use Canadian examples.

For this second Canadian edition, we have cited topical examples throughout the text of how Canadian companies adapted financial policies to the Great Recession of 2008–09. We have also expanded coverage of such topics as break-even analysis, vertical and horizontal analysis, and cash flow statements.

Throughout each chapter, Activities and Self-Assessment Questions encourage students to become active learners by thinking about important issues and checking their understanding of key topics. We have again significantly increased the number of Review Questions and Problems and Cases at the ends of the chapters (except Chapter 1) and on the Companion Website.

Calculations in the original U.K. edition were done using financial tables. We have increased the number of financial tables presented in Appendix A, and have applied them to working out the Examples in the book. At the same time, we appreciate the widespread use of other calculating tools in the workplace; consequently, material for Excel has been prepared for the book and provided on the Companion Website. Please see below under Features for details.

Organization

In Chapter 1, we begin by considering the role of financial management in helping a business achieve its objectives within a good ethical and corporate governance environment.

In Chapters 2, 3, and 4, we consider how accounting is used in financial management. Chapter 2 reviews important accounting concepts and the four types of financial statements, and also introduces some income-tax concepts that may affect decision making. In Chapter 3, we examine the way in which financial plans are prepared and the role of pro forma financial statements in helping managers assess future outcomes. We proceed in Chapter 4 to develop techniques to analyze financial statements that are also applicable in analyzing pro forma financial statements.

Chapters 5, 6, and 7 are concerned with techniques used in investment decision making. Chapter 5 reviews the important concepts of the time value of money, which are needed to evaluate cash flows properly. Chapter 6 introduces several methods that can be used to assess and monitor investment projects. Chapter 7 looks at ways to deal with the problem of risk when evaluating investment proposals.

Chapters 8 to 11 examine various aspects of the financing decision. Chapter 8 provides an overview of the many sources of funds available to a business. Chapter 9 concentrates on issues and costs of obtaining long-term funds and includes a section on the lease-versus-buy decision. In Chapter 10, we then examine issues surrounding the appropriate mix of funds within the capital structure of a company. Finally, we conclude this part in Chapter 11 with a discussion of factors that should be considered when deciding between the retention of profits and their distribution to shareholders in the form of dividends.

In Chapter 12, we look at ways in which managers can exert financial control over the working capital of a business. We examine all of the elements of working capital (cash, receivables, inventory, and payables) and discuss various techniques for controlling them.

In Chapter 13, we evaluate the effectiveness of various methods for measuring and managing shareholder wealth and explore their links to the strategic objectives of a business.

Finally, in Chapter 14, we examine the topic of mergers and acquisitions, drawing on our understanding of investment appraisal methods, financing, and capital market operations discussed earlier. We consider the effect of merger proposals on shareholder wealth and the ways in which mergers may be evaluated.

Features

The following features have been carefully prepared and integrated into the book to facilitate learning and enhance your understanding of financial management.

- **Learning Outcomes**   Numbered points listed at the beginning of each chapter and referenced within the chapter show what you can expect to learn from that chapter. In the body of the chapter, each Learning Outcome number (abbreviated L.O. #) appears in the margin next to the relevant heading or paragraph.

- **Introduction**   A chapter introduction previews each chapter, preparing you for the material ahead.

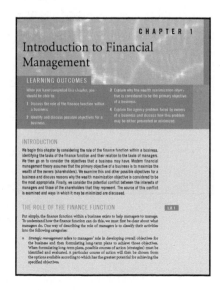

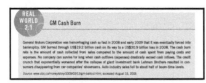

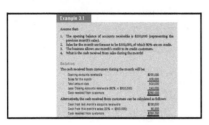

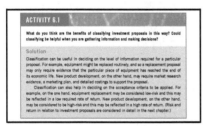

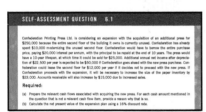

■ **Key terms**   Key terms and concepts are boldfaced where they are first introduced and defined in the chapter. A list of Key Terms is provided near the end of each chapter and all the key terms, along with their definitions, are collated in a Glossary near the back of the book.

■ **Equations**   Important equations are highlighted and numbered in the body of the chapter. For easy reference, they are also presented in a List of Equations near the end of each chapter.

■ **Real World boxes**   Illustrative examples drawn from real companies are integrated throughout the text. They highlight the practical application by real businesses of Canadian accounting and financial techniques, and provide valuable insights from the real world.

■ **Examples**   At frequent intervals throughout the chapters, numerical examples of the material being discussed give you a step-by-step approach to follow through to the solution.

■ **Activities**   These short questions, integrated throughout each chapter, allow you to check your understanding of the material. Activities require you to review or critically consider certain topics or to perform a short numerical calculation. A suggested answer is given immediately after each activity.

■ **Self-Assessment Questions**   Most chapters include two self-assessment questions at significant points. These allow you to attempt a more comprehensive question before tackling the end-of-chapter Problems and Cases. Complete solutions are provided near the back of the book in Appendix B.

■ **Summary**   At the end of each chapter, a point-form summary, organized by main heading within the chapter, highlights the material covered and provides a quick reminder of the main issues.

■ **Review Questions**   Every chapter contains five short review questions that encourage you to review or critically assess your understanding of the main topics covered. Answers to all the review questions are provided on the Companion Website.

■ **Problems and Cases** Most chapters contain 20 or more questions arranged in ascending order of difficulty, including those found on the Companion Website. These problems and cases are mostly quantitative and serve to further test your understanding of the material. Solutions to the even-numbered problems and cases are provided on the Companion Website.

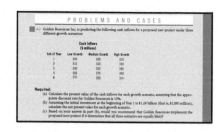

■ **Financial Tables** Five financial tables are provided near the back of the book in Appendix A.

■ **Excel Templates and Spreadsheets** Excel material has been prepared for the book by Colin Kovacs of Algonquin College. It consists of templates with explanations for various types of problems (e.g., net present values, internal rates of return, taxes, capital cost allowance, loan amortizations, and annuities) plus spreadsheets for specific Problems and Cases in the book. The material itself is provided on the Companion Website and is keyed to the book by means of special icons placed in the margins.

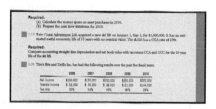

HOW TO USE THIS BOOK

We have ordered the contents of the book in what we believe is a logical sequence and, for this reason, we suggest that you work through the book in the order in which it is presented. Every effort has been made to ensure that earlier chapters do not refer to concepts or terms that are not explained until a later chapter. If you work through the chapters in a different order, you will probably encounter concepts and points that were explained previously but which you have missed.

Chapter 2 (Accounting—The Language of Business) and Chapter 5 (The Time Value of Money) cover material that you may have already studied in other courses. In that case, these chapters can serve as a refresher of important material for you.

Whether you are using the book as part of a lecture/tutorial based course or as the basis for a more independent form of study, we recommend you follow broadly the same approach.

We have integrated numerous activities, questions, and exercises for self-assessment throughout the book. If you methodically work through this material, you will be able to check your understanding and obtain immediate feedback. We strongly encourage you to attempt all the Activities, Self-Assessment Questions, and Review Questions before consulting the solutions. As we noted above under Features, solutions are also provided on the Companion Website for the even-numbered Problems and Cases. Please also note that we have provided additional Self-Test Questions on the Companion Website (as described below under Supplements).

We also encourage you to make use of the Excel templates and spreadsheets provided on the Companion Website. These tools are prevalent in the workplace.

Supplements

The following supplements have been carefully prepared to assist instructors and students in using this book.

The **Instructor's Resource CD-ROM** consists of the following five items:

■ An **Instructor's Solution Manual**, prepared by Paul Hurley, presents answers to all the Review Questions and solutions to all the Problems and Cases in the book and the Additional Problems and Cases on the Companion Website.

■ A computerized test bank (known as **Pearson TestGen**) provides multiple-choice questions for each chapter. Each question is accompanied by the correct answer, the relevant page number(s) in the book, the level of difficulty (1 = Easy, 2 = Moderate, and 3 = Challenging), the skill required (recall or applied), and the question type (quantitative or qualitative).

Pearson TestGen enables instructors to view and edit the test bank questions, generate tests, and print the tests in a variety of formats. Powerful "search and sort" functions make it easy to locate questions and arrange them in any order desired. TestGen also enables instructors to administer tests on a local area network, have the tests graded electronically, and have the results prepared in electronic or printed reports. Pearson TestGen is compatible with Windows or Macintosh systems.

■ A **Test Item File** provides the same test bank in a printer-friendly Word format.
■ An **Image Library** provides electronic versions of all the numbered figures and tables in the book.
■ **Excel Templates and Spreadsheets** are also available to students on the Companion Website, as mentioned above under Features.

Finally, an open-access **Companion Website (www.pearsoned.ca/atrill)** has been specially created for this book. It contains the following material:

■ Answers to all Review Questions
■ Solutions to the even-numbered Problems and Cases
■ Additional Problems and Cases not included in the text book
■ Excel Templates and Spreadsheets keyed to the book
■ Self-Test Questions for each chapter. You can attempt the questions, send your answers to the electronic grader, and receive instant feedback.

ACKNOWLEDGMENTS

We are grateful to the following instructors who provided formal reviews of drafts of the manuscript for the second Canadian edition:

David Birkett (University of Guelph)
Andrea Chance (University of Guelph)
Iona Green (Acadia University)
Keith Jensen (Vancouver Island University)
Susan Kelsall (Humber College)
Mahesh Kumar (Camosun College)
Raymond Leung (University of the Fraser Valley)
Maggie Liu (University of Winnipeg)
Carol Meissner (Georgian College)
Dale Northey (Fleming College)
Joe Pidutti (Durham College)

We hope that you will find this book helpful.

Peter Atrill
Paul Hurley
2010

CHAPTER 1

Introduction to Financial Management

LEARNING OUTCOMES

When you have completed this chapter, you should be able to:

1 Discuss the role of the finance function within a business.

2 Identify and discuss possible objectives for a business.

3 Explain why the wealth maximization objective is considered to be the primary objective of a business.

4 Explain the agency problem faced by owners of a business and discuss how this problem may be either prevented or minimized.

INTRODUCTION

We begin this chapter by considering the role of the finance function within a business, identifying the tasks of the finance function and their relation to the tasks of managers. We then go on to consider the objectives that a business may have. Modern financial management theory assumes that the primary objective of a business is to maximize the wealth of the owners (shareholders). We examine this and other possible objectives for a business and discuss reasons why the wealth maximization objective is considered to be the most appropriate. Finally, we consider the potential conflict between the interests of managers and those of the shareholders that they represent. The source of this conflict is examined and ways in which it may be minimized are discussed.

THE ROLE OF THE FINANCE FUNCTION

L.O. 1

Put simply, the finance function within a business exists to help managers to manage. To understand how the finance function can do this, we must first be clear about what managers do. One way of describing the role of managers is to classify their activities into the following categories:

■ *Strategic management* refers to managers' role in developing overall objectives for the business and then formulating long-term plans to achieve those objectives. When formulating long-term plans, possible courses of action (strategies) must be identified and evaluated. A particular course of action will then be chosen from the options available according to which has the greatest potential for achieving the specified objectives.

- *Operations management* refers to the day-to-day decision making and control that managers undertake. Managers must ensure that events conform to the plans that have been made and take appropriate actions to see that this occurs.
- *Risk management* refers to the way in which risks faced by the business are controlled or managed. Risks may arise from the nature of the business operations and/or the way in which the business is financed.

As we can see from Figure 1.1, these three categories do not represent separate and distinct areas. They are interrelated and overlaps arise between categories. When considering a particular strategy, for example, managers must also make a careful assessment of the risks involved and how these risks may be managed. Similarly, when making operational decisions, managers must try to ensure they fit within the strategic plans that have been formulated.

FIGURE 1.1   The Overlapping Role of Managers

The finance function is concerned with helping managers in each of the three areas. The key tasks undertaken by the finance function are set out in Figure 1.2 and described below.

- *Financial planning.*   The likely effect of proposals on the financial performance of the business is a vitally important input to the overall planning process. By developing pro forma financial statements (including cash budgets, income statements, and balance sheets), as well as other financial estimates, the viability of proposed courses of action

FIGURE 1.2   The Four Main Tasks of the Finance Function

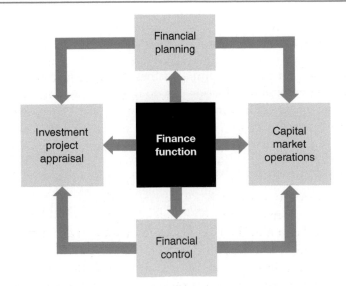

can be evaluated. In addition, future strategies have to be implemented and investment projects financed. It is important, therefore, to be able to identify and assess possible sources of financing available. When choosing among different financing options, consideration must be given to the overall financial structure of the business. This involves achieving the appropriate balance between long-term and short-term financing and between the financing contribution of shareholders (equity) and that of lenders (debt). Not all financing requirements are derived from external sources: some funds may be internally generated. An important source of internally generated funds is profits, and the extent to which the business reinvests profits rather than distributing them in the form of dividends is another important issue.

- *Investment project appraisal.* Assessing the profitability and riskiness of proposed investment projects is another important input to the overall planning process. By appraising projects in this way, managers can make more informed decisions concerning either their acceptance or rejection, or their prioritization.

- *Capital market operations.* The business may try to raise funds from the capital markets and so finance department staff should understand how these markets work. There must be an appreciation of how financing can be raised through the markets, how securities (shares and bonds) are priced, and how the markets are likely to react to proposed investment and financing plans.

- *Financial control.* Once plans are put into action, managers must ensure that things stay on course. Finance department staff can provide information on matters such as the profitability of investment projects, levels of working capital, and cash flows, which can be relayed to managers as a basis for evaluating performance and, where necessary, taking corrective action.

The links between the tasks of managers and the tasks of the finance function are many and varied. Strategic management decisions, for example, may require input from the finance department on issues relating to financial planning, investment project appraisal, and capital market operations. Operations management may require input on issues relating to financial planning, investment project appraisal, and financial control. Risk management may require input on issues relating to all of the tasks identified above.

THE ESSENTIAL FEATURES OF FINANCIAL MANAGEMENT

In the early years of its development, financial management was really an offshoot of accounting. The purpose of accounting is to measure *how money has been spent* as a result of past decisions. In contrast, finance is concerned with *how money should be spent* by helping managers in all areas of the company make correct decisions today in order to achieve the desired future results. Much of the early work in finance was descriptive, and arguments were based on casual observation rather than any clear theoretical framework. However, over the years, financial management has been increasingly influenced by economic theories, and the reasoning applied to particular issues has become more rigorous and analytical. Indeed, such is the influence of economic theory that modern financial management is often viewed as a branch of applied economics.

Economic theories concerning the efficient allocation of scarce resources have been developed into decision-making tools for management. This involves taking account of both the time dimension and the risks associated with management decision making. An investment decision, for example, must look at both the time period over which the investment extends and the degree of risk associated with the investment. This fact has led to financial management being described as the *economics of time and risk*.

Economic theories have also helped us to understand the importance of **capital markets**—such as stock markets, bond markets, and banks—to a business. Capital markets have a vital role to play in bringing together borrowers and lenders, in allowing investors to select the type of investment that best meets their risk requirements, and in helping to evaluate the performance of businesses through the prices assigned to their shares.

Canadian bond markets are over-the-counter markets, meaning there is a network of dealers connected by computers and telephones. The bond market is not housed in a physical location like the Toronto Stock Exchange (TSX). A major player in the Canadian bond market is the federal government, with outstanding marketable bonds, treasury bills, Canada savings bonds, and other debt amounting to about $395 billion at the end of 2008.[1] The federal government has not had to issue much new debt in recent years as it incurred a surplus for about a decade through 2009. However, a deficit was projected for 2010 due to the recent recession. Provincial and territorial governments also issue bonds, as do public utilities.

The TMX Group operates the Toronto Stock Exchange, the TSX Venture Exchange, and the Montreal Exchange. There are about 3,700 companies listed on the TMX. Through nine months in 2009, new equity issued amounted to $45 billion. The market capitalization of all companies listed with the TMX Group was $1.7 trillion. The traded value of shares amounted to almost $1.1 trillion.[2]

REAL WORLD 1.1 contains an extract from an article by Professor Dimson of London Business School. It neatly sums up the essence of modern financial management.

REAL WORLD 1.1

Finance on the Back of a Postage Stamp

Here is one student's summary of his finance course . . . Time is money . . . Don't put all your eggs in one basket . . . You can't fool all the people all of the time.

■ The idea that time is money refers to the fact that a sum of money received now is worth more than the same sum paid in the future. This gives rise to the principle that future cash flows should be discounted, in order to calculate their present value.

■ You can reduce the risk of an investment if you don't put all your eggs in one basket. In other words, a diversified portfolio of investments is less risky than putting all your money in a single asset. Risks that cannot be diversified away should be accepted only if they are offset by a higher expected return.

■ The idea that you can't fool all of the people all of the time refers to the efficiency of financial markets. An efficient market is one in which information is widely and cheaply available to everyone and relevant information is therefore incorporated into security prices. Because new information is reflected in prices immediately, investors should expect to receive only a normal rate of return. Possession of information about a company will not enable an investor to outperform the market. The only way to expect a higher expected return is to be exposed to greater risk.

These three themes of discounted cash flow, risk and diversification, and market efficiency lie at the very heart of most introductory finance courses.

Each of these themes will be considered in this book.

Source: E. Dimson, "Assessing the Rate of Return," *Financial Times* Mastering Management Series, supplement issue, no. 1, 1995, p. 13.

---

[1] Statistics Canada website: www40.statcan.gc.ca/l01/cst01/govt03a-eng.htm, accessed March 13, 2010.

[2] TMX Website: www.tmx.com/en/listings/listing_with_us/canadian_market.html, accessed March 13, 2010.

THE OBJECTIVES OF A BUSINESS

`L.O. 2`

A key idea underpinning modern financial management is that the primary objective of a business is **shareholder wealth maximization**. In a market economy, the shareholders will provide funds to a business in the expectation that they will receive the maximum possible increase in wealth for the level of risk that must be faced. When we use the term *wealth* in this context, we are referring to the *market value of the common shares*. The market value of the shares will, in turn, reflect the future returns the shareholders will expect to receive *over time* from the shares and the level of risk involved. Note that we are concerned not with maximizing shareholders' returns over the short term, but rather with providing the highest possible returns over the long term.

Wealth Maximization or Profit Maximization?

`L.O. 3`

Wealth maximization is not the only financial objective that a business can pursue. Profit maximization is often suggested as an alternative objective for a business. Profit maximization is different from wealth maximization in a number of important respects, as we shall see. However, before we consider these differences, we must first decide what we mean by the term *profit*.

There are various measures of profit that could be maximized, including the following:

- Operating profit (that is, earnings before interest and taxation)
- Earnings before tax
- Net income
- Net income available to common shareholders
- Net income per common share—also called *earnings per share (EPS)*.

These different possible measures of profit may pose problems as the evaluation of a particular opportunity can vary according to the choice of profit measure used. This point is illustrated in Activity 1.1.

ACTIVITY 1.1

Pointon Ltd. has the following long-term capital and annual profits:

Capital invested (100,000 common shares)	$100,000
Net income	$15,000

It is considering issuing 20,000 new common shares for $20,000 and investing the amount raised in an opportunity that provides a profit after tax of $2,000.

What should the managers do if the objective of the business is:

(a) To maximize net income available to common shareholders?
(b) To maximize net income per common share (or earnings per share, EPS)?

Solution

Although the net income available to common shareholders will be increased by the investment to $17,000 (i.e., $15,000 + $2,000), the net income per share will be decreased. (The current EPS is $0.15 [i.e., $15,000/100,000], whereas the expected EPS on the

▶

> new investment is $0.10 [i.e., $2,000/20,000]. Therefore overall EPS would fall to $0.14 [i.e., ($15,000 + $2,000)/(100,000 + 20,000)]). An objective of maximizing net income available to shareholders would therefore lead to a decision to invest, whereas an objective of maximizing net income per common share would lead to a decision to reject the opportunity.

Profit maximization is usually seen as a short-term objective, whereas wealth maximization is a long-term objective. There can be a conflict between short-term and long-term performance. It would be quite possible, for example, to maximize short-term profits at the expense of long-term profits, as shown in Activity 1.2.

ACTIVITY 1.2

How might the managers of a business increase short-term profits at the expense of long-term profits?

Solution

The managers may reduce operating expenses by:

- Cutting research and development expenditure
- Cutting staff training and development
- Buying lower-quality materials
- Cutting quality-control mechanisms.

These policies may all have a beneficial effect on short-term profits but may undermine the long-term competitiveness and performance of a business.

In recent years, many businesses have been criticized for failing to consider the long-term implications of their policies on the wealth of the owners. REAL WORLD 1.2 gives some examples of how an emphasis on short-term profits can have a damaging effect.

REAL WORLD 1.2

Short-Term Gains, Long-Term Problems

Companies that are publicly traded on a stock exchange must report their financial results on a quarterly basis. Results can greatly affect a firm's share price, depending on whether they meet, beat, or fall short of expectations, as conveyed by stock market analysts' forecasted estimates. This volatility in share prices often leads management to focus on short-term results in order to keep the share price high.

For example, two of the Big 3 North American automobile firms filed for bankruptcy protection in 2009 in part because they were having difficulty adjusting to the era of high gasoline prices. They earned record profits early in the new millennium. In recent years they have fallen on hard times, with large, gas-guzzling SUVs (sport–utility vehicles) not selling well. It seems the car companies were satisfied to make high profits in the short term without worrying too much about where oil prices were heading in the long term. The auto companies have had lots of warning, as this is not the first time high oil prices have significantly affected them in the past 35 years. They are now scrambling to keep up with consumer preferences for smaller, more fuel-efficient cars.

Another example of putting the short term ahead of the long term may be companies' use of automated telephone systems at the expense of direct human interaction with customers. Their bottom line results may temporarily improve as they save on salaries, but consumer frustration may eventually lead to lost sales.

A final problem with the use of profit maximization as an objective is that it fails to take account of risk. As we will discuss in some detail later, the higher the level of risk, the higher the expected return required by investors for a particular investment. This means that, logically, a profit maximization policy should lead managers to invest in high-risk projects. Such a policy, however, may not reflect the needs of the shareholders. When considering an investment, shareholders are concerned with both *risk* and the *long-run returns* that they expect to receive. Only a wealth maximization objective takes both of these factors into account. Managers who pursue this objective will choose investments that provide the highest returns in relation to the risks involved.

To Maximize or to Satisfy?

Even if we reject the use of profit and accept shareholder wealth as an appropriate financial objective, we may still question whether the *maximization* of shareholder wealth is appropriate. Accepting this objective implies that the needs of the shareholders are paramount. Shareholders are not the only ones who have a financial interest in a business, however. A business can be viewed as a coalition of various interest groups, with each group having a "stake" in the business, as shown in Activity 1.3.

ACTIVITY 1.3

What stakeholder groups may have a financial interest in a business?

Solution

The following groups may be seen as being stakeholders:

- Shareholders
- Employees
- Bondholders
- Bankers
- Managers
- Suppliers
- Customers
- The community.

This is not an exhaustive list. You may have thought of other examples.

If we take a broader view of the business, shareholders simply become one of a number of stakeholder groups whose needs have to be satisfied. It can be argued that, instead of seeking to maximize the returns to shareholders, the managers should try to provide each stakeholder group with a *satisfactory return*. The term **satisficing** has been used to describe this particular business objective. Although this objective may sound appealing, there are practical problems associated with its use.

Within a market economy, strong competitive forces ensure that failure to maximize shareholder wealth will not be tolerated for long. Competition for the funds provided by shareholders and competition for managers' jobs should ensure that the interests of the shareholders prevail. If the managers of a business do not provide the expected increase in shareholder wealth, the shareholders have the power to replace the existing management team with a new team that is more responsive to shareholder needs. Alternatively, the shareholders may decide to sell their shares in the business (and reinvest in other businesses that provide better returns in relation to the risks involved). The sale of shares in the business is likely to depress the market price of the shares, which management will have to rectify in order to avoid the risk of takeover. This can only be done by pursuing policies that are consistent with the needs of shareholders.

Do the above arguments mean that the interests of shareholders are all that managers must consider and that the interests of other stakeholders are irrelevant? The answer is almost certainly no. Satisfying the needs of the other stakeholder groups will often be consistent with the need to maximize shareholder wealth. A dissatisfied workforce, for example, may result in low productivity or strikes, which will in turn have an adverse effect on the shareholders' investment in the business. This kind of interdependence has led to the argument that the needs of other stakeholder groups must be viewed as constraints within which shareholder wealth should be maximized.

Viewing the needs of the other stakeholders as constraints that must be satisfied is a rather neat way of reconciling the objective of shareholder wealth maximization with the interests of other stakeholders. It assumes, however, that a business should *maximize* the wealth of shareholders but provide only a *satisfactory return* to other stakeholders. Whether or not this assumption is considered valid will involve a value judgment being made. It is important, however, to recognize the implications of ignoring the needs of shareholders in a competitive market economy. It is likely that all other stakeholder groups will suffer if the share price performance of the business falls below the expectations of the shareholders.

A final argument made in support of the wealth maximization objective is that, even if we accept the view that wealth maximization is not necessarily appropriate, the models that are based on this objective may still be useful for management decision making. By employing these models, managers can identify the most appropriate course of action from the shareholders' viewpoint and can see the costs borne by shareholders if a different (that is, non-wealth-maximizing) course of action is decided upon. The managers would then have to account to shareholders for their decision.

Wealth Maximization and Mission Statements

A business will often express its ultimate purpose in the form of a **mission statement**. These statements are widely published and frequently adorn the annual reports and websites of businesses. Mission statements are usually concise and try to convey the essence of the business. REAL WORLD 1.3 provides examples of businesses that proclaim a commitment to maximizing shareholder wealth.

Mission Possible: Maximize Profits

Canadian Imperial Bank of Commerce (CIBC) lists one of its key performance drivers as:

To generate strong total returns for our shareholders.

Intrawest Corp., one of the leading destination resort and adventure-travel companies in the world, undertook a strategic review in 2006 to maximize shareholder value and set the stage for a new era of growth. One business strategy adopted by the company is to maximize profits from real estate sales.

Sources: CIBC 2008 Annual Report, page 1. Intrawest Corp. 2006 Annual Report, pages 1 and 8.

Wealth Maximization and Ethical Behaviour

The importance of maximizing shareholder wealth has been given added impetus in recent years. One of the effects of the global deregulation of markets and of technological change has been to provide investors with greater opportunities to increase their returns. Investors are now able to move their funds around the world with comparative ease. This has increased competition among businesses for investment funds and has put managers under greater pressure to produce returns that are attractive in international—rather than merely national—terms.

Given these pressures, there is a risk that shareholder wealth maximization may be pursued by managers using methods that are not acceptable to the community. Examples may include paying bribes to government officials to secure contracts, employing child labour in developing countries to minimize production costs, or polluting the environment to avoid the cost of emission controls. Some managers may feel that such behaviour is acceptable because all is fair in business. However, the responsibility "to maximize the wealth of shareholders does not mean that managers are being asked to act in a manner which absolves them from the considerations of morality and simple decency that they would readily acknowledge in other walks of life."[3]

Thus, when considering a particular course of action, managers should ask themselves whether it conforms to accepted moral standards, whether it treats people unfairly, and whether it has the potential for harm. It can be argued that wealth maximization and ethical behaviour need not conflict; indeed, high ethical standards may be a necessary condition for wealth maximization. A business that treats customers, suppliers, and employees fairly and with integrity is more likely to flourish over the longer term. Some support for this view is set out in **REAL WORLD 1.4**.

---

[3] H. Rose, "Tasks of the Finance Function," *Financial Times* Mastering Management Series, supplement issue no. 1, 1995, p. 11.

Ethical Investing

Nearly 65% of socially responsible mutual funds outperformed their benchmarks in 2009. Funds focusing on large companies outperformed their peer group by about 6%.

Source: Social Investment Forum: http://socialinvest.org/news/releases/pressrelease.cfm?id=151, accessed March 13, 2010.

Businesses often proclaim their commitment to high standards of ethics and social responsibility in their dealings and develop appropriate policies to guide managers and employees in carrying out their work. REAL WORLD 1.5 provides an example of one such business and offers an insight into the sorts of policies that may be adopted.

Ethics and Social Reporting at Canadian Tire

Canadian Tire noted the following accomplishments in its 2008 annual report:

- Company-wide energy and carbon assessment
- Most stores using low-energy lighting
- Electronic central energy management pilot program established at Mark's Work Wearhouse stores
- Zero-waste initiative at head office
- Company-wide waste assessment.

Source: Canadian Tire 2008 Annual Report, page 18.

Ethics and Finance

Integrity and ethical behaviour are particularly important within the finance function, where many opportunities for unethical practice exist. Although there may be rules in place to try to prevent unethical behaviour, these will only provide a partial answer. The financial staff themselves must appreciate the importance of ethical behaviour in building long-term relationships for the benefit of all those connected with the business. It is not surprising that senior financial officers regard integrity as the most valued attribute of financial staff.

To demonstrate their commitment to integrity and ethical behaviour, some businesses provide a code of ethics for their employees. REAL WORLD 1.6 provides an example of one such code.

In the face of such scandalous corporate frauds as the high-profile bankruptcies of Enron and WorldCom, securities regulators in the U.S. and Canada have attempted to legislate improved integrity and ethical behaviour. Penalties for failure to provide better corporate governance include massive fines and jail time. In the United States, the *Sarbanes-Oxley Act* (SOX) requires senior executives of public companies to certify the effectiveness of internal controls designed to prevent fraud. SOX requires public companies and their auditors to report on the effectiveness of internal controls designed over financial reporting.

REAL WORLD 1.6   Royal Bank's Code of Conduct

The Royal Bank of Canada's Code of Conduct includes the following principles:

- Upholding the law
- Confidentiality
- Fairness
- Corporate responsibility
- Honouring our trust in you
- Objectivity
- Integrity
- Individual responsibility.

The code was updated in 2008 to clarify employee use of the internet, sharing of information with third parties, and contacts for reporting irregularities.

Sources: www.rbc.com/responsibility/governance/principles.html#codeofconduct, accessed March 13, 2010, and the Royal Bank's 2008 Annual Report, page 20.

Bill 198 in Canada is modelled on the U.S. legislation. Both acts aim to improve investor confidence by improving the quality and reliability of financial statements. In a survey, 270 chief financial officers (CFOs) in Canada were asked what they thought the likely impact of the increased corporate governance would be. Figure 1.3 provides the results of the survey in which executives were allowed more than one answer. Nearly 30% of Canadian CFOs thought that the legislation mandating tougher internal controls would lead to a more ethical business environment.

REAL WORLD 1.7 describes the very serious results of not complying with the corporate laws for one well-known individual.

REAL WORLD 1.7   Lord Conrad Black Convicted

Conrad Black, former CEO of Hollinger International Inc., former Canadian citizen, and now member of the British aristocracy, was sentenced to six and a half years in prison on December 10, 2007, for mail fraud and obstruction of justice. The mail fraud convictions involved cheques mailed in the United States to Lord Black as part of various non-compete agreements. The obstruction of justice charge involved Lord Black removing 13 boxes of material from his Toronto offices in 2005 in violation of a court order. This was filmed by security cameras. In July of 2010, Black was released on bail pending a review of his conviction by a U.S. appeals court later that year.

Sources: Paul Waldie, "Why he fell," *Globe and Mail,* July 14, 2007, and CBC News, "Conrad Black gets bail." *CBCNews.ca,* July 19, 2010.

FIGURE 1.3   Impact of Increased Corporate Governance

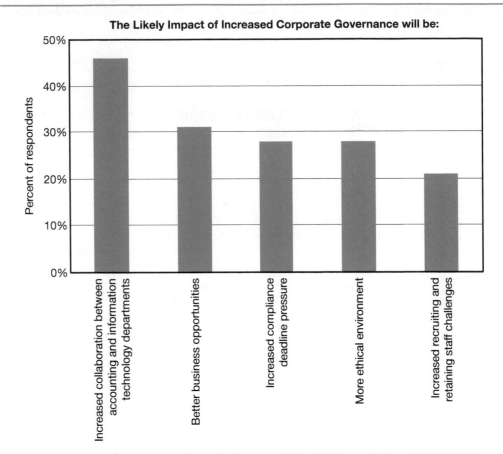

Source: Robert Half International Inc., *Next Generation Accountant: A New Outlook on a Timeless Profession,* 2005.

L.O. 4   CORPORATE GOVERNANCE AND THE AGENCY PROBLEM

In recent years, the issue of **corporate governance** has generated much debate. The term is used to describe the ways in which companies are directed and controlled. The issue of corporate governance is important because, in larger companies, those who own the company (that is, the shareholders) are not usually involved in the day-to-day control of the business. The shareholders employ professional managers to manage the company for them. Senior managers may, therefore, be viewed as *agents* of the shareholders (who are the *principals*).

Given this agent–principal relationship, it may seem reasonable to assume that the best interests of shareholders will guide the senior executives' decisions. However, in practice this does not always occur. Executives may be more concerned with pursuing their own interests, such as increasing their pay and perks (expensive cars and overseas trips, for example) and improving their job security and status. As a result, a conflict can occur between the interests of shareholders and the interests of senior managers; this is known as an **agency problem**.

It can be argued that in a competitive market economy, this agency problem should not persist over time. The competition for the funds provided by shareholders and for the top corporate jobs referred to earlier should ensure that the interests of the shareholders will prevail. However, if competitive forces are weak, or if information concerning management's activities is not available to shareholders, the risk of agency problems will be increased. Shareholders must be alert to such risks and should take steps to ensure that the managers operate the business in a manner that is consistent with shareholder needs. Activity 1.4 explores the role shareholders may play in this regard.

ACTIVITY 1.4

What kinds of actions might be taken to ensure that the executive team acts in accordance with the shareholders' interests?

Solution

Two types of actions are employed in practice:

1. The shareholders may insist on closely monitoring the actions of the managers and the way in which the resources of the business are used.
2. The shareholders may introduce incentive plans for executives that link their compensation to the share performance of the business. In this way, the interests of managers and shareholders will become more closely aligned.

The first option is fine in theory, but can be both difficult to implement and costly. Many businesses are now extremely large and their shareholders (who may individually own only a very small proportion of the shares of the business) may find it difficult to act collectively with other shareholders. However, if they try to monitor manager behaviour on an individual basis, the costs will be high in relation to the benefits. In such a situation, doing nothing may be a better option for a shareholder.

Incentive plans can also be difficult to implement and costly. A common form of incentive plan is to give managers **share options**. These options give managers the right, but not the obligation, to purchase shares in the business at an agreed price at some future date. If the current market value of the shares exceeds the agreed price at that date, the managers will gain by exercising the options. Activity 1.5 explores the problems associated with share options.

ACTIVITY 1.5

What problems may arise with share options as a form of management incentive? Are share prices influenced solely by managers' actions?

Solution

Movements in the price of the shares of the business may be influenced by a variety of factors such as interest rates, inflation, and taxation policy, over which the managers have no control. These factors can, however, have a significant effect on the rewards that managers receive where share options are used.

CORPORATE GOVERNANCE AND ECONOMIC PERFORMANCE

Where managers pursue their own interests at the expense of the shareholders, it is clearly a problem for the shareholders. However, it may also be a problem for society. If shareholders feel their funds are likely to be mismanaged, they will be reluctant to invest. A shortage of funds will mean that fewer investments can be made and the costs of funds will increase as businesses compete for whatever funds are available. Thus, a lack of concern for shareholders can have a profound effect on the performance of the economy.

To avoid these problems, most competitive market economies have a framework of rules to help monitor and control the behaviour of directors. These rules are usually based around three guiding principles:

- *Disclosure.* This lies at the heart of good corporate governance. An Organisation for Economic Co-operation and Development (OECD) report summed up the benefits of disclosure as follows:

  > Adequate and timely information about corporate performance enables investors to make informed buy-and-sell decisions and thereby helps the market reflect the value of a corporation under present management. If the market determines that present management is not performing, a decrease in stock (share) price will sanction management's failure and open the way to management change.[4]

- *Accountability.* This involves defining the roles and duties of the directors and executives and establishing an adequate monitoring process. Corporate law requires that directors and executives of a business act in the best interests of shareholders. This means, among other things, that they must not try to use their position and knowledge to make gains at the expense of the shareholders. The law also requires publicly traded companies (those with shares listed on a stock exchange) to have their annual financial statements independently audited. The purpose of an independent audit is to lend credibility to the financial statements prepared by the directors.

- *Fairness.* Directors and senior management should not be able to benefit from access to inside information that is not available to shareholders. As a result, both the law and the stock exchange place restrictions on the ability of directors and senior management to deal in the shares of the business. One example of these restrictions is that the directors cannot buy or sell shares immediately before the announcement of the final results of the business for a year or before the announcement of a significant event such as a planned merger or the resignation of the chief executive. This would constitute insider trading, which is illegal.

Strengthening the Framework of Rules

The number of rules designed to safeguard shareholders has increased considerably over the years. This has been in response to weaknesses in corporate governance procedures, which have been exposed through well-publicized business failures and frauds, including excessive pay increases to directors and senior managers and evidence that some financial reports were being massaged so as to mislead shareholders.

Directors

Outside directors do not work full-time in the company, but act solely in the role of director. This contrasts with executive directors, who are salaried employees. For

---

[4] Organisation for Economic Co-operation and Development, *Corporate Governance: Improving Competitiveness and Access to Capital in Global Markets*, OECD Report by Business Sector Advisory Group on Corporate Governance, 1998.

example, the chief financial officer (CFO) in most large companies is a full-time employee. This person is a member of the board of directors and, as such, takes part in decision making at the board level. At the same time, he or she is responsible for managing the departments of the company that act on those board decisions as far as the finance function is concerned.

Executive directors can become too embroiled in the day-to-day management of the company to be able to take the broad view. For executive directors, conflicts can arise between their own interests and those of the shareholders. The advantage of outside directors can be that they are much more independent of the company than their executive colleagues. Outside directors are paid by the company for their work, but this would normally form only a small proportion of their total income. This gives them an independence that the executive directors may not have. Outside directors are often senior managers in other businesses or people who have had significant experience in such roles.

REAL WORLD 1.8 lists several initiatives adopted under the most significant securities legislation in the U.S. since the Securities and Exchange Commission was created in 1934 during the depths of the Great Depression.

REAL WORLD 1.8

The U.S. *Sarbanes-Oxley Act* 2002

Some key elements of the *Sarbanes-Oxley Act* include:

- Creation of the Public Company Accounting Oversight Board
- Requirement that public companies must evaluate and disclose the effectiveness of their internal controls
- Requirement that chief executive officers (CEOs) and chief financial officers (CFOs) must certify the financial reports
- Improved auditor independence due to having banned certain types of (consulting) work by the auditors
- Enhanced criminal and civil penalties for violating securities laws
- Employee protections for corporate fraud whistleblowers.

Sources: www.sec.gov/about/laws/soa2002.pdf, accessed July 15, 2007; www.sec.gov/about/whatwedo.shtml, accessed April 17, 2007.

Strengthening the framework of rules has improved the quality of information available to shareholders, resulted in better checks on the powers of directors, and provided greater transparency in corporate affairs. However, rules can only be a partial answer. A balance must be struck between the need to protect shareholders and the need to encourage the entrepreneurial spirit of directors—which could be stifled under too many rules. This implies that rules should not be too tight, and so unscrupulous directors may still find ways around them.

REAL WORLD 1.9 shows corporate governance responsibilities at Rogers Communications, a diversified Canadian communications company.

Corporate Governance at Rogers

Corporate governance responsibilities at Rogers are subdivided into seven committees: Audit, Corporate Governance, Nominating, Compensation, Executive, Finance, and Pension. The audit committee is responsible for the integrity of the financial statements. The nominating committee helps ensure the Board of Directors is properly constituted to carry out its responsibilities. The compensation committee recommends senior management compensation and develops succession plans. The finance committee reviews the Company's investment strategies and its debt/equity structure.

Source: Rogers Communications 2009 Annual Report, p. 129.

The Rise of Shareholder Activism

Although a framework of rules is important to good corporate governance, it is equally important for shareholders to play their part by actively monitoring and controlling the behaviour of directors. In the past, shareholders have been criticized for being too passive and for allowing the directors too much independence; however, there is evidence that shareholders are beginning to play a more active role. This has coincided with the growing power of financial institutions, such as insurance businesses, pension funds, investment trusts, and banks. These institutions now own, or manage on behalf of individual shareholders, the majority of shares listed on the stock exchanges.

Financial institutions are often committed to the long-term success of the businesses in which they invest, even though this may not be through choice. This is because selling the shares of a poorly managed business may not always be a realistic option. There are at least two reasons for this. First, where the financial institution invests on behalf of individuals, such as an investment in mutual funds, there may be an obligation to match the performance of a stock market index by investing in the businesses that make up the index. In such a situation, it may not be possible to sell the shares of a particular business without deviating from the index. Second, the number of shares that a financial institution holds in a particular business can be very large indeed, and it may not be possible to sell such a large investment in the business without incurring heavy losses. In both cases, therefore, it may be better to try to influence the actions and decisions of managers by exercising (or threatening to exercise) the voting rights attached to the shares rather than selling the shares.

While financial institutions may intervene publicly to curb blatant mismanagement or excesses, they often exert their power in less public, more subtle, ways. For example, they may improve corporate governance procedures within a business by ensuring that outside directors are appointed who can be relied upon to ensure that necessary changes are made.

A particularly rich source of contention between shareholders and directors is executive pay. In recent years there have been some very public disagreements over one particular aspect of directors' remuneration: compensation payments available to directors who lose their jobs. REAL WORLD 1.10 explores the issue of executive bonuses in a time of recession—another contentious issue.

REAL WORLD 1.10

Canadian Bank Executive Bonuses

The Canadian banks stand out as pillars of strength during the Great Recession of 2008–09 and the subsequent recovery. So bonuses for executives at Canadian banks continue to be large because they continue to perform well and did not require government bailouts like so many of their international competitors. For example, in March 2010, the CEO of Scotiabank received a deferred share bonus of $1.5 million and the CEO at the National Bank got a $1.4 million bonus for exceeding objectives.

Sources: www.investmentexecutive.com/client/en/News/DetailNews.asp?Id=52628&cat=149&IdSection=149&PageMem= &nbNews= and http://nationalbankofcanada.corpfreespeech.com/national-bank-ceo-gets-big-bonus, accessed March 13, 2010.

SUMMARY

The main points in this chapter may be summarized as follows:

The Role of the Finance Function

- Helps managers in carrying out their tasks of strategic management, operations management, and risk management
- Helps managers in each of these tasks through financial planning, investment project appraisal, capital market operations, and financial control

The Essential Features of Financial Management

- Is influenced by economic theory
- Has been described as the economics of time and risk

The Objectives of a Business

Shareholder Wealth Maximization

- Is assumed to be the primary objective of a business
- Is a long-term rather than a short-term objective
- Takes account of both risk and the long-term returns that investors expect to receive
- Must take account of the needs of other stakeholders
- Is often proclaimed in the mission statements of businesses

Ethical Behaviour

- Need not conflict with the maximization of shareholder wealth objective
- May be set out in policies and codes
- Is particularly important in the finance function

Corporate Governance and the Agency Problem

- Agency problem may exist between shareholders and managers
- May be overcome or minimized by monitoring the activities of directors and/or aligning directors' interests to those of shareholders
- Has led to legislation to help monitor and control the behaviour of directors

Corporate Governance and Economic Performance

The Rise of Shareholder Activism

- Has coincided with the growing importance of financial institutions as investors in firms listed on stock exchanges
- Has provided some counterweight to directors' and senior management's excesses

KEY TERMS

Capital markets
Shareholder wealth maximization
Satisficing
Mission statement

Corporate governance
Agency problem
Share options

REVIEW QUESTIONS

Answers to the Review Questions can be found on the Companion Website that accompanies this text at www.pearsoned.ca/atrill.

1.1 What are the main tasks of the finance function within a business?

1.2 Why is the maximization of wealth viewed as superior to profit maximization as a business objective?

1.3 Some managers, if asked what the main objective of their business is, may simply state, "To survive!" What do you think of this as a primary objective?

1.4 Some businesses try to overcome the agency problem referred to in the chapter by using an incentive pay plan that is based on the growth of profits over a period. What are the drawbacks of this type of compensation plan?

1.5 Do you think an investment mutual fund that restricts its investment to environmentally friendly companies (green investments) can outperform mutual funds unrestricted in where they invest their money? Why?

Accounting—The Language of Business

When you have completed this chapter, you should be able to:

1 Understand asset, liability, shareholders' equity, working capital, revenue, expense, and dividend as accounting terms.

2 Contrast cash accounting with accrual accounting, discuss the matching principle, and explain the difference between revenues/expenses and cash flows.

3 Prepare and explain the main purpose of each of the four main financial statements—income statement, statement of retained earnings, balance sheet, and cash flow statement.

4 Explain the difference between depreciation and capital cost allowance.

5 Describe how corporate taxes are determined.

INTRODUCTION

In this chapter we review key accounting topics that you may have already encountered in a previous financial accounting course, but here you will see the role of accounting in a corporate finance setting. Although knowledge of accounting is important in corporate finance, you should note that the purpose of *accounting* is to understand how money *has been spent*. The goal of *finance* is to understand how money *should be spent* in the future. We discuss the main financial statements—income statement, statement of retained earnings, balance sheet, and cash flow statement—within a financing framework, and examine working capital and cash flow issues. Since taxation is an important fact to consider in decision making, we discuss depreciation, capital cost allowance, and the impact of each on corporate taxes.

THE FUNDAMENTAL ACCOUNTING EQUATION

The fundamental accounting equation, also sometimes called the balance sheet equation, is shown as Equation 2.1.

$$\text{Assets} = \text{Liabilities} + \text{Shareholders' equity} \qquad 2.1$$

The balances of the individual components in this equation continually change in order to keep the equation in balance. For example, assume that a company acquired a new machine asset. In order to keep the fundamental accounting equation in balance, one or a combination of the following events must also simultaneously occur with the new asset purchase:

1. Another asset balance must decrease, such as cash, if the machine is fully paid for
2. Liabilities must increase, such as accounts payable or loans payable, if the machine is bought on credit
3. Shareholders' equity must increase, such as common shares, if the machine is paid for by issuing common shares to the seller.

L.O. 1   SIGNIFICANT ACCOUNTING TERMS

Asset

An **asset** is anything the company *owns* that is expected to provide future benefits. Assets may be tangible (such as land, buildings, furniture, and fixtures) or intangible (such as patents, copyrights, or trademarks). Current assets include cash, as well as other items that are expected to be turned into cash in less than one year (such as accounts receivable and inventory). Also included in current assets are regular expenses that have been prepaid with cash (such as prepaid rent or prepaid insurance).

In contrast to current assets, long-term assets last longer than one year. Long-term assets are sometimes also called capital assets, non-current assets, fixed assets, or property, plant, and equipment. A company with extra cash available may convert it to a long-term asset by acquiring bonds or shares of another company in order to earn a higher return. Thus a company (or individual) may own a bond asset with the intention of holding it to maturity and receiving semi-annual interest payments throughout that time.

If a company uses all of its cash and draws on its bank overdraft position, then cash will cross the line into negative territory and appear on the balance sheet as a current liability.

Accumulated depreciation is grouped with the assets because it represents the total amount of depreciation subtracted from an asset.

Liability

A **liability** is an amount that the company *owes*. If a company must deliver cash to an outside party at some point in the future, this is a liability. A current liability must be paid within one year. Examples of current liabilities include accounts payable, accrued wages and salaries payable, and income taxes payable. Typical examples of long-term liabilities, with due dates longer than one year, are bank loans payable, bonds and debentures payable, and mortgages payable.

Shareholders' Equity

A corporation's **shareholders' equity** is the residual amount belonging to the share-holders and includes contributed capital and retained earnings. If a corporation has incurred larger losses than profits throughout its history, the retained earnings will be in a deficit (negative) position. Contributed capital consists mainly of cash received from the sale of new common shares and preferred shares. Sometimes preferred shares are classified as a liability on the balance sheet if they mostly have debt characteristics. The common share account consists of net cash amounts received by the company from its owners, the shareholders, upon the sale of its shares. The retained earnings account generally is the accumulated total of all the net income or earnings the company has made since its inception, minus the total of all dividends paid to shareholders.

Sometimes a company will use excess cash to buy back its own shares in the marketplace, especially when it feels that its shares are undervalued in the stock market. This transaction reduces both cash and common shares. It should also provide a boost to earnings per share as the number of shares outstanding is reduced. We will see the calculation of earnings per share below the income statement in the Red River Ltd. financial statements in the following pages. We will also encounter more on share repurchases in Chapter 11.

Working Capital

Working capital is defined in Equation 2.2 as current assets less current liabilities.

$$\text{Working capital} = \text{Current assets} - \text{Current liabilities} \qquad 2.2$$

Working capital is a measure of the cash available to the company during the next year, and might suggest a need for further borrowing if working capital is too low. Working capital will be discussed again in Chapter 4 when we study financial ratios.

Revenues

Revenues include sales of the company's goods and fees charged for services performed. Revenue accounts increase retained earnings. It is very important for revenues to be entered into the books in the correct accounting period. Companies are sometimes tempted to illegally speed up the reporting of future revenues by reporting them in the current accounting period. This happened at Nortel Networks, causing several reissuings of the company's financial statements.

Expenses

It is sometimes helpful to think of **expenses** as assets that were used up in the accounting period being reviewed. Expenses reduce retained earnings. Expenses should include all the costs incurred in order to produce the revenues for that accounting period. This includes the cost of goods sold, selling expenses, and administrative expenses, as well as depreciation and amortization expense, interest expense, and income tax expense. As with revenues, it is important for expenses to be reported in the correct accounting period. Companies might be tempted to underreport expenses by sliding them into future periods, thereby increasing net income for the current period.

Dividends

Dividends are a transfer of assets (usually cash payments) made by a business to its owners, the shareholders. Dividends reduce retained earnings. The total amount of retained earnings is usually the maximum amount of dividends that may be declared by the board of directors. You will learn more about dividend policy in Chapter 11.

L.O. 2   ACCRUAL ACCOUNTING, CASH FLOWS, AND THE MATCHING PRINCIPLE

Probably the earliest accounting systems simply recorded cash transactions because credit had not yet been invented. Once credit was established, an agreement had to be established on whether to report the revenue when the sale occurred or when the cash was collected. Accountants eventually agreed to report all revenues when the goods were delivered to or picked up by the customer. In the case of services, the revenue is generally earned when the service is completed. The extension of credit and the collection of cash related to a sale is a financing issue, not a revenue issue. Accrual accounting involves reporting a sale when the customer receives the goods or services without regard to when the cash is actually collected. So, a sale on credit is just as good as a cash sale, as far as revenue reporting is concerned.

Similarly, under accrual accounting principles, expenses are reported in the period when incurred, whether or not the cash is paid. Amortization and depreciation expense never directly involves cash but must continue to be reported; it is an apportionment of the cost of a capital asset over many years. For example, depreciation expense on a factory building with a 25-year estimated useful economic life is reported in the current year's income statement, even though it was acquired for cash 20 years ago. The factory was used to produce products that were sold to generate revenue in the current period, so the depreciation expense is reported. See Example 2.1 for a comparison of cash flows and expenses.

Many calculations for decision-making purposes in finance require the use of cash flows. For example, in determining whether a company should acquire a new machine, we need to estimate the future cash flows for each year over the estimated useful life of the machine based on future sales of products the machine will produce.

Another very important idea in accounting is the **matching principle**: *expenses are matched to revenues.* In every accounting period, expenses incurred in that period to achieve those revenues are reported. The matching principle is the reason why it is very important to slot revenues and expenses into the correct accounting period prior to preparing the financial statements.

Example 2.1   Cash Flows versus Expenses

Fizzy Drinks paid $3 million cash on January 2, Year 1, to buy an empty warehouse. Company executives assign $1 million of the purchase price to the land on which the building stands and $2 million to the building. The building is expected to last 20 years, at which time it will be replaced with a new building on the same land. Fizzy's year-end is December 31, Year 1.

The expense for Year 1 associated with this purchase is not equal to the $3 million cash paid. Since land is considered not to wear out, except for a mining or oil and gas company, there is no expense related to the $1 million cost of the land. The only expense is the depreciation expense associated with spreading the cost of the building over the 20 years of its expected useful life. One way to report depreciation expense is to make it equal for every year. This is called straight-line depreciation, and in this case it amounts to $2 million ÷ 20 years = $100,000 per year for 20 years. So by accrual accounting standards, there is a $100,000 expense every year for 20 years even though cash was involved only in the first year, as shown in Table 2.1.

▶

TABLE 2.1   Cash Flows versus Expenses for Fizzy's Warehouse Purchase

										($ millions)										
Year	1	2	3	4	5	6	7	8	9	10	11	12	13	14	15	16	17	18	19	20
Cash Flows																				
Land	−1.0																			
Building	−2.0																			
Expenses																				
depreciation expense	0.1	0.1	0.1	0.1	0.1	0.1	0.1	0.1	0.1	0.1	0.1	0.1	0.1	0.1	0.1	0.1	0.1	0.1	0.1	0.1

Activity 2.1 compares accounting revenues with cash receipts.

ACTIVITY 2.1

Fizzy Drinks, with a year-end of December 31, sold $300,000 of goods on December 15, Year 1. The terms of the sale included delivery of half the goods on December 30 and the remainder on January 15, Year 2. The terms of the sale called for payments by the customer of one-third of the amount in each month starting on January 15, Year 2.

Required:
Prepare an analysis of this transaction comparing monthly revenues and cash flows.

Solution

	Dec. Year 1	Jan. Year 2	Feb. Year 2	Mar. Year 2
Sales revenue	$150,000	$150,000		
Cash collections		100,000	$100,000	$100,000

Since half of the goods were delivered in December and the other half in January, the revenues are split half and half. You may not think that this revenue split is very important, but because the fiscal year-end is December 31, it means that half the revenue is reported in fiscal Year 1 and the other half in fiscal Year 2. Improperly reporting revenues distorts net income and could cause the firm's share price to increase or decrease significantly. Quarterly and annual financial results are very important in accounting because they are widely reported in the media and affect share prices.

FINANCIAL STATEMENTS

L.O. 3

Although companies prepare monthly financial statements and report quarterly results in the media, we will focus mostly on the annual financial statements. Annual financial statements are prepared by the company's management from the shareholders' point of view. Shareholders (both current and prospective), bondholders, and bankers are interested in the financial statements of a company. Figure 2.1 shows a sample income statement for a sports equipment company with several stores in western Canada.

FIGURE 2.1 Sample Income Statement

Red River Limited
Income Statement
for the year ended December 31, 2010
(in $ thousands)

Sales		500
Less: Cost of goods sold		280
Gross profit		220
Less: Selling expenses	5	
Distribution expenses	10	
Depreciation expenses	35	
Administration expenses	70	120
Operating income		100
Add: Gain on sale of land and building		20
Earnings before interest and taxes (EBIT)		120
Less: Interest expense		10
Earnings before income taxes (EBT)		110
Less: Income tax expense (40% × 110)		44
Net income		66

Note 1: *Earnings per share (EPS) Calculation*

Net income (from above)	66
Less: Dividends on preferred shares	
($0.02 × 100,000 preferred shares)	2
Net income available to common shareholders	64
Earnings per share (EPS) ($64,000 ÷ 1 million shares)	$0.064

Note 2: *Effect on EPS of a potential share buy-back plan*
Assume Red River acquired 100,000 of its own shares at the beginning of 2011 in the stock market. This leaves only 900,000 common shares outstanding in 2011. If net income available to common shareholders for 2011 remained at $64,000, the 2011 EPS would be $64,000 ÷ 900,000 shares = $0.071. This represents a 10.9% [($0.071 − 0.064) ÷ $0.064] increase in EPS simply because of the reduction in the number of shares outstanding.

Income Statement

Overview

The **income statement** measures the earnings (profit or loss) of a company during a given period. It is like the summary highlights reel of a hockey game. It shows how the company performed during the period. Notice from the title of the income statement in Figure 2.1 that it is for the year ended December 31, 2010, meaning that it measures income from January 1, 2010, to December 31, 2010.

An easy way to remember the income statement is to think about it in terms of a simple equation. Equation 2.3 expresses the income statement.

$$\text{Net income} = \text{Revenues} - \text{Expenses} \qquad \text{2.3}$$

Companies that sell goods must either manufacture or buy them. Either way, when those goods are sold, the cost of those goods sold often is reported separately from all other expenses in the cost of goods sold line on the income statement. This allows us to measure the gross profit, defined as sales less the cost of goods sold. These types of firms are, at least partly, trading companies. They buy or make something and sell it for a profit. Gross profit is an important measure because firms must use it to pay all other expenses, such as selling, distribution, administration, interest, and income tax expenses. Service firms—such as law, accounting, and marketing firms—do not sell a product and will not have a cost of goods sold line in the income statement.

Notes 1 and 2, below the income statement in Figure 2.1, calculate the earnings per share (EPS) for 2010 and hypothetically for 2011, assuming a share buy-back. As shown, EPS is obtained by dividing the net income, net of any preferred share dividend, by the number of shares outstanding. EPS is an important measure of the firm's quarterly and annual results as it is widely reported in the financial media and can have a large impact on the firm's share price. For example, if the EPS is below analysts' expectations, owners will often sell the shares en masse, driving down the share price. One way to increase EPS, all things being equal, is to reduce the number of outstanding shares through a share buy-back, as shown in Note 2.

Explanation

- Notice that the date for the income statement reads "for the year ended" and, therefore, covers the period January 1, 2010, to December 31, 2010.
- Sales are revenues from selling sports equipment. The sum for each individual sale is given by the price of the product sold and the quantity of items sold. Equation 2.4 is the sales equation.

$$\text{Sales} = \text{Price} \times \text{Quantity} \qquad 2.4$$

- Cost of goods sold is the cost to make or purchase the products that were sold.
- Gross profit equals sales less cost of goods sold from inventory.
- Selling expenses include sales salaries, commissions, and advertising costs.
- Distribution expenses are the cost of shipping products from warehouses to the stores and to the customers.
- Administrative costs include office expenses and salaries.
- Gain on sale of land and building is the profit on the sale of land (cost: $30,000) and a building (cost: $50,000; accumulated depreciation: $10,000) for $90,000 that was reported on the balance sheet at a net of $70,000 ($30,000 + $50,000 − $10,000). This produced a $20,000 gain (i.e., $90,000 − $70,000). The accounts for land, building, and accumulated depreciation on the building were all reduced by this transaction.
- Interest expense of $10,000 is calculated as 10% of the $100,000 bond debt (see balance sheet).
- Income tax expense of $44,000 is calculated as 40% of $110,000, the earnings before income taxes (EBT) (but after interest expenses).
- EPS is net income available to common shareholders divided by number of shares outstanding.

Figure 2.2 shows a sample statement of retained earnings.

Statement of Retained Earnings

Overview

This **statement of retained earnings** measures the changes in retained earnings from one period to the next. It can be expressed as Equation 2.5.

$$\begin{aligned} \text{Closing retained earnings} = \ & \text{Opening retained earnings} \\ & + \text{Net income} - \text{Dividends} \qquad 2.5 \end{aligned}$$

FIGURE 2.2   Sample Statement of Retained Earnings

Red River Limited
Statement of Retained Earnings
for the year ended December 31, 2010
(in $ thousands)

Opening retained earnings, January 1		87
Add: Net income		66
Less: Dividends		
Preferred shares ($0.02 x 100,000 shares)	2	
Common shares ($0.018 x 1,000,000)	18	20
Closing retained earnings, December 31		133

The term *retained earnings* stems from the fact that net income less dividends is the net amount of earnings that are retained within the business. The retained earnings account is one of the components of shareholders' equity because these profits belong to the common shareholders. Companies generally consider the amount in retained earnings as the maximum amount that could be declared for dividends. However, do not think of retained earnings as cash: they only represent the shareholders' claim on company assets. Sometimes the board of directors will limit the use of or set aside a portion of retained earnings for capital project allocations, thereby further limiting the size of potential future dividends. This is not the same as setting aside cash. It merely limits the size of future dividends and announces management's future intentions, usually disclosed in a note accompanying the financial statements. Funds for capital projects, including limiting dividend payouts in order to retain more cash for expansion plans, is considered in Chapters 8 and 10.

Explanation

- Notice that the date for the statement of retained earnings also reads "for the year ended" and also covers the period January 1, 2010, to December 31, 2010.
- The opening retained earnings balance is obtained from last year's balance sheet.
- Net income is the amount from the income statement.
- Dividends on preferred shares and common shares are declared by the board of directors. The preferred share dividend is fixed at $0.02 per preferred share. The common share dividend for 2010 was $0.018 per common share and, unlike the preferred dividend, will likely increase as future profits increase.
- Closing retained earnings agrees to this year's retained earnings in the shareholders' equity section of the balance sheet.

Balance Sheet

Overview

The **balance sheet** shows the financial position of the company at a point in time. It is like the scoreboard at the end of a hockey game. The balance sheet shows the result—what the company owns (assets), what it owes (liabilities), and what is left over for the shareholders' equity. In Figure 2.3, the balance sheet shows the financial position of the company at the close of business on December 31, 2010. The next day, in the case of a merger between two companies, for example, the balance sheet might look completely different.

FIGURE 2.3   Sample Balance Sheet

Red River Limited
Balance Sheet
as at December 31, 2010
(in $ thousands)

Current assets

Cash		20
Accounts receivable	25	
Less: Allowance for doubtful accounts	3	22
Inventory		110
Total current assets		152

Property, plant, and equipment

Land		200	
Buildings	300		
Less: accumulated depreciation—Buildings	170	130	
Furniture and fixtures	75		
Less: accumulated depreciation—F. & F.	25	50	
Vehicles	30		
Less: accumulated depreciation—Vehicles	10	20	
Net property, plant, and equipment			400

Total assets	552

Current liabilities

Accounts payable	10	
Wages payable	4	
Income taxes payable	5	
Total current liabilities		19

Long-term liabilities

Bonds payable, 10%, due 2020	100
Total liabilities	119

Shareholders' equity

Preferred shares (100,000 shares outstanding)	100	
Common shares (1 million shares outstanding)	200	
Retained earnings	133	
Total shareholders' equity		433
Total liabilities + shareholders' equity		552

Figure 2.3 shows a sample balance sheet. The balance sheet does not normally reflect what the company is worth. That is a far more complex question that will be addressed later in the text. The non-financial assets are reported at cost or depreciated cost. For example, land that cost $10 million 20 years ago may now be worth $100 million, but that increased value is not reported on the balance sheet. The balance sheet generally uses the cost principle, in which assets are reported at cost less accumulated depreciation. Similarly a $20 million building might be reported on the balance sheet 15 years later at $5 million (i.e., $20 million cost − $15 million accumulated depreciation), even though it would have a fair value of $150 million if sold today. However, as noted later in this chapter, in the international financial reporting standards (IFRS) section, the strict adherence to the cost principle will soon be relaxed. This will give companies the choice of reporting these assets at net fair value or depreciated cost.

Explanation

- Notice the change in the date reference here. The balance sheet in Figure 2.3 reads "as at December 31, 2010." This means it is valid only on one day.
- Current assets are assets that last for less than one year. These include cash or items likely to be turned into cash or used up within a year.
- Cash includes petty cash on hand at the company offices to pay incidental expenses plus cash in the company's bank accounts.
- Accounts receivable are amounts related to credit sales that will hopefully soon be collected, usually within 30 to 60 days.
- Allowance for doubtful accounts is a deduction from accounts receivable in recognition that some customers will not pay their bills.
- Inventory is the cost of goods available for sale that have not yet been sold.
- Property, plant, and equipment are assets used in the operation of the business. They are expected to last longer than one year.
- Land is the cost of the land owned by the company, including land on which the company's buildings are located. Usually when the company buys a building, it agrees to one price that includes both the building and the land. So the price paid must be analyzed by the company and split into a land cost and a building cost. The reason for splitting the cost this way is that land is considered to last forever and therefore does not need to be depreciated.
- Buildings represents the cost allocated to constructing or buying the buildings. Buildings generate depreciation expense on the income statement every year until they are fully depreciated.
- Accumulated depreciation–Buildings is the total amount of depreciation expense taken by the company in all the years since it has owned the buildings. In Red River's case, the buildings are over half depreciated (i.e., $\$170{,}000 \div \$300{,}000 \times 100\% = 56.7\%$).
- Furniture and fixtures is the cost of the office and store furniture, and store shelving.
- Accumulated depreciation–Furniture and fixtures shows that Red River's furniture and fixtures are one-third depreciated (i.e., $\$25{,}000 \div \$75{,}000 = 33.3\%$).
- The vehicles account is the cost of company cars and trucks.
- Accumulated depreciation–Vehicles indicates that Red River's vehicles are also one-third depreciated (i.e., $\$10{,}000 \div \$30{,}000 = 33.3\%$).
- Net property, plant, and equipment includes the total of long-term assets for Red River, less accumulated depreciation. Other companies may also have intangible assets, such as patents.
- Total assets are the total unamortized (undepreciated) cost of all the assets owned by the company.
- Current liabilities are amounts the company must repay within one year.
- Accounts payable is the amount owing for goods the company has purchased, including inventory and regular credit items for the office and store.
- Wages payable is the amount owing to the company's employees for work completed. The fact that the company owes wages to its employees does not signify that it is in financial trouble and cannot pay its workers. It simply means that the balance sheet was prepared between payday dates, so there are wage liabilities in existence until payday comes around. The matching principle, together with the accrual accounting method, dictates that these wage expenses and wages owing be recognized in the income statement and balance sheet respectively.
- Income taxes payable is the amount owing to the government for income taxes. Income taxes payable is always a current liability because the government will not wait very long to get its money.
- Total current liabilities is the total amount to be repaid in the next year.

- Long-term liabilities are amounts to be repaid more than one year into the future.
- Bonds payable, 10%, due 2020, is the amount of long-term bonds issued by the company at 10% interest.
- Total liabilities are the sum of current and long-term liabilities owed by the company.
- Shareholders' equity includes common shares, preferred shares, and retained earnings.
- Preferred shares, as noted earlier, have a stated dividend amount, which is $0.02 per preferred share for Red River.
- Common shares, which currently receive a dividend of $0.018 per share, as noted earlier, can expect to see the dividend grow as the firm's net income increases.
- Retained earnings are the sum of all net income less dividends over all the years the company has been in business.
- Total shareholders' equity is the residual amount left over for the shareholders, after subtracting the debt from the assets owned. Where preferred shares exist, the preferred share amount is also deducted from total assets to arrive at the total shareholders' equity available to common shareholders.
- Total liabilities and shareholders' equity equals total assets.

SELF-ASSESSMENT QUESTION   2.1

The Prince George Airport Authority has the following unsorted trial balance for December 31, 2010. All accounts are shown and all have normal account balances.

Accounts payable	$ 47,000
Land	100,000
Cash	25,000
Salaries expenses	300,000
Hangars	275,000
Bonds payable, due 2020	200,000
Airplanes	450,000
Accumulated depreciation–Hangars	100,000
Common shares	200,000
Accounts receivable	70,000
Revenues	1,200,000
Accumulated depreciation–Airplanes	100,000
Gas expenses	670,000
Retained earnings, January 1, 2010	203,000
Dividends	100,000
Depreciation expense	60,000

Required:

(a) Prepare an income statement for the year ended December 31, 2010.
(b) Prepare a statement of retained earnings for the year ended December 31, 2010.
(c) Prepare a balance sheet as at December 31, 2010.

Figure 2.4 shows a sample cash flow statement.

FIGURE 2.4   Sample Cash Flow Statement

Red River Limited
Cash Flow Statement
for the year ended December 31, 2010
(in $ thousands)

Cash flows from operating activities		
Net income (from income statement)	66	
Add (deduct) non-cash items:		
Depreciation expense *	35	
Gain on sale of land and buildings *	(20)	
Decrease in accounts receivable **	5	
Increase in inventory **	(10)	
Increase in current liabilities **	<u>4</u>	
Increase in cash from operating activities		80
Cash flows from investing activities		
Proceeds from the sale of land and buildings **	90	
Purchase of new land **	(40)	
Purchase of new furniture and fixtures **	(10)	
Purchase of new vehicles **	<u>(20)</u>	
Increase in cash from investing activities		20
Cash flows from financing activities		
Decrease in long-term bonds payable **	(70)	
Dividends paid (from statement of retained earnings)	<u>(20)</u>	
Decrease in cash from investing activities		<u>(90)</u>
Total increase in cash (80 + 20 − 90)		10
Cash at January 1, 2010		<u>10</u>
Cash at December 31, 2010 (agrees to balance sheet cash)		<u>20</u>

* from income statement
** see Figure 2.6 Analysis of Balance Sheet Changes between December 31, 2009 and 2010

Cash Flow Statement

Template for Cash Flow

Overview

The **cash flow statement** shows the sources and uses of cash for the company throughout the period. It shows investors and bankers where the company got its money during the period and what was done with it. The finance professional offers advice to management on what to do with cash to increase shareholder wealth. Such advice could be to reduce debt, to give cash back to the shareholders by way of dividends or share buybacks, or to make further investments in the business. Investors and bankers will analyze the cash flow statement to assess the performance of the company and the uses of its cash, including re-investment in property, plant, and equipment to generate future profits. Only transactions involving cash appear in the statement. For example, assume a company sells land for a $5,000 down payment and holds a $95,000 mortgage for the remainder of the selling price. Only $5,000 will appear in the cash flow statement, because the mortgage does not involve cash.

The cash flow statement is very important because many of the decision making concepts in finance deal with cash flows. The cash flow statement is divided into three sections:

1. Cash flows from operating activities
2. Cash flows from investing activities
3. Cash flows from financing activities.

Cash flows from operating activities   Cash flows from operating activities measure the amount of cash generated by the main business activities of the company, such as cash received from customers and cash paid for inventory purchases.

Direct Method Cash Flow Statement

The cash flow statement can be prepared directly from actual cash flows and grouped by operating, investing, and financing activities. The direct method alters the presentation of the operating activities section of the cash flow statement so that it reports cash inflows from customers and cash outflows to various groups such as suppliers, employees, insurance companies, and government for income taxes. Example 2.2 shows the preparation of a cash flow statement using the direct method.

Example 2.2

2012 data for the Ottawa Hot Air Balloon company are provided below.

Ottawa Hot Air Balloon Company

Cash balance at January 1, 2012	$ 400,000
Cash balance at December 31, 2012	$ 500,000

Other information for 2012

Salaries paid	$ 300,000
Inventory purchases	$ 600,000
Hydro invoices paid	$ 40,000
Cash received from bank loan	$ 300,000
Collections from customers	$ 1,140,000
Purchase of a machine	$ 400,000

Required:

Prepare a cash flow statement for 2012 for the Ottawa Hot Air Balloon Company.

Solution

Ottawa Hot Air Balloon Company
Cash Flow Statement
Year ended December 31, 2012

Operating activities		
Cash inflows		
Collections from customers	$1,140,000	
Cash outflows		
Salaries paid	(300,000)	
Inventory purchases	(600,000)	
Hydro invoices paid	(40,000)	
Net cash flows from operating activities		$200,000
Investing activities		
Purchase of a machine		(400,000)
Financing activities		
New bank loan		300,000
		100,000
Cash balance at January 1, 2012		400,000
Cash balance at December 31, 2012		$500,000

Indirect Method Cash Flow Statement

Most Canadian companies use the indirect method to prepare the cash flow statement because it is easier to do. This method uses the accrual basis net income as the starting point and requires several adjustments to convert it to cash flows. Prominent among these adjustments is the need to add back the non-cash depreciation and amortization expenses, deduct gains, and add back losses on the sale of capital assets. Figure 2.5 summarizes the impact of the changes in account balances under the indirect method used to prepare the cash flow statement.

FIGURE 2.5   Cash Flow Summary Chart

For the Indirect Method

Cash Inflow		Cash Outflow
	Operating Activities	
Current asset decreases		Current asset increases
Current liability increases		Current liability decreases
Net income		Net loss
	Investing Activities	
Property, plant, equipment, and intangible assets sold		Property, plant, equipment, and intangible assets purchased
	Financing Activities	
		Dividends paid
New shares sold (issued)		Company shares purchased
New bonds sold (issued)		Company bonds repaid

Cash flows from investing activities   This section of the cash flow statement indicates how much cash was spent during the past year on acquiring new capital assets, such as land, buildings, and equipment. It also shows how much cash was received from sales of old capital assets. Companies must continually make new investments in long-term capital assets in order to remain productive; cash from investing activities will typically be a negative figure, meaning net new assets were acquired.

Cash flows from financing activities   This section of the cash flow statement shows all cash inflows from issuing new shares and new long-term debt as well as all cash outflows from paying down long-term debt, buying back shares from investors, and paying dividends.

Figure 2.6 shows balance sheet changes between 2009 and 2010 for Red River Limited.

Explanation

Cash flows from operating activities

- Net income is the starting point in the measurement of cash flows from operating activities. Then a series of non-cash adjustments are made to convert net income to cash flow:
    - Amortization and depreciation expense from the income statement is added back to net income since it is a non-cash expense on the income statement. For cash flow purposes, amortization and depreciation expense is cancelled out (negative in the income statement's net income and positive in the cash flow statement adjustment).

FIGURE 2.6   Analysis of Balance Sheet Changes between December 31, 2009 and 2010

Red River Limited
Balance Sheets
as at
(in $ thousands)

	12/31/2010		12/31/2009		Change	Add: Land sold	Add: Buildings sold	Total Change
Current assets								
Cash		20		10	10			10
Accounts receivable	25		30		(5)			(5)
Less: Allowance for doubtful accounts	(3)	22	(3)	27	-			-
Inventory		110		100	10			10
Total current assets		152		137				
Property, plant, and equipment								
Land		200		190	10	30		40*
Buildings	300		350		(50)		50	-*
Less: Accumulated depreciation—Buildings	(170)	130	(157)	193	NA			
Furniture and fixtures	75		65		10			10
Less: Accumulated depreciation—F. & F.	(25)	50	(20)	45	NA			
Vehicles	30		10		20			20
Less: Accumulated depreciation—Vehicles	(10)	20	(3)	7	NA			
Net property, plant, and equipment		400		435				
Total assets		552		572				
Current liabilities								
Accounts payable		10		8	2			
Wages payable		4		3	1			
Income taxes payable		5		4	1			
Total current liabilities		19		15	4			4
Long-term liabilities								
Bonds payable, 10%, due 2020		100		170	(70)			(70)
Total liabilities		119		185				
Shareholders' equity								
Preferred shares (100,000 shares)		100		100	-			
Common shares (1 million shares)		200		200	-			
Retained earnings		133		87				
Total shareholders' equity		433		387				
Total liabilities + shareholders' equity		552		572				

*See Calculations in the *Cash flows from investing activities* section.

- The gain on the sale of the land and buildings is similarly cancelled out (positive in the income statement and negative in the cash flow statement adjustment) because the entire cash sale price of $90,000, which includes the $20,000 gain, is included as proceeds from the sale in the cash flows from investing activities. The gain would be double-counted if it were not cancelled out.
- The $5,000 decrease in accounts receivable during the year shown in Figure 2.6 represents a cash inflow (+) since more receivables were collected.
- The $10,000 increase in inventory during the year (Figure 2.6) represents a cash outflow (−) to pay for more inventory.
- The $4,000 increase in current liabilities (Figure 2.6) represents a cash inflow (+) since cash was saved by not paying for these debts.

Cash flows from investing activities

- As noted above, the entire sales price for the land and buildings is shown as an increase (+) in cash from investing activities.
- In this section of the cash flow statement, we learn that Red River acquired new land for $40,000, new furniture and fixtures for $10,000, and new vehicles for $20,000.
- The latter two are easy to understand as straightforward purchases. The amounts are obtained by comparing account balances as shown in Figure 2.6.
- Recall from page 25 that land costing $30,000 and a building costing $50,000 with accumulated depreciation of $10,000 were sold in 2010 for $90,000. When assets are sold, the analysis involves another step. You must compare the asset's ending balance with its adjusted opening balance after deducting the cost of the asset sold as follows:

Land		
Land at 12/31/2010		$ 200
Land at 12/31/2009	$ 190	
Cost of land sold in 2010	30	
Adjusted land at 2009		160
New land purchased in 2010		$ 40

Buildings		
Buildings at 12/31/2010		$ 300
Buildings at 12/31/2009	$ 350	
Cost of buildings sold in 2010	50	
Adjusted buildings at 2009		300
New buildings purchased in 2010		nil

See Figure 2.6 where the land and buildings sold adjustments are included in the worksheet to arrive at the total change for these accounts as shown above.

- If you only compared the land balance at the end of 2010 and 2009, you might think Red River had acquired land for $10,000. By taking into account that the company also sold $30,000 worth of land, you realize it must have also bought new land for $40,000 ($10,000 + 30,000 as shown in Figure 2.6).
- Similarly, the analysis shows no buildings were purchased in 2010. The decline in the account balance is entirely accounted for by the sale.

Cash flows from financing activities

- Red River spent $70,000 (Figure 2.6) to retire a portion of its long-term bonds and another $20,000 to pay for the dividends.

Conclusion

- Overall, cash inflows from operations generated $80,000, cash inflows from investing activities resulted in another $20,000, and $90,000 was spent on paying off some long-term bonds and paying the dividend. The net result was a $10,000 increase in cash (i.e., $80,000 + $20,000 − $90,000), which was added to the $10,000 cash balance at the beginning of the year to arrive at the $20,000 cash amount appearing on the year-end balance sheet.
- Overall, Red River generated a significant positive cash flow in 2010 and used it to pay down its long-term debt. Red River can expect to be debt-free within two years if this trend continues, since its total long-term debt is only $100,000.

Example 2.3 shows an example of using the indirect method to prepare a cash flow statement.

Example 2.3

Preparing a Cash Flow Statement

In 2010, Portage la Prairie Kayak Corp. (PPK) sold some land at cost and added an addition to their building. PPK earned a net income of $47,000 and paid dividends of $75,000 in 2010. Depreciation expense for the building was $15,000, for the furniture was $11,000, and for the equipment was $20,000.

Portage la Prairie Kayak Corp.
Balance Sheet
as at December 31,

	2010	2009
Current assets		
Cash	$ 120,000	$ 169,000
Accounts receivable	54,000	43,000
Inventory	24,000	33,000
Total current assets	198,000	245,000
Property, plant, and equipment		
Land	54,000	67,000
Buildings, net	320,000	250,000
Furniture, net	41,000	32,000
Equipment, net	140,000	123,000
Total property, plant, and equipment	555,000	472,000
Total assets	$ 753,000	$ 717,000
Current liabilities		
Accounts payable	$ 69,000	$ 75,000
Long-term liabilities		
Bonds payable	259,000	259,000
Total liabilities	328,000	334,000
Shareholders' equity		
Common shares	200,000	130,000
Retained earnings	225,000	253,000
Total shareholders' equity	425,000	383,000
Total liabilities and shareholders' equity	$ 753,000	$ 717,000

Required:

(a) Prepare an analysis to determine the cost of the addition to the building and how much furniture and equipment was acquired in 2010.

(b) Prepare the cash flow statement for 2010.

Solution

(a)

	Buildings	Furniture	Equipment
2010	$ 320,000	$ 41,000	$ 140,000
2009	250,000	32,000	123,000
Less: 2010 depreciation	(15,000)	(11,000)	(20,000)
2009 adjusted balance	235,000	21,000	103,000
Purchases 2010 balance less 2009 adjusted balance	$85,000	$20,000	$37,000

(b)

Portage la Prairie Kayak Corp.
Balance Sheet
as at December 31,

	2010	2009	Difference
Current assets			
Cash	$ 120,000	$ 169,000	$ (49,000)
Accounts receivable	54,000	43,000	11,000
Inventory	24,000	33,000	(9,000)
Total current assets	198,000	245,000	
Property, plant, and equipment			
Land	54,000	67,000	(13,000)
Buildings, net	320,000	250,000	70,000
Furniture, net	41,000	32,000	9,000
Equipment, net	140,000	123,000	17,000
Total, property, plant, and equipment	555,000	472,000	
Total assets	$ 753,000	$ 717,000	
Current liabilities			
Accounts payable	$69,000	$ 75,000	(6,000)
Long-term liabilities			
Bonds payable	259,000	259,000	–
Total liabilities	328,000	334,000	
Shareholders' equity			
Common shares	200,000	130,000	70,000
Retained earnings	225,000	253,000	
Total shareholders' equity	425,000	383,000	
Total liabilities and shareholders' equity	$ 753,000	$ 717,000	

Portage la Prairie Kayak Corp.
Cash Flow Statement
for the year ended December 31, 2010

Cash flows from operating activities		
Net income	$ 47,000	
Add back: Depreciation ($15,000 + 11,000 + 20,000)	46,000	
	93,000	
Less: Increase in accounts receivable	(11,000)	
Add: Decrease in inventory	9,000	
Less: Decrease in accounts payable	(6,000)	
Increase in cash from operating activities		$ 85,000
Cash flows from investing activities		
Proceeds from sale of land	$ 13,000	
New building purchased	(85,000)	
New furniture purchased	(20,000)	
New equipment purchased	(37,000)	
Decrease in cash from investing activities		(129,000)

Cash flows from financing activities		
New shares issued	70,000	
Dividends paid	(75,000)	
Decrease in cash from financing activities		(5,000)
Total decrease in cash		(49,000)
Cash at January 1, 2010		169,000
Cash at December 31, 2010		$ 120,000

SELF-ASSESSMENT QUESTION   2.2

In 2010, North Battleford Gypsum Ltd. (NBG) sold some furniture for $40,000. This furniture had cost NBG $50,000 and had $40,000 accumulated depreciation associated with it. The financial statements are as follows:

North Battleford Gypsum Ltd.
Income Statement
for the year ended December 31, 2010

Sales	$	2,000,000
Cost of goods sold		940,000
Gross profit		1,060,000
Add: Gain on sale of furniture		30,000
Less: Depreciation expense		(64,000)
Less: Other expenses		(220,000)
Net income	$	806,000

North Battleford Gypsum Ltd.
Statement of Retained Earnings
for the year ended December 31, 2010

Retained earnings, Jan. 1	$	561,000
Net income		806,000
Less: Dividends		(643,000)
Retained earnings, Dec. 31	$	724,000

North Battleford Gypsum Ltd.
Balance Sheet
as at December 31

	2010		2009	
Cash	$	350,000	$	267,000
Accounts receivable		221,000		180,000
Inventory		362,000		300,000
Land		428,000		300,000
Buildings		728,000		728,000
Accumulated depreciation—Buildings		(354,000)		(320,000)
Furniture and equipment		276,000		296,000

▶

Accumulated depreciation—F. & E.	(150,000)	(175,000)
Trucks	163,000	140,000
Accumulated depreciation—Trucks	(50,000)	(35,000)
Total assets	$ 1,974,000	$ 1,681,000
Accounts payable	$ 300,000	$ 420,000
Bonds payable, 2020	450,000	350,000
Common shares	500,000	350,000
Retained earnings	724,000	561,000
Total liabilities and shareholders' equity	$ 1,974,000	$ 1,681,000

Required:

(a) Prepare an analysis of the furniture and equipment account to determine how much was purchased in 2010.

(b) Prepare the 2010 cash flow statement for NBG.

REAL WORLD 2.1 shows the importance of cash flows to a business that was once the largest company in the world.

REAL WORLD 2.1

GM Cash Burn

General Motors Corporation was hemorrhaging cash so fast in 2008 and early 2009 that it was eventually forced into bankruptcy. GM burned through US$19.2 billion cash on its way to a US$30.9 billion loss in 2008. The cash burn rate is the amount of cash collected from sales compared to the amount of cash spent from paying costs and expenses. No company can survive for long when cash outflows (expenses) drastically exceed cash inflows. The credit crunch that exponentially worsened after the collapse of giant investment bank Lehman Brothers resulted in consumers disappearing from car companies' showrooms. Auto industry sales fell to about half of boom-time levels.

Source: www.cbc.ca/money/story/2009/03/12/gm-bailout.html, accessed August 15, 2009.

INTERNATIONAL FINANCIAL REPORTING STANDARDS (IFRS) IN CANADA

Starting in 2011, publicly listed Canadian companies adopted international financial reporting standards (IFRS), as used by much of the world, to prepare financial statements. Private enterprises can choose to use IFRS or a set of made-in-Canada accounting guidelines, which will permit some simplifications to ease the burden on small companies. Previously, Canada's own generally accepted accounting principles (GAAP) developed differently from other countries to meet our local business conditions. However, with the increasing globalization of the world's economies, it no longer makes sense for Canada to have its own set of accounting rules. After all, our equity markets represent less than 4% of the global markets.

The International Accounting Standards Board (IASB) has been working for many years to develop high quality, understandable, and international financial reporting standards (IFRSs) for general purpose financial statements. This harmonization of accounting standards throughout the world will make it easier for investors and bankers to compare financial results and make investment decisions. Harmonization will also save the companies time and money because they will only have to prepare one set of financial statements. Consider the current situation of a large Canadian company that has its shares listed on the Toronto Stock Exchange, the New York Stock Exchange, and the London Stock Exchange and has been preparing three sets of financial statements to satisfy the requirements of each exchange. Under the IFRS, this company will need to prepare only one set of financial statements.

One significant accounting difference under IFRS is that companies will be able to choose to report inventory and property, plant, and equipment, such as land and buildings, at fair value. For example, a Canadian bank with an office tower in downtown Toronto, built in the 1970s for $30 million, will be able to report it on the balance sheet at its appraised fair value of $550 million under the IFRS standards. All of a sudden the bank's assets and shareholders' equity will dramatically increase. Companies will have to think carefully about this because writing up the building to $550 million will result in higher depreciation expenses, as the higher building amount will have to be depreciated. This will depress future earnings for years to come.

A minor difference involves a name change. **Amortization** is the general term for the allocation of the cost of a long-term capital asset to the income statement as an expense and is also used for intangible assets like patents. IFRS uses the term **depreciation** with respect to the cost allocation for property, plant, and equipment such as buildings, machines, trucks, and cars. *Depletion* is used for cost allocation of natural resources in the mining and oil industries. All three terms have the same meaning. Canadian GAAP had virtually eliminated the term depreciation over the past twenty years, but now we will see its return under IFRS. However, we will probably see depreciation and amortization used interchangeably during the transition period to IFRS; this text will use *depreciation*.

INCOME TAXES

Corporate Taxes

L.O. 5

Income taxes are an unusual type of expense because they are based on net income, which is determined by subtracting expenses from revenues. Net income serves as the starting point in the determination of income taxes payable and then income tax expense. Net income is adjusted to arrive at taxable income according to the legal requirements of the *Income Tax Act*. The income taxes payable are determined using Equation 2.6.

Template for Tax

$$\text{Taxes payable} = \text{Corporate tax rate} \times \text{Taxable income} \qquad 2.6$$

The current federal tax rate for Canadian-controlled private corporations that qualify for the small business deduction is 11%. Otherwise, the federal tax rate is 18% for corporations. Similarly, each province has a lower tax rate for qualifying small businesses and a higher tax rate for other companies. For example, the Ontario lower tax rate is 4.5%; the regular rate is 12%. This brings the total federal and Ontario provincial tax rate for corporations qualifying for the small business deduction rate to 15.5%; otherwise it is 30%. Figure 2.7 compares Ontario tax rates with those of British Columbia.

DEPRECIATION AND CAPITAL COST ALLOWANCE

L.O. 4

As noted earlier, *depreciation* is an accounting term referring to the allocation of the cost of a long-term capital asset to the income statement as an expense. For example, a $20 million building, with an estimated useful economic life of 20 years and no residual value, results in $1 million depreciation expense to be reported in the income statement every year for 20 years.

Template for CCA

Considerable judgment is involved in using estimated values, such as useful economic life and residual value of the asset. If another company uses an economic useful life of 10 years for a similar building, its depreciation expense is $2 million per year, twice as high as its competitor's.

FIGURE 2.7   Selected Tax Rates

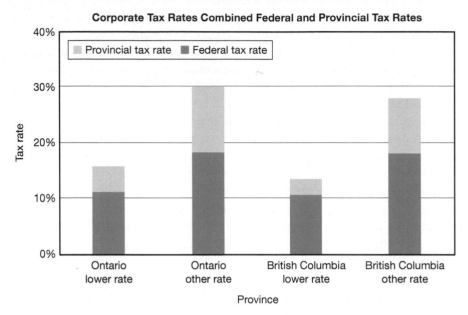

Source: www.cra-arc.gc.ca/tx/bsnss/tpcs/crprtns/rts-eng.html, accessed March 20, 2010.

The taxation authority wanted to remove this judgment factor in determining corporate income taxes, so it devised the **capital cost allowance (CCA)** method. CCA is the tax return's equivalent to depreciation expense. CCA is optional and probably is not taken in a year where the company has a taxable loss, but depreciation expense must be reported every year. Another major difference is that the *Income Tax Act* specifies the maximum CCA rate that can be used to calculate the CCA deduction, thereby removing the judgment factor involved in determining an asset's economic useful life.

CCA is calculated on a pooled asset basis. This also differs from depreciation, which is calculated on an individual asset basis. The tax act specifies various asset classes and their CCA rate. Most buildings fit into class 1 with a 4% CCA rate, trucks and cars are class 10 with a 30% CCA rate, and manufacturing equipment is class 43, also having a 30% CCA rate.

Table 2.2 presents a 10-year comparison between the amount of CCA taken in the tax return on a $100,000 machine and depreciation expense taken in the income statement. The CCA rate for this machine is 20% (class 8). Capital cost allowance works on a declining balance basis, with the half-year rule in effect for the year in which the asset

TABLE 2.2   10-Year Comparison between CCA and Depreciation

Year	Opening UCC	CCA @ 20%	Closing UCC	Depreciation (straight-line over 10 years)	Net book value
1	$ 100,000	$ 10,000	$ 90,000	$ 10,000	$ 90,000
2	90,000	$ 18,000	72,000	10,000	80,000
3	72,000	$ 14,400	57,600	10,000	70,000
4	57,600	$ 11,520	46,080	10,000	60,000
5	46,080	$ 9,216	36,864	10,000	50,000
6	36,864	$ 7,373	29,491	10,000	40,000
7	29,491	$ 5,898	23,593	10,000	30,000
8	23,593	$ 4,719	18,874	10,000	20,000
9	18,874	$ 3,775	15,099	10,000	10,000
10	15,099	$ 3,020	12,080	10,000	0

is acquired. The maximum amount of CCA that could be claimed for the machine in the first year is 1/2 × 20% × $100,000 = $10,000. Now the balance in the machine account for tax purposes has declined to $100,000 − 10,000 = $90,000. The $90,000 remaining balance is the amount that is undepreciated for tax purposes and is called the undepreciated capital cost (UCC) of the machine. For the second year, the maximum CCA deduction is 20% × UCC balance = 20% × $90,000 = $18,000.

One difference in Table 2.2 is that the CCA rate is 20% while the depreciation rate is 100% ÷ 10 years = 10%. Another big difference in this example is that depreciation expense is constant over 10 years. At that point, depreciation expense ends because the asset is fully depreciated. On the other hand, CCA is calculated on a declining balance method. The CCA amount gradually declines each year (except for the increase in the second year caused by the application of the half-year rule in the first year), because the same CCA rate is applied to a declining UCC balance. CCA would continue past year 10 if the machine is kept, while the depreciation would be zero for those years.

Unless explicitly stated to the contrary, most problems, cases, examples, and situations described in this text assume that the amount of CCA taken in a year is the same as the depreciation reported. The reason for making this simplifying assumption is to clearly focus on the particular issue we are studying, without complicating it too much with extra tax issues.

Disposal of the only asset in a CCA class

Theoretically, the CCA will go on forever, as long as there are assets remaining in the CCA class, because the UCC balance never quite gets to zero. However, when the last asset in a CCA class is sold, there are usually income tax implications because the CCA class has been terminated. Depending on the selling price of the asset, there are four possible income tax scenarios as shown in Figure 2.8.

FIGURE 2.8   Sale of the Last Asset in a CCA Class   Four Situations

Case 1:

No further tax impact	Year	UCC
UCC	10	$12,080
Asset sold for its UCC amount	11	(12,080)
		nil

Case 2:

Terminal loss reduces taxes	Year	UCC
UCC	10	$12,080
Asset sold for less than its UCC amount	11	6,000
Terminal loss		$6,080
Tax rate		40%
Tax savings (40% × $6,080)		$2,432

Case 3:

CCA recapture increases taxes	Year	UCC
UCC	10	$12,080
Asset sold for more than its UCC amount		
(but not more than its original cost)	11	100,000
CCA recapture		$87,920
Tax rate		40%
Additional taxes (40% × $87,920)		$35,168

Case 4:

Capital gains plus CCA recapture increases taxes	Year	UCC
Everything in Case 3 applies plus:		
Asset sold for more than its original cost	11	$150,000
Original cost		100,000
Capital gain		$50,000
Taxable capital gain rate		50%
Taxable capital gain		$25,000
Tax rate		40%
Additional capital gains taxes (40% × $25,000)		$10,000
Total additional taxes (Case 3 + Case 4)		$45,168

In Case 2, the tax saving on this terminal loss is the tax rate, T, times the terminal loss, as shown in Equation 2.7.

$$\text{Tax saving} = \text{Tax rate, T} \times \text{Terminal loss} \qquad 2.7$$

In Case 3, CCA recapture applies to any selling price above the UCC amount of $12,080 up to the original cost of $100,000. The CCA recapture amount increases for higher selling prices and increases the additional taxes to be paid. The rationale for having to pay more income taxes is that the company must not have paid enough taxes in the past, due to its CCA deductions being too high in past tax returns (although within legal limits). The evidence for this conclusion is that the machine has not really been depreciated down to $12,080, since it was sold for such a high price.

In Case 4, there are two components generating additional taxes—the capital gain and the CCA recapture from Case 3. Capital gains are valued highly by both individuals and corporations because only half of the capital gain is subject to income tax. Therefore, the taxable capital gain in this case is 50% × $50,000 = $250,000.

If other assets remain in the same tax class, then 50% of any capital gain is added to taxable income in the usual manner, and the rest of the proceeds are used to reduce the UCC of the class, so that future CCA is reduced. Activity 2.2 extends this example for the case of an asset class having more than one asset.

ACTIVITY 2.2

Assume the data in Table 2.2 represented two different machines instead of one machine. Consider each of the following situations independently.

Required:

(a) What is the tax impact of selling one machine at the beginning of Year 11 for $7,000?

(b) What is the tax impact of scrapping one of the machines because it is worn out?

(c) What is the tax impact of selling one of the machines for $25,000?

▶

Solution

Since there are two machines in this tax class, these transactions do not result in an empty UCC class. The results are shown in Figure 2.9.

FIGURE 2.9   Sale of an Asset That Is Not the Last Asset in a CCA Class

a: Sold one machine for $7,000 (less than UCC)

CCA is reduced	Year	UCC
Ending UCC	10	$12,080
Less: Proceeds from sale	11	7,000
Adjusted opening balance	11	$ 5,080
Less: CCA @ 20%	11	1,016
Ending balance	11	$ 4,064

b: One machine is scrapped

CCA is unreduced	Year	UCC
Ending UCC	10	$12,080
Less: CCA @ 20%	11	2,416
Ending balance	11	$ 9,664

c: Sold one machine for $25,000 (more than UCC)

CCA is zero	Year	UCC
Ending UCC	10	$12,080
Less: Proceeds from sale	11	25,000
Adjusted opening balance	11	(12,920)
CCA recaptured	11	12,920
Adjusted opening balance	11	nil
CCA	11	nil

(a) The proceeds from the sale reduce the UCC in this asset class. So the CCA is reduced to $1,016 compared to $2,416 (20% × $12,080) if there had been no sale.

(b) Since no proceeds were involved in scrapping the machine, the opening UCC balance is unaffected. So CCA continues just as if the machine had never been scrapped.

(c) Selling one machine for $25,000 results in recaptured CCA of $12,920. This will increase income taxes payable in Year 11 by $5,158 (40% × $12,920). Further CCA will not be available since the UCC balance is zero for this class.

Taxable Income

We have already seen that depreciation expense is one of the major adjustments needed to transform accounting net income into taxable income on the company's tax return. Depreciation expense is not permitted in the *Income Tax Act*. However, as we have seen earlier, a similar deductible expense, called capital cost allowance, is permitted. This is an example of a temporary difference between accounting and taxable income. It is temporary because at the end of the economic life of the assets the temporary difference disappears.

Other adjustments often include moving from an accrual basis in accounting to a cash basis in the tax return. The government does not want a company to lower its tax bill by making high estimates for its expenses. These estimated expenses, which are required in accounting, are often not deductible in the tax return. Instead, only the cash payments are tax-deductible. Two examples of this are estimated warranty expenses and pension expense. Only actual cash warranty expenses paid, not estimates, are allowable deductions in the tax return. Similarly, the actual cash pension funding paid to the company's pension fund trustee, not the unfunded portion of the expense, is tax-deductible.

Another adjustment for corporations is that dividends received from other Canadian corporations are not taxable. Since corporations pay dividends out of after-tax income, taxes have already been paid for these dividends. So, they are not taxed again in the hands of another corporation.

As noted previously, capital gains are a valuable source of income because only half of the capital gain is included in taxable income.

Activity 2.3 focuses on determining taxable income and taxes payable.

ACTIVITY 2.3

The Montreal Furniture Company Ltd. earned an accounting income before income taxes of $550,000 in 2010. Depreciation expense was $100,000. The capital cost allowance permitted in 2010 is $150,000. This is the only temporary difference between accounting net income and taxable income. The combined federal and provincial tax rate is 40%.

Required:

(a) Calculate taxable income for Montreal Furniture for 2010.
(b) Calculate income taxes payable for Montreal Furniture for 2010.

Solution

(a)	Accounting income before income taxes	$550,000
	Adjustments to determine taxable income:	
	Add back: Non-deductible depreciation expense	100,000
	Deduct: CCA for 2010	(150,000)
	Taxable income for 2010	$500,000
(b)	Taxable income for 2010 (from part (a))	$500,000
	Tax rate for 2010	40%
	Taxes payable for 2010 (40% × $500,000)	$200,000

Tax Loss Carry-Backs and Carry-Forwards

Since net income and taxable income can be negative in a year with a loss, income tax payable and income tax expense can in fact also be negative. Firms can carry a taxable loss back to the previous three years and obtain a refund of the taxes paid in these years. If the loss is so large that it cannot all be used up against the previous three years' taxable income, the unused loss can be carried forward and used in any of the next 20 years to reduce taxable income. This creates a future income tax asset because real cash savings are created by deducting the current year's loss carry-forward from future income. Accounting issues in the preparation of income taxes are often complex and confusing; we are only touching on them in this text. Students specializing in finance or accounting will usually take an entire course dedicated to this subject.

REAL WORLD 2.2 shows how one company was able to reduce its loss before income taxes by applying tax loss carry-back and carry-forwards.

Cott Corp. Has Negative Income Tax

Cott Corp. is one of the world's largest soft drink companies. Cott is a Canadian company with its head office in Pointe-Claire, Quebec. Executive offices are located in Mississauga, Ontario, and Tampa, Florida.

Cott Corporation
Consolidated Statements of (Loss) Income
for the years ended
(in millions of U.S. dollars, except share and per share data)

	December 27, 2008	December 29, 2007	December 30, 2006
Loss before income taxes	$ 142.3	$ 85.3	$ 33.8
Income tax benefit	(19.5)	(13.9)	(16.3)
Net loss	$ 122.8	$ 71.4	$ 17.5

Losses were reduced each year by the income tax benefit. Some of this represents an actual cash refund from the government of taxes previously paid ($9.6 million in 2008) and some represents a future tax reduction, which is a benefit.

Source: 2008 Cott Corp. Annual Report.

Individual Taxes

Canada has a progressive income tax system in place for individuals. That is, the higher your income, the higher your tax rate. In addition to the federal rates, provincial and territorial income tax rates range from 14% to 17.95% depending on the tax bracket and the jurisdiction. Table 2.3 shows selected 2009 federal, Manitoba, and combined income tax brackets for various amounts of taxable income.

Figure 2.10 shows a graph of the federal and provincial marginal tax rates for Manitoba and Nova Scotia for a person earning $30,000 and a person earning $150,000.

The higher tax rate percentage only applies to the income amount starting at the tax rate's lower threshold level. Income up to this threshold point is taxed at the previous tax bracket's rate. For example, assume Jackie Bishop from Winnipeg, Manitoba, earned a gross income of $80,000, which reduced to a taxable income of $70,000 in 2009 after deductions. $70,000 falls into the fourth tax bracket, with a 39.40% combined tax rate in Table 2.3.

TABLE 2.3   2009 Federal and Provincial Marginal Income Tax Rates for Manitoba

Taxable Income	Federal Tax Rate	Manitoba Tax Rate	Combined Federal and Provincial Marginal Tax Rate
$0–$31,000	15%	10.80%	25.80%
$31,000–$40,725	15%	12.75%	27.75%
$40,725–$67,000	22%	12.75%	34.75%
$67,000–$81,452	22%	17.40%	39.40%
$81,452–$126,264	26%	17.40%	43.40%
Over $126,264	29%	17.40%	46.40%

FIGURE 2.10   Marginal Tax Rates for 2009

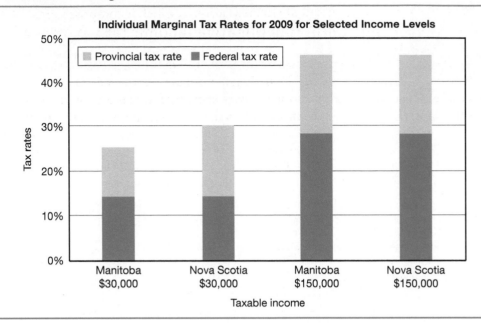

However, this rate only applies to the income amount from $67,000 up to $70,000. The first $31,000 of income is taxed at only 25.80%, and so on.

The complete calculation of income taxes payable for Jackie Bishop is shown below. Notice there are four tax classes involved for this individual.

	Combined Federal and Provincial Marginal Tax Rate	Marginal Income	Combined Federal and Provincial Taxes Payable
On the first $31,000	25.80%	$31,000.00	$7,998.00
On the next $40,725 − $31,000 = $10,725	27.75%	10,725.00	$2,976.19
On the next $67,000 − $40,725 = $26,275	34.75%	26,275.00	$9,130.56
On the last $70,000 − $67,000 = $3,000	39.40%	3,000.00	$1,182.00
Total taxes payable			$21,286.75

The average tax rate is given by Equation 2.8:

$$\text{Average tax rate} = \frac{\text{Total taxes payable}}{\text{Gross income}} \qquad 2.8$$

Jackie Bishop's average tax rate is $21,286.75 ÷ $80,000 × 100% = 26.61%. The marginal tax rate is given by Equation 2.9:

$$\text{Marginal tax rate} = \text{Tax rate on the last dollar of income} \qquad 2.9$$

Jackie Bishop's marginal tax rate is 39.40%, considerably higher than her average tax rate. The marginal tax rate should always be used for making decisions. For instance, assume that Jackie is offered the chance to work overtime. If accepted, it would boost her income to $95,000 and her taxable income to $85,000. Notice that this amount puts her into the 43.40% marginal tax bracket for some of the overtime. Since, for a portion of the overtime worked, she only gets to keep 56.6% (i.e., 100% − 43.40%) of the dollars earned, she might decide to refuse the overtime work.

Dividends

Recall that dividends are paid out of retained earnings, which is comprised of the accumulated net income (after tax) less previous dividends. So, dividends are paid from after-tax earnings.

To alleviate the double taxation on dividends, individual shareholders receive a dividend tax credit on dividends from eligible Canadian corporations. The way this works for 2009 on the tax return is that cash dividends received are grossed up 145% to determine taxable dividends. Then the tax rate is applied to the taxable dividend to determine the tax on the dividends. Finally the dividend tax credit of 18.9655% of taxable dividends is deducted from the taxes to arrive at the net tax on the dividend. For example, here is the tax calculation for someone in a combined federal/provincial 40% tax bracket who receives a $5,000 dividend from an eligible Canadian corporation.

Cash dividend	$ 5,000.00
Taxable dividends =	
Grossed up dividend (145% × $5,000)	$ 7,250.00
Marginal tax rate	40%
Tax on dividends (40% × $7,250)	$ 2,900.00
Less: Dividend tax credit (18.9655% × $7,250)	$(1,375.00)
Net taxes paid on dividends	$ 1,525.00
Effective tax rate on dividends =	
Net taxes/Dividends = $1,525/5,000)	30.50%

As a result, dividends are taxed more lightly (30.50%) than ordinary income (40%) in the hands of individuals.

SUMMARY

Significant Accounting Terms

- Asset: something the company owns.
- Liability: amount the company owes.
- Shareholders' equity: residual amount belonging to the shareholders.
- Working capital: current assets less current liabilities.
- Revenues: sales earned when the product is delivered to the customer or the job is completed.
- Expenses: costs incurred to generate the sales. Expenses are matched to revenues.
- Dividends: distribution of profits to the shareholders.

Accrual Accounting, Cash Flows, and the Matching Principle

- Accrual accounting
  - Reporting sales when made, not when the cash is collected.
  - Reporting expenses when incurred, not when paid.

- Cash flows: the measurement and timing of cash inflows and cash outflows in a business.
- Matching principle: expenses in a period are matched to the same period in which the related revenues were generated.

Financial Statements

- Income statement: measures the earnings of a company during a period.
- Statement of retained earnings: measures the changes in retained earnings for the period.
- Balance sheet: presents the financial position of the company at a certain date by showing its assets, liabilities, and shareholders' equity.
- Cash flow statement: shows where cash was obtained and where it was spent during the period.

Depreciation and Capital Cost Allowance

■ Amortization and depreciation: the apportionment of part of the cost of an asset each year to the income statement as an expense.

■ Capital cost allowance: the tax return's equivalent to depreciation expense.

■ CCA rates are specified in the *Income Tax Act* for various asset classes.

■ CCA presents additional tax complications at the end of the useful life of an asset and especially when the entire asset class is terminated.

Income Taxes

■ Taxable income is determined by starting with net income and making adjustments to arrive at taxable income.

■ Taxes payable equal the sum of, for each tax bracket, the applicable tax rate multiplied by the applicable slice of taxable income.

KEY TERMS

Asset	Expenses	Balance sheet
Liability	Dividends	Cash flow statement
Shareholders' equity	Matching principle	Amortization and depreciation
Working capital	Income statement	Capital cost allowance
Revenues	Statement of retained earnings	(CCA)

LIST OF EQUATIONS

2.1 Assets = Liabilities + Shareholders' equity

2.2 Working capital = Current assets − Current liabilities

2.3 Net income = Revenues − Expenses

2.4 Sales = Price × Quantity

2.5 Closing retained earnings = Opening retained earnings + Net income − Dividends

2.6 Taxes payable = Corporate tax rate × Taxable income

2.7 Tax saving = Tax rate × Terminal loss

2.8 Average tax rate $= \dfrac{\text{Total taxes payable}}{\text{Gross income}}$

2.9 Marginal tax rate = Tax rate on the last dollar of income

REVIEW QUESTIONS

Answers to the Review Questions can be found on the Companion Website that accompanies this text at www.pearsoned.ca/atrill.

2.1 Why is the shareholders' equity section of the balance sheet sometimes called the residual?

2.2 What makes the balance sheet balance?

2.3 Does the matching principle mean that expenses have to equal revenues? Explain.

2.4 Explain why net income is not the same as taxable income.

2.5 "Executives would prefer to show lower earnings per share because the company's tax bill will be reduced." Discuss.

PROBLEMS AND CASES

2.1 Your company is reviewing the following accounts:

Bonds payable	Inventory
Dividends	Accounts payable
Cash	Accounts receivable
Accumulated depreciation–Cars	Income taxes payable
Common shares	Net income

Required:

Group the preceding accounts as asset, liability, or shareholders' equity accounts.

2.2 Complete the following summary income statements for the year ended December 31, 2010, by calculating the missing numbers.

	A Company	B Company	C Company	D Company	E Company
Sales	_____	450,000	700,000	_____	9,458,000
Cost of goods sold	1,050,000	300,000	_____	90,900	_____
Gross profit	_____	_____	200,000	(3,000)	4,958,000
Expenses	750,000	60,000	_____	_____	_____
Net income	200,000	_____	(100,000)	(48,000)	1,079,000

2.3 (a) Complete the following income statements for the year ended December 31, 2010, by calculating the missing information.

	A Company	B Company	C Company	D Company	E Company
Sales	850,000	_____	500,000	_____	7,000,000
Cost of goods sold	_____	300,000	300,000	125,000	3,500,000
Gross profit	350,000	475,000	_____	225,000	_____
Expenses:					
Selling expenses	85,000	150,000	_____	70,000	1,500,000
Administrative expenses	125,000	_____	80,000	60,000	800,000
Depreciation expense	45,000	50,000	40,000	60,000	_____
Total expenses	_____	400,000	_____	_____	_____
EBIT	_____	_____	30,000	_____	800,000
Interest expense	10,000	_____	20,000	50,000	100,000
EBT	_____	50,000	_____	_____	_____
Income tax expense	_____	_____	4,000	(6,000)	_____
Net income	51,000	30,000	_____	_____	420,000

(b) Assuming there are no adjustments from the income statements to the tax return, calculate the income tax rate for each company.

(c) Provide a reason why company D has a negative income tax expense.

2.4 Jazz Inc. has the following statements of retained earnings for the years ended December 31, 2008 to December 31, 2010.

	2010	2009	2008	2007
Statement of Retained Earnings				
Retained earnings, 1/1	_____	_____	300,000	
Net income (loss)	(75,000)	_____	100,000	
Dividends paid	_____	56,000	45,000	
Retained earnings, 12/31	290,000	400,000	_____	300,000

Jazz Inc. has the following condensed balance sheets as at December 31 from 2008 to 2010.

	2010	2009	2008
Condensed Balance Sheet			
Current assets	150,000	_____	125,000
Property, plant, and equipment	700,000	800,000	635,000
Other assets	40,000	50,000	_____
Total assets	_____	_____	_____
Current liabilities	100,000	_____	89,000
Long-term debt	_____	400,000	250,000
Total liabilities	400,000	550,000	_____
Common shares	_____	_____	_____
Retained earnings	_____	_____	_____
Total shareholders' equity	_____	_____	_____
Total liabilities and shareholders' equity	_____	_____	_____

Required:

(a) Complete the statement of retained earnings for each year from 2008 to 2010.
(b) Complete the balance sheet for each year from 2008 to 2010, given that the common shares balance for Jazz Inc. was $200,000 in all three years.

2.5 The Jamery Goods Company has the following account balances:

Bonds payable, due 2016	$100,000
Inventory	30,000
Dividends	10,000
Accounts payable	20,000
Cash	200,000
Accounts receivable	60,000
Accumulated depreciation–Cars	30,000
Income taxes payable	15,000
Common shares	120,000
Net income	50,000
Cars	75,000
Opening retained earnings	40,000

Required:

Prepare a statement of retained earnings using whichever of the preceding accounts you need from the December 31, 2010, books of the Jamery Goods Company.

2.6 Using the data from Problem and Case 2.5, prepare a balance sheet as at December 31, 2010, for the Jamery Goods Company.

2.7 Flex Motors shows the following account balances on March 31, 2010.

Cash	$ 16,450
Accounts payable	8,230
Unearned royalty fees	5,000
Selling expenses	45,000
Dividends declared	3,500
Interest payable	6,000
Administrative expenses	25,000
Accumulated depreciation—Buildings	56,000
Cost of goods sold	135,000
Depreciation expense	14,000
Common shares	250,000
Retained earnings	55,720
Motor revenues	325,000
Buildings	450,000
Accounts receivable	17,000

Required:

(a) Prepare an income statement for the month ending March 31, 2010. Ignore income taxes.
(b) Prepare a statement of retained earnings for the month ending March 31, 2010.
(c) Prepare a balance sheet as at March 31, 2010.

2.8 The following Trial Balance exists at December 31, 2010 for Hockey Consultants Inc.

Hockey Consultants Inc.
Trial Balance
December 31, 2010

Accounts	Debit ($000s)	Credit ($000s)
Accounts payable		12,000
Accounts receivable	50,000	
Building, net	500,000	
Cash	30,000	
Consulting fees earned		550,000
Hydro expense	35,000	
Insurance expense	18,000	
Land	200,000	
Unearned consulting fees		150,000
Office salaries expense	45,000	
Prepaid insurance	9,000	
Sales salaries expense	65,000	
Supplies expense	8,000	
Common shares		200,000
Retained earnings		123,000
Dividends	75,000	
Totals	1,035,000	1,035,000

Required:

Prepare an income statement, statement of retained earnings, and a balance sheet for Hockey Consultants Inc.

2.9 Below is the Trial Balance for the MicroHard Company as at December 31, 2010.

MicroHard Company
Trial Balance
December 31, 2010

Accounts	Debit ($000s)	Credit ($000s)
Accounts payable		12,000
Accounts receivable	50,000	
Building	500,000	
Cash	30,000	
Bonds payable		327,000
Accumulated depreciation—Buildings		125,000
Land used in operations	150,000	
Notes receivable	40,000	
Notes payable		300,000
Common shares		100,000
Retained earnings		163,000
Patents	207,000	
Land not used in operations	50,000	
Totals	1,027,000	1,027,000

Notes: $20,000 of the Notes payable is due to be repaid on November 30, 2011.
$5,000 of the Notes receivable is due by November 30, 2011.

Required:

Prepare a formal balance sheet for MicroHard Company.

2.10 Laurier Baseball Inc. sells baseballs to minor league teams. Below is some data for 2010.

Unit sales price	$ 7.00
Unit cost of goods sold price	5.50
Fixed costs:	
Depreciation expense	270,000
Rent expense	500,000
Salaries	250,000
Commission expense	10% of sales revenues
Quantity sold	2,000,000

Required:

Construct an income statement for Laurier Baseball Inc. for 2010.

2.11 You have been employed for six months in the marketing department at Joe's Transports Ltd. Joe has asked for your advice on how to invest the firm's $100,000 in liquid cash since you are the most recent graduate on staff. He wants to invest in the trucking industry since that is what he understands best. He also feels the economy is improving and trucking industry profits will soar.

He has provided you with the following condensed financial statements for 2010. Healthy Movers does all the moving for its clients while Al's Co-Haul business, although less expensive, expects its clients to move the small items themselves. Healthy's shares sells for $10 per share and Al's shares sells for $2.25 per share on the Toronto Stock Exchange. Healthy's websites indicate that its long-term debt is due in five years. Al's long-term debt is due in six months.

Healthy Movers Ltd.   Al's Co-Haul Co.
Condensed Income Statements
for the year ended December 31, 2010

	$	$
Sales	550,000	800,000
Expenses	750,000	700,000
Net income	(200,000)	100,000

Healthy Movers Ltd.   Al's Co-Haul Co.
Condensed Balance Sheet
as at December 31, 2010

	$	$
Current assets	75,000	140,000
Property, plant, and equipment	350,000	500,000
Total assets	425,000	640,000
Current liabilities	32,000	200,000
Long-term debt	125,000	300,000
Total liabilities	157,000	500,000
Common shares	120,000	50,000
Retained earnings	148,000	90,000
Total shareholders' equity	268,000	140,000
Total liabilities and shareholders' equity	425,000	640,000

Required:

Recommend which company would make the better investment for Joe.

2.12

Medicine Hat ArtGlass Ltd.
Income Statement
for the year ended December 31, 2010

Sales	$	120,000
Cost of goods sold		70,000
Gross profit		50,000
Less: Loss on sale of truck		(3,000)
Less: Depreciation expense		(11,000)
Less: Other expenses		(74,800)
Net loss	$	(38,800)

Medicine Hat ArtGlass Ltd.
Statement of Retained Earnings
for the year ended December 31, 2010

Retained earnings, Jan. 1	$	76,300
Net loss		(38,800)
Less: Dividends		(20,000)
Retained earnings, Dec. 31	$	17,500

Medicine Hat ArtGlass Ltd.
Balance Sheet
as at December 31

	2010	2009
Cash	$ 62,000	$ 75,000
Accounts receivable	15,000	18,500
Inventory	47,000	42,000
Land	50,000	50,000
Buildings	145,000	145,000
Lees: Accumulated depreciation—Buildings	(110,000)	(105,000)
Furniture and equipment (F. & E.)	30,000	24,000
Less: Accumulated depreciation—F. & E.	(12,000)	(11,000)
Trucks	36,000	50,000
Less: Accumulated depreciation—Trucks	(22,000)	(26,000)
Total assets	$ 241,000	$ 262,500
Accounts payable	$ 49,000	$ 35,000
Taxes payable	4,500	6,200
Bonds payable, 2018	75,000	50,000
Common shares	95,000	95,000
Retained earnings	17,500	76,300
Total liabilities and shareholders' equity	$ 241,000	$ 262,500

Required:

(a) Calculate the difference in account balances for the balance sheet accounts between 2009 and 2010 for MHA.

(b) Prepare the cash flow from operating activities section of the cash flow statement for MHA for 2010.

2.13 Use the data in Problem and Case 2.12.

Required:

(a) Prepare a calculation to prove the net loss on the sale of the truck.

(b) Prepare the cash flow from investing activities section of the cash flow statement for MHA for 2010.

2.14 Use the data in Problem and Case 2.12.

Required:

Prepare the cash flow from financing activities section of the cash flow statement for MHA for 2010.

2.15 Use your answers to Problems and Cases 2.12 through 2.14.

Required:

(a) Prepare a summary cash flow statement showing only a single line for each of the three activity sections of the cash flow statement for MHA for 2010 and reconciling it to opening and closing cash for 2010.

(b) Did it work? Did you get the 2010 cash balance on the balance sheet? If not, check each activity section in the previous three questions and try to correct your error.

(c) Briefly explain in one sentence what happened to cash at MHA in 2010.

2.16 In 2010, the Moosonee Beer Company reported net income of $46,340, paid $20,000 in dividends, and incurred depreciation expense of $10,000, $4,200, and $2,000 on its buildings, furniture, and equipment respectively. The balance sheets for the years ended December 31, 2010 and 2009 are shown below.

	2010	2009
Current assets		
Cash	$ 25,560	$ 28,000
Accounts receivable	15,000	10,000
Inventory	45,980	60,000
Total current assets	86,540	98,000
Property, plant, and equipment		
Land	100,000	10,000
Buildings, net	250,000	260,000
Furniture, net	75,800	80,000
Equipment, net	54,600	42,000
Total, property, plant, and equipment	480,400	392,000
Intangible assets		
Patents	42,000	-
Total assets	$ 608,940	$ 490,000
Current liabilities		
Accounts payable	$ 22,600	$ 30,000
Long-term liabilities		
Bonds payable	120,000	120,000
Total liabilities	142,600	150,000
Shareholders' equity		
Common shares	400,000	300,000
Retained earnings	66,340	40,000
Total shareholders' equity	466,340	340,000
Total liabilities and shareholders' equity	$ 608,940	$ 490,000

Required:
Prepare the 2010 cash flow statement for the Moosonee Beer Company.

2.17 In 2010, Sudbury Wolverine Comics Ltd. (SWC) sold some furniture for $6,000. It had cost $10,000 and had accumulated depreciation of $4,000 associated with it. In the same year, SWC also sold a truck for $12,000 (cost: $54,000; accumulated depreciation $45,000).

Sudbury Wolverine Comics Ltd.
Income Statement
for the year ended December 31, 2010

Sales	$ 900,000
Cost of goods sold	350,000
Gross profit	550,000
Add: Gain on sale of truck	3,000
Less: Depreciation expense	(65,000)
Less: Other expenses	(67,000)
Net income	$ 421,000

Sudbury Wolverine Comics Ltd.
Statement of Retained Earnings
for the year ended December 31, 2010

Retained earnings, Jan. 1	$ 106,500
Net income	421,000
Less: Dividends	(12,500)
Retained earnings, Dec. 31	$ 515,000

Sudbury Wolverine Comics Ltd.
Balance Sheet
as at December 31

	2010	2009
Cash	$ 135,000	$ 63,500
Accounts receivable	210,000	120,000
Inventory	145,000	110,000
Land	120,000	120,000
Buildings	400,000	350,000
Accumulated depreciation—Buildings	(125,000)	(110,000)
Furniture and equipment	110,000	120,000
Accumulated depreciation—F. & E.	(55,000)	(49,000)
Trucks	325,000	254,000
Accumulated depreciation—Trucks	(100,000)	(105,000)
Total assets	**$ 1,165,000**	**$ 873,500**
Accounts payable	$ 100,000	$ 87,000
Bonds payable, 2025	300,000	430,000
Common shares	250,000	250,000
Retained earnings	515,000	106,500
Total liabilities and shareholders' equity	**$ 1,165,000**	**$ 873,500**

Required:
   (a) Calculate the gain or loss on the sale of the truck and on the sale of the furniture.
   (b) Calculate the cost of the new trucks purchased.
   (c) Prepare the 2010 statement of cash flow.

2.18 Trail Mixer Corp. earned net income of $200,000 and paid dividends of $80,500 in 2010. Depreciation expense in 2010 was: Buildings $10,000; Furniture $7,500; Equipment $14,000; and amortization expense on the copyrights was $4,000. The comparative balance sheets are shown below for 2010 and 2009.

Trail Mixer Corp.
Balance Sheet

	2010	2009
Current assets		
Cash	$ 36,500	$ 54,000
Accounts receivable	34,000	40,000
Inventory	50,000	40,000
Total current assets	120,500	134,000
Property, plant, and equipment		
Land	65,000	55,000
Buildings, net	400,000	250,000
Furniture, net	65,000	56,000
Equipment, net	125,000	86,000
Total, property, plant, and equipment	655,000	447,000
Intangible assets		
Copyrights	96,000	76,000
Total assets	$ 871,500	$ 657,000
Current liabilities		
Accounts payable	$ 40,000	$ 60,000
Long-term liabilities		
Bonds payable	300,000	185,000
Total liabilities	340,000	245,000
Shareholders' equity		
Common shares	200,000	200,000
Retained earnings	331,500	212,000
Total shareholders' equity	531,500	412,000
Total liabilities and shareholders' equity	$ 871,500	$ 657,000

Required:
  (a) Calculate the money spent on asset purchases in 2010.
  (b) Prepare the cash flow statement for 2010.

2.19 Rain Coast Adventures Ltd. acquired a new ski lift on January 1, Year 1, for $1,500,000. It has an esti-
     mated useful economic life of 10 years with no residual value. The ski lift has a CCA rate of 20%.

Required:
Compare accounting straight-line depreciation and net book value with tax return CCA and UCC for the 10-year
life of the ski lift.

2.20 Tim's Bits and Drills Inc. has had the following results over the past five fiscal years.

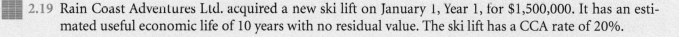

	2006	2007	2008	2009	2010
Net income	$100,000	$150,000	$200,000	$250,000	$300,000
Taxable income	$ 52,000	$ 75,000	$ 98,000	$121,000	$144,000
Tax rate	30%	34%	45%	48%	28%

Required:

    (a) Calculate income taxes payable for each year.

    (b) Describe two things that might cause the difference between net income and taxable income.

2.21 On January 1, 2010 Hudson Semiconductor Limited acquired a new wafer pressing machine at a cost of $500,000. The estimated economic life of this machine is 10 years, at which time it can be sold for $10,000 scrap value. Hudson uses the straight-line depreciation method. This machine qualifies for a capital cost allowance of 30%. The corporate tax rate is 35%.

Required:

    (a) Calculate the amount of depreciation expense for 2010.

    (b) Calculate the capital cost allowance for 2010.

    (c) How much tax saving did Hudson receive in 2010 as a result of purchasing the new machine?

2.22

Required:

Using the data provided in Problem and Case 2.21, complete the required questions for the year 2011.

2.23 Maritime Breweries Limited reported the following results for 2010.

Earnings before income taxes	$5,025,000
Depreciation expense	$1,250,000
UCC—Buildings, Jan. 1, 2010	$ 3,000,000
CCA rate—Buildings	4%
UCC—Machines, Jan. 1, 2010	$5,600,000
CCA rate—Machines	20%
UCC—Vehicles, Jan. 1, 2010	$ 800,000
CCA rate—Vehicles	30%

Required:

    (a) Calculate taxable income for 2010.

    (b) Calculate taxes payable for 2010, assuming a corporate tax rate of 35%.

2.24 The president of Fallen Down Gold Mines stated, "The company does not have sufficient cash to pay its $2 million dividend in 2010." During his speech, he said that cash inflows from operations are expected to be $2,500,000, cash outflows from investing are expected to be $(1,400,000), and cash inflows from financing are expected to be $500,000.

Required:

    (a) How might you determine whether the president's statement is accurate?

    (b) What is the minimum amount of the opening cash balance required in order to pay the $2 million dividend and remain with a cash balance of $350,000 at the end of this year?

CHAPTER 3

Financial Planning and Pro Forma Financial Statements

LEARNING OUTCOMES

When you have completed this chapter, you should be able to:

1 Explain the role of pro forma financial statements in the planning process.

2 Prepare pro forma financial statements for a business and explain their usefulness for decision-making purposes.

3 Use breakeven analysis techniques.

4 Discuss the strengths and weaknesses of the percent-of-sales method as an alternative method of preparing forecast financial statements.

5 Explain the ways in which managers can use pro forma financial statements to consider the problems of risk and uncertainty.

6 Explain how managers use the pro forma financial statements and cash budgets for control purposes.

INTRODUCTION

In this chapter, we take a look at pro forma financial statements. These statements play an important role in the planning process and, in particular, in assessing the impact of management decisions on the performance and position of a business. We shall see how these statements are prepared and what issues are involved in their preparation.

PLANNING FOR THE FUTURE

In this section, we briefly examine the planning process within a business and then, in later sections, go on to consider the ways in which those plans are expressed in financial terms.

Developing plans for a business involves the following key steps as depicted in Figure 3.1:

1. *Establishing the aims and objectives of the business, such as being the low-cost provider of goods in our segment of the marketplace, or selling the highest quality goods, or offering the best choice of products.* These should provide a clear sense of direction.
2. *Identifying the options available, such as opening new stores, carrying new product lines, or foreign expansion.* This will involve collecting information, which can be extremely time consuming, particularly when the business is considering entering new markets or investing in new technology.

3. *Evaluating the options and making a selection.* Each option must be examined to see whether it fits with the objectives and to assess whether it is feasible to provide the resources required. The effect of each option on the future financial performance of the business must also be considered. It is in this final part—the financial evaluation of the various options—that pro forma financial statements have a valuable role to play.

FIGURE 3.1 Steps in the Planning Process

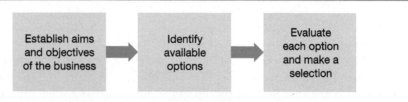

L.0. 1 THE ROLE OF PRO FORMA FINANCIAL STATEMENTS

Pro forma financial statements describe the predicted financial outcome of a particular course of action. By showing the financial implications of certain decisions, managers should be able to allocate resources in a more efficient and effective manner. REAL WORLD 3.1 discusses a pro forma financial disclosure for the merger of two large Canadian energy companies.

REAL WORLD 3.1 Suncor Buys Petro Canada

On August 3, 2009, Suncor Energy of Calgary completed a merger with Petro Canada. A press release showed that Suncor prepared pro forma financial statements for the combined companies. These pro forma statements indicated the combined companies would have a strong balance sheet. Total debt would be only 29.6% of assets. Furthermore, the combined companies will be large enough to compete globally. Suncor is a large player in the Canadian oil sands at Fort McMurray, Alberta.

Source: Suncor Energy website: www.suncor.com/en/newsroom/2418.aspx?id=2375, accessed August 18, 2009.

The pro forma financial statements will normally comprise:

- A pro forma income statement
- A pro forma statement of retained earnings
- A pro forma balance sheet.

In addition, a cash budget is usually prepared. When taken together, these documents will provide a comprehensive picture of likely future performance and position. Pro forma statements are projections of what management expects or hopes will happen in the future. As such, pro forma financial statements cannot be audited in the usual sense of the word. Investors should keep this in mind when reading pro forma financial information.

The preparation of pro forma statements will provide valuable insight into the probable effect of the particular course of action on the future financial performance of the business. Where, for example, a business is considering a move to increase market share, managers will need to know the likely effect on profits and whether the resources are adequate to sustain the planned growth in sales.

When managers are developing plans for the future, they typically use a forecast horizon of three to five years and prepare pro forma financial statements for each year of the forecast period for each option being considered. When we examine the preparation of these statements later in the chapter, however, we shall deal with a shorter time period for the sake of simplicity. The main principles of preparation are not affected by the particular forecast horizon.

For pro forma financial statements to be useful, they should be as reliable as possible. The shorter the forecast horizon, the more accurate the forecast is likely to be. Other techniques used to analyze key variables affecting accuracy (such as sensitivity analysis, scenario analysis, and simulations) are discussed later in the chapter.

Pro forma financial statements are prepared for management purposes. Only on rare occasions, such as when new financing is being sought, will external parties see these statements. The reasons for keeping the statements within the business are often that publication may damage the competitive position of the business or that the statements may be misunderstood by investors. Some large businesses do, however, publish key figures based on projections that have been made; these figures are usually forecast sales and profit figures for the forthcoming three, six, or twelve months. REAL WORLD 3.2 discusses the sales and earnings per share forecast figures for a major phone company.

Bell Canada Raises 2009 EPS Forecast

BCE, otherwise known as Bell Canada, of Montreal, issued a press release on August 6, 2009, that raised their revenue and earnings per share forecast for the rest of the year. In February, BCE had forecast EPS to grow around 5%. Only four months later, the year was going so well that BCE raised its EPS guidance to between $2.40 and $2.50. This represents an increase of between 7% and 11%. BCE is Canada's largest telecommunications company.

Source: BCE News Release, http://www.bce.ca/en/news/releases/corp/2009/08/06/75186.html, accessed August 18, 2009.

PREPARING PRO FORMA FINANCIAL STATEMENTS

L.O. 2

In the sections that follow, we look at some of the issues involved in developing pro forma financial statements. Because the main purpose of this chapter is to discuss the preparation of pro forma statements and their usefulness, we shall deal fairly briefly with the forecasting issues.

Preparing pro forma financial statements involves four major steps:

1. Identify the factors that will affect the pro forma statements
2. Forecast the sales for the period
3. Forecast the remaining elements of the financial statements
4. Prepare the pro forma financial statements.

Step 1: Identify the Factors That Provide a Framework for the Pro Forma Statements

Opportunities and Threats

External factors such as changes in government policy and in key economic factors can have a significant effect on future performance. In particular, expected changes to the following must be identified:

- Corporate income tax rate
- Interest rates
- Inflation rate
- GDP growth rate.

A great deal of published information is usually available to help identify these expected changes. Take care, however, to ensure that the particular impact of any changes on the business is properly taken into account. When estimating the likely rate of inflation, for example, separately consider each major category of item affected by inflation. Using an average rate of inflation for all items is usually inappropriate, as levels of inflation can vary significantly between items.

Strengths and Weaknesses

Internal factors cover policies and agreements to which the business is committed. Examples include:

- Capital expenditure commitments
- Financing agreements
- Inventory policies
- Credit period allowed to customers
- Payment policies for accounts payable
- Accounting policies (for example, depreciation rates)
- Dividend policy.

Dividend policy may require some clarification. For large businesses at least, a target level of dividends is often established, from which managers are usually reluctant to deviate. The target may be linked to the level of profits for the particular year and/or to dividends paid in previous years. (This issue is discussed in more detail in Chapter 11.)

Step 2: Forecast the Sales for the Period

The usual starting point is to forecast sales for the period. Sales are regarded as a key element within the financial statements, because the level of sales will normally determine the level of operating activity for the period. This means that other elements of the financial statements—such as inventory, receivables, and payables—are influenced by the level of sales.

Producing a reliable sales forecast involves understanding the competitive environment and deciding upon a particular approach to forecasting. Each of these is considered below.

The Competitive Environment

To understand the likely competitive environment, managers must examine the general economic conditions, the industry in which the business operates, and the potential threat posed by major competitors.

- *General economic conditions.* Most businesses are affected by economic cycles. During an upturn in a cycle, sales and profits will increase and businesses will increase their scale of operations. During a downturn in a cycle, sales and profits will decrease and businesses will decrease their scale of operations. The particular phase of the economic cycle can, therefore, exert a significant influence on sales.

The economy has a history of going through these types of ups and downs (business cycles). Governments and business managers need to have a good grasp of macro-economics. A company does not want to be pursuing a significant expansion, such as building a new factory, when the economy goes into a recession. If a company gets caught unawares in the midst of a downturn in the economy, a good strategy is to mothball the project until the economy rights itself. Companies will cut back on capital expenditures during a recession to conserve cash.

A severe global recession occurred in 2008–2009. It was the worst recession since the end of World War II in 1945. Some commentators have called it the first credit recession. People stopped buying because they could not get credit (or loans) from the banks to buy things. Companies were then forced to lay off workers because sales had dropped. REAL WORLD 3.3 shows some examples of sales declines at Canadian businesses during the second quarter of 2009. The lack of credit after the collapse of the big investment bank Lehman Brothers dramatically worsened the recession already underway as panicked banks stopped lending even to each other.

REAL WORLD 3.3

Sales Slump in a Recession

As shown below, some companies can lose a significant portion of their business during a recession. Both Gildan, in the clothing business, and CN Rail incurred double-digit sales declines during the April–June 2009 quarter. Canadian Tire's business was more stable during the recession.

Sales Declines in 2009 versus 2008

	Gildan		Canadian Tire		CN Rail	
	First Quarter of 2009	Second Quarter of 2009	First Quarter of 2009	Second Quarter of 2009	First Quarter of 2009	Second Quarter of 2009
Sales	−16.68%	−19.17%	−3.68%	−5.14%	−3.53%	−15.11%

Source: Compiled from interim financial reports obtained at www.sedar.com/, accessed August 19, 2009.

On the other hand, the Great Depression of the 1930s originated as a demand-based slow-down. Layoffs far greater than those of the 2008–2009 severe recession ensued. At the trough of the Depression well over 20% of the workforce had been idled. With so many out of work, consumers did not have much money to spend so aggregate demand in the economy fell. The governments of the day made policy errors such as increasing tariffs, sparking trade wars, and increasing taxes, which further reduced demand.

That is why we saw governments respond so vigorously to the Great Recession of 2008–2009 with stimulus packages. Economists have learned from the past and the hope is to revive the credit markets and stimulate demand.

- *The industry.* Carefully examine the industry factors that can influence sales, including:
  - Market size and growth prospects
  - Level of competition within the industry
  - Bargaining power of customers
  - Threat of substitute products or services.

- *Competitive analysis.*   Estimate the threat posed by major competitors, through **competitor profiling**. This involves developing a profile of each major competitor by gathering information about its:
  - Goals and strategies
  - Resources (including financial, technological, and human resources)
  - Products and/or services being developed
  - Strategic partnerships and joint ventures with other businesses that affect market power
  - Cost structures, profits, and sales.

This information can help in assessing a major competitor's ability to upset the business's sales plans and initiatives. Competitive information is not always easy to obtain, as businesses are reluctant to release information that may damage their competitive position. Nevertheless, there are sources of information that can be used to help build a picture of competitors, such as their published financial statements (which are obligatory for publicly traded companies), media reports, industry reports, physical observation, and information gathered from customers and suppliers.

Forecasting Approaches

Once the competitive environment is understood, an approach to forecasting sales must be selected. There are two main approaches to sales forecasting:

1. *Subjective approach.*   This approach normally relies on the views of the sales force or sales managers. It is a bottom-up approach that involves aggregating forecasts from those with specialist knowledge of particular products, services, or market segments. It is often useful for fairly short forecasting horizons. However, take care to ensure that sales forecasts are realistic.
2. *Objective approach.*   This approach relies on statistical techniques or, in the case of very large businesses (such as multinational automobile manufacturers), econometric models. These techniques and models can range from simple extrapolation of past trends to extremely sophisticated models that incorporate a large number of variables with complex interrelationships.

It may be useful to use more than one approach. By using sales managers' forecasts and statistical analysis, a cross-check on the accuracy of the forecast figures may be achieved. In addition, the sales forecast, however derived, may be modified if senior managers believe that proper account has not been taken of external and internal factors and the competitive environment.

Step 3: Forecast the Remaining Elements of the Financial Statements

Once the level of sales has been estimated, the items appearing in the cash budget, income statement, statement of retained earnings, and balance sheet will be forecast.

Forecasting Operating Costs

Let us begin by considering how operating costs can be forecast. It was mentioned earlier that the level of sales will have an influence on many other items in the financial statements, including certain costs. However, not all costs relating to a business will vary with the level of sales. Although some costs vary in direct proportion to the level of sales, other costs are unaffected by the level of sales during a period. Activity 3.1 considers the different types of costs.

ACTIVITY 3.1

Try to identify two costs that are likely to vary in direct proportion to the level of sales, and two costs that are likely to stay constant no matter what the level of sales.

Solution

Costs of goods sold, royalty payments to authors, and sales force commissions are examples of costs that vary in direct proportion to sales output. These are referred to as variable costs. Other costs—such as depreciation, rent, insurance, and salaries—may stay fixed during a period, no matter what the level of sales generated. These are referred to as fixed costs.

Some costs have both a variable and a fixed element and so may vary partially with sales output. These are referred to as **mixed costs**. These costs may be identified by examining past records of the business. Heating and lighting costs may be examples of a mixed cost. A certain amount of heating and lighting will be incurred no matter what the level of sales. If, however, overtime is being worked due to heavy demand, these costs will increase. Mixed costs can be broken down into their fixed and variable elements (perhaps using a statistical technique such as regression analysis). Once this has been done, the total variable costs and total fixed costs can be established. By splitting costs into their fixed and variable elements, it is possible to forecast the likely impact of a particular level of sales output much more reliably.

As the total costs of a business have both a variable and a fixed element, they will rise directly, but not proportionately, with the level of output. The behaviour of total costs in relation to the level of activity is shown in Figure 3.2.

The forecast of sales and operating costs—along with forecasts of corporate tax rates, interest rates, and dividend policy—will provide the basis for preparing the forecast income statement and statement of retained earnings for the period.

FIGURE 3.2   Graph of Total Cost Against the Level of Activity

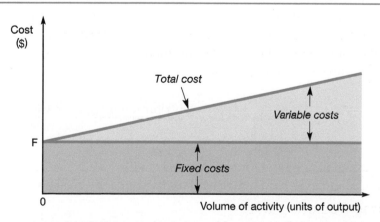

The bottom part of the graph represents the fixed cost element. To this is added the wedge-shaped top portion, which represents the variable costs. The two parts together represent total costs. At zero level of output, the variable costs are zero so total costs equal fixed costs. As activity increases so do the total costs, but only because variable costs increase.

L.O. 3

Breakeven (B/E) Analysis

A company's breakeven point occurs when its sales equal its costs; that is, its net income is zero. A breakeven analysis can be done for the company as a whole, but often it is useful to determine the breakeven point for a particular product line. The breakeven point can be determined as dollars of sales, but it is often helpful to divide the sales by the selling price to obtain the number of units the company must sell to break even.

Breakeven analysis is especially useful in determining whether a new product for the company might be successful. By comparing the breakeven number of units it needs to sell with the size of the overall market, management can determine whether this product has a realistic chance of earning a profit for the company.

For example, assume that CFL Apparel Ltd. is a small business that produces and sells officially licensed football apparel in Canada. CFL Apparel has gathered the following information on its best seller, a football jersey.

Official Football Jersey Data		
Selling Price (SP)	$	100
Variable costs (VC)	$	60
Fixed costs (FC)	$	500,000

Equation 3.1 shows that the contribution margin is the difference between the selling price and the variable cost for a jersey.

$$\text{Contribution margin (CM)} = \text{SP} - \text{VC} \qquad \text{3.1}$$

So the contribution margin for CFL Apparel is $100 - $60 = $40.

Since the breakeven point occurs when total revenues exactly match total costs, Equation 3.2 shows how to calculate the breakeven point in terms of number of units.

$$\text{Breakeven point for number of units} = \frac{\text{Fixed costs}}{\text{Contribution margin}} = \frac{\text{FC}}{\text{CM}} \qquad \text{3.2}$$

The B/E units for CFL Apparel = $500,000 ÷ $40 = 12,500 units.

Equation 3.3 expresses the contribution margin as a percentage of sales. This is known as the contribution margin ratio.

$$\text{Contribution margin ratio} = \frac{\text{Contribution margin}}{\text{Sales}} = \frac{\text{CM}}{\text{Sales}} \qquad \text{3.3}$$

The contribution margin ratio for CFL Apparel is $40 ÷ $100 = 40%.
The contribution margin ratio can be used to determine the breakeven sales as shown in Equation 3.4.

$$\text{Breakeven sales} = \frac{\text{Fixed costs}}{\text{Contribution margin ratio}} = \frac{\text{FC}}{\text{CM ratio}} \qquad \text{3.4}$$

The B/E sales for CFL Apparel = $500,000 ÷ 40% = $1,250,000.

Equation 3.5 also shows how to calculate the breakeven sales.

Breakeven sales = Breakeven sales units × Unit sales price   3.5

For CFL Apparel, the breakeven sales is 12,500 units × $100 unit selling price = $1,250,000, as shown in the income statement in Activity 3.2 and as obtained with Equation 3.4.

ACTIVITY 3.2

Prove that the breakeven point really is 12,500 units by preparing an income statement for CFL Apparel for sales of 12,500 units.

Solution

CFL Apparel Ltd.
Breakeven Income Statement

Sales (12,500 × $100)		$1,250,000
Variable costs (12,500 × $60)	$ 750,000	
Fixed costs	500,000	
Total costs		1,250,000
Net income		nil

It is possible to solve the breakeven point graphically as shown in Figure 3.3. First, you should generate data points as shown in Table 3.1. For example, at zero unit sales you still have the fixed costs. At sales of 2,000 units, sales are 2,000 × $100 = $200,000. Fixed costs are $500,000 plus variable costs of 2,000 units × $60 = $120,000. Total costs amount to $620,000. There is a net loss of $200,000 minus $620,000 = $(420,000).

FIGURE 3.3   Breakeven Chart

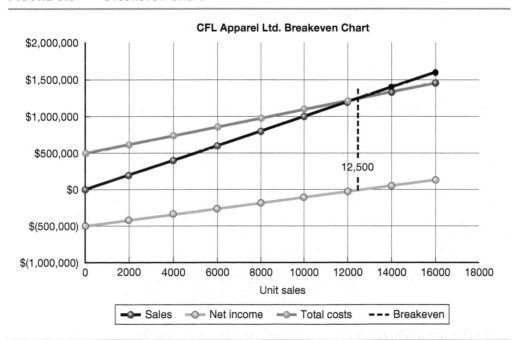

TABLE 3.1   Data for Breakeven Chart

Unit sales	Sales	Total Costs	Net Income (Loss)
0	$ 0	$ 500,000	$(500,000)
2,000	200,000	620,000	(420,000)
4,000	400,000	740,000	(340,000)
6,000	600,000	860,000	(260,000)
8,000	800,000	980,000	(180,000)
10,000	1,000,000	1,100,000	(100,000)
12,000	1,200,000	1,220,000	(20,000)
14,000	1,400,000	1,340,000	60,000
16,000	1,600,000	1,460,000	140,000

Then the graph is drawn. Figure 3.3 shows that the breakeven point can be read from the graph in two ways. Once you become confident in using this technique, you do not not have to use both methods, although one serves to check on the other.

1. The breakeven unit sales point is the point at which the sales line crosses the total costs line. You can see from the dashed line on the graph that the breakeven point is at 12,500 units.
2. The second way to see the breakeven point is to read the point at which the net income line becomes zero. This occurs at 12,500 units. By definition, when net income is zero, that is the breakeven point.

SELF-ASSESSMENT QUESTION   3.1

Lizard Gameware Inc. has created a new dinosaur game with the following price and cost characteristics:

Selling price (SP)	$ 46
Variable costs (VC)	$ 21
Fixed costs (FC)	$130,000

Required:

(a) Calculate the breakeven point in units for the game.
(b) Draw a breakeven graph for the new game.

Operating Leverage

Operating leverage refers to the idea that a small increase in sales may have a large impact on earnings before interest and taxes (EBIT). If a firm has a relatively high fixed cost structure, its operating leverage is higher compared to a firm with relatively more variable costs. The reason for its higher leverage is that it is able to spread its fixed costs over more sales to achieve a lower cost per unit sold than the firm with more variable costs. More sales go directly to the bottom line (EBIT).

Equation 3.6 shows how to calculate operating leverage.

$$\text{Operating leverage} = \frac{\% \text{ Change in EBIT}}{\% \text{ Change in sales}} \qquad 3.6$$

In Figure 3.4, House Ltd. has an increase in sales of 20% [($600,000 − $500,000) ÷ $500,000] and an increase in EBIT of 50% [($300,000 − $200,000) ÷ $200,000]. The

FIGURE 3.4   Illustration of Operating Leverage

	Tree Limited			House Limited		
	2010	**2011**	**Percent Change**	**2010**	**2011**	**Percent Change**
Sales	$500,000	$600,000	20%	$500,000	$600,000	20%
Fixed Costs	200,000	200,000		300,000	300,000	
EBIT	$300,000	$400,000	33%	$200,000	$300,000	50%
Operating Leverage		33%/20%	1.67		50%/20%	2.5

operating leverage for House is 2.5 (50% ÷ 20%) using Equation 3.6. Similarly, Tree Ltd. has an increase in sales of 20% and an increase in EBIT of 33% [($400,000 − $300,000) ÷ $300,000]. The operating leverage for Tree is 1.67 (33% ÷ 20%) using Equation 3.6.

The reason for the higher operating leverage at House is that it had a 60% fixed cost structure in 2010 ($300,000 ÷ $500,000 − 60%) compared to only 40% at Tree ($200,000) ÷ $500,000 = 40%). Both companies enjoyed the classic economic benefit of spreading their fixed costs over more units of sales, but House benefited more than Tree because it has more fixed costs.

Forecasting Assets, Liabilities, and Capital

The level of sales will have an effect on the level of some assets and liabilities held. When sales increase, there will be an automatic increase in some items See Activity 3.3.

ACTIVITY 3.3

Can you think of two items (in both assets or liabilities) that will increase automatically as a result of an increase in the level of sales?

Solution

An increase in the level of sales is likely to lead to:

■ An increase in accounts receivable, and
■ An increase in inventory to meet the increase in demand.

An increase in the level of sales should also lead to:

■ An increase in accounts payable as a result of increased purchases, and
■ An increase in accrued expenses as a result of increased costs.

The particular policies adopted by the business (for example, to offer customers a one-month credit period or to hold inventory equivalent to two months' sales) can help determine the amounts of current assets and current liabilities held at the end of the forecast period. These amounts are needed to prepare the forecast balance sheet.

An increase in sales may also lead to an increase in long-term capital assets if the business is already being operated at full capacity. If this is not the case, an increase in sales may simply absorb excess capacity. A temporary decrease in sales will probably have no effect on the level of capital assets.

Long-term debt and common shares will not increase automatically with increases in sales. These amounts, which appear on the balance sheet, will remain unchanged unless management decides otherwise. However, retained earnings will change as a result of any profits (losses) and dividends for the period, and therefore retained earnings have an indirect relationship to sales.

Forecasting Cash Budget Items

A cash budget is useful because it helps to identify changes in the liquidity of a business over time. Cash has been described as the lifeblood of a business. It is vital for a business to have sufficient liquid resources to meet its obligations. Failure to maintain an adequate level of liquidity can have disastrous consequences for the business. The cash budget helps to assess the impact of expected future events on the cash balance as well as other working capital items like accounts receivable and accounts payable that appear on the pro forma balance sheet. So the cash budget is a first step toward preparing the pro forma balance sheet. It will identify periods where there are cash surpluses and cash deficits and will allow managers to plan for these occurrences. Where there is a cash surplus, managers should consider the profitable investment of the cash. Where there is a cash deficit, managers should consider the ways in which this can be financed.

The main sources of cash inflows and outflows are set out in Figure 3.5.

FIGURE 3.5   The Main Sources of Cash Inflows and Outflows

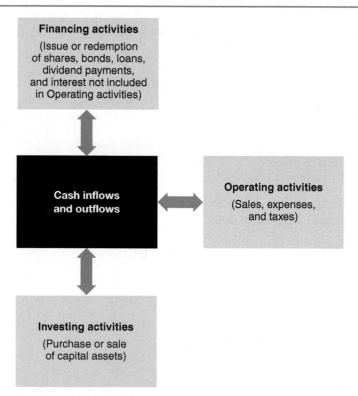

The direction of the arrows indicates that both inflows and outflows arise for each source.

When preparing the cash budget for a fairly short period, such as six months, it is often useful to provide a monthly breakdown of the cash inflows and outflows. This helps managers to closely monitor changes in the cash position of the business. The further the business projects its cash budget into the future, however, the more difficult it becomes to provide a monthly breakdown.

Cash flow used in finance to make decisions looks to the future as opposed to the formal cash flow statement covered in Chapter 2, which only covers the past. Once the sales, costs, and changes to the assets and liabilities have been forecast, all of the information needed to forecast the cash budget items for the period is available. It is a relatively simple matter to identify cash received from customers, payments to suppliers, payments for operating costs, and the cash flow effects of changes in assets and liabilities.

Example 3.1 below provides a simple demonstration of how this may be done. The amount of cash that is forecast to be received from customers is calculated to illustrate the process.

Example 3.1

Assume that:

1. The opening balance of accounts receivable is $200,000 (representing the previous month's sales).
2. Sales for the month are forecast to be $300,000, of which 80% are on credit.
3. The business allows one month's credit to its credit customers.
4. What is the cash received from sales during the month?

Solution

The cash received from customers during the month will be:

Opening accounts receivable	$200,000
Sales for the month	300,000
Total amount due	500,000
Less: Closing accounts receivable (80% × $300,000)	240,000
Cash received from customers	$260,000

Alternatively, the cash received from customers can be calculated as follows:

Cash from last month's accounts receivable	$200,000
Cash from this month's sales (20% × $300,000)	60,000
Cash received from customers	$260,000

A similar approach can be taken for other cash budget items mentioned.

Example 3.2 shows another cash budget.

Example 3.2   A Cash Budget

Flex Systems Inc. starts the year on January 1, 2010, with $35,000 cash in the bank. Credit sales for November and December 2009, and January, February, and March 2010 were $15,000, $20,000, $15,000, $20,000, and $35,000 respectively. It has been the traditional pattern that 70% of sales are collected in the month following the sale and the remainder is collected in the second month following the sale. Monthly cash expenses are $25,000.

Required:
Prepare a cash budget for the first three months of 2010 showing opening cash, cash collections, cash expenditures, and closing balance.

Solution

	Nov. 2009	Dec. 2009	Jan. 2010	Feb. 2010	Mar. 2010
Sales	$15,000	$20,000	$15,000	$20,000	$35,000
Opening cash			$35,000	$28,500	$20,000
Collections					
70% of 1 month ago			14,000	10,500	14,000
30% of 2 months ago			4,500	6,000	4,500
Total collections			18,500	16,500	18,500
Payments			(25,000)	(25,000)	(25,000)
Ending cash		$35,000	$28,500	$20,000	$13,500

The January 2010 cash collections consist of 70% of the December 2009 sales (i.e., 70% × $20,000 = $14,000) plus 30% of the November 2009 sales (i.e., 30% × $15,000 = $4,500), for a total cash inflow of $18,500. Analyzing the December 2009 sales balance of $20,000, we see that $14,000 (i.e., 70%) is collected in January and $6,000 (i.e., 30%) is collected in February.

To illustrate the preparation of the cash budget and the pro forma financial statements, consider Example 3.3—the solution to which will be presented over the next several pages.

Example 3.3

Designer Dresses Limited is a small business to be formed by James and William Clark to sell an exclusive range of dresses from a boutique in a fashionable area of Toronto. On January 1, they plan to invest a total of $50,000 cash to acquire 25,000 shares each in the business ($1 per share). Of this, $30,000 is to be invested in new equipment in January. The equipment is to be depreciated over three years on the straight-line basis (the scrap value is assumed to be zero at the end of the equipment's life). The straight-line basis of depreciation allocates the total amount evenly over the life of the asset. In this case, a half-year's depreciation is to be charged in the first six months. The sales and purchases projections for the business are as follows:

	Jan.	Feb.	Mar.	Apr.	May	Jun.	Total
Sales ($000)	10.2	30.6	30.6	40.8	40.8	51.0	204.0
Purchases of							
inventory ($000)	20.0	30.0	25.0	25.0	30.0	30.0	160.0
Other costs ($000)[*]	9.0	9.0	9.0	9.0	9.0	9.0	54.0

[*]Other costs include wages but exclude depreciation.

The sales will all be made by credit card. The credit card business will take one month to pay and will deduct its fee of 2% of gross sales before paying amounts due to Designer Dresses. One month's credit is allowed by suppliers. Other costs shown above do not include rent of $10,000 per quarter, payable on January 1 and April 1. All other costs will be paid in cash. Closing inventory at the end of June is expected to be $58,000. No dividends will be paid.

Ignore taxation. For your convenience you are advised to work to the nearest thousand dollars.

Required:

(a) Prepare a cash budget for the six months to June 30.
(b) Prepare a pro forma income statement for the six months to June 30.
(c) Prepare a pro forma statement of retained earnings for the six months to June 30.
(d) Prepare a pro forma balance sheet at June 30.

(Note that, for the sake of simplicity, the example considers only one course of action and all of the forecast figures are provided for use in preparing the pro forma financial statements. This should help in understanding the main principles of preparing pro forma financial statements.)

There is no set format for the cash budget, as it is normally used for internal purposes only. Managers are free to decide on the form of presentation that best suits their needs. Activity 3.4 (see page 74) shows a cash budget for Designer Dresses Limited for the six months to June 30. This format seems to be widely used.

We can see from Activity 3.4 that:

■ Immediately below the monthly total for cash inflows, the cash outflows are set out and a monthly total for these is also shown.
■ The difference between the monthly totals of cash inflows and outflows is the *net cash flow* for the month.
■ If we add this net cash flow to the opening cash balance, which has been brought forward from the previous month, we obtain the closing cash balance. (This will become the opening cash balance in the next month.)

When preparing a cash budget, two questions must be asked concerning each item of information that is presented:

1. *Does the item of information concern a cash transaction (that is, does it involve cash inflows or outflows)?* If the answer to this question is no, then the information should be ignored when preparing this statement. For example, depreciation expense does not involve cash. If the item involves cash then ask:
2. *When did the cash transaction take place?* It is important to identify the particular month in which cash is collected or paid. Where sales and purchases are made on credit, the cash flows will often take place after the month in which the sale or purchase takes place.

Problems in preparing cash budgets usually arise because these two questions have not been properly addressed. It is worth emphasizing that the format used is for internal reporting purposes only and differs from the formal cash flow statement we saw in Chapter 2.

ACTIVITY 3.4

Prepare the cash budget for Designer Dresses Limited for each month of the six months ending June 30 using the information contained in Example 3.3.

Solution

The pro forma cash budget for the six months to June 30 is:

Designer Dresses Limited
Pro Forma Cash Budget
for the six months ending June 30

	Jan. ($000)	Feb. ($000)	Mar. ($000)	Apr. ($000)	May. ($000)	Jun. ($000)
Cash inflows						
Issue of shares	50					
Collections of accounts receivable	–	10	30	30	40	40
Total inflows	50	10	30	30	40	40
Cash outflows						
Payment of accounts payable	–	20	30	25	25	30
Other cash costs	9	9	9	9	9	9
Rent payments	10	–	–	10	–	–
Equipment purchases	30	–	–	–	–	–
Total outflows	49	29	39	44	34	39
Net cash flow	1	(19)	(9)	(14)	6	1
Opening cash balance	–	1	(18)	(27)	(41)	(35)
Closing cash balance	1	(18)	(27)	(41)	(35)	(34)

Notes

1. The receipts from credit sales will arise one month after the sale has taken place. Hence, cash from January's sales of 10.2 will be collected in February, less the 2% credit card fee, rounded. Similarly, accounts payable are paid one month after the goods have been purchased.
2. The closing cash balance for each month is obtained by adding to (or subtracting from) the opening balance, the net cash flow for the month.
3. The closing cash balance for June, $(34), appears on the June 30 pro forma balance sheet as a bank overdraft.

Companies will not normally collect all accounts receivable amounts in the month following the sale even if credit terms require customers to pay within 30 days. Usually, these amounts are spread over several months. Some are never collected and become bad debts that are written off. In addition, companies may sometimes delay payment to suppliers in an effort to conserve cash. In general, considerable attention must be paid to understanding the exact timing of cash flows in a business. Example 3.4 illustrates some timing issues connected with accounts receivable and accounts payable.

Example 3.4

Akawzi Ltd. is in the early stages of developing a cash budget for next year. Akawzi has recently completed its projected monthly sales and purchase requirements for next year. Twenty percent of total sales are expected to be cash sales, with 40% of total sales to be collected in the month following the sale and the remainder one month after that. Bad debts are negligible. Thirty percent of purchases are cash purchases, 40% will be paid one month after purchase, and the remainder will be paid in the second month after purchase.

Activity 3.5 asks you to consider the timing of cash flows for sales and inventory purchases.

ACTIVITY 3.5

Given that sales for Akawzi Ltd., in thousands, for January are $100 and purchases, in thousands, for January are $150, prepare the cash receipt and cash payment schedule for the first three months of the year using the January data only.

	Total	Jan.	Feb.	Mar.
Cash Receipts				
Sales				
January	$100	$20	$40	$40
Cash Payments				
Purchases				
January	$150	$45	$60	$45

Solution

January cash sales total 20% × $100 = $20. February collections of the January sales amount to 40% × $100 = $40. Finally, March collections of the January sales total 40% × $100 = $40.

In a similar fashion for purchases, payments in January are 30% × $150 = $45. Payments in February for the January purchases amount to 40% × $150 = $60. Finally, March payments for January's purchases are 30% × $150 = $45.

This activity represents the first lines in the Cash Receipts and Cash Payments section shown in Activity 3.6 with other months layered in.

As you can see in Activity 3.6, the timing of cash inflows and cash outflows is fairly straightforward. For each month, cash flows from sales and purchases are spread over three months. For each month, total sales equal the total amount eventually collected, since bad debts are negligible in this example. For instance, total sales are $120 for February. This sum is collected in amounts of $24 in February, $48 in March, and $48 in April, for a total of $120, exactly equal to the February sales. The same goes for purchases, which, for example, are $224 for December. These are paid as follows: $67 in December, $90 in January, and $67 in February for a total amount paid of $224. This equals the total December purchases.

ACTIVITY 3.6

Sales, in thousands, for Akawzi Ltd. are forecast to be $100 in January. Sales are expected to grow by $20 (thousand) each month. Inventory purchases, in thousands, are forecast to be $150 in January and only $84 in February. Thereafter purchases are expected to grow by $14 (thousand) each month.

Required:

Prepare the monthly cash budget for Akawzi Ltd. for next year's sales and purchases given that Akawzi starts the year with $50 (thousand) cash in the bank. Be sure to show, for each month, the collection of its accounts receivable, total monthly receipts, payment for its purchases, total payments, and net cash flows.

Solution

Akawzi Ltd
Cash Budget
($ thousands)

Sales	Total Sales	Jan.	Feb.	Mar.	Apr.	May	Jun.	Jul.	Aug.	Sep.	Oct.	Nov.	Dec.	Jan.	Feb.	Total Cash Collections
Cash Receipts						Cash Inflows From Sales										
Jan.	100	20	40	40												100
Feb.	120		24	48	48											120
Mar.	140			28	56	56										140
Apr.	160				32	64	64									160
May	180					36	72	72								180
Jun.	200						40	80	80							200
Jul.	220							44	88	88						220
Aug.	240								48	96	96					240
Sep.	260									52	104	104				260
Oct.	280										56	112	112			280
Nov.	300											60	120	120		300
Dec.	320												64	128	128	320
Total Receipts Per Month		20	64	116	136	156	176	196	216	236	256	276	296	248	128	2,520

Purchases	Total Purchases	Jan.	Feb.	Mar.	Apr.	May	Jun.	Jul.	Aug.	Sep.	Oct.	Nov.	Dec.	Jan.	Feb.	Total Cash Payments
Cash Payments						Cash Outflows From Purchases										
Jan.	150	45	60	45												150
Feb.	84		25	34	25											84
Mar.	98			29	39	30										98
Apr.	112				34	44	34									112
May	126					38	50	38								126
Jun.	140						42	56	42							140
Jul.	154							46	62	46						154
Aug.	168								50	67	51					168
Sep.	182									55	72	55				182
Oct.	196										59	78	59			196

▶

Nov.	210										63	84	63		210
Dec.	224											67	90	67	224
Total Payments Per Month	45	85	108	98	112	126	140	154	168	182	196	210	153	67	1,844
Net Cash Flows Per Month	(25)	(21)	8	38	44	50	56	62	68	74	80	86	95	61	676
Cash at Beginning of Month	50	25	4	12	50	94	144	200	262	330	404	484	570	656	
Cash at the End of Month	25	4	12	50	94	144	200	262	330	404	484	570	656	726	

In this example, Akawzi has negative cash flow in January and February. The remainder of the year generates positive cash flows. All companies need to prepare cash budgets to determine if a cash crunch is developing in any particular month. This gives management notice that either short-term financing (such as bank loans) or longer-term financing (involving the issue of new bonds or even shares) is needed. On the other hand, if the cash budget shows a surplus of cash developing through the year, management needs to consider how best to utilize this cash in order to earn a return on it for shareholders. REAL WORLD 3.4 discusses cash flow projections at three famous companies during a period of crisis.

REAL WORLD 3.4   GM, Chrysler, Ford Negative Cash Flow

December 2008 was crunch time for the North American auto industry. Sales and cash flow budgets showed the Big 3—GM, Chrysler, and Ford—were burning through cash so quickly that many feared they would declare bankruptcy. Banks were not lending, so the industry turned to government for help. General Motors of Canada requested loans from Canadian federal and provincial governments of $2.4 billion, with $800 million of that needed urgently. Chrysler said they needed $1.6 billion while Ford requested a $2 billion line of credit. In the United States, the House of Representatives passed a bill to provide $14 billion in emergency loans to the auto industry. In the end, both GM and Chrysler were forced into bankruptcy anyway.

Source: CBC News. "U.S. automaker bailout deal passes in House of Representatives." December 12, 2008. www.cbc.ca/money/story/2008/12/10/usautobailout.html, accessed August 20, 2009.

SELF-ASSESSMENT QUESTION   3.2

Alberto Vitali owns and operates LillyPad Home Furniture Ltd. in Toronto. At year-end (December 31, 2010) during its second year in business, LillyPad had $2,000 in the bank. Monthly sales average $20,000, of which 10% are cash sales and the rest are sold on account. Five percent of the receivables are never collected and must be written off. The remainder is collected evenly over the two months following the sale. Inventory purchases average $10,000 per month and are paid evenly in the two months following the purchase. Monthly rent is $1,000. Monthly salaries average $3,500. Sales commissions are 5% of sales excluding bad debts, paid in the month of the sale.

Required:

(a) Prepare a monthly cash budget for 2011. Your calculations should be done to two decimal places.
(b) State your conclusions concerning cash flows for 2011.

Step 4: Prepare the Pro Forma Financial Statements

Having prepared forecasts for the various elements of the financial statements, the final step is to include them in the pro forma financial statements. How we prepare these statements will be considered in some detail in the following section.

Figure 3.6 summarizes the steps in the planning process just described.

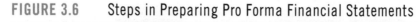

FIGURE 3.6   Steps in Preparing Pro Forma Financial Statements

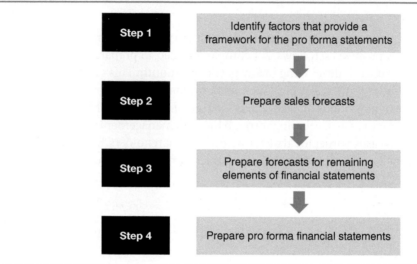

Preparing the Pro Forma Statements: An Example

We can now turn our attention to the preparation of the following pro forma financial statements:

■ The pro forma income statement
■ The pro forma statement of retained earnings
■ The pro forma balance sheet.

The methods and principles used for pro forma financial statements are the same as those for historical financial statements, which were reviewed in Chapter 2. The only real difference lies in the fact that the statements are prepared using *forecast* information rather than *actual* information.

PRO FORMA INCOME STATEMENT

A pro forma income statement provides insight into the anticipated level of future profits or losses, which can be defined as the difference between the anticipated levels of sales and expenses. Recall from Chapter 2 that sales made on credit will normally be recognized *before* the cash is actually received.

The format of the pro forma income statement for Designer Dresses Limited for the six months to June 30 appears in Activity 3.7:

ACTIVITY 3.7

Prepare the pro forma income statement for Designer Dresses Limited for the six months to June 30 using the information from Example 3.3.

Solution

Designer Dresses Limited
Pro Forma Income Statement
for the six months ended June 30
(in $ thousands)

Sales		204
Less: Cost of goods sold:		
Opening inventory	0	
Plus: Purchases	160	
Goods available for sale	160	
Less: Closing inventory	58	
Cost of goods sold		102
Gross profit		102
Less: Credit card expenses	4	
Rent expense	20	
Depreciation of equipment	5	
Other expenses	54	83
Earnings before taxes		19
Less: Income tax expense		
(ignored)		0
Net income		19

Notes
1. The credit card expense is shown explicitly as an expense rather than netted against sales because this provides more information to the income statement user.
2. This company uses the periodic inventory system to determine its cost of goods sold. This method assumes that what is not remaining in inventory has been sold.

PRO FORMA STATEMENT OF RETAINED EARNINGS

The pro forma statement of retained earnings computes the closing balance in retained earnings, which will appear on the pro forma balance sheet. It uses the opening balance in the retained earnings account (obtained from the last period's closing balance), adds the net income from the pro forma income statement, and deducts the projected level of dividends that will be paid to shareholders to arrive at the closing balance in retained earnings.

The format of the pro forma statement of retained earnings for Designer Dresses Limited is shown in Activity 3.8.

ACTIVITY 3.8

Prepare the pro forma statement of retained earnings for Designer Dresses Limited for the six months ended June 30 using the information in Example 3.3.

Solution

Designer Dresses Limited
Pro Forma Statement of Retained Earnings
for the six months ended June 30
(in $ thousands)

Opening balance in retained earnings as at January 1	0
Plus: Net income for the six months ended June 30	19
Less: Dividends paid during the six months ended June 30	0
Closing balance in retained earnings as at June 30	19

PRO FORMA BALANCE SHEET

The pro forma balance sheet reveals the end-of-period balances for assets, liabilities, and shareholders' equity. It should normally be the last of the four statements to be prepared. This is because the other statements will produce information to be used when preparing the pro forma balance sheet. The pro forma cash budget determines the end-of-period cash balance for inclusion under current assets (or where there is a negative balance, for inclusion under current liabilities). The pro forma income statement calculates the projected profit (loss) for the period for inclusion in the pro forma statement of retained earnings. In turn, the pro forma statement of retained earnings provides the ending balance of retained earnings for inclusion under the equity section of the balance sheet. It is important to remember that the accumulated depreciation must also be taken into account when preparing the property, plant, and equipment section of the pro forma balance sheet. The format of the pro forma balance sheet for Designer Dresses Limited as at June 30 is shown in Activity 3.9.

ACTIVITY 3.9

Prepare the pro forma balance sheet for Designer Dresses Limited for the six months ended June 30 using the information in Example 3.3.

Solution

Designer Dresses Limited
Pro Forma Balance Sheet
as at June 30
(in $ thousands)

Assets

Current assets

Accounts receivable	50	
Inventory	58	
Total current assets		108

▶

Property, plant, and equipment

Furniture and fixtures	30	
Less: Accumulated depreciation	_5_	
Total property, plant, and equipment		_25_
Total assets		<u>133</u>
Current liabilities		
Bank overdraft	34	
Accounts payable	<u>30</u>	
Total current liabilities		64
Shareholders' equity		
Common shares	50	
Retained earnings	<u>19</u>	
Total shareholders' equity		69
Total liabilities and shareholders' equity		<u>133</u>

Note: The accounts receivable figure represents the June sales of $51 less the 2% credit card fee. Similarly, the accounts payable figure represents June purchases.

PRO FORMA FINANCIAL STATEMENTS AND DECISION MAKING

The finished pro forma financial statements should be examined with a critical eye. There is a danger that the figures will be too readily accepted. Forecast figures are unlikely to be completely accurate and it is important to form an opinion as to how much they can be relied upon. Thus, managers should ask such questions as:

- How were the forecasts developed?
- What underlying assumptions have been made? Are those assumptions valid?
- Have all relevant items been included?

Only when the managers have received satisfactory answers to these questions should they use the statements for decision making purposes.

Unfortunately, pro forma financial statements do not come with clear decision rules indicating whether a proposed course of action should go ahead. Managers must rely on their judgment. To help form this judgment, they may examine the statements for answers to the following questions:

- Are the cash flows satisfactory? Can they be improved by changing policies or plans (for example, delaying capital expenditure decisions involving the purchase of new property, plant, and equipment, or requiring customers to pay more quickly)?
- Is there a need for additional financing? Is it feasible to obtain the amount required?
- Can any surplus funds be profitably reinvested?
- Is the level of projected profit satisfactory in relation to the risks involved? If not, what could be done to improve matters?

■ Are the sales and individual expense items at a satisfactory level?
■ Is the financial position at the end of the period acceptable?
■ Is the level of borrowing acceptable? Is the business too dependent on borrowing?

Activity 3.10 evaluates a pro forma financial statement using this criteria.

ACTIVITY 3.10

Evaluate the pro forma financial statements of Designer Dresses Limited. Pay particular attention to the projected profitability and liquidity of the business.

Solution

The pro forma cash budget on page 73 reveals that the business will have a negative balance in its bank accounts—also known as a bank overdraft—throughout most of the period under review. The maximum overdraft requirement will be $41,000 in April. The business will be heavily dependent on bank financing in the early months. This situation should not last for too long provided the business achieves, and then maintains, the level of projected profit and provided it does not invest heavily in further assets.

The business is expected to generate a profit of 9.3 cents for every $1 of sales (i.e., Net income/Sales = $19/$204 × 100% = 9.3%). The profit of $19,000 on the original outlay of $50,000 by the owners seems high. It represents a 38% return (i.e., $19,000/$50,000 × 100%). However, the business may be of a high-risk nature and therefore the owners will be looking to make high returns. As this is a new business, it may be very difficult to project into the future with any accuracy. Thus, the basis on which the projections have been made requires careful investigation.

Some further points regarding profitability can be made. It is not clear from the question whether the wages (under "other costs" in the income statement) include any compensation for the owners. If no compensation for their efforts has been included, the level of profit shown may be overstated. It may not be possible to extrapolate the projected revenues and expenses for the six-month period in order to obtain a projected profit for the year. It is likely that the business is seasonal in nature and, therefore, the next six-month period may be quite different.

Activity 3.11 provides an opportunity to prepare and assess a cash budget and pro forma income statement.

ACTIVITY 3.11

Dalgleish Ltd. is a wholesale supplier of stationery. In recent months, the business has experienced liquidity problems. The business has an overdraft of $126,000 at the end of November 2010, and the bank has been pressing for a reduction in this overdraft over the next six months. The business is owned by the Dalgleish family, who are unwilling to obtain a long-term loan. Accounts receivable stood at $120,000 at the end of November, 2010. Accounts payable for inventory purchases were $145,000.

▶

The following projections for the six months ended May 31, 2011, are available concerning the business:

1. Sales and inventory purchases for the six months ended May 31, 2011, will be as follows:

	Sales ($000)	Purchases ($000)
December	160	150
January	220	140
February	240	170
March	150	110
April	160	120
May	200	160
	1,130	850

2. 70% of sales are on credit and 30% are for cash. Credit sales are collected in the following month. All purchases are paid in one month.
3. Wages are $40,000 for each of the first three months. However, this will increase by 10% from March 2011 onward. All wages are paid in the month they are incurred.
4. The gross profit percentage on goods sold is 30% (therefore, the cost of goods sold is 70%).
5. Administration expenses are expected to be $12,000 in each of the first four months and $14,000 in subsequent months. These figures include a monthly charge of $4,000 in respect of depreciation of property, plant, and equipment assets. Administration expenses are paid in the month they are incurred.
6. Selling expenses are expected to be $8,000 per month, except for May 2011 when an advertising campaign costing $12,000 will be paid for. The advertising campaign will commence at the beginning of June 2011. Selling expenses are paid for in the month they are incurred.
7. A dividend of $20,000 will be declared and paid in December 2010.
8. The business intends to purchase, and pay for, new equipment at the end of April 2011 for $28,000. It will be delivered in June 2011.

Required:

(a) Prepare a cash budget projection for Dalgleish Ltd. for each of the six months to May 31, 2011.
(b) Prepare a pro forma income statement for the six months to May 31, 2011.
(c) Briefly discuss ways in which the business might reduce the bank overdraft as required by the bank.

Solution

(a) The cash budget projection for the six months to May 31, 2011, is:

	Dec. ($000)	Jan. ($000)	Feb. ($000)	Mar. ($000)	Apr. ($000)	May ($000)
Cash inflows						
Credit sales	120	112	154	168	105	112
Cash sales	48	66	72	45	48	60
Total inflows	168	178	226	213	153	172

Cash outflows

Purchases	145	150	140	170	110	120
Admin. expenses	8	8	8	8	10	10
Wages	40	40	40	44	44	44
Selling expenses	8	8	8	8	8	20
Equipment	–	–	–	–	28	–
Dividend	20	–	–	–	–	–
Total outflows	221	206	196	230	200	194
Net cash flow	(53)	(28)	30	(17)	(47)	(22)
Opening balance	(126)	(179)	(207)	(177)	(194)	(241)
Closing balance	(179)	(207)	(177)	(194)	(241)	(263)

(b) The pro forma income statement is:

Dalgleish Ltd.
Pro Forma Income Statement
for the six months ended May 31, 2011
(in $ thousands)

Sales		1,130
Less: Cost of goods sold (70% of sales)		791
Gross profit (30% of sales)		339
Wages (3 × $40 + 3 × $44)	252	
Selling expenses (excl. ad campaign, which starts in June) (6 × $8)	48	
Administration expenses (incl. depreciation) (4 × $12 + 2 × $14)	76	376
Net loss		(37)

Note that the advertising campaign relates to the next financial period and will therefore be charged to the income statement of that period. It will appear on the balance sheet at the end of May as a prepaid expense (advertising) asset.

(c) You might have thought of a number of possible options. The following (or perhaps some combination of these) might be feasible:

- Inject cash by selling new shares to the Dalgleish family or others
- Reduce inventory levels
- Delay purchase/payment of equipment
- Sell non-current assets
- Increase the proportion of cash sales
- Accelerate the collection of accounts receivable
- Delay payment of accounts payable to suppliers
- Delay payment of dividend
- Look for ways to reduce expenses since the company is operating at a loss.

(Note that the Dalgleish family has ruled out the possibility of obtaining a loan.) Each of the above options has advantages and disadvantages and these must be carefully assessed before a final decision is made. A decision must be made soon, however, as the cash flow trend is worsening.

PERCENT-OF-SALES METHOD

L.O. 4

Template for Pro Forma
Statements

An alternative approach to preparing a forecast income statement and balance sheet is the **percent-of-sales method**. This is a less thorough approach to forecasting than the approach discussed above. It assumes that most items appearing in the income statement and balance sheet vary according to the level of sales. As a result, these financial statements can be prepared by expressing most items as a percentage of the sales for the forecast period.

To use this method, an examination of past records needs to be undertaken to see by how much items vary with sales. It may be found, for example, that inventory levels have been around 30% of sales in previous periods. If the sales for the forecast period are, say, $10 million, the level of inventory will be forecast as $3 million (i.e., 30% × $10 million). The same approach will be used for other items.

Shown below is a brief summary of how key items appearing in the income statement and balance sheet are derived.

Income Statement

The percent-of-sales method assumes that the following income statement items can be expressed as a percentage of sales:

- All operating expenses
- The net profit figure, which is the difference between sales and expenses.

However:

- Corporate tax and dividends are assumed to vary with the level of net profit and so are expressed as a percentage of the net profit figure.

Balance Sheet

The percent-of-sales method assumes that the following balance sheet items can be expressed as a percentage of sales:

- Current assets that increase with sales, such as inventory and accounts receivable
- Current liabilities that increase with sales, such as accounts payable and accrued expenses
- Cash (as a pro forma cash budget is not prepared to provide a more accurate measure of cash).

However:

- Property, plant, and equipment will only be expressed as a percentage of sales if they are already operating at full capacity—otherwise they will not usually change
- Long-term liabilities and shareholders' equity, including retained earnings, will not be expressed as a percentage of sales but will be based on figures at the beginning of the forecast period (unless changes are made as a result of management decisions).

Example 3.5 on page 86 provides a comprehensive example of the percent-of-sales method.

Identifying the Financing Gap

When sales increase, there is a risk that the business will outgrow its current financing. The forecast increase in assets may exceed the forecast increase in liabilities and the retained earnings; a financing gap may arise because the initial pro forma balance sheet does not balance. The additional financing required by the business will be the amount necessary to make the balance sheet balance, and includes obtaining new loans and issuing new equity (shares), which we will see later, in Chapter 8.

An Example of the Percent-of-Sales Method

Example 3.5

The financial statements for Burrator Limited for the year just ended are as follows:

Burrator Limited
Income Statement
for the year ended December 31, 2010
(in $ thousands)

Sales		800
Less: Cost of goods sold		600
Gross profit		200
Less: Selling expenses	80	
Distribution expenses	20	
Other expenses	20	120
Earnings before taxes		80
Less: Income tax expense (25%)		20
Net income		60

Burrator Limited
Statement of Retained Earnings
for the year ended December 31, 2010
(in $ thousands)

Opening retained earnings, January 1	350
Add: Net income	60
Less: Dividends paid or declared	(30)
Closing retained earnings, December 31	380

Burrator Limited
Balance Sheet
as at December 31, 2010
(in $ thousands)

Current assets		
Cash	20	
Accounts receivable	200	
Inventory	320	
Total current assets		540
Property, plant, and equipment, net		160
Total assets		700
Current liabilities		
Accounts payable	240	
Income taxes payable	20	
Total current liabilities		260

Shareholders' equity

Common shares	60	
Retained earnings	380	
Total shareholders' equity		440
Total liabilities and shareholders' equity		700

The following information is relevant for 2011:

1. Sales are expected to be 10% higher than in 2010.
2. The property, plant, and equipment of the business are currently operating at full capacity.
3. The corporate tax rate will be the same as in 2010 and 50% of the tax expense will be paid in 2011.
4. The business intends to maintain the same dividend rate as in 2010.
5. Any financing gap will be filled by obtaining a long-term loan from the bank.

Required:

Prepare a pro forma income statement and statement of retained earnings for the year ended December 31, 2011 using the percent-of-sales method. (Assume that 2010 provides a useful guide to past experience.)

Solution

To prepare the pro forma income statement, we calculate each expense as a percentage of sales for 2010 and then use this percentage to forecast the equivalent expense in 2011. Tax and dividends are calculated using the same percentage of the profit as in 2010.

Burrator Limited
Pro Forma Income Statement
for the year ended December 31, 2011
(in $ thousands)

Sales (800 × 1.10)		880
Less: Cost of sales [(600 ÷ 800) = 75% × Sales]		660
Gross profit (25% × Sales)		220
Less: Selling expenses 80 ÷ 800 = (10% × Sales)	88	
Distribution expenses 20 ÷ 800 = (2.5% × Sales)	22	
Other expenses 20 ÷ 800 = (2.5% × Sales)	22	132
Earnings before taxes		88
Less: Income tax expense		
(25% × Earnings before taxes)		22
Net income		66

Burrator Limited
Pro Forma Statement of Retained Earnings
for the year ended December 31, 2011
(in $ thousands)

Opening retained earnings, January 1	380
Add: Net income	66
Less: Dividends paid or declared	
(50% × Net income)	(33)
Closing retained earnings, December 31	413

Activity 3.12 illustrates the use of the pro forma balance sheet to determine the size of the financing gap.

ACTIVITY 3.12

(a) **Prepare the pro forma balance sheet of Burrator Limited as at December 31, 2011.**
(b) **What is the size of Burrator's financing gap?**

Solution

(a) The pro forma balance sheet is as follows:

Burrator Limited
Pro Forma Balance Sheet
as at December 31, 2011
(in $ thousands)

Current assets

Cash 20 ÷ 800 = (2.5% of sales)	22	
Accounts receivable 200 ÷ 800 = (25% of sales)	220	
Inventory 320 ÷ 800 = (40% of sales)	352	
Total current assets		594

Property, plant, and
equipment (net) 160 ÷ 800 = (20% of sales)   176
Total assets   770

Current liabilities

Accounts payable 240 ÷ 800 = (30% of sales)	264	
Income taxes payable (50% × $22)	11	
Total current liabilities	275	

Long-term liabilities

Bank loan payable (balancing figure)   22

Total liabilities   297

Shareholders' equity

Common shares	60	
Retained earnings (from statement of retained earnings)	413	
Total shareholders' equity		473
Total liabilities and shareholders' equity		770

(b) The financing gap is $22,000. This is the figure needed to balance the pro forma balance sheet. Therefore, Burrator needs to borrow $22,000.

The advantage of the percent-of-sales method is that the task of preparing the pro forma financial statements becomes much easier. It can provide an approximate figure for the financing required without the need to prepare a projected cash budget. It can also help reduce the time and cost of forecasting every single item appearing in the pro forma income statement and balance sheet. This can be of real benefit, particularly for large businesses.

The problem with this method, however, is that it takes the relationships between particular items and sales as being fixed. The forecasts prepared are based on relationships that have existed in the past. These relationships may change over time because of changes in strategic direction (for example, launching completely new products) or because of changes in management policies (for example, liberalizing credit terms to customers).

PRO FORMA FINANCIAL STATEMENTS AND RISK

L.O. 5

When making estimates concerning the future, there is always a chance that things will not turn out as expected. The likelihood that what is expected to occur will not actually occur is referred to as **risk** and this will be considered in some detail in Chapter 7. However, it is worth taking a little time at this point to consider the ways in which managers may deal with the problem of risk in the context of pro forma financial statements. We consider the following three risk reduction methods:

1. Sensitivity analysis
2. Scenario analysis
3. Simulations.

1. Sensitivity Analysis

Sensitivity analysis is a useful technique to employ when evaluating the contents of pro forma financial statements. This involves taking a single variable (for example, volume of sales) and examining the effect of changes in the chosen variable on the likely performance of the business. By examining the shifts that occur, it is possible to determine what effect changes in the projected outcomes will have on the company's finances. Although only one variable is examined at a time, a number of variables that are considered to be important to the performance of a business may be examined consecutively.

One form of sensitivity analysis is to pose a series of "What if . . . ?" questions. If we take sales as an example, the following "What if . . . ?" questions may be asked:

- What if sales volume is 5% higher than expected?
- What if sales volume is 10% lower than expected?
- What if sales price is reduced by 15%?
- What if sales price could be increased by 20%?

In answering these questions, it is possible to develop a better feel for the effect of forecast inaccuracies on the final outcomes. However, this technique does not assign probabilities to each possible change, nor does it consider the effect on projected outcomes of more than one variable at a time.

2. Scenario Analysis

Another approach is to prepare pro forma financial statements according to different possible states of the world. For example, managers may wish to examine pro forma financial statements prepared on the following bases:

- An optimistic view of likely future events
- A pessimistic view of likely future events
- A most likely view of future events.

This approach is referred to as **scenario analysis** and, unlike sensitivity analysis, it will involve changing a number of variables simultaneously in order to portray a possible state of the world. To help in assessing the level of risk involved, it would be useful to know the likelihood of each state of the world occurring. The most pessimistic scenario is usually referred to as the worst case scenario.

3. Simulations

The **simulation** approach creates a distribution of possible values to key variables in the pro forma financial statements, and a probability of occurrence is attached to each value. A computer is used to generate pro forma statements on the basis of the selected values for each variable. Many iterations, involving many combinations of the key variables, may produce many pro forma financial statements.

From the huge amount of information produced, a range of likely outcomes may be determined and the probability of each outcome identified. For example, many computations may indicate that the expected profit for the following period will fall within the range of $100,000–$500,000. This information may help managers decide whether the expected level of performance is satisfactory.

This approach is claimed to make managers think carefully about the relationships between the key variables in the pro forma statements. In practice, however, there is a danger that carrying out simulations will lead to a rather mechanical approach to dealing with risk. Undue emphasis may be placed on carrying out trials and producing their results, and insufficient emphasis may be given to a more critical evaluation of the underlying assumptions and issues.

L.O. 6

HOW MANAGERS USE PRO FORMA FINANCIAL STATEMENTS AND CASH FLOW BUDGET FOR CONTROL PURPOSES

Managers should compare their department's monthly results with the estimated amounts included in the pro forma financial statements and cash budget. In this way early action can be taken by the company to address areas of concern. For example, if January's sales increased by only 4% compared to the forecasted 10% increase, management knows very early on that the company is not meeting its sales goals. Then management can limit increases in expenses so that they reflect the new reality. This month-by-month monitoring of actual results versus expected results helps to keep the company on track financially.

Furthermore, management can consider questions about why the company is not meeting its pro forma projections. For example, has the competition lowered its prices resulting in lost sales for the company? Management can consider lowering its own prices for certain products. The pro forma financial statements and cash budgets can be updated to see how such a decision would affect the company.

SELF-ASSESSMENT QUESTION 3.3

Pro Forma Financial Statements

Quardis Ltd. is an importer of high-quality laser printers. Selected balance sheet accounts, in thousands, for Quardis as at May 31, 2010, are:

Inventory	$24	Land	$220
Buildings	240	Accumulated depreciation—Buildings	30
Furniture and fixtures	35	Accumulated depreciation—Furniture and fixtures	10
Bank loan payable to		Common shares	200
First Nations' Bank	125	Retained earnings	144

▶

The following forecast information is available for the year ended May 31, 2011:

1. Sales are expected to be $280,000 for the year. Sixty percent of sales are on credit and it is expected that, at year-end, three months' credit sales will be outstanding. Sales revenues accrue evenly over the year.

2. Purchases of inventory during the year will be $186,000 and will accrue evenly over the year. All purchases are on credit, and at year-end it is expected that two months' purchases will remain unpaid.

3. Furniture and fixtures costing $25,000 will be purchased and paid for during the year. Depreciation is charged at 10% on the cost of furniture and fixtures held at year-end.

4. Depreciation is charged on the buildings at 2% of the cost.

5. On June 1, 2010, $30,000 of the loan from the First Nations' Bank is to be repaid. Interest is at the rate of 13% per annum. All interest accrued during the fiscal year is paid on May 31 of each year.

6. Inventory at year-end is expected to be 25% higher than at the beginning of the year.

7. Wages for the year will be $34,000. It is estimated that $4,000 of this total will remain unpaid at year-end.

8. Other overhead expenses for the year (excluding those mentioned above) are expected to be $21,000. It is expected that $3,000 of this total will still be unpaid at year-end.

9. A dividend of $0.05 per share will be paid during the year. There are 200,000 shares outstanding.

10. Corporate tax is payable at the rate of 35% per annum. Corporate tax outstanding at the beginning of the year will be paid during the year. Half of the corporate tax relating to the year will also be paid during the year.

All calculations should be shown to the nearest thousand dollars.

Required:

(a) Prepare a pro forma income statement for the year ended May 31, 2011.
(b) Prepare a pro forma statement of retained earnings for the year ended May 31, 2011.
(c) Prepare a pro forma balance sheet as at May 31, 2011.
(d) Comment on the significant features revealed by these pro forma financial statements.

Note: A pro forma cash budget is not required. The cash figure in the pro forma balance sheet will be the balancing figure.

SUMMARY

Planning for the Future

- Developing plans involves:
  - Establishing aims and objectives
  - Identifying the options available
  - Evaluating the options and making a selection.

The Role of Pro Forma Financial Statements

- Pro forma financial statements help in evaluating the options available.

Preparing Pro Forma Financial Statements

- Involves a four-stage process:
  - Identifying the external and internal factors that provide a framework for the forecast statements
  - Forecasting sales for the period by analyzing the competitive environment and using an appropriate forecasting approach

- Forecasting the remaining elements of the financial statements
- Preparing the pro forma financial statements.

■ The pro forma financial statements normally prepared are:
- The pro forma cash budget
- The pro forma income statement
- The pro forma statement of retained earnings
- The pro forma balance sheet.

■ The pro forma cash budget is usually broken down into monthly periods.

Pro Forma Financial Statements and Decision Making

■ The pro forma statements should be checked for reliability before using them for decision making purposes.

■ The pro forma statements do not provide clear decision rules for managers, who must employ judgment.

Percent-of-Sales Method

■ Provides a less rigorous approach to forecasting

■ Assumes that most items on the income statement and balance sheet vary with sales

■ Calculates any financing gap by reference to the amount required to make the balance sheet balance

■ A financing gap arises when the pro forma balance sheet does not intially balance

■ Makes the preparation of forecast statements easier and less costly but assumes that relationships between individual items and sales that held in the past will also hold in the future.

Pro Forma Financial Statements and Risk

■ Three methods of dealing with risk are:
- Sensitivity analysis
- Scenario analysis
- Simulations.

KEY TERMS

Pro forma financial statements
Competitor profiling
Variable costs

Fixed costs
Mixed costs
Percent-of-sales method
Risk

Sensitivity analysis
Scenario analysis
Simulation

LIST OF EQUATIONS

3.1 Contribution margin (CM) = SP − VC

3.2 Breakeven point for number of units $= \dfrac{\text{Fixed costs}}{\text{Contribution margin}} = \dfrac{\text{FC}}{\text{CM}}$

3.3 Contribution margin ratio $= \dfrac{\text{Contribution margin}}{\text{Sales}} = \dfrac{\text{CM}}{\text{Sales}}$

3.4 Breakeven sales $= \dfrac{\text{Fixed costs}}{\text{Contribution margin ratio}} = \dfrac{\text{FC}}{\text{CM ratio}}$

3.5 Breakeven sales = Breakeven sales units × Unit sales price

3.6 Operating leverage $= \dfrac{\text{\% Change in EBIT}}{\text{\% Change in sales}}$

REVIEW QUESTIONS

Answers to the Review Questions can be found on the Companion Website that accompanies this text at www.pearsoned.ca/atrill.

3.1 In what ways might pro forma financial statements help a business that is growing quickly?

3.2 "The future is uncertain and so pro forma financial statements will almost certainly prove to be inaccurate. It is, therefore, a waste of time to prepare them." Comment.

3.3 Why would it normally be easier to prepare pro forma financial statements for an existing business than for a new one?

3.4 Why is the sales forecast normally of critical importance to the preparation of pro forma financial statements?

3.5 Why are depreciation expenses excluded from net income when preparing the cash budget?

PROBLEMS AND CASES

3.1

Product	A	B	C	D
Fixed costs	$ 9,000,000	$ 540,000	$ 11,000	$ 15,000
Contribution margin	150	3,000	20	3

Required:
Calculate the breakeven point in units for each product.

3.2 You have gathered the following data for your new line of engagement rings.

Sales	$ 10,000,000	
Fixed costs	8,000,000	
Variable costs	6,000,000	
Mixed costs	2,000,000	60% fixed; 40% variable
Unit sales	2,000	

Required:
  (a) Calculate the unit selling price.
  (b) Calculate the total variable costs.
  (c) Calculate the total fixed costs.
  (d) Calculate the breakeven point.
  (e) Prepare the breakeven income statement.

3.3 Betty-Lou Tsu owns and operates Betty's Gourmet Milkshakes. Here is the financial data from last year. She has come to you for help in calculating the breakeven point for her business.

Sales	$ 2,000,000
Fixed costs	1,200,000
Variable costs	800,000
Unit sales	400,000

Required:
  (a) Calculate the breakeven point in unit sales.
  (b) Prepare a breakeven chart for her business.

3.4 The following companies in the movie business produced these results over the past two years.

	Toronto Animations Limited		Halifax Productions Inc.	
	2009	2010	2009	2010
Sales	$1,200,000	$1,800,000	$700,000	$1,050,000
Fixed costs	400,000	400,000	300,000	300,000
EBIT	$ 800,000	$1,400,000	$400,000	$ 750,000

Required:
Determine which company has the higher operating leverage.

3.5 All-Season Gloves Ltd. finished December 2010 with a balance of $450,000 in its accounts receivable. January's sales are forecast to be $560,000 (90% on credit) and are expected to grow by 2% per month for the entire year. Assume all amounts are collected in the month following the sale.

Required:
Calculate the sales, the ending balance in accounts receivable, and the cash received for each month in 2011.

3.6 Four Seasons Boots Ltd. had sales in November 2010 of $538,255. Ten percent of the sales were cash sales, with 70% of the credit sales collected one month after the sale, 25% collected two months after the sale, and 5% written off as bad debts. Sales are expected to grow by 2% per month between December 2010 and the end of 2011.

Required:
(a) Prepare a cash inflow budget for each month in 2011.
(b) Show the collection and write-off results for January's sales.

3.7 Diamond Drillers Inc. had sales in December of $60,000. Sales are expected to grow at 5% per month for the foreseeable future because of increased oil field drilling. All sales are on credit and are collected in the month following the sale. Inventory purchases for January are expected to be $40,000 per month, growing at 6% per month. Because of credit problems over the last year, Diamond Drillers must pay cash for its purchases. Operating expenses are $30,000 per month. There is a tax payment of $5,000 due in May.

Required:
(a) Prepare a monthly analysis of the cash inflows and the cash outflows for Diamond Drillers Inc. for the January to June period.
(b) Assuming Diamond Drillers ended December with $40,000 cash in the bank, when do you expect a bank loan to be needed?

3.8 Alice's Wholesale Ltd. is trying to plan its cash flows for the next year. On January 2, 2011, it has $7,000 in the bank. On average, 50% of sales each month are collected in the following month, with the remainder collected in the second following month. All sales are on credit. On average, 40% of purchases each month are paid in the following month, with the remainder paid in the second month following the purchase. The monthly data are shown below.

| | 2010 | | 2011 | | | | | | | | | | | |
	Nov.	Dec.	Jan.	Feb.	Mar.	Apr.	May	Jun.	Jul.	Aug.	Sep.	Oct.	Nov.	Dec.
Sales	5,000	7,000	8,000	9,000	10,000	11,000	12,000	13,000	14,000	15,000	16,000	17,000	18,000	19,000
Purchases	7,000	8,000	9,000	10,000	11,000	12,000	13,000	14,000	15,000	16,000	17,000	18,000	19,000	20,000

Required:

    (a) Determine the monthly cash balance at the end of every month in 2011.

    (b) Will the cash run out?

3.9 Proton Drinks wants to estimate the amount of cash needed for dividends in 2010. Sales will likely grow by 40%. The percentage of sales for variable costs will increase to 40%. Dividends will be bumped up to 50% of net income.

	2009	2010
Sales	$ 300,000	_____
Variable costs	100,000	_____
Fixed costs	75,000	_____
Net income	$ 125,000	_____
Dividends	$ 50,000	_____

Required:

Complete the pro forma income statement and dividend data for 2010.

3.10 The income statements for the Fresh Sandwich Company for 2009 and 2010 are given below. Your boss wants you to prepare a pro forma income statement for 2011 using the same percentage increases as last year for sales, purchases, closing inventory, maintenance expenses, and other expenses. Rent and depreciation are fixed expenses.

	2009 ($000)		2010 ($000)	
Sales		1,031.00		1,278.44
Less: Cost of sales:				
Opening inventory	32.00		56.00	
Plus: purchases	820.00		967.60	
Goods available for sale	852.00		1,023.60	
Less: Closing inventory	56.00		62.72	
Cost of sales		796.00		960.88
Gross profit		235.00		317.56
Less: Maintenance expenses	43.00		57.62	
Rent expenses	65.00		65.00	
Depreciation	45.00		45.00	
Other expenses	12.00	165.00	12.60	180.22
Earnings before taxes		70.00		137.34
Less: Income tax expense (40%)		28.00		54.94
Net income		42.00		82.40

Required:

    (a) Calculate the percentage increase between 2009 and 2010 for sales, purchases, closing inventory, maintenance expenses, and other expenses.

    (b) Prepare the pro forma income statement for 2011.

3.11 Pro Martin Shoes, which operates one store in Guelph, Ontario, is forecasting next year's income statement results based on a preliminary 10% increase in sales.

	2009	2010
Sales	$ 300,000	_____
Variable costs	200,000	_____
Fixed costs	65,000	_____
Net income	$ 35,000	_____

Required:

(a) Complete the 2010 pro forma income statement using the 10% sales increase figure.

(b) Explain whether the store owner should be satisfied about next year's forecast for his store given that several Canadian bank economists are forecasting a recession that will include a 5% contraction in the economy in 2010?

3.12 Your assistant has prepared the following pro forma income statement for 2010. He used your forecast sales figure as the starting point. The administrative expenses are fixed except for salaries, which are expected to increase 3%. The cost of goods sold and selling expenses vary in direct proportion to the sales. You are surprised by the larger forecast loss for 2010.

	2009		2010	
Sales		$ 700,200		$ 875,250
Cost of goods sold		300,000		390,000
Gross profit		400,200		485,250
Selling expenses				
Sales commissions	$ 70,020		$ 80,000	
Delivery expenses	105,030		112,000	
Patent royalties expenses	35,010		40,000	
Total selling expenses		210,060		232,000
Administrative expenses				
Salaries	$ 120,000		$ 135,000	
Rent expense	60,000		72,000	
Insurance expense	12,000		14,400	
Total administrative expenses		192,000		221,400
Net income		$ (1,860)		$ (31,850)

Required:

(a) Re-do the 2010 pro forma income statement to correct your assistant's work.

(b) Explain what percentage increase amounts you used to develop the corrected pro forma income statement.

3.13 East Coast Pipelines Ltd. had the following income statement data for the month of December 2010.

East Coast Pipelines Ltd.
Income Statement
for the month ended December 31, 2010
(in $ thousands)

Sales		750
Less: Cost of goods sold:		
Opening inventory	50	
Plus: Purchases	600	
Goods available for sale	650	
Less: Closing inventory	75	
Cost of goods sold		575
Gross profit		175
Less: Maintenance expenses	20	
Rent expense	20	
Depreciation	30	
Other expenses	35	105
Earnings before taxes		70
Less: Income tax expense (40%)		28
Net income		42

Sales are expected to increase in 2011 by 10% each month. Purchases and closing inventory will increase by 12% per month. Maintenance expenses will increase by 7% per month. Other expenses will increase by 15% per month. Rent and depreciation expenses are fixed expenses.

Required:

(a) Prepare pro forma income statements for each of the first six months of 2011.

(b) What do the pro forma income statements indicate?

3.14 Choice Designs Ltd. operates a small group of wholesale/retail carpet stores in Alberta and British Columbia. The balance sheet is below:

Choice Designs Ltd.
Balance Sheet
as at May 31, 2010
(in $ thousands)

Current assets			
Cash		165	
Accounts receivable		220	
Inventory		240	
Total current assets			625
Property, plant, and equipment			
Land		150	
Buildings	450		
Less: Accumulated depreciation	100	350	
Furniture and fixtures	140		
Less: Accumulated depreciation	80	60	
Total property, plant, and equipment			560
Total assets			1,185
Current liabilities			
Accounts payable		268	
Income taxes payable		166	
Total current liabilities			434
Shareholders' equity			
Common shares		500	
Retained earnings		251	
Total shareholders' equity			751
Total liabilities and shareholders' equity			1,185

As a result of falling profits, the directors of the business would like to completely renovate each store during June 2010 at a total cost of $300,000. However, before making such a large capital expenditure commitment, they require financial projections for the forthcoming year.

The following information is available concerning the year ending May 31, 2011:

- The forecast sales for the year are $1,400,000 and the gross profit is expected to be 30% of sales. Eighty percent of all sales are on credit. At present the average collection period is six weeks but it is likely that this will change to eight weeks in the forthcoming year.
- At the year-end, inventory is expected to be 25% higher than at the beginning of the year.
- During the year the company intends to pay $40,000 for a fleet of delivery vans.
- Administration expenses for the year are expected to be $225,000 (including $12,000 for depreciation of buildings and $38,000 for depreciation of furniture and fixtures). Selling expenses are expected to be $85,000 (including $10,000 for depreciation of delivery vans).

■ All purchases are on credit. It has been estimated that the average payment period taken will be 12 weeks during the forthcoming year.

■ Income taxes for the year are expected to be $34,000. Half of this will be paid during the year and the remaining half will be outstanding at the year-end.

■ Dividends declared and paid for the year are expected to be $0.06 per share.

■ There are 500,000 shares outstanding.

All calculations should be made to the nearest thousand dollars.

Required:

(a) Prepare a pro forma income statement for the year ended May 31, 2011.

(b) Prepare a pro forma statement of retained earnings for the year ended May 31, 2011.

(c) Prepare a pro forma balance sheet as at May 31, 2011.

Note: The cash balance will be the balancing figure.

3.15 Prolog Ltd. is a small wholesaler of powerful microcomputers. In recent months, it has been selling 50 machines a month at a price of $2,000 each. These machines cost $1,600 each. A new model has just been launched and this is expected to offer greatly enhanced performance. Its selling price and cost will be the same as for the old model. From the beginning of January 2011, sales are expected to increase at a rate of 20 machines each month until the end of June 2011, when sales will amount to 170 units per month. They are expected to continue at that level thereafter. Operating costs, including depreciation of $2,000 a month, are forecast as follows:

	Jan.	Feb.	Mar.	Apr.	May	Jun.
Operating costs ($000)	6	8	10	12	12	12

Prolog expects to receive no credit for operating costs. Additional shelving for storage costing $12,000 will be bought, installed, and paid for in April. Corporate tax of $25,000 is due at the end of March. Prolog expects that customers will take two months to pay. To give its customers a good level of service, Prolog plans to hold enough inventory at the end of each period to fulfill anticipated demand in the following month. The computer manufacturer, however, grants one month's credit to Prolog. Prolog Ltd.'s balance sheet is shown below.

Prolog Ltd.
Balance Sheet
as at December 31, 2010
(in $ thousands)

Current assets		
Accounts receivable	200	
Inventory	112	
Total current assets		312
Property, plant, and equipment		80
Total assets		392
Current liabilities		
Bank overdraft	68	
Accounts payable	112	
Income taxes payable	25	
Total current liabilities		205
Shareholders' equity		
Common shares	10	
Retained earnings	177	
Total shareholders' equity		187
Total liabilities and shareholders' equity		392

Required:

  (a) Prepare a projected cash budget for Prolog Ltd., showing the cash balance or required overdraft for each month in the six months ending June 30, 2011.

  (b) State briefly what further information a banker would require from Prolog before granting additional overdraft privileges for the anticipated expansion of sales.

3.16 Changes Ltd. owns a chain of eight stores selling fashion accessories. In the past the business maintained a healthy cash balance. However, this has fallen in recent months, and at the end of September 2010 the company had an overdraft of $70,000. In view of this, Changes Ltd.'s president has asked you to prepare a cash forecast for the next six months. You have collected the following data:

	Oct. ($000)	Nov. ($000)	Dec. ($000)	Jan. ($000)	Feb. ($000)	Mar. ($000)
Sales forecast	140	180	260	60	100	120
Purchases	160	180	140	50	50	50
Wages and salaries	30	30	40	30	30	32
Rent	–	–	60	–	–	–
Other expenses	20	20	20	20	20	60
Renovations	–	–	–	80	–	–

Inventory at October 1 amounted to $170,000 and accounts payable was $70,000. The purchases in October, November, and December are contractually committed, and those in January, February, and March are the minimum necessary to restock with spring fashions. Cost of goods sold is 50% of sales and suppliers allow one month's credit on purchases. Taxes of $90,000 are due on January 1. Other expenses include depreciation of $10,000 per month. Rent expense is paid six months in advance, in June and December.

Required:

  (a) Calculate the forecast cash balance at the end of each month, for the six months ended March 31, 2011.

  (b) Calculate the projected inventory levels at the end of each month for the six months to March 31, 2011.

  (c) Prepare a pro forma income statement for the six months ended March 31, 2011.

  (d) What problems might Changes Ltd. face in the next six months and how would you attempt to overcome them?

(Hint: A forecast of inventory flows is required to answer part (b). This will be based on the same principles as a cash flow budget, that is, inflows and outflows with opening and closing balances.)

3.17 Kwaysar Limited sells television satellite dishes both to retail outlets and directly to the public. The balance sheet is as follows:

**Kwaysar Limited
Balance Sheet
as at May 31, 2010
(in $ thousands)**

Current assets		
Cash	120	
Accounts receivable	52	
Inventory	44	
Total current assets		216
Property, plant, and equipment		
Land	75	
Buildings	275	
Less: Accumulated depreciation	(60)	215
Furniture and fixtures	80	
Less: Accumulated depreciation	(42)	38
Total property, plant, and equipment		328
Total assets		544
Current liabilities		
Accounts payable	32	
Accrued overhead	12	44
Long-term liabilities		
Bank loan payable		48
Total liabilities		92
Shareholders' equity		
Common shares	200	
Contributed capital	80	
Retained earnings	172	
Total shareholders' equity		452
Total liabilities and shareholders' equity		544

In the second half of the financial year ended May 31, 2010, the business generated a net income of $62,400 and sales of $525,000. It is believed that this level of performance will be repeated in the forthcoming six-month period, provided the business does not implement any changes to its marketing strategy. The business is determined to increase its market share, however, and is considering the adoption of a new marketing strategy that has been developed by the marketing department. The main elements of the new strategy are as follows:

1. The selling price of each satellite dish will be reduced to $90. At present each dish is sold for $120.
2. There will be an increase in the amount of advertising costs incurred by the business. Advertising costs will increase from $6,500 per month to $12,000 per month.
3. Retail outlets will be allowed to pay for satellite dishes three months after delivery. At present, customers are allowed one month's credit. Those retail outlets that continue to pay within one month will, for future sales, be given a 2% discount.

The marketing department believes that, due to the new strategy, sales in each of the first three months to retail outlets will rise to 1,000 units and sales to the public will rise to 300 units. Thereafter, sales each month will be 1,200 units and 400 units respectively.

Assuming the strategy is adopted, the following forecast information is available:

1. The purchase of satellite dishes will be made at the beginning of each month and will be sufficient to meet that month's sales. Each satellite dish costs $50. Suppliers are paid one month after the month of purchase.
2. Depreciation will be charged on buildings at 2% per year on cost and for furniture and fixtures at 15% per year on cost.
3. Motor vehicles costing $80,000 will be acquired and paid for immediately. These are required to implement the new strategy and will be depreciated at 30% per year on cost.
4. Wages will be $18,000 per month and will be paid in the month in which they are incurred.
5. Advertising costs will be paid for in the month incurred.
6. Other overhead costs (excluding costs mentioned above) will be $14,000 per month and will continue to be paid for one month after the month in which they are incurred.
7. The loan of $48,000 will be repaid in July 2010.
8. Sales direct to the public will continue to be paid for in cash. No credit will be allowed.
9. It is estimated that 50% of retail sales will continue to be on one month's credit and 50% will be on three months' credit.

Ignore taxation.

Required:
Assuming that the new marketing strategy is adopted:
(a) Prepare a pro forma income statement for the six-month period ended November 30, 2010. (A monthly breakdown of profit is not required.)
(b) Prepare a projected cash budget for the six-month period ended November 30, 2010. (A monthly breakdown of cash flows is not required.)
(c) Comment on the financial results of Kwaysar Limited for the six-month period to November 30, 2010

3.18 Newtake Records Limited owns a chain of 14 stores selling CDs and DVDs. At the beginning of June, the business had an overdraft of $35,000, and the bank has asked for this to be eliminated by the end of November of the same year. As a result, the directors of the business have recently decided to review their plans for the next six months in order to comply with this requirement.

The following forecast information was prepared for the business some months earlier:

	May ($000)	Jun. ($000)	Jul. ($000)	Aug. ($000)	Sep. ($000)	Oct. ($000)	Nov. ($000)
Expected sales	180	230	320	250	140	120	110
Purchases	135	180	142	94	75	66	57
Admin. expenses	52	55	56	53	48	46	45
Selling expenses	22	24	28	26	21	19	18
Payment of taxes	–	–	–	22	–	–	–
Loan and interest payments	5	5	5	5	5	5	5
Store upgrades	–	–	14	18	6	–	–

Notes:

1. Inventory held at June 1 was $112,000. The business believes it is necessary to maintain a minimum inventory level of $40,000 over the period ended November 30 of the same year.
2. Suppliers sell on terms of 30 days for payment. The first three months' purchases are subject to a contractual agreement that must be honoured.
3. The gross profit margin is 40%.
4. All sales income is received in the month of sale. However, 50% of customers pay with a credit card. The charge made by the credit card business to Newtake Records Limited is 3% of the sales value.

These charges are in addition to the selling expenses identified above. The credit card business pays Newtake Records Limited in the month of sale.

5. The business has a bank loan that it is paying off in monthly installments of $5,000 per month. The interest element represents 20% of each installment.

6. Administration expenses are paid when incurred. This item includes a charge of $15,000 each month in respect of depreciation.

7. Selling expenses are payable in the following month.

Required:

(a) Prepare a cash budget for the six months ended November 30 that shows the cash balance at the end of each month.

(b) Calculate the projected inventory levels at the end of each month for the six months ended November 30.

(c) Prepare a pro forma income statement for the six months ended November 30. (A monthly breakdown of profit is not required.)

(d) What problems is Newtake Records Limited likely to face in the next six months? Can you suggest how the business might deal with these problems?

3.19 It is November 2010 and you have been asked to work on next year's cash budget for the Far Flung Sports Company. You have gathered the following information:

Estimated December 31, 2010, cash balance	$1,500,000
Estimated Data for 2011:	
Total sales for 2011	$32,500,000
Percent of total sales in January	8%
Percent of total sales in June, July, and August, spread evenly	60%
Percent of total sales in the eight remaining months, spread evenly	32%
Percent of monthly sales that are cash sales	10%
Percent of monthly credit sales that are collected one month after the sale	25%
Percent of monthly credit sales that are collected two months after the sale	50%
Percent of monthly credit sales that are collected three months after the sale	25%
Annual depreciation expense	$500,000
Quarterly capital expenditures, paid quarterly starting in March	$80,000
Annual income tax expense, paid quarterly starting in February	$400,000
Monthly wages and salaries	$500,000
Annual purchases, made proportionately according to sales	$22,500,000
Percent of monthly purchases that are cash purchases	5%
Percent of monthly credit purchases that are paid one month after purchase	50%
Percent of monthly credit purchases that are paid two months after purchase	20%
Percent of monthly credit purchases that are paid three months after purchase	30%
Annual rent expense, paid monthly	$120,000

Required:

(a) Prepare a monthly cash budget for 2011 and the first quarter of 2012. Prepare your calculations to one decimal.

(b) Evaluate the month-end cash figures that the cash budget predicts.

3.20 The Lavalle Ladies Legends (LLL), a professional hockey team playing in the Canadian Hockey League, is preparing an outline forecast of its pro forma income statement for 2010. The president of the team thinks it is most likely that she can increase ticket sales by 20% in 2010. League officials believe that revenues can grow by as much as 40%. However, if some of the top players in the league defect to a European league, sales may drop to only 80% of the 2009 levels.

	2009	2010 Most Likely	2010 Optimistic View	2010 Pessimistic View
Sales	1,200,000			
Variable costs	500,000			
Fixed costs	600,000			
Net income	100,000			

Required:

(a) The president has asked you to prepare a scenario analysis of the 2010 income statement similar to the outline shown above.

(b) Advise the president in her negotiations with a food concessions supplier who is willing to offer a 5% discount if LLL guarantees to buy at least $100,000 worth of food during the 2010 hockey season. In 2009 LLL bought $90,000 worth of food.

CHAPTER 4

Analyzing and Interpreting Financial Statements

LEARNING OUTCOMES

When you have completed this chapter, you should be able to:

1 Identify the major categories of ratios that can be used for analysis purposes.

2 Calculate important ratios for assessing the financial performance of a business, and explain the significance of the ratios calculated.

3 Use horizontal and vertical analysis to assess the trends in the financial performance of a company.

4 Discuss the limitations of ratios as a tool of financial analysis.

INTRODUCTION

In this chapter we consider the analysis and interpretation of the financial statements. We will see how financial (or accounting) ratios can help in assessing the financial health of a business. We will also discuss the problems that are encountered when applying this technique.

Financial ratios can be used to examine various aspects of financial performance, and are widely used for planning and control purposes. As we will see in later chapters, they can be very helpful to managers in a wide variety of decision areas, such as profit planning, working capital management, financial structure, and dividend policy.

FINANCIAL RATIOS

Financial ratios provide a quick and relatively simple means of assessing the financial health of a business. A ratio simply relates one figure appearing in the financial statements to some other figure appearing there (for example, net income in relation to capital employed) or, perhaps, to some resource of the business (for example, net income per employee, or sales revenue per square metre of counter space).

Ratios can be very helpful when comparing different businesses' financial health. Differences may exist between businesses in the scale of operations, and so a direct comparison of the profits generated by each business may be misleading. By expressing net income in relation to some other measure (for example, sales revenue), the problem of scale is eliminated. A business with a profit of $10,000 and sales revenue of $100,000 can be compared with a much larger business with a profit of $80,000 and sales revenue of $1,000,000 by the use of a simple ratio. The net income to sales revenue ratio for the smaller business is 10% [i.e., ($10,000/$100,000) × 100%], and the same ratio for the larger business is 8% [i.e., ($80,000/$1,000,000) × 100%]. These ratios can be directly compared, whereas comparison of the absolute profit figures would be less meaningful.

The need to eliminate differences in scale through the use of ratios can also apply when evaluating the performance of the same business over time.

By calculating a small number of ratios, it is often possible to develop a good picture of a business's performance. The ratios can highlight financial strengths and weaknesses, and so it is not surprising that ratios are widely used by those who have an interest in businesses and business performance. However, ratios provide only the starting point for further analysis. Changes in a particular ratio may be due to a variety of factors and a ratio cannot, by itself, explain why certain strengths or weaknesses exist, or why certain changes have occurred. Only a detailed investigation will reveal these underlying reasons.

Ratios can be expressed in various forms—for example, as a percentage or as a proportion. The way that a particular ratio is presented will depend on the needs of those who will use the information. Although it is possible to calculate a large number of ratios, only a few, based on key relationships, tend to be helpful to a particular user. Many ratios that could be calculated from the financial statements (for example, rent expense in relation to current assets) may not be considered because there is no clear or meaningful relationship between the two items.

There is no generally accepted list of ratios that can be applied to financial statements, nor is there a standard method of calculating many ratios. Variations in both the choice of ratios and their calculation will be found in practice. However, it is important to be consistent in how ratios are calculated for comparison purposes. The ratios discussed below are widely used because many consider them to be important for decision-making purposes.

FINANCIAL RATIO CLASSIFICATION

`L.O. 1`

Ratios can be grouped into categories, each of which relates to a particular aspect of financial performance. Five broad categories provide a useful basis for explaining the nature of the financial ratios to be dealt with.

- *Profitability.* Profitability ratios measure a business's success in creating wealth for its owners. They express the profits made (or figures bearing on profit, such as overheads) in relation to other key figures in the financial statements or to some business resource.
- *Efficiency.* Some ratios measure the efficiency with which particular resources have been used within the business. These ratios are also referred to as activity ratios.
- *Liquidity.* It is vital to the survival of a business that there be sufficient cash available to meet debts that must be paid in the near future. Some liquidity ratios examine the relationship between cash and other current assets held and payables due in the near future.
- *Financial leverage.* This is the relationship between the shareholders' contribution to the business's financing and the amount contributed by others in the form of loans. The amount of leverage has an important effect on the degree of risk associated with a business. Leverage is, therefore, something that managers must consider when making financing decisions. Leverage ratios tend to highlight the extent to which the business uses debt to finance its operations.
- *Investment.* Certain ratios are concerned with assessing the returns and performance of shares held in a particular business from the perspective of shareholders who are not involved with the management of the business.

The analyst must be clear who the target users are and why they need the information. Different users of financial information are likely to have different information needs, which will in turn determine which ratios they find useful. For example, shareholders are likely to be interested in their returns in relation to the level of risk associated with their investment. Thus profitability, investment, and leverage ratios will be of particular interest. Long-term lenders are concerned with the long-term viability of the business, so the business's profitability and leverage ratios are likely to be of particular interest. Short-term lenders, such as suppliers of goods and services on credit, may be interested in the business's ability to repay the amounts owing in the short term. As a result, the liquidity ratios should be of interest to them.

THE NEED FOR COMPARISON

Merely calculating a ratio will not tell us very much about the position or performance of a business. For example, if a ratio revealed that the business was generating $10,000 in sales revenue per employee, it would not be possible to determine from this information alone whether this particular level of performance was good, bad, or indifferent. Only when we compare this ratio with some benchmark can the information be interpreted and evaluated. Activity 4.1 considers different types of benchmarks.

ACTIVITY 4.1

Can you think of any benchmarks that could be used to compare with a ratio you have calculated from the financial statements of a particular period?

Solution

You might have thought of the following bases:

- *Past periods.* By comparing the ratio we have calculated with the same ratio, but for a previous period, it is possible to detect whether there has been an improvement or deterioration in performance. Indeed, it is often useful to track particular ratios over time (say, five or ten years) to see whether it is possible to detect trends.
- *Similar businesses.* In a competitive environment, a business must consider its performance in relation to that of other businesses operating in the same industry. Survival may depend on the ability to achieve comparable levels of performance. Thus it is very useful to compare a particular ratio with the ratio achieved by similar businesses during the same period.
- *Planned or budgeted performance.* Ratios may be compared with the targets that management developed before the start of the period under review. Comparing planned performance with actual performance may therefore be useful for revealing the level of achievement attained.

Planned performance is likely to be the most valuable benchmark for the managers to assess their own business. Businesses tend to develop planned ratios for each aspect of their activities. When planning, a business may usefully take account of its own past performance and that of other businesses. There is no reason, however, why a particular business should seek to achieve either its own previous performance or that of other businesses. Neither of these may be seen as an appropriate target.

Analysts outside the business do not normally have access to the business's plans. For these people, past performance and the performance of other similar businesses may be the only practical benchmarks.

KEY STEPS IN FINANCIAL RATIO ANALYSIS

When undertaking ratio analysis, analysts follow a sequence of steps:

1. *Identify the key indicators and relationships that require examination.* In carrying out this step, the analyst must be clear *who* the target users are and *why* they need the information. We saw earlier that different types of users of financial information are likely to have different information needs that will, in turn, determine which ratios they find useful.
2. *Calculate ratios that are considered appropriate* for the particular users and the purpose for which they require the information.
3. *Interpret and evaluate the ratios.* Interpretation involves examining the ratios along with an appropriate basis for comparison and any other information that may be relevant. The ratios' significance can then be established. Evaluation involves judging the value of the information uncovered in the calculation and interpretation of the ratios. Whereas calculation is usually straightforward, interpretation and evaluation are more difficult and often require high levels of skill. This skill can only really be acquired through much practice.

Figure 4.1 summarizes this.

FIGURE 4.1 The Three Key Steps of Financial Ratio Analysis

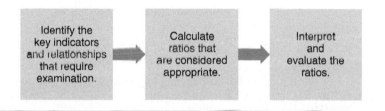

Examples of key metrics investors might use in steps 1 and 2 are:

Retail:
- Percentage growth in same-store sales
- New store opening trends (expansion plans)
- Gross profit margin trends.

Newer companies:
- Times interest earned
- Debt/equity ratio.

Mining companies:
- Demand and price trend for the underlying commodity
- New mine openings.

CALCULATING THE RATIOS

L.O. 2

Example 4.1 provides a set of financial statements from which we can calculate important ratios.

Example 4.1

The following financial statements and analyses relate to Alexis Corporation, which operates in the wholesale carpet business:

Alexis Corporation
Balance sheets
as at March 31,

| | 2010 | | 2009 | | | |
	($ millions)	Vertical Analysis %	($ millions)	Vertical Analysis %	Horizontal Analysis % Change	Horizontal Analysis Calculations
Current assets						
Cash	0	0.00%	4	0.38%	−100.00%	(0−4)/4
Accounts receivable (273/1,266)*	273	21.56%	240	22.77%	13.75%	(273−240)/240
Inventory (406/1,266)	406	32.07%	300	28.46%	35.33%	(406−300)/300
Total current assets (679/1,266)	679	53.63%	544	51.61%	24.82%	(679−544)/544
Property, plant, and equipment						
Land (100/1,266)	100	7.90%	100	9.49%	0.00%	(100−100)/100
Buildings (net) (327/1,266)	327	25.83%	281	26.66%	16.37%	(327−281)/281
Equipment (net) (160/1,266)	160	12.64%	129	12.24%	24.03%	(160−129)/129
Total property, plant, and equipment (587/1,266)	587	46.37%	510	48.39%	15.10%	(587−510)/510
Total assets (1,266/1,266)	1,266	100.00%	1,054	83.25%	20.11%	(1266−1054)/1054
Current liabilities						
Bank overdraft (76/1,266)	76	6.00%	0	0.00%		N/A
Accounts payable (314/1,266)	314	24.80%	221	20.97%	42.08%	(314−221)/221
Income taxes payable (2/1,266)	2	0.16%	30	2.84%	−93.33%	(2−30)/30
Dividends payable (40/1,266)	40	3.16%	40	3.79%	0.00%	(40−40)/40
Total current liabilities (432/1,266)	432	34.12%	291	27.60%	48.45%	(432−291)291
Long-term liabilities						
Bonds payable, (9%) (300/1,266)	300	23.70%	200	18.98%	50.00%	(300−200)/200
Total liabilities (732/1,266)	732	57.82%	491	46.58%	49.08%	(732−491)/491
Shareholders' equity						
Common shares (Note 1) (300/1,266)	300	23.70%	300	28.46%	0.00%	(300−300)/300
Retained earnings (234/1,266)	234	18.48%	263	24.95%	−11.03%	(234−263)/263
Total shareholders' equity (534/1,266)	534	42.18%	563	53.42%	−5.15%	(534−563)/563
Total liabilities and shareholders' equity (1,266/1,266)	1,266	100.00%	1,054	100.00%	20.11%	(1,266−1,054)/1,054

*2010 vertical analysis calculation

Alexis Corporation
Income Statements
for the year ended March 31,

	2010		2009			
	($ millions)	Vertical Analysis %	($ millions)	Vertical Analysis %	Horizontal Analysis % Change	Horizontal Analysis Calculations
Sales (Note 2) (2,681/2,681)	2,681	100.00%	2,240	100.00%	19.69%	(2,681−2,240)/2,240
Less: Cost of goods sold (Note 3) (2,272/2,681)	2,272	84.75%	1,745	77.90%	30.20%	(2,272−1,745)/1,745
Gross profit (409/2,681)	409	15.25%	495	22.10%	−17.37%	(409−495)/495
Less: Operating costs (362/2,681)	362	13.50%	252	11.25%	43.65%	(362−252)/252
Earnings before interest and taxes (EBIT) (47/2,681)	47	1.75%	243	10.85%	−80.66%	(47−243)/243
Less: Interest expense (32/2,681)	32	1.19%	18	0.80%	77.78%	(32−18)/18
Earnings before taxes (15/2,681)	15	0.56%	225	10.05%	−93.33%	(15−225/225
Less: Income tax expense (4/2,681)	4	0.15%	60	2.68%	−93.33%	(4−60)/60
Net income (11/2,681)	11	0.41%	165	7.37%	−93.33%	(11−165)/165

Alexis Corporation
Statements of Retained Earnings
for the year ended March 31,
(in $ millions)

	2010	2009
Opening retained earnings, April 1	263	138
Add: Net income	11	165
Less: Dividends declared	40	40
Closing retained earnings, March 31 (Note 4)	234	263

Notes:

1. The market value of the 600 million shares outstanding on March 31 was $1.50 for 2010 and $2.50 for 2009.
2. All sales and purchases were made on credit.
3. Cost of goods sold details are as follows:

	(in $ millions)	
	2010	2009
Opening inventory	300	241
Plus: Purchases (Note 2)	2,378	1,804
Goods available for sale	2,678	2,045
Less: Closing inventory	406	300
Cost of goods sold	2,272	1,745

4. Closing balance appears on the balance sheet.
5. The business employed 13,995 staff at March 31, 2009, and 18,623 at March 31, 2010.
6. At April 1, 2008, the total shareholders' equity stood at $438 million, long-term debt was $200 million, and current liabilities were $400 million.

HORIZONTAL AND VERTICAL ANALYSIS

Before we start our detailed look at the ratios for Alexis Corporation (in Example 4.1), it is helpful to take a quick look at what information is obvious from the financial statements. This will usually reveal some issues that the ratios may not be able to identify. It may also highlight some points that could help us in our interpretation of the ratios.

L.O. 3

Horizontal Analysis

Horizontal analysis compares financial statements between two or more years. An analysis covering a longer period helps to understand the trend better. Example 4.1 shows the percentage increase or decrease between account balances for 2009 compared to 2010. The percentage change from 2009 to 2010 is calculated as: (2010 Balance − 2009 Balance) ÷ 2009 Balance. Horizontal analysis can shed light on trends from one year to the next. Some comments on the horizontal analysis of various accounts are as follows:

- *Reduction in the cash balance.*   The cash balance fell 100% from $4 million to a zero balance between 2009 and 2010. In fact, there is a cash overdraft of $76 million in current liabilities in 2010. The bank may be pressuring the business to reverse this, which could raise difficulties.

- *Major expansion in the elements of working capital.*   Inventory increased by about 35% [i.e., ($406 − $300) ÷ $300 × 100%], receivables by about 14%, and accounts payables by about 42% between 2009 and 2010. These are major increases, particularly in inventory and payables (which are linked because the inventory is all bought on credit—see Note 2).

- *Expansion of property, plant, and equipment.*   These have increased by about 15% [i.e., ($587 − $510) ÷ $510 × 100%] over the year. However, as the closing figure reflects the position after depreciation for the year has been deducted, the amount actually invested in those assets during the year will be higher than the difference between the opening and closing figures. We are not told when these new assets were added, but it is quite possible that it was well into the year. This could mean that not much benefit was reflected in terms of additional sales revenue or cost savings during 2010. Sales revenue, in fact, expanded by about 20% (from $2,240 million to $2,681 million), more than the expansion in capital assets.

- *Apparent debt capacity.*   Bonds payable increased 50% in 2010. Comparing either the property, plant, and equipment assets or the net assets with the long-term debt implies that the business may well be able to offer security on further borrowing. This is because potential lenders usually look at the value of assets that can be offered as security, when assessing loan requests. Lenders seem particularly attracted to land and buildings as security. For example, at March 31, 2010, land and buildings had a balance sheet value of $427 million, but long-term borrowing was only $300 million (though there was also an overdraft of $76 million). Balance sheet values are not normally market values, of course. Land and buildings tend to have a market value higher than their balance sheet value owing to inflation in property values.

- *Lower profit.*   Although sales revenue expanded by 20% between 2009 and 2010, both cost of goods sold and operating costs rose by a greater percentage, leaving both gross profit and, particularly, net income significantly reduced. The level of staffing, which increased by about 33% (from 13,995 to 18,623), may have greatly affected the operating costs. (Without knowing when during 2010 the additional employees were recruited, we cannot be sure of the effect on operating costs.) Increasing staffing by 33% must put an enormous strain on management, at least in the short term. It is not surprising, therefore, that 2010 was not a good year for the business.

Vertical Analysis

L.O. 3

Vertical analysis can help you compare results at different companies. Vertical analysis is within one year, while horizontal analysis is over two or more years. However, to arrive at a clearer picture, the analyst should review the trend in various ratios over several years. Vertical analysis on the balance sheet calculates the percentage of each account to total assets. For the income statement, everything is usually calculated as a percentage of sales. Example 4.1 shows a vertical analysis trend over two years: 2010 and 2009.

Summary of Horizontal and Vertical Analysis

To summarize, the managers of Alexis Corporation would use horizontal and vertical analyses to determine whether the company is on track with its expansion plans. For example, the vertical analysis for 2009 indicates buildings were 22.60% of assets. In 2010, buildings were 25.83% of assets. Either buildings were acquired or constructed, or other assets declined. Then the horizontal analysis shows that the account value for buildings increased 16.37%.

Significant increases in inventory, property, plant, and equipment, and the number of employees have strained the company's cash position. In light of this, management needs to consider some additional sources of long-term financing—perhaps the issuing of new shares or new debt, either bonds or bank loans.

Investors would be concerned by the decline in profitability. The gross profit percentage in 2010 of 15.25% was significantly lower than the 22.10% gross profit in 2009. The company has expanded. Now it needs to deliver the results to the bottom line by showing increased sales and profits.

SELF-ASSESSMENT QUESTION   4.1

Robert Paddle Inc. developed and sold a new paddle, known as the Bobby Oar, in 2010. Here are the financial results for the last two years.

Robert Paddle Inc.
Balance Sheets
as at December 31,

	2010	2009
Current assets		
Cash	$ 100,000	$ 71,000
Accounts receivable	254,000	340,000
Inventory	300,000	210,000
Total current assets	654,000	621,000
Property, plant, and equipment		
Land	235,000	100,000
Buildings (net)	652,000	342,000
Equipment (net)	137,500	122,000
Total property, plant, and equipment	1,024,500	564,000
Intangible assets		
Patents	26,000	11,000
Total assets	$ 1,704,500	$ 1,196,000

▶

Current liabilities

Accounts payable	$ 85,000	$ 95,000
Income taxes payable	12,433	22,467
Total current liabilities	97,433	117,467

Long-term liabilities

Bonds payable	142,000	264,000
Total liabilities	239,433	381,467

Shareholders' equity

Common shares	1,000,000	650,000
Retained earnings	465,067	164,533
Total shareholders' equity	1,465,067	814,533
Total liabilities and shareholders' equity	$ 1,704,500	$ 1,196,000

Robert Paddle Inc.
Income Statements
for the year ended December 31,

	2010	2009
Sales	$ 724,300	$ 610,000
Less: Cost of goods sold	500,000	356,000
Gross profit	224,300	254,000
Less: Operating costs	134,600	110,690
Earnings before interest and taxes (EBIT)	89,700	143,310
Less: Interest expense	15,000	25,000
Earnings before taxes	74,700	118,310
Less: Income tax expense	30,000	42,500
Net income	$ 44,700	$ 75,810

Required:

(a) Prepare a horizontal and vertical analysis for Robert Paddle Inc.

(b) Did the new product improve the company's performance?

PROFITABILITY

The following ratios may be used to evaluate the profitability of the business:

- Return on equity
- Return on capital employed
- Operating profit margin
- Gross profit margin.

Return on Equity

The **return on equity (ROE)** compares the amount of profit for the period available to the owners, with the owners' average stake in the business during that same period. The ratio (which is normally expressed in percentage terms) is express in Equation 4.1:

$$\text{Return on equity} = \frac{\text{Net income after preferred dividends (if any)}}{\text{Average shareholders' equity}} \times 100\% \quad \text{4.1}$$

Shareholders' equity consists of common shares plus retained earnings.

The net income after any preferred dividend is used in calculating the ratio, as this figure represents the amount of profit that is left for the owners (that is, the common shareholders).

In the case of Alexis Corporation, the ratio for the year ended March 31, 2009, is:

$$ROE = \frac{165}{(438 + 563)/2} \times 100\% = 33.0\%$$

Note that, in calculating the ROE, the average of the figures for shareholders' equity at the beginning and the end of the year has been used (see Activity 4.2). It is preferable to use an average figure, as this might be more representative: shareholders' equity did not have the same total throughout the year, yet we want to compare it with the profit earned during the whole period. We know, from Note 6, that the total of the shareholders' equity at April 1, 2008, was $438 million. By a year later, however, it had risen to $563 million, according to the balance sheet as at March 31, 2009.

The easiest approach to calculating the average amount of shareholders' equity is to take a simple average based on the opening and closing figures for the year. This is often the only information available, as is the case here. Where the beginning-of-year figure is not available, it is usually acceptable to use just the year-end figure, provided that this approach is adopted consistently. This is generally valid for all ratios that combine a figure for a period (such as net income) with one taken at a point in time (such as shareholders' equity). Activity 4.2 calculates ROE for the following year.

ACTIVITY 4.2

Calculate the ROE for Alexis for the year ended March 31, 2010.

Solution

Net income for 2010 is $11 (page 109) while shareholders' equity is $563 for 2009 and $534 for 2010 (page 108).
   The ROE for 2010 is:

$$ROE = \frac{11}{(563 + 534)/2} \times 100\% = 2.0\%$$

Businesses seek to generate as high as possible a value for ROE, provided that it is not achieved at the expense of potential future returns by, for example, taking on more risky activities. We need to find out why ROE declined so much in 2010. As we look at other ratios, we should find some clues.

REAL WORLD 4.1 shows the Bank of Canada's response to excessive risk-taking.

REAL WORLD 4.1   Bank of Canada Wants to Fight Excessive Risk-Taking

Mark Carney, governor of the Bank of Canada, stated in August 2009 that he would like additional powers from the federal government to combat financial market instability caused by excessive risk-taking. Many U.S. banks made large bets on the financial markets with their own money. This is known as proprietary trading and it involved such esoteric financial instruments as derivatives, credit default swaps, and asset-backed securities. Some insurance companies insured some of these financial instruments. When the markets turned bad, these "investments" generated such large losses that the banks' shareholders' equity was wiped out and the banks became insolvent. The

▶

results were a disaster for many banks and investors. The financial debacle spilled over onto "Main Street," affecting average citizens—many companies downsized their workforce to cope with the decreased demand for goods and services worldwide.

The Bank of Canada is currently restricted by government to maintaining inflation within a 0%–2% range. This mandate expired in 2011. In 2008 and 2009, the financial market crash started with a U.S. sub-prime mortgage collapse. This eventually resulted in the worst global recession since the end of World War II. Carney thinks central bankers may have done too good a job as inflation-fighters. The long period of benign inflation since the mid-1980s created low interest rates and a false sense of security that encouraged Wall Street traders to take excessive risks to earn high bonuses. The low interest rates allowed banks to borrow money at practically no cost (almost zero interest rate in Japan) and make investments elsewhere with the borrowed money to try to generate profits.

Mr. Carney wants to be able to raise interest rates, a monetary policy tool, to cool off future financial market bubbles even at the cost of permitting increased inflation.

Source: www.cbc.ca/money/story/2009/08/22/carney-powers.html, accessed August 26, 2009.

Return on Capital Employed

The **return on capital employed (ROCE)** is a fundamental measure of business performance. This ratio expresses the relationship between the earnings before interest and taxes generated during a period and the average long-term capital invested in the business during that period.

The ratio is expressed in percentage terms in Equation 4.2:

$$\text{Return on capital employed} = \frac{\text{Earnings before interest and taxes}}{\text{(Average shareholders' equity + Average preferred shares + Average long-term debt)}} \times 100\% \quad \text{4.2}$$

Note that in this case, that the profit figure used is the earnings *before* interest and taxation. This is because the ratio attempts to measure the returns to all suppliers of long-term capital before any deductions for interest payable to lenders or payments of dividends to shareholders are made.

For the year ended March 31, 2009, the ratio for Alexis is:

$$\text{ROCE} = \frac{243}{[(438 + 200) + (563 + 200)]/2} \times 100\% = 34.7\%$$

ROCE is considered by many to be a primary measure of profitability. It compares inputs (capital invested) with outputs (profit), which is important in assessing how effectively funds have been used. Once again, an average figure for capital employed should be used where the information is available. Activity 4.3 calculates ROCE for the following year.

ACTIVITY 4.3

Calculate the **ROCE** for Alexis Corporation for the year ended March 31, 2010.

Solution

Earnings before interest and taxes for 2010 is $47. The other figures are taken from page 108. For 2010, the ratio is:

$$\text{ROCE} = \frac{47}{[(563 + 200) + (534 + 300)]/2} \times 100\% = 5.9\%$$

This ratio tells much the same story as ROE: namely a poor performance in 2010, with the return on capital employed being less than the rate that the business has to pay for most of its borrowed funds (that is, 9% for the bonds).

REAL WORLD 4.2 shows financial ratios used by banks as a basis for setting profitability targets.

REAL WORLD 4.2

Big Banks Employ Profit Targets

2008 was a very challenging year. Many companies omitted publishing financial targets in their annual reports in part because they had missed past targets so badly. Canadian banks were generally forthcoming. All the banks fell short on growing their return on equity (ROE) and earnings per share (EPS).

	ROE		EPS Growth	
	2008	Target	2008	Target
Royal Bank of Canada	18%	20%	(19%)	7%–10%
Bank of Nova Scotia	17%	20%–23%	(24%)	7%–12%
Toronto-Dominion Bank	n/a	n/a	(15%)	7%–10%
Bank of Montreal	13%	17%–20%	(8.5%)	10%–15%

Source: 2008 annual reports.

Operating Profit Margin

The **operating profit margin ratio** relates the earnings before interest and taxes (EBIT) for the period to the sales revenue during that period. The ratio is expressed in Equation 4.3:

$$\text{Operating profit margin} = \frac{\text{Earnings before interest and taxes}}{\text{Sales revenue}} \times 100\% \qquad \text{4.3}$$

EBIT is used in this ratio as it represents the profit from business operations before the interest costs are taken into account. This is often regarded as the most appropriate measure of operational performance, when used as a basis of comparison, because differences arising from the way in which the business is financed will not influence the measure.

For the year ended March 31, 2009, Alexis's operating profit margin ratio is:

$$\text{Operating profit margin} = \frac{243}{2,240} \times 100\% = 10.8\%$$

This ratio compares one output of the business (profit) with another output (sales revenue). The ratio can vary considerably between types of business. For example, on the one hand, supermarkets tend to operate on low prices and, therefore, low operating profit margins in order to stimulate sales and thereby increase the total amount of profit generated. Jewellers, on the other hand, tend to have high operating profit margins, but have much lower levels of sales volume. Factors such as the degree of competition, the type of customer, the economic climate, and the industry characteristics (such as the level of risk) will influence the operating profit margin of a business. Activity 4.4 calculates operating profit margin.

ACTIVITY 4.4

Calculate the operating profit margin for Alexis Corporation for the year ended March 31, 2010.

Solution

Earnings before interest and taxes is $47 in 2010, and sales are $2,681, both from page 109. The operating profit margin for 2010 is:

$$\text{Operating profit margin} = \frac{47}{2,681} \times 100\% = 1.8\%$$

Once again, Alexis showed a very weak performance compared with that of 2009. After paying the cost of the carpets sold and other expenses of operating the business, for every $1 of sales revenue an average of 10.8 cents (that is, 10.8%) was left as profit in 2009; for 2010, this had fallen to only 1.8 cents for every $1. Thus, the poor ROE and ROCE ratios were partially—or perhaps wholly—due to a high level of expenses relative to sales revenue. The next ratio should provide us with a clue as to how the sharp decline in these ratios occurred.

REAL WORLD 4.3 shows margins at several Canadian companies over a five-year period.

Margin Variations at Selected Retailers

	2008	2007	2006	2005	2004
Lululemon gross profit margin	50.7%	53.7%	51.2%	51.1%	52.3%
Gildan gross profit margin	32.2%	32.1%	32.6%	31.1%	29.0%
Tim Hortons operating margin	21.7%	22.4%	22.9%	19.6%	23.9%
Loblaw operating margin	3.4%	2.5%	1.0%	5.1%	6.3%

Lululemon, the Vancouver-based high-end seller of yoga-inspired athletic wear, achieves margins in the 50% range because it markets both high-quality and lifestyle goods. Gildan, being more of a mass-market T-shirt and sock wholesaler, earns smaller margins. Tim Hortons' margins are even smaller. Loblaw, in the grocery business, has the smallest margins, but when applied to huge sales volume, the company turns a reasonable profit.

It is important for a company to try to maintain and improve its margins. You can see Loblaw's difficulties are reflected in its fluctuating operating margins as it ran into trouble trying to diversify into non-food products to meet competition from Wal-Mart.

Source: various annual reports.

Gross Profit Margin

The **gross profit margin ratio** relates the gross profit of the business to the sales revenue generated for the same period. Gross profit represents the difference between sales revenue and the cost of sales. The ratio is therefore a measure of profitability in buying (or producing) and selling goods before any other expenses are taken into account. As cost of goods sold represents a major expense for many businesses, a change in this ratio can have a significant effect on the bottom line (that is, the net income for the year). The gross profit margin ratio is calculated in Equation 4.4:

$$\text{Gross profit margin} = \frac{\text{Gross profit}}{\text{Sales revenue}} \times 100\% \qquad 4.4$$

For the year ended March 31, 2009, the ratio for Alexis Corporation is:

$$\text{Gross profit margin} = \frac{495}{2,240} \times 100\% = 22.1\%$$

Activity 4.5 calculates the ratio for the following year.

ACTIVITY 4.5

Calculate the gross profit margin for Alexis Corporation for the year ended March 31, 2010.

Solution

Gross profit for 2010 is $409, while sales are $2,681, from page 109:
The gross profit margin for 2010 is:

$$\text{Gross profit margin} = \frac{409}{2,681} \times 100\% = 15.3\%$$

The decline in this ratio means that gross profit was lower *relative* to sales revenue in 2010 than it had been in 2009. Bearing in mind that:

$$\text{Gross profit} = \text{Sales revenue} - \text{Cost of goods sold}$$

This means that cost of goods sold was higher *relative* to sales revenue in 2010 than in 2009. This could mean that sales prices were lower and/or that the purchase cost of goods sold had increased. It is possible that both sales prices and cost of goods sold prices had decreased, but with sales prices having fallen at a greater rate than cost of goods sold prices. Similarly, they may both have increased, but with sales prices having increased at a lesser rate than costs of the goods sold.

Clearly, part of the decline in the net profit margin ratio is linked to the dramatic decline in the gross profit margin ratio. After paying for the carpets sold, from each $1 of sales revenue there were 22.1 cents left to cover other operating expenses and leave a profit in 2009, whereas there were only 15.3 cents left over in 2010.

The profitability ratios for the business over the two years can be set out as follows:

	2010 (%)	2009 (%)
Return on equity	2.0	33.0
Return on capital employed	5.9	34.7
Operating profit margin	1.8	10.8
Gross profit margin	15.3	22.1

Activity 4.6 explores the significance of different profitability ratios.

ACTIVITY 4.6

What can you conclude from a comparison of the declines in the operating profit and gross profit margin ratios?

Solution

We can see that the decline in the operating profit margin was 9% (that is, from 10.8% to 1.8%), whereas the decline in the gross profit margin was only 6.8% (that is, from 22.1% to 15.3%). This can only mean that operating expenses were greater—compared with sales revenue—in 2010 than they had been in 2009. Thus, the declines in both ROE and ROCE were caused partly by the business incurring higher inventory purchasing costs relative to sales revenue, and partly through higher operating expenses relative to sales revenue. We would need to compare these actual ratios with the planned ratios before we could usefully assess the business's success.

The analyst must now carry out some investigation to discover what caused the increases in both cost of goods sold and operating costs, relative to sales revenue, from 2009 to 2010. This will involve checking on what has happened with sales and inventory prices over the two years. Similarly, it will involve looking at each of the individual expenses that make up operating costs to discover which ones were responsible for the increase, relative to sales revenue. Other ratios—for example, staff costs (wages and salaries) to sales revenue—could be calculated in an attempt to isolate the cause of the change from 2009 to 2010. In fact, as we discussed in the overview of the financial statements, the increase in staffing may well account for most of the increase in operating costs.

REAL WORLD 4.4 shows return on capital employed and return on equity over a four-year period at Encana.

REAL WORLD 4.4

Encana Tries to Improve ROCE and ROE

In 2005, Encana, a large natural gas company based in Calgary, sold $4 billion of non-core assets in an attempt to improve return on capital employed and return on equity. Did it work? Both ROCE and ROE improved significantly in 2006, declined below 2005 levels in 2007, and improved in 2008. Some of the 2008 increased returns were the result of high oil prices, which peaked at $147 per barrel, and natural gas prices that topped out at $13.61 per dekatherm.

	2008	2007	2006	2005
ROCE	20%	16%	25%	17%
ROE	27%	21%	34%	23%

Source: Encana 2006 and 2008 Annual Reports.

EFFICIENCY

Efficiency ratios examine the ways in which various resources of the business are managed. The following ratios consider some of the more important aspects of resource management:

- Average inventory turnover period
- Average collection period for receivables
- Average payment period for payables
- Sales revenue to capital employed
- Sales revenue per employee.

Average Inventory Turnover Period

Inventory often represents a significant investment for a business. For some types of businesses (for example, manufacturers and retailers), inventory may account for a substantial proportion of the total assets held. The **average inventory turnover period** measures the average period for which inventory is being held. The ratio is calculated in Equation 4.5:

$$\text{Average inventory turnover period} = \frac{\text{Average inventory held}}{\text{Cost of goods sold}} \times 365 \qquad 4.5$$

The average inventory for the period can be calculated as a simple average of the opening and closing inventory levels for the year. However, in the case of a highly seasonal business, where inventory levels may vary considerably over the year, a monthly average may be more appropriate.

In the case of Alexis Corporation, the inventory turnover period for the year ended March 31, 2009, is:

$$\text{Average inventory turnover period} = \frac{(241 + 300)/2}{1,745} \times 365 = 56.6 \text{ days}$$

This means that, on average, the inventory held is being turned over every 56.6 days. So, a carpet bought by the business on a particular day would, on average, have been sold about eight weeks later. A business will normally prefer a short inventory turnover period to a long one, as funds tied up in inventory cannot be used for other purposes. In judging the amount of inventory to carry, the business must consider such things as the likely demand for the inventory, the possibility of supply shortages, the likelihood of price increases, the amount of storage space available, and the perishability of the inventory. At the individual store level, store managers responsible for ordering inventory should strive to minimize the inventory held without jeopardizing sales. This would result in a lower average inventory turnover period and would eventually increase company profitability. The management of inventory is considered in more detail in Chapter 12.

This ratio is sometimes expressed in terms of months rather than days. Multiplying by 12 rather than 365 will achieve this.

Activity 4.7 calculates average inventory turnover period.

ACTIVITY 4.7

Calculate the average inventory turnover period for Alexis Corporation for the year ended March 1, 2010.

Solution

Inventory data is from page 108. Cost of goods sold for 2010 is $2,272
The average inventory turnover period for 2010 is:

$$\text{Average inventory turnover period} = \frac{(300 + 406)/2}{2,272} \times 365 = 56.7 \text{ days}$$

Thus the average inventory turnover period is virtually the same in both years.

Average Collection Period for Receivables

A business will usually be concerned with how long it takes for customers to pay the amounts owing. The speed of payment can have a significant effect on the business's cash flow. The **average collection period for receivables** calculates how long, on average, credit customers take to pay the amounts they owe to the business. The ratio is expressed in Equation 4.6:

$$\frac{\text{Average collection period}}{\text{for receivables}} = \frac{\text{Average accounts receivable}}{\text{Credit sales revenue}} \times 365 \qquad \text{4.6}$$

A business will normally prefer a shorter average settlement period to a longer one as, once again, funds are being tied up that may be used for more profitable purposes. Though this ratio can be useful, it is important to remember that it produces an average figure for the number of days for which receivables are outstanding. This average may be badly distorted by, for example, a few large customers who are very slow or very fast payers.

Since all sales made by Alexis Corporation are on credit, the average collection period for receivables for the year ended March 31, 2009, is:

$$\text{Average collection period for receivables} = \frac{240}{2,240} \times 365 = 39.1 \text{ days}$$

As no figures for opening accounts receivable are available, only the year-end accounts receivable figure is used. This is common practice. Activity 4.8 calculates the average collection period.

ACTIVITY 4.8

Calculate the average collection period for Alexis Corporation's receivables for the year ended March 31, 2010. (In the interest of consistency, use the year-end receivables figure rather than an average figure.)

▶

Solution

Accounts receivable is $273 (p. 108), while sales are $2,681.
The average collection period for 2010 is:

$$\text{Average collection period for receivables} = \frac{273}{2,681} \times 365 = 37.2 \text{ days}$$

On the face of it, this reduction in the average collection period is welcome. It means that less cash was tied up in receivables for each dollar of sales revenue in 2010 than in 2009. The desirability of the reduction might be questioned only if the reduction were achieved at the expense of customer satisfaction or at a high direct financial cost. For example, the reduction might have been a result of chasing customers too vigorously for payment, or a result of incurring higher costs (such as discounts allowed to customers who pay quickly).

Average Payment Period for Payables

The **average payment period for payables** measures how long, on average, the business takes to pay its suppliers. The ratio is calculated in Equation 4.7:

$$\text{Average payment period for payables} = \frac{\text{Average accounts payable}}{\text{Credit purchases}} \times 365 \qquad \text{4.7}$$

This ratio provides an average figure, which, like the average collection period for receivables ratio, can be distorted by the payment period for one or two large suppliers.

As accounts payable provide a free source of financing for the business, it is perhaps not surprising that some businesses attempt to increase their average payment period. However, such a policy can be taken too far and result in a loss of support from the suppliers. We return to the issues concerning the management of accounts receivable and accounts payable in Chapter 12.

For the year ended March 31, 2009, Alexis's average payment period is:

$$\text{Average payment period for payables} = \frac{221}{1,804} \times 365 = 44.7 \text{ days}$$

Once again, the year-end figure rather than an average figure for accounts payable has been used in the calculations. Activity 4.9 completes the calculation for the following year.

ACTIVITY 4.9

Calculate the average payment period for payables for Alexis Corporation for the year ended March 31, 2010. (For the sake of consistency, use a year-end figure for payables.)

Solution

Acounts payable is $314 (p. 108), while purchases are $2,378 (Note 3, p. 109).
The average payment period for 2010 is:

$$\text{Average payment period for payables} = \frac{314}{2,378} \times 365 = 48.2 \text{ days}$$

There was an increase, between 2009 and 2010, in the average length of time that elapsed between buying inventory and paying for it. On the face of it, this is beneficial because the business is using free loans provided by suppliers. If, however, this is alienating the suppliers, the longer payment period is not necessarily advantageous to Alexis.

Sales Revenue to Capital Employed

The **sales revenue to capital employed** ratio (or net asset turnover ratio) examines how effectively the assets of the business are being used to generate sales revenue. It is calculated in Equation 4.8:

$$\frac{\text{Sales revenue to}}{\text{capital employed}} = \text{Net asset turnover}$$

$$= \frac{\text{Sales revenue}}{(\text{Average long-term liabilities} + \text{Average shareholders' equity})}$$

$$= \frac{\text{Sales revenue}}{(\text{Average total assets} - \text{Average current liabilities})} \quad 4.8$$

Recall from Chapter 2 that these two versions of Equation 4.8 are identical since the denominators form the balance sheet equation (Assets = Liabilities + Shareholders' equity). Preferred shares, if any, are included in total shareholders' equity.

Generally speaking, a higher sales revenue to capital employed (net asset turnover) ratio is preferred. A higher ratio will normally suggest that the capital invested in assets is being used more productively in the generation of revenue. However, a very high ratio may suggest that the business is overtrading on its assets; that is, it has insufficient capital (assets) to sustain the level of sales revenue achieved. (Overtrading is discussed in more detail later in this chapter.) When comparing this ratio for different businesses, such factors as the age and condition of assets held, the valuation bases for assets, and whether assets are rented or purchased outright can complicate interpretation.

From Note 6 on page 109, shareholders' equity of $438 plus long-term debt of $200 totals to $638 for 2008. For 2009, total assets of $1,054 less current liabilities of $291 gives $763. For the year ended March 31, 2009, this ratio for Alexis Corporation is as follows:

$$\text{Sales revenue to capital employed} = \frac{2,240}{(638 + 763)/2} = 3.20 \text{ times}$$

Activity 4.10 calculates the sales revenue to capital employed ratio for the following year.

ACTIVITY 4.10

Calculate the sales revenue to capital employed ratio for Alexis Corporation for the year ended March 31, 2010.

▶

Solution

For 2010, total assets of $1,266 less current liabilities of $432 gives $834.
The sales revenue to capital employed ratio for 2010 is:

$$\text{Sales revenue to capital employed} = \frac{2,681}{(763 + 834)/2} = 3.36 \text{ times}$$

This seems to be an improvement, since in 2010 more sales revenue ($3.36) was being generated for each $1 of capital employed than was the case in 2009 ($3.20). Provided that overtrading is not an issue, this is to be welcomed.

Sales Revenue per Employee

The **sales revenue per employee** ratio relates sales revenue to a particular business resource, that is, labour. It provides a measure of the productivity of the workforce. The ratio is expressed in Equation 4.9:

$$\text{Sales revenue per employee} = \frac{\text{Sales revenue}}{\text{Number of employees}} \qquad 4.9$$

Generally, businesses would prefer to have a high value for this ratio, implying that they are using their staff efficiently. Marketing managers and human resources staff should keep the sales revenue per employee ratio in mind when hiring plans are being developed. Sometimes managers' bonuses depend on the value of these types of ratios.

The number of employees is given in Note 5 on page 109. For the year ended March 31, 2009, the ratio for Alexis Corporation is:

$$\text{Sales revenue per employee} = \frac{\$2,240,000,000}{13,995} = \$160,057$$

Activity 4.11 calculates the sales revenue per employee for the following year.

ACTIVITY 4.11

Calculate the sales revenue per employee for Alexis Corporation for the year ended March 31, 2010.

Solution

The ratio for 2010 is:

$$\text{Sales revenue per employee} = \frac{\$2,681,000,000}{18,623} = \$143,962$$

This represents a fairly significant decline and probably merits further investigation. As we discussed previously, the number of employees has increased quite notably (by about 33%) during 2010, and the analyst will probably try to discover why this has not generated sufficient additional sales revenue to maintain the ratio at its 2009 level. It could be that the additional employees were not hired until late in the year ended March 31, 2010.

The efficiency, or activity, ratios for Alexis Corporation may be summarized as follows:

	2010	2009
Average inventory turnover period	56.7 days	56.6 days
Average collection period for receivables	37.2 days	39.1 days
Average payment period for payables	48.2 days	44.7 days
Sales revenue to capital employed (net asset turnover)	3.36 times	3.20 times
Sales revenue per employee	$143,962	$160,057

Activity 4.12 compares these efficiency ratios.

ACTIVITY 4.12

What do you conclude from a comparison of the efficiency ratios over the two years?

Solution

Maintaining the inventory turnover period at the 2009 level seems reasonable, although whether this period is satisfactory can probably only be assessed by looking at the business's planned inventory holding period. The inventory holding period for other businesses operating in carpet retailing—particularly those regarded as the market leaders—may have been helpful in formulating the plans. On the face of things, a shorter collection period for receivables and a longer payment period for payables are both desirable. On the other hand, these may have been achieved at the cost of alienating both customers and suppliers. The increased net asset turnover ratio seems beneficial, provided that the business can manage this increase. The decline in the sales revenue per employee ratio is undesirable but, as we have already seen, is probably related to the dramatic increase in the level of staffing. As with the inventory turnover period, these other ratios need to be compared with the planned or budgeted standard of efficiency.

THE RELATIONSHIP BETWEEN PROFITABILITY AND EFFICIENCY

In our earlier discussions concerning profitability ratios, we saw that return on capital employed (ROCE), Equation 4.2, is regarded as a key ratio by many businesses.

This ratio can be broken down into two elements, as shown in Figure 4.2. The first ratio is the operating profit margin ratio, and the second is the sales revenue to capital employed (net asset turnover) ratio, which we discussed earlier.

FIGURE 4.2   The Main Elements Comprising the ROCE Ratio

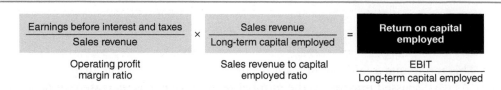

By breaking down the ROCE ratio in this manner, we highlight the fact that the overall return on funds used within the business will be determined both by the profitability of sales and by the efficient use of capital.

Example 4.2 demonstrates that a relatively low operating profit margin can be compensated for by a relatively high sales revenue to capital employed ratio, and a relatively low sales revenue to capital employed ratio can be compensated for by a relatively high operating profit margin. In many areas of retail and distribution (for example, supermarkets and delivery services), the operating profit margins are quite low, but the ROCE can be high, provided that the assets are used productively.

Example 4.2

Consider the following information concerning two different businesses operating in the same industry:

	Antler Ltd.	Baker Ltd.
EBIT	$ 20 million	$ 15 million
Long-term capital employed	$100 million	$ 75 million
Sales revenue	$200 million	$300 million

The ROCE for both businesses is identical (20%). However, the manner in which the return was achieved by each business was quite different. In the case of Antler, the operating profit margin is 10% and the sales revenue to long-term capital employed ratio is 2 times (so, ROCE = 10% × 2 = 20%). In the case of Baker, the operating profit margin is 5% and the sales revenue to long-term capital employed ratio is 4 times (and so, ROCE = 5% × 4 = 20%).

Activity 4.13 analyzes the ROCE ratio for Alexis Corporation.

ACTIVITY 4.13

Show how the ROCE ratio for Alexis Corporation can be analyzed into the two elements for each of the years 2009 and 2010.

What conclusions can we draw from your figures?

Solution

	Equation 4.2		Equation 4.3		Equation 4.8
	ROCE	=	Operating profit margin	×	Sales revenue to capital employed
2009	34.7%	=	10.8%	×	3.20
2010	5.9%	=	1.8%	×	3.36

Thus the relationship among the three ratios holds for Alexis Corporation for both years. The small rounding differences arise because the three ratios are stated above only to one or two decimal places.

Though the business was more effective at generating sales (sales revenue to capital employed ratio increased) from 2009 to 2010, this ratio was well below the level necessary to compensate for the sharp decline in the effectiveness of each sale (operating profit margin). As a result, the 2010 ROCE was well below the 2009 value.

SELF-ASSESSMENT QUESTION   4.2

Both Ali Limited and Bhaskar Corp. operate electrical stores throughout the Maritimes. The financial statements of each business for the year ended June 30, 2010, are as follows:

Balance Sheets
as at June 30, 2010
(in $ thousands)

	Ali Limited		Bhaskar Corp.	
Current assets				
Cash	84.6		91.6	
Accounts receivable	176.4		321.9	
Inventory	592.0		403.0	
Total current assets		853.0		816.5
Property, plant, and equipment				
Land	160.0		210.0	
Buildings, net	200.0		300.0	
Plant and equipment, net	87.0		91.2	
Total property, plant, and equipment		447.0		601.2
Total assets		1,300.0		1,417.7
Current liabilities				
Accounts payable	271.4		180.7	
Income taxes payable	16.0		17.4	
Dividends payable	135.0		95.0	
Total current liabilities		422.4		293.1
Long-term liabilities				
Bonds payable		190.0		250.0
Total liabilities		612.4		543.1
Shareholders' equity				
Common shares	320.0		250.0	
Retained earnings	367.6		624.6	
Total shareholders' equity		687.6		874.6
Total liabilities and shareholders' equity		1,300.0		1,417.7

Income Statements
for the year ended June 30, 2010
(in $ thousands)

	Ali Limited		Bhaskar Corp.	
Sales		1,478.1		1,790.4
Less: Cost of goods sold				
Opening inventory	480.8		372.6	
Plus: Purchases	1,129.5		1,245.3	
Goods available for sale	1,610.3		1,617.9	
Less: Closing inventory	592.0		403.0	

▶

Cost of goods sold	1,018.3	1,214.9
Gross profit	459.8	575.5
Less: Operating expenses	308.5	408.6
Earnings before interest and taxes	151.3	166.9
Interest expenses	19.4	27.5
Earnings before taxes	131.9	139.4
Less: Income tax expense	32.0	34.8
Net income	99.9	104.6

Statements of Retained Earnings
for the year ended June 30, 2010
(in $ thousands)

	Ali Limited	Bhaskar Corp.
Opening retained earnings, July 1	402.7	615.0
Add: Net income	99.9	104.6
Less: Dividends declared	(135.0)	(95.0)
Closing retained earnings, June 30	367.6	624.6

Notes
1. All purchases and sales were on credit.
2. The market value of the shares on June 30, 2010, was $6.50 for Ali Limited and $8.20 for Bhaskar Corp.
3. Ali Limited has 320,000 shares outstanding, and Bhaskar Corp. has 250,000 shares outstanding.

Required:

For each business, calculate three ratios that are concerned with profitability and three that are concerned with efficiency (six ratios in total). What can you conclude about the ratios you calculated?

LIQUIDITY

Liquidity ratios are concerned with the ability of the business to meet its short-term financial obligations. The following ratios are widely used:

- Current ratio
- Acid test ratio.

Current Ratio

The **current ratio** compares the business's liquid assets (that is, cash and those assets that will soon be turned into cash) with the current liabilities. The ratio is calculated in Equation 4.10:

$$\text{Current ratio} = \frac{\text{Current assets}}{\text{Current liabilities}} \qquad 4.10$$

Some people suggest that there is an ideal current ratio (usually 2 times, or 2:1) for all businesses. However, this fails to take into account the fact that different types of businesses require different current ratios. For example, on the one hand, a manufacturing business will often have a relatively high current ratio because it is necessary to hold inventories of finished goods, raw materials, and work in progress. It will also normally sell goods on credit, thereby incurring receivables. A supermarket chain, on the other hand, will have a relatively low ratio, as it will hold only fast-moving inventories of finished goods and will generate mostly cash sales revenue.

The higher the ratio, the more liquid the business is considered to be. As liquidity is vital to the survival of a business, a higher current ratio might be thought to be preferable to a lower one. If a business has a very high ratio, however, funds might be tied up in cash or other liquid assets that could be used more productively elsewhere.

As at March 31, 2009, the current ratio of Alexis is:

$$\text{Current ratio} = \frac{544}{291} = 1.9 \text{ times (or 1.9:1)}$$

Activity 4.14 calculates the current ratio for the following year.

ACTIVITY 4.14

Calculate the current ratio for Alexis as at March 31, 2010.

Solution

For 2010, current assets are \$679 and current liabilities are \$432, from page 108. The current ratio as at March 31, 2010, is:

$$\text{Current ratio} = \frac{679}{432} = 1.6 \text{ times (or 1.6:1)}$$

Though this is a decline from 2009 to 2010, it is not necessarily a matter of concern. The next ratio may provide a clue as to whether there seems to be a problem.

Acid Test Ratio

The **acid test ratio** is very similar to the current ratio, but it represents a more stringent test of liquidity. It can be argued that, for many businesses, inventory cannot be converted into cash quickly. (Note that in the case of Alexis, the inventory turnover period was about 57 days in both years.) Because of the delay in converting inventory to cash, it may be better to exclude this particular asset from any measure of liquidity. The acid test ratio is a variation of the current ratio, but it excludes inventory.

The minimum level for this ratio is often stated as 1.0 times—or 1:1; that is, current assets (excluding inventory) equals current liabilities. In many highly successful businesses that are regarded as having adequate liquidity, however, it is not unusual for the acid test ratio to be below 1.0 without causing particular liquidity problems.

The acid test ratio is calculated in Equation 4.11:

$$\text{Acid test ratio} = \frac{\text{Current assets} - \text{Inventory}}{\text{Current liabilities}} \qquad 4.11$$

The acid test ratio for Alexis as at March 31, 2009, is:

$$\text{Acid test ratio} = \frac{544 - 300}{291} = 0.8 \text{ times (or 0.8:1)}$$

We can see that the liquid current assets do not quite cover the current liabilities, and so the business might be experiencing some liquidity problems. Activity 4.15 finds the acid test ratio for the following year.

ACTIVITY 4.15

Calculate the acid test ratio for Alexis as at March 31, 2010.

Solution

Inventory for 2010 is $406.
The acid test ratio as at March 31, 2010, is:

$$\text{Acid test ratio} = \frac{679 - 406}{432} = 0.6 \text{ times (or } 0.6{:}1)$$

The 2010 ratio is significantly below that for 2009. The 2010 level may well be a cause for concern. The rapid decline in this ratio should lead to steps being taken, at least, to stop further decline.

The liquidity ratios for the two-year period may be summarized as follows:

	2010	2009
Current ratio	1.6	1.9
Acid test ratio	0.6	0.8

Activity 4.16 considers these ratios.

ACTIVITY 4.16

What do you conclude from the liquidity ratios set out above?

Solution

Though it is not really possible to make a valid judgment without knowing the budgeted ratios, there appears to have been an alarming decline in liquidity. This is indicated by both of these ratios. The apparent liquidity problem may, however, be planned, short-term, and linked to the expansion in non-current assets and staffing. It may be that when the benefits of the expansion are realized, liquidity will improve. On the other hand, short-term creditors (suppliers) may become anxious when they see signs of weak liquidity. This anxiety could lead to steps being taken by creditors to press for payment, and this could cause problems for Alexis Corporation.

LEVERAGE

Financial leverage occurs when a business is financed, at least in part, by borrowing, instead of by funds provided by the owners (the shareholders). A business's degree of leverage (that is, the extent to which it is financed from sources that require a fixed return) is an important factor in assessing risk. Where a business borrows heavily, it takes on a commitment to pay interest charges and make capital repayments. This can be a significant financial burden; it can increase the risk of the business becoming insolvent. Nevertheless, most businesses are leveraged to some extent.

Given the risks involved, we may wonder why a business would want to take on debt. One reason may be that the owners have insufficient funds and therefore the only way to finance the business adequately is to borrow from others. Another reason is that leverage can be used to increase the returns to owners. This is possible provided the returns generated from borrowed funds exceed the cost of paying interest. The issue of leverage is important and we leave a detailed discussion of this topic until Chapter 10.

Two ratios are widely used to assess leverage:

- Leverage ratio
- Times interest earned ratio.

Leverage Ratio

The **leverage ratio** measures the contribution of long-term lenders to the long-term capital structure of a business. It may be calculated as in Equation 4.12:

$$\text{Leverage ratio} = \frac{\text{Long-term (non-current) debt}}{\text{Shareholders' equity} + \text{Long-term (non-current) debt}} \times 100\% \qquad 4.12$$

The leverage ratio for Alexis as at March 31, 2009, is:

$$\text{Leverage ratio} = \frac{200}{(563 + 200)} \times 100\% = 26.2\%$$

This ratio reveals a degree of leverage that would not normally be considered to be very high.

Activity 4.17 calculates the leverage ratio for the following year.

ACTIVITY 4.17

Calculate the leverage ratio of Alexis as at March 31, 2010.

Solution

Long-term debt is $300 and total shareholders' equity is $534 for 2010. See page 108. The leverage ratio as at March 31, 2010, is:

$$\text{Leverage ratio} = \frac{300}{(534 + 300)} \times 100\% = 36.0\%$$

This ratio reveals a substantial increase in the degree of leverage over the year.

Times Interest Earned Ratio

The **times interest earned ratio** measures the amount of profit available to cover interest expense. The ratio may be calculated as in Equation 4.13:

$$\text{Times interest earned ratio} = \frac{\text{Earnings before interest and taxes}}{\text{Interest expense}} \qquad 4.13$$

The ratio for Alexis Corporation for the year ended March 31, 2009, is:

$$\text{Times interest earned ratio} = \frac{243}{18} = 13.5 \text{ times}$$

This ratio shows that the level of profit is considerably higher than the level of interest expense. Thus, a significant decrease in profits could occur before profit levels would fail to cover interest payments. The lower the level of profit coverage, the greater the risk to lenders that interest payments will not be met, and the greater the risk to the shareholders that the lenders will take action against the business to recover the interest due.

Activity 4.18 calculates the times interest earned ratio for the following year.

ACTIVITY 4.18

Calculate the times interest earned ratio of Alexis Corporation for the year ended March 31, 2010.

Solution

EBIT for 2010 is $47 while interest expense is $32.
The times interest earned ratio for 2010 is:

$$\text{Times interest earned ratio} = \frac{47}{32} = 1.5 \text{ times}$$

Alexis Corporation's leverage ratios are:

	2010	2009
Leverage ratio	36.0%	26.2%
Times interest earned ratio	1.5 times	13.5 times

Activity 4.19 compares these two ratios.

ACTIVITY 4.19

What do you conclude from a comparison of the leverage ratios over the two years?

Solution

The leverage ratio altered significantly. This is mainly due to the substantial increase in the long-term debt during 2010, which has had the effect of increasing the relative contribution of long-term lenders to the financing of the business.

The times interest earned ratio has declined dramatically, from a position where profit covered interest 13.5 times in 2009, to one where profit covered interest only 1.5 times in 2008. This was partly caused by the increase in borrowing in 2010, but mainly caused by the dramatic decline in profitability in that year. The latter situation looks hazardous; even a small decline in future profitability in 2011 would leave the business with insufficient profit to cover the interest payments. The leverage ratio at March 31, 2010, would not necessarily be considered to be very high for a business that was operating successfully. It is the low profitability that is the problem.

Without knowing what the business planned these ratios to be, it is not possible to reach a totally valid conclusion on Alexis Corporation's leverage.

REAL WORLD 4.5 shows leverage ratios for several Canadian corporations.

Some Leverage Ratios

The long-term debt (LTD) to shareholders' equity plus long-term debt ratio, Equation 4.12, of five well-known Canadian companies is shown below.

	LTD to shareholders' equity plus LTD	
	2008	2007
BCE	37%	38%
Telus	47%	40%
Encana	28%	30%
CN Rail	41%	35%
Canadian Tire	28%	30%

Source: 2008 annual reports.

INVESTMENT RATIOS

Various ratios designed to help investors assess the returns on their investment are available. The following are widely used:

- Dividend payout ratio
- Dividend yield ratio
- Earnings per share
- Price/earnings ratio.

Dividend Payout Ratio

The **dividend payout ratio** measures the proportion of earnings that a business pays out to shareholders in the form of dividends. The ratio is calculated in Equation 4.14:

$$\text{Dividend payout ratio} = \frac{\text{Annual dividends to common shareholders for the year}}{\text{Net income available to common shareholders}} \times 100\% \qquad 4.14$$

In the case of common shares, the earnings available for dividends will normally be the net income after any preferred dividends announced during the period. This ratio is normally expressed as a percentage.

Alexis Corporation's dividend payout ratio for the year ended March 31, 2009, is:

$$\text{Dividend payout ratio} = \frac{40}{165} \times 100\% = 24.2\%$$

The information provided by this ratio is often expressed slightly differently as the **dividend cover ratio**. Here, the calculation is expressed in Equation 4.15:

$$\text{Dividend cover ratio} = \frac{\text{Net income available to common shareholders}}{\text{Annual dividends to common shareholders}} \qquad 4.15$$

In the case of Alexis Corporation for 2009, the dividend cover ratio is $165/40 = 4.1$ times. That is to say, the earnings available for dividends cover the actual dividends just over four times.

Activity 4.20 calculates the dividend payout ratio for the following year.

ACTIVITY 4.20

Calculate the dividend payout ratio of Alexis Corporation for the year ended March 31, 2010.

Solution

In 2010, dividends were $40 and net income was $11.
The ratio for 2010 is:

$$\text{Dividend payout ratio} = \frac{40}{11} \times 100\% = 363.6\%$$

This would normally be considered to be a very alarming increase in the ratio over the two years. Paying a dividend of $40 million on net income of only $11 million in 2010 would probably be regarded as very imprudent.

Dividend Yield Ratio

The **dividend per share** is a ratio that divides the dividends announced for a period by the number of shares outstanding. From Note 1 on page 109, there were 600 million shares outstanding and the share price was $2.50 for 2009. For Alexis Corporation, for the year ended March 31, 2009:

$$\text{Dividend per share} = \frac{\text{Dividend declared}}{\text{Number of shares}} = \frac{\$40}{600} = \$0.067$$

The **dividend yield ratio** relates the dividend on a share to its current market value. This can help investors to assess the cash return on their investment in the business. The ratio is expressed in Equation 4.16:

$$\text{Dividend yield ratio} = \frac{\text{Dividend per share}}{\text{Market value per share}} \times 100\% \qquad 4.16$$

The dividend yield ratio is also expressed as a percentage. The dividend yield for Alexis Corporation for the year ended March 31, 2009, is:

$$\text{Dividend yield} = \frac{\$0.067}{\$2.50} \times 100\% = 2.7\%$$

Activity 4.21 calculates the dividend yield for the following year.

ACTIVITY 4.21

Calculate the dividend yield for Alexis Corporation for the year ended March 31, 2010.

Solution

The dividend yield for Alexis Corporation for the year ended March 31, 2010 is:

$$\text{Dividend yield} = \frac{\$0.067^*}{\$1.50^{**}} \times 100\% = 4.5\%$$

*$40/600 = $0.067
**From Note 1, page 109.

The dividend yield increased because the share price has dropped. The higher yield is likely to help put a floor under the share price as investors buy the shares for their dividend.

Earnings per Share

The **earnings per share (EPS)** ratio relates the earnings generated by the business and available to common shareholders during a period to the number of shares outstanding. For common shareholders, the amount available will be represented by the net income (less any preferred dividend, where applicable). The ratio for common shareholders is calculated in Equation 4.17:

$$\text{Earnings per share} = \frac{\text{Net income available to common shareholders}}{\text{Number of common shares outstanding}} \qquad 4.17$$

In the case of Alexis, the earnings per share for the year ended March 31, 2009, are as follows:

$$\text{EPS} = \frac{\$165}{600} = \$0.275$$

Many investment analysts regard the EPS ratio as a fundamental measure of share performance. The trend in earnings per share over time is used to help assess the investment potential of a business's shares. Though it is possible to make total profits rise through common shareholders investing more in the business, this will not necessarily mean that the profitability *per share* will rise as a result.

It is not usually very helpful to compare the earnings per share of one business with those of another. Differences in capital structure (degree of leverage) can render any such comparison meaningless. However, it can be very useful to monitor the changes that occur in this ratio for a particular business over time. Activity 4.22 calculates the ratio for Alexis, for the following year.

ACTIVITY 4.22

Calculate the earnings per share of Alexis Corporation for the year ended March 31, 2010.

Solution

The earnings per share for the year ended March 31, 2010, are:

$$EPS = \frac{\$11}{600^*} = \$0.018$$

*From Note 1, page 109.

The EPS has declined from $0.275 to $0.018. There is a significant negative for the share price.

Price/Earnings Ratio

The **price/earnings (P/E) ratio** relates the market value of a share to the earnings per share. This ratio can be calculated as in Equation 4.18:

$$\text{Price/earnings ratio} = \frac{\text{Market value per share}}{\text{Earnings per share}} \qquad 4.18$$

From Note 1 on page 109, the share price in 2009 was $2.50. The P/E ratio for Alexis Corporation as at March 31, 2009, is:

$$\text{P/E ratio} = \frac{\$2.50}{\$0.275} = 9.1 \text{ times}$$

This ratio reveals that the capital value of the share is 9.1 times higher than its current level of earnings. The ratio is a measure of market confidence in the future of a business. The higher the P/E ratio, the greater the confidence in the future earning power of the business and, consequently, the more investors are prepared to pay in relation to the earnings stream of the business.

P/E ratios provide a useful guide to market confidence concerning the future and they can, therefore, be helpful when comparing different businesses. However, differences in accounting policies between businesses can lead to different profit and earnings per share figures, and this can distort comparisons.

Often P/E ratios are used to help investors determine whether a business's share price is expensive or inexpensive. For example, if the average P/E ratio for a Toronto Stock Exchange (TSX) listed company is 20.9, then you might figure that shares with a P/E ratio of 12.0 are a bargain and shares with a P/E ratio of 30 are too expensive. However, sometimes shares with a high P/E ratio are a better investment because their sales and profits are growing rapidly compared with the average company. Investors are confident that the company can maintain this tremendous growth rate and they bid up the price of the shares. Thus the high P/E ratio is justified by the high growth rates. One of Canada's fastest growing firms, Research In Motion (RIM), maker of the BlackBerry wireless smartphone, was accorded a P/E ratio of 20.5 in 2009, compared to 20.9 for the TSX composite index.[1] So in this respect, RIM shares in 2009 could have been considered cheap.

---

[1] *Source:* www.tsx.com/en/index.html, accessed August 27, 2009.

Activity 4.23 calculates the P/E ratio of Alexis Corporation for the year ended March 31, 2010.

ACTIVITY 4.23

Calculate the P/E ratio of Alexis Corporation for the year ended March 31, 2010.

Solution

The P/E ratio of Alexis Corporation as at March 31, 2010, is:

$$\text{P/E ratio} = \frac{\$1.50^*}{\$0.018} = 83.3 \text{ times}$$

*From Note 1, page 109.

The P/E ratio has increased, making Alexis shares very expensive on a P/E basis. Investors would perceive Alexis to be a high-risk company.

The investment ratios for Alexis Corporation over the two-year period are as follows:

	2010	2009
Dividend payout ratio	363.6%	24.2%
Dividend yield ratio	4.5%	2.7%
Earnings per share	$0.018	$0.275
Price/earnings ratio	83.3 times	9.1 times

Activity 4.23 examines the significance of these investment ratios.

ACTIVITY 4.24

What do you conclude from the investment ratios set out above? Explain why the share price has not fallen as much as it might have, considering the very poor (relative to 2009) operating performance in 2010.

Solution

Although the EPS has fallen dramatically, and the dividend payment for 2010 seems very imprudent, the share price seems to have held up remarkably well (falling from $2.50 to $1.50). This means that dividend yield and P/E value for 2010 look better than those for 2009. This is an anomaly of these two ratios, which stems from using a forward-looking value (the share price) in conjunction with historic data (dividends and earnings). Share prices are based on investors' assessments of the business's future. At the end of 2010 the market was not happy with Alexis, relative to 2009, given that the share price had fallen by $1 a share. On the other hand, the share price has not fallen as much as profits. Investors believe that the business will perform better in the future than it did in 2010, perhaps because the large expansion in assets and employee numbers that occurred in 2010 will yield benefits in the future that the business was not able to generate during 2010.

REAL WORLD 4.6 gives some information about the shares of several large, well-known Canadian businesses. This type of information is provided on a daily basis by several newspapers, notably the *Globe and Mail*, although for the most part, newspapers have now moved detailed stock tables online.

Stock Market Data for Some Well-Known Businesses

The following stock market quotes from companies trading on the TSX were compiled from the website of StockHouse Canada: www.stockhouse.com. This website has free membership. You enter a company's ticker symbol or name to obtain a great deal of trading information, some of which is shown below.

Ticker Symbol	52 week High	Low	Price	Change	Volume	Bid/Ask
BNS	50.59	23.99	47.58	0.91	3,037,672	47.58/47.59
ECA	79.97	41.36	57.26	(0.03)	1,627,637	57.25/57.26
G	44.90	17.77	39.23	0.80	1,134,297	39.25/39.26
L	37.57	26.12	33.20	(0.20)	481,011	33.19/33.22
MFC	39.40	9.02	22.38	(0.48)	2,824,984	22.37/22.38
RIM	135.55	44.23	79.82	(2.13)	806,258	79.93/79.96

- *Ticker Symbol.*   A stock symbol is used rather than the company name when an order is placed with a broker. For example: BNS–Bank of Nova Scotia, ECA–Encana, G–Goldcorp, L–Loblaw, MFC–Manulife Financial Corporation, and RIM–Research In Motion.
- *52-Week High/Low.*   The highest and lowest closing price for the shares in the last year (stated in dollars).
- *Current Intraday Price.*   The latest price at which the stock traded (in dollars). Often there is a 20-minute delay in the prices websites can provide, so this is the price as of 20 minutes ago.
- *Change.*   The change in the intraday price from the previous day's close (in dollars).
- *Volume.*   The number of shares traded so far today.
- *Bid/Ask.*   The bid is the highest price potential buyers have bid on the stock, while the ask is the lowest price potential sellers have demanded for their shares. So the bid price is lower than the ask price. The greater the spread between the bid and ask prices, the more inefficient the market for that particular stock is. No transaction will occur until there is a meeting of the minds on the price. Also given, although not shown above, is the number of bids and asks.

Source: www.stockhouse.com/, accessed August 27, 2009.

REAL WORLD 4.7 compares some investment ratios between different industries.

Investment Ratios by Industry

Investment ratios can vary significantly between businesses and between industries. To give some indication of the range of variations that occur, the average dividend yield ratios and average P/E ratios for listed businesses in 13 different industries plus the S&P TSX composite index are shown in Figures 4.3 and 4.4 respectively.

These ratios are calculated from the current market value of the shares and the most recent year's dividend paid (in the case of the dividend yield ratio) or earnings per share (in the case of the P/E ratio).

Some industries tend to pay out lower dividends than others, leading to lower dividend yield ratios. Gold miners tend to invest heavily in developing new mines, hence their tendency to pay low dividends compared with their share prices. Utilities tend to invest less heavily than gold miners, hence their rather higher level of dividend yields. Some of the inter-industry differences in the dividend yield ratio can be explained by the nature of the calculation of the ratio.

▶

The prices of shares at any given moment are based on expectations of their economic futures; dividends are actual past events. A business that had a good year recently may have paid a dividend that, in the light of investors' assessment of the business's economic future, may be high (a high dividend yield).

FIGURE 4.3   Average Dividend Yields by Industry

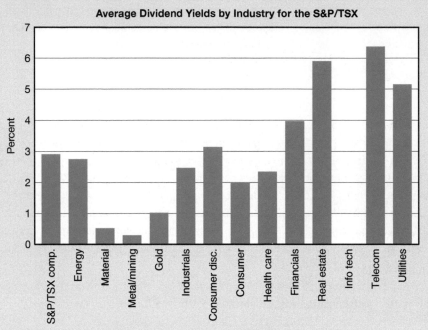

Source: Adapted from data obtained at the TSX website: http://cxa.marketwatch.com/TSX/en/Market/marketactivitycan.aspx, accessed August, 27, 2009.

FIGURE 4.4   Average Price/Earnings Ratios by Industry

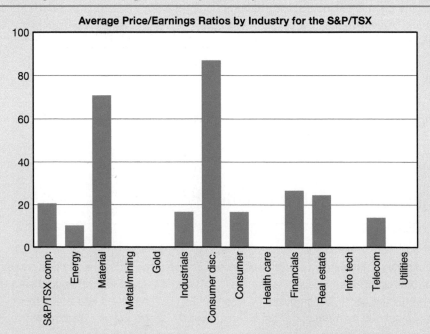

Source: Adapted from data obtained at the TSX website: http://cxa.marketwatch.com/TSX/en/Market/marketactivitycan.aspx, accessed August, 27, 2009.

Businesses that have a high share price relative to their recent earnings have high P/E ratios. Several industries do not have a P/E in the graph because their earnings became losses in the Great Recession of 2008 and 2009.

Government agencies have made industry data available to anyone. Owners and prospective entrepreneurs developing a business plan can go online and get industry statistics for comparison to their situation. This of course can lead a company to modify its business practices in an effort to emulate successful companies. REAL WORLD 4.8 examines industry statistics in the pub industry.

REAL WORLD 4.8 — Industry Averages for Pubs

Statistics Canada has made it relatively easy for companies to compare their economic performance with the industry average for their particular industry. At this website, www.ic.gc.ca/eic/site/pp-pp.nsf/eng/Home, you can generate reports on many different industry classifications and compare the average results to your company. Simply select Create a Report and enter the industry code, which can be looked up if you do not know it.

The selected data below are for industry classification number 7224—Drinking Places (Alcoholic Beverages) for 2006, the latest year available at the time of writing. Other data not shown here are also available on the website reports, including average income statements and balance sheets for the whole industry, for the bottom half of companies and the upper half, as well as the upper quartile (the top 25% of companies in this industry). Other report choices can be made at the discretion of the user.

Industry averages for key financial ratios are shown below. The debt ratio, total liabilities ÷ total assets, is 29% higher for the bottom half companies (0.9 − 0.7)/0.7) × 100. All the debt ratios including interest amounts are much worse for the lower tier companies.

Small Business Profiles—Canada 2006
Drinking Places (Alcoholic Beverages)
NAICS Number: 7224

	Whole Industry	Lower Half	Upper Half	Top Quartile (25%)
Number of Businesses	4,239			
Revenue Range:				
Low Value ($ 000)	30	30	367	744
High Value ($ 000)	5,000	367	5,000	5,000
Financial Ratios:				
Current ratio	1.0	0.8	1.0	1.0
Debt to equity ratio	2.9	6.2	2.5	2.2
Interest coverage ratio	2.9	0.4	3.6	4.0
Debt ratio	0.7	0.9	0.7	0.7
Revenue to equity ratio	7.9	8.5	7.8	7.6
Revenue to closing inventory ratio	35.0	33.6	35.2	33.6
Current debt to equity (%)	128.4	229.2	112.8	106.9
Net profit to equity (%)	21.0	(12.3)	26.1	28.2
Net fixed assets to equity (%)	215.3	411.5	184.9	171.0
Gross margin (%)	50.9	53.5	50.5	49.9
Return on total assets (%)	8.2	1.0	10.5	11.6
Collection period for accounts receivable (days)	4.8	6.3	4.5	4.3

Source: Based on Statistics Canada, 2006 Small Business Profiles – Canada – NAICS number 7224 – Drinking Places (Alcoholic Beverages), retrieved on Industry Canada Website, SME Benchmarking Tool at this url address: http://www.ic.gc.ca/eic/site/pp-pp.nsf/eng/Home (Extracted on August 2, 2009).

SELF-ASSESSMENT QUESTION   4.3

Use the same data for Ali Limited and Bhaskar Corp. as in Self-Assessment Question 4.2 on pages 126–127.

Required:
For each business, calculate two ratios that are concerned with liquidity, leverage, and investment (six ratios in total). What can you conclude about the ratios you calculated?

FINANCIAL RATIOS AND THE PROBLEM OF OVERTRADING

Overtrading occurs when a business is operating at a level of activity that cannot be supported by the amount of funds that have been invested. An example is a business that has inadequate cash to fund the level of receivables and inventory necessary for the level of sales revenue that it is achieving. This situation usually reflects a poor level of financial control over the business.

The reasons for overtrading are varied. It may occur in young, expanding businesses that fail to prepare adequately for the rapid increase in demand for their goods or services. It may also occur in businesses whose managers may have miscalculated the level of expected sales demand or failed to control escalating project costs. It may occur as a result of a fall in the value of money (inflation), causing more funds to be invested in inventory and receivables, even when there is no expansion in the real volume of trade. It may occur when the owners are unable to inject further funds into the business or to persuade others to invest in the business. Whatever the reason for overtrading, the problems that it brings must be dealt with if the business is to survive.

Overtrading results in liquidity problems such as exceeding borrowing limits, or slow repayment of lenders and creditors. It can also result in suppliers withholding supplies, thereby making it difficult to meet customer demand. The managers of the business might be forced to direct all their efforts to dealing with immediate and pressing problems, such as finding cash to meet interest charges due or paying wages. Longer-term planning becomes difficult and managers may spend their time going from crisis to crisis. At the extreme, a business may fail because it cannot meet its debt obligations.

To deal with an overtrading problem, a business must ensure that the funds available are commensurate with the level of operations. If a business that is overtrading is unable to raise new funds, it should cut back its level of operations to be in line with the funds available. Although this may mean lost sales and lost profits in the short term, it may be necessary to ensure survival over the longer term. Activity 4.25 explores the signs of overtrading.

ACTIVITY 4.25

If a business is overtrading, would the following be higher or lower than normally expected?

(a) Current ratio
(b) Average inventory turnover period
(c) Average collection period for receivables
(d) Average payment period for payables

Solution

A business that is overtrading would show the following:

(a) The current ratio would be lower than normally expected. This is a measure of liquidity, and lack of liquidity is an important symptom of overtrading.

(b) The average inventory turnover period would be lower than normally expected. When a business is overtrading, the level of inventory held will be low because of the problems of financing inventory. In the short term, sales revenue may not be badly affected by the low inventory levels and therefore inventory will be turned over more quickly.

(c) The average collection period for receivables may be lower than normally expected. When a business is suffering from liquidity problems, it may chase customers more vigorously in order to improve cash flows.

(d) The average payment period for payables may be higher than normally expected. The business may try to delay payments to suppliers because of the liquidity problems.

TREND ANALYSIS

It is often helpful to see whether ratios are indicating trends. Key ratios can be plotted on a graph to provide a simple visual display of changes occurring over time. The trends occurring within a business may, for example, be plotted against trends for rival businesses or for the industry as a whole for comparison purposes. An example of trend analysis is shown in REAL WORLD 4.9.

REAL WORLD 4.9

Trend Setting

In Figure 4.5, the return on equity (ROE) ratio is plotted for three Canadian banks—Royal Bank of Canada (RBC), Bank of Montreal (BMO), and the Canadian Imperial Bank of Commerce (CIBC) over an eight-year period. While return on equity at RBC and BMO is quite similar and trending gently upward, it is much more erratic at CIBC and even turned negative in 2005 and 2008.

The ROE ratio is plotted for the financial years 2001–2008 for all three companies on the same graph, enabling an easy visual comparison.

▶

FIGURE 4.5   Return on Equity at Three Big Banks

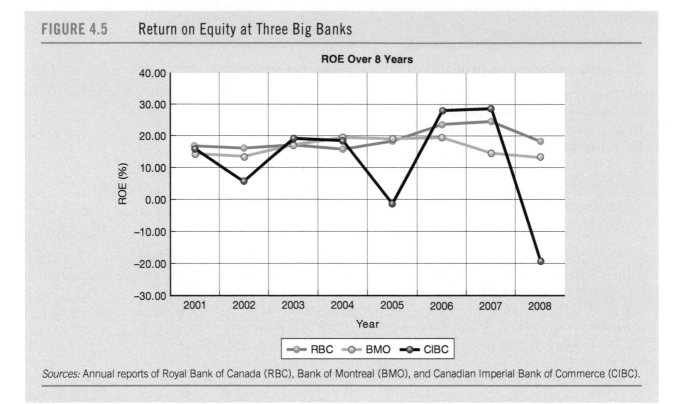

Sources: Annual reports of Royal Bank of Canada (RBC), Bank of Montreal (BMO), and Canadian Imperial Bank of Commerce (CIBC).

Activity 4.26 considers CIBC's negative return on equity.

ACTIVITY 4.26

Using the graph in Figure 4.5, what do you think might have caused CIBC to have a negative return on equity in 2005 and again in 2008 while the other banks had good results?

Solution

Some company-specific event must have affected CIBC's return on equity. In 2005, it was a US$2.4 billion settlement in regard to an Enron-related class-action lawsuit that arose when the latter went bankrupt. While admitting no wrongdoing, CIBC agreed to settle the suit to eliminate the uncertainties and expense of a lengthy litigation. In 2008, CIBC recorded large market-to-market write-downs, including a $4.2 billion loss on structured credit write-downs. We will encounter this idea of company-specific risk again in Chapter 9 when we discuss diversifiable and non-diversifiable risk.

Source: Adapted from CBC News, www.cbc.ca/money/story/2005/08/02/CIBC-enron050802.html, accessed July 19, 2007, and CIBC's 2008 Annual Report.

Many larger businesses publish certain key financial ratios as part of their annual reports to help users identify significant trends. These ratios typically cover several years' activities. REAL WORLD 4.10 is based on extracts from tables of key performance measures of BCE, the well-known Canadian communications company, which were published in its 2008 annual report.

Key Performance Measures at BCE

After long being known as a blue-chip company, BCE suffered a recent decline in fortunes due to increased competition from wireless, cable, and internet telephony. BCE's risk profile has worsened in recent years, as shown by fluctuating earnings per share and return on equity results. Companies would prefer to have smooth growth in both these ratios, since that is what the stock market values the most and rewards with a higher share price. The earnings before interest, taxes, depreciation, and amortization (EBITDA) margin does not seem to be the problem, as it has held steady at around 40%. BCE's operating margin seems to bounce around between 15% and 21%. ROE and EPS fell significantly in 2008. Expenses were up due to restructuring charges, including an $810 million charge for layoffs. BCE raised its dividend in 2005 and again in 2007. The dividend had been eliminated in 2008 as it was thought BCE would be acquired by a private equity group led by the Ontario Teachers' Pension Fund. The takeover bid was initiated in 2007 and only fell through in December 2008, at which time BCE reinstated the quarterly dividend. In February 2009, BCE announced it would increase the dividend by 5%. We will see more on dividend theory in Chapter 11.

	2008	2007	2006	2005	2004
EBITDA* margin (%)	39.6	39.4	38.7	39.2	40.4
Operating margin (%)	16.2	19.6	18.9	21.3	15.5
ROE (%)	5.6	30.0	15.7	14.9	12.6
EPS ($)	1.01	4.87	2.25	2.04	1.65
Dividends per share ($)	0.73	1.46	1.32	1.32	1.20

*Earnings before interest, taxes, depreciation, and amortization.

Source: BCE 2008 Annual Report.

Managers use trend analysis techniques to spot areas where changes are required. For example, trend analysis may indicate that the company's current ratio is deteriorating. (Recall that the current ratio is current assets divided by current liabilities.) Management may decide to obtain more funds by obtaining a long-term bank loan or by issuing some new shares. Both options improve the current ratio by increasing cash. Further improvement to the current ratio could be made by paying off some of the current liabilities.

The value of trend analysis is that it allows managers to act sooner rather than later; they can achieve the best deals available at the right time without having to rush into things at the last minute. For example, they might obtain a long-term bank loan to take advantage of a low interest rate environment, using the cash to pay off the accounts payable balance. In this way, trend analysis can help managers solve problems before they become crises, in this case by substituting long-term debt for current liabilities.

USING RATIOS TO PREDICT FINANCIAL FAILURE

Financial ratios based on current or past performance are often used to help predict the future. However, both the choice of ratios and the interpretation of results normally depend on the judgment and opinion of the analyst. In recent years, however, attempts have been made to develop a more rigorous and systematic approach to the use of ratios for prediction purposes. In particular, researchers have shown an interest in the ability of ratios to predict the financial failure of a business.

By *financial failure*, we mean a business either going out of business or being severely adversely affected by its inability to meet its financial obligations. It is often referred to as "going bust" or "going bankrupt." This, of course, concerns all those connected with the business.

Using Single Ratios

Many methods and models employing ratios have now been developed that claim to predict future financial failure. Early research focused on the examination of ratios on an individual basis to see whether they were good or bad predictors of financial failure. A particular ratio (for example, the current ratio) for a business that had failed was tracked over several years leading up to the date of the failure. This was to see whether it was possible to say that the ratio had showed a trend that could have been taken as a warning sign.

William Beaver carried out the first research in this area.[2] He calculated the average (mean) of various ratios for 79 businesses that had actually failed, over the 10-year period leading up to their failure. Beaver then compared these average ratios with similarly derived ratios for a sample of 79 businesses that did not fail over this period. Beaver found that some ratios exhibited a marked difference between the failed and non-failed businesses for up to five years prior to failure. This is shown in Figure 4.6.

To explain Figure 4.6, let us take a closer look at graph (a). This plots a ratio: cash flow (presumably the operating cash flow figure, taken from the cash flow statement) divided by total debt. For the non-failed businesses, this stayed fairly steady at about +0.45 over the period. For the failed businesses, however, this was already well below the non-failed businesses—at about +0.15—even five years before those businesses eventually failed. It then declined steadily until, by one year before the failure, it was less than −0.15. Note that the scale of the horizontal axis shows the most recent year (Year 1) on the left and the earliest year (Year 5) on the right. Graphs (b) to (f) show a similar picture for five other ratios. In each case, there is a deteriorating average ratio for the failed businesses as the time of failure approaches, even for graph (c), which shows dramatically rising debt levels for failed businesses.

What is shown in Figure 4.6 implied that failure could be predicted by careful assessment of the trend shown by particular key ratios. Research by M.E. Zmijewski, using a sample of 72 failed and 3,573 non-failed businesses over a six-year period, found that failed businesses were characterized by lower rates of return, higher leverage, lower levels of coverage for their fixed interest payments, and more variable returns on shares.[3] While we may not find these results very surprising, it is interesting to note that Zmijewski, like a number of other researchers in this area, did not find liquidity ratios particularly useful in predicting financial failure. Intuition might have led us (wrongly, it seems) to believe that the liquidity ratios would have been particularly helpful in this context.

---

[2] William H. Beaver, "Financial Ratios as Predictors of Failure," in *Empirical Research in Accounting: Selected Studies*, supplement to *Journal of Accounting Research*, Autumn 1966, pp. 71–111.

[3] M.E. Zmijewski, *Predicting Corporate Bankruptcy: An Empirical Comparison of the Extent of Financial Distress Models*, Research Paper, State University of New York, 1983.

FIGURE 4.6   Average (Mean) Ratios of Failed and Non-Failed Businesses

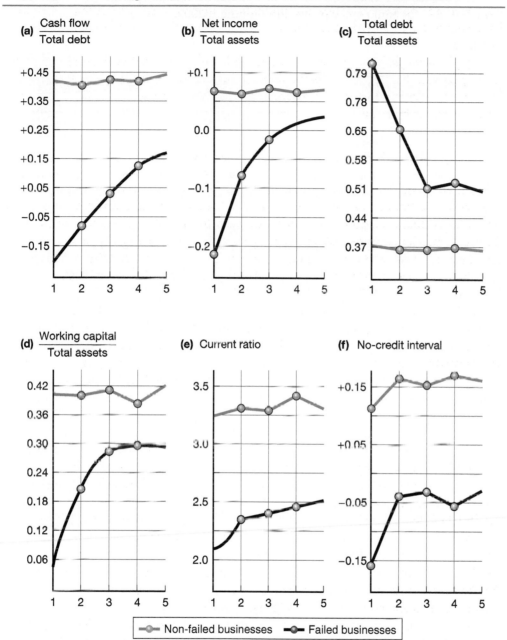

Each of the ratios (a) to (f) above indicates a marked difference in the average ratio between the sample of failed businesses and a matched sample of non-failed businesses. The vertical scale of each graph is the average value of the particular ratio for each group of businesses (failed and non-failed). The horizontal axis is the number of years before failure. Thus, Year 1 is the most recent year and Year 5 is the earliest of the years. For each of the six ratios, the difference between the average for the failed and the non-failed businesses can be detected five years prior to the failure of the former group.

Source: W.H. Beaver, "Financial ratios as predictors of failure," *Empirical Research in Accounting: Selected Studies,* supplement to *Journal of Accounting Research,* 1966, pp. 71–111. *Journal of Accounting Research.* Published by Blackwell Publishing on behalf of The Institute of Professional Accounting, Graduate School of Business, University of Chicago.

REAL WORLD 4.11 examines a ratio at General Motors Corporation, the giant auto firm that filed for bankruptcy protection on June 1, 2009.

REAL WORLD 4.11

Did GM Fit the Bill?

Did the cash flow to total debt ratio, shown in graph (a) in Figure 4.6, predict a bankruptcy filing by GM? Yes it did, as shown below. The total cash flow from operations ÷ total debt ratio was −18% in 2005 and −11% in 2006. We can see by the graph in Figure 4.6 that cash flow to total debt for failed companies turned negative two years before bankruptcy was filed. GM reversed the ratio in 2007 but it fell again into significant negative territory in 2008. Furthermore, the Z-scores are well below the 1.81 level that predicts companies that tend to fail. It might be said that GM hung on longer than most failed businesses. For more on GM's ratios, see Problem and Case 4.25.

Cash flow from operations	2008	2007	2006	2005
—Automotive	$ (13,133)	$ 5,643	$ 5,557	$ 36
—Financing and Insurance	$ 1,068	$ 2,088	$ (17,316)	$(16,892)
Total cash flow	$ (12,065)	$ 7,731	$ (11,759)	$(16,856)
Long-term debt and other long-term liabilities	$100,654	$109,040	$111,044	$ 93,225
Total cash flow to total debt	**−12%**	**7%**	**−11%**	**−18%**

_Z_-score Ratios	2008	2007	2006	2005
Working capital ÷ Total assets	(0.36)	(0.00)		
Retained earnings ÷ Total assets	(0.78)	(0.26)		
EBIT ÷ Total assets	(0.29)	(0.01)		
Market value of shares* ÷ Total liabilities	—	—		
Sales ÷ Total assets	1.6	1.2	1.1	0.4
_Z_-score	**(0.85)**	**0.81**		

*No longer available on Yahoo! Finance.

Source: GM annual reports: www.sec.gov/Archives/edgar/data/40730/000119312509045144/d10k.htm, accessed Aug 28, 2009.

Using Combinations of Ratios

We may also wish to test whether two ratios (say, the current ratio and the return on capital employed) can help to predict failure. To do this, we can calculate these ratios, first for a sample of failed businesses and then for a matched sample of non-failed businesses. From these two sets of data, we can produce a scatter diagram that plots each business according to these two ratios, to produce a single coordinate. Figure 4.7 illustrates this approach. Using the observations plotted on the diagram, we try to identify the boundary between the failed and the non-failed businesses. This is the diagonal line in Figure 4.7.

We can see that those businesses to the bottom left of the line are predominantly failed ones, and those to the upper right are predominantly non-failed ones. Note that

FIGURE 4.7 Scatter Diagram Showing the Distribution of Failed and Non-Failed Businesses

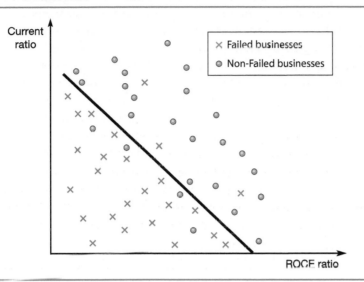

there is some overlap between the two populations. The boundary produced is unlikely, in practice, to eliminate *all* errors. Some businesses that fail may fall on the side of the boundary with non-failed businesses, and vice versa. However, the boundary will *minimize* the misclassification errors.

The boundary shown in Figure 4.7 can be expressed in the form:

$$Z = a + (b \times \text{Current ratio}) + (c \times \text{ROCE})$$

where a is a constant and b and c are weights to be attached to each ratio. A weighted average or total score (Z) is then derived. The weights given to the two ratios will depend on the slope of the line and its absolute position.

Z-Score Models

Edward Altman was the first to develop a model using financial ratios to predict financial failure.[4] His model, the Z-score model, is based on five financial ratios and is as follows:

$$Z = 1.2a + 1.4b + 3.3c + 0.6d + 1.0e$$

where: a = Working capital/Total assets
b = Retained earnings/Total assets
c = Earnings before interest and taxes/Total assets
d = Market value of common and preferred shares/Total liabilities at book value
e = Sales revenue/Total assets.

In developing this model, Altman carried out experiments using a paired sample of failed businesses and non-failed businesses and collected relevant data for each business for five years prior to failure. He found that the model represented by the formula above was able to predict failure for up to two years before it occurred. However, the predictive accuracy of the model became weaker the longer the time before failure.

---

[4] Edward I. Altman, "Predicting financial distress of companies: revisiting Z-score and Zeta models," working paper, New York University, June 2000.

The ratios used in this model were identified by Altman through a process of trial and error, as there is no underlying theory of financial failure to help guide researchers in their selection of appropriate ratios. According to Altman, those businesses with a Z-score of less than 1.81 tended to fail, and the lower the score the greater the probability of failure. Those with a Z-score greater than 2.99 tended not to fail. Those businesses with a Z-score between 1.81 and 2.99 were difficult to classify. However, the model was able to classify 95% of the businesses correctly overall. Altman based his model on U.S. businesses.

In recent years, this model has been updated and other models, using a similar approach, have been developed throughout the world. In the UK, Richard Taffler developed separate Z-score models for different types of business.[5]

The prediction of financial failure is not the only area where research into the predictive ability of ratios has taken place. Researchers have also developed ratio-based models that claim to assess the vulnerability of a business to takeover by another. This is another area of importance to all those connected with the business.

L.O. 4   LIMITATIONS OF RATIO ANALYSIS

Although ratios offer a quick and useful method of analyzing the performance of a business, they are not without their problems and limitations. Some of the more important limitations are as follows:

- *Accounting conventions.*   It must always be remembered that ratios are based on financial statements, and the results of ratio analysis are dependent on the quality of these underlying statements. Ratios will inherit the limitations of the financial statements on which they are based. An example would be whether research and development costs are capitalized or expensed.
- *Creative accounting.*   Despite the proliferation of accounting rules and the independent checks that are imposed, there is evidence that the management of some companies has employed particular accounting policies or structured particular transactions to portray the company's financial performance unfairly. This practice is referred to as **creative accounting**, and it can pose a major problem for those seeking to estimate the financial health of a business.

Activity 4.27 considers the motivations for creative accounting.

ACTIVITY 4.27

Why might the management of a business engage in creative accounting?

Solution

Management might engage in creative accounting to:

- Get around restrictions (for example, to report sufficient profit to pay a dividend)
- Avoid government action (for example, the taxation of excessive profits)
- Hide poor management decisions
- Achieve sales or profit targets, thereby ensuring that performance bonuses are paid
- Attract new financing by showing a healthy financial position
- Satisfy the demands of major investors concerning levels of return
- Deliver on the guidance statements already made to the market.

---

[5] Richard Taffler, "The Assessment of Company Solvency and Performance Using a Statistical Model: A Comparative UK-Based Study," *Accounting and Business Research*, Autumn 1983, pp. 295–307.

Creative accounting was significantly involved in the fraud perpetrated by management at Enron and WorldCom that led to those companies' spectacular downfall. The U.S. has reacted to these and other huge business failures by passing the *Sarbanes-Oxley Act* (SOX) of 2002, which bolsters internal controls that help prevent creative accounting, requires CEOs and CFOs to certify financial reports, and increases jail terms and fines for willful misstatements.

The particular methods that unscrupulous managers use to manipulate the financial statements are many and varied. They can involve overstatement of revenues and asset values, manipulation of expenses, and concealment of losses and liabilities.

Overstatement of revenues has been a particularly popular goal of creative accounting. The methods used often involve the early recognition of sales revenue or the reporting of sales transactions that have no real substance. REAL WORLD 4.12 notes a famous defunct Canadian theatrical company whose founders were perpetrating an accounting fraud.

REAL WORLD 4.12　Fraud at Livent

Livent Inc. founder Garth Drabinsky was sentenced on August 5, 2009, to seven years in jail and his partner got six years for their part in an accounting scheme that defrauded investors of $500 million in the 1990s. Livent consistently understated expenses and manipulated income and cash flows. Livent was very well known in Canada and on Broadway in New York City for such theatrical hits as *Kiss of the Spider Woman, The Phantom of the Opera*, and a revival of *Showboat*.

Source: www.cbc.ca/money/story/2009/03/25/livent-decision-fraud.html, accessed August 28, 2009.

When examining the financial statements of a business, a number of checks may be carried out to help gain a feel for their reliability. These can include checks to see whether:

- The reported profits are significantly higher than the operating cash flows for the period, which may suggest that profits have been overstated
- The income tax expense is low in relation to reported profits, which may suggest, again, that profits are overstated, although there may be other, more innocent, explanations
- There have been any changes in accounting policies over the period, particularly in key areas such as revenue recognition, inventory valuation, and depreciation
- The accounting policies adopted are in line with those adopted by the rest of the industry
- The auditors' report gives a clean bill of health to the financial statements
- The small print—that is, the notes to the financial statements—is not being used to hide significant events or changes. The notes to the financial statements are even more important than ever under IFRS because of the greater reporting requirements.

Although such checks are useful, they are not guaranteed to identify creative accounting practices, some of which may be very deeply seated.

Other factors that may limit the usefulness of the results obtained from employing ratio analysis include:

- *Inflation.*　A persistent (though recently less severe) problem is that the financial results of businesses can be distorted as a result of inflation. One effect of inflation is that the values of assets on the balance sheet held for any length of time may bear little resemblance to current fair values. Generally speaking, the book value of assets will be understated in current terms during a period of inflation as assets are usually recorded at their original cost (less any amounts written off for depreciation). This means that comparisons, either between businesses or between periods, will be hindered. A difference in return on capital employed may simply be owing to the fact that assets in one of the balance sheets being compared were acquired more recently (ignoring the effect of depreciation on the asset values). Another effect of inflation is to distort the measurement of profit. Sales revenue for a period is often reported against expenses from an earlier period because there is often a time lag between acquiring a particular resource and using it in the business. For example, inventory may be acquired in one period and sold in a later period. During a period of inflation, this will mean that the costs do not reflect current prices. The cost of goods sold figure is based on the historical cost of the inventory concerned. As a result, costs will be understated in the current income statement and this, in turn, means that profit will be overstated. One effect of this will be to distort the profitability ratios discussed earlier.

- *Ratios versus absolute size.* It is important not to rely exclusively on ratios, thereby losing sight of information contained in the underlying financial statements. In comparing one figure with another, ratios measure *relative* performance and therefore provide only part of the picture. For example, Business A may generate $1 million profit and have a return on capital employed of 15%, and Business B may generate $100,000 profit and have an ROCE of 20%. Although Business B has a higher level of *profitability*, as measured by ROCE, it generates lower total profits.
- *The basis for comparison.* No two businesses will be identical, and the greater the differences between the businesses being compared, the greater the limitations of ratio analysis. Also, differences in such matters as accounting policies, financing methods (leverage levels), and financial year-ends will add to the problems of evaluation.
- *Balance sheet ratios.* Because the balance sheet is only a snapshot of the business at a particular moment in time, any ratios based on balance sheet figures, such as the liquidity ratios above, may not be representative of the financial position of the business for the year as a whole. For example, it is common for a seasonal business to have a financial year-end that coincides with a low point in business activity. Thus inventory and receivables may be low at the balance sheet date, and the liquidity ratios may also be low as a result. A more representative picture of liquidity can only be gained by taking additional measurements at other points in the year.

SUMMARY

Financial Ratios

- Ratios compare two related figures, usually both from the same set of financial statements.
- Ratios are an aid to understanding what the financial statements portray.
- Ratio analysis is an inexact science and so results must be interpreted cautiously.
- Past periods, the performance of similar businesses, and planned performance are often used to provide benchmark ratios.

- A brief overview of the financial statements can often provide insights that may not be revealed by ratios or may help in their interpretation.

Financial Ratio Classification

Profitability Ratios—Concerned with Effectiveness at Generating Profit

- Return on equity (ROE)
- Return on capital employed (ROCE)

- Operating profit margin
- Gross profit margin.

Efficiency Ratios—Concerned with Efficiency of Using Assets/Resources

- Average inventory turnover period
- Average collection period for receivables
- Average payment period for payables
- Sales revenue to capital employed
- Sales revenue per employee.

Liquidity Ratios—Concerned with the Ability to Meet Short-Term Obligations

- Current ratio
- Acid test ratio.

Leverage Ratios— Concerned with the Relationship Between Equity and Debt Financing

- Leverage ratio
- Times interest earned ratio.

Investment Ratios—Concerned with Returns to Shareholders

- Dividend payout ratio
- Dividend yield ratio
- Earnings per share
- Price/earnings ratio.

Financial Ratios and the Problem of Overtrading

- Overtrading occurs when a business operates at a level of activity that it is insufficiently funded to sustain.

Trend Analysis

- Individual ratios can be tracked (for example, plotted on a graph) to detect trends.

Using Ratios to Predict Financial Failure

Ratios can be used to predict financial failure by:

- Looking at just one ratio over time
- Looking at several ratios, put together in a model, over time (such as with Z-scores).

Limitations of Ratio Analysis

- Ratios are only as reliable as the financial statements from which they derive.
- Creative accounting can distort the portrayal of financial health.
- Inflation can also distort the information.
- Ratios have restricted vision.
- It can be difficult to find a suitable benchmark (for example, another business) to compare with.
- Some ratios could mislead due to the snapshot nature of the balance sheet.

KEY TERMS

Horizontal analysis	Average collection period for receivables	Leverage ratio
Vertical analysis		Times interest earned ratio
Return on equity (ROE)	Average payment period for payables	Dividend payout ratio
Return on capital employed (ROCE)		Dividend cover ratio
Operating profit margin ratio	Sales revenue to capital employed	Dividend per share
Gross profit margin ratio	Sales revenue per employee	Dividend yield ratio
Average inventory turnover period	Current ratio	Earnings per share (EPS)
	Acid test ratio	Price/earnings (P/E) ratio
	Financial leverage	Overtrading
		Creative accounting

LIST OF EQUATIONS

Four Profitability Ratios

$$4.1 \quad \text{Return on equity} = \frac{\text{Net income after preferred dividends (if any)}}{\text{Average shareholders' equity}} \times 100\%$$

$$= \frac{\text{Net income} - \text{Preferred dividends}}{(\text{Average common shares} + \text{Average retained earnings})} \times 100\%$$

4.2 Return on capital employed

$$= \frac{\text{Earnings before interest and taxes}}{(\text{Average shareholders' equity} + \text{Average preferred shares} + \text{Average long-term debt})} \times 100\%$$

4.3 Operating profit margin $= \dfrac{\text{Earnings before interest and taxes}}{\text{Sales revenue}} \times 100\%$

4.4 Gross profit margin $= \dfrac{\text{Gross profit}}{\text{Sales revenue}} \times 100\%$

Five Efficiency Ratios

4.5 Average inventory turnover period $= \dfrac{\text{Average inventory held}}{\text{Cost of goods sold}} \times 365$

4.6 Average collection period for receivables $= \dfrac{\text{Average accounts receivable}}{\text{Credit sales revenue}} \times 365$

4.7 Average payment period for payables $= \dfrac{\text{Average accounts payable}}{\text{Credit purchases}} \times 365$

4.8 Sales revenue to capital employed $=$ Net asset turnover

$$= \frac{\text{Sales revenue}}{(\text{Average long-term liabilities} + \text{Average shareholders' equity})}$$

$$= \frac{\text{Sales revenue}}{(\text{Average total assets} - \text{Average current liabilities})}$$

4.9 Sales revenue per employee $= \dfrac{\text{Sales revenue}}{\text{Number of employees}}$

Two Liquidity Ratios

4.10 Current ratio $= \dfrac{\text{Current assets}}{\text{Current liabilities}}$

4.11 Acid test ratio $= \dfrac{\text{Current assets} - \text{Inventory}}{\text{Current liabilities}}$

Leverage Ratios

4.12 Leverage ratio $= \dfrac{\text{Long-term (non-current) debt}}{\text{Shareholders' equity} + \text{Long-term (non-current) debt}} \times 100\%$

4.13 Times interest earned ratio $= \dfrac{\text{Earnings before interest and taxes}}{\text{Interest expense}}$

Five Investment Ratios

4.14 Dividend payout ratio $= \dfrac{\text{Annual dividends to common shareholders for the year}}{\text{Net income available to common shareholders}} \times 100\%$

4.15 Dividend cover ratio $= \dfrac{\text{Net income available to common shareholders}}{\text{Annual dividends to common shareholders}}$

4.16 Dividend yield ratio $= \dfrac{\text{Dividend per share}}{\text{Market value per share}} \times 100\%$

4.17 Earnings per share $= \dfrac{\text{Net income available to common shareholders}}{\text{Number of common shares outstanding}}$

4.18 Price/earnings ratio $= \dfrac{\text{Market value per share}}{\text{Earnings per share}}$

REVIEW QUESTIONS

Answers to the Review Questions can be found on the Companion Website that accompanies this text at www.pearsoned.ca/atrill.

4.1 Some businesses operate on a low operating profit margin (for example, a supermarket chain). Does this mean that the return on capital employed from the business will also be low?

4.2 What potential problems arise for the external analyst from the use of balance sheet figures in the calculation of financial ratios?

4.3 Is it responsible to publish financial analyses of businesses that are in financial difficulties? What are the potential problems of doing this?

4.4 Identify and discuss three reasons why the P/E ratios of two businesses operating within the same industry may differ.

4.5 The times interest earned ratio for Burlington Perfumes Inc. is 3.0, but the current ratio is only 1.2. Discuss future prospects for Burlington, given that the industry average for these ratios is 2.1 for both. Suggest a plan for Burlington.

4.6 Describe three problems that could arise from comparing a ratio with one from a past period.

4.7 Describe three problems that could arise from trying to compare a ratio with one from a competitor.

4.8 Describe a problem that could arise from trying to compare a ratio with one from a budget.

PROBLEMS AND CASES

4.1 You are considering buying a franchise operation in The Tree Pruning Company. One of your friends in a nearby city has had one for two years. She shared her results, below:

The Tree Pruning Company
Income Statements
for the year ended December 31,

	2010	2009
Sales	$ 75,000	$ 62,000
Less: Cost of goods sold	37,000	30,000
Gross profit	38,000	32,000
Less: Operating costs	28,000	24,000
Earnings before interest and taxes (EBIT)	10,000	8,000
Less: Interest expense	3,000	5,000
Earnings before taxes	7,000	3,000
Less: Income tax expense	2,800	1,200
Net income	$ 4,200	$ 1,800

Required:
(a) Prepare a horizontal and vertical analysis on the income statement.
(b) Should you buy a franchise?

4.2 In 2010, Borden Formal Wear Inc. paid $100 million in dividends. Here are the comparative balance sheets for the latest two years.

Borden Formal Wear Inc.
Balance Sheets
as at December 31,

	(in $ millions) 2010	(in $ millions) 2009
Current assets		
Cash	10	12
Accounts receivable	10	13
Inventory	25	65
Total current assets	45	90
Property, plant, and equipment		
Land	50	40
Buildings (net)	250	250
Equipment (net)	100	88
Total property, plant, and equipment	400	378
Total assets	445	468
Current liabilities		
Accounts payable	28	23
Long-term liabilities		
Bank loans	75	60
Total liabilities	103	83
Shareholders' equity		
Common shares	124	124
Retained earnings	218	261
Total shareholders' equity	342	385
Total liabilities and shareholders' equity	445	468

Required:

(a) Prepare a horizontal and vertical analysis on the balance sheet.

(b) How did the business do in 2010?

4.3 Canadian Yogurt Inc. (CYI) had the following results over the past two years.

Canadian Yogurt Inc.
Balance sheets
as at December 31,

	2010	2009
Current assets		
Cash	$ 150,000	$ 110,000
Accounts receivable	240,000	200,000
Inventory	123,000	100,000
Total current assets	513,000	410,000

Property, plant, and equipment

Land	90,000	110,000
Buildings (net)	370,000	300,000
Equipment (net)	520,000	400,000
Total property, plant, and equipment	980,000	810,000
Total assets	$ 1,493,000	$ 1,220,000
Current liabilities		
Accounts payable	$ 110,000	$ 130,000
Other payables	45,000	20,000
Total current liabilities	155,000	150,000
Long-term liabilities		
Bank loans	500,000	400,000
Total liabilities	655,000	550,000
Shareholders' equity		
Common shares	658,000	500,000
Retained earnings	180,000	170,000
Total shareholders' equity	838,000	670,000
Total liabilities and shareholders' equity	$ 1,493,000	$ 1,220,000

Canadian Yogurt Inc.
Income Statements
for the year ended December 31,

	2010	2009
Sales	$ 220,000	$ 188,000
less: Cost of goods sold	90,000	73,000
Gross profit	130,000	115,000
Less: Operating costs	85,000	69,000
Earnings before interest and taxes (EBIT)	45,000	46,000
Less: Interest expense	25,000	20,000
Earnings before taxes	20,000	26,000
Less: Income tax expense	10,000	12,000
Net income	$ 10,000	$ 14,000

Required:

(a) Prepare a horizontal and vertical analysis of the balance sheet and the income statement.

(b) What conclusions can you draw from your analysis?

(c) Refer to the following data for the yogurt industry and explain if your opinion of Canadian Yogurt's performance in 2010 changes from your answer in part (b).

Industry Data

% Change in 2010 over 2009

Cash	10%
Interest expense	30%
Sales	5%
Net income	−50%
Long-term liabilities	30%

4.4 The following data have been selected from the annual report of Graphic Chips Limited.

	($000)		($000)
Sales (80% on credit)	2,550	Cost of goods sold	1,750
EBIT	250	Net income	140
Accounts receivable	400	Long-term debt	300
Common shares	1,200	Retained earnings	800

Required:

Calculate the following ratios:

(a) Gross profit margin
(b) Operating profit margin
(c) Sales revenue to capital employed
(d) Leverage ratio
(e) Average collection period for receivables
(f) Times interest earned, assuming income tax expense was nil
(g) Return on equity
(h) Return on capital employed.

4.5 Northern Electric Corporation has the following common share data:

Share price	$60.00
P/E ratio	20.0
Dividend Yield	4%

Required:

Calculate the following:

(a) EPS
(b) Dividend per share
(c) Dividend payout ratio.

4.6 The current ratio for Arrow Industries is 2.0 and the acid test ratio is 1.0. Current assets total $200,000 and cost of goods sold was $1,000,000.

Required:

(a) Calculate the amount of inventory on Arrow's balance sheet.
(b) Determine the average inventory turnover period.

4.7 The following is a condensed balance sheet for the Albinitree Corporation.

Albinitree Corporation
Balance Sheet
as at December 31, 2010

Assets	($000)
Cash	50,000
Accounts receivable	90,000
Inventory	65,000
Land	130,000
Property, plant, and equipment (net)	95,000
Total assets	430,000

Liabilities

Accounts payable	25,000
Taxes payable	65,000
Accrued wages payable	50,000
Bonds payable (due in 2020)	150,000
Total liabilities	290,000

Shareholders' equity

Common shares	80,000
Retained earnings	60,000
Total shareholders' equity	140,000
Total liabilities and shareholders' equity	430,000

Sales totalled $500 million, with 90% on credit; gross profit was $220 million; purchases were $300 million, with 70% on credit; and Albinitree employed 4,000 employees.

Required:
Calculate the following:

(a) Current ratio
(b) Acid test ratio
(c) Sales revenue per employee
(d) Leverage ratio
(e) Sales revenue to capital employed
(f) Inventory at the start of the year
(g) Average inventory turnover period
(h) Gross profit margin
(i) Average collection period for receivables
(j) Average payment period for payables.

4.8 There are four independent supermarkets in an isolated city in Northern Ontario. In your capacity as a banker, you have obtained the following financial data for all four companies:

	East Co.	West Co.	North Co.	South Co.
EBIT	$ 75,660	$ 320,000	$ 50,300	$ 140,000
Sales	600,000	2,600,000	420,000	1,200,000
Total assets	200,000	1,600,000	950,000	1,800,000

Required:

(a) Calculate the operating profit margin for each store and for the supermarket industry in the city as a whole.
(b) Calculate the return on capital employed for each store and for the supermarket industry in the city as a whole, assuming current liabilities are negligible.

4.9 Set out below are ratios relating to three different businesses. Each business operates within a different industrial sector.

Ratio	A Co.	B Co.	C Co.
Operating profit margin	3.6%	9.7%	6.8%
Sales revenue to capital employed	2.4 times	3.1 times	1.7 times
Inventory turnover period	18 days	n/a	44 days
Collection period for receivables	2 days	12 days	26 days
Current ratio	0.8 times	0.6 times	1.5 times

Required:

State, with reasons, which of the above is:

    (a) A holiday tour operator

    (b) A supermarket chain

    (c) A food manufacturer.

4.10 Victoria Ltd. and Halifax Ltd. are both engaged in retailing, but they seem to approach it differently, according to the following information:

Ratio	Victoria Ltd.	Halifax Ltd.
Return on capital employed (ROCE)	20%	17%
Return on equity (ROE)	30%	18%
Average collection period for receivables	63 days	21 days
Average payment period for payables	50 days	45 days
Gross profit margin	40%	15%
Operating profit margin	10%	10%
Inventory turnover period	52 days	25 days

Required:

Describe what this information indicates about the differences in approach between the two businesses. If one of them prides itself on personal service and one of them on competitive prices, which do you think is which, and why?

4.11 Creative Advertising constructs, maintains, and sells advertising for highway billboard signs. Use the information in the following financial statements for the next five problems and cases.

Creative Advertising Limited
Income Statement
for the year ended December 31,

	2010	2009
Sales	$ 400,000	$ 350,000
Cost of goods sold	210,000	185,000
Gross profit	$ 190,000	$ 165,000
Expenses (excluding interest)	75,000	55,000
EBIT	$ 115,000	$ 110,000
Interest expense	20,000	20,000
EBT	$ 95,000	$ 90,000
Income tax expense (40%)	38,000	36,000
Net income	$ 57,000	$ 54,000
Preferred dividends	2,000	2,000
Net income available to common shareholders	$ 55,000	$ 52,000

Creative Advertising Limited
Statement of Retained Earnings
for the year ended December 31,

	2010	2009
Opening retained earnings	$ 35,000	$ (7,000)
Net income available to common shareholders	55,000	52,000
Dividends to common shareholders	10,000	10,000
Closing retained earnings	$ 80,000	$ 35,000

Creative Advertising Limited
Balance Sheet
as at December 31,

	2010	2009
Assets		
Current assets		
Cash	$ 25,000	$ 15,000
Accounts receivable	50,000	40,000
Inventory	50,000	45,000
Total current assets	125,000	100,000
Property, plant, and equipment	500,000	400,000
Intangible assets	50,000	35,000
Total assets	$ 675,000	$ 535,000
Liabilities		
Current liabilities		
Accounts payable	$ 75,000	$ 50,000
Long-term liabilities		
long-term liabilities (10%)	200,000	150,000
Preferred shares (2%)	100,000	100,000
Total long-term liabilities	300,000	250,000
Total liabilities	375,000	300,000
Shareholders' equity		
Common shares	200,000	200,000
Retained earnings	100,000	35,000
Total shareholders' equity	300,000	235,000
Total liabilities and shareholders' equity	$ 675,000	$ 535,000

Required:
(a) Calculate the four profitability ratios for Creative Advertising Limited for 2010.
(b) What can you conclude from these ratios?

4.12 Use the data in Problem and Case 4.11. The notes to the financial statements indicated that 80% of the sales for Creative Advertising Limited were credit sales. Inventory purchases, 90% of which were on credit, were $215,000 in 2010 and $200,000 in 2009. On average there were 325 employees throughout 2010.

Required:
(a) Calculate the five efficiency ratios for Creative Advertising Limited for 2010.
(b) What can you conclude from these ratios?

4.13

Required:
(a) Use the data in Problem and Case 4.11. Calculate the two liquidity ratios for Creative Advertising Limited for 2010.
(b) What can you conclude from these ratios?

4.14

Required:

(a) Use the data in Problem and Case 4.11. Calculate the leverage ratio and the times interest earned ratio for Creative Advertising Limited for 2010. Treat the preferred shares the same as long-term debt as they can be converted into an equal amount of debt.

(b) What can you conclude from these ratios?

4.15

Required:

(a) Use the data in Problem and Case 4.11. Calculate five investment ratios, including the dividend cover ratio, for Creative Advertising Limited for 2010, given that there was an average of 50,000 shares outstanding during the year. Share prices averaged $10.50 per share throughout 2010 and also closed at $10.50 at year-end.

(b) What can you conclude from these ratios?

4.16

Required:

(a) Use the data in Problem and Case 4.11. Redo Problems and Cases 4.11 to 4.15 for 2009. Where an average figure is needed, assume the opening amount and closing amounts are the same. Creative Advertising's share price averaged $13.25 during 2009 and the shares also closed at $13.25 on December 31, 2009. Other data remains the same. For instance, 80% of sales are on credit and 90% of the $185,000 inventory purchases were on credit.

(b) What can you conclude from these ratios?

4.17

Required:

Use your answers to Problems and Cases 4.11 to 4.16 to summarize the results for all the ratios for 2009 and 2010. Discuss the results of your ratio analysis. Recommend any action you think Creative Advertising should take, if any.

4.18 The financial statements of Helena Beauty Products Ltd. are presented below.

Helena Beauty Products Ltd.
Income Statements
for the year ended September 30,

	2010		2009
	(in $ thousands)		
Sales (all on credit)	3,840		3,600
Less: Cost of goods sold:			
Opening inventory	400		320
Plus: Purchases	2,350		2,240
Goods available for sale	2,750		2,560
Less: Closing inventory	500		400
Cost of goods sold	2,250		2,160
Gross profit	1,590		1,440
Less: Expenses	1,500		1,360
Net income	90		80

Helena Beauty Products Ltd.
Balance Sheets
as at September 30,

	2010	2009
	(in $ thousands)	
Current assets		
Cash	4	8
Accounts receivable	960	750
Inventory	500	400
Total current assets	1,464	1,158
Property, plant, and equipment	1,860	1,900
Total assets	3,324	3,058
Current liabilities	450	390
Shareholders' equity		
Common shares	1,766	1,650
Retained earnings	1,108	1,018
Total shareholders' equity	2,874	2,668
Total liabilities and shareholders' equity	3,324	3,058

Required:

Using six ratios, comment on the profitability (three ratios) and efficiency (three ratios) of the business as revealed by the financial statements. Assume there is no interest or taxes.

4.19 Threads Limited manufactures nuts and bolts, which are sold to industrial users. The abbreviated financial statements for 2010 and 2009 are as follows.

Threads Limited
Income Statements
for the year ended June 30,

	2010		2009	
	(in $ thousands)			
Sales		1,200		1,180
Less: Cost of goods sold		750		680
Gross profit		450		500
Operating expenses	208		200	
Depreciation	75		66	
Interest	8	291	–	266
Earnings before taxes		159		234
Income tax expense		48		80
Net income		111		154

Threads Limited
Balance Sheets
as at June 30,

	2010	2009
	(in $ thousands)	
Current assets		
Cash	4	3
Accounts receivable	156	102
Inventory	236	148
Total current assets	396	253
Property, plant, and equipment (net)	687	702
Total assets	1,083	955
Current liabilities		
Bank overdraft	122	81
Accounts payable	76	60
Income taxes payable	24	40
Other accrued liabilities	16	18
Total current liabilities	238	199
Long-term liabilities		
Bank loan	50	–
Total liabilities	288	199
Shareholders' equity		
Common shares	500	500
Retained earnings	295	256
Total shareholders' equity	795	756
Total liabilities and shareholders' equity	1,083	955

Threads Limited
Statements of Retained Earnings
for the year ended June 30,

	2010	2009
	(in $ thousands)	
Opening retained earnings, July 1	256	172
Add: Net income	111	154
Less: Dividends paid	(72)	(70)
Closing retained earnings, June 30	295	256

Required:

(a) Assuming that all sales and purchases are on credit, and that the interest expense relates to the long-term debt, calculate the following financial ratios for 2009 and 2010 (using year-end figures for balance sheet items):

    (i)   Return on capital employed
    (ii)   Operating profit margin
    (iii) Gross profit margin
    (iv) Current ratio

(v)   Acid test ratio

(vi)   Collection period for receivables

(vii)   Payment period for payables

(viii) Inventory turnover period.

(b) Comment on the performance of Threads Limited from the viewpoint of a business considering supplying a substantial amount of goods to Threads Limited on usual credit terms.

4.20 Genesis Ltd. was incorporated in 2007 and has grown rapidly over the past three years. The rapid rate of growth has created problems for the business that management has found difficult to deal with. Recently, a firm of management consultants has been asked to help the company overcome these problems.

In a preliminary report to management, the management consultants state: "Most of the difficulties faced by the business are symptoms of an underlying problem of overtrading."

The most recent financial statements of the business are set out below.

Genesis Ltd.
Balance Sheet
as at October 31, 2010
(in $ thousands)

Current assets		
Accounts receivable	104	
Inventory	128	
Total current assets		232
Property, plant, and equipment		
Land		200
Buildings	330	
Less: Accumulated depreciation	88	242
Plant and equipment	168	
Less: Accumulated depreciation	52	110
Trucks	118	
Less: Accumulated depreciation	54	64
Total property, plant, and equipment		622
Total assets		854
Current liabilities		
Bank overdraft	358	
Accounts payable	184	
Income taxes payable	8	
Total current liabilities		550
Long-term liabilities		
Bonds payable (10%, secured)		120
Total liabilities		670
Shareholders' equity		
Common shares	60	
Retained earnings	124	
Total shareholders' equity		184
Total liabilities and shareholders' equity		854

Genesis Ltd.
Income Statement
for the year ended October 31, 2010
(in $ thousands)

Sales		1,640
Less: Opening inventory	116	
Plus: Purchases	1,260	
Goods available for sale	1,376	
Less: Closing inventory	128	
Cost of goods sold		1,248
Gross profit		392
Less: Selling and distribution expenses	204	
Administration expenses	92	
Interest expenses	44	340
Earnings before taxes		52
Less: Income tax expense		16
Net income		36

Genesis Ltd.
Statement of Retained Earnings
for the year ended October 31, 2010
(in $ thousands)

Opening retained earnings, November 1	92
Add: Net income	36
Less: Dividends paid	(4)
Closing retained earnings, October 31	124

Note
1. All purchases and sales were on credit.

Required:

(a) Explain the term *overtrading* and state how overtrading might arise for a business.
(b) Discuss the kinds of problems that overtrading can create for a business.
(c) Calculate and discuss *five* financial ratios that might be used to establish whether or not the business is experiencing overtrading.
(d) State the ways in which a business may overcome the problem of overtrading.

4.21 You are managing a live performance theatre in Saskatoon called Community Arts Theatre (CAT). Your theatre has had two successful seasons and you would like to compare your results to other Canadian *small businesses* in the performing arts and spectator sports industry.

Here are some of CAT's financial data that you are concerned about.

Current ratio	1.5
Debt to equity ratio	5.0
Interest coverage ratio	2.0
Net profit to equity (%)	10.0%
Net fixed assets to equity (%)	150.0%
Gross margin (%)	80%
Return on total assets (%)	2.5%
Collection period for accounts receivable (days)	35.0

Required:
Discuss CAT's financial results. To obtain comparison data, go to the website www.ic.gc.ca/eic/site/pp-pp.nsf/eng/Home, click on Create a Report, and compare your theatre results to the averages in Canada—incorporated business for the Whole Industry, Lower Half, Upper Half, and Top Quartile (top 25%). You will have to click the drop-down arrow to find the correct industry for your comparison.

4.22

Required:
(a) Find annual reports of General Motors on Google for recent years and collect sufficient data from 2005 to 2008 to compute ratios (b), (c), (d), and (e) in Figure 4.6 on page 145.
(b) Determine whether the ratios were predicting GM's bankruptcy filing.

CHAPTER 5

The Time Value of Money

LEARNING OUTCOMES

When you have completed this chapter, you should be able to:

1 Explain the time value of money and how it is affected by interest rates, risk, and inflation.

2 Calculate the future value of an investment today (a single amount), and calculate the present value of a future payment or future receipt.

3 Calculate the present value of a series of equal future payments and calculate the future value of a series of equal investments (an annuity).

4 Calculate the present value of a series of unequal future payments and calculate the future value of a series of unequal investments.

INTRODUCTION

"Time is money." In this chapter we will investigate the relationship between time and money. An amount of money to be received one year from now is not as valuable as—and is therefore worth less than—the same amount received today. If we are to make sound business decisions, we must take into account the changing value of money over different time periods. In considering revenues and costs that occur at different times, it is important that we use numbers that represent one point in time. This chapter will show how to calculate the value of a stream of payments, both now (the present value) and at a point in the future (the future value). Finally, we will see how to determine the implicit interest rate in a stream of payments or receipts.

L.O. 1

THE TIME VALUE OF MONEY, INTEREST RATES, RISK, AND INFLATION

To identify the main factors that affect the value of money over time, let's consider the following example. Suppose the Billingsgate Battery Company is considering buying a new machine that will improve productivity and increase profits. The total cash flows arising from the new machine include a cash outflow (representing the cost of the new machine), and annual cash inflows (representing the cash profit from the sale of products produced by the new machine). Cash flow can be obtained by adding back the amortization expense to the net profit. A further cash inflow may result from the disposal sale of the machine at the end of its useful life. These cash flows are illustrated as follows:

Time		($000)
Immediately	Cost of machine	(100)
1 year's time	Net profit before depreciation	20
2 years' time	Net profit before depreciation	40
3 years' time	Net profit before depreciation	60
4 years' time	Net profit before depreciation	60
5 years' time	Net profit before depreciation	20
5 years' time	Disposal proceeds	20

We could simply add up the cash inflows (total $220,000) and compare them with the cash outflows ($100,000). This would lead us to the conclusion that the project is profitable by $120,000. Of course, this doesn't explain the complete story, because time is involved. The cash outflow (payment) will occur immediately if the project is undertaken. The inflows (receipts) will happen over a range of later times.

The time factor is an important issue because people do not normally see $100 paid out now as equivalent in value to $100 receivable in a year's time. If we were to be offered $100 in 12 months, provided that we paid $100 now, we would consider it a poor deal. Activity 5.1 explores the time factor.

ACTIVITY 5.1

Why would you see $100 to be received in a year's time as unequal in value to $100 to be paid immediately? (There are basically three reasons.)

Solution

$100 to be received in a year is unequal to $100 to be paid immediately because of:

- Interest lost
- Risk
- Inflation.

Interest Lost

By placing the $100 on deposit in a bank at the end of the year we could have our money back and have interest as well. Thus, unless the opportunity to invest will offer similar returns, we shall be incurring an *opportunity cost*. An opportunity cost occurs where one course of action (for example, making an investment in a computer) deprives us of the opportunity to derive some benefit from an alternative action (for example, putting the money in the bank).

For Billingsgate Battery Company, the return from investing in the machine must be better than that from having money in the bank. If the bank offered a better return, the business would become wealthier by depositing the money in the bank.

Risk

Risk occurs when things may not turn out as expected. Activity 5.2 explores what might go wrong.

ACTIVITY 5.2

Can you suggest some areas where things could go other than according to plan in the Billingsgate Battery Company example?

Solution

Some problems might be:

- The machine might not work as well as expected; it might break down, leading to loss of the service.
- Sales of the product or service may not reach the expected levels.
- Labour costs may prove to be higher than was expected.
- The disposal proceeds of the machine could prove to be less than was estimated.

It is important to remember that the decision about whether to invest in the machine must be made *before* any of these things are known. Ultimately, however, we have to decide whether or not to leap into the dark and accept the risk, if we want the opportunity to make profitable investments.

Normally, people expect to receive greater returns where they perceive risk to be a factor. One such example is that banks tend to charge higher rates of interest to borrowers whom the bank perceives as more risky. Those who can offer good security for a loan, and who can point to a regular source of income, tend to be charged fairly low rates of interest.

For Billingsgate Battery Company, it is not enough to say that we should not recommend the investment unless its returns are higher than a bank deposit's. Clearly, we should want returns above the level of bank deposit interest rates, because the logical equivalent to investing in the machine is not to put the money on deposit but to make an alternative investment that is risky.

It is not possible to know how risky a particular project is, and therefore how large this **risk premium** should be. It is usually necessary to make some judgment on these questions and we consider this point in more detail in Chapter 7.

Inflation

If you are deprived of $100 for a year, when you go to spend that money it will not buy as many goods and services as it would have done a year earlier. Generally, prices rise in a healthy economy. The loss in the purchasing power of money, or **inflation**, occurs over time. Clearly, the investor needs this loss of purchasing power to be compensated for if the investment is to be made. This is on top of a return that takes account of what could have been gained from an alternative investment of similar risk.

In practice, interest rates in the market tend to take inflation into account. Rates that are offered on mortgages to home owners and to bank depositors include an allowance for the rate of inflation that is expected in the future.

Actions of a Logical Investor

The logical investor, who is seeking to increase his or her wealth, will only be prepared to make investments that will compensate for the loss of interest and purchasing power of the money invested and for the fact that the returns expected may not materialize (there is risk). This is usually assessed by seeing whether the proposed investment will yield a return that is greater than the basic rate of interest (which would include an allowance for inflation) plus a risk premium. These three factors (interest lost, risk, and inflation) are shown in Figure 5.1.

FIGURE 5.1   Three Factors Influencing the Required Returns from Investors

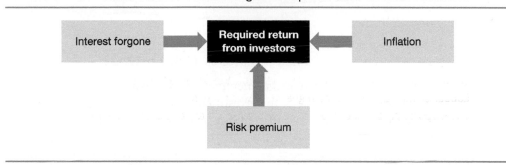

Naturally, investors need at least the minimum returns before they are prepared to invest. Usually it is the investment with the highest percentage return that will make the investor most wealthy.

For Billingsgate Battery Company, the return on the machine investment also has to exceed the returns offered by alternative investments.

TIME VALUE CALCULATIONS INVOLVING A SINGLE AMOUNT

Future Value

Consider the situation of Elin Shu, who wishes to contribute $2,000 into a guaranteed 7% compound interest educational savings account in the name of her newborn nephew. Elin wants to know how much will be in the account in 19 years, when her nephew is expected to enroll in a college or university.

To solve problems like this, it is often helpful to sketch a timeline. Time = 0 represents the time now; in other words, the present time. Since the $2,000 investment is made now, it is placed at the left, at Time = 0.

$2,000		??
0	Time	19
	(Years)	

As a general rule, any time you "move" money to the right, known as **compounding**, you are calculating the **future value (FV)** of an amount. Future value is the value of an amount invested today at some point in the future. Future value is dependent on the interest rate and the number of years involved. In a **compound interest** investment, like this one, interest is earned on the interest as well as on the principal. In a **simple interest** investment, the total interest earned this year is only the interest on the initial investment.

In a future value table (Table A1 in Appendix A), the interest rate is listed at the top of each column. The number of periods, usually years, is listed on the left side at

L.O. 2

Template for TVM Calculations in Excel

the beginning of each row. In this case, the interest rate (r) is 7% and the number of years (n) is 19. We go across the columns until we reach the 7% column. Then we go down the 7% column until we reach the $n = 19$ row. This gives a future value factor of 3.6165. Equation 5.1 shows how to calculate the future value amount using a future value table.

$$\text{Future value amount} = \text{Future value factor} \times \text{Present amount} \qquad 5.1$$

Therefore,

$$\text{Future value amount} = 3.6165 \times \$2{,}000 = \$7{,}233$$

After 19 years, Elin's $2,000 gift to her nephew will be worth $7,233. The total amount of interest earned over the life of the investment is $5,233 (i.e., $7,233 − $2,000). Activity 5.3 explores the future value of different investment options for Elin's gift.

ACTIVITY 5.3

Use a future value table to

(a) Calculate the amount that will be in her nephew's account and the total interest earned, if Elin finds a better account that pays 10% compounded annually for 19 years.

(b) Calculate the amount that will be in her nephew's account and the total interest earned, if Elin initially contributes $5,000 at 7% compounded annually.

(c) Calculate how much Elin would have to contribute at 7% compounded annually and the total interest earned, if she wants to have $35,000 in the account after 19 years.

Solution

(a) The balance in the account will be:

Future value amount = 6.1159 × $2,000 = $12,232

The total interest earned will be $10,232 ($12,232 − $2,000).

An increase in the interest rate of three percentage points increases the end result by almost $5,000.

(b) The balance in the account will be:

Future value amount = 3.6165 × $5,000 = $18,083

The total interest earned will be $13,083.

A $3,000 increase in the initial investment increases the end result by almost $10,850.

(c) Required end result = $35,000

Future value factor at $r = 7\%$ and $n = 19$ is 3.6165.

Therefore, the initial investment must be: $35,000 ÷ 3.6165 = $9,678.

The total interest earned will be $25,322.

Each of these activities is an example of compound interest at work. The initial investment is made and it earns interest during the first year. This continues compounding over the life of the investment.

Did you notice that part (c) of this activity required us to work backwards? In fact, part (c) could have been done using a *present value factor* instead of a future value factor. Let's now turn to the concept of present value.

SELF-ASSESSMENT QUESTION   5.1

For each situation, the deposit is made today. Interest is compounded annually.

	a	b	c	d	e	f
Deposit	$1,000	$2,000	$4,000	$10,000	$25,000	$100,000
Interest rate	5%	6%	7%	8%	10%	12%
Years	5	6	10	20	25	30

Required:
Calculate the final balance on deposit at the end of the period for each situation.

Rule of 72

Equation 5.2 is the rule of 72. It tells approximately how long it takes for money to double.

> Number of years for money to double = 72 ÷ Compound interest rate   5.2

This is a very handy rule that gives a quick feeling for the value of an investment. For example, in Self-Assessment Question 5.1, case (c), the interest rate is 7%. Using Equation 5.2, we have: 72 ÷ 7 = 10.2 years. So money will double in a little over 10 years at 7%. The solution to case (c) shows a future value factor of 1.9672 (almost 2, a double) for 10 years, and the balance is $7,868.80, almost double from the initial deposit of $4,000.

Present Value

Reconsider part (c) of Activity 5.3. Elin wants to know how much she must contribute now in order to have $35,000 in 19 years at a 7% interest rate. The following timeline diagram depicts the situation.

```
|??                        $35,000|
0           Time              19
         (Years)
```

Anytime you "move" money to the left, also known as **discounting**, you are calculating the **present value (PV)** of the amount. Present value is dependent on the interest rate (**discount rate**) and the number of years involved. In this situation, the terms *discount rate* and *interest rate* can be used interchangeably. When a company is determining the present value of risky investment projects, such as the acquisition of a new machine, it might use the current interest rate as a starting point and adjust it higher for risk in order to obtain the discount rate. Equation 5.3 shows how to calculate the present value amount using a present value table.

> Present value amount = Present value factor × Future amount   5.3

We look up the present value factor in a present value table (Table A2 in Appendix A). At the intersection of the *r* = 7% interest column and the *n* = 19 period row we get the present value factor of 0.2765.

Therefore, present value amount = 0.2765 × 35,000 = $9,678.

This is the same result as obtained in part (c) of Activity 5.3, but here we solved the question a different way. Often there are several ways to look at a problem. Activity 5.4 explores present value.

ACTIVITY 5.4

(a) **A furniture store, advertising no interest for one year, offers you a flat-screen television for $1,500, to be paid in one year. Calculate how much the television is worth today if the current interest rate is 9%, and the amount of interest you would save if you had the cash to buy it today.**

(b) **Calculate how much you have to contribute now as a single lump sum amount at 5% compounded annually, if you need $500,000 in order to retire in 30 years. Also determine the amount of interest this investment will earn over 30 years.**

Solution

(a) The television is worth (in terms of cash value):

Present value amount with interest rate r = 9% and n = 1 is

$$0.9174 \times \$1,500 = \$1,376$$

The store should be indifferent to receiving $1,376 now or $1,500 in one year with interest rates at 9%. This means that if you had the cash, the store should accept a cash offer of $1,376 now for the television. You save the difference, which is the interest, of $124.

(b) Required end result = $500,000

Present value amount with interest rate r = 5% and n = 30 is

$$0.2314 \times \$500,000 = \$115,700.$$

In order to retire with $500,000 in the bank, you need to invest $115,700 at 5% compounded annually now. This may seem to be a relatively small initial contribution as the total interest earned over the 30 years amounts to $384,300. But in the next section, which deals with annuities, we will see that very small annual contributions can grow very large with the power of compound interest. The secret is to make annual contributions.

SELF-ASSESSMENT QUESTION   5.2

You have recently won the world lottery and have to choose your prize from among many different options. For example, option (a) lets you receive $1 million after two years assuming the interest rate is 3%.

	a	b	c	d	e	f
Prize ($)	1,000,000	1,500,000	2,000,000	3,000,000	5,000,000	10,000,000
Interest rate	3%	6%	9%	12%	16%	20%
Years	2	5	9	15	20	40

Required:

Calculate the present value for each option and choose the best prize.

TIME VALUE CALCULATIONS INVOLVING EQUAL ANNUAL AMOUNTS (ANNUITIES)

L.O. 3

An **annuity** is a series of equal payments or receipts at a constant interest rate, r, at equal time intervals over a specified time period. For an **ordinary annuity**, each payment or receipt starts at the end of the period. Table A3 in Appendix A contains future value factors for an ordinary annuity, and Table A4 has present value factors for an ordinary annuity.

An **annuity due** has payments or receipts at the beginning of each period. Since every payment or receipt is made one year earlier than in the case of an ordinary annuity, each amount receives an extra year of interest, compared to an ordinary annuity. We can convert the factor for an ordinary annuity to an annuity due factor by multiplying it by $(1 + r)$. A common example of an annuity due is a lease. Most leases require the first payment be made on the day the lease is signed—in other words, at the beginning of the period. This is true for car leases. Apartment leases are slightly different because they often require first and last month's rent to be paid on the day the lease is signed. Equation 5.4 shows how to convert an ordinary annuity factor to an annuity due factor.

$$\text{Annuity due factor} = \text{Ordinary annuity factor} \times (1 + r) \qquad 5.4$$

Future Value

Elin Shu now wishes to contribute $500 annually, starting one year from now, into a guaranteed 7% compound interest educational savings account in the name of her newborn nephew. Elin wants to know how much will be in the account in 19 years, when her nephew is expected to enroll in a college or university.

This is an ordinary annuity since the payments start at the end of each period. The annuity timeline is as follows:

	$500	$500	etc.	$500	$500
0	1	2	...	18	19

Time
(Years)

Since all monies are being "moved" to the right, this is a future value question and compounding will occur.

Equation 5.5 shows the annuity formula. It looks very similar to Equation 5.1 for a single amount.

$$\text{Future value amount} = \text{Future value annuity factor} \times \text{Annual payment or receipt} \qquad 5.5$$

In this case, $r = 7\%$ and $n = 19$. Use Table A3 in Appendix A for the future value ordinary annuity factor. At the intersection of the $r = 7\%$ column and the $n = 19$ row, we find the future value ordinary annuity factor of 37.3790.

$$\text{Future value amount} = 37.3790 \times \$500 = \$18,690$$

Therefore, after 19 years, Elin's annual $500 gift to her nephew will have compounded to $18,690. The total interest amounts to $18,690 − (19 × $500) = $9,190. The amount of interest over the life of the investment can be confirmed, albeit with a slight rounding error, by preparing a schedule showing contributions and interest for each year as follows:

Investment Schedule 7%

Year-end	Contribution ($)	Interest ($)	Balance ($)
1	500.00	–	500.00
2	500.00	35.00	1,035.00
3	500.00	72.45	1,607.45
4	500.00	112.52	2,219.97
5	500.00	155.40	2,875.37
6	500.00	201.28	3,576.65
7	500.00	250.36	4,327.01
8	500.00	302.89	5,129.90
9	500.00	359.09	5,988.99
10	500.00	419.23	6,908.22
11	500.00	483.58	7,891.80
12	500.00	552.43	8,944.23
13	500.00	626.09	10,070.32
14	500.00	704.92	11,275.24
15	500.00	789.27	12,564.51
16	500.00	879.52	13,944.03
17	500.00	976.08	15,420.11
18	500.00	1,079.41	16,999.52
19	500.00	1,189.96	18,689.48
Total	9,500.00	9,189.48	

Notice that the first contribution, made at year-end, does not attract any interest in Year 1. In subsequent years, the interest is equal to 7% times the previous year's balance. For example, Year 8's interest of $302.89 is calculated as 7% × Year 7's balance of $4,327.01.

Suppose Elin were to start making the annual contributions now, at the time of her nephew's birth, rather than waiting until the baby is one year old. The timeline would look as follows:

$500	$500	$500	etc.	$500	
0	1	2	...	18	19

Time
(Years)

This is now an annuity due because the payments start at the beginning of each period. We can use Equation 5.3 to convert the future value ordinary annuity factor to an annuity due factor.

For $r = 7\%$ and $n = 19$, we have:

Future value amount for the annuity due = 37.3790 × (1 + 0.07) × $500
= $19,998

This is an increase of $1,308, which is equal to the future amount of the ordinary annuity, $18,690 times another year of interest, at 7% = $1,308. Activity 5.5 explores different scenarios for the future value of Elin's gift.

ACTIVITY 5.5

(a) Calculate the amount that will be in her nephew's account if Elin finds a better account that pays 10% compounded annually for 19 years and she contributes $500 per year starting on the child's date of birth.

(b) Calculate the amount that will be in her nephew's account after 19 years, if Elin contributes $1,000 per year at 7% compounded annually, starting on the child's first birthday.

(c) Calculate how much Elin has to contribute each year, starting on the child's date of birth, at 7% compounded annually if she wants to have $35,000 in the account after 19 years.

Solution

(a) The balance in the account will be:

$$\text{Future value amount} = 51.1591 \times 1.10 \times \$500 = \$28,137.51$$

An increase of three percentage points in the interest rate increases the end result by $8,139.

(b) The balance in the account will be:

$$\text{Future value amount} - 37.3790 \times \$1,000 = \$37,379$$

A doubling of the annual contribution from $500 to $1,000 also doubles the end result.

(c) Required end result = $35,000. Future value factor at $r - 7\%$ and $n = 19$ is 37.3790. The annual investment must be:

$$\$35,000 \div (37.3790 \times 1.07) = \$875$$

SELF-ASSESSMENT QUESTION   5.3

For each situation, which covers a series of annual deposits, the first deposit is made today. Interest is compounded annually.

	a	b	c	d	e	f
Annual deposit ($)	500	1,000	1,500	2,000	2,500	3,000
Interest rate	3%	6%	9%	12%	16%	20%
Years	2	5	9	15	20	40

Required:
Calculate the future value for each case if:

(a) the annual deposit is made at the end of each year.
(b) the annual deposit is made at the beginning of each year.

Present Value

Suppose your uncle gives you $50 every six months for 10 years, starting in six months. You are wondering what this gift will cost your uncle, if the current annual compound interest rates are 10%.

The following timeline diagram depicts the situation.

??	$50	$50	etc.	$50
0	1	2	. . .	20

Time
(Six-month intervals)

Notice that $n = 20$ because you will receive 20 payments (twice a year for 10 years). This is a present value question because we are moving money to the left. It is an ordinary annuity because the payments start in six months, not now.

Equation 5.6 describes how to calculate the present value of an ordinary annuity.

$$\text{Present value amount} = \text{Present value annuity factor} \times \text{Annual payment or receipt} \qquad 5.6$$

There are 20 semi-annual periods. So, $n = 20$ and $r = 10\% \div 2 = 5\%$. We use Table A4 in Appendix A for $r = 5\%$ and $n = 20$ to obtain the present value ordinary annuity factor of 12.4622.

$$\text{Present value amount} = 12.4622 \times \$50 = \$623.11$$

The gift would have cost your uncle $623.11.

Suppose your uncle said that at the end of 10 years he would also give you $1,000. To recalculate the total value of the gift, you must add the present value of the $1,000 to the present value of the $50 annuity.

The $1,000 gift is not an annuity because it only happens once. So, we use Table A2 for $n = 20$ and $r = 10\% \div 2 = 5\%$ and Equation 5.3:

$$\text{Present value amount} = \text{Present value factor} \times \text{Future amount}$$

$$\text{Present value amount} = 0.3769 \times \$1,000 = \$376.90$$

The total value today of the semi-annual $50 gift and the $1,000 gift in 10 years is $623.11 + $376.90 = $1,000.01.

SELF-ASSESSMENT QUESTION   5.4

For each situation, which covers a series of deposits, the first deposit is made today. Interest is compounded annually.

	a	b	c	d	e	f
Payment ($)	500	1,000	1,500	2,000	2,500	3,000
Interest rate	3%	6%	9%	12%	16%	20%
Years	2	5	9	15	20	40

Required:

Calculate the present value for each case if:

(a) the annual payment is made at the end of each year.
(b) the annual payment is made at the beginning of each year.

Bonds

The interest rate on a bond is called the **coupon rate**. If the coupon rate is the same as the current interest rate, the bond should sell for its face value. For example, a $1,000 bond with a coupon rate of 10% would sell for $1,000 if the prevailing interest rate was also 10%. So, your uncle really gives you a $1,000 bond in the previous discussion.

The market price or fair value of a bond is the present value of its coupon interest payments plus the present value of the face amount, or principal, of the bond discounted at the current interest rate.

Bonds that are unsecured long-term loans are also known as **debentures**. These unsecured bonds are backed only by the government or corporation's commitment to repay the loan. The federal government, provincial and territorial governments, and corporations issue long-term bonds, which are bought by individuals and other corporations as investments. Most bonds have a fixed maturity date, such as 10, 20, or 30 years, at which time the principal is returned and investors get their money back. In the meantime, investors have been receiving interest payments, usually semi-annually.

Bond Markets

Although the stock market gets all the publicity, the bond markets in Canada are in fact many times larger. Some days the dollar trading value is up to 35 times larger in the bond markets than in all of the stock exchanges in Canada.[1] REAL WORLD 5.1 takes a look at the size of the bond market in Canada today. Bond markets are discussed further in Chapter 8.

Bonds in Canada

The two main issuers of bonds in Canada are corporations and governments. However, the size of the corporate bond market has been growing, while the size of the government bond market has been shrinking. Many Canadian governments—and especially the federal government—have run surpluses and paid down their outstanding debt in the recent past.

As the table and the graph show, the dollar amount of long-term corporate bonds has risen about 10.47% [($274,099 − 248,127) ÷ 248,127] over the past four years. Over the same period, the dollar amount of long-term government debt has fallen by about 11.69% [($261,040 − 295,605) ÷ 295,605].

Table of Canadian long-term corporate and Canadian government bonds

($ millions)

	2004	2005	2006	2007	2008
Corporate Bonds and debentures	248,127	258,158	254,938	262,291	274,099
Government Bonds and debentures	295,605	280,011	272,672	266,406	261,040

▶

---

[1] For more information on the bond markets, see https://www.credentialdirect.com/Education/ilc/ BondMarket.aspx.

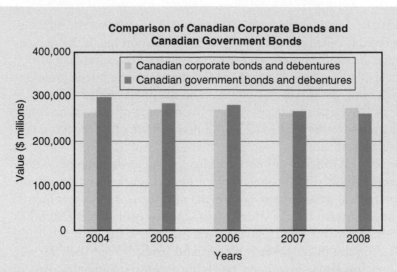

Comparison of Canadian Corporate Bonds and Canadian Government Bonds

- Canadian corporate bonds and debentures
- Canadian government bonds and debentures

Sources: Statistics Canada, www40.statcan.ca/l01/cst01/fin22.htm?sdi=bonds, accessed September 18, 2009; and Statistics Canada, www40.statcan.ca/l01/cst01/govt35a.htm?sdi=bonds, accessed September 18, 2009.

Bonds at a Discount or Premium

Bonds are very sensitive to interest rates, which in turn are affected by inflation. Rising interest rates cause the market price of all bonds to fall because the fixed coupon rates make the old bonds less valuable. Conversely, falling interest rates cause all existing bond prices to rise. So, bond prices rise and fall in a similar fashion to stock prices, although usually they are not as volatile.

To illustrate the fluctuating bond price concept, consider the previous example, in which your uncle gave you a bond. Now assume that the market interest rate increases to 11% and the bond must be sold. If the seller tries to get $1,000 for the bond no one will buy it, because it only pays 10% interest when the market rate is 11%. To compensate for the increased market interest rate, the price of the bond must fall sufficiently below $1,000 that a prospective buyer will earn an implicit 11% return. The bond is sold at a discount to its face value (below $1,000) in this case.

What happens to the market price of a 10% bond if interest rates drop to 9%? The price of a bond rises. The rationale for bond prices rising when the prevailing interest rate drops is that a 10% bond is more valuable in a 9% interest world. There is a greater demand for high coupon bonds and this drives the price of the bond upward so that the yield to maturity falls to the current 9% interest rate. Activities 5.6 and 5.7 explore the fair value of your uncle's gift, and Activity 5.8 uses the same principles to evaluate the terms of a hockey player's contract.

ACTIVITY 5.6

(a) Recalculate the fair value of your uncle's gift of a bond (with the coupon rate of 10% compounded semi-annually), if the current annual interest rate is 12%.

(b) Recalculate the fair value of your uncle's gift of a bond (with the coupon rate of 10% compounded semi-annually), if the current annual interest rate is 6%.

Solution

(a) With $n = 20$ and $r = 12\% \div 2 = 6\%$, we calculate the present value of the interest receipts and the present value of the face value of the bond separately and add these together. Note that because the coupon rate on the bond has

▶

remained unchanged at 10% compounded semi-annually, the semi-annual interest receipts remain unchanged at $50.

Present value of interest receipts   = 11.4699 × $50   = $573.50
Present value of bond face amount = 0.3118 × $1000 = $311.80
Total present value of the bond $885.30

Your uncle's 10% bond gift to you is worth $885.30 when the prevailing interest rate is 12%.

(b)   With $n = 20$ and $r = 6\% \div 2 = 3\%$, we have:

Present value of interest receipts   = 14.8775 × $50   = $ 743.88
Present value of bond face amount = 0.5537 × $1,000 = $ 553.70
Total present value of the bond $1,297.58

Your uncle's 10% bond gift to you is worth $1,297.58 when the prevailing interest rate is 6%.

ACTIVITY 5.7

Can you summarize the results from Activity 5.6 and make a general statement about bond coupon rates and market interest rates, ignoring risk factors?

Solution

Whenever the market interest rate is higher than the bond's coupon rate, the bond sells at a discount to its face value. A bond discount, defined as the face value of the bond less the fair value of the bond, occurs when a bond sells for less than its face value. We saw in Activity 5.6 that a $1,000, 10% bond sells for only $885.30, a discount of $114.70, when the current interest rate is 12%. This makes sense, because you might ask yourself why anyone would pay full price for a bond that pays two percentage points below the current going interest rate. In fact, the bond is discounted so that its yield to maturity exactly matches the current interest rate, 12%.

Similarly, *whenever the market interest rate is lower than the bond's coupon rate, the bond sells at a premium to its face value.* A bond premium, defined as the fair value of the bond less the face value of the bond, occurs when a bond sells for more than its face value. The bond is more valuable because in a time when interest rates are low, it is paying a higher interest rate. So the $1,000 bond is bid up to $1,297.58, a premium of $297.58, which puts its yield to maturity at exactly the current market interest rate of 6%.

We saw in the initial calculations of the present value of your uncle's gift that a $1,000, 10% bond is worth exactly $1,000 when the current interest rate is 10% (ignoring a $0.01 rounding error, because the present value factors in the tables are also rounded).

ACTIVITY 5.8

Boris Karmalov, the number-one draft choice of the Edmonton Oilers, has asked you to evaluate various contract offers made by the team. The team has offered him the following mutually exclusive deals (meaning he can choose only one of these deals):

(a) $4,000,000 payable immediately for a three-year contract, with no further payments

(b)   Annual payments of $1,500,000 for each of the three years, starting immediately

(c)   Annual payments of $1,600,000 for each of the three years, starting one year from now

(d)   A signing bonus of $500,000 immediately and semi-annual payments of $700,000 over three years starting in six months.

▶

Required:

Assuming the annual interest rate is expected to remain at 10% over the next three years, which contract should Boris sign?

Solution

The present values of the various cash flows must be determined in order to answer Boris's question. Since option (d) involves semi-annual payments, the semi-annual interest rate is 10% ÷ 2 = 5%. It turns out that option (b), as shown below, is the best contract for Boris, because it provides the highest present value of $4,103,385.

	a	b	c	d
Bonus ($)				500,000
Payment ($)	4,000,000	1,500,000	1,600,000	700,000
Interest rate	0%	10%	10%	5%
Years (except half-years for **d**)	0	3	3	6
Present Value Annuity Factor	1	2.4869	2.4869	5.0757
Annuity due factor	n/a	1.10	n/a	n/a
Present Value—Contract ($)	4,000,000	4,103,385	3,979,040	4,052,990

Limitations of Using Present Value Tables

1. Many discount rates are not included in the tables' interest rates. Example 5.1 below has a car lease with a monthly interest rate of 0.333% for 4 years. The tables do not have an interest rate column for 0.333% nor do they contain a row for the 48th period (4 years × 12 months per year). Linear interpolation can be used when you are between rows and columns, but it is only an approximation.
2. Tables are rounded to four decimals. This will result in round-off differences when compared to computer or calculator answers.
3. Annuity tables cannot handle a constant growth annuity because then the annual amounts are different and it does not appear even to be an annuity.

Leases

Template for Loan
Amortization

As noted earlier, almost all leases are annuities due because the first payment is required at the beginning of the period—the day the lease is signed. A good example is a car lease, considered in Example 5.1. Most people know that when they buy a car they must negotiate the best price available; the same goes for car leases. You should negotiate the best price and residual value available, which then determines what the monthly payment is going to be. Activity 5.9 explores another leasing situation.

Example 5.1

Car Leasing

Upon graduating and being hired, you decide to lease a brand-new car. The car's list price is $38,000, but you have negotiated a $35,000 price with a present value residual of $13,448.88 using an annual interest rate of 4%. This gives a monthly interest rate of 4% ÷ 12 = 0.333%. So the net value being leased is $21,551.12 (i.e., $35,000.00 − $13,448.88). In Ontario, HST of 13% is added onto the net lease value of the car. This is one of the advantages of leasing—you do not pay tax on the residual value. With taxes included, this brings the total amount leased to $24,352.76 ($21,551.12 × 1.13). With the same monthly interest rate of 0.33%, the monthly payment amounts to $548.04 over a 48-month lease term.

The complete, exact car lease loan amortization schedule is presented on page 181. Notice the constant monthly payment, the declining monthly interest charge and loan balance, and the final zero loan balance. The first payment immediately reduces the loan balance in an annuity due. In the second month there is an interest charge of 0.333% × the previous loan balance of $23,804.73.

Car Lease Loan Amortization Schedule

Month	Payment ($)	0.333% Interest ($)	Loan Balance ($)
			24,352.76
1	548.04		23,804.73
2	548.04	79.35	23,336.04
3	548.04	77.79	22,865.79
4	548.04	76.22	22,393.97
5	548.04	74.65	21,920.59
6	548.04	73.07	21,445.62
7	548.04	71.49	20,969.07
8	548.04	69.90	20,490.93
9	548.04	68.30	20,011.20
10	548.04	66.70	19,529.87
11	548.04	65.10	19,046.93
12	548.04	63.49	18,562.38
13	548.04	61.87	18,076.22
14	548.04	60.25	17,588.44
15	548.04	58.63	17,099.03
16	548.04	57.00	16,608.00
17	548.04	55.36	16,115.32
18	548.04	53.72	15,621.00
19	548.04	52.07	15,125.04
20	548.04	50.42	14,627.42
21	548.04	48.76	14,128.14
22	548.04	47.09	13,627.20
23	548.04	45.42	13,124.59
24	548.04	43.75	12,620.30
25	548.04	42.07	12,114.33
26	548.04	40.38	11,606.68
27	548.04	38.69	11,097.33
28	548.04	36.99	10,586.29
29	548.04	35.29	10,073.54
30	548.04	33.58	9,559.08
31	548.04	31.86	9,042.91
32	548.04	30.14	8,525.02
33	548.04	28.42	8,005.40
34	548.04	26.68	7,484.05
35	548.04	24.95	6,960.96
36	548.04	23.20	6,436.13
37	548.04	21.45	5,909.54
38	548.04	19.70	5,381.21
39	548.04	17.94	4,851.11
40	548.04	16.17	4,319.24
41	548.04	14.40	3,785.61
42	548.04	12.62	3,250.19
43	548.04	10.83	2,712.99
44	548.04	9.04	2,174.00
45	548.04	7.25	1,633.21

46	548.04	5.44	1,090.61
47	548.04	3.64	546.21
48	548.04	1.82	0.00

ACTIVITY 5.9

You are the owner and operator of a CD and DVD store in Jeansville's only shopping mall. An enterprising entrepreneur has offered to sell you new shelving for $20,000. Alternatively, you could lease the shelving for 10 years by making annual payments starting immediately, calculated at an interest rate of 8%. After 10 years, you get to keep the shelving at no extra cost.

(a) Calculate the annual payments required to lease the shelving.
(b) How much interest is paid over the life of the lease?

Solution

(a) $20,000 = \text{Present value annuity factor}_{(r = 8\%, \, n = 10)} \times (1 + r) \times \text{Annual payment}$

Annual payment = $20,000 ÷ (6.7101 × 1.08)
Annual payment = $20,000 ÷ 7.2469
Annual payment = $2,759.80

(b) The total interest paid over the life of the lease is $2759.80 × 10 years − $20,000 = $7,598.

Annuities and Capital Asset Purchases

Companies often pay for major purchases like capital assets over time. For example, a company may have a $500,000, 12% mortgage on its store building that requires semi-annual payments over a 10-year period, starting six months from now. To determine the semi-annual payment, look up the present value of an ordinary annuity factor in Table A4 (Appendix A) for $r = 12\% \div 2 = 6\%$ and $n = 10 \times 2 = 20$. This factor is 11.4699. So the semi-annual mortgage payment is $500,000 ÷ 11.4699 = $43,592.36. Activity 5.10 explores annual payments and annuities.

ACTIVITY 5.10

Hudson Company buys 10 hectares of land for $15 million, making a $3 million down payment immediately and financing the remainder over the next 10 years at 10% interest with annual payments starting in one year. In this case, the principal financed is $12 million (i.e., the $15 million cost less the $3 million down payment).

(a) Calculate the annual payments required to pay for the land described above.
(b) How much interest is paid over the 10-year annuity?
(c) Can you suggest a couple of ways to get the annual payment down?

Solution

(a) The payments for the land represent an ordinary annuity because they are made at the end of each year. So we have:

$12,000,000 = \text{Present value annuity factor}_{(r = 10\%, \, n = 10)} \times \text{Annual payment}$
Annual payment = $12,000,000 ÷ 6.1446
Annual payment = $1,952,934.28

▶

(b) The total interest paid over the 10-year annuity is $1,952,934.28 × 10 years − $12,000,000 = $7,529,342.84, more than half the cost of the land.

(c) There are basically three ways to lower the annual payment:

  (i) Negotiate a lower price for the land and keep the same down payment.

  (ii) Increase the size of the down payment. This would lower the annual payment, because a smaller amount would be financed.

  (iii) Negotiate a lower interest rate with the seller of the land. A lower interest rate would give a larger present value annuity factor, thereby lowering the annual payment.

The ways to lower the payment in part (c) of Activity 5.10 are always valid—the higher the down payment, the smaller the principal being financed; the smaller the principal, the lower the annual payment. The annual payment of $1,952,934.28 is called a blended payment because it is partly a repayment of principal and partly a payment of interest. In all of these types of loans, the amount of interest included in the early payments is much higher than the interest included in the final payments. This is reasonable, because in the early years the size of the loan from the seller of the land is much higher than in the later years when many payments have been made. Activity 5.11 calculates the interest in this scenario.

ACTIVITY 5.11

Using the purchase of land data from Activity 5.10, calculate the amount of interest included in the payment at the end of the first year.

Solution

Principal outstanding during the first year	$12,000,000
Interest rate	10%
Interest for the first year	$ 1,200,000

Therefore, $1,200,000 of the first payment of $1,952,934.28 is interest.

Sometimes purchases can be negotiated in which only the interest is paid and no principal is paid until later. This is a simple interest case. Activity 5.12 considers an alternative repayment plan for the Hudson Company's land purchase.

ACTIVITY 5.12

Assume that the purchase terms for the land acquired in Activities 5.10 and 5.11 required only interest payments at the end of each of the first five years, after which half of the outstanding principal must be paid, with the same arrangements for the second half of the 10-year loan term. Use the purchase of land data from above.

(a) Calculate the annual interest payments during the first five years.

(b) Calculate the loan balance outstanding during the last five years.

(c) Calculate the annual interest payments during the last five years.

(d) Determine the total interest paid over the 10-year period under this loan arrangement.

> **Solution**
>
> (a) The annual interest payments are 10% × $12 million = $1,200,000 for the first five years.
>
> (b) $6 million of the principal is repaid at the end of the fifth year, so the outstanding loan balance is $6 million.
>
> (c) The annual interest payments are 10% × $6 million = $600,000 for the last five years.
>
> (d) The total interest paid during the 10-year period under this type of loan is 5 × $1,200,000 + 5 × $600,000 = $9,000,000. This is higher than the $7.53 million paid under the blended annual payment terms, discussed in Activity 5.10, part (b), because the amount of the loan remains higher for a longer period of time.

SELF-ASSESSMENT QUESTION　5.5

LawnCare Ltd. needs to buy a new machine for its factory. Three payment choices are available to LawnCare, shown below as A, B, and C.

	A	B	C
Down payment	$ 0	$10,000	$20,000
Annual payments	$75,000	$70,000	$65,000
Annual payments start date	In 1 year	In 1 year	In 1 year
Length of payments	10 years	10 years	10 years
Interest rate	7%	7%	7%

Required:
What payment choice should LawnCare select? Show all calculations.

TIME VALUE CALCULATIONS INVOLVING UNEQUAL ANNUAL AMOUNTS

Let us now return to the Billingsgate Battery Company example. We should recall that the cash flows expected from this investment are:

Time		($000)
Immediately	Cost of machine	(100)
1 year's time	Net profit before amortization	20
2 years' time	Net profit before depreciation	40
3 years' time	Net profit before depreciation	60
4 years' time	Net profit before depreciation	60
5 years' time	Net profit before depreciation	20
5 years' time	Disposal proceeds	20

Let us assume that, instead of making this investment, the business could make an alternative investment with similar risk and obtain a return of 20% a year.

To calculate the *net present value* (*NPV*) of the project as a whole, use a discount factor of 20% in Table A2 (Appendix A) because the cash flow amounts vary from year to year.

Time	1 Cash Flow ($000)	2 Present Value Factor (20%) From Table A2	3 = 1 × 2 PV ($000)
Immediately (time 0)	(100)	1.0000	(100.00)
1 year's time	20	0.8333	16.67
2 years' time	40	0.6944	27.78
3 years' time	60	0.5787	34.72
4 years' time	60	0.4823	28.94
5 years' time	20	0.4019	8.04
5 years' time	20	0.4019	8.04
		NPV	24.19

The net present value of this project of buying a machine for $100,000 is positive $24,190. For the time being, you should be sure to understand the calculations and note that a positive net present value is better than a negative result. In Chapter 6, we will learn more about net present value in relation to making investment decisions.

A faster way to solve problems involving unequal amounts is to utilize spreadsheet software rather than factor tables. The use of spreadsheet software greatly simplifies the calculation of net present value, especially when the cash flow amounts are unequal.

Figure 5.2 shows diminishing present value factors for each year into the future and Activity 5.13 explores net present value.

FIGURE 5.2   Present Value of $1 Receivable at Various Times in the Future, Assuming an Annual Discount Rate of 20%

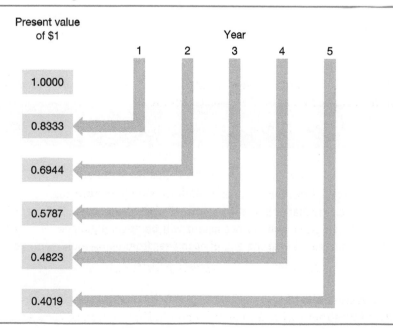

ACTIVITY 5.13

What is the net present value of the following project, assuming a 14% opportunity cost of financing (discount rate)? You should use the discount table (Table A2) in Appendix A.

Time		($000)
Immediately	Cost of machine	(150)
1 year's time	Net saving before depreciation	30
2 years' time	Net saving before depreciation	30
3 years' time	Net saving before depreciation	30
4 years' time	Net saving before depreciation	30
5 years' time	Net saving before depreciation	30
6 years' time	Net saving before depreciation	30
6 years' time	Disposal proceeds from the machine	30

Solution

The calculation of the NPV of the project is as follows:

Time	Cash Flows	Discount Factor (14%, from Table A2)	Preset Value
	($000)		($000)
Immediately	(150)	1.0000	(150.00)
1 year's time	30	0.8772	26.32
2 years' time	30	0.7695	23.09
3 years' time	30	0.6750	20.25
4 years' time	30	0.5921	17.76
5 years' time	30	0.5194	15.58
6 years' time	30	0.4556	13.67
6 years' time	30	0.4556	13.67
		NPV	(19.66)

This project has a negative net present value of $19,660.

SELF-ASSESSMENT QUESTION   5.6

Karena Oberne is considering buying a machine from one of three suppliers. Although she is convinced that each of these machines will do a reasonable job, she only has $10,000 to spend. The manufacturers are having difficulty determining a price for the machine, because it will be specially made. However, they have provided cash flow savings, shown on page 187, at the end of each year from using their machine. The current interest rate is 5%.

►

Cash Flow Savings

Year	Machine A ($)	Machine B ($)	Machine C ($)
1	2,000	1,500	1,000
2	500	2,000	1,300
3	0	1,000	1,600
4	0	4,000	1,900
5	7,000	500	2,200
6	2,000	1,000	2,500
7	1,000	500	2,800
8	500	300	3,100
9	0	0	3,400
10	0	0	3,700

Required:

Which machine should be the least expensive?

SUMMARY

The Time Value of Money, Interest Rates, Risk, and Inflation

The time value of money involves using present value and future value techniques to discount future cash flow income streams at an appropriate interest rate (discount rate).

- Present value is what future cash flows are worth today.
- Present value involves moving money to the left along the timeline.
- Future value is what current and future cash flows are worth at some point farther into the future.
- Future value involves moving money to the right along the timeline.
- No monies can be added or subtracted unless they are revalued into the same point in time (the same time zone, we might say).

The discount rate used to discount future cash flow streams is influenced by current interest rates, the risk level of the investment, and the inflation rate.

- The discount rate will increase if interest rates increase.
- The discount rate will increase if the perceived risk level of the investment increases.
- The discount rate will increase if inflation increases, in part because rising inflation usually results in rising interest rates.

Time Value Calculations Involving a Single Amount, and Time Value Calculations Involving Equal Annual Amounts (Annuities)

It is important to distinguish between a single amount and an annuity, which is a series of equal amounts.

- A one-time amount, sometimes called a lump sum, uses the future value table (Table A1) or the present value table (Table A2) in Appendix A.
- An annuity, which is a series of equal amounts, uses the future value of an annuity table (Table A3) or the present value of an annuity table (Table A4) in Appendix A.
- Using the wrong table will result in a wrong answer.
- Use the same tables for an annuity due and adjust your answer by $(1+r)$.

Time Value Calculations Involving Unequal Annual Amounts

A series of unequal cash flow amounts can be discounted by treating each amount as a single lump sum amount. Therefore, you cannot use annuity factor tables when the amounts are unequal.

- When cash flows are unequal, we must treat each cash flow item as a single lump sum amount and use the present value table (Table A2 in Appendix A).

KEY TERMS

Risk	Simple interest	Annuity due
Risk premium	Discounting	Coupon rate
Inflation	Present value (PV)	Debentures
Compounding	Discount rate	Bond discount
Future value (FV)	Annuity	Bond premium
Compound interest	Ordinary annuity	

LIST OF EQUATIONS

5.1 Future value amount = Future value factor × Present amount

5.2 Number of years for money to double = 72 ÷ Compound interest rate

5.3 Present value amount = Present value factor × Future amount

5.4 Annuity due factor = Ordinary annuity factor × $(1 + r)$

5.5 Future value amount = Future value annuity factor × Annual payment or receipt

5.6 Present value amount = Present value annuity factor × Annual payment or receipt

REVIEW QUESTIONS

Answers to the Review Questions can be found on the Companion Website that accompanies this text at www.pearsoned.ca/atrill.

5.1 When asked about his salary of $60,000 and earning more money than the president of the United States, Babe Ruth, a famous baseball player in the 1920s, is reported to have said that he'd had a better year than the president. When you graduate and start earning $70,000 per year, does that mean you are having a better year than Babe Ruth?

5.2 Explain the difference between an ordinary annuity and an annuity due, when renting an apartment.

5.3 Provide a name to describe each of the cash inflow streams in the table at the bottom of this page.

5.4 What would you expect to happen to the net present value of a project if the Bank of Canada unexpectedly raised the bank rate, which affects all other interest rates?

5.5 An investment advisor has suggested that your mother buy bonds because they won't decrease in value and are safer than stocks. Comment on this investment advice.

Time	Situation A	Situation B	Situation C	Situation D
0	0	100	200	0
1	100	100	400	0
2	100	100	600	0
3	100	0	0	2,000

PROBLEMS AND CASES

5.1

Required:
Calculate the present values of the following cash flows:

(a) $100,000 to be received in 10 years at a discount rate of 6%
(b) $50,000 to be received in 5 years at a discount rate of 1%
(c) $75,000 to be received in 8 years at a discount rate of 5%.

5.2

Required:
Calculate the future values of the following cash flows. Round the table factors to two decimal places.

(a) $25,000 deposited now for 30 years at an interest rate of 9%
(b) $10,000 deposited now for 20 years at an interest rate of 12%
(c) $5,000 deposited now for 50 years at an interest rate of 7%.

5.3

Required:
Calculate the present values of the following cash flows:

(a) $1,000 to be received every year, starting one year from now, for 25 years at a discount rate of 8%
(b) $2,500 to be received every year, starting one year from now, for 15 years at a discount of 7%.

5.4 Shares of Exem Radiator Limited (ERL), a government-controlled company, currently sell for $45.00 on the Toronto Stock Exchange. ERL pays an annual dividend of $8.00 per share at year-end. Government scientists have announced a breakthrough that they say will make radiators obsolete in 10 years, at which time the shares in ERL would become worthless. Interest rates are expected to fluctuate between 3% and 8% over the next 10 years.

Required:
Use present value calculations to determine whether it makes sense for you to buy shares in Exem Radiator Limited.

5.5 The Rambooie Music Company (RMC) has a dilemma. A customer wants RMC to sell it 7,000 CDs at a gross margin of $8.00 each year for five years with payment at the beginning of the year. That is the only way it will buy 7,000 CDs each year from RMC. Otherwise, the customer will only buy 10,000 CDs at a gross margin of $10.00 per CD this year, with payment up front, and another 10,000 CDs in year 5 with payment at the beginning of year 5. In the intervening three years, the customer will buy CDs from another supplier. Use 6% as the interest rate.

Required:
Calculate which option is better for RMC.

5.6 Whispering Pines Golf Club is trying to decide the best course of action for its fleet of new golf carts. Whispering Pines can buy premium tires at a cost of $10,000 per cart. These tires last four years and then must be replaced. It is expected the prices for the tires will not change. A cart is expected to last sixteen years, at which time it is replaced. The second option is to buy regular tires at a cost of $5,100 and replace them every two years. Use 3% as the interest rate.

Required:

Determine the better option by preparing a present value calculation for the cost of the tires for the sixteen-year economic life of the golf cart.

5.7 Summertime Fun Limited (SFL) is evaluating the purchase of a new rocket roller coaster. The initial cost is $1 million with annual maintenance fees equal to 10% of the annual revenues. Annual revenues are expected to be $200,000. The ride should last for 10 years and must be purchased now to be ready for next year. Use a 7% discount rate.

Required:

Calculate the present value of future revenues and the present value of all costs to determine whether SFL should purchase this new ride.

5.8 Rad Footwear is investigating a new line of athletic shoes. The company needs the present value of the future revenue stream to exceed $3 million at a discount rate of 5%. The annual revenue stream, starting one year from now, is as follows:

Years	Revenues
1	350,000
2	420,000
3	550,000
4	510,000
5	430,000
6	390,000
7	330,000
8	250,000

Required:

Determine whether the new line of athletic shoes will achieve the company's goals.

5.9

Required:

Calculate the future values of the following cash flows:

(a) $200 to be deposited in a bank account every year, starting now, for 30 years at an interest rate of 5%
(b) $350 to be deposited in a bank account every year, starting now, for 18 years at an interest rate of 7%

5.10 Montreal Comedy Clubs Limited (MCC) has enjoyed success and now has $500,000 to invest for eighteen months in either bonds or shares before it starts construction on a new club in Vancouver. See the relevant data below. You can ignore taxes since the government has declared a two-year tax holiday for entertainment companies in Canada.

Investment	$500,000.00
Share price—Now	$ 80.00
Estimated Share price—In 18 months	$ 85.00
Quarterly Dividend per share	$ 2.00
Semi-annual bond interest	$ 35,000.00
Prevailing interest rate	12%

Required:

Prepare calculations and make a recommendation as to which is the better investment for MCC.

5.11

Required:

Start with $350,000 savings. Prepare calculations to compare the "rule of 72" estimated time for money to double with the actual time it takes for money to double, for the following interest rates:

(a) 5%   (c) 14%

(b) 10%   (d) 20%.

5.12 On January 1, 2009, the Government of Canada introduced a new tax-free savings account (TFSA). This allows individuals to contribute up to $5,000 to a TFSA each year. While the contribution is not deductible, all earnings are tax free and will never be taxed. You have decided to contribute the maximum amount every year, starting immediately on January 1, 2009. Use an interest rate of 3%.

Required:

Calculate your account balance after 5, 8, 10, 15, 20, and 30 years.

5.13 A new machine costing $250,000 will provide the following cash flows:

Year	Amount
0	(250,000)
1	30,000
2	60,000
3	95,000
4	125,000
5	60,000
6	3,000
7	(25,000)
8	20,000
9	40,000
10	15,000
11	2,000

Required:

Calculate the net present value of these cash flows using a discount rate of 10%.

5.14 You have just turned 25 years of age and accepted your first position after graduation. You understand the power of compound interest and wish to save for early retirement at age 55.

Required:

How much should you contribute *annually* to your registered retirement savings plan (RRSP), starting one year from now, in order to accumulate $2 million by the time you retire? Assume an interest rate of (a) 8% and (b) 16%.

5.15 Your aunt recently won the lottery and has a difficult choice to make. She has come to you for help in deciding whether she should accept an immediate cash payment of $3.5 million, or instead take an annual payment of $200,000 for life, starting immediately. She is 50 years old. Currently the best interest rate you can get in a guaranteed investment certificate is 4%.

Required:

Assuming you do not expect interest rates to change, what should you advise your aunt to do if:

(a) She expects to live another 25 years?
(b) She expects to live another 30 years?

5.16 The Oakville Yacht Society has the following lump-sum payments to make to members.

	Lump-Sum Payments			
	A	B	C	D
Amount to be paid	$ 100,000	$ 75,000	$ 320,000	$ 400,000
Discount rate	4%	10%	8%	12%
Years to due date	5	3	10	12.5
Compounding	annual	semi-annual	annual	quarterly

Required:
Calculate the present value for each lump-sum payment.

5.17 The City of Moose Jaw has a budget surplus and can afford to set aside money today to fund future projects connected with the city's infrastructure.

	Projects			
	A	B	C	D
Future amount needed	$20,000	$25,000	$30,000	$35,000
Discount rate	9%	8%	5%	8%
Years	4	6	6	5
Compounding	annual	semi-annual	annual	quarterly

Required:
Calculate the amount the city will have available when each project starts.

5.18 You are planning your finances for college. Your parents started a registered educational savings plan (RESP) for you when you were born by contributing $2,000. Each year thereafter they contributed $1,000 to the RESP on your birthday, and will continue to do so until you turn 19 years of age.

You have just turned 13, and have saved $2,000 from your paper route. You wish to augment your RESP by contributing your money as well. The day after your thirteenth birthday, you start working after school for a dry cleaner. You expect to contribute $3,000 a year on your birthday starting one year from now for the next six years, from age 14 to 19.

The government matches 20% of all contributions to the RESP. Your parents think that the annual costs of a three-year college program—including tuition, residence, books, food, and incidentals—will be $35,000 per year, payable at the beginning of the year, by the time you start college on your nineteenth birthday.

Required:
(a) Assuming an average 7% interest rate throughout, prepare a year-by-year analysis of the cash flows, including interest and college costs, into and out of the RESP to the day of your twenty-first birthday, by which time you will have completed your three-year college program.
(b) What is the minimum annual scholarship needed to cover the deficit? Assume a 7% interest rate and that the scholarship is paid at the beginning of your second and third years.

5.19 You work in the accounting department of a major flat-screen television manufacturer. Demand for your product is very high. These televisions sell for $2,000 each. An offer has arrived on your desk from a major retailer to buy 100,000 televisions with 10 equal annual payments of $22 million starting immediately. The current interest rate is 5%.

Required:
What is the present value of the order? Do you advise your employer to accept or to reject it?

5.20 There are two investments you can make with $150,000: (1) Buy a small house and live in it for 15 years. House prices are expected to rise 3% per year over that period. (2) Invest in the stock market, focusing on capital gains. After 15 years, the expected value of your investment in the stock market is $350,000.

Required:

Ignoring taxes and the cost of renting an apartment, which is the better investment?

5.21 You have a choice of investing $50,000 in a 12%, 10-year semi-annual bond, or in shares of TIM Inc., paying a quarterly dividend of $1.00 per share starting the quarter after you buy them. TIM shares currently sell for $25.00 per share.

Required:

Which is the better investment, assuming the current interest rate is 8% and assuming you would hold the TIM shares for 10 years, at which time they would be worth $75 each?

5.22 You have negotiated your best price and have just signed on the dotted line to buy your first car. The payments are $500 per month starting immediately for four years and two months at a 12% interest rate.

Required:

How much did the car cost?

5.23 Burnaby Bricks Ltd. (BBL) pays cash for everything. BBL is saving to buy a machine for five different projects. Interest is compounded annually in each of the following cases.

	a	b	c	d	e
Bank account ($)	25,000	40,000	100,000	240,000	500,000
Interest rate	5%	8%	12%	14%	16%
Years	5	8	12	16	20

Required:

(a) Calculate the annual deposits that must be made at the end of each year.
(b) Calculate the annual deposits that must be made at the beginning of each year.

5.24 The B.C. Port Authority is considering acquiring a new ferry at a cost of $122 million. Equal payments are to be made annually over 40 years and the implied interest rate is 5%.

Required:

(a) Calculate the annual payment, assuming the first payment is made the day the purchase agreement is signed.
(b) Calculate the annual payment, assuming the first payment is made one year after the purchase agreement is signed.
(c) If the ferry carries 310,000 passengers per year and charges $20 per ride, calculate the present value of the revenue stream. To simplify the calculations, assume the money is collected at year-end every year.
(d) Does the acquisition of the new ferry make economic sense? Explain.

5.25 Your company is negotiating to acquire a new head office building listed for $25 million. The owner has proposed the following payment plan for the next 20 years:

■ There would be a 20% down payment and annual payments for the next 10 years of $1.8 million, starting one year from now.
■ For Years 11 through 15, the annual payments balloon to $3 million.
■ For Years 16 through 20, the annual payments would decline to $400,000.

Required:

(a) Should your company accept this offer if the interest rate is 6% for real estate?
(b) Determine the breakeven interest rate for the given payment plan, assuming that the fair value of the building is equal to its list price.

CHAPTER 6

Making Capital Investment Decisions

INTRODUCTION

In this chapter we first study an overview of the investment decision-making process. We see ways in which managers can oversee capital investment projects and how they exert control and reviews throughout the life of the project. Then we look at how businesses can make decisions involving investments in new plant, machinery, buildings, and similar non-current assets. The general principles that apply to assessing investments in these types of assets can also be applied to investments in the shares of businesses, whether by another business or by a private individual. We examine four major investment appraisal methods and consider evidence relating to the use of these methods in practice.

L.O. 1 THE PROCESS OF INVESTMENT DECISION MAKING

Managers must consider six stages in making investment decisions, as shown in Figure 6.1.

Stage 1: Determine Investment Funds Available

Often there will not be sufficient funds to finance all the profitable investment opportunities available. When this occurs, some form of **capital rationing** has to be undertaken. This means that managers are faced with the task of deciding on the most profitable use of the investment funds available. To ensure that competing projects are prioritized correctly, some modification to the NPV decision rule (to accept all projects with a positive NPV) is necessary. This point is discussed further in the next chapter.

FIGURE 6.1   The Six Stages of Managing the Investment Decision

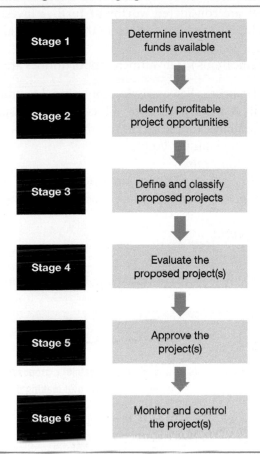

Stage 2: Identify Profitable Project Opportunities

An important part of the investment process is the search for profitable investment opportunities. A business should adopt a systematic approach toward identifying investment opportunities. The range of available investment opportunities is likely to include developing new products or services, improving existing products or services, entering new markets, and investing to increase capacity or efficiency. The search for new opportunities will often involve looking outside the business to identify changes in technology, customer demand, and market conditions.

It is important that the business's investments should mesh with its strategic plans. The business should seek out investment projects that use its strengths (such as management expertise in a particular activity) to exploit opportunities (for example, an expansion of the market). At the same time, investment projects that are selected should avoid exposing the business's weaknesses (such as a shortage of suitably skilled labour) to threats (for example, other businesses hiring your skilled staff).

The search for new opportunities is likely to be more successful where there is a culture that encourages employees at all levels to submit proposals. Some businesses will encourage investment ideas through the reward and appraisal bonus systems operating for employees.

Stage 3: Define and Classify Proposed Projects

This stage of the process aims to convert promising ideas into full-blown proposals. A two-stage process is often adopted. The first stage involves collecting enough information to allow a preliminary screening. Many proposals trip on this first hurdle because it soon becomes clear that they are unprofitable or unacceptable for other reasons. Proposals that are considered worthy of further investigation continue to the second stage, developing the ideas further so that more detailed screening can be carried out.

The following classifications for investment opportunities are also useful:

- *New product development.* For example, Apple Inc. has transformed the music industry with its iPod and iTunes store, released the very successful iPhone and now the iPad. These changes are so significant that Apple has dropped "Computer" from its name and is now simply "Apple Inc."
- *Improving existing product sales.*
- *Reducing costs.* For example, purchasing a new machine may reduce the costs incurred from scrap, reworking, product labour costs, maintenance costs, and quality inspection.
- *Replacement of equipment.*
- *Welfare and safety.*

Activity 6.1 explores the benefits of classifying investment proposals.

ACTIVITY 6.1

What do you think are the benefits of classifying investment proposals in this way? Could classifying be helpful when you are gathering information and making decisions?

Solution

Classification can be useful in deciding on the level of information required for a particular proposal. For example, equipment might be replaced routinely, and so a replacement proposal may only require evidence that the particular piece of equipment has reached the end of its economic life. New product development, on the other hand, may require market research evidence, a marketing plan, and detailed costings to support the proposal.

Classification can also help in deciding on the acceptance criteria to be applied. For example, on the one hand, equipment replacement may be considered low-risk and this may be reflected in a low required rate of return. New product development, on the other hand, may be considered to be high-risk and this may be reflected in a high rate of return. (Risk and return in relation to investment proposals are considered in detail in the next chapter.)

Stage 4: Evaluate the Proposed Project(s)

A detailed evaluation may involve answering these key questions:

- What is the nature and purpose of the project?
- Does the project align with the overall objectives of the business?
- How much financing is required? Does this fit with the funds available?
- What other resources (such as expertise, IT, and factory space) are required for successful completion of the project?
- How long will the project last and what are its key stages?
- What is the expected pattern of cash flows?
- What are the major problems associated with the project and how can they be overcome?

- What is the NPV and/or IRR of the project? Both NPV and IRR are covered later in this chapter. How does this compare with other opportunities available?
- Have risk and inflation been taken into account in the appraisal process and, if so, what are the results?

Managers proposing a new project may also be evaluated. In some cases, senior managers may decide not to support a project that appears profitable on paper if they lack confidence in the ability of key managers to see it through to completion.

Stage 5: Approve the Project(s)

Approval may be authorized at different levels of management according to the type of investment and amount of financing required. For example, a plant manager may have authority to accept investment projects up to a maximum of $100,000, and beyond this amount, authority from a capital expenditure committee of senior managers and directors may be required.

Stage 6: Monitor and Control the Project(s)

Well-managed businesses continually reassess existing projects. Progress reports should provide information relating to the actual cash flows for each stage of the project, which can then be compared against the forecast figures. The reasons for significant variations should be ascertained, and corrective action taken where possible. In extreme cases, managers may even abandon the project if circumstances appear to have changed dramatically for the worse.

REAL WORLD 6.1 shows the size of project cuts by Canadian energy firms during the Great Recession of 2008–2009.

REAL WORLD 6.1   Recession Delays in the Oil Sands

During the recession of 2008–2009, the price of a barrel of oil dropped from $147 to below $40. Many large projects in the Canadian oil sands were delayed or cancelled. Here are some big cuts:

Company	Size ($ billions)	Action
Suncor	3	Delayed
Teck Cominco	24	Delayed
Nexen	3	Delayed
BA Energy	4	Cancelled

Most estimates are that oil needs to be around $80 to $100 per barrel for these projects to make economic sense.

Source: CBCnews.CA at: www.cbc.ca/money/story/2009/02/27/f-oilsands-challenges.html, accessed Sept. 2, 2009.

Key non-financial measures (such as physical output, spoilage rate, and customer satisfaction scores) may also be used to monitor performance. Completion target dates should be monitored carefully. Project management techniques (for example, critical path analysis) should be employed wherever possible.

A **post-completion audit** is a review of the project performance in order to see whether it met expectations. The audit should evaluate financial costs and benefits, and non-financial measures of performance, such as the ability to meet deadlines and levels of quality achieved.

Regular use of a post-completion audit will encourage managers to use realistic estimates. Where over-optimistic estimates are used in an attempt to secure project approval, the managers responsible will find themselves accountable at the post-completion audit stage. Activity 6.2 explores the drawbacks of post-completion audits.

ACTIVITY 6.2

Can you think of any drawbacks to post-completion audits? Could they have an adverse effect on manager behaviour?

Solution

A post-completion audit may inhibit managers from proposing and supporting projects that carry a high level of risk. If things go wrong, they could be blamed. This may result in only low-risk projects being submitted for consideration.

In addition, managers may feel threatened by the post-completion audit investigations and so might not cooperate fully with the audit team.

If a post-completion audit is seen by managers as simply a device to assign blame, then the problems mentioned in Activity 6.2 are more likely to occur. However, if it is used as a constructive tool whose main objective is to learn from experience, the problems mentioned need not arise.

REAL WORLD 6.2 shows that most businesses now employ post-completion audits.

L.O. 2   THE NATURE OF INVESTMENT DECISIONS

The essential feature of investment decisions is *time*. An investment is typically one large amount and the benefits arrive as a series of smaller amounts over a fairly protracted period.

Investment decisions tend to be of crucial importance to the business because:

■ *Large amounts of resources are often involved.*
■ *It is often difficult and/or expensive to bail out of an investment once it has been undertaken.* For example, a hotel business may invest in a new hotel complex, which would have limited second-hand value to another potential user with different needs.

REAL WORLD 6.3 indicates the level of annual investment for a number of well-known Canadian businesses. In nearly all of these businesses, the scale of investment is very significant. Most *capital* asset investment also requires a higher level of *current* asset investment to support it (additional inventories, for example), meaning that the real scale of investment is even greater than indicated. Activity 6.3 considers the decision making surrounding capital investments.

Capital Investment Post-Completion Audits

A 1996 survey of capital budgeting techniques concluded that internal controls have significantly improved to prevent cost overruns during the implementation of the project. In addition, post-completion audits of capital projects are now standard with 72% of respondents conducting such reviews. If managers know a post-completion audit will be conducted, it may encourage them to submit more realistic capital budget proposals.

Source: Richard Pike, "A Longitudinal Survey on Capital Budgeting Practices," *Journal of Business Finance and Accounting,* January 1996, Volume 23, Issue 1, pp. 79–92.

Large Capital Investments

The size of capital investment is large in terms of both sales and capital assets held at the start of the year. In 2008, Waterloo, Ontario-based Research In Motion (RIM), maker of the BlackBerry smart phone, increased its assets by 89%. That is nearly a doubling. Three years ago its assets increased by 85%.

It is interesting to compare 2008 with 2005. All companies shown below, except for RIM, slowed their capital investment growth in 2008 to cope with the recession. As we also saw in Real World 6.1 with the Canadian oil sands, cutting capital expenditures to save cash is a normal response to a recession.

Capital Investment by Canadian Firms

| | 2005 | | 2008 | |
| | As a Percentage of: | | | |
Company	Annual Sales	Capital Assets	Annual Sales	Capital Assets
BCE	17.9%	16.2%	4.6%	4.4%
Encana	48.5%	30.8%	−1.5%	−1.2%
Gildan	13.2%	40.7%	4.7%	15.6%
Research In Motion	8.7%	85.2%	5.7%	89.1%
Loblaw	4.2%	16.3%	0.3%	1.2%
Pason Systems	42.0%	76.5%	5.0%	7.6%
Shoppers Drug Mart	3.5%	40.5%	3.3%	28.0%

Source: 2005 and 2008 annual reports of companies listed.

ACTIVITY 6.3

When managers are making decisions involving capital investments, what should the decision seek to achieve?

Solution

Investment decisions must be consistent with the objectives of the particular business. For a private sector business, maximizing the wealth of the shareholders is usually assumed to be the key objective.

METHODS OF INVESTMENT APPRAISAL

The use of cash flows to appraise investment projects is the main subject of this chapter. Research shows that basically four methods are used in practice by businesses throughout the world to evaluate investment opportunities. They are:

- Accounting rate of return (ARR)
- Payback period (PP)
- Net present value (NPV)
- Internal rate of return (IRR).

To help us to examine each of the methods, it is useful to consider how each of them would cope with a particular investment opportunity. In Chapter 5 we calculated the net present value of an investment project by Billingsgate Battery Company. Example 6.1 shows how those cash flows were derived.

Example 6.1

Billingsgate Battery Company has carried out some research showing that the business could provide a standard product that it has recently developed.

Production of the product would require investment in a machine that would cost $100,000, payable immediately. Sales would take place throughout the next five years. At the end of that time, it is estimated that the machine could be sold for $20,000.

Sales of the product, in units, would be expected to occur as follows:

	Number of Units
Next year	5,000
Second year	10,000
Third year	15,000
Fourth year	15,000
Fifth year	5,000

It is estimated that each unit could be sold for $12, and that the relevant (variable) costs would total $8 a unit.

Each unit of product sold will generate a net cash inflow of $4 (i.e., $12 − $8). The total net cash flows (receipts less payments) for each year would be as follows:

Time		($000)
Immediately	Cost of machine	(100)
1 year's time	Net profit before depreciation ($4 × 5,000)	20
2 years' time	Net profit before depreciation ($4 × 10,000)	40
3 years' time	Net profit before depreciation ($4 × 15,000)	60
4 years' time	Net profit before depreciation ($4 × 15,000)	60
5 years' time	Net profit before depreciation ($4 × 5,000)	20
5 years' time	Disposal proceeds from the machine	20

▶

The net profit before deducting depreciation (that is, before non-cash items) equals the net amount of cash flowing into the business. Apart from that, all of this business's expenses cause cash to flow out of the business. Sales revenues lead to cash flowing in.

Example 6.1 assumes that the cash from sales is received—and the cash for the costs of providing those sales is paid—at the end of each year. (This is clearly unlikely to be true in real life. Money will have to be paid to employees for salaries and wages on a weekly or a monthly basis. Customers will pay within a month or two of buying the product. On the other hand, making the assumption probably does not lead to a serious distortion. It is a simplifying assumption that is often made in real life, and it will make things more straightforward for us now. We should be clear, however, that there is nothing about any of the four approaches that *demands* this assumption be made.)

ACCOUNTING RATE OF RETURN (ARR)

L.O. 4

The **accounting rate of return (ARR)** method takes the average accounting profit that the investment will generate and expresses it as a percentage of the average investment made over the life of the project. Thus as Equation 6.1 shows:

$$\text{Accounting rate of return} = \frac{\text{Average annual profit}}{\text{Average investment to earn that profit}} \times 100\% \quad \text{6.1}$$

In our example, the average annual profit *before depreciation* over the five years is $40,000 [i.e., ($20,000 + $40,000 + $60,000 + $60,000 + $20,000)/5]. Assuming straight-line depreciation (that is, equal annual amounts), the annual depreciation charge will be $16,000 [i.e., ($100,000 − $20,000)/5]. Thus the average annual profit *after depreciation* is $24,000 (i.e., $40,000 − $16,000).

The average investment over the five years can be calculated as follows:

$$\frac{\text{Average}}{\text{investment}} = \frac{\text{Machine's beginning-of-period value} + \text{Machine's end-of-period value}}{2}$$

Continuing with our average investment calculation, we get:

$$\text{Average investment} = \frac{\text{Cost of machine} + \text{Disposal value}}{2}$$

$$= \frac{\$100,000 + \$20,000}{2} = \$60,000$$

Thus, the ARR of the investment is:

$$\text{ARR} = \frac{\$24,000}{\$60,000} \times 100\% = 40\%$$

To decide whether the 40% return is acceptable, we need to compare this percentage return with the minimum rate required by the business.

Activity 6.4 outlines another example of the ARR method.

ACTIVITY 6.4

Chaotic Industries is considering an investment in a fleet of 10 delivery vans to take its products to customers. The vans will cost $15,000 each to buy, payable immediately. The annual maintenance and operating costs are expected to total $20,000 for each van (including the driver's salary). The vans are expected to operate successfully for six years, at the end of which period they will all have to be sold, with disposal proceeds expected to be about $3,000 a van. At present, the business uses a commercial carrier for all of its deliveries. It is expected that this carrier will charge a total of $230,000 each year for the next five years to undertake the deliveries.

What is the ARR of buying the vans? (Note that cost savings are as relevant a benefit from an investment as are net cash inflows.)

Solution

The vans will save the business $30,000 a year [i.e., $230,000 − ($20,000 × 10)], before depreciation, in total.

Thus, the inflows and outflows will be:

Time		($000)
Immediately	Cost of vans	(150)
1 year's time	Net saving before depreciation	30
2 years' time	Net saving before depreciation	30
3 years' time	Net saving before depreciation	30
4 years' time	Net saving before depreciation	30
5 years' time	Net saving before depreciation	30
6 years' time	Net saving before depreciation	30
6 years' time	Disposal proceeds from the vans (10 × 3)	30

The total annual depreciation expense (assuming a straight-line approach) will be $20,000 [i.e., ($150,000 − $30,000)/6]. Thus, the average annual saving, after depreciation, is $10,000 (i.e., $30,000 − $20,000).

The average investment will be:

$$\text{Average investment} = \frac{\$150,000 + \$30,000}{2} = \$90,000$$

Thus, the ARR of the investment is:

$$\text{ARR} = \frac{\$10,000}{\$90,000} \times 100\% = 11.1\%$$

ARR and ROCE

We should note that ARR and the return on capital employed (ROCE) ratio take the same approach to performance measurement, in that they both relate accounting profit to the cost of the assets invested to generate that profit. We saw in Chapter 4 that ROCE is a popular means of assessing the performance of a business, as a whole, *after* the fact (i.e., year-end). ARR is an approach that assesses the potential performance of a particular investment, taking the same approach as ROCE, *before the fact.*

Managers using the ARR method must have a minimum target ARR in mind. The decision rules should be:

- For any project to be acceptable, it must achieve the target ARR.
- If the business can choose only one of several viable projects that achieve the target ARR, the project with the highest ARR should be selected.

Advantages of ARR

ROCE is a widely used measure of business performance. ARR is consistent with this overall approach to measuring business performance. Managers feel comfortable with using measures expressed in percentage terms as ARR does.

Problems with ARR

1. ARR Ignores Time Value of Money

Activity 6.5 explores ARR method in relation to time factor.

ACTIVITY 6.5

What is ARR's major defect? Consider the three competing projects—A, B, and C—whose cash flows are shown below. All three of these involve investment in a machine that is expected to have no residual value at the end of the five years. Note that all of the projects have the same total net profits over the five years.

Time		A ($000)	B ($000)	C ($000)
Immediately	Cost of machine	(160)	(160)	(160)
1 year's time	Net profit after depreciation	20	10	160
2 years' time	Net profit after depreciation	40	10	10
3 years' time	Net profit after depreciation	60	10	10
4 years' time	Net profit after depreciation	60	10	10
5 years' time	Net profit after depreciation	20	160	10

Solution

The problem with ARR is that it almost completely ignores the time factor. In this example, exactly the same ARR would have been computed for each of the three projects.

Since the same total profit over the five years arises in all three of these projects (i.e., $200,000) and the average investment in each project is $80,000 (i.e., $160,000/2), this means that each case will give rise to the same ARR of 50% (i.e., $40,000/$80,000).

However, in terms of the time value of money, Project C is the best choice because of the huge net profit before depreciation in Year 1. Project A would rank second, and Project B would come a poor third. Any appraisal technique that is not capable of distinguishing between these three situations is seriously flawed.

2. ARR Can Lead to an Illogical Decision

There are further problems associated with the use of ARR. Example 6.2 illustrates a paradox that may arise when using this method. This paradox results from the approach taken to derive the average investment in a project.

Example 6.2

How to Increase ARR by Throwing Money Away!

To illustrate the unusual results that ARR can produce, assume that you have submitted an investment proposal to your department head based on the following information:

Cost of equipment	$200,000
Estimated residual value of equipment	$ 40,000
Average annual profit before depreciation	$ 48,000
Estimated life of project	10 years
Annual straight-line depreciation charge	$ 16,000 [($200,000 − $40,000)/10]

The ARR of the project will be:

$$ARR = \frac{(\$48,000 - \$16,000)}{[(\$200,000 + \$40,000)/2]} \times 100\% = 26.7\%$$

You are told by your department head, however, that the minimum ARR for investment projects of this nature is 27%. To improve the ARR, all you have to do is agree to give the piece of equipment away at the end of its useful life rather than sell it. The residual value of the equipment will then be zero and the annual depreciation charge will become [($200,000 − $0)/10] = $20,000 a year. Your revised ARR calculation will then be as follows:

$$ARR = \frac{(\$48,000 - \$20,000)}{[(\$200,000 + \$0)/2]} \times 100\% = 28\%$$

Obviously, however, it does not make business sense to give away a piece of equipment that has some value at the end of its useful economic life.

3. ARR Is Based on the Accounting Profit, Not the Future

Another problem is that ARR is based on the use of accounting profit. When measuring performance over the whole life of a project, however, it is cash flows rather than accounting profits that are important. Accounting profit, on the other hand, is more appropriate for reporting achievement on a periodic basis, such as a year or half-year.

4. ARR Measures Relative Size and Not Absolute Size of the Return

The ARR method can also create problems when considering competing investments of different sizes, as shown in Activity 6.6.

ACTIVITY 6.6

Sinclair Wholesalers Limited is currently considering opening a new sales outlet in Ottawa. Two possible sites have been identified for the new outlet.

- Site A has floor space of 30,000 square metres. It will require an average investment of $6 million, and will produce an average profit of $600,000 a year.

- Site B has floor space of 20,000 square metres. It will require an average investment of $4 million, and will produce an average profit of $500,000 a year.

What is the ARR of each investment opportunity? Which site would you select, and why?

Solution

The ARR of Site A is $600,000/$6 million = 10%. The ARR of Site B is $500,000/ $4 million = 12.5%. Thus, Site B has the higher ARR. However, in terms of the absolute profit generated, Site A is the more attractive. It might be better to choose Site A even though the percentage return is lower. It is the absolute size of the return rather than the relative (percentage) size that is important.

PAYBACK PERIOD (PP)

Template for Payback and Discounted Payback

The **payback period (PP)** is the length of time it takes for an initial investment to be repaid out of the net cash inflows from a project. Since it takes time into account, the PP method seems to go some way toward overcoming the timing problem of ARR—or at least at first glance it does.

It will be three years before the $100,000 expenditure is covered by the inflows in the Billingsgate Battery Company example. This is still assuming that the cash flows occur at year-ends. The payback period can be derived by calculating the cumulative cash flows as follows:

Time		Net Cash Flows ($000)	Cumulative Cash Flows ($000)	
Immediately	Cost of machine	(100)	(100)	
1 year's time	Net profit before depreciation	20	(80)	(−100 + 20)
2 years' time	Net profit before depreciation	40	(40)	(−80 + 40)
3 years' time	Net profit before depreciation	60	20	(−40 + 60)
4 years' time	Net profit before depreciation	60	80	(20 + 60)
5 years' time	Net profit before depreciation	20	100	(80 + 20)
5 years' time	Disposal proceeds	20	120	(100 + 20)

We can see that the cumulative cash flows become positive at the end of the third year. Had we assumed that the cash flows arise evenly over the year, the precise payback period would be:

$$2 \text{ years} + (\$40,000/\$60,000) = 2.67 \text{ years}$$

where $40,000 represents the cash flow still required at the beginning of the third year to repay the initial expenditure, and $60,000 is the projected cash flow during the third year. A manager using PP would need to have a maximum payback period in mind. The decision rules to be used are:

- For any project to be acceptable, it must fall within the maximum payback period.
- Where there are competing projects that meet the maximum payback period requirement, the project with the shortest payback period should be selected.

If Billingsgate Battery Company had a maximum payback period of three years, the project would be acceptable. Activity 6.7 determines the payback period for the Chaotic Industries project.

ACTIVITY 6.7

What is the payback period of the Chaotic Industries project from Activity 6.4 (page 202)?

Solution

The inflows and outflows are expected to be:

Time		Net Cash Flows ($000)	Cumulative Net Cash Flows ($000)	
Immediately	Cost of vans	(150)	(150)	
1 year's time	Net saving before depreciation	30	(120)	(−150 + 30)
2 years' time	Net saving before depreciation	30	(90)	(−120 + 30)
3 years' time	Net saving before depreciation	30	(60)	(−90 + 30)
4 years' time	Net saving before depreciation	30	(30)	(−60 + 30)
5 years' time	Net saving before depreciation	30	0	(−30 + 30)
6 years' time	Net saving before depreciation	30	30	(0 + 30)
6 years' time	Disposal proceeds from the vans	30	60	(30 + 30)

The payback period here is five years (when the cumulative Net Cash flows reach 0).

Advantages of PP

It is quick and easy to calculate, and can easily be understood by managers. The logic of using PP is that projects that can recover their cost quickly are economically more attractive than those with longer payback periods. That is, PP emphasizes liquidity. PP is probably an improvement on ARR with respect to the timing of the cash flows. PP is not, however, the whole answer to the problem.

Problems with PP

The PP method is not concerned with the profitability of projects; it is concerned simply with their payback period. Thus cash flows arising beyond the payback period are ignored.

PP only looks at the risk that the project will end earlier than expected. What about, for example, the risk that the demand for the product may be less than expected?

PP's key deficiency, however, is that it is not linked to promoting increases in the wealth of the business. PP will tend to recommend undertaking projects that pay for themselves quickly, as illustrated in Activity 6.8.

ACTIVITY 6.8

In what respect is PP not satisfactory as a means of assessing investment opportunities? Consider the cash flows arising from three competing projects:

Time		Project 1 ($000)	Project 2 ($000)	Project 3 ($000)
Immediately	Cost of machine	(200)	(200)	(200)
1 year's time	Net profit before depreciation	40	10	80
2 years' time	Net profit before depreciation	80	20	100
3 years' time	Net profit before depreciation	80	170	20
4 years' time	Net profit before depreciation	60	20	200
5 years' time	Net profit before depreciation	40	10	500
5 years' time	Disposal proceeds	40	10	20
		140	40	720

Solution

The PP for each project is three years, and so the PP method would regard the projects as being equally acceptable. It cannot distinguish between those projects that pay back a significant amount early in the three-year payback period and those that do not.

In addition, this method ignores cash flows after the payback period. A decision maker concerned with maximizing shareholder wealth would prefer Project 3 in the table above because the cash flows come in earlier (most of the cost of the machine has been repaid by the end of the second year) and they are greater in total.

NET PRESENT VALUE (NPV)

Template for NPV and IRR

To make sensible investment decisions, we need a method of appraisal that:

- Considers *all* of the costs and benefits of each investment opportunity
- Makes a logical allowance for the *timing* of those costs and benefits.

The **net present value (NPV)** method provides us with this.

Consider the Billingsgate Battery Company example again. The cash flows are shown below. Recall from Chapter 5 that we calculated the net present value of these cash flows as positive $24,190 using a discount rate of 20%.

		1	2 PV Factor	3 = 1 + 2 PV
Time		**($000)**	**20%**	**($000)**
Immediately	Cost of machine	(100)	(1.0000)	(100.00)
1 year's time	Net profit before depreciation	20	0.8333	16.67
2 years' time	Net profit before depreciation	40	0.6944	27.78
3 years' time	Net profit before depreciation	60	0.5787	34.72
4 years' time	Net profit before depreciation	60	0.4823	28.94
5 years' time	Net profit before depreciation	20	0.4019	8.04
5 years' time	Disposal proceeds	20	0.4019	8.04
			NPV	24.19

The decision rules are:

- For any project to be acceptable, the NPV must be positive.
- Where there are competing projects with positive NPVs, the one that gives the highest positive NPV should be accepted.

In this case, the NPV is positive (and there are no competing projects), so we should accept the project and buy the machine. The reasoning behind this decision rule is quite straightforward. Given the investment opportunities available to the business, investing in the machine will make the business $24,190 better off.

NPV is explored in Activity 6.9 and 6.10.

ACTIVITY 6.9

What is the *maximum* the Billingsgate Battery Company would be prepared to pay for the machine, given the potential benefits of owning it?

Solution

The business would be prepared to pay up to $124,190 (i.e., the current cost of $100,000 plus the current NPV of $24,190), since the wealth of the owners of the business would be increased up to this price—although the business would prefer to pay as little as possible.

ACTIVITY 6.10

Recall the Chaotic Industries example, with the following cash flows:

Time		($000)
Immediately	Cost of vans	(150)
1 year's time	Net Saving before depreciation	30
2 years' time	Net Saving before depreciation	30
3 years' time	Net Saving before depreciation	30
4 years' time	Net Saving before depreciation	30
5 years' time	Net Saving before depreciation	30
6 years' time	Net Saving before depreciation	30
6 years' time	Disposal proceeds from the vans	30

▶

In Chapter 5, we determined the net present value of these cash flows as negative $19,660 using a discount rate of 14%. How would you interpret this result?

Solution

The fact that the project has a negative NPV means that the present values of the benefits from the investment are worth less than the cost of entering into it. Any cost up to $130,340 (i.e., the cost of $150,000 minus the NPV of $19,660) would be worth paying, but not $150,000.

The Discount Rate and the Cost of Capital

The appropriate discount rate to use in NPV assessments is the opportunity cost of funds. This is, in effect, the cost to the business of the funds that it will use to finance the investment, if it goes ahead. This will normally be the cost of the mixture of funds (shareholders' funds and debt) used by the business. This is usually known as the **cost of capital**. We will discuss this in more detail in Chapter 10.

Why NPV Is Superior to ARR and PP

NPV is a better method of appraising investment opportunities than either ARR or PP because it fully takes account of each of the following:

- *The timing of the cash flows.* By discounting the various cash flows, NPV takes account of the time value of money. NPV considers financing costs because it uses the cost of capital as discount rate.
- *The whole of the relevant cash flows.* NPV includes all of the relevant cash flows, unlike the PP method.
- *The objectives of the business.* NPV is the only method of appraisal that considers the wealth of the shareholders of a business. (Positive net present values enhance wealth; negative net present values reduce it.)

However, it should be noted that many business owners find the payback period method more intuitive than the net present value method.

INTERNAL RATE OF RETURN (IRR)

This is the last of the four major methods of investment appraisal that are found in practice. It is quite closely related to the NPV method in that, like NPV, it also involves discounting future cash flows. The **internal rate of return (IRR)** is the breakeven discount rate that makes NPV = 0. If the discount rate is higher than the IRR, the NPV will be negative. If the discount rate is lower than the IRR, then the NPV will be positive.

IRR is expressed as a percent, like an interest rate. Managers often have an intuitive understanding of IRR because it produces the yield (percentage return) for an investment project, which can then be compared to the firm's weighted average cost of capital (covered in detail in Chapter 10) and to current interest rates. For example, if analysis of a project's cash flows reveals an IRR of 24%, and the firm's cost of capital is 15%, while current interest rates sit at 10%, then it is immediately obvious that this appears to be a very good project. Example 6.3 and Activity 6.11 demonstrate the use of IRR.

Example 6.3

North West Pizza is considering the acquisition of a new high-heat oven for $105,000. If the oven is acquired, cash flows will improve by $40,000 per year for three years, at which time the oven will be scrapped.

Required:

(a) List the annual cash flows for this project, assuming they will be received at the end of each year.
(b) Determine the internal rate of return for this project.

Solution

(a) The cash flows are:

Year	Cost of Machine ($000)	Cash Profits ($000)	Net Cash Flows ($000)
0	(105)		(105)
1		40	40
2		40	40
3		40	40

(b) The internal rate of return can be estimated by guessing an IRR and computing the net present value to see if NPV is zero. If NPV is positive, adjust the IRR guess higher and re-compute NPV. If NPV is negative, adjust the IRR guess lower and re-compute NPV. This iterative process requires us to keep adjusting our guess for IRR until we get an NPV of zero.

Let's try a guess of 6% for IRR. Therefore the NPV at a discount rate of 6% is:

	6%
PV ordinary annuity factor, $n = 3, r = 6\%$	2.6730
	($000)
PV cash inflows ($40 × factor)	106.92
PV cash outflow	(105.00)
NPV	1.92

At a 6% discount rate, the NPV is $1,920. Since it is positive, we know the IRR must be higher in order to decrease the NPV to zero.

So let us now try a discount rate of 8%.

	8%
PV ordinary annuity factor, $n = 3, r = 8\%$	2.5771
	($000)
PV cash inflows ($40 × factor)	103.084
PV cash outflow	(105.00)
NPV	−1.916

At 8%, the NPV is negative $1,916. We have almost exactly "surrounded" the zero NPV level with $1,920 above and $1,916 below. It looks like the IRR is going to be 7%. To prove this, we repeat the calculations for a third time.

	7%
PV ordinary annuity factor, $n = 3, r = 7\%$	2.6243
	($000)
PV cash inflows ($40 × factor)	104.972
PV cash outflow	(105.00)
NPV	−0.028

The NPV is negative $28, which is close enough to zero to consider 7% to be a valid estimate of the internal rate of return for this project. The actual IRR turns out to be 6.99%, so our iterative estimation process is very accurate indeed.

ACTIVITY 6.11

Kawartha Lakes Delivery Ltd. is considering buying a new truck for $56,000. The truck will improve cash flows by $20,000 for each of the next four years, and then will be scrapped for no salvage value. Determine the internal rate of return for this project assuming all cash inflows are received at the end of the year. (*Hint:* Try 10% first.)

Year	Cost of Machine	Cash Profits	Net Cash Flows
			($000)
0	(56)		(56)
1		20	20
2		20	20
3		20	20
4		20	20

Solution

	Discount Rate, r%		
	10%	20%	16%
PV ordinary annuity factor, $n = 4$, various r%	3.1699	2.5887	2.7982
	($000)	($000)	($000)
PV cash inflows ($20 × factor)	63.398	51.774	55.964
PV cash outflow	(56.000)	(56.000)	(56.000)
NPV	7.398	−4.226	−0.036

Notice that this solution guessed 10% first and 20% second before trying 16%. After two attempts, you can estimate IRR by using a method called **interpolation** as long as you have one positive and one negative NPV. The method would be employed as follows:

Interpolation

Difference in discount rates from 10% to 20%	10%
Difference in NPV between 10% and 20% [7.398 − (−4.226)]	11.624
Difference to get NPV from 7.398 to 0	7.398
Pro-rated difference in discount rates (7.398 ÷ 11.624) × 10%	6.36%
Plus: Add on the base discount rate	10%
Interpolated IRR	16.36%

You can think of interpolation as a measure of distances, like on a road map. The distance from 10% to 20% is 10%. The distance from an NPV of $7,398 to an NPV of $(4,226) is $11,624. The distance from an NPV of $7,398 to an NPV of $0 is $7,398. Therefore, we need to start on the discount road map at 10% and move along it a distance of 6.36% up to 16.36% in order to get to an NPV of zero.

Interpolation suggests that our third guess for IRR should be 16%, which, as it turns out, is confirmed as the correct IRR by the net present value calculation. Activity 6.12 explores what NPV can tell us about IRR.

ACTIVITY 6.12

We should recall that, when we discounted the cash flows of the Billingsgate Battery Company machine investment opportunity at 20%, we found that the NPV was a positive figure of $24,190. What does the NPV of the machine project tell us about the IRR of the investment?

Solution

The fact that the NPV is positive when discounting at 20% implies that the IRR of the project is more than 20%. The fact that the NPV is a large figure implies that the actual rate of return is quite a lot more than 20%.

For Billingsgate Battery Company, let us try a higher rate—say, 30%—and see what happens:

Time	Cash Flow ($000)	Discount Factor* 30%	PV ($000)
Immediately (time 0)	(100)	1.000	(100.00)
1 year's time	20	0.769	15.38
2 years' time	40	0.592	23.68
3 years' time	60	0.455	27.30
4 years' time	60	0.350	21.00
5 years' time	20	0.269	5.38
5 years' time	20	0.269	5.38
		NPV	(1.88)

* Rounded to three decimal places
Because future cash flow projections have no guarantee of absolute precision, notice that the discount factors are rounded to three decimals. In some later examples and solutions, two decimals will be used.

In increasing the discount rate from 20% to 30%, we have reduced the NPV from positive $24,190 to negative $1,880. We can conclude that the IRR of Billingsgate Battery Company's machine project is very slightly below 30%. Further trials could lead us to the exact

FIGURE 6.2   The Relationship between the NPV and IRR Methods

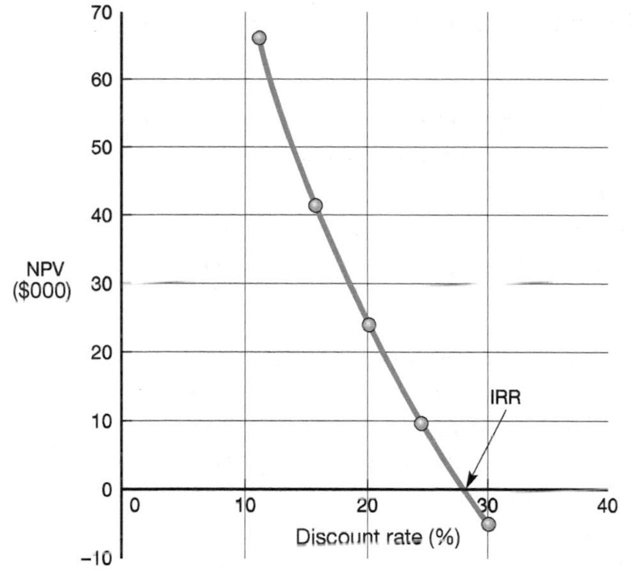

rate, but there is probably not much point, given the likely inaccuracy of the cash flow estimates. It is probably good enough, for practical purposes, to say that the IRR is about 30%.

The relationship between NPV and IRR is shown graphically in Figure 6.2 using the information relating to the Billingsgate Battery Company.

As the discount rate increases, there is a corresponding decrease in the NPV of the project. IRR is the discount rate at the point where the NPV line crosses the horizontal axis because that is where NPV – 0.

Activity 6.13 explores the IRR for the Chaotic Industries project.

ACTIVITY 6.13

What is the internal rate of return of the Chaotic Industries project? You should use the discount table in Appendix A or a spreadsheet. (*Hint:* Remember that you already know the NPV of this project, negative $19,670, calculated at a discount rate of 14%.)

Solution

Since we know that, at a 14% discount rate, the NPV is a relatively large negative figure, our next trial is using a lower discount rate—say, 10%:

Time	Cash Flows ($000)	Discount Factor* (10%, from the table)	Present Value ($000)
Immediately	(150)	1.000	(150.00)
1 year's time	30	0.909	27.27
2 years' time	30	0.826	24.78
3 years' time	30	0.751	22.53
4 years' time	30	0.683	20.49
5 years' time	30	0.621	18.63
6 years' time	30	0.565	16.95
6 years' time	30	0.565	16.95
		NPV	(2.40)

* Rounded to three decimal places

This figure is close to zero NPV. However, the NPV is still negative and so the precise IRR will be a little below 10%.

In answering Activity 6.13, we were fortunate in using a discount rate of 10% for our second iteration, as this happened to be very close to the IRR figure. But what if we had used 6%? This discount factor will provide us with a large positive NPV, as we shall see below.

Time	Cash Flows ($000)	Discount Factor* (6%, from the table)	Present Value ($000)
Immediately	(150)	1.000	(150.00)
1 year's time	30	0.943	28.29
2 years' time	30	0.890	26.70
3 years' time	30	0.840	25.20
4 years' time	30	0.792	23.76
5 years' time	30	0.747	22.41
6 years' time	30	0.705	21.15
6 years' time	30	0.705	21.15
		NPV	18.66

*Rounded to three decimal places

By interpolation, we have:

Trial	Discount Factor	Net Present Value ($000)
1	14%	(19.66)
2	6%	18.66
Difference	8%	38.32

The change in NPV for every 1% change in the discount rate will be:

$$\frac{38.32}{8} = 4.79\%$$

The reduction in the 14% discount rate required to achieve a zero NPV would therefore be:

$$\frac{19.66}{4.79} = 4.10\%$$

The IRR is therefore:

$$14.00\% - 4.10\% = 9.90\%$$

Note that this approach, another variation of *interpolation,* assumes a straight-line relationship between the discount rate and NPV. We can see from Figure 6.2 on page 213, however, that this assumption is not strictly correct. Nevertheless, over a relatively short range, this simplifying assumption is not usually a problem and so we can still arrive at a reasonable approximation.

The minimum required IRR is often referred to as the *hurdle rate.* It is usually the firm's weighted average cost of capital (WACC), which is discussed in detail in Chapter 10. The following decision rules should be applied:

■ For any project to be acceptable, it must exceed the minimum IRR requirement
■ Where there are competing projects, the one with the highest IRR should be selected.

REAL WORLD 6.4 lists the IRRs expected from the investment projects of a large business.

Suncor Targets 15%

Suncor Energy of Calgary targets a minimum 15% rate of return on capital projects. For 2008, Suncor's new projects achieved a threshold of 22.5% despite the ongoing recession. Suncor is a major player in Canada's Athabasca oil sands region. Suncor grew larger in 2009 when it acquired Petro-Canada.

Source: Suncor website: http://documents.suncor.com/default.aspx?cid=1195&lang=1, accessed September 2, 2009.

Limitations of IRR

The main disadvantage of IRR is the fact that it does not correctly address the question of wealth generation. It could therefore lead to the wrong decision being made. The IRR approach would, for example, always consider an IRR of 25% to be preferable to an IRR of 20%, assuming an opportunity cost of capital of 15%. Although accepting the project with the higher percentage return will often generate more wealth, this may not always be the case because IRR completely ignores the *scale of investment*. With a 15% cost of capital, $15 million invested at 20% [i.e., $15 million (20% − 15%) = $0.75 million] would make us richer than $5 million invested at 25% [i.e., $5 million (25% − 15%) = $0.50 million]. IRR does not recognize this. NPV is better to use than IRR.

A further problem with the IRR method is that it has difficulty handling projects with unconventional cash flows. Some projects may have both positive and negative cash flows in the future. Such a pattern of cash flows can result in there being more than one IRR, as shown in Example 6.4, or even no IRR at all.

Example 6.4

Let us assume that a project had the following pattern of cash flows:

Time	Cash Flows ($000)
Immediately	(4,000)
1 year's time	9,400
2 years' time	(5,500)

These cash flows will give a zero NPV at both 10% and 25%. Thus, we will have two IRRs, which can be confusing for decision makers. Assume, for example, that the minimum acceptable IRR is 15%. Should the project be accepted or rejected?

Figure 6.3 shows the NPV of the above project for different discount rates.

FIGURE 6.3   Two IRRs
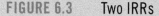

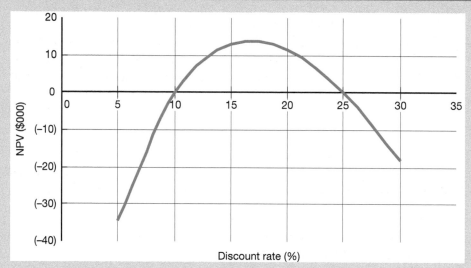

The points at which the graphed NPV line crosses the horizontal axis line are the IRRs. The figure shows two IRRs: the NPV of the project is zero when the discount rate is 10%, and also when the discount rate is 25%.

SOME PRACTICAL POINTS

When undertaking an investment appraisal, there are several practical points that we should bear in mind:

■ *Sunk costs.*   As with all decisions, we should only take account of **relevant costs** in our analysis. This means that only costs that vary with the decision should be considered. Thus, all sunk costs should be ignored as they occurred in the past and cannot vary with the decision. An example is research and development costs incurred *before* the evaluation of a new product.

■ *Common future costs.*   It is not only past costs that do not vary with the decision; some future costs may also be the same. Take, for example, a trucking business that is going to buy a new truck, and the decision lies between two different models. The truck will require a driver, no matter which truck is chosen. So the cost of employing the driver is thus irrelevant to the decision as to which truck to buy. If, however, the decision was whether to operate an additional truck or not, the cost of employing the additional driver would be relevant. This is because it would then be a cost that would vary with the decision made.

■ *Opportunity costs.*   Opportunity costs arising from benefits forgone must be taken into account. Thus, for example, when considering a decision concerning whether or not to continue to use a machine already owned by the business, the salvage value of the machine might be an important **opportunity cost**.

These three points concerning costs are brought together in Activity 6.14.

ACTIVITY 6.14

An independent garage has an old car that it bought a week ago for $3,000. The car needs a tune-up and safety inspection, costing $300, before it can be sold. This would take two hours by a worker who is paid $12 an hour. At present the garage is short of work, but the owners are reluctant to lay off any workers or even to cut down their basic working week because labour is difficult to find and an upturn in repair work is expected soon.

Without the tune-up and safety inspection, the car still could be sold for parts for an estimated $3,500. What is the minimum price at which the garage should sell the car, with a tune-up and safety inspection, to avoid incurring a loss? (Ignore any timing differences in receipts and payments.)

Solution

The minimum price is the amount required to cover the relevant costs of the job. At this price, the business will make neither a profit nor a loss. Any price below this amount will result in a reduction in the wealth of the business. Thus, the minimum price is:

	($)
Opportunity cost of the car	3,500
Cost of the tune-up and safety	300
Total	3,800

The original cost of the car is a sunk cost and is, therefore, irrelevant. However, we are told that, without the tune-up and safety inspection, the car could be sold for $3,500. This is the opportunity cost of the car, which represents real benefits forgone, and should be taken into account.

The cost of the tune-up and safety inspection is relevant because, if the work is done, the garage will have to pay $300 but will pay nothing if the job is not done.

The labour cost is irrelevant because the same common future cost will be incurred whether the worker undertakes the work or not.

- *Taxes.* Investors will be interested in the after-tax returns generated. Unless tax is formally taken into account, the wrong decision could easily be made. A significant complication is that rarely does depreciation cost equal capital cost allowance, the tax return's equivalent of depreciation. So, the adjustment is to add book depreciation and subtract off taxes paid, as follows:

Sales	xxx	
Less: Expenses (including depreciation)	xx	
EBIT	xxx	
Add back: Non-cash depreciation expense	xx	
Cash flows from operations		xxx
Less: Tax payment:		
Net profits excluding taxes	xxx	
Add back: Non-deductible depreciation expense	xx	
Less: Capital cost allowance	(xx)	
Taxable income	xxx	
Tax rate (assumed)	40%	
Less tax payment		(xx)
After-tax cash flow		xxx

■ *Cash flows, not profit flows.*   We have seen that for the NPV, IRR, and PP methods, it is cash flows rather than profit flows that are relevant to the evaluation of investment projects.

Some adjustment should be made to take account of changes in working capital. For example, launching a new product may give rise to an increase in the net cash investment made in receivables, inventories, and payables, requiring an immediate outlay of cash. This outlay for additional working capital (current assets less current liabilities) should be shown in the NPV calculations as part of the initial cost. However, at the end of the life of the project, the additional working capital will be released. This disinvestment (resulting in an inflow of cash at the end of the project) should also be taken into account at the point at which it is received.

■ *Interest payments.*   When using discounted cash flow techniques, interest payments should not be taken into account in deriving the cash flows for the period. The discount factor already adjusts for the costs of financing.

■ *Other factors.*   Investment decision making must not be viewed as simply a mechanical exercise. Broader issues connected to the decision might have to be considered, but might be difficult or impossible to quantify. For example, a regional bus company might be considering an investment in a new bus to serve a particular route. Although the NPV calculations may reveal that a loss will be made on the investment, it may be that by not investing in the new bus, and therefore not operating the route, the renewal of the company's licence to operate will be put at risk. In such a situation, the licence issue is more important than the calculations.

The reliability of the forecasts and the validity of the assumptions used in the evaluation will also have a bearing on the final decision. We shall see in the following chapter that various techniques take account of risk and assess sensitivity to any inaccuracies in the figures used.

Example 6.5 provides some additional insight into relevant costs.

Example 6.5

Thunder Tools Ltd. specializes in mining equipment. A few years ago, Thunder spent $45,000 on some vacant land on which to build a second workshop. Since now is a slow period and Thunder does not wish to lay experienced employees off, the current workshop has idle capacity for its workforce. Therefore, Thunder is now considering an expansion plan for building the new workshop on the vacant land. However, if the decision is made not to expand, the vacant land could be sold for $47,000 now. Materials would cost $200,000. Ten of Thunder's current employees, each paid at the rate of $4,000 per month, would construct the workshop building. It would take one month to complete the construction. After-tax cash flows from additional sales would amount to $50,000 per year for the next five years. Assume each of these amounts is received at year-end. After five years, it is expected there will be no need for the second worksite due to slowing demand for mining equipment. The land and building are expected to be sold for $60,000 ($50,000 for land and $10,000 for the building) at that time.

Required:

(a) Prepare a schedule of the relevant cash flows under the assumption that Thunder will proceed with construction of the new building.
(b) Calculate the net present value of these cash flows, assuming a discount rate of 8%.

(c) Now assume that the fair value of the land at the beginning of the project remains at $45,000 and the land cannot be sold, according to city bylaw, until the end of the fifth year, when it would fetch $50,000. How would this affect the net present value?

Solution

(a) and (b)

The land cost of $47,000 represents an opportunity cost. If Thunder decides against the expansion, then it has the option of selling the land for $47,000. By expanding, Thunder can no longer sell the land and therefore has forgone the use of $47,000. This is accounted for by showing $-$47,000 cash outflow at time = 0. The relevant cash flows and the net present value calculations are shown below:

Year	Materials Cost ($)	Land	Building Salvage ($)	After-Tax Cash Flows ($)	Net Cash Flows ($)	Present Value Factor	Present Value ($)
0	(200,000)	(47,000)			(247,000)	1.0000	(247,000)
1				50,000	50,000	0.9259	46,295
2				50,000	50,000	0.8573	42,865
3				50,000	50,000	0.7938	39,690
4				50,000	50,000	0.7350	36,750
5		50,000	10,000	50,000	110,000	0.6806	74,866
						NPV	(6,534)

The net present value of this project is negative $6,534. The project should not proceed.

Some of the cash flows mentioned in the question are not relevant to the analysis:

■ The labour cost should not be included in the decision-making process because these employees were not going to be laid off and therefore would be paid anyway.

■ The original cost for the land is not relevant to the decision-making process because it is an old cost (a sunk cost). The relevant cost is the $47,000 selling price that could be achieved if the expansion did not proceed.

(c) If the land cannot be sold until the end of the fifth year, the land costs would not be relevant. Furthermore, the $50,000 for which the land could be sold at the end of five years would be obtained whether or not the expansion plan proceeds. So we can ignore the land costs in the NPV calculation.

Year	Materials Cost ($)	Land ($)	Building Salvage ($)	After-Tax Cash Flows ($)	Net Cash Flows ($)	Present Value Factor	Present Value ($)
0	(200,000)				(200,000)	1.0000	(200,000)
1				50,000	50,000	0.9259	46,295
2				50,000	50,000	0.8573	42,865
3				50,000	50,000	0.7938	39,690
4				50,000	50,000	0.7350	36,750
5			10,000	50,000	60,000	0.6806	40,836
						NPV	6,436

Now, with a positive net present value (although not a large amount), it looks like the project should go ahead.

Activity 6.15 brings together several aspects of capital investment decision making.

ACTIVITY 6.15

The directors of Manuff Steel Ltd. are considering closing one of the business's factories. There has been a reduction in the demand for the products made at the factory in recent years, and management is not optimistic about the long-term prospects for these products. The factory is situated in Northern Ontario, in an area where unemployment is high.

The factory is leased, and there are still four years of the lease remaining. Management is uncertain as to whether the factory should be closed immediately or at the end of the period of the lease. Another business has offered to sublease the premises from Manuff at a rental of $40,000 a year for the remainder of the lease period.

The machinery and equipment at the factory cost $1,500,000, and are reported on the balance sheet at a net book value of $400,000. In the event of immediate closure, the machinery and equipment could be sold for $220,000. The working capital at the factory is $420,000, and could be liquidated for that amount immediately, if required. Alternatively, the working capital can be liquidated in full at the end of the lease period. Immediate closure would result in severance payments to employees of $180,000.

If the factory continues in operation until the end of the lease period, the following operating profits (losses) are expected:

	Year 1 ($000)	Year 2 ($000)	Year 3 ($000)	Year 4 ($000)
Operating profit (loss)	160	(40)	30	20

The above figures include a charge of $90,000 a year for depreciation of machinery and equipment. The residual value of the machinery and equipment at the end of the lease period is estimated at $40,000.

Severance payments are expected to be $150,000 at the end of the lease period if the factory continues in operation. The business has an annual cost of capital of 12%. Ignore taxation.

Required:

(a) Determine the relevant cash flows arising from a decision to continue operations until the end of the lease period rather than to close immediately.
(b) Calculate the net present value of continuing operations until the end of the lease period, rather than closing immediately.
(c) What other factors might management take into account before making a final decision on the timing of the factory closure?
(d) State, with reasons, whether the business should continue to operate the factory until the end of the lease period.

Solution

(a) Relevant cash flows for Manuff

	Year 0 ($000)	Year 1 ($000)	Year 2 ($000)	Year 3 ($000)	Year 4 ($000)
Operating cash flows (Note 1)		250	50	120	110
Sale of machinery (Note 2)	(220)				40
Severance costs (Note 3)	180				(150)
Sublease rentals (Note 4)		(40)	(40)	(40)	(40)
Working capital invested (Note 5)	(420)				420
	(460)	210	10	80	380

▶

(b) Discount rate 12%	1.000	0.8929	0.7972	0.7118	0.6355
Present value	(460.00)	187.51	7.97	56.94	241.49
Net present value	33.91				
(Sum of present values)					

(c) Other factors that may influence the decision include:

- *The overall strategy of the business.*   The business may need to set the decision within a broader context. It may be necessary to manufacture the products made at the factory because they are an integral part of the business's product range. The business may wish to avoid layoffs in an area of high unemployment for as long as possible.
- *Flexibility.*   A decision to close the factory is probably irreversible. If the factory continues, however, there may be a chance that the prospects for the factory will brighten in the future.
- *Creditworthiness of sublessee.*   The business should investigate the creditworthiness of the sublessee. Failure to receive the expected sublease payments would make the closure option far less attractive.
- *Accuracy of forecasts.*   The forecasts made by the business should be examined carefully. Inaccuracies in the forecasts or any underlying assumptions may change the expected outcomes.

(d) The NPV of the decision to continue operations rather than close immediately is positive. The factory should therefore continue in operation rather than close down.

Notes
1. Each year's operating cash flows are calculated by adding back the depreciation charge for the year to the operating profit for the year. In the case of the operating loss, the depreciation charge is deducted.
2. In the event of closure, machinery could be sold immediately. Thus an opportunity cost of $220,000 is incurred if operations continue because the company loses the opportunity to sell the machinery if the plant is kept open.
3. By continuing operations, there will be a saving in immediate severance costs of $180,000. However, severance costs of $150,000 will be paid in four years' time.
4. By continuing operations, the opportunity to sublease the factory will be forgone.
5. Immediate closure would mean that working capital could be liquidated. By continuing operations this opportunity is forgone. However, working capital can be liquidated in four years' time.

SELF-ASSESSMENT QUESTION   6.1

Confederation Printing Press Ltd. is considering an expansion with the acquisition of an additional press for $250,000 because the entire second floor of the building it owns is currently unused. Confederation has already spent $10,000 modernizing the unused second floor. Confederation would have to borrow the entire purchase price, paying $20,000 interest per annum, with the principal to be repaid at the end of 10 years. The press would have a 10-year lifespan, at which time it could be sold for $25,000. Additional annual net income after depreciation of $22,500 per year is expected to be $50,000 if Confederation goes ahead with the new press purchase. Confederation could lease the second floor for $12,000 per year if it decides not to proceed with the new press. If Confederation proceeds with the expansion, it will be necessary to increase the size of the paper inventory by $23,000. Accounts receivable will also increase by $15,000 due to increased sales.

Required:

(a) Prepare the relevant cash flows associated with acquiring the new press. For each cash amount mentioned in the question that is not a relevant cash flow item, provide a reason why that is so.
(b) Calculate the net present value of the expansion plan using a 16% discount rate.

INVESTMENT APPRAISAL IN PRACTICE

Many surveys have been conducted into the methods of investment appraisal used by businesses. They have tended to show that:

- Businesses are using more than one method to assess each investment decision
- The discounting methods (NPV and IRR) are increasingly being used over time, with these two becoming the most popular in recent years
- ARR and PP have continuing popularity, despite their theoretical shortcomings and the rise in popularity of the discounting methods
- There is a tendency for larger businesses to use the discounting methods, and to use more than one method in respect of each decision.

REAL WORLD 6.5 shows the percentage of businesses that use these investment appraisal methods.

REAL WORLD 6.5

Capital Budgeting in Practice

The IRR and NPV methods are widely used by U.S. businesses. Nevertheless, theoretically incorrect methods like payback and ARR continue to have a following, with the payback method still used by a majority of U.S. businesses.

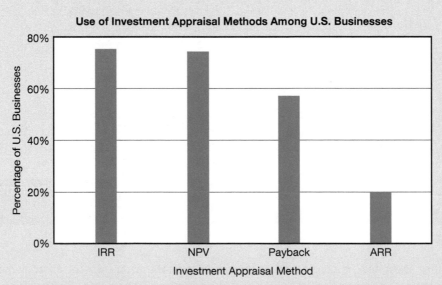

Use of Investment Appraisal Methods Among U.S. Businesses

Source: Based on information in "How do CFOs make capital budgeting and capital structure decisions?", R. Graham and C. Harvey, Journal of Applied Corporate Finance, vol. 15, no. 1, 2002, as cited in *Financial Management for Decision Makers*, Peter Atrill, 5th Ed., FT Prentice Hall, 2009.

Activity 6.16 outlines the popularity of the payback method for making investment decisions.

ACTIVITY 6.16

Earlier in the chapter, we discussed the theoretical limitations of the payback method. How do you explain the fact that it still seems to be popular for investment appraisal among businesses?

▶

> **Solution**
>
> A number of possible reasons may explain this finding:
>
> - PP is easy to understand and use.
> - It can avoid the problems of forecasting far into the future.
> - It gives emphasis to the early cash flows when there is greater certainty concerning the accuracy of their predicted value.
> - It emphasizes the importance of liquidity. Where a business has liquidity problems, a short payback period for a project is likely to appear attractive.

PP can provide a convenient—although rough and ready—assessment of the profitability of a project, in the way that it is used in REAL WORLD 6.6.

Scotiabank's Key Criteria

Scotiabank assesses all major capital deployment initiatives through the lenses of impact on EPS, return on invested capital, expected payback period, and internal rate of return based on discounted cash flows.

Source: Scotiabank 2008 Annual Report.

The popularity of PP may suggest a lack of sophistication among managers concerning investment appraisal, especially for smaller businesses.

The survey evidence suggests that many businesses use more than one method to appraise investments, especially NPV and IRR. IRR may be as popular as NPV, despite its shortcomings, because it expresses outcomes in percentage terms rather than in absolute terms.

REAL WORLD 6.7 shows how a well-known Canadian gold mining company uses NPV.

The Greening of Gold at Goldcorp

Vancouver-based Goldcorp Inc., an international gold mining company, uses net present value techniques to determine the size of the liability it should report for future reclamation costs for mines, including site rehabilitation and long-term treatment and monitoring costs.

Source: Goldcorp 2008 Annual Report.

SELF-ASSESSMENT QUESTION   6.2

Beacon Chemicals Limited is considering buying some equipment to produce a new chemical named X14. The new equipment's capital cost is estimated at $100,000 with no salvage value at the end of five years. If its purchase is approved now, the equipment can be bought and production can commence by the end of this year. $50,000 has already been spent on research and development. Estimates of sales in litres, selling price, and costs arising from the operation of the new equipment appear below:

	Year 1	Year 2	Year 3	Year 4	Year 5
Sales price ($/L)	100	120	120	100	80
Sales volume (L)	800	1,000	1,200	1,000	800
Variable costs ($/L)	50	50	40	30	40
Fixed costs ($000)	30	30	30	30	30

If the equipment is bought in order to produce X14, sales of some existing products will be lost, and this will result in lost cash profits of $15,000 a year over the equipment's life.

The accountant has informed you that the fixed costs include depreciation of $30,000 a year on the new equipment. A separate study has indicated that if the new equipment were bought, additional overheads (excluding depreciation) arising from producing the chemical would be $8,000 a year. Production would require additional working capital of $30,000.

For the purposes of your initial calculations, ignore taxation.

Required:

(a) Determine the relevant annual cash flows associated with buying the equipment.
(b) Compute the payback period.
(c) Calculate the net present value using a discount rate of 8%.

Hint: You should deal with the investment in working capital by treating it as a cash outflow at the start of the project and an inflow at the end.

INVESTMENT DECISIONS AND HUMAN BEHAVIOUR

An investment project will often gather support among managers as it is being developed. The greater the level of support, the greater the potential for bias in the information used to evaluate the project. This may mean that future cash flows are overestimated or the risks associated with the project are underestimated. It is important to recognize that investment decisions are made by individuals who may have their own interests to satisfy.

Triple Bottom Line Accounting

Triple bottom line accounting seeks to influence the behavioural side of the investment decision by adding environmental and social responsibility performance reporting into the mix alongside traditional financial performance. Triple bottom line reporting can be summarized as "People, Planet, and Profit." "People" refers to fair business practices by corporations toward labour, community, and region. "Planet" refers to sustainable environmental practices. In 2007, the United Nations passed a resolution ensuring that triple bottom line accounting became the standard for urban and community accounting.

SUMMARY

The Process of Investment Decision Making

Management of the investment project has six stages:

1. Determine investment funds available—dealing with capital rationing problems, if necessary
2. Identify profitable project opportunities
3. Define and classify proposed projects
4. Evaluate the proposed project(s)
5. Approve the project(s)
6. Monitor and control the project(s) using a post-completion audit approach.

Accounting Rate of Return (ARR)

- Accounting rate of return (ARR) is the average accounting profit from the project expressed as a percentage of the average investment.
- Decision rules: Projects with an ARR above a defined minimum are acceptable; the greater the ARR, the more attractive the project becomes.
- Conclusions on ARR:
  - ARR does not relate directly to shareholders' wealth—it can lead to illogical conclusions
  - ARR takes almost no account of the timing of cash flows
  - ARR ignores some relevant information and may consider some information that is irrelevant
  - ARR is relatively simple to use
  - ARR is much inferior to NPV.

Payback Period (PP)

- Payback period (PP) is the length of time that it takes for the cash outflow for the initial investment to be repaid out of resulting cash inflows.
- Decision rules: Projects with a PP up to a defined maximum period are acceptable; the shorter the PP, the more desirable.

- Conclusions on PP:
  - PP does not relate to shareholders' wealth; it ignores cash flows after the payback date
  - PP takes little account of the timing of cash flows (time value of money)
  - PP ignores much relevant information
  - PP does not always provide clear signals and can be impractical to use
  - PP is much inferior to NPV, but it is easy to understand and can offer a liquidity insight, which might be the reason for its widespread use.

Net Present Value (NPV)

- Net present value (NPV) is the sum of the discounted values of the net cash flows from the investment.
- Decision rules: All positive NPV investments enhance shareholders' wealth; the greater the NPV, the greater the enhancement and the more desirable.
- Conclusions on NPV:
  - NPV relates directly to the shareholders' wealth objective
  - NPV considers the timing of cash flows
  - NPV takes all relevant information into account
  - NPV provides clear signals and is practical to use.

Internal Rate of Return (IRR)

- Internal rate of return (IRR) is the discount rate, which, when applied to the cash flows of a project, causes the project to have a zero NPV.
- IRR represents the average percentage return on the investment, taking account of the fact that cash may be flowing in and out of the project at various points in its life.

■ Decision rules: Projects that have an IRR greater than the cost of capital are acceptable; the greater the IRR, the more attractive the project.

■ IRR cannot normally be calculated directly unless a financial calculator or spreadsheet formula is used; a trial and error approach is often necessary when using a calculator.

■ Conclusions on IRR:
  • IRR does not relate directly to shareholders' wealth. It usually gives the same signals as NPV but can mislead where there are competing projects of different sizes
  • IRR considers the timing of cash flows

• IRR takes all relevant information into account
• There is the problem of multiple IRRs when there are unconventional cash flows
• IRR is inferior to NPV.

Investment Appraisal in Practice

■ All four methods identified are widely used
■ The discounting methods (NPV and IRR) show a steady increase in usage over time
■ Many businesses use more than one method
■ Larger businesses seem to be more sophisticated in their choice and use of appraisal methods than smaller ones.

KEY TERMS

Capital rationing	Payback period (PP)	Interpolation
Post-completion audit	Net present value (NPV)	Relevant costs
Accounting rate of return (ARR)	Cost of capital	Opportunity cost
	Internal rate of return (IRR)	

LIST OF EQUATION

6.1   Accounting rate of return $= \dfrac{\text{Average annual profit}}{\text{Average investment to earn that profit}} \times 100\%$

REVIEW QUESTIONS

Answers to the Review Questions can be found on the Companion Website that accompanies this text at www.pearsoned.ca/atrill.

6.1 Why is the net present value method of investment appraisal considered to be theoretically superior to other methods that are found in practice?

6.2 The payback method has been criticized for not taking the time value of money into account. Could this limitation be overcome? If so, would this method then be preferable to the NPV method?

6.3 Research indicates that the IRR method is a more popular method of investment appraisal than the NPV method. Why might this be?

6.4 Why are cash flows rather than profit flows used in the IRR, NPV, and PP methods of investment appraisal?

6.5 Prairie Computers Limited (PCL) has three projects it could implement with the following cost and NPV profiles.

	Cost ($)	NPV ($)
Project A	400,000	75,000
Project B	450,000	125,000
Project C	625,000	195,000

However, PCL has only $1 million available to spend on capital projects. Define capital rationing and explain how it fits into this situation.

6.6 You are a new graduate employed at a small manufacturing company. The president has asked for your advice on a suggestion made by a senior manager that would make the company $1 million wealthier. The company would buy a new machine for $1 million to make NBA-endorsed basketballs. The machine would last 10 years and generate sales of $300,000 per year. Annual material, labour, and maintenance costs would be $100,000 per year. No other cost is anticipated. Advise the president.

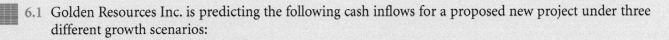

PROBLEMS AND CASES

6.1 Golden Resources Inc. is predicting the following cash inflows for a proposed new project under three different growth scenarios:

Cash Inflows
($ millions)

End of Year	Low Growth	Medium Growth	High Growth
1	300	300	300
2	310	320	330
3	330	350	380
4	355	375	460
5	370	390	500

Required:

(a) Calculate the present value of the cash inflows for each growth scenario, assuming that the appropriate discount rate for Golden Resources is 10%.

(b) Assuming the initial investment at the beginning of Year 1 is $1.28 billion (that is, $1,280 million), calculate the net present value for each growth scenario.

(c) Based on your answer in part (b), would you recommend that Golden Resources implement the proposed new project, if it determines that all three scenarios are equally likely?

6.2 Manitoba Railroad Limited (MRL) is considering spending $522 million to add new locomotives and train cars. It is estimated that the trains will last 15 years and have an estimated salvage value of $50 million at the end of 15 years. Expected annual revenue increases before depreciation for the first five years are $75 million, for the next five years are $50 million, and for the last five years are $40 million. MRL's cost of capital is 7%.

Required:

(a) Calculate:
   (i)   Accounting rate of return
   (ii) Payback period
   (iii) Net present value
   (iv) Internal rate of return.

(b) State, with reasons, your recommendation to MRL concerning implementation of this project.

6.3 Berry Chips Inc. (BCI) is considering acquiring a new semiconductor fabricator. The machine costs $985,000, will last for eight years, and has a salvage value of $45,000. The forecasted net revenue stream is as shown. For simplicity, assume all net revenues are received at the end of the year. BCI uses a discount rate of 9%.

Year 1	Cost	Cash Inflows	Salvage Value	Net Cash Inflows
0	$985,000	$	$	$
1		75,000		
2		90,000		
3		220,000		
4		280,000		
5		210,000		
6		175,000		
7		160,000		
8		110,000	45,000	

Required:
   (a) Use the net present value method to determine whether BCI should buy the machine.
   (b) Name two things that would have to change for you to change your decision. Assume cash flows cannot change.

6.4

Required:
Use the data from Problem and Case 6.3 to recalculate part (a) using a discount rate of 7%.

6.5

Required:
Use the data in (and your solutions to) Problems and Cases 6.3 and 6.4 to determine the internal rate of return for BCI.

6.6 You are considering the following three projects.

	Project A	Project B	Project C
Discount rate	10%	3%	6%
Year	Net Cash Inflows	Net Cash Inflows	Net Cash Inflows
0	$(300,000)	$(32,000)	$(87,000)
1	80,000	9,000	30,000
2	40,000	9,000	35,000
3	60,000	9,000	12,000
4	150,000	9,000	45,000

Required:
   (a) Calculate the net present value of each project.
   (b) Determine the internal rate of return for each project.

6.7 Prairie Eateries Limited (PEL) is considering the following projects. PEL uses straight-line depreciation.

	Projects			
	A	B	C	D
Net profit increases before depreciation	$16,000	$25,000	$35,000	$42,000
Cost	$50,000	$80,000	$250,000	$500,000
Salvage value	$10,000	–	$50,000	$40,000
Economic life in years	5	8	10	20

Required:
Calculate the accounting rate of return for each project.

6.8

Required:
Use the data in Problem and Case 6.7 to calculate the payback period for each project.

6.9

Required:
Use the data in Problem and Case 6.7 to calculate the net present value for each project using a discount rate of 12%. For simplicity, assume the cash flows occur at the end of the year, except for the original cost of the project.

6.10

Required:
Use the data in Problem and Case 6.7 to calculate the internal rate of return for each project. For simplicity, assume the cash flows occur at the end of the year, except for the original cost of the project.

6.11 Moncton Semiconductors Corporation (MSC) is considering spending an additional $4 million to expand its computer chip factory to increase production of its best-selling product. The expansion will begin producing revenue in one year. MSC has already spent $500,000 studying the upgrade. The following data applies:

	Year 1	Year 2	Year 3	Year 4
Sale price per chip ($)	10	15	25	20
Estimated unit sales	100,000	125,000	140,000	110,000
Variable costs per chip ($)	2	3	3	2.50
Fixed costs ($)	200,000	200,000	200,000	200,000

The fixed costs stem from depreciation expenses and overhead. Overhead will increase by $20,000 per year as a result of the expansion. It is estimated that this expansion will cannibalize some existing sales, resulting in a lost profit contribution of $35,000 per year. Additional working capital of $40,000 will be required if the expansion proceeds.

Required:
(a) Determine the net relevant cash flows for proceeding with the expansion.
(b) Determine the payback period.
(c) Calculate the net present value using a discount rate of 5% and determine if the project should proceed.

6.12 Island Fabricating Limited is contemplating an investment project with the following cash flows:

Year	Net Cash Flow ($ thousands)
0	(120,000)
1	310,000
2	(200,000)

Required:

(a) Calculate the net present value of the project using a discount rate of 8%.
(b) Calculate the internal rate of return.
(c) Can you find another internal rate of return?
(d) Should the project be accepted?

6.13 The Ottawa Micro Brewery Company (OMB) is examining four expansion projects. OMB has adjusted the cost of capital to reflect the risk level of each project. The cash flows, which occur at year end, are as follows:

Project Cash Flows
(thousands of dollars)

Cost of Capital	8%	4%	2%	10%
Year	Project 1	Project 2	Project 3	Project 4
0	$ (620)	$ (160)	$ (500)	$ (230)
1	120	30	80	50
2	120	30	80	50
3	120	30	80	50
4	120	30	80	50
5	120	30	80	50
6	120	30	80	50
7	120	30	80	50

Required:

(a) Calculate the net present value for each project.
(b) Which project should OMB choose if it can only do one project?

6.14 Fredericton Allied Networks (FAN) is reviewing three projects. FAN has adjusted the cost of capital to reflect the risk level of each project. The cash flows, which occur at year end, are as follows:

Project Cash Flows
(thousands of dollars)

Cost of Capital	8%	5%	3%
Year	Project 1	Project 2	Project 3
0	$ (200)	$ (160)	$ (310)
1	20	30	50
2	40	50	30
3	60	42	20
4	50	38	50
5	40	22	80
6	30	14	67
7	20	5	35
8	10	3	15

Required:
  (a) Calculate the net present value for each project.
  (b) Which project should FAN choose if it can only do one project?
  (c) Without doing any further calculations, determine the internal rate of return for Project 1.

6.15 The directors of Mylo Ltd. are currently considering two mutually exclusive investment projects. Both projects are concerned with the purchase of a new plant. The following data are available for each project:

	Project 1 ($)	Project 2 ($)
Cost (immediate expenditure)	100,000	60,000
Expected annual net profit (loss):		
Year 1	29,000	18,000
2	(1,000)	(2,000)
3	2,000	4,000
Estimated residual value of the plant	7,000	6,000

The business has an estimated cost of capital of 10%, and uses the straight-line method of depreciation for all non-current (fixed) assets when calculating net profit. Neither project would increase the working capital of the business. The business has sufficient funds to meet all capital expenditure requirements.

Required:
  (a) Calculate for each project:
      (i) The net present value
      (ii) The approximate internal rate of return
      (iii) The payback period.
  (b) State which, if any, of the two investment projects Mylo should accept, and why.
  (c) State, in general terms, which method of investment appraisal you consider to be most appropriate for evaluating investment projects, and why.

6.16 Arkwright Mills Corporation is considering expanding its production of a new yarn, code name X15. The plant is expected to cost $1 million and have a life of five years and no residual value. It will be bought, paid for, and ready for operation on December 31, Year 0. $500,000 has already been spent on development costs of the product, and this has been reflected in the income statement in the year it was incurred.
      The following results are projected for the new yarn:

	($ millions)				
	Year 1	Year 2	Year 3	Year 4	Year 5
Sales	1.2	1.4	1.4	1.4	1.4
Costs, including depreciation	1.0	1.1	1.1	1.1	1.1
Profit before tax	0.2	0.3	0.3	0.3	0.3

Tax is charged at 50% on annual profits (before tax and after capital cost allowance, which exactly matches depreciation in this case) and paid one year in arrears. Depreciation of the plant has been calculated on a straight-line basis. Additional working capital of $0.6 million will be required at the beginning of the project and released at the end of Year 5. You should assume that all cash flows occur at the end of the year in which they arise.

Required:

(a) Prepare a statement showing the incremental cash flows of the project relevant to a decision concerning whether or not to proceed with the construction of the new plant.

(b) Calculate the net present value of the project using a 10% discount rate.

(c) Calculate the payback period to the nearest year. Explain the meaning of this term.

6.17 The accountant of your business has recently become ill from overwork. In his absence, his assistant has prepared some calculations of the profitability of a project, which are to be discussed soon at the board meeting of your business. His work, which is set out below, includes some errors of principle. You can assume that the statement below includes no arithmetical errors.

	Year 1 ($000)	Year 2 ($000)	Year 3 ($000)	Year 4 ($000)	Year 5 ($000)	Year 6 ($000)
Sales revenue	–	450	470	470	470	470
Less: Costs						
Materials	–	126	132	132	132	132
Labour	–	90	94	94	94	94
Overhead	–	45	47	47	47	47
Depreciation	–	120	120	120	120	120
Working capital	180	–	–	–	–	–
Interest on working capital	–	27	27	27	27	27
Write-off of development costs	–	30	30	30	–	–
Total costs	180	438	450	450	420	420
Profit (loss)	(180)	12	20	20	50	50

$$\frac{\text{Total profit (loss)}}{\text{Cost of equipment}} = \frac{\$(28,000)}{\$600,000} = \text{Return on investment (4.7\%)}$$

You ascertain the following additional information:

1. The cost of equipment value includes $100,000, which is the book value of an old machine. If it were not used for this project, it would be scrapped with a zero net realizable value. New equipment costing $500,000 will be purchased on December 31, Year 0. You should assume that all other cash flows occur at the end of the year to which they relate.

2. The development costs of $90,000 have already been spent.

3. Overhead has been costed at 50% of direct labour, which is the business's normal practice. An independent assessment has suggested that incremental overhead is likely to amount to $30,000 a year.

4. The business's cost of capital is 12%.

Ignore taxes in your answer.

Required:

(a) Prepare a corrected statement of the incremental cash flows arising from the project. Where you have altered the assistant's figures, you should attach a brief note explaining your alterations.

(b) Calculate:
  (i) The project's payback period
  (ii) The project's net present value as at December 31, Year 0.

(c) Write a memo to the board advising on the acceptance or rejection of the project.

6.18 The Saskatchewan Benders are a professional baseball team that has enjoyed considerable success in recent years. As a result, the team has accumulated $10 million to spend on its further development. The board of directors is currently considering two mutually exclusive options for spending the funds available.

The first option is to acquire another player. The team manager has expressed a keen interest in acquiring Basil (Bazza) Ramsey, a pitcher, who currently plays for a rival team. The rival team has agreed to release the player immediately for $10 million if required. A decision to acquire Bazza Ramsey would mean that the existing pitcher, Vinnie Smith, could be sold to another team. The Benders have recently received an offer of $2.2 million for this player. This offer is still open but will only be accepted if Bazza Ramsey joins the Benders. If this does not happen, Vinnie Smith will be expected to stay on with the team until the end of his playing career in five years' time. During this period, Vinnie will receive an annual salary of $400,000 and a loyalty bonus of $200,000 at the end of his five-year period with the team.

Assuming Bazza Ramsey is acquired, the team manager estimates additional gate receipts of $2.5 million in the first year and $1.3 million in each of the four following years. There will also be an increase in advertising revenues of $1.2 million for each of the next five years if the player is acquired. At the end of five years, the player can be sold to a baseball team for $1 million. During his period with the Benders, Bazza will receive an annual salary of $800,000 and a loyalty bonus of $400,000 after five years.

The second option is for the baseball team to improve its ground facilities. The west stand could be extended and executive box seating could be built for businesses wishing to offer corporate hospitality to clients. These improvements would also cost $10 million and would take one year to complete. During this period, the west stand would be closed, resulting in a reduction of gate receipts of $1.8 million. However, gate receipts for each of the following four years would be $4.4 million higher than current receipts. In five years' time, the team has plans to sell the existing stadium and to move to a new one nearby. Improving the stadium is not expected to affect its value when it comes to be sold. Payment for the improvements will be made when the work has been completed at the end of the first year. Whichever option is chosen, the board of directors has decided to take on additional stadium staff. The additional wage bill is expected to be $350,000 a year over the next five years.

The team has a cost of capital of 10%. Ignore taxation.

Required:

(a) Calculate the incremental cash flows arising from each of the options available to the Saskatchewan Benders.

(b) Calculate the net present value of each of the options.

(c) On the basis of the calculations made in part (b) above, which of the two options would you choose and why?

(d) Discuss the validity of using the net present value method in making investment decisions for a professional baseball team.

6.19 Haverhill Engineers Ltd. manufactures components for the car industry. It is considering automating its line for producing crankshaft bearings. The automated equipment will cost $700,000. It will replace equipment with a scrap value of $50,000 and a net book value of $180,000.

At present, the line has a capacity of 1.25 million units per year but typically it has only been run at 80% of capacity because of the lack of demand for its output. The new line has a capacity of 1.4 million units per year. Its life is expected to be five years and its scrap value at that time will be $100,000.

The accountant has prepared the following cost estimates based on the expected output of 1,000,000 units per year:

	Old Line (per unit) ($)	New Line (per unit) ($)
Materials	0.40	0.36
Labour	0.22	0.10
Variable overheads	0.14	0.14
Fixed overheads	0.44	0.20
	1.20	0.80
Selling price	1.50	1.50
Profit per unit	0.30	0.70

Fixed overheads include depreciation on the old machine of $40,000 per year and $120,000 for the new machine. It is considered that, for the business overall, fixed overhead is unlikely to change.

The introduction of the new machine will enable inventory to be reduced by $160,000. The business uses 10% as its cost of capital. Ignore taxes.

Required:

(a) Prepare a statement of the incremental cash flows arising from the project.
(b) Calculate the project's net present value.
(c) Calculate the project's approximate internal rate of return.
(d) Explain the terms *net present value* and *internal rate of return*. State which method you consider to be preferable, giving reasons for your choice.

6.20 A $1,000, 10%, eight-year bond, compounded semi-annually, sells for $900. What is the current interest rate? *Hint:* You can think of this as an internal rate of return question.

CHAPTER 7

Making Capital Investment Decisions: Further Issues

LEARNING OUTCOMES

When you have completed this chapter, you should be able to:

1 Explain the modifications to the simple NPV decision rules that are required (a) when there is capital rationing or (b) when competing projects of unequal duration are compared.

2 Discuss the effect of inflation on investment appraisal and explain how inflation may be taken into account.

3 Discuss the nature of risk and explain why it is important in the context of investment decisions.

4 Describe the main approaches to the measurement of risk and discuss their limitations.

INTRODUCTION

This chapter deals with a number of important issues relating to the application of the investment appraisal methods considered in Chapter 6. In practice, there are certain circumstances that call for a modification to the simple NPV decision rules learned in Chapter 6. In this chapter, we consider three such circumstances.

As well, we consider the problems that inflation creates for the evaluation of investment decisions. We also consider ways in which we can adjust for the effects of inflation when undertaking discounted cash flow analysis.

Finally, we consider the problem of risk in the context of investment decision making. We shall see that methods proposed for dealing with risk vary greatly in their level of sophistication.

INVESTMENT DECISIONS WHEN FUNDS ARE LIMITED

L.O. 1(a)

We saw in Chapter 6 that projects with a positive NPV should be undertaken if the business wishes to maximize shareholder wealth. However, what if there are insufficient funds available to undertake all the projects with a positive NPV? Where capital is rationed, the basic NPV rules mentioned in Chapter 6 require modification. To illustrate the modifications required, let us consider Example 7.1.

Example 7.1

Unicorn Engineering Ltd. is considering three possible investment projects: X, Y, and Z. The expected pattern of cash flows for each project is as follows:

	Project Cash Flows		
	X ($ millions)	Y ($ millions)	Z ($ millions)
Initial cost	(8)	(9)	(11.0)
1 year's time	5	5	4.0
2 years' time	2	3	4.0
3 years' time	3	3	5.0
4 years' time	4	5	6.5

The business has a cost of capital of 12% and the investment budget for the year that has just begun is restricted to $12 million. Each project is divisible (that is, it is possible to undertake part of a project if required).

Which investment project(s) should the business undertake?

Solution

If the cash flows for each project are discounted using the cost of capital as the appropriate discount rate, the NPVs are:

	Project X			Project Y			Project Z		
Year	Cash ($ millions)	PV Factor* 12%	PV ($ millions)	Cash ($ millions)	PV Factor* 12%	PV ($ millions)	Cash ($ millions)	PV Factor* 12%	PV ($ millions)
0	(8)	1.00	(8.0)	(9)	1.00	(9.0)	(11.0)	1.00	(11.0)
1	5	0.89	4.5	5	0.89	4.5	4.0	0.89	3.6
2	2	0.80	1.6	3	0.80	2.4	4.0	0.80	3.2
3	3	0.71	2.1	3	0.71	2.1	5.0	0.71	3.6
4	4	0.64	2.6	5	0.64	3.2	6.5	0.64	4.2
PV of cash inflows			10.8			12.2			14.6
		NPV	2.8		NPV	3.2		NPV	3.6

*Rounded to two decimal places

It is tempting to think that the best approach to dealing with the limited availability of capital would be to rank the projects according to their NPVs. Thus, Project Z would be ranked first, Project Y would be ranked second, and Project X would be ranked last. Given that $12 million is available, this would lead to the acceptance of Project Z ($11 million) and part of Project Y ($1 million). The total NPV from the $12 million invested would, therefore, be:

$$\$3.6 \text{ million} + \frac{\$3.2 \text{ million}}{9 \text{ million}} \times \$1 = \$4 \text{ million}$$

$$\text{or } \$3.6 \text{ million} + \frac{1}{9} \times \$3.2 \text{ million} = \$4 \text{ million}$$

However, this solution would not represent the most efficient use of the limited capital available.

The best approach, when projects are divisible, is to maximize the *present value per dollar of scarce financing*. By dividing the present values of the future cash inflows by the cost or expenditure for each project, a figure that represents the present value per dollar of scarce capital is obtained. This figure provides a measure that is known as the **profitability index** as shown in Equation 7.1.

$$\text{Profitability index} = \frac{\text{Present values of future cash inflows}}{\text{Cost for the project}} \qquad 7.1$$

An alternative version of the profitability formula is shown in Equation 7.2:

$$\text{Profitability index} = \frac{\text{Cost for the project} + \text{NPV of the project}}{\text{Cost for the project}} \qquad 7.2$$

Using the information in the example, the following figures would be obtained for the profitability index for each project. (*Note:* The top parts of the fractions represent the future cash flows *before* deducting the investment costs, or alternatively, represent the cost plus the NPV of the project.)

	Project X	Project Y	Project Z
PV of cash inflows (or Cost + NPV)	10.8	12.2	14.6
Cost	8.0	9.0	11.0
Profitability index:	= 1.35	1.36	= 1.33

All of the projects provide a profitability index greater than 1. The profitability index will always be greater than 1 where the NPV from the project is positive.

Activity 7.1 explores additional aspects of the profitability index.

ACTIVITY 7.1

What does the profitability index calculated in Example 7.1 suggest about the relative profitability of the projects? What would be the NPV of the $12 million invested, assuming the profitability index approach is used?

Solution

The above calculations indicate that Project Y provides the highest present value per dollar of scarce capital and so should be ranked first. Project X should be ranked second, and Project Z should be ranked third. To maximize the use of the limited funds available ($12 million), the business should, therefore, undertake all of Project Y ($9 million) and part of Project X ($3 million).

The total NPV of the $12 million invested would be $3.2 million + (3/8 × $2.8 million) = $4.3 million. Note that this figure is higher than the total NPV obtained where projects were ranked according to their absolute NPVs.

There may be a need for projects to be financed over more than one year and limits may be placed on the availability of capital in each year. In such circumstances, there will be more than one constraint to consider. A mathematical technique known as **linear programming** can be used to maximize the NPV, given that not all projects with a positive NPV can be undertaken. This technique adopts the same approach as that just illustrated (that is, it maximizes the NPV per dollar of scarce capital). Computer software is available to undertake the analysis required for this kind of multi-period rationing problem.

Non-Divisible Investment Projects

The profitability index approach is only suitable where projects are divisible. Where this is not the case, the problem must be looked at in a different way. Where projects are not divisible, the investment project (or combination of whole projects) that will produce the highest NPV for the limited financing available should be selected, as illustrated in Activity 7.2.

ACTIVITY 7.2

Recommend a solution for Unicorn Engineering Ltd. if the investment projects are not divisible (that is, it is impossible to undertake part of a project) and the financing available is:

(a) $12 million
(b) $18 million
(c) $20 million.

Solution

(a) If the capital available is $12 million, only Project Z should be recommended as this would provide the highest NPV ($3.6 million) for the funds available for investment.

(b) If the capital available is $18 million, Projects X and Y should be recommended as this would provide the highest NPV ($6 million).

(c) If the capital available is $20 million, Projects Y and Z should be recommended as this would provide the highest NPV ($6.8 million).

Mutually Exclusive Projects

A business may be considering investment projects that are mutually exclusive. For example, a business may be able to invest in either one project or another, but not both. In this kind of situation, the possible combinations available within the financing limit should be compared to see which provides the highest NPV, as illustrated in Activities 7.3 and 7.4.

ACTIVITY 7.3

What investment solution should be recommended if all three projects are divisible but the business can select *either* Project X *or* Project Z (that is, they are mutually exclusive)? Assume the capital available is $12 million.

▶

Solution

In this case, the combinations that are possible within the $12 million financing limit should be compared. There are really only two combinations:

1. Project Y plus part of Project X, or
2. Project Y plus part of Project Z.

The outcomes from each combination are as follows:

	Combination 1		Combination 2	
	Cost ($ millions)	NPV ($ millions)	Cost ($ millions)	NPV ($ millions)
Project Y	9	3.2	9	3.2
Project X (3/8 of total)	3	1.1	–	–
Project Z (3/11 of total)	–	–	3	1.0
	12	4.3	12	4.2

The calculations reveal that the first combination is better, as it has a slightly higher NPV.

ACTIVITY 7.4

Assume the budget limit is $18 million rather than $12 million. What would the recommended combination be now?

Solution

The calculations are as follows:

	Combination 1		Combination 2	
	Cost ($ millions)	NPV ($ millions)	Cost ($ millions)	NPV ($ millions)
Project Y	9	3.2	9	3.2
Project X (whole)	8	2.8	–	–
Project Z (9/11)	–	–	9	2.9
	17	6.0	18	6.1

The calculations now reveal that the second combination is better, as it would give a slightly higher NPV.

COMPARING PROJECTS WITH UNEQUAL DURATION

L.O. 1(b)

On occasion, a business may find itself in a position where it has to decide between two (or more) competing projects that have different life spans. Example 7.2 and Activity 7.5 show how to deal with this situation.

Example 7.2

Khan Engineering Ltd. has the opportunity to invest in two competing machines:

Cash flows

	Machine A ($000)	Machine B ($000)
Initial cost	(100)	(140)
1 year's time	50	60
2 years' time	70	80
3 years' time	–	32

The business has a cost of capital of 10%.

State which of the two machines, if either, should be acquired.

Solution

One way to tackle this problem is to assume that the machines form part of a repeated chain of replacement and to compare the machines using the shortest-common-period-of-time approach. If we assume that investment in Machine A can be repeated every two years and that investment in Machine B can be repeated every three years, the *shortest common period of time* over which the machines can be compared is six years (that is, 2 × 3).

The first step in this process of comparison is to calculate the NPV for each project over their expected lives. Thus, the NPV for each project will be as follows:

	Cash Flows ($000)	Discount Rate 10%	Present Value ($000)
Machine A			
Initial cost	(100)	1.00*	(100.0)
1 year's time	50	0.91	45.5
2 years' time	70	0.83	58.1
		NPV	3.6
Machine B			
Initial cost	(140)	1.00	(140.0)
1 year's time	60	0.91	54.6
2 years' time	80	0.83	66.4
3 years' time	32	0.75	24.0
		NPV	5.0

*Rounded to two decimals.

The next step is to calculate the NPV arising for each machine, over a six-year period, assuming the machines are replaced at the end of their economic life. That is, investment in Machine A will be repeated three times, and investment in Machine B will be repeated twice during the six-year period.

This means that, for Machine A, the NPV over the six-year period will be equal to the NPV above (that is, $3,600) plus equivalent amounts two years and four years later. The calculation using Table A2 in Appendix A (in thousands of dollars) will be:

$$NPV = \$3.6 + \$3.6 \times 0.826 + \$3.6 \times 0.683 = \$9.1$$

These calculations can be shown in the form of a diagram as in Figure 7.1.

FIGURE 7.1   NPV for Machine A Using a Common Period of Time

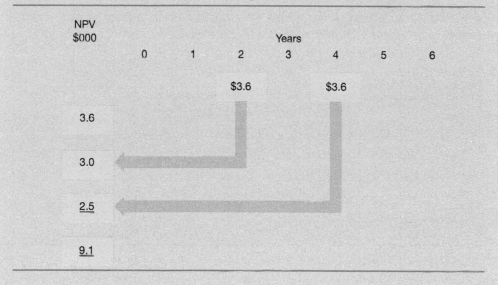

ACTIVITY 7.5

What is the NPV for Machine B over the six-year period? Which machine is the better buy?

Solution

In the case of Machine B, the NPV over the six-year period will be equal to the NPV in Example 7.2 plus the equivalent amount three years later. The calculation will be:

$$NPV = \$5.0 + \$5.0 \times 0.751 = \$8.8$$

The calculations set out earlier suggest that Machine A is the better buy, as it will have the higher NPV over the six-year period.

AN ALTERNATIVE APPROACH

When investment projects have a longer lifespan than those in the examples, the calculations required using this method can be time consuming. Fortunately, another method can be used that avoids the need for laborious calculations. This approach uses the annuity concept to solve the problem. Recall that an **annuity** is simply an investment that pays a constant sum each year over a period of time.

The second approach to solving the problem of competing projects that have unequal lives is based on the annuity principle. Put simply, the **equivalent-annual-annuity approach** converts the NPV of a project into an annual annuity stream over its expected life. This conversion is carried out for each competing project and the one that provides the highest annual annuity is the most profitable project, as illustrated in Activity 7.6.

ACTIVITY 7.6

Use Table A5 in Appendix A to calculate the equivalent annual annuity for each machine referred to in Example 7.2. Which machine is the better buy?

Solution

The equivalent annual annuity for Machine A over two years is:

$$\$3.6 \times 0.5762 = \$2.07$$

The equivalent annual annuity for Machine B over three years is:

$$\$5.0 \times 0.4021 = \$2.01$$

Machine A is, therefore, the better buy as it provides the higher annuity value. This is consistent with the finding of the shortest-common-period-of-time approach described earlier.

SELF-ASSESSMENT QUESTION   7.1

Choi Ltd. is considering the purchase of a new photocopier that could lead to considerable cost savings. Two machines on the market are suitable for the business. The two machines have the following costs and expected cost savings:

	Cost Savings	
	Lo-tek	Hi-tek
	($)	($)
Initial cost	(10,000)	(15,000)
1 year's time	4,000	5,000
2 years' time	5,000	6,000
3 years' time	5,000	6,000
4 years' time	–	5,000

The business has a cost of capital of 12% and will have a continuing need for the chosen machine. Use present value factors to four decimals.

Required:

(a) Evaluate each machine using both the shortest-common-period-of-time approach and the equivalent-annual-annuity approach.

(b) Which machine would you recommend and why?

The NPV Approach and the Ability to Delay

In recent years there has been some re-evaluation of the NPV approach. One important criticism is that conventional theory does not recognize the fact that, in practice, it is often possible to delay making an investment decision. This ability to delay can have a profound effect on the final investment decision. Activity 7.7 explores the benefits of delay.

ACTIVITY 7.7

What are the possible benefits of delaying an investment decision?

Solution

By delaying, it may be possible to acquire more information concerning the likely outcome of the investment proposal. If a business decides not to delay, the investment decision, once made, may be irreversible. This may lead to losses if conditions prove unfavourable.

If managers do not exercise their option to delay, there may be an opportunity cost in the form of the benefits lost from later information. This opportunity cost can be large, and so failure to take this into account may lead to grossly incorrect investment decisions. One way of dealing with this problem is to modify the NPV decision rule so that the present value of the future cash flows must exceed the initial expenditure *plus* any expected benefits from delaying the decision in order to obtain additional information. These benefits will often be difficult to quantify, however.

THE PROBLEM OF INFLATION   L.O. 2

Although the rate of inflation may change over time, there has been a persistent tendency for the general price level to rise in most economies. It is important to recognize this phenomenon when evaluating investment projects, as inflation will have an effect on both the cash flows and the discount rate over the life of the project.

REAL WORLD 7.1 discusses the relatively rare opposite of inflation, deflation. During a period of inflation, the amount of money needed to acquire resources will rise over time, and the business may seek to pass on any increase to customers in the form of higher prices. Inflation will also affect the cost of financing the business, as investors seek to protect their investment from a decline in purchasing power by demanding higher returns. As a result of these changes, the cash flows and discount rates relating to the investment project will be affected.

REAL WORLD 7.1   **2008 Deflation Threat**

Deflation is falling prices for goods and services. Deflation is an insidious economic disease because it causes people to defer spending. After all, why would you buy a house or a car or a refrigerator now when you can get one cheaper next year?

▶

Deflation reared its ugly head when the markets and the economy crashed in 2008 and early 2009. This created a credit crunch brought on by the collapse of the U.S. housing market. A mortgage crisis ensued as customers defaulted. This contributed to bringing down some big international banks such as Lehman Brothers. The world financial system was rocked to the core. All of a sudden, governments around the world realized that a 1930s-type depression could occur and with it a serious collapse in the price of everything because many people lacked a job or money to spend. Governments, having learned from their inaction in the 1930s, responded with massive stimulus packages in late 2008 to jump-start the economy.

Source: CBC.ca www.cbc.ca/world/story/2008/12/16/interest-rate.html, accessed September 6, 2009.

To deal with the problem of inflation in the appraisal of investment projects, two possible approaches can be used:

- *Include inflation in the calculations* by adjusting annual cash flows by the expected rate of inflation, and by using a discount rate that is also adjusted for inflation. This will mean estimating the actual monetary cash flows expected from the project and using a market rate of interest that will take inflation into account. This is the approach favoured by large and medium-sized businesses.
- *Exclude inflation from the calculations* by adjusting cash flows accordingly and by using a "real" discount rate that does not include any element to account for inflation.

Both methods, properly applied, will give the same result. However, small businesses are more likely not to make any adjustments for inflation.

In practice, inflation is likely to affect the various items that make up the net cash flows differently. This means that separate adjustments for each of the monetary cash flows will be necessary. Activity 7.8 explores the effects of inflation.

ACTIVITY 7.8

Why is inflation likely to have different effects on the various items making up the net cash flow of a business?

Solution

Costs may increase at different rates. For example, labour costs may rise more quickly than materials costs if labour is in greater demand than the materials being used. Also, the price of oil rises and falls due to supply and demand considerations and geo-political events. Certain costs may be fixed over time (for example, lease payments) and may therefore be unaffected by inflation over the period of the project.

In a competitive environment, a business may be unable to pass all of the increase in costs on to customers and so will have to absorb some of the increase by reducing profits. Thus, cash inflows from sales may not fully reflect the rise in the costs of the various inputs.

To determine the real cash flows from a project, it will be necessary to calculate the monetary cash flows relating to each item and then deflate these amounts by the *general* rate of inflation. This adjustment will provide us with the *current general purchasing power* of the cash flows. This measure of general purchasing power is of more relevance to investors than if the cash flows were deflated by a specific rate of inflation relevant to each type of cash flow. Similarly, the real discount rate will be determined by deflating the market rate of interest by the *general* rate of inflation.

REAL WORLD 7.2 discusses how a large Canadian gold mining company considers inflation.

REAL WORLD 7.2

Inflation Planning at Barrick Gold

Barrick Gold Corporation of Toronto, one of the world's largest gold producers, thinks that the amount of monetary stimulus injected into the global economy by countries such as the U.S., China, the European Union, Great Britain, and Canada, to name a few, will eventually result in higher gold prices and inflation. However, inflationary pressures on capital costs have eased in the teeth of the recession of 2008–2009.

Source: Barrick 2008 Annual Report.

RISK AND INVESTMENT DECISIONS

L.O. 3

Risk arises where the future is unclear and where a range of possible future outcomes exists. As the future is uncertain, there is a chance (or risk) that estimates made concerning the future will not occur. Risk is particularly important in the context of investment decisions because of:

- The relatively long time scales involved—there is more time for things to go wrong between the decision point and the end of the project
- The size of the investment—if things do go wrong, the impact can be both significant and lasting.

In this chapter the words *risk* and *uncertainty* are used interchangeably.

RISK MEASUREMENT METHODS

L.O. 4

In the sections that follow, we will focus on the more useful and systematic approaches that help managers with risk. Crude methods of dealing with risk are not recommended. These include shortening the required payback period and employing conservative cash flows.

Sensitivity Analysis

A popular way of assessing the level of risk is to carry out **sensitivity analysis**. This method involves an examination of key input values in order to see how changes in each input might influence the likely outcomes. One form of sensitivity analysis involves posing a series of "What if . . . ?" questions. For example:

- What if sales volume is 5% higher than expected?
- What if sales volume is 10% lower than expected?

By answering these "What if . . . ?" questions, the managers will establish a range of possible outcomes to consider, which can be useful for investment appraisal purposes as well as for profit planning.

FIGURE 7.2   Factors Affecting the Sensitivity of NPV Calculations for a New Machine

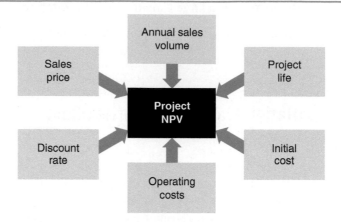

The margin of safety for each key factor can be examined to see how much it could change before the project became unprofitable for that reason alone.

Suppose that the NPV for an investment in a machine to provide a particular service is estimated to be a positive value of $50,000. To carry out sensitivity analysis on this investment proposal, each of the key input factors—cost of the machine, sales volume and price, operating costs, life of the machine, and discount rate—is considered in turn. For each factor, we will calculate the highest adverse value that it could have before the NPV figure became negative (that is, we will find the value for the factor at which NPV is zero). The difference between the value for that factor at which the NPV is zero and the estimated value represents the margin of safety for that particular factor. The process is summarized in Figure 7.2.

Example 7.3 illustrates sensitivity analysis.

Example 7.3

Saluja Property Developers Ltd. intends to bid at an auction, to be held today, for an old house that has fallen into disrepair. The auctioneer believes that the house will be sold for about $450,000. The business wishes to renovate the property and to divide it into condominiums to be sold for $150,000 each. The renovation will be in two stages.

Stage 1 will cover the first year of the project. It will cost $500,000 and the six condos completed during this stage are expected to be sold for a total of $900,000 at the end of the first year.

Stage 2 will cover the second year of the project. It will cost $300,000 and the three remaining condos are expected to be sold at the end of the second year for a total of $450,000.

The cost of renovation is subject to an agreed figure with local builders; however, there is some uncertainty over the remaining input values.

The business estimates its cost of capital at 12% a year.

Required:

(a) What is the NPV of the proposed project?
(b) Assuming none of the other inputs deviates from the best estimates provided:
   (i)   What is the margin of safety for the purchase price of the old house?

(ii)   What cost of capital would cause the project to have a zero NPV?

(iii)   What is the margin of safety for the $150,000 selling price of the condos?

(c)   Is the level of risk associated with the project high or low?

Solution

(a)   The NPV of the proposed project is as follows:

	Cash Flows ($)	Discount Factor 12%	Present Value ($)
Year 1 ($900,000 − $500,000)	400,000	0.893*	357,200
Year 2 ($450,000 − $300,000)	150,000	0.797	119,550
Less: Initial cost			(450,000)
		NPV	26,750

*Rounded to three decimals.

(b)   (i)   The margin of safety is the change in a particular variable that results in a zero NPV. Therefore, auction price for the old house would have to be $26,750 higher than the current estimate (that is, the amount of the estimated NPV). This would make a total price of $476,750, which is a margin of safety of about 6% above the current estimated price. Saluja Property Developers should not bid more than this amount at the auction.

(ii)   As there is a positive NPV, the cost of capital that would cause the project to have a zero NPV must be higher than 12%. Let us try 20%.

	Cash Flows ($)	Discount Factor 20%	Present Value ($)
Year 1 ($900,000 − $500,000)	400,000	0.833	333,200
Year 2 ($450,000 − $300,000)	150,000	0.694	104,100
Less: Initial outlay			(450,000)
		NPV	(12,700)

As the NPV, using a 20% discount rate, is negative, the breakeven cost of capital must lie somewhere between 12% and 20%. A reasonable approximation is obtained as follows:

	Discount Rate (%)	NPV ($)
	12	26,750
	20	(12,700)
Difference	8	39,450

The change in NPV for every 1% change in the discount rate will be:

$$\frac{39,450}{8} = 4,931$$

The reduction in the 20% discount rate required to achieve a zero NPV would therefore be:

$$\frac{12,700}{4,931} = 2.6\%$$

The cost of capital (that is, the discount rate) would, therefore, have to be 17.4% (i.e., 20.0% − 2.6%) for the project to have a zero NPV.

This calculation is, of course, the same as that used in Chapter 6 when calculating the IRR of the project. In other words, 17.4% is the IRR of the project.

(iii) To obtain a zero NPV, the sale price of each condo must be reduced so that the NPV is reduced by $26,750. In Year 1, six condos are sold, and in Year 2, three condos are sold. The discount factor for Year 1 is 0.893 and for Year 2 it is 0.797. We can derive the fall in value per condo (Y), to give a zero NPV, by using the equation:

$$(6Y \times 0.893) + (3Y \times 0.797) = \$26,750$$

$$Y = \$3,452$$

The sale price of each condo necessary to obtain a zero NPV is therefore:

$$\$150,000 - \$3,452 = \$146,548$$

This represents a margin of safety of about 2.3% below the estimated selling price of a condo.

(c) These calculations indicate that the auction price would have to be about 6% above the estimated price before a zero NPV is obtained. The margin of safety is, therefore, not very high for this factor. The calculations also reveal that the price of the luxury condos would only have to fall by 2.3% from the estimated price before the NPV is reduced to zero. Hence, the margin of safety for this factor is even smaller. However, the cost of capital is less sensitive to changes and there would have to be an increase from 12% to 17.4% before the project produced a zero NPV.

It seems from these calculations that the sale price of the condos is the most sensitive of the three inputs examined. A careful re-examination of the market value of the condos seems appropriate before a final decision is made.

Suppliers or bankers may assess risks by performing a sensitivity analysis to determine whether the client business is a good credit risk. REAL WORLD 7.3 shows how two Canadian businesses employ sensitivity analysis, and Activity 7.9 prepares a sensitivity analysis for three different factors.

REAL WORLD 7.3

Sensitivity Analysis at RIM and Telus

Research In Motion (RIM), based in Waterloo, Ontario, and maker of the BlackBerry smartphone, notes the following:

■ A 10% increase in warranty expenses will decrease net income by 1%.

Telus Corporation, a large Vancouver-based telecommunications company, notes that:

■ A 10% favourable change in the exchange rate between the Canadian and U.S. dollars would increase net income by $7 million (0.62%).

■ A 1/4% (25 basis points) decrease in interest rates would add $3 million (0.27%) to net income.

Sources: Research In Motion 2009 Annual Report and Telus 2008 Annual Report.

ACTIVITY 7.9

A business has the opportunity to invest $12 million immediately in new plant and equipment in order to produce a new product. The product will sell at $80 each and it is estimated that 200,000 units of the product can be sold in each of the next four years. Variable costs are $56 a unit and additional fixed costs (excluding depreciation) are $1 million in total. The residual value of the plant and machinery at the end of the life of the product is estimated to be $1.6 million. The business has a cost of capital of 12%.

Required:

(a) Calculate the NPV of the investment proposal. Round present value factors to two decimals.
(b) Prepare a separate sensitivity analysis to calculate the margin of error for each of the following factors
    (i)   Initial cost of plant and equipment
    (ii) Discount rate
    (iii) Residual value of the plant and equipment.

Solution

(a) Annual operating cash flows are as follows:

	($ millions)	($ millions)
Sales (200,000 × $80)		16.0
Less: Variable costs (200,000 × $56)	11.2	
Fixed costs	1.0	12.2
Operating cash flows		3.8

Estimated cash flows are as follows:

	Year 0 ($ millions)	Year 1 ($ millions)	Year 2 ($ millions)	Year 3 ($ millions)	Year 4 ($ millions)
Plant and equipment	(12.0)	–	–	–	1.6
Operating cash flows	–	3.8	3.8	3.8	3.8
	(12.0)	3.8	3.8	3.8	5.4

The NPV of the project is:

	Year 0 ($ millions)	Year 1 ($ millions)	Year 2 ($ millions)	Year 3 ($ millions)	Year 4 ($ millions)
Cash flows	(12.0)	3.8	3.8	3.8	5.4
Discount rate (12%)	1.0	0.89	0.80	0.71	0.64
Present value	(12.0)	3.38	3.04	2.70	3.46
NPV	0.58 (sum across present value row)				

(b) (i)   The increase required in the initial cost of plant and equipment to achieve an NPV of zero will be $0.58 million (as the plant and equipment are already expressed in present value terms). This represents a 4.8% increase ($0.58 million/$12 million) on the current estimated figure of $12 million.

▶

(ii) Using a discount rate of 14%, the NPV of the project is:

	Year 0 ($ millions)	Year 1 ($ millions)	Year 2 ($ millions)	Year 3 ($ millions)	Year 4 ($ millions)
Cash flows	(12.0)	3.8	3.8	3.8	5.4
Discount rate (14%)	1.0	0.88	0.77	0.68	0.59
Present value	(12.0)	3.34	2.92	2.58	3.18

NPV   0.02   (sum across present value row)

This is very close to an NPV of zero and so 14% is the approximate figure. This is 16.7% [(14% − 12%)/12%] higher than the cost of capital.

(iii) The fall in the residual value of the plant and equipment (R) that will lead to a zero NPV is:

(R × Discount factor at the end of four years) − NPV of the project = 0

By rearranging this equation, we have:

(R × Discount factor at the end of four years) = NPV of the project

R × 0.64 = $0.58 million

R = $0.58 million/0.64

R = $0.90 million

This represents a 43.8% [i.e., ($0.90 million − $1.60 million)/$1.60 million] decrease in the current estimated residual value.

Sensitivity analysis is, in essence, a form of *breakeven analysis*. The point at which the NPV is zero is the point at which the project breaks even.

Sensitivity analysis should help managers to gain a feel for the investment project as they will be able to see the margin of safety for each factor. They should also be able to identify highly sensitive factors, which require careful study and which are also likely to require more detailed information. Sensitivity analysis can also be useful in directing the actions of managers. Where a project outcome has been identified as being highly sensitive to changes in a key factor, managers may decide to formulate plans to deal with possible variations from the estimated outcome.

Although sensitivity analysis is undoubtedly a useful tool for managers, it has two major drawbacks:

■ It does not give managers clear decision rules concerning acceptance or rejection of the project. This means that managers must rely on their own judgment.
■ It is a static form of analysis. Only one factor is considered at a time while the rest are held constant. In practice, however, it is likely that more than one factor value will differ from the best estimates provided.

Scenario Analysis

A slightly different approach, which overcomes the problem of dealing with a single variable at a time, is **scenario analysis**. We may recall from Chapter 3 that this approach changes a number of variables simultaneously so as to provide a particular state of the world, or scenario, for managers to consider. A popular form of scenario analysis is to provide three different states of the world, or scenarios, which are:

■ An optimistic view of likely future events
■ A pessimistic view of likely future events
■ A most likely view of future events.

The approach is open to criticism because it does not indicate the likelihood of each scenario occurring, nor does it identify the other possible scenarios that might occur. Nevertheless, the portrayal of optimistic and pessimistic scenarios may be useful in providing managers with some feel for the downside risk and upside potential associated with a project.

Simulations

The starting point for carrying out a **simulation** exercise is to model the investment project. This involves identifying the key factors affecting the project and their inter-relationships. Thus, the cash flows will have to be modelled to reveal the key factors influencing both the cash receipts and the cash payments and their interrelationships.

Let us illustrate this point using a simple example. The cash received from sales may be modelled by Equation 7.3:

$$\text{Sales revenue} = \text{Selling price per unit} \times (\text{Market share} \times \text{Market size}) \quad \text{7.3}$$

The modelling process will also require equations showing the factors determining the cash expenses and the interrelationships between these factors. The relationship between the cash inflows and outflows must also be modelled. As investment projects usually extend over more than one year, there may also be a need to model the relationship between the cash flows occurring in different periods. Thus, a fairly large number of equations may be required to model even a fairly simple investment project proposal.

Once the key factors have been identified and their relationships have been modelled, the next step is to specify the possible values for each of the factors within the model. A computer is then used to select one of the possible values from each distribution on a random basis. It then generates projected cash flows using the selected values for each factor. This process represents a single trial. The process is then repeated using other values for each factor until many possible combinations of values for the key factors have been considered. The results of the repeated sampling allow us to obtain a probability distribution of the values of the cash flows for the project. Figure 7.3 summarizes these three steps.

The use of simulations is meant to help managers in two ways. First, the process of building a model helps managers to understand more fully the nature of the project

FIGURE 7.3   The Main Steps in Simulation

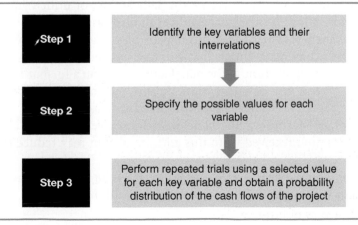

Step 1 — Identify the key variables and their interrelations

Step 2 — Specify the possible values for each variable

Step 3 — Perform repeated trials using a selected value for each key variable and obtain a probability distribution of the cash flows of the project

and the issues that must be resolved. Second, it provides managers with a distribution of project outcomes that can be used to assess the riskiness of the project. However, these potential benefits must be weighed against the potential problems of producing simulations.

Simulations can be costly and time-consuming. Furthermore, there are usually problems in modelling the relationship between factors and in establishing the distribution of outcomes for each factor. The more complex the project, the more complex these problems are likely to be.

RISK PREFERENCES OF INVESTORS

So far, the methods discussed have sought to identify the level of risk associated with a project. However, the attitude of investors toward risk must also be determined. Unless they know how investors are likely to react to the presence of risk in investment opportunities, managers cannot really understand which opportunities will be most attractive to investors.

In theory, investors may display three possible attitudes toward risk. They may be:

- **Risk-seeking investors.**   Some investors prefer a gamble. Given two projects with the same expected return but with different levels of risk, the risk-seeking investor would choose the project with the higher level of risk.
- **Risk-neutral investors.**   Some investors are indifferent to risk. Thus, given two projects with the same expected return but with different levels of risk, the risk-neutral investor would have no preference. Both projects provide the same expected return and the fact that one project has a higher level of risk would not be an issue.
- **Risk-averse investors.**   Some investors are averse to risk. Given two projects with the same expected return but with different levels of risk, a risk-averse investor would choose the project that has a lower level of risk.

Evidence suggests that the vast majority of investors are risk-averse. It is important to appreciate that being risk-averse does *not* mean that an investor will not be prepared to take on risky investments. It means, rather, that investors will require compensation in the form of higher returns from projects that have higher levels of risk. An explanation as to why this is the case can be found in *utility theory*.

Risk and Utility Theory

Utility theory assumes you can measure the satisfaction, or utility, you receive from money in the form of utils of satisfaction. Let us also assume that you are penniless. If a rich benefactor gives you $1,000, this may bring you a great deal of satisfaction as it will allow you to buy many things that you have yearned for. Let us say it provides you with 20 utils of satisfaction. If the benefactor gives you a further $1,000, this may also bring you a great deal of satisfaction, but not as much as the first $1,000, since some of your essential needs have now been met. Let us say, therefore, it provides you with 10 utils of satisfaction. If the benefactor then gives you a further $1,000, the additional satisfaction received from this additional sum may reduce to, say, 6 utils, and so on.

The expression *diminishing marginal utility of wealth* means that additional satisfaction declines with each additional amount of wealth received.

The relationship between the level of satisfaction received and the amount of wealth received can be expressed in the form of a **utility function**. For a risk-averse individual, the utility function, when shown graphically, would take the shape of an upward-sloping concave curve, as shown in Figure 7.4.

FIGURE 7.4   Utility Function for a Risk-Averse Individual

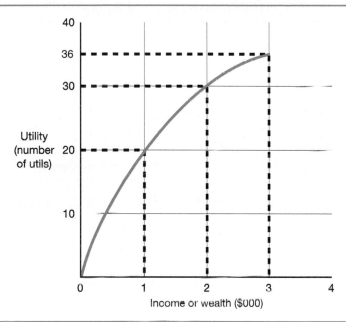

An individual with wealth of, say, $2,000 would receive satisfaction from this amount of 30 utils. If, however, the wealth of the individual fell by $1,000 for some reason, the loss of satisfaction would be greater than the satisfaction gained from receiving an additional $1,000. We can see that the loss of satisfaction from a fall in wealth of $1,000 would be 10 utils, whereas the gain in satisfaction from receiving an additional $1,000 would only be 6 utils. A risk averse individual will only accept the risk in exchange for the prospect of higher returns.

The particular shape of the utility curve will vary among individuals. Some individuals are likely to be more risk-averse than others. The more risk-averse an individual is, the more concave the shape of the curve will become. However, this general concave curve shape will apply to all risk-averse individuals.

The practical value of utility theory is limited. In the real world, managers may make decisions based on their own attitudes toward risk rather than those of investors, or make assumptions about the risk preferences of investors.

Risk-Adjusted Discount Rate

For almost all investors, the higher the level of risk associated with a project, the higher the required rate of return. The **risk-adjusted discount rate** is based on this simple relationship between risk and return. Thus, when evaluating investment projects, managers will increase the NPV discount rate to factor in the increased risk. In other words, a *risk premium* will be required for risky projects; the higher the level of risk, the higher the risk premium.

The risk premium is usually added to a risk-free rate of return in order to derive the total return required. The risk-free rate is normally taken to be equivalent to the rate of return from long-term government bonds. In practice, a business may divide projects up into risk categories (for example, low, medium, and high risk) and then assign a risk premium to each risk category. The cash flows from a particular project will then be discounted using a rate based on the risk-free rate plus the appropriate risk premium. This relationship between risk and return is illustrated in Figure 7.5.

FIGURE 7.5   The Relationship between Risk and Return

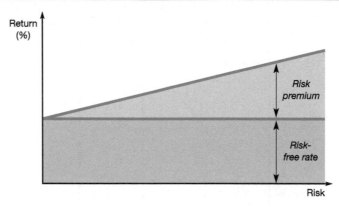

The more risky the project, the higher the risk premium.

The use of a risk-adjusted discount rate provides managers with a single-figure outcome that can be used when making a decision either to accept or to reject a project. Moreover, managers are likely to have an intuitive grasp of the relationship between risk and return and may well feel comfortable with this technique. However, there are practical difficulties with implementing this approach, as illustrated in Activity 7.10.

ACTIVITY 7.10

Can you think of what the practical problems with this approach might be?

Solution

Subjective judgment is required when assigning an investment project to a particular risk category and then in assigning a risk premium to each category. The choices made will reflect the personal views of the managers responsible and these may differ from the views of the shareholders they represent. The choices made can, nevertheless, make the difference between accepting and rejecting a particular project. (Chapter 10 outlines a more sophisticated approach to deriving a risk premium that does not rely on subjective judgment.)

Expected Values and Risk Assessment

A further method of assessing risk is through the use of *statistical probabilities*. It may be possible to identify a range of possible outcomes and to assign a probability of occurrence to each one of the outcomes in the range. Using this information, we can derive an **expected value**, which is a weighted average of the possible outcomes where the probabilities are used as weights. To illustrate this method in relation to an investment decision, let us consider Example 7.4.

Example 7.4

Patel Properties Ltd. has the opportunity to acquire a lease on a block of apartments that has only two years remaining before it expires. The cost of the lease would be $1,000,000. The occupancy rate is currently around 70% and the apartments are rented almost exclusively to naval personnel. There is a large naval base located nearby and there is little other demand for the apartments. The occupancy rate will change in the remaining two years of the lease depending on the outcome of a defence review. The navy is currently considering three options for the naval base. These are:

- Option 1. Increase the size of the base by closing down a naval base in another region and transferring the naval personnel to the base located near the apartments.
- Option 2. Close down the naval base near the apartments and leave only a skeleton staff there for maintenance purposes. The personnel would be moved to a base in another region.
- Option 3. Leave the naval base open but reduce staffing levels by 20%.

The directors of Patel Properties Ltd. have estimated the following net cash flows for each of the two years under each option and the probability of their occurrence:

	($)	Probability
Option 1	800,000	0.6
Option 2	120,000	0.1
Option 3	400,000	<u>0.3</u>
		<u>1.0</u>

Note: The sum of the probabilities is 1.0 (that is, it is certain that one of the possible options will be chosen). The business has a cost of capital of 10%.

Required:
Should the business purchase the lease on the block of apartments?

Solution

To answer the question, the **expected net present value (ENPV)** of the proposed investment can be calculated. To do this, the weighted average of the possible outcomes for each year must first be calculated. This involves multiplying each cash flow by its probability of occurrence (as the probabilities are used as weights). The expected annual net cash flows will be:

	Cash Flows ($)	Probability	Expected Cash Flows ($)
Option 1	800,000	0.6	480,000
Option 2	120,000	0.1	12,000
Option 3	400,000	0.3	<u>120,000</u>
Expected cash flows in each year			<u>612,000</u>

▷

Having derived the expected annual cash flows in each year, they can be discounted using a rate of 10% to reflect the cost of capital.

	Expected Cash Flows ($)	Discount Rate 10%	Expected Present Value ($)
Year 1	612,000	0.909*	556,308
Year 2	612,000	0.826	505,512
			1,061,820
Less: Initial investment			1,000,000
Expected net present value (ENPV)			61,820

*Rounded to three decimals.

We can see that the ENPV is positive. Hence, the wealth of shareholders is expected to increase if the lease is purchased. (However, the size of the ENPV is small in relation to the initial investment and so the business may wish to think again about the key assumptions used in the analysis before a final decision is made.)

The ENPV approach has the advantage of producing a single-figure outcome and of having a clear decision rule to apply (that is, if the ENPV is positive, the business should invest; if ENPV is negative, it should not).

However, using an average figure can obscure the underlying risk associated with the project. Simply deriving the ENPV, as in Example 7.4, can be misleading. Without some idea of the individual possible outcomes and their probability of occurring, the managers are in the dark. If either Option 2 or 3 were to occur, the NPV of the investment would be negative (wealth destroying). It is 40% probable that one of these options will occur, so this is a significant risk. Only if Option 1 were to occur (60% probable) would investing in the apartments represent a good decision.

None of this should be taken to mean that the investment in the apartments should not be made: the situation is simply that the managers must make a judgment even though the actual outcome is uncertain. Thus, where the ENPV approach is being used, it is a good idea to reveal to managers the different possible outcomes and the probability attached to each outcome. By so doing, the managers will be able to gain an insight to the downside risk attached to the project. This point is further illustrated by Activity 7.11.

ACTIVITY 7.11

Ukon Ltd. is considering two competing projects:

- Project A has a 0.8 probability of producing a negative NPV of $500,000, a 0.1 probability of producing a positive NPV of $1.0 million, and a 0.1 probability of producing a positive NPV of $5.5 million.
- Project B has a 0.2 probability of producing a positive NPV of $125,000, a 0.3 probability of producing a positive NPV of $250,000, and a 0.5 probability of producing a positive NPV of $300,000.

What is the expected net present value (ENPV) of each project?

▶

Solution

The ENPV of Project A is:

Probability ($)	NPV ($)	Expected Value ($)
0.8	(500,000)	(400,000)
0.1	1,000,000	100,000
0.1	5,500,000	550,000
	ENPV	250,000

The ENPV of Project B is:

Probability	NPV ($)	Expected Value ($)
0.2	125,000	25,000
0.3	250,000	75,000
0.5	300,000	150,000
	ENPV	250,000

Although the ENPVs of both projects in Activity 7.11 are identical, this does not mean that the business will be indifferent about which project to undertake. Project A has a high probability of losing money, whereas Project B will probably make money under either possible outcome. If we assume that investors are risk averse, they will prefer the business to take on Project B, as this will provide the same level of expected return as Project A but at a lower level of risk.

Event Tree Diagrams

When a range of possible outcomes can arise from a particular investment opportunity, it is sometimes helpful to identify each of the possible outcomes by preparing an **event tree diagram**. Probabilities may be assigned to each of the events or outcomes identified and if individual outcomes can occur in different combinations, we can calculate the probability of each possible combination by multiplying together the probabilities associated with the individual outcomes.

Example 7.5 provides an illustration of how an event tree may be constructed for an investment project with possible outcomes that can be combined in different ways.

Example 7.5

Zeta Computing Services Ltd. has recently produced some software for a client organization. The software has a life of two years and will then become obsolete. The cost of developing the software was $60,000. The client organization has agreed to pay a licence fee of $80,000 a year for the software if it is used in only one of its two divisions and $120,000 a year if it is used in both of its divisions. The client may use the software for either one or two years in either division but will definitely use it in at least one division in each of the two years.

Zeta Computing Services Ltd. believes there is a 0.6 chance that the licence fee received in any one year will be $80,000 and a 0.4 chance that it will be $120,000.

Required:

Produce an event tree diagram for the project.

Solution

FIGURE 7.6   Event Tree Diagram Showing Different Possible Project Outcomes

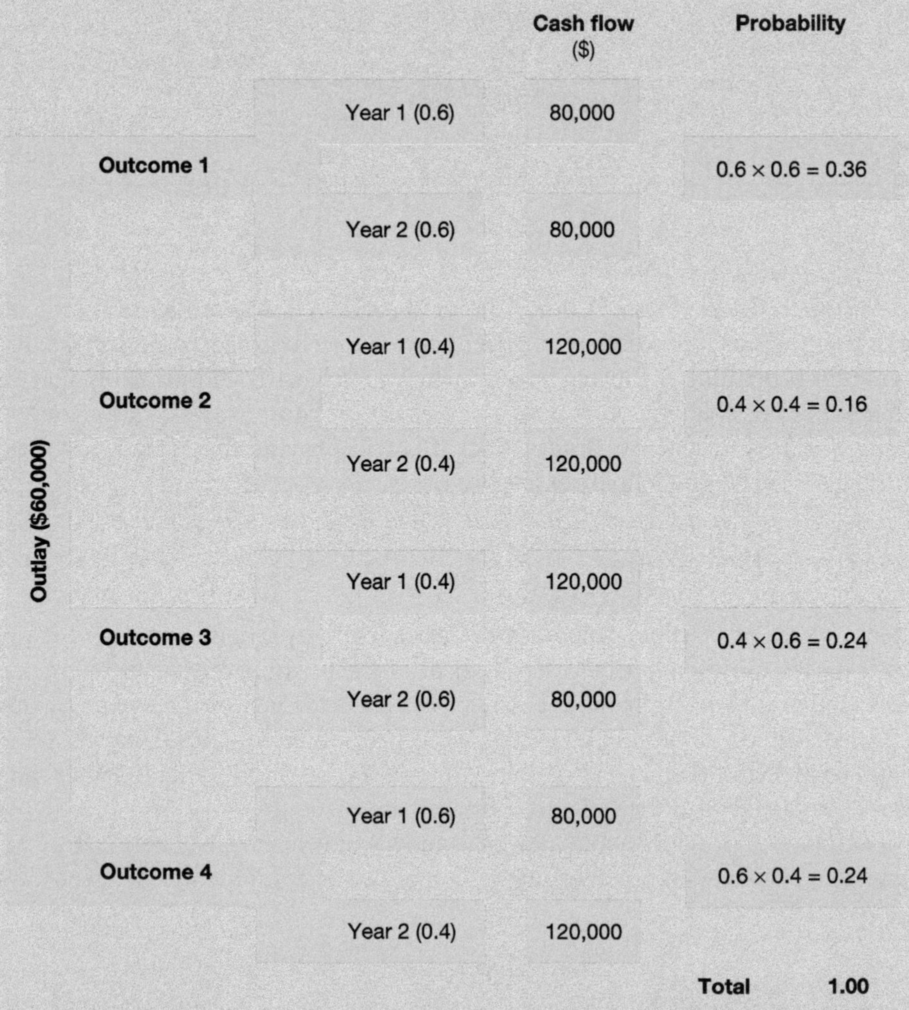

		Cash flow ($)	Probability
	Year 1 (0.6)	80,000	
Outcome 1			0.6 × 0.6 = 0.36
	Year 2 (0.6)	80,000	
	Year 1 (0.4)	120,000	
Outcome 2			0.4 × 0.4 = 0.16
	Year 2 (0.4)	120,000	
	Year 1 (0.4)	120,000	
Outcome 3			0.4 × 0.6 = 0.24
	Year 2 (0.6)	80,000	
	Year 1 (0.6)	80,000	
Outcome 4			0.6 × 0.4 = 0.24
	Year 2 (0.4)	120,000	
		Total	**1.00**

Outlay ($60,000)

Each outcome is represented by a branch and each branch has subsidiary branches. The sum of the probabilities attached to the outcomes must equal 1.00.

As you can see from the event tree diagram in Figure 7.6, the four possible outcomes attached to this project and their probabilities of occurrence (p) are as follows:

Outcome		Probability
1	Year 1 cash flow $80,000 ($p = 0.6$) and Year 2 cash flow $80,000 ($p = 0.6$). The probability of both years having cash flows of $80,000 will be ($0.6 \times 0.6$)	= 0.36
2	Year 1 cash flow $120,000 ($p = 0.4$) and Year 2 cash flow $120,000 ($p = 0.4$). The probability of both years having cash flows of $120,000 will be ($0.4 \times 0.4$)	= 0.16
3	Year 1 cash flow $120,000 ($p = 0.4$) and Year 2 cash flow $80,000 ($p = 0.6$). The probability of this sequence of cash flows occurring will be (0.4×0.6)	= 0.24
4	Year 1 cash flow $80,000 ($p = 0.6$) and Year 2 cash flow $120,000 ($p = 0.4$). The probability of this sequence of cash flows occurring will be (0.6×0.4)	= 0.24
		1.00

Activity 7.12 explores risk assessment using ENPV and NPV.

ACTIVITY 7.12

Kernow Cleaning Services Ltd. provides street-cleaning services for local municipalities in Southern Ontario. The work is currently labour intensive and few machines are used. However, the business is considering buying a fleet of street-cleaning vehicles at a total cost of $540,000. The vehicles have a life of four years and are likely to provide a considerable saving of labour costs. Estimates of the likely labour savings and their probability of occurrence are listed below:

	Estimated Savings ($)	Probability of Occurrence
Year 1	80,000	0.3
	160,000	0.5
	200,000	0.2
Year 2	140,000	0.4
	220,000	0.4
	250,000	0.2
Year 3	140,000	0.4
	200,000	0.3
	230,000	0.3
Year 4	100,000	0.3
	170,000	0.6
	200,000	0.1

Estimates for each year are independent of other years. The business has a cost of capital of 10%.

▶

Required:

(a) **Calculate the expected net present value (ENPV) of the street-cleaning machines.**

(b) **Calculate the net present value (NPV) of the worst possible outcome and the probability of its occurrence.**

Solution

(a) **Step 1:** Calculate the expected annual cash flows.

Year 1	($)	Year 2	($)
$80,000 $\times$ 0.3	24,000	$140,000 $\times$ 0.4	56,000
$160,000 $\times$ 0.5	80,000	$220,000 $\times$ 0.4	88,000
$200,000 $\times$ 0.2	40,000	$250,000 $\times$ 0.2	50,000
	144,000		194,000

Year 3	($)	Year 4	($)
$140,000 $\times$ 0.4	56,000	$100,000 $\times$ 0.3	30,000
$200,000 $\times$ 0.3	60,000	$170,000 $\times$ 0.6	102,000
$230,000 $\times$ 0.3	69,000	$200,000 $\times$ 0.1	20,000
	185,000		152,000

Step 2: Calculate the expected net present value (ENPV).

Period	Expected Cash Flow ($)	Discount Rate 10%	Expected PV ($)
0	(540,000)	1.000*	(540,000)
1	144,000	0.909	130,896
2	194,000	0.826	160,244
3	185,000	0.751	138,935
4	152,000	0.683	103,816
		ENPV	(6,109)

*Rounded to three decimals.

(b) The worst possible outcome can be calculated by taking the lowest values of savings each year, as follows.

Period	Cash Flow ($)	Discount Rate 10%	PV ($)
0	(540,000)	1.000*	(540,000)
1	80,000	0.909	72,720
2	140,000	0.826	115,640
3	140,000	0.751	105,140
4	100,000	0.683	68,300
		NPV	(178,200)

*Rounded to three decimals.

The probability of occurrence can be obtained by multiplying together the probability of each of the worst outcomes above, that is, 0.3 $\times$ 0.4 $\times$ 0.4 $\times$ 0.3 = 0.014 (or 1.4%). Thus, the probability of occurrence is 1.4%, which is very low.

RISK AND THE STANDARD DEVIATION

Suppose that two projects have a large number of possible outcomes and we are able to identify each possible outcome and assign a probability to it. This would mean that we could plot a probability distribution of the outcomes that could take the form of a continuous curve for each project, such as the ones shown in Figure 7.7.

FIGURE 7.7   Probability Distribution of Two Projects with the Same Expected Value

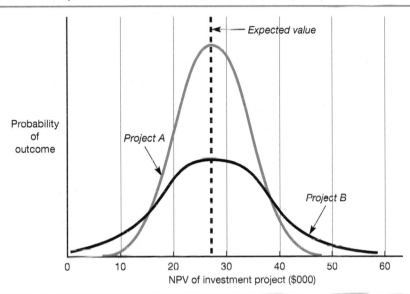

The particular shape of the curve is likely to vary between investment projects. However, note that Project A has a range of possible values that is much more tightly distributed around the expected value than Project B, even though both projects have the same expected value.

This difference in the shape of the two probability distributions can provide us with a useful indicator of risk. The graph shows that the tighter the distribution of possible future values, the greater the chance that the actual value will be close to the expected value. This means there is less downside risk associated with Project A (but also less upside potential). We can say, therefore, that *the tighter the probability distribution of outcomes, the lower the risk associated with the investment project*. Project A will be considered a less risky venture than Project B.

The variability of possible future values associated with a project can be measured using a statistical measure called the **standard deviation**. This is a measure of spread that is based on deviations from the mean, or expected value. To demonstrate how the standard deviation is calculated, let us consider Example 7.6.

Example 7.6

Telematix Limited is considering two mutually exclusive projects: Cable and Satellite. The possible NPVs for each project and their associated probabilities are as follows:

Cable		Satellite	
NPV ($ millions)	Probability of Occurrence	NPV ($ millions)	Probability of Occurrence
10	0.1	15	0.6
20	0.5	20	0.2
25	0.4	40	0.2

Step 1. The ENPV for each project must be calculated. In the case of the Cable project, the ENPV is as follows:

(a) NPV ($ millions)	(b) Probability of Occurrence	(c) = (a) × (b) ENPV ($ millions)
10	0.1	1.0
20	0.5	10.0
25	0.4	10.0
		21.0

Step 2. Calculate the deviations around the ENPV by deducting the expected NPV from each possible outcome. For the Cable project, the following set of deviations will be obtained:

(a) Possible NPV ($ millions)	(b) ENPV ($ millions)	(c) = (a) − (b) Deviation ($ millions)	Squared Deviations ($ millions)
10	21	−11	121
20	21	−1	1
25	21	4	16
		Variance	138

The standard deviation is:

$$\text{Standard deviation} = \sqrt{\text{Variance}}$$

For the Cable project, the standard deviation is:

$$\text{Standard deviation} = \sqrt{\$138 \text{ million}} = \$11.75 \text{ million}$$

The higher the standard deviation for a particular investment project, the greater the spread, or variability, of possible outcomes and, therefore, the greater the risk. This is illustrated in Activity 7.13.

ACTIVITY 7.13

Calculate the standard deviation for the Satellite project. Which project has the higher level of risk?

Solution

Follow the steps outlined in Example 7.6.
Step 1. Calculate the ENPV:

(a) NPV ($ millions)	(b) Probability of Occurrence	(c) = (a) × (b) ENPV ($ millions)
15	0.6	9.0
20	0.2	4.0
40	0.2	8.0
		21.0

Step 2. Calculate the deviations around the ENPV:

(a) Possible NPV ($ millions)	(b) ENPV ($ millions)	(c) = (a) × (b) Deviation ($ millions)	Squared Deviations ($ millions)
15	21	−6	36
20	21	−1	1
40	21	19	361
		Variance	398

Step 3. Standard deviation = $\sqrt{\$398 \text{ million}}$

= \$19.95 million

The Satellite project has the higher standard deviation and, therefore, the greater variability of possible outcomes. Hence, it has the higher level of risk.

SELF-ASSESSMENT QUESTION   7.2

Dynamic Capital Inc. is considering investing in either Project 1 or Project 2. Dynamic has gathered the following data concerning the projects:

	Project 1		Project 2	
	NPV	Probability	NPV	Probability
	$100	0.4	$69	0.6
	60	0.3	55	0.3
	13	0.3	40	0.1

Required:

Which project is the better investment for Dynamic? Show all calculations.

THE STANDARD DEVIATION AND THE NORMAL DISTRIBUTION

If the distribution of possible outcomes has a symmetrical bell shape when plotted on a graph, it is referred to as a **normal distribution**. In Figure 7.8 we can see an example of a normal distribution, in which approximately 68%, 95%, and 100% of possible outcomes fall within one, two, and three standard deviations, respectively, from the mean or expected value. There is little chance of an outcome being more than three standard deviations away from the mean. In practice, distributions of data often display a bell-curve pattern.

Even when the possible outcomes do not form a precisely symmetrical bell shape, or normal distribution, these rules can still be reasonably accurate. We shall see how these rules may be useful in interpreting the level of risk associated with a project.

FIGURE 7.8 The Normal Distribution and Standard Deviations

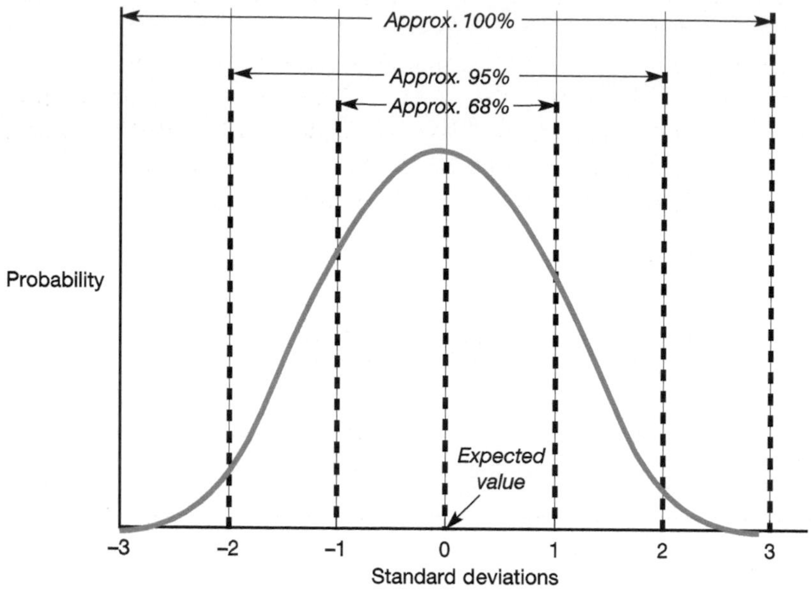

The Expected Value–Standard Deviation Rules

If investors are risk-averse, they will be seeking either the highest level of return for a given level of risk or the lowest level of risk for a given level of return. The following decision rule can, therefore, be applied where the possible outcomes for investment projects are normally distributed:

> *Where there are two competing projects, X and Y, Project X should be chosen when the expected return of Project X is equal to, or greater than, that of Project Y, and the standard deviation of Project X is not higher than that of Project Y.*

The **expected value–standard deviation rules**, as they are known, do not cover all possibilities. For example, the rules cannot help us discriminate between two projects where one has both a higher expected return and a higher standard deviation. Nevertheless, they provide some help for managers, as demonstrated in Activity 7.14.

ACTIVITY 7.14

Refer back to Example 7.6 on page 261. Which project should be chosen and why? (Assume the possible outcomes are normally distributed.)

Solution

The Cable and Satellite projects have identical expected net present values. However, the Cable project has a much lower standard deviation, indicating less variability of possible outcomes. Applying the decision rule mentioned above, this means that the Cable project should be selected. A risk-averse investor would prefer the Cable project as it provides the same expected return for a lower level of risk.

Measuring Probabilities

Probabilities may be derived using either an objective or a subjective approach. **Objective probabilities** are based on information gathered from experience. For example, the transport manager of a business operating a fleet of trucks may be able to provide information concerning the possible life of a newly purchased truck based on the record of similar trucks acquired in the past. **Subjective probabilities** are based on opinion and should be used where past data are either inappropriate or unavailable.

Despite these problems, we should not dismiss the use of probabilities. They help to make explicit some of the risks associated with a project and can help managers to appreciate the uncertainties that must be faced. REAL WORLD 7.4 provides an example of the use of probabilities to assess cash flows.

REAL WORLD 7.4

Probabilities Used at Barrick Gold

Toronto-based Barrick Gold estimates expected future cash flows using a probability-weighted approach. Annual updates, including probabilities, are assigned to estimates of projected future revenues, costs of production, and capital expenditures.

Source: Barrick Gold Corporation 2008 Annual Report.

PORTFOLIO EFFECTS AND RISK REDUCTION

So far, our consideration of risk has looked at the problem from the viewpoint of an investment project being undertaken in isolation. However, in practice, a business will normally invest in a range, or *portfolio*, of projects rather than a single project. This approach to investment provides a potentially useful way of reducing risk. The problem with investing all available funds in a single project is, of course, that an unfavourable outcome could have disastrous consequences for the business. By investing in a variety of projects, an adverse outcome from a single project is less likely to have severe repercussions. The old saying, "Don't put all your eggs in one basket," is still the best advice concerning investment policy.

Investing in a range of different projects is referred to as **diversification**, and by holding a diversified portfolio of investment projects, the total risk associated with the business can be reduced.

In theory, it is possible to combine two risky investment projects so as to create a portfolio of projects that is riskless. To illustrate this point, let us consider Example 7.7.

Example 7.7

Stein Company has the opportunity to invest in two investment projects in Transylvania. The possible outcomes from each project will depend on whether the ruling party of the country wins or loses the next election. The NPV from each project under each outcome is estimated as follows:

	Project 1 NPV ($ millions)	Project 2 NPV ($ millions)
Ruling party wins	(20)	30
Ruling party loses	40	(30)

What should the business do to manage the risks involved in each project?

Solution

By investing in *both* projects, the business's total NPV under each outcome will be as follows:

	Project 1 NPV ($ millions)	Project 2 NPV ($ millions)	Total Returns ($ millions)
Ruling party wins	(20)	30	10
Ruling party loses	40	(30)	10

We can see that, whatever the outcome of the election, the total NPV for the business will be the same (that is, $10 million). Although the possible returns from each project vary according to the results of the election, they are inversely related and the total returns will be stabilized.

Companies may find inversely related capital investment projects by seeking geographical, industry, and other types of diversification. As risk can be diversified away in this manner, the relationship between the returns from individual investment projects is an important issue for managers.

The Coefficient of Correlation

A business may eliminate the variability in total returns by investing in projects whose returns are inversely related, such as in Example 7.7. Ideally, a business should invest in a variety of investment projects so that when certain projects generate low (or negative) returns, other projects are generating high returns, and vice versa. It is possible to measure the degree to which the returns from individual projects are related by using the **coefficient of correlation**. This coefficient ranges along a continuum between +1 and −1.

When the coefficient for two projects, X and Y, is positive, it means that increases in the returns from Project X will be accompanied by increases in returns from Project Y: the higher the positive measure, the stronger the relationship between the returns of the two projects. A coefficient of +1 indicates a perfect positive correlation and this means that the returns are moving together in perfect step. Figure 7.9 shows the returns for two investment projects that have a perfect positive correlation.

If the coefficient of correlation is negative, increases in the returns from Project X will be accompanied by decreases in the returns from Project Y. A coefficient of −1 indicates a perfect negative correlation between two projects. In other words, the projects' returns will move together in perfect step, but in *opposite directions*.

If the coefficient of correlation between the returns of two projects is 0, this means that the returns from Project X and Project Y move independently of one another and so there is no relationship between them.

Our examination of the coefficient of correlation suggests that, in order to eliminate risk completely, a business should invest in projects whose returns are perfectly negatively correlated. When this is done, the variability in returns between projects will cancel out and risk is completely diversified away. Unfortunately, in the real world, projects whose returns are perfectly negatively correlated are extremely difficult to find. Nevertheless, risk can still be diversified away to some extent by investing in projects

FIGURE 7.9   Two Projects Whose Returns Have a Perfect Positive Correlation

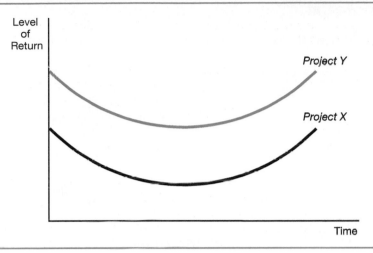

whose returns do not have a perfect positive correlation. Provided the correlation between projects is less than +1, some offsetting will occur. The further the coefficient of correlation moves away from +1 and toward −1 on the scale, the greater this offsetting effect will be.

Activities 7.15 and 7.16 explore negative correlation.

ACTIVITY 7.15

Suppose the returns from Project Y had a perfect negative correlation with those of Project X. Draw a graph depicting the relationship between the two projects.

Solution

The graph for two investment projects whose returns are perfectly negatively correlated is shown in Figure 7.10.

FIGURE 7.10   Two Projects Whose Returns Have a Perfect Negative Correlation

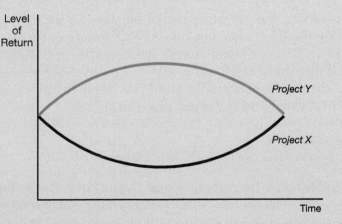

When the returns from Project Y are low, the returns from Project X are high, and vice versa.

ACTIVITY 7.16

Should the managers of a business seek project diversification as their primary objective?

Solution

The answer is no. Even if two projects could be found whose returns had a perfect negative correlation, this does not necessarily mean that they should be pursued. The expected returns from the projects must also be considered when making any investment decision.

One potential problem of diversification is that a range of different projects can create greater project management problems. Managers will have to deal with a variety of different projects with different technical and resource issues to resolve. The greater the number of projects, the greater the management problems are likely to be.

REAL WORLD 7.5 provides examples of diversification in practice.

REAL WORLD 7.5

Diversification at Gildan (T-Shirts) and CAE (Flight Simulators)

Gildan Inc., a Montreal-based T-shirt and socks maker, has embarked on a strategy to diversify its sales from strictly wholesale into the mass-market retail channel. Gildan has also recently diversified its manufacturing facilities to the low-cost Caribbean region.

CAE Inc., also from Montreal, is diversifying its revenue base away from the volatility of new aircraft deliveries. Today 30% of CAE's revenue comes from new aircraft deliveries and the rest is derived from more stable sources like pilot training and military simulation products. CAE's revenue stream is globally diversified with one third coming from the U.S., one third from Europe, and the remainder from the rest of the world.

Sources: Gildan 2008 Annual Report and CAE 2009 Annual Report.

Diversifiable and Non-Diversifiable Risk

The benefits of risk diversification can be obtained by increasing the number of projects within the investment portfolio. As each investment project is added to the portfolio, the variability of total returns will diminish, providing that the projects are not perfectly correlated. However, there are limits to the benefits of diversification due to the nature of the risks faced. The total risk relating to a particular project can be divided into two types: diversifiable risk and non-diversifiable risk. As the names suggest, it is only the former type of risk that can be eliminated through diversification.

The two types of risk can be described as follows:

■ **Diversifiable risk** is the part of the total risk that is specific to the project, such as changes in key personnel, legal regulations, and the degree of competition. By spreading available funds between investment projects, it is possible to offset adverse outcomes occurring in one project against beneficial outcomes in another. (Diversifiable risk is also referred to as avoidable risk, or unsystematic risk.)

■ **Non-diversifiable risk** is the part of the total risk that is common to all projects and which, therefore, cannot be diversified away. This element of risk arises from general market conditions and will be affected by such factors as the rate of inflation, the general level of interest rates, exchange rate movements, and the rate of growth within the economy. (Non-diversifiable risk is also referred to as unavoidable risk, or systematic risk.)

Companies can attempt to manage risk by actively using hedging programs. Financial derivatives, such as forward contracts, help governments, corporations, and individuals to manage risk. A currency forward contract can help a company manage its foreign currency exchange rate risk, by locking in a future exchange rate today. A forward contract is an agreement to deliver a specified amount of foreign currency at a future date at a predetermined exchange rate, decided upon today. Currency forward contracts are acquired at no up-front expense. The expense is in effect embedded in the future exchange rate specified in the contract. Example 7.8 shows how a foreign currency hedge is used to limit risk.

Example 7.8

CeeJay's Diner, a Canadian firm, wants to borrow US$1 million, at 5% interest for one year from the First Bank of Chicago to take advantage of the lower interest rate south of the border. At the time it takes out the loan, the exchange rate is C$1 = US$0.9500—one Canadian dollar buys 95 U.S. cents. CeeJay's plans to convert the borrowed US$1 million into C$1,052,631.58 and use it to open new restaurants in Canada.

Using its crystal ball, CeeJay's estimates that, one year from now, the exchange rate will be C$1 = US$0.8500. CeeJay's will need C$1,176,470.59 (i.e., US$1 million ÷ US$0.8500) in order to buy US$1 million to pay back the loan, ignoring the interest expense. The company will have lost almost C$124,000 on the fluctuating currency exchange rate.

Alternatively, on the date the loan is arranged, CeeJay's could acquire a forward contract to deliver US$1 million at a locked-in exchange rate of C$1 = US$0.9300 one year from now. When the forward contract is executed in one year, the US$1 million will cost only C$1,075,268.82 (i.e., US$1,000,000 ÷ US$0.9300), using the locked-in hedge rate. The forward contact would save CeeJay's C$101,201.77 (C$1,176,470.59 − C$1,075,268.82).

In Figure 7.11, the relationship between the level of portfolio risk and the size of the portfolio is shown. As the number of projects increases, the diversifiable element of total risk is reduced. This does not mean, necessarily, that a business should invest in a large number of projects. Many of the benefits from diversification can often be reaped from investing in a relatively small number of projects. In Figure 7.11, we can see the additional benefits from each investment project diminish quite sharply. This suggests that a business with a moderate number of projects may gain very little from further diversification.

Non-diversifiable risk is based on general economic conditions and therefore all businesses will be affected. However, certain businesses are more sensitive to changes in economic conditions than others. For example, during a recession, some types of businesses will be badly affected, whereas others will be only slightly affected, as illustrated in Activity 7.17.

FIGURE 7.11   Reducing Risk Through Diversification

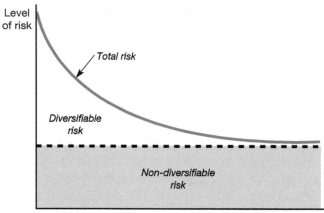

Number of investment projects

ACTIVITY 7.17

Provide two examples of businesses that are likely to be:

(a) badly affected by an economic recession
(b) only slightly affected by an economic recession.

Solution

(a) The types of business that are likely to be badly hit by recession will include those selling expensive or luxury goods and services, such as:

- hotels and restaurants
- travel companies
- house builders and construction
- airlines
- jewellers.

(b) The types of business that are likely to be only slightly affected by recession will include those selling essential goods and services, such as:

- gas and electricity suppliers
- basic food retailers and producers
- undertakers.

The businesses that are likely to be badly affected by an economic recession will usually have a cyclical pattern of profits. Thus, during a period of economic growth, these businesses may make large profits, and during periods of recession they may incur large losses. The businesses that are likely to be only slightly affected will tend to have a fairly stable pattern of profits over the economic cycle.

The distinction between diversifiable and non-diversifiable risk is an important issue that we shall return to when considering the cost of capital in Chapter 10.

Risk Assessment in Practice

Surveys of North American businesses suggest that risk assessment methods have become more widely used over time. These surveys, described in **REAL WORLD 7.6**, also suggest that sensitivity analysis and personal experience are the most popular methods of assessing risk.

Assessing Risk in Canada and the United States

The following table examines the extent to which various risk assessment methods are used in Canada and the United States.

Technique	Canada (%)	United States (%)
Sensitivity analysis	60	52
Adjust the payback period	28	14
Adjust the discount rate (hurdle rate)	49	47
Adjust projected cash flows	35	33
Quantify based on personal experience	63	50
Quantify based on other companies' experience in same industry	22	10

The table shows that executives in North America rely heavily on personal experience when assessing risk in capital budgeting. Then, sensitivity analyses are performed, most likely by adjusting the discount rate and/or the cash flows. Differences between Canada and the U.S. are likely accounted for by the difference in company sizes in the two countries, with larger companies less likely to use the payback period method and other companies' experience.

Source: Janet D. Payne, Will Carrington Heath, and Lewis R. Gale, "Comparative Financial Practice in the US and Canada: Capital Budgeting and Risk Assessment Techniques," *Financial Practice & Education*, Spring/Summer 1999, Vol. 9 Issue 1, pp. 16–24, 9p, 6 charts; (*AN 2259377*).

SUMMARY

Investment Decisions When Funds Are Limited

- Managers should maximize the present value per dollar of scarce financing
- The profitability index provides a measure of the present value per dollar of scarce financing
- Where funding requirements extend beyond a single period, linear programming can be used to maximize NPV.

Comparing Projects with Unequal Duration

- Can be dealt with by assuming the projects form part of a repeat chain of replacement and then make comparisons using the shortest-common-period-of-time approach
- Alternatively, the equivalent-annual-annuity approach converts the NPV of a project into an annual annuity stream over its expected life.

The Problem of Inflation

- Include inflation by adjusting the annual cash flows and the discount rate to take account of price increases
- Or, exclude inflation by adjusting the cash flow to real terms and by using a real discount rate.

Risk and Investment Decisions

- Risk is important because of the long time scales and amounts involved in investment decisions
- Various methods of dealing with risk are available.

Sensitivity Analysis

- Provides an assessment, taking each input factor in turn, of how much each one can vary from estimate before a project is not viable
- Provides useful insights to projects
- Does not give a clear decision rule, but provides an impression
- Considers only one input factor at a time.

Scenario Analysis

- Changes a number of variables simultaneously to provide a particular state of the world
- Usually three different states—optimistic, pessimistic, and most likely—are evaluated
- Does not indicate the likelihood of each state occurring or the other possible states that may occur.

Simulations

- Managers identify the key variables of the project and their key relationships
- Possible values are attached to each factor and a computer is used to select one of the possible values randomly to produce a projected cash flow
- The process is repeated many times to obtain a probability distribution of the values of the cash flows
- Can be costly and time consuming.

Risk Preferences of Investors

- Given a choice between two projects with the same expected return but with different levels of risk:
  - Risk-seeking investors will choose the project with the higher level of risk
  - Risk-neutral investors will have no preference
  - Risk-averse investors will choose the project with the lower level of risk.
- Most investors appear to be risk-averse.

Risk-Adjusted Discount Rate

- Most investors will require a risk premium for risky projects
- Using a risk-adjusted discount rate, where a risk premium is added to the risk-free rate, is a logical response to risk.

Expected Values and Risk Assessment

- The expected net present value (ENPV) approach:
  - Assigns probabilities to possible outcomes; probabilities may be subjective (based on opinion) or objective (based on evidence)
  - Uses the expected value—the weighted average of the possible outcomes where the probabilities are used as weights
  - Provides a single value and a clear decision rule, although the single ENPV figure can hide the real risk
  - Should be supported by information on the range of possible outcomes.

Risk and the Standard Deviation

- Standard deviation is a measure of spread based on deviations from the mean
- Standard deviation provides a measure of risk.

Portfolio Effects and Risk Reduction

- By holding a diversified portfolio of investment projects, the total risk associated with the business can be reduced
- Ideally, a business should undertake a variety of projects, so that when certain projects generate low returns, others generate high returns
- Only diversifiable risk can be eliminated through diversification.

KEY TERMS

Linear programming
Profitability index
Shortest-common-period-
of-time approach
Annuity
Equivalent-annual-annuity
approach
Risk
Sensitivity analysis
Scenario analysis

Simulation
Risk-seeking investors
Risk-neutral investors
Risk-averse investors
Utility function
Risk-adjusted discount rate
Expected value
Expected net present value
(ENPV)
Event tree diagram

Standard deviation
Normal distribution
Expected value–standard
deviation rules
Objective probabilities
Subjective probabilities
Diversification
Coefficient of correlation
Diversifiable risk
Non-diversifiable risk

LIST OF EQUATIONS

7.1 Profitability index $= \dfrac{\text{Present value of future cash inflows}}{\text{Cost for the project}}$

7.2 Profitability index $= \dfrac{\text{Cost for the project} + \text{NPV of the project}}{\text{Cost for the project}}$

7.3 Sales revenue $=$ Selling price per unit $\times$ (Market share $\times$ Market size)

REVIEW QUESTIONS

Answers to the Review Questions can be found on the Companion Website that accompanies this text at **www.pearsoned.ca/atrill**.

7.1 What is risk and why is it an important issue for investment decision making?

7.2 There is evidence to suggest that some businesses fail to consider inflation in investment decisions. Does this really matter given that, in recent years, the level of inflation has been low?

What would be the effect on NPV calculations (that is, would NPV be overstated or understated) if inflation is dealt with incorrectly by:

(a) Discounting nominal cash flows at real discount rates?

(b) Discounting real cash flows at a nominal discount rate?

7.3 What practical problems arise when using the risk-adjusted discount rate to deal with the problem of risk?

7.4 Explain why the standard deviation may be useful in measuring risk.

7.5 Exclusive Luggage Limited Enterprises (ELLE), a retailing organization, is considering opening stores in Calgary, New York, and Paris. Explain, with reasons, what ELLE is trying to accomplish with regard to risk. How does this relate to the concepts of diversifiable risk and non-diversifiable risk?

PROBLEMS AND CASES

7.1 Quebec Lasers Limited (QLL) is expanding rapidly and has the opportunity to invest in four projects. The forecast cash flows for each project are as follows:

Project cash flows
($ thousands)

Year	Project 1	Project 2	Project 3	Project 4
0	(500)	(400)	(300)	(100)
1	300	150	120	60
2	200	170	200	45
3	150	90	90	25

QLL has a cost of capital of 12% and an investment budget for the year of $600,000.

Required:
(a) Calculate the net present value (NPV) to two decimal places and profitability index to three decimal places for each project.
(b) Which investment project(s) should QLL undertake, assuming all projects are divisible?
(c) Which investment project(s) should QLL undertake, assuming all projects are non-divisible?
(d) Which investment project(s) should QLL undertake, assuming all projects are divisible but Projects 3 and 4 are mutually exclusive?

7.2 Kamloops Gold Breakers (KGB) needs to acquire one of three crushers. KGB uses a discount rate of 6% to evaluate investment decisions. The crushers have the following investment cash flows:

Machine cash flows
($ thousands)

Year	Machine 1	Machine 2	Machine 3
0	(400)	(600)	(900)
1	165	190	140
2	165	190	140
3	165	190	140
4		190	140
5			140
6			140
7			140
8			140
9			140
10			140
11			140
12			140

Required:
(a) Use the shortest-common-period-of-time approach to determine which, if any, machine should be acquired.
(b) Use the equivalent-annual-annuity approach to determine which, if any, machine should be acquired.
(c) Did (a) and (b) give you the same decision?

7.3 Canuck Enterprises Limited (CEL) is considering investing in a new machine with the following cash flow data:

Year	New Machine Cash Flows ($ thousands)
0	(900)
1	300
2	300
3	300
4	300

CEL enjoys a 10% cost of capital.

Required:
(a) What is the NPV of the proposed investment in the new machine?
(b) By how much would the price paid for the machine have to change to cause the investment to have a zero NPV?
(c) By how much would the cost of capital have to change to cause the investment to have a zero NPV?
(d) Assuming they are to remain equal for all years, by how much would the annual cash inflows have to change to cause the investment to have a zero NPV?
(e) State any conclusions you can make from your sensitivity analysis.

7.4 The Signal Hill Society (SHS) is considering two large-scale computer investments with the following year-end cash flow patterns. SHS would like you to perform a sensitivity analysis of these projects in relation to the cost of capital, the estimated cost of the project, and the estimated cash flows themselves.

		Project cash flows (millions of dollars)	
	Cost of capital	12%	12%
	Year	Project 1	Project 2
Estimated cost	0	$(530)	$(400)
Estimated cash inflows	1	190	140
Estimated cash inflows	2	190	140
Estimated cash inflows	3	190	140
Estimated cash inflows	4	190	140

Required:
(a) Calculate the net present value of each project.
(b) Which project is more sensitive to the estimated cost?
(c) Calculate the internal rate of return for each project.
(d) Which project is more sensitive to the discount rate?
(e) Determine the revenues that would cause each project to have a zero net present value. Keep the cost of capital at 12% and the cost unchanged from the original data for this analysis.
(f) Which project is more sensitive to estimated cash flow projections?
(g) Which project is riskier, based on your sensitivity analysis?

7.5 Wu and Chu Chocolates Emporium (WCCE) is considering the acquisition of new production equipment. Based on medical studies extolling the health benefits of daily chocolate intake, demand is expected to grow. WCCE has assembled the following data concerning the possible expansion:

New Machine Cash Flows
($ thousands)

Year	High Growth	Medium Growth	Low Growth
0	(600)	(600)	(600)
1	200	150	100
2	300	200	125
3	350	300	150
4	270	200	100
Probability	40%	30%	30%

The cost of capital for WCCE is 14%.

Required:

(a) Calculate the expected cash inflow for each year and determine the expected net present value, NPV.

(b) Should WCCE buy the new machine?

7.6 Saskatchewan Aeronautics Corporation (SAC) is considering two mutually exclusive projects with the following net present value profiles:

	Project 1		Project 2	
NPV ($ millions)	Probability		NPV ($ millions)	Probability
100	20%		50	50%
75	10%		45	40%
10	70%		40	10%

Required:

(a) Calculate the expected net present value for each project.

(b) Calculate the standard deviation for each project.

(c) Which project should SAC accept? Why?

7.7 Lee Caterers Ltd. is about to make an investment in new kitchen equipment. It is considering whether to replace the existing kitchen equipment with cook/freeze or cook/chill technology. The following cash flows are expected from each form of technology:

	Cook/Chill ($000)	Cook/Freeze ($000)
Initial cost	(200)	(390)
1 year's time	85	88
2 years' time	94	102
3 years' time	86	110
4 years' time	62	110
5 years' time	–	110
6 years' time	–	90
7 years' time	–	85
8 years' time	–	60

The business would expect to replace the new equipment purchased with similar equipment at the end of its life. The cost of capital for the business is 10%.

Required:
Which type of equipment should the business invest in? Use both approaches considered in the chapter to support your conclusions and round present value factors to two decimals.

7.8 D'Arcy Builders Ltd. is considering three possible investment projects: A, B, and C. The expected pattern of cash flows for each project is:

Project Cash Flows

	A	B	C
	($000)	($000)	($000)
Initial cost	(17)	(20)	(24)
1 year's time	11	12	9
2 years' time	5	7	9
3 years' time	7	7	11
4 years' time	6	6	13

The business has a cost of capital of 10% and the capital expenditure budget for next year is $25 million.

Required:
Which investment project(s) should the business undertake, assuming:

(a) Each project is divisible?
(b) Each project is non-divisible?

Round present value factors to two decimals.

7.9 Simonson Engineers Limited is considering building a new plant in Indonesia to produce goods for the Southeast Asian market. To date, $450,000 has been invested in market research and site surveys. The cost of building the plant will be $9 million and it will be in operation and paid for in one year's time. Estimates of the likely cash flows from the plant and their probability of occurrence are set out as follows:

	Estimated Cash Flows ($ millions)	Probability of Occurrence
Year 2	2.0	0.2
	3.5	0.6
	4.0	0.2
Year 3	2.5	0.2
	3.0	0.4
	5.0	0.4
Year 4	3.0	0.2
	4.0	0.7
	5.0	0.1
Year 5	2.5	0.2
	3.0	0.5
	6.0	0.3

Estimates for each year are independent of each other. The cost of capital for the business is 10%. Round present value factors to three decimals.

Required:

    (a) Calculate the expected net present value of the proposed plant.

    (b) Calculate the net present value of the worst possible outcome and the probability of its occurrence.

    (c) Should the business invest in the new plant? Why?

7.10 Acadian Controls Limited (ACE) is designing a new switching device and is very unsure of just how successful it will be. The project will cost $300,000. Ace uses a 10% discount rate. Ace has derived the following annual year-end cash flow options regarding the project.

	Annual Cash Flows $	Probability
Option 1	20,000	20%
Option 2	45,000	10%
Option 3	75,000	50%
Option 4	92,000	10%
Option 5	130,000	10%
		100%

Required:

    (a) Calculate the expected net present value of the project.

    (b) What probability does the project have of being successful?

    (c) Would you recommend proceeding with the project?

7.11 Nimby Corporation is considering two mutually exclusive projects: Delphi and Oracle. The possible NPVs for each project and their associated probabilities are as follows:

Delphi		Oracle	
NPV ($ millions)	Probability of Occurrence	NPV ($ millions)	Probability of Occurrence
20	0.2	30	0.5
40	0.6	40	0.3
60	0.2	65	0.2

Required:

    (a) Calculate the expected net present value and the standard deviation associated with each project.

    (b) Which project would you select and why? State any assumptions you have made in coming to your conclusions.

    (c) Discuss the limitations of the standard deviation as a measure of project risk.

7.12 Portage Mainframes Limited (PML) is studying the following three projects.

Project 1		Project 2		Project 3	
NPV ($ thousands)	Probability	NPV ($ thousands)	Probability	NPV ($ thousands)	Probability
320	15%	100	40%	50	10%
450	22%	200	30%	250	50%
650	55%	300	10%	300	30%
900	8%	400	20%	700	10%
	100%		100%		100%

Required:
  (a) Calculate the expected net present value for each project
  (b) Calculate the variance for each project
  (c) Calculate the standard deviation for each project.

7.13 You have obtained cash flow data for the following projects.

| | Cash Flows | | |
Year	Project 1	Project 2	Project 3
1	230.00	210.00	260.00
2	260.00	290.00	220.00
3	290.00	270.00	230.00
4	270.00	205.00	240.00
5	210.00	188.00	250.00

Required:
  (a) Calculate the average cash flow for each project over its five-year life
  (b) Calculate the cash flow variance for each project
  (c) Calculate the cash flow standard deviation for each project.

7.14 The YellowBelly Corporation (YBC) is trying to budget sales for its new wireless device, known by the code name SapSucker. YBC's market research has garnered the following data:

Revenues	Probability
$30,000,000	10%
32,000,000	20%
34,000,000	25%
34,000,000	30%
36,000,000	10%
38,000,000	5%
	100%

Required:
  (a) Calculate the expected revenue for the SapSucker.
  (b) Calculate the standard deviation for the SapSucker's revenues.
  (c) Provide the Director of Market Research with a 95% range of revenues for the new product. Assume a normal distribution for revenues.

7.15 The Green Machine Experience (GME), a local rhythm and blues band, has developed the following data for its prospective income statement. All sales and expenses are paid in cash.

Probability	50%	20%	30%
Sales	180,000	140,000	220,000
Commission expenses	10,008	7,784	12,232
Salaries	20,000	20,000	20,000
Rent	15,000	15,000	15,000
Depreciation expense	22,000	22,000	22,000
Total expenses	67,008	64,784	69,232
Net income	112,992	75,216	150,768

Required:

(a) Calculate the expected cash flows for GME
(b) Calculate the standard deviation for GME's cash flows
(c) Provide a 95% range of cash flows. Assume a normal distribution for revenues.

7.16 Truro United Technologies Limited (TUT) is a company that has been in business for years and has already achieved its desired risk profile. TUT has four projects under consideration with the following characteristics. TUT can implement only two projects because of limited funds available.

	Expected NPV	Standard Deviation
Project 1	200	40
Project 2	180	35
Project 3	170	30
Project 4	160	25

Project	Correlation Coefficient
1 and 2	0.90
1 and 3	0.80
1 and 4	0.85
2 and 3	0.80
2 and 4	−0.65
3 and 4	0.40

Required:

Which two projects do you recommend TUT implement?

7.17 Plato Pharmaceuticals Ltd. has invested $300,000 to date in developing a new type of insect repellent. The repellent is now ready for production and sale, and the marketing manager estimates that the product will sell 150,000 bottles a year over the next five years. The selling price of the insect repellent will be $5 a bottle and variable costs are estimated to be $3 a bottle. Fixed costs (excluding amortization) are expected to be $200,000 a year. This figure is made up of $160,000 additional fixed costs and $40,000 fixed costs relating to the existing business that will be apportioned to the new product.

In order to produce the repellent, machinery and equipment costing $520,000 will have to be purchased immediately. The estimated residual value of this machinery and equipment in five years' time is $100,000. The business calculates depreciation on a straight-line basis.

The business has a cost of capital of 12%. Ignore taxes. Use present value factors to four decimals.

Required:

(a) Calculate the net present value of the product.
(b) Undertake sensitivity analysis to show by how much the following factors would have to change before the product ceased to be worthwhile.
   (i)   The discount rate
   (ii) The initial cost of machinery and equipment
   (iii) The net operating cash flows
   (iv) The residual value of the machinery and equipment.

CHAPTER 8

Financing a Business 1: Sources of Funds

LEARNING OUTCOMES

When you have completed this chapter, you should be able to:

1 Identify the main sources of external financing available to a business and explain the advantages and disadvantages of each source.

2 Discuss the factors to be taken into account when choosing an appropriate source of financing.

3 Identify the main sources of internal financing available to a business and explain the advantages and disadvantages of each source.

INTRODUCTION

This is the first of two chapters that examine the financing of businesses. In this chapter, we identify the main sources of financing available to businesses and discuss the main features of each source. We also consider the factors to be taken into account when choosing among the various sources of financing that are available.

In Chapter 9, we go on to examine capital markets, including the role and efficiency of stock exchanges and the ways in which new shares can be issued. We also consider the ways in which smaller businesses, which do not have access to most stock exchanges, may try to raise funds.

SOURCES OF FINANCING

External sources of financing are those that require the agreement of someone beyond the directors and managers of the business. Thus, on the one hand, financing from an issue of new shares is an external source because it requires the agreement of potential shareholders. *Internal sources of financing,* on the other hand, do not require agreement from other parties and arise from management decisions. Thus, retained earnings are a source of internal financing because management has the power to retain earnings without the agreement of the shareholders (whose profits they are!).

There are *long-term* and *short-term* sources of external financing. In practice, these terms are not tightly defined, but for clarity we will use the accounting definition: long-term financing is due for repayment after one or more years, whereas short-term financing must be repaid within approximately one year.

L.O. 1

SOURCES OF EXTERNAL FINANCING

Figure 8.1 summarizes the main sources of long-term and short-term external financing available to a business.

FIGURE 8.1   The Major External Sources of Financing

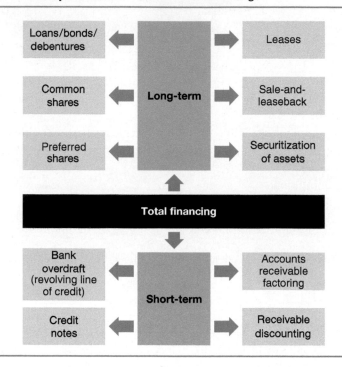

LONG-TERM SOURCES OF EXTERNAL FINANCING

The major sources of long-term external financing are:

- Common shares, including:
    - Warrants and options
- Preferred shares
- Debt financing, including:
    - Loans
    - Bonds and debentures
    - Mortgages
    - Foreign borrowing
    - Strip bonds
    - Convertible bonds
    - Leases
    - Sale-and-leaseback arrangements
    - Securitization of assets.

Common Shares

Common shares form the backbone of the financial structure of a business. Common share capital represents a business's risk capital. There is no fixed rate of dividend and common shareholders will receive a dividend only if profits available for distribution still remain after other investors (preferred shareholders and lenders) have received their returns in the form of dividend payments or interest. If the business is dissolved, the common shareholders will receive any proceeds from asset disposals only after lenders and creditors—and preferred shareholders—have received their entitlements. Because of the high risks associated with this form of investment, common shareholders will normally require the business to provide a comparatively high rate of return.

Although common shareholders have a limited loss liability, based on the amount they have invested, the potential returns from their investment are unlimited. This is because, after preferred shareholders and lenders have received their returns, all the remaining profits will go to the common shareholders. Thus, their downside risk is limited, whereas their upside potential is not. Common shareholders exercise control over the business through their voting rights. This gives them the power both to elect the directors and to remove them from office.

From the business's perspective, common shares can be a valuable form of financing because, at times, it is useful to be able to avoid paying a dividend, as illustrated in Activity 8.1.

ACTIVITY 8.1

Under what circumstances might a business find it useful to avoid paying a dividend?

Solution

Two circumstances spring to mind. An expanding business may prefer to retain funds in order to fuel future growth. A business in financial difficulty may need the funds to meet its operating costs and so may find paying a dividend a real burden.

Although a business financed by common shares can avoid making cash payments to shareholders when it is not prudent to do so, the market value of the shares may go down. The cost to the business of financing through common shares may become higher if shareholders feel uncertain about future dividends. It is also worth pointing out that the business does not obtain any tax relief on dividends paid to shareholders, whereas interest on debt is tax-deductible.

Warrants and Options

Holders of **warrants and stock options** have the right, but not the obligation, to acquire common shares in a business at a given price (the exercise price). In the case of both convertible bonds and warrants, the price at which shares may be acquired is usually higher than the market price of those common shares at the time of issue. The warrant will usually state the number of shares that the holder may purchase and the time limit within which the option to buy shares can be exercised. Occasionally, perpetual warrants are issued that have no set time limits. Warrants do not confer voting rights or entitle the holders to make any claims on the assets of the business. They are neither shares nor debt and represent a form of financial derivative. A **financial derivative** is any form of financial instrument—based on shares or bonds—that can be used by investors to increase their returns or reduce risk.

To the business issuing the warrants, they represent a source of funds (the proceeds of selling the warrants). However, they can also represent an incentive for investors to purchase bonds in a business. Share warrants are often provided as a sweetener to accompany the issue of bonds. The issue of warrants in this way may enable the business to offer lower rates of interest on the bond or to negotiate less restrictive loan conditions. Warrants enable investors to benefit from any future increases in the business's common share price, without having to buy the shares themselves. Activity 8.2 considers when warrants and options may be exercised.

ACTIVITY 8.2

Under what circumstances will the holders of warrants exercise their option to purchase?

Solution

Holders will exercise this option only if the market price of the shares exceeds the exercise price within the time limit specified. If the exercise price is higher than the market price, it will be cheaper for the investor to buy the shares in the market.

Because warrants often have an intrinsic value, they may be detachable, which means that they can be sold separately from the bond. The warrants of businesses whose shares are listed on a stock exchange are often themselves listed, providing a ready market for buying and selling the warrants.

Issuing warrants to lenders may be particularly useful for businesses that are considered to be relatively risky. Lenders in such businesses may feel that a new project offers them opportunities for loss but no real opportunity to participate in any upside potential from the risks undertaken. By receiving share warrants, lenders are given the opportunity to participate in future gains, which may make them more prepared to support risky projects.

Warrants have a leverage element, which means that changes in the value of the underlying shares can lead to a disproportionate change in value of the warrants. This makes them a speculative form of investment. To illustrate this leverage element, suppose that a share had a current market price of $2.50 and that an investor was able to exercise an immediate option to purchase a single share in the business at $2.00. The value of the warrant, in theory, would be $0.50 (that is, $2.50 − $2.00). Let us further suppose that the price of the share rose by 10% to $2.75 before the warrant option was exercised. The value of the warrant would now rise to $0.75 (that is, $2.75 − $2.00), which represents a 50% increase in value. The leverage is five-fold—a 10% increase in the share price results in a 50% increase in the warrant. This leverage effect can, of course, operate in the opposite direction as well.

Warrant holders become common shareholders by paying cash to the company for the shares. If the warrant holders hold bonds as well, then their status as lenders is unaffected by exercising their right to buy the shares bestowed by the warrant. Thus they become both common shareholders of and lenders to the business.

Preferred Shares

Preferred shares offer investors a lower level of risk than common shares. Provided there are sufficient profits available, preferred shares will normally be given a fixed rate of dividend each year and preferred dividends will be paid before common dividends are paid. If a business is dissolved, the claims of preferred shareholders may be given priority over those of common shareholders. (The business's particular documents of incorporation will state the precise rights of preferred shareholders in this respect.) Activity 8.3 compares the level of return associated with preferred shares to that of common shares.

ACTIVITY 8.3

Would you expect the returns to preferred shares to be higher or lower than those to common shares?

Solution

Because of the lower level of risk associated with preferred shares (preferred shareholders have priority over common shareholders regarding dividends, and sometimes capital repayment), investors will be offered a lower level of return than that normally expected by common shareholders.

Preferred shareholders are not usually given voting rights, although these may be granted where the preferred dividend is in arrears.

Various types of preferred shares may be issued. *Cumulative preferred shares* give investors the right to receive arrears of dividends that have arisen as a result of there being insufficient profits in previous periods. The unpaid amounts will accumulate and will be paid when sufficient profits have been generated. *Non-cumulative preferred shares* do not give investors this right. Thus, if a business is not in a position to pay the preferred dividend due for a particular period, the preferred shareholder loses the right to receive that dividend. *Participating preferred shares* give investors the right to a further share in the profits available for dividend after they have been paid their fixed rate and after common shareholders have been awarded a dividend. *Redeemable preferred shares* allow the business to buy back the *shares* from shareholders at some agreed future date. Redeemable preferred shares are seen as a lower-risk investment than non-redeemable shares and so tend to carry a lower dividend. A business can also issue redeemable common shares, but these are rare in practice. Activity 8.4 compares the market price volatility of common and preferred shares.

ACTIVITY 8.4

Which market price would you expect to be the more volatile: common shares or preferred shares? Why?

Solution

The dividends of preferred shares tend to be fairly stable over time, and there is usually an upper limit on the returns that can be received. As a result, the share price, which reflects the expected future returns from the share, will normally be less volatile than that of common shares.

Preferred share capital is similar to bonds insofar as both offer investors a fixed rate of return. In fact, relatively recent accounting pronouncements require preferred shares that are likely to be redeemed to be classified as liabilities on the balance sheet, rather than as shareholders' equity. However, preferred shares are a far less popular form of fixed-return capital than bonds. An important reason for this is that dividends paid to preferred shareholders are not deductible in the tax return of the business, whereas interest paid to lenders is deductible. From the perspective of the common shareholders, it is preferable for prior claims to be deductible for income tax purposes as this will leave a larger residual amount for them.

In Chapter 9, we shall look at the role of the stock exchange in raising funds from issuing shares and the methods used by larger businesses to make share issues.

Debt Financing

There are many forms of debt financing a business may undertake, as outlined in the following pages.

Loans

Most businesses rely on loans, as well as shares, to finance operations. Lenders enter into a contract with the business in which the rate of interest, dates of interest payments, capital repayments, and security for the loan are clearly stated. This means that if a business is successful, the lenders will not benefit from this success beyond the fact that their claim will become more secure. If, on the other hand, the business experiences financial difficulties, the lenders may receive less than the terms of their contract with the business.

The major risk facing those who invest in debt is that the business will default on interest payments and capital repayments. To protect themselves against this risk, lenders often seek some form of **security** from the business. This may take the form of assets pledged either by a **fixed charge** on particular assets held by the business, or a **floating charge**, which hangs over the whole of the business's assets. A floating charge will become fixed on particular assets in the event the business defaults on its obligations. Activity 8.5 explores the advantage of floating charges over fixed charges.

ACTIVITY 8.5

What do you think is the advantage for the business of having a floating charge rather than a fixed charge on its assets?

Solution

A floating charge on assets will allow the managers of the business greater flexibility in their day-to-day operations than a fixed charge. Assets can be sold without the permission of the lenders.

Not all assets will be acceptable to investors as a form of security. Assets to be pledged must normally be non-perishable, be capable of being sold easily, and be fairly high in value relative to their size. Land and buildings normally meet these criteria and so are often favoured by lenders. The availability of asset-based security means that lenders, in the event of default, have the right to seize the assets pledged and sell these in order to obtain the amount owing. Any amounts remaining from the proceeds of the sale, after the investors' claims have been satisfied, will be returned to the business.

Lenders may seek further protection through the use of **loan covenants**. These are obligations, or restrictions, on the business that form part of the loan contract. Such covenants may impose:

- The right of lenders to receive particular financial reports concerning the business
- An obligation to buy insurance on the assets that are offered as security
- A restriction on the right to incur further loans without prior permission of the existing lenders
- A restriction on the ability of the managers of the business to sell certain assets held
- A restriction on the level of dividend payments or level of payments made to directors
- Minimum acceptable levels of liquidity or maximum acceptable levels of leverage.

Any breach of these restrictive covenants can have serious consequences for the business; the lender may demand immediate repayment of the loan. REAL WORLD 8.1 provides an example of a restrictive covenant placed on a revolving line of credit for a well-known Canadian beverage company.

REAL WORLD 8.1

Cott's Restrictive Covenant

Cott Corporation, a large Canadian beverage company, has a revolving line of credit of up to $250 million. However, the amount it can borrow is based on the value of its accounts receivable, inventory, and fixed assets. At the end of 2008, Cott had borrowed $118.3 million of a possible $163.8 million based on those assets. This left an excess borrowing capacity of $45.5 million. However, a restrictive covenant states that the fixed charge coverage ratio must be at least 1.1 to 1 if the excess borrowing capacity falls to fewer than $30 million. Cott noted that if the excess borrowing capacity had dropped below $30 million, it would not have met the covenant's ratio requirement. In this event lenders could seize Cott's cash to pay down the line of credit debt.

Source: Cott Corp. 2008 Annual Report.

One common form of long-term loan is the **term loan**. This type of loan is offered by banks and other financial institutions, and is usually tailored to the needs of the client business. The amount of the loan, the time period, the repayment terms, and the interest payable are all open to negotiation and agreement, which can be very useful. For example, where all of the funds to be borrowed are not required immediately, a business may agree with the lender that funds are drawn only as and when required. This means that interest will be paid only on amounts drawn and the business will not have to pay interest on amounts borrowed that are temporarily surplus to requirements. Term loans tend to be inexpensive to set up (from the borrower business's perspective) and can be quite flexible as to conditions.

Bonds and Debentures

Bonds that are unsecured long-term loans are also known as **debentures**. These unsecured bonds are backed only by faith in the government's or corporation's ability to repay the loan. The federal, provincial, territorial, and other levels of government, as well as corporations, issue long-term bonds that are bought by individuals and other corporations as investments. Most bonds have a fixed maturity date, such as 10, 20, or 30 years, at which time the principal is returned and investors get their money back. In the meantime, investors receive interest payments, usually semi-annually.

As we saw in Chapter 5, bonds are very sensitive to interest rates, which in turn are affected by inflation. Rising interest rates cause the market price of all bonds to fall because the fixed coupon rates make the old bonds less valuable. Conversely, falling interest rates cause all existing bond prices to rise. So, bond prices rise and fall in a similar fashion to stock prices, although usually they are not as volatile.

Some bonds contain a call provision. This allows the corporation to call the bonds, usually after a suitable interval such as five years, and pay off the principal. Normally a call premium is associated with bonds having a call provision, so that investors receive an amount higher than the face value when the bond is called. The extra amount above face value is called a call premium. A retractable bond is similar, except in this case the retractable feature gives the investor the option of forcing the corporation to pay back the full principal of the bond, with the investor forgoing future interest payments. Bonds with callable and retractable features protect both the issuer and the investor from the vagaries of interest rate fluctuations by allowing early termination of the bond.

The use of security and loan covenants can significantly lower the risk to which lenders are exposed and may make the difference between a successful and an unsuccessful bond issue. They can also lower the cost of debt to the business as the required rate of return for lenders will vary according to the perceived level of risk of a business defaulting on its obligations.

It is possible for a business to issue bonds that are subordinated to (that is, ranked below) other outstanding bonds, similar to a second mortgage on a house. This means that holders of this form of debt will not receive interest payments or capital repayments until the claims of senior lenders (that is, lenders ranked above the subordinated lenders) have been satisfied. Any restrictive covenants imposed by senior lenders relating to the issue of further debt will often ignore the issue of **subordinated loans** as this should not pose a threat to their claims. Holders of subordinated bonds will normally expect to be compensated for the higher risks involved by a higher level of interest payment than that given to senior lenders.

The secondary bond market in Canada—where you can buy and sell bonds that have already been issued—is an over-the-counter (OTC) market of investment dealers and banks. There is no physical market for trading bonds, unlike the stock exchange for trading shares. Instead, brokers use computer networks to execute trades. Only convertible bonds are traded on the Toronto Stock Exchange (TSX). These are hybrid securities because they can be converted into shares at a given price or quantity at the bondholder's option. Because of their OTC nature, bond markets are likely not as efficient as stock markets. Often the spread between the bid price from a buyer and the ask price or offer price from a seller is relatively large compared to spreads for shares in the stock market, especially for the small, individual retail investor. Consequently, small retail investors may prefer to invest in bonds through a mutual fund or an exchange-traded fund.

Mortgages

A **mortgage** is a form of loan that is secured on an asset, typically property. Financial institutions such as banks, insurance businesses, and pension funds are often prepared to lend to businesses on this basis. The mortgage may be over a long period (20 years or more).

Foreign Borrowing

Companies are not restricted to borrowing in Canada. They can choose to borrow in places like the United States, the United Kingdom, or the European Union. Foreign borrowing introduces another risk factor—currency exchange risk. As we saw in Chapter 7, foreign borrowing can become very expensive when the Canadian dollar declines in value relative to the foreign currency. As discussed there, a way to mitigate the risk is to implement a hedging policy for all foreign currency borrowings. Using this strategy, a firm acquires a forward contract on the date the loan was initiated at a locked-in exchange rate for the amount of foreign currency needed to repay the loan or bond. Thus, there are no exchange rate surprises.

In the last few years, especially since the 30% foreign ownership limitations were lifted for the big Canadian pension funds as well as for registered retirement savings plans (RRSPs), many foreign firms have looked to Canada to meet their borrowing needs. These "maple bonds" are denominated in Canadian dollars and sold by foreign companies to Canadians. European companies have found this idea attractive because Canada has very low interest rates, having run a federal government surplus for a number of years, and the euro has been appreciating against the Canadian dollar. So, foreign firms save two ways—once on interest rates and again on the euro appreciation.

Eurobonds are unsecured bonds issued by listed businesses (and other large organizations) in various countries, and the funds are raised internationally. Despite their name, eurobonds are not always denominated in euros. A Canadian business may issue a eurobond that is denominated in U.S. dollars. (It is quite common for eurobonds to be issued in U.S. dollars, although they may also be issued in other major currencies.) They are bearer bonds (that is, the owner of the bond is not registered and the holder of the bond certificate is regarded as the owner) and interest is normally paid (without tax deductions) annually.

Eurobonds are part of an emerging international capital market and they are not subject to regulations imposed by authorities in particular countries. This may explain, in part, the fact that the cost of servicing eurobonds is usually lower than the cost of servicing similar domestic bonds. Numerous financial institutions throughout the world have created a market for eurobonds, where holders of eurobonds are able to sell them to buyers. Eurobonds are usually issued by businesses to large banks and other financial institutions, which may either retain them as an investment or sell them to their clients.

The extent of borrowing by Canadian businesses in foreign currencies has expanded greatly in recent years. Businesses are often attracted to eurobonds because of the size of the international capital market. Access to a large number of international investors is likely to increase the chances of a successful financing. In addition, the lack of regulation in the eurobond market means that national restrictions regarding loans may be overcome. REAL WORLD 8.2 provides an example of foreign borrowing by several well-known Canadian businesses.

Foreign Borrowing by Canadian Companies

Many Canadian companies have diversified their borrowing over the years, especially by accessing the U.S. credit markets and/or issuing eurobond debt. The following table shows the range of foreign borrowing by well-known Canadian firms:

Company	Long-Term Debt Percentage In Foreign Currency
Encana (US$)	75
Torstar (US$)	18
Canadian National Railway (US$)	81
Loblaw (US$)	16

By accessing foreign credit markets, companies can lower their cost of capital and reach new investors. Diversifying the investor base is important to companies, as it increases their flexibility when they need to raise capital.

However, by taking on foreign denominated debt, companies must also manage the currency risk. It would be unwise to have significant U.S. dollar debt when the Canadian dollar is declining in value. The firm would have to pay an increasing amount in Canadian dollars, which would buy less and less in U.S. dollars, just to keep up with the interest payments, not to mention the actual debt retirement problem at maturity. As noted previously, many companies attempt to reduce risk by hedging their exposure to foreign currency exchange rate fluctuations.

Source: Various 2008 annual reports.

Activity 8.6 compares the return on bonds to that of preferred shares. The risk/return characteristics of bond, preferred share, and common share financing are shown graphically in Figure 8.2.

ACTIVITY 8.6

Both bonds and preferred shares provide fixed returns to investors. Would you expect the bond returns to be higher or lower than the preferred share returns?

Solution

Investors will normally view bonds as being less risky than preferred shares. Lenders have priority over any claims from preferred shareholders, and will usually have security for their loans. As a result of the lower level of risk associated with bonds, investors are usually prepared to accept a lower rate of return.

FIGURE 8.2   The Risk/Return Characteristics of Long-Term Sources of Financing

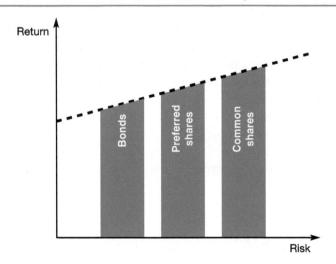

The higher the level of risk, the higher the expected returns from investors will be.

Strip Bonds

A business may issue bonds at a discount to their face value. Thus, a business may issue bonds at $80 for every $100 of nominal value. These are referred to as **zero coupon bonds** or **strip bonds** as the coupons have been stripped away from the bond. *Strip bonds* also refers to normal bonds where the coupons have been stripped and are sold separately from the bond itself, which thus becomes the strip bond. Although buyers will receive no interest during the period of the loan, they will receive a gain when the bond is finally redeemed at the full $100. The yield to maturity (as it is referred to) is often quite high and, when calculated on an annual basis, may compare favourably with returns from other forms of bonds with the same level of risk. Furthermore, strip bonds eliminate the reinvestment problem of what to do with the semi-annual interest receipts. The yield to maturity is locked in until the bond matures.

Strip bonds may have particular appeal to businesses with short-term cash flow problems. They receive an immediate injection of cash and there are no significant cash outflows associated with the bond until the maturity date. From an investment perspective, the situation is reversed. Strip bonds are likely to appeal to investors who do not have short-term cash flow needs since the return is received on maturity of the loan. However, strip bonds can often be traded if required, which will not affect the borrower but will enable the investor to obtain cash.

Convertible Bonds

A **convertible bond** (or debenture) gives an investor the right to convert the bond into common shares at a given future date and at a specified price. The investor remains a lender to the business and will receive interest on the amount of the loan until such time as the conversion takes place. The investor is not obliged to convert the bond or debenture to common shares. This will be done only if the market price of the shares at the conversion date exceeds the agreed conversion price.

An investor may find this form of investment a useful hedge against risk (that is, it can reduce the level of risk). This may be particularly useful when investment in a new business is being considered. If the business is successful, the investor can then decide to convert the investment into common shares.

There is a difference in status within a business between holders of a convertible bond and holders of a bond with share warrants attached if both groups decide to exercise their right to convert. Convertible bondholders become common shareholders and are no longer lenders to the business. They will have used the value of the bond to buy the shares. As noted earlier, a holder of a bond with warrants attached becomes both a common shareholder and a bondholder once the warrants are exercised.

A business may also find this form of financing useful. If the business is successful, the bond becomes self-liquidating as investors will exercise their option to convert and there will be no redemption costs. The business may also be able to offer a lower rate of interest to investors because they expect future benefits to arise from the conversion However, there will be some dilution of control and possibly a dilution of earnings for existing shareholders if holders of convertible loans exercise their option to convert.

REAL WORLD 8.3 sets out details of one particular convertible loan issue.

REAL WORLD 8.3   AECON Issues Convertible Debt

AECON Group Inc., Canada's largest publicly traded construction company, announced in September 2009, that it would issue $150 million of convertible debentures. The debentures bear an annual 7% interest rate, with interest paid semi-annually and can be converted into common shares at a price of $19 per share. Two days later the shares traded at $11.55, so the share price needs to appreciate significantly for the conversion feature to come into play. The shares last traded at $19 in January 2008.

Source: AECON website at: www.aecon.com/News_Releases/news09080901.aspx.

Measuring the Riskiness of Bonds   A number of credit rating agencies—including DBRS, Moody's Investor Services, and Standard and Poor's Corporation (S&P)—rate bonds issued by businesses by categories according to the level of default risk: the lower the risk of default, the higher the rating category assigned to the bond. The ratings used by the leading agencies are very similar and are described in **REAL WORLD 8.4**. To arrive at an appropriate bond rating, an agency will rely on the use of both published and unpublished information, interviews with key executives, and visits to the business's premises. The rating classification assigned to the bond will be derived from an assessment of all the relevant information obtained.

Debt Rating Categories by Various Debt-Rating Agencies

A number of other ratings services are available. The following chart gives equivalent ratings for different rating services.

Equivalent Credit Ratings

Credit Risk	Moody's*	Standard & Poor's**	Fitch IBCA**	DBRS***
INVESTMENT GRADE				
Highest quality	Aaa	AAA	AAA	AAA
High quality (very strong)	Aa	AA	AA	AA
Upper medium grade (strong)	A	A	A	A
Medium grade	Baa	BBB	BBB	BBB
NOT INVESTMENT GRADE				
Lower medium grade (somewhat speculative)	Ba	BB	BB	BB
Low grade (speculative)	B	B	B	B
Poor quality (may default)	Caa	CCC	CCC	CCC
Most speculative	Ca	CC	CC	CC
No interest being paid or bankruptcy petition filed	C	C	C	C
In default	C	D	D	D

*The ratings from Aa to Ca by Moody's may be modified by the addition of a 1, 2, or 3 to show relative standing within the category.

**The ratings from AA to CC by Standard & Poor's and Fitch IBCA may be modified by the addition of a plus or minus sign to show relative standing within the category.

***The ratings from AA to CC by DBRS may be modified by the addition of an h, m, or l (high, middle, low) to show relative standing within the category.

Sources: Securities Industry and Financial Markets Association (SIFMA), www.investinginbonds.com/learnmore.asp?catid= 46&id=8, accessed August 6, 2007; and DBRS, www.dbrs.com/intnlweb/jsp/common/infoPage.faces, accessed February 13, 2007.

Once the bonds have been assigned to a particular category, they will tend to remain in that category unless there is a significant change in circumstances.

Junk Bonds (High-Yield Bonds)   As noted above, bonds in any of the first four categories identified in Real World 8.4 are generally considered to be of high quality (investment grade), and some financial institutions are restricted by their rules to

ACTIVITY 8.7

Does it really matter if the bonds of a business are downgraded to junk bond status?

Solution

A downgrade to junk bond status is usually regarded as serious because it may well increase the cost of capital, especially for future borrowing. Investors are likely to seek higher returns to compensate for the perceived increase in default risk.

investing only in these bond categories. Bonds rated below these first four categories are often rather disparagingly called **junk bonds**. In many cases, junk bonds initially had a high rating but, because the business suffered misfortune, were downgraded. Activity 8.7 discusses the significance of a downgrade to junk bond status.

REAL WORLD 8.5 describes the effect that bond downgrades can have on an investor.

Manulife Hurt by Others' Downgrades

Manulife, Canada's largest insurance company, expected to take a $250 million write-off in its third quarter, 2008, financial statements. Fifty million dollars of this was a reserve for losses resulting from credit downgrades on bonds and other investment assets it owns. When a ratings agency downgrades a company's debt, the bonds fall in price because of the greater risk of default. Since Manulife is the investor, it incurred losses on these investments. On August 5, 2010 Manulife reported a $2.4 billion loss for its second quarter. Although its product lines were profitable, its investments generated non-cash charges of $1.7 billion from stock market declines and $1.5 billion from interest rate declines affecting its bond portfolio.

Source: CBC News.ca, www.cbc.ca/money/story/2008/10/13/manulife-loss.html, accessed September 11, 2009 and www.cbc.ca/money/ story/2010/08/05/manulife-earnings.html, accessed September 21, 2010.

In addition to increasing the cost of capital, a downgrade to junk bond status can adversely affect business relationships. REAL WORLD 8.6 lists dividend cuts some Canadian companies made in 2009.

Dividend Cuts in 2009

Listed below are some Canadian companies that cut their dividend payments to conserve cash in 2009 as a way of coping with the severe recession.

Company	% Dividend Cut	Date Cut Announced
Manulife	50%	August 6, 2009
Biovail Corp.	76%	May 6, 2009
Russel Metals	44%	February 23, 2009
Torstar	50%	February 26, 2009

Source: various CBC.ca stories: www.cbc.ca/money/story/2009/08/06/manulife-dividend-earnings.html, accessed September 11, 2009.

Not all junk bonds start life as investment-grade securities. Since the 1980s, bonds with an initial low rating have been issued by some American businesses. These types of bonds provide investors with high interest rates to compensate for the high level of default risk. Businesses that issue junk bonds are usually less financially stable than those offering investment-grade bonds, and may offer lower levels of security and weaker bond covenants than those normally associated with standard bond agreements. As junk bonds provide relatively high levels of returns to investors, they are also referred to as **high-yield bonds**.

Junk bonds, or high-yield bonds, became very popular in the United States as they allowed some businesses to raise funds that were not available from other sources. Within a fairly short space of time, a market for this form of debt developed. Although junk bonds are used by many businesses to finance everyday needs (such as investment in inventory, receivables, and non-current assets), they came to the attention of the public through their use in financing hostile takeovers. In some cases, a small business would take on very high levels of debt through the use of junk bonds in order to finance a takeover of a larger business. Once the takeover was achieved, non-core assets of the larger business would often be sold off in order to repay the junk bondholders.

The European market for junk bonds is approximately one-tenth the size of the U.S. market. Perhaps this is because European investors tend to view common shares as a high-risk/high-return investment, and view bonds as a form of low-risk/low-return investment. Junk bonds are a hybrid form of investment, lying somewhere between common shares and conventional bonds.

Activity 8.8 considers how businesses decide between preferred shares and debt.

ACTIVITY 8.8

We have considered two major forms of long-term financing: preferred shares and debt (usually bonds). Both forms of financing require the business to provide a particular rate of return to investors. What are the factors that may be taken into account by a business when deciding between these two sources of funds?

Solution

The main factors are as follows:

- Preferred shares have a higher rate of return than bonds. From the investors' point of view, preferred shares are more risky. The amount invested cannot be secured and the return is paid after the returns paid to lenders.
- A business has a legal obligation to pay interest and make capital repayments on bonds at the agreed dates. It will usually make every effort to meet its obligations, as failure to do so can have serious consequences, as mentioned earlier. Failure to pay a preferred dividend, on the other hand, is less important. There is no legal obligation to pay if profits are not available for distribution. Although failure to pay a preferred dividend may prove embarrassing for the business, and may make it difficult to persuade investors to buy future preferred share issues, the preferred shareholders will have no redress against the business if there are insufficient profits to pay the dividend due.
- It was mentioned earlier that interest on loans is allowed to be deducted from profits for taxation purposes, whereas preferred dividends cannot be deducted. As a result, the cost of capital for bonds is usually much less than the cost of capital for preferred shares.
- The issuance of bonds may result in the management of a business having to accept some restrictions on its freedom of action. Bonds often contain covenants that can be onerous. However, no such restrictions can be imposed by preferred shareholders.

Public Issues of Common Shares, Preferred Shares, and Bonds REAL WORLD 8.7 provides a graphical representation of the relative importance of the principal types of securities: common shares and preferred shares are compared to bonds.

REAL WORLD 8.7

New Financing by Canadian Businesses

Figure 8.3 plots annual dollar amounts of bonds and shares issued in Canada in recent years. Over that period companies have generally issued more debt than equity.

FIGURE 8.3 Financing by Canadian Corporations, 2004–2009

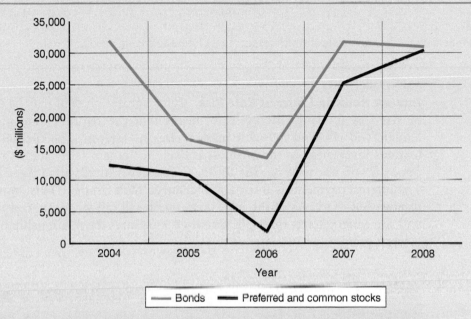

Source: Adapted from the Statistics Canada website: www40.statcan.ca/l01/cst01/fin34.htm, accessed September 11, 2009.

SELF-ASSESSMENT QUESTION 8.1

You are employed as a manager at a consulting firm that provides advice to small and medium-sized companies on how to manage their financing needs. The following three companies, which have similar balance sheets, have asked for your advice.

Balance Sheets
as at December 31, 2010
(in $ millions)

	Oak Ltd.	Elm Ltd.	Birch Ltd.
Assets			
Current assets	20	10	10
Property, plant, and equipment	40	55	50
Total assets	60	65	60

Current liabilities	5	5	10
Long-term liabilities	45	30	10
Total liabilities	50	35	20
Shareholders' equity			
Common shares	2	22	10
Retained earnings	8	8	30
Total shareholders' equity	10	30	40
Total liabilities and shareholders' equity	60	65	60

Required:

Provide recommendations for each company with respect to its future financing needs.

Interest Rates and Interest Rate Risk   Interest rates on debt may be either floating or fixed. A **floating interest rate** means that the required rate of return from lenders will rise and fall with market rates of interest. The market value of the lender's investment in the business is likely to remain fairly stable over time. The opposite will normally be true for loans and debentures with a **fixed interest rate**. The interest payments will remain unchanged with rises and falls in market rates of interest but the value of the loan investment will fall when interest rates rise, and will rise when interest rates fall. Activity 8.9 explores the relationship between fixed-interest bond value and interest rates.

ACTIVITY 8.9

Why do you think the value of fixed-interest bonds will rise and fall with rises and falls in interest rates?

Solution

Recall from Chapter 5 calculations that investors will be prepared to pay less for a bond that pays a rate of interest below the market rate of interest and will be prepared to pay more for a bond that pays a rate of interest above the market rate of interest.

Movements in interest rates can be a significant issue for businesses that have high levels of borrowing. A business with a floating rate of interest may find that interest rate rises will place real strains on cash flows and profitability. Conversely, a business that has a fixed rate of interest will find that, when interest rates are falling, it will not enjoy the benefits of lower interest charges. To reduce or eliminate these risks, a business may enter into a **hedging arrangement**. This is an attempt to reduce or eliminate risk by taking some form of counteraction in the same manner that forward contracts attempt to hedge foreign currency exchange rate risk, as we saw earlier.

To hedge against the risk of interest rate movements, various devices may be used. One popular device is the **interest rate swap**: an arrangement between two businesses whereby each business assumes responsibility for the other's interest payments. Typically, it involves a business with a floating interest rate loan swapping interest payment obligations with a business with a fixed interest rate loan. A swap agreement can be undertaken through direct negotiations with another business, but it is usually easier to negotiate through a bank or other financial intermediary. Although there is an agreement to swap interest payments, the legal responsibility for these payments will still rest with the business that entered into the original loan agreement. Thus, the borrowing business may continue to make interest payments to the lender in line with the loan agreement. However, at the end of an agreed period, the two parties to the swap agreement will make a compensating cash adjustment between themselves.

A swap agreement can be a useful hedging device where there are different views concerning future movements in interest rates. For example, a business with a floating rate agreement may believe that interest rates are going to rise, whereas a business with a fixed rate agreement may believe that interest rates are going to fall. However, swap agreements may also be used to exploit imperfections in the capital markets. It is sometimes the case that one business has an advantage over another when negotiating interest rates for a fixed loan agreement, but would prefer a floating loan agreement, whereas the other business is in the opposite position. When this occurs, both businesses can benefit from a swap agreement.

REAL WORLD 8.8 describes an interest rate swap that subsequent events showed was unnecessary.

REAL WORLD 8.8

Telus Tries to Swap Out of a Risk

Telus Corporation, a major Vancouver-based telecommunications company, has 8% US$1.9 billion notes due in 2011. Telus entered into a cross-currency interest rate swap agreement to convert these notes effectively to an 8.493% fixed interest rate and a fixed exchange rate of 1US$ = 1.5327C$. In retrospect, this financial manoeuvre appears to have backfired as the Canadian prime interest rate stands at 0.5% and the U.S. dollar exchange rate is around C$1.08 at the time of writing. Telus would have been better off not hedging this risk.

Source: Telus 2008 Annual Report.

Leases

Instead of buying an asset (such as a piece of equipment) directly from a supplier, a business may arrange for another business (typically a financial institution such as a bank) to buy it and then **lease** it to the business. The business that purchases the asset and leases it out is known as the *lessor* and the business that leases the asset is known as the *lessee.*

A lease is in essence a form of lending, because had the lessee borrowed the funds and then used them to buy the asset itself, the effect would have been much the same. The lessee would have use of the asset but would also have a financial obligation to the lender—just as with a leasing arrangement.

Although, with leasing, legal ownership of the asset remains with the financial institution (the lessor), a lease agreement transfers to the user (the lessee) virtually all the rewards and risks that are associated with the item being leased. The lease agreement covers a significant part of the life of the item being leased and, often, cannot be cancelled. In accounting terms, a capital lease would appear on both sides of the lessee's balance sheet—as both a long-term asset and a long-term liability—for an amount equal to the present value of the lease payments. REAL WORLD 8.9 gives an example of the use of leasing by ACE Aviation, the parent company of Air Canada.

REAL WORLD 8.9

Leasing Aircraft at ACE Aviation

Many airlines use leasing to acquire new airplanes. ACE Aviation leased 41 airplanes. The net amount capitalized for the leased aircraft on ACE's balance sheet was almost $1.32 billion. WestJet, by comparison, leases 24 aircraft. This has a value of $645 million, but for technical accounting reasons it does not appear on the balance sheet.

Source: Air Canada and WestJet 2008 annual reports.

A lease may sometimes be an **operating lease**, where the rewards and risks of ownership stay with the owner (the lessor) and where the lease is short-term. An example of an operating lease is where a builder rents some earth-moving equipment for a week.

Leasing is popular for many reasons, including:

- *Ease of borrowing.*   Leasing may be arranged more easily than other forms of long-term financing. A lessor may be prepared to lease assets to a new business without a track record if the lessor retains ownership or can use the leased assets as security for the amounts owing.
- *Cost.*   Leasing agreements may be offered at reasonable cost. As the asset leased is used as security, standard lease arrangements can be applied and detailed credit checking of lessees may be unnecessary.
- *Flexibility.*   Leasing can help provide flexibility where there are rapid changes in technology. If an option to cancel can be incorporated into the lease, the business can avoid the risk of obsolescence.
- *Cash flows.*   Leasing means that large cash outflows can be avoided. In some cases, it is possible to arrange for low lease payments to be made in the early years of the asset's life, when cash inflows may be low, and for these to increase over time as the asset generates positive cash flows.

REAL WORLD 8.10 shows the importance of lease financing over recent years.

REAL WORLD 8.10

Leasing in Canada

Figure 8.4 charts the growth in lease financing by Canadian businesses. Leasing has steadily grown in Canada over the past five years, despite both GM and Chrysler stopping their leasing programs due to the severe recession.

▶

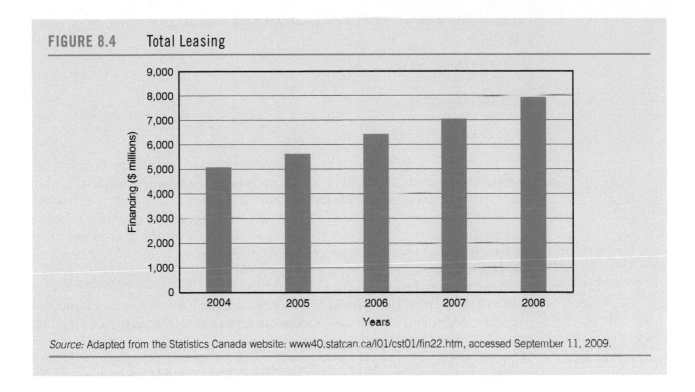

FIGURE 8.4   Total Leasing

Source: Adapted from the Statistics Canada website: www40.statcan.ca/l01/cst01/fin22.htm, accessed September 11, 2009.

Sale-and-Leaseback Arrangements

A **sale-and-leaseback arrangement** involves a business raising funds by selling an asset to a financial institution. The sale is accompanied by an agreement to lease the asset back to the business to allow it to continue to use the asset. The lease payment is a business expense that is allowable against profits for taxation purposes.

A corporation's head office building is often the asset that is the subject of such an arrangement. When this is the case, there are usually rent reviews at regular intervals throughout the period of the lease, and the amounts payable in future years may be difficult to predict. At the end of the lease agreement, the business must either try to renew the lease or find alternative premises. Although the sale of the premises will result in an immediate injection of cash for the business, it will lose benefits from any future capital appreciation on the property. Where a capital gain arises on the sale of the premises to the financial institution, a liability for taxation may also arise.

A sale-and-leaseback agreement can be used to help a business focus on its core competencies.

Securitization

Securitization involves bundling together illiquid financial or physical assets of the same type in order to provide backing for issuing interest-bearing securities, such as bonds. This financing method was first used by U.S. banks, which bundled together residential mortgage loans in order to provide asset backing for the issue of bonds to investors. (Mortgage loans held by a bank are financial assets that offer future benefits to the bank in the form of interest receivable.) The bonds issued were considered to be low-risk as they were also backed by a guarantee from the bank. It was therefore possible for a bank to offer lower rates of interest on the bonds issued than the interest accruing to the mortgage loans that provided the asset backing.

Securitization has now spread beyond the banking industry and has become an important source of financing for businesses in a wide range of industries. Future benefits from a variety of illiquid assets are now used as backing for bond issues, including:

- Credit card receipts
- Rental income from university accommodation
- Ticket sales for sports teams
- Royalties from music copyright
- Consumer installment contracts.

The effect of securitization is to capitalize the claims to these future benefits. This capitalized amount is then sold to investors, through the financial markets, to raise funds for the business holding the claims.

Securitized assets tend to be of good quality with regular and predictable income streams. To reassure investors, however, the assets offered may be higher in value than the securities issued (known as *overcollateralization*) or some form of credit insurance may be available from a third party, such as a bank.

In addition to being a useful source of financing, a securitization issue may be used to help manage risk. Where, for example, a bank has lent large amounts to a particular industry sector, it can reduce its exposure to the sector by bundling together some of the outstanding loan contracts and making a securitization issue. However, risks were underestimated for the U.S. sub-prime mortgage market and the asset-backed commercial paper (ABCP) markets in Canada, which caused large losses for investors in 2007, and led to a recession.

SHORT-TERM SOURCES OF EXTERNAL FINANCING

A short-term source of borrowing is one that is available for a short time period (less than one year).

Bank Overdrafts

A **bank overdraft** (or a revolving line of credit) enables a business to maintain a negative bank account balance. It represents a very flexible form of borrowing as (subject to bank approval) the size of an overdraft can be increased or decreased according to the financing requirements of the business. It is relatively inexpensive to arrange and interest rates are often very competitive. The rate of interest charged on an overdraft will vary, however, according to how creditworthy the bank perceives the customer to be. It is also fairly easy to arrange—sometimes all that is needed is a telephone call. In view of these advantages, it is not surprising that this is an extremely popular form of short-term financing.

Banks prefer to grant overdrafts that are self-liquidating; that is, the funds applied will result in cash inflows that will extinguish the overdraft balance. The banks may ask for forecast cash flow statements from the business to see when the overdraft will be repaid and how much funds are required. The bank may also require some form of security on amounts advanced.

One potential drawback with this form of financing is that it is repayable on demand. This may pose problems for a business that is illiquid. However, many businesses operate for many years using an overdraft. This form of borrowing, though in theory regarded as short-term, can often become a long-term source of financing.

Credit Notes

A **credit note** is similar, in some respects, to an IOU ("I owe you"). It is a written agreement that is addressed by one person to another, requiring the payer to pay a particular amount at some future date. Credit notes are offered by a buyer to a supplier in exchange for goods. The supplier who accepts the credit note may either keep it until the date the payment is due (this is usually between 60 and 180 days after the note is first drawn up) or may present it to a bank for payment. The bank will usually be prepared to pay the supplier the face value of the note, less a discount, and will then collect the full amount of the note from the buyer at the specified payment date. The advantage of using a credit note is that it allows the buyer to delay payment for the goods purchased but provides the supplier with an opportunity to receive immediate payment from a bank if required. Nowadays, credit notes are not widely used for transactions within Canada, but they are still used for overseas transactions.

Accounts Receivable Factoring

Accounts receivable factoring is a service offered by a financial institution known as a factor. Many of the large factors are subsidiaries of commercial banks. Receivables factoring involves the factor taking over the invoicing and accounts receivable collection for a business. In addition to operating normal credit control procedures, a factor may offer to undertake credit investigations and advise on the creditworthiness of customers. It may also offer protection for approved credit sales. Two main forms of factoring agreement exist:

- *Recourse factoring,* where the factor assumes no responsibility for bad debts arising from credit sales.
- *Non-recourse factoring,* where, for an additional fee, the factor assumes responsibility for bad debts up to an agreed amount.

The factor is usually prepared to make an advance to the business of around 80% of approved accounts receivable. This advance is usually paid immediately after the goods have been supplied to the customer. The balance of the receivable, less any deductions for fees and interest, will be paid after an agreed period or when the receivable is collected. The charge made for the factoring service is often around 2–3% of the total factored accounts receivables. Any advances made to the business by the factor will attract a rate of interest similar to the rate charged on bank overdrafts.

Receivables factoring is, in effect, outsourcing the accounts receivable to a specialist subcontractor. Many businesses find a factoring arrangement very convenient. It can result in savings in credit management and can create more certain cash flows. It can also release the time of key personnel for more profitable ends. This may be extremely important for smaller businesses that rely on the talent and skills of a few key individuals. However, there is a possibility that some will see a factoring arrangement as an indication that the business is experiencing financial difficulties. For this reason, some businesses try to conceal the factoring arrangement by collecting outstanding debts on behalf of the factor.

Not all businesses will find factoring arrangements the answer to their financing problems. Factoring agreements may not be possible to arrange for very small businesses (those with sales of less than $100,000) because of the high set-up costs. In addition, businesses engaged in certain sectors (such as retailers or building contractors, where trade disputes are part of the business culture) may find that factoring arrangements are simply not available.

Figure 8.5 shows the factoring process.

FIGURE 8.5   The Factoring Process

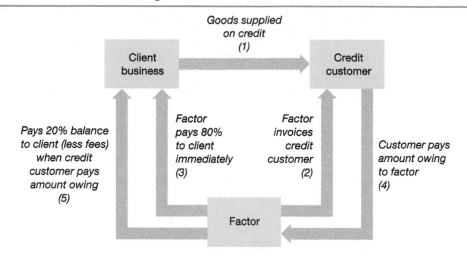

The figure shows the three main parties to the factoring agreement. The client business will sell goods on credit and the factor will take responsibility for invoicing the customer and collecting the amount owing. The factor will then pay the client business the invoice amount, less fees and interest, in two stages. The first stage represents 80% of the invoice value and will be paid immediately after the goods have been delivered to the customer. The second stage will represent the balance outstanding and will usually be paid when the customer has paid the factor the amount owing.

Source: After McLaney and Atrill (2004), Fig. 15.6.

When considering a factoring agreement, the costs and likely benefits arising must be identified and carefully weighed. Example 8.1 illustrates how this may be done.

Example 8.1

Mayo Computers Ltd. has annual sales of $20 million before taking into account bad debts of $0.1 million. All sales made by the business are on credit and, at present, credit terms are negotiable by the customer. On average, the collection period for accounts receivable is 60 days. The business is currently reviewing its credit policies to see whether more efficient and profitable methods could be used.

Mayo is considering whether it should factor its accounts receivable. The accounts receivables department has recently approached a factoring business, which has agreed to provide an advance equivalent to 80% of the receivables (where the accounts receivable figure is based on an average collection period of 40 days) at an interest rate of 12%. The factoring business will undertake collection of the receivables and will charge a fee of 2% of receivables for this service. The factoring service is also expected to eliminate bad debts and will lead to credit administration savings of $90,000. The collection period for receivables will be reduced to an average of 40 days, which is equivalent to that of Mayo's major competitors.

Mayo currently has an overdraft of $4.8 million at an interest rate of 14% a year. The bank has recently written to the business, stating that it would like to see a reduction in this overdraft.

In evaluating the factoring arrangement, it is useful to begin by considering the cost of the existing arrangements:

Existing Arrangements

	($000)
Bad debts written off each year	100
Interest cost of average receivables outstanding	
[($20 million × 60/365) × 14%]	460
Total cost	560

The cost of the factoring arrangement can now be compared with the above:

Factoring Arrangement

	($000)
Factoring fee ($20 million × 2%)	400
Interest on factor loan (assuming 80% advance	
(80% × $20 m = $16 m) and reduction in average	
credit period) [($16 million × 40/365) × 12%]	210
Interest on overdraft (remaining 20% of receivables	
[20% × $20 m = $4 m] financed in this way)	
[($4 million × 40/365) × 14%]	61
	671
Less: Savings in credit administration	90
Cost of factoring	581

The above calculations show that the net additional cost of factoring for the business would be $21,000 (i.e., $581,000 – $560,000). So, Mayo would be better off to continue with the existing arrangements.

SELF-ASSESSMENT QUESTION   8.2

Sudbury Shoes Limited (SSL) is considering factoring its accounts receivable to improve its cash flow. Shortfalls in collecting the receivables are met by a short-term revolving line of credit. The controller has gathered the following data to help make the decision:

Annual credit sales	$2,000,000
Average collection period	30 days
Industry average collection period	15 days
Average annual bad debt write-offs	$20,000
Revolving line of credit financing charge	8%
Factor data:	
Advance on accounts receivable	90%
Collection fee on credit sales	3.0%
Collection period assumption:	
Industry average collection period	15 days
Interest rate	6%
Annual bad debt write-offs	$2,000
Administrative savings	$20,000

Required:

(a) Calculate the cost of SSL's continuing to collect its own accounts receivable.
(b) Calculate the cost of SSL's factoring the accounts receivable.
(c) What would you suggest that SSL do?

Receivables Discounting

Receivables discounting involves a business approaching a factor or other financial institution for a loan based on a proportion of the face value of accounts receivable outstanding. If the institution agrees, the amount advanced is usually 75–80% of the value of the approved receivables outstanding. The business must agree to repay the advance within a relatively short period—perhaps 60 or 90 days. The responsibility for collecting the accounts receivable outstanding remains with the business and repayment of the advance is not dependent on the receivables being collected. Receivables discounting will not result in such a close relationship developing between the business and the financial institution as occurs with factoring. It may be a one-time arrangement, whereas factoring usually involves a longer-term arrangement between the client and the financial institution.

Nowadays, receivables discounting is a much more important source of funds to businesses than factoring. There are three main reasons for this.

- It is a confidential form of financing about which the business's customers will know nothing.
- The service charge for receivables discounting is only about 0.2–0.3% of receivables, compared to 2.0–3.0% of receivables for factoring.
- Many businesses are unwilling to relinquish control of their customers' records. Customers are an important resource of the business and many businesses wish to retain control over all aspects of their relationship with their customers.

Factoring and invoice discounting are forms of **asset-based financing**, as the accounts receivable asset is used as security for the cash advances received by the business.

L.O. 2　CHOOSING AN APPROPRIATE SOURCE OF FINANCING

Having decided that some form of borrowing is required to finance the business, managers must then decide whether long-term borrowing or short-term borrowing is more appropriate. Some of the many issues that should be taken into account when making this decision are described below.

Matching

The business may attempt to match the type of borrowing with the nature of the assets held. Thus, long-term borrowing might finance assets that form part of the permanent operating base of the business, including property, plant, and equipment and a certain level of current assets. This leaves assets held for a short period (such as current assets required to meet seasonal increases in demand) to be financed by short-term borrowing, because short-term borrowing tends to be more flexible in that funds can be raised and repaid at short notice. Figure 8.6 shows this funding division graphically and Activity 8.10 considers different alternatives.

Flexibility

Short-term borrowing may be a useful means of postponing a commitment to take on a long-term loan. This may be seen as desirable if interest rates are high and it is

FIGURE 8.6   Short-Term and Long-Term Financing Requirements

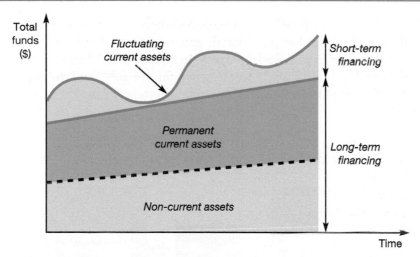

Source: After McLaney and Atrill (2004), Fig. 15.8.

ACTIVITY 8.10

Some businesses may have a less cautious financing position than shown in Figure 8.6, and others may have a more cautious one. How would the diagram differ under each of these options?

Solution

A less cautious position would mean relying on short-term financing to help fund part of the permanent capital base, so the arrow labelled *short-term financing* would expand downwards. A more cautious position would mean relying on long-term financing to help fund the fluctuating assets of the business, so the arrow labelled *long-term financing* would expand upwards.

---

forecast that they will fall in the future. Short-term borrowing does not usually incur penalties if there is early repayment of the amount outstanding, whereas some form of financial penalty may be levied if long-term loans are repaid early.

Renewal Risk

Short-term borrowing has to be renewed more frequently than long-term borrowing. This may create problems for the business if it is already in financial difficulties or if there is a shortage of funds available for lending.

Interest Rates

Interest payable on long-term financing is often higher than for short-term financing, as lenders require a higher return where their funds are locked up for a long period. This fact may make short-term borrowing a more attractive source of funds for a business. However, there may be other costs associated with borrowing (arrangement fees, for example) that need to be taken into account. The more frequently that borrowings must be renewed, the higher these costs will be.

L.O.3
INTERNAL SOURCES OF FINANCING

In addition to external sources of financing, there are certain internal sources of financing that a business may use to generate funds for particular activities. These sources usually have the advantage of being relatively flexible. They may also be obtained quickly—particularly working capital sources—and do not require the permission of other parties. The main sources of internal funds are summarized in Figure 8.7.

FIGURE 8.7   Major Internal Sources of Financing

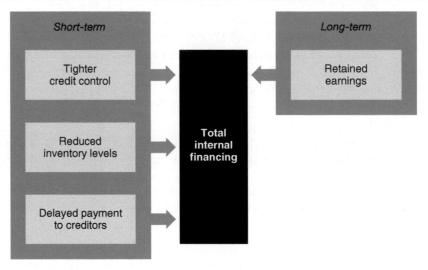

Source: After McLaney and Atrill (2004), Fig. 15.1.

Long-Term Sources of Internal Financing

Retained Earnings

Retained earnings are the major source of financing (internal or external) for most businesses. By retaining profits within the business rather than distributing them to shareholders in the form of dividends, the funds of the business are increased. However, recall from Chapter 2 that retained earnings does not necessarily mean that the company has a pot of cash to spend—this is discussed in Activity 8.11.

ACTIVITY 8.11

Are retained earnings a free source of financing for the business?

Solution

It is tempting to think that retained earnings are a cost-free source of funds for a business. However, this is not the case. If profits are reinvested rather than distributed to shareholders, those shareholders cannot reinvest the profits in other investments. They will therefore expect a rate of return from the profits reinvested that is equivalent to what they would have received if the funds had been invested in another opportunity with the same level of risk.

The reinvestment of profit rather than the issuing of new shares can be a useful way of raising funds from common share investors. There are no issue costs associated with retaining profits. With new shares, the issue costs may be substantial and there may be uncertainty over the success of the issue. Retaining profits will have no effect on the control of the business by existing shareholders. On the other hand, when new shares are issued to outside investors, existing shareholders will experience some dilution of control.

The retention of profits is something that is determined by the directors of the business. They may find it easier simply to retain profits rather than to ask investors to subscribe to a new share issue. Retained earnings are already held by the business and so it does not have to wait to receive the funds. Moreover, there is often less scrutiny when profits are being retained for reinvestment purposes than when new shares are being issued. Investors and their advisers will closely examine the reasons for any new share issue.

A problem with the use of profits as a source of financing, however, is that the timing and level of future profits cannot always be reliably determined. Some shareholders may prefer profits to be retained by the business rather than distributed in the form of dividends. By ploughing back profits, it may be expected that the business will expand and share values will increase as a result. In Canada, only 50% of capital gains are taxed. (Canadian business owners with capital gains of fewer than $500,000 would not be taxed at all on those gains.) A further advantage of capital gains over dividends is that the shareholder has a choice as to when the gain is realized. Research suggests that investors may be attracted to particular businesses according to the dividend/retention policies that they adopt. This point is considered in more detail in Chapter 10.

Retained Earnings and Pecking Order Theory

It has been argued that businesses have a pecking order when increasing long-term financing. This pecking order can be summarized as follows:

- Retained earnings will be used to finance the business if possible
- Where retained earnings are insufficient, or unavailable, debt will be used
- Where debt is insufficient, or unavailable, shares will be used.

A plausible explanation for this pecking order is that the managers of the business have access to information that investors do not. Let us suppose that the managers have reliable information indicating that the prospects for the business are better than predicted by the market. This means that shares will be undervalued and, so, to raise funds by an issue of new shares under such circumstances would involve selling them at an undervalued price. This would, in effect, result in a transfer of wealth from existing shareholders to those investors who acquire the new shares. Hence, the managers, who are employed to act in the best interests of existing shareholders, will prefer to rely on retained earnings, followed by debt, instead. Activity 8.12 explores why managers would not release this information to the market.

ACTIVITY 8.12

Why should the managers not simply release any inside information to the market to allow the share price to rise and so make it possible to issue shares at a fair price?

Solution

There are at least two reasons why this might not be a good idea:

- It may be time-consuming and costly to persuade the market that the prospects of the business are better than current estimates. Investors may not believe what the managers tell them.
- It may provide useful information to competitors about future developments.

Let us now suppose that the managers of a business have access to bad news about the future. If the market knows that the business will rely on retained earnings and debt when in possession of good news, it will assume that the issue of new shares can be taken as an indication that the business is in possession of bad news. Investors are, therefore, likely to consider the shares of the business currently overvalued and not to be interested in buying new shares. (There is some evidence to show that the value of shares will fall when a new share issue is announced.) Hence, this situation will again lead managers to favour retained earnings followed by debt, with new shares as a last resort.

The pecking order theory may well help explain the heavy reliance of businesses on retained earnings as a source of long-term financing, but it will not be the only influence on the financing decision. There are other factors to be taken into account when deciding on an appropriate source of financing, as we shall see in Chapter 10.

Short-Term Sources of Internal Financing

Figure 8.7 (p. 306) reveals that the major forms of short-term internal financing are:

- Tighter credit control
- Reduced inventory levels
- Delayed payments to creditors.

Tighter Credit Control

By exerting tighter control over receivables, it may be possible for a business to reduce the proportion of assets held in this form and so release funds for other purposes. Having funds tied up in receivables represents an opportunity cost in that those funds could be used for profit-generating activities. It is important, however, to weigh the benefits of tighter credit control against the likely costs in the form of lost customers and lost sales. To remain competitive, a business must consider the needs of its customers and the credit policies adopted by rival businesses within the industry. We examine this further in Chapter 12. Activity 8.13 involves weighing the costs of tighter credit control against the likely future benefits.

ACTIVITY 8.13

H. Rusli Ltd. provides a car valet service for car rental businesses when their cars are returned after being rented. Details of the service costs are as follows:

	Per car	
	($)	($)
Car valet charge		20
Less: Variable costs	14	
Fixed costs	4	18
Net profit		2

Sales revenue is $10 million a year and is all on credit. The average credit period taken by the car rental businesses is 45 days, although the terms of credit require payment within 30 days. Bad debts are currently $100,000 a year. Receivables are financed by a bank overdraft costing 15% a year.

▶

The firm's credit control department believes it can eliminate bad debts and can reduce the average collection period to 30 days if new credit control procedures are implemented. These will cost $50,000 a year and are likely to result in a reduction in sales of 5% a year.

Should the business implement the new credit control procedures?

To answer this activity, it is useful to compare the current cost of accounts receivable with the costs under the proposed approach.

Solution

The current cost of accounts receivable is:

	($)
Bad debts	100,000
Overdraft [($10 million × 45/365) × 15%]	184,931
	284,931

The cost of accounts receivable under the new policy will be:

	($)
Overdraft [(95% × $10 million) × (30/365) × 15%]	117,123
Cost of control procedures	50,000
Net cost of lost sales [($10 million/$20 × 5%)($20 − $14*)]	150,000
	317,123

The above figures reveal that the business will be worse off if the new policies are adopted.

*The loss will be the contribution from the valet service, that is, the difference between the valet charge and the variable costs. The fixed costs are ignored as they do not vary with the decision.

Reduced Inventory Levels

This is an internal source of funds that may prove attractive to a business. As with receivables, holding inventory imposes an opportunity cost on a business as the funds tied up cannot be used for other opportunities. By holding less inventory, businesses make funds available for those opportunities. However, a business must try to ensure there is sufficient inventory available to meet likely future sales demand. Failure to do so will result in lost customers and lost sales revenue.

The nature and condition of the inventory held will determine whether it is possible to exploit this form of financing. A business may be overstocked as a result of poor buying decisions in the past. This may mean that a significant proportion of inventory held is slow moving or obsolete and cannot, therefore, be reduced easily.

Delayed Payments to Creditors

By providing a period of credit, suppliers are in effect offering a business an interest-free loan. If the business delays payment, the period of the loan is extended and funds are retained within the business for other purposes. This may be a cheap form of financing for a business, although this is not always the case. If a business fails to pay within the agreed credit period, there may be significant costs: for example, the business may find it difficult to buy on credit if it has a reputation as a slow payer.

Example 8.2 shows the opportunity cost of not taking a discount when one is offered.

Example 8.2

Sometimes firms are offered a discount by suppliers as an incentive to pay their invoice early. For example 2/10, n30 (read as 2/10 net 30) gives a customer 30 days to pay the invoice but offers a 2% discount incentive if it is paid within 10 days of the invoice date.

Consider two firms buying $10,000 of office equipment with terms 2/10, n30. Firm A takes the discount and pays $9,800 on the tenth day. Firm B ignores the discount and pays $10,000 on the 30th day. In effect, Firm B has borrowed $9,800 from the supplier for an extra 20 days (days 11–30) at a cost of $200. It turns out that this is a very expensive way to borrow funds.

The effective annual interest rate can be calculated on the 20-day loan as follows:

$$\left[1 + \left(\frac{\text{Discount\%}}{(100\% - \text{Discount\%})}\right)\right]^{\frac{365}{\text{Days to pay} - \text{Discount period}}} - 1$$

$$= \left[1 + \left(\frac{2\%}{(100\% - 2\%)}\right)\right]^{\frac{365}{30-10}} - 1$$

$$= 44.59\%$$

Depending on the terms, firms are usually well advised to take all discounts offered even if they have to use a line of credit to borrow the funds needed to pay the invoice. This calculation also shows why many firms feel that it is too expensive to offer a cash discount to customers.

SELF-ASSESSMENT QUESTION   8.3

Helsim Ltd. is a wholesaler and distributor of electrical components. The most recent financial statements of the business revealed the following:

Helsim Ltd.
Income Statement
for the year ended May 31, 2010
(in $ millions)

Sales		14.2
Less: Opening inventory	3.2	
Plus: Purchases	8.4	
Goods available for sale	11.6	
Less: Closing inventory	3.8	
Cost of goods sold		7.8
Gross profit		6.4
Less: Selling and distribution expenses	2.1	
Administration expenses	3.0	
Interest expenses	0.8	5.9
Earnings before taxes		0.5
Less: Income tax expense		0.2
Net income		0.3

▶

Helsim Ltd.
Statement of Retained Earnings
for the year ended May 31, 2010
(in $ millions)

Opening retained earnings, June 1	1.5
Add: Net income	0.3
Less: Dividends paid	(0.0)
Closing retained earnings, May 31	1.8

Helsim Ltd.
Balance Sheet
as at May 31, 2010
(in $ millions)

Current assets		
Cash	0.1	
Accounts receivable	3.6	
Inventory	3.8	
Total current assets		7.5
Property, plant, and equipment		
Land	1.0	
Buildings, net	2.8	
Equipment, net	0.9	
Vehicles, net	0.5	
Total property, plant, and equipment		5.2
Total assets		12.7
Current liabilities		
Bank overdraft	3.6	
Accounts payable	1.8	
Total current liabilities		5.4
Long-term liabilities		
Debentures (secured on the land)		3.5
Total liabilities		8.9
Shareholders' equity		
Common shares	2.0	
Retained earnings	1.8	
Total shareholders' equity		3.8
Total liabilities and shareholders' equity		12.7

Note: No dividends have been paid to common shareholders for the past three years.

In recent months, suppliers have been pressing for payment. The president has, therefore, decided to reduce the level of accounts payable to an average of 40 days outstanding. In order to achieve this, he has decided to approach the bank with a view to increasing the overdraft to finance the necessary payments. The business is currently paying 12% interest on the overdraft.

Required:

(a) Comment on the liquidity position of the business.
(b) Calculate the amount of financing required in order to reduce accounts payable, as shown on the balance sheet, to an average of 40 days outstanding.
(c) State, with reasons, how you consider the bank would react to the proposal to allow an increased overdraft.
(d) Evaluate four sources of financing (internal or external, but excluding a bank overdraft) that may be used to finance the reduction in accounts payable and state, with reasons, which of these you consider the most appropriate.

SUMMARY

Sources of Financing

- Long-term sources of financing are not due for repayment within one year, whereas short-term sources are due for repayment within one year.
- External sources of financing require the agreement of someone beyond the directors and managers of the business, whereas internal sources of financing do not require the compliance of outsiders.
- The higher the level of risk associated with investing in a particular form of financing, the higher the level of return that will be expected by investors.

Long-Term Sources of External Financing

- Sources of external long-term financing are common shares, preferred shares, and debt, which includes loans, bonds, leases, and securitization of assets.
- Common shares are normally considered to be the most risky form of investment and, therefore, provide the highest expected returns to investors.
- Warrants and stock options give holders the right, but not the obligation, to buy common shares at a given price, and are often used as a sweetener to accompany a loan issue.
- Preferred shares normally provide returns somewhere between those offered by common shares and debt.
- Debt is normally the least risky and provides the lowest expected returns to investors.
- Debt is relatively low risk because lenders are often offered security for their loan; furthermore, covenants in the loan contract often impose restrictions on the actions of managers, which help protect the lenders.
- There are different types of debt, including term loans, bonds, debentures, mortgages, eurobonds, and strip bonds.
- Convertible bonds give investors the right to convert the bonds to common shares at a given future date and at a specified price. This will be done if the market price at the conversion date exceeds the specified price.
- A number of credit-rating agencies categorize bonds issued by businesses according to the level of default risk.
- Junk bonds are those that do not fall within the investment grade categories established by the credit-rating agencies.

- Interest rates may be floating or fixed.
- Interest rate risk may be reduced, or eliminated, through the use of hedging arrangements such as interest rate swaps.
- A lease is, in essence, a form of lending that gives the lessee the use of an asset over most of its useful life in return for payment of a lease rental.
- A sale-and-leaseback arrangement involves the sale of an asset to a financial institution accompanied by an agreement to lease the asset back to the business.
- Securitization involves bundling together homogeneous, illiquid assets to provide backing for the issue of bonds.

Short-Term Sources of External Financing

- The main sources of external short-term financing are bank overdrafts, accounts receivable factoring, and invoice discounting.
- Bank overdrafts are flexible and cheap but are repayable on demand.
- Receivable factoring and invoice discounting both use the receivables of a business as a basis for borrowing, with the latter being more popular because of relative cost and flexibility.

Choosing an Appropriate Source of Financing

- When considering the choice between long-term and short-term sources of borrowing, factors such as matching the type of borrowing with the nature of the assets held, the need for flexibility, refunding risk, and interest rates should be taken into account.

Internal Sources of Financing

- An internal source of long-term financing is retained earnings. It is by far the most important source of new long-term financing (internal or external) for Canadian businesses.
- Retained earnings are not a free source of financing as investors will require levels of return from retained earnings similar to those from common shares.
- The main short-term sources of internal financing are tighter credit control of receivables, reduced inventory levels, and delayed payments to creditors.

KEY TERMS

Warrants and stock options
Financial derivative
Security
Fixed charge
Floating charge
Loan covenants
Term loan
Debentures
Subordinated loans
Mortgage

Eurobonds
Strip bonds (or zero coupon
   bonds)
Convertible bond
Junk bonds (or high-yield
   bonds)
Floating interest rate
Fixed interest rate
Hedging arrangement
Interest rate swap

Lease
Operating lease
Sale-and-leaseback
   arrangement
Securitization
Bank overdraft
Credit note
Accounts receivable factoring
Receivables discounting
Asset-based financing

REVIEW QUESTIONS

Answers to the Review Questions can be found on the Companion Website that accompanies this text at www.pearsoned.ca/atrill.

8.1 What are warrants and what are the benefits to a business of issuing warrants?

8.2 "Convertible bonds are really a form of delayed equity." Do you agree? Discuss.

8.3 What are the benefits of an interest rate swap agreement and how does it work?

8.4 Distinguish between invoice discounting and receivables factoring.

8.5 Identify the main differences between non-cumulative preferred shares, common shares, and bonds.

PROBLEMS AND CASES

8.1 Your friend has asked you for some advice about investing in corporate bonds. He shows you the following summary based on bond market quotes in the newspaper. All of these bonds currently pay interest.

Company	Price per $100 of Bonds ($)	Yield
Joiner Industries	93.21	10%
K-Pit Co.	82.20	22%
LMO Industries	104.30	9%
Smith Diamonds Ltd.	52.40	35%
Hope Inc.	142.90	7%

Required:

(a) Which of these bonds is likely to be convertible?

(b) What is your best estimate of the market rate of interest?

(c) Rank these bonds according to the ranking system used by DBRS as described in Real World 8.4 on page 292.

8.2 The three companies shown below have gathered data to determine whether they should factor their accounts receivable.

	Larry Ltd.	Curly Ltd.	Moe Ltd.
Average annual accounts receivables	$375,000	$125,000	$65,000
Average collection period in days	42	55	75
Annual bad debt write-offs	$22,000	$8,000	$6,000
Marginal interest rate for accounts receivables	10%	15%	7%
% factor fee on receivables	10%	6%	4%
% of receivables advanced by factor	90%	80%	85%
Interest rate charged by factor	5%	2%	3%
Reduced collection period with factor in days	20	25	30
Annual accounts receivable credit administration savings	$2,000	$6,000	$5,000

Required:

Prepare calculations for each company to determine the total cost of collecting its own receivables.

8.3

Required:

Use the data in Problem and Case 8.2 to prepare calculations for each company to determine the total cost of factoring its accounts receivable.

8.4

Required:

Use the data in (and your solutions to) Problems and Cases 8.2 and 8.3 to determine for each company whether it should factor its accounts receivable.

8.5 Côté Biologique Limitée (CBL) is considering factoring its accounts receivable to improve its cash flow. Shortfalls in collecting the receivables are met by a short-term revolving line of credit. The controller has gathered the following data to help her make the decision:

Annual credit sales	$10,000,000
Average collection period	50 days
Industry average collection period	30 days
Average annual bad debt write-offs	$100,000
Revolving line of credit financing charge	12%
Factor data:	
Advance on accounts receivable	70%
Collection fee on credit sales	1.5%
Collection period assumption:	
Industry average collection period	30 days
Interest rate	9%
Annual bad debt write-offs	$55,000
Administrative savings	$40,000

Required:

(a) Calculate the cost of CBL continuing to collect its own accounts receivable.
(b) Calculate the cost of CBL factoring the accounts receivable.
(c) What would you suggest that CBL do?
(d) Would your decision change if the advance on the receivables was 90% instead of 70%?

8.6 The three companies shown below have gathered data to determine whether they should factor their accounts receivable.

	One Ltd.	Two Ltd.	Three Ltd.
Average annual accounts receivables	$3,000,000	$750,000	$1,500,000
Average collection period in days	70	90	100
Annual bad debt write-offs	$100,000	$40,000	$25,000
Marginal interest rate for accounts receivables	10%	12%	9%
% factor fee on receivables	5%	8%	6%
% of receivables advanced by factor	70%	90%	85%
Interest rate charged by factor	4%	2%	3%
Reduced collection period with factor in days	30	20	25
Annual accounts receivable credit administration savings	$3,000	$5,000	$3,000

Required:

Prepare calculations to determine whether any of these companies would be better off to factor its receivables.

8.7 The following companies are trying to decide whether to change their accounts receivables collection policy.

	Three Rivers Industries	Twin Peaks Ltd.	Single Signals Inc.
Current receivables policy			
Unit sale price	$125	$250	$550
Contribution margin per unit	$50	$62	$140
Units sold per year on credit	120,000	75,000	25,000
Average collection period in days	72	60	100
Bad debts per year	$175,000	$149,000	$160,000
Interest rate on line of credit	11%	7%	9%
Proposed new receivables policy			
Revised average collection period in days	50	30	70
Cost	$89,000	$45,000	$60,000
% reduction in unit sales	10%	7%	4%

Required:

Compute the cost of the current receivables policy for each company.

8.8

Required:

Use the data in Problem and Case 8.7 to compute the cost of switching to a new accounts receivables policy for each company.

8.9

Required:

Use the data in Problem and Case 8.7 and 8.8 to determine which company should change its accounts receivables policy.

8.10 The following companies are considering a change in their accounts receivables policy.

	Alpha Industries	Beta Ltd.	Gamma Inc.
Current receivables policy			
Unit sale price	$400	$860	$190
Contribution margin per unit	$130	$300	$90
Units sold per year on credit	75,000	22,000	130,000
Average collection period in days	60	90	100
Bad debts per year	$200,000	$300,000	$400,000
Interest rate on line of credit	13%	9%	10%
Proposed new receivables policy			
Revised average collection period in days	30	60	45
Cost	$45,000	$100,000	$60,000
% reduction in unit sales	5%	5%	7%

Required:

Determine whether the proposed change in accounts receivables policy is beneficial to any of these companies.

8.11 Intercity Commuters Limited (ICL) flies people between Victoria and Vancouver. Last year an average $100 flight had a $35 contribution margin and $5 fixed costs per customer. Credit sales totalled $2,500,000 with an average collection period of 70 days and $50,000 in bad debts. The company maintains a revolving line of credit at a 10% interest rate.

ICL is looking at expanding its credit collection efforts by hiring an additional person at an annual salary of $35,000. ICL estimates that bad debts could be reduced by 75% and the average collection period reduced to 30 days. However, the more stringent credit terms would likely reduce sales by 7%.

Required:

Should the business implement the new credit controls?

8.12 The three companies shown below have gathered data to determine whether they should factor their accounts receivable.

	Great Ski Ltd.	Rich Yard Inc.	Bob Ore Mines
Current receivables policy			
Unit sale price	$30	$160	$55
Contribution margin per unit	$14	$50	$25
Annual sales on credit	$345,000	$820,000	$1,500,000
Average collection period in days	50	75	120
Bad debts per year	$17,000	$24,000	$70,000
Interest rate on line of credit	11%	7%	12%
Proposed new receivables policy			
Revised average collection period in days	20	30	60
Cost	$30,000	$20,000	$60,000
% reduction in sales	3%	8%	5%

Required:
Prepare calculations to determine whether any of these companies would be better off to factor its receivables.

8.13 Jiminez Skill Shops Limited (JSSL) acquired inventory of $5,000 with terms of 1/5 n30. JSSL maintains access to a line of credit at a bank at 12% interest.

Required:
Should JSSL use its line of credit to take the discount or not?

8.14 Your company normally pays early on its accounts payable in order to take advantage of any discount offered. However, now you would like to slow down payments because your company has been slow to collect on its own accounts receivables. Your company's five most prominent suppliers offer the following terms:

		Payment Terms			
Supplier	1	2	3	4	5
Terms	1/10/n30	2/10/n40	1/5/n60	2/20/n60	3/10/n60

Required:
Which supplier should your company choose to delay payment and forgo taking the discount?

8.15 Crosby Gloves Ltd. is considering a number of options.

Required:
Provide reasons why Crosby might decide to:

(a) Lease rather than buy an asset that is to be held for long-term use
(b) Use retained earnings to finance growth rather than issue new shares
(c) Repay a long-term loan earlier than the specified repayment date.

8.16 H. Brown Ltd. produces a range of central heating systems for sale to builders. As a result of increasing demand for the business's products, management has decided to expand production. The cost of acquiring new plant and machinery and the increase in working capital requirements are planned to be financed by a mixture of long-term and short-term borrowing.

Required:

(a) Discuss the major factors that should be taken into account when deciding on the appropriate mix of long-term and short-term borrowing necessary to finance the expansion program.
(b) Discuss the major factors that a lender should take into account when deciding whether to grant a long-term loan to the business.
(c) Identify three restrictions that might be included in a long-term loan agreement, and state the purpose of each.

8.17 Securitization is now used in a variety of different industries. In the music industry, for example, rock stars such as David Bowie, Michael Jackson, and Iron Maiden have used this form of financing to their benefit.

Required:

(a) Explain the term *securitization*.
(b) Discuss the main features of this form of financing and the benefits of using securitization.

8.18 Raphael Ltd. is a small engineering business that has annual credit sales revenue of $2.4 million. In recent years, the business has experienced credit control problems. The average collection period for sales has risen to 50 days even though the stated policy of the business is for payment to be made within 30 days. In addition, 1.5% of sales are written off as bad debts each year. The accounts receivable are currently financed through a bank overdraft, which has an interest rate of 12% a year.

The business has recently communicated with a factor that is prepared to make an advance to the business equivalent to 80% of receivables, based on the assumption that customers will, in future, adhere to a 30-day payment period. The interest rate for the advance will be 11% a year. The factor will take over the credit control procedures of the business and this will result in a saving to the business of $18,000 a year; however, the factor will charge 2% of sales revenue for this service. The use of the factoring service is expected to eliminate the bad debts incurred by the business.

Required:

Calculate the net cost of the factor agreement to the business and state whether the business should take advantage of the opportunity to factor its accounts receivables.

8.19 Cybele Technology Ltd. is a software business owned and managed by two computer software specialists. Although sales have remained stable at $4 million per year in recent years, the level of receivables has increased significantly. A recent financial report submitted to the owners indicates an average collection period for receivables of 60 days compared with an industry average of 40 days. The level of bad debts has also increased in recent years and the business now writes off approximately $20,000 of bad debts each year.

The recent problems experienced in controlling credit have led to a liquidity crisis for the business. At present, the business finances its receivables by a bank overdraft bearing an interest rate of 14% a year. However, the overdraft limit has been exceeded on several occasions in recent months and the bank is now demanding a significant decrease in the size of the overdraft. To comply with this demand, the owners of the business have approached a factor who has offered to make an advance equivalent to 85% of receivables, based on the assumption that the level of receivables will be in line with the industry average. The factor will charge a rate of interest of 12% a year for this advance. The factor will take over the sales ledger of the business and, for this service, will charge a fee based on 2% of sales. The business believes that the services offered by the factor should eliminate bad debts and should lead to administrative cost savings of $26,000 per year.

Required:

(a) Calculate the effect on the net income of Cybele Technology Ltd. of employing a receivables factor. Discuss your findings.

(b) Discuss the potential advantages and disadvantages for a business that employs the services of a receivables factor.

Financing a Business 2: Raising Long-Term Funds

INTRODUCTION

In this chapter, we continue our examination of the ways in which businesses may raise long-term funds. We begin by looking at the role of stock exchanges in raising funds for large businesses, and then go on to consider whether shares listed on a stock exchange are efficiently priced. We shall see that the efficiency with which a stock exchange prices shares has important implications for the financing of a business. To complete our discussion of stock exchanges, we discuss the different ways in which common shares may be issued.

Smaller businesses do not have access to stock exchanges and so must look elsewhere to raise long-term financing. In this chapter, we discuss some of the main providers of long-term financing for smaller businesses.

A STOCK EXCHANGE

L.O. 1

In the sections that follow, we examine the role that a **stock exchange** plays in raising long-term financing for businesses and discuss some of the key features of financial markets. We then go on to examine the extent to which shares, or other financial claims such as convertible bonds, are efficiently priced by a stock exchange.

The Role of a Stock Exchange

A stock exchange acts as an important *primary* and *secondary* capital market for businesses. As a primary market, its main function is to enable businesses to raise new capital. Thus, businesses may use a stock exchange to raise funds by issuing shares to new or existing shareholders. In order to issue shares through a stock exchange, a business must be listed with the exchange, and so must meet fairly stringent requirements concerning size, profit history, and information disclosure. REAL WORLD 9.1 provides some information regarding Canadian stock exchanges and details of the listing requirements for the Toronto Stock Exchange and TSX Venture Exchange.

REAL WORLD 9.1

Canadian Stock Exchanges and Listing Requirements

As of May 2008, the TMX Group owns and operates the three Canadian stock exchanges:

■ *Montreal Exchange (MX).*   The MX is Canada's oldest stock exchange and specializes in the derivatives markets. Derivatives, which include forward contracts, are used by businesses to hedge various risks such as foreign exchange risks.
■ *Toronto Stock Exchange.*   The Toronto Stock Exchange is the main Canadian stock exchange and started over 150 years ago. It is the stock exchange for Canada's larger, more established companies.
■ *TSX Venture Exchange.*   The TSX Venture Exchange is Canada's stock exchange for junior and emerging companies, providing access to public venture capital to facilitate their growth. The TSX Venture Exchange also focuses on attracting international junior companies, even posting its listing requirements on the website in Chinese.

The TMX Group has 4,013 companies listed with a total market capitalization of $1.3 trillion on the Toronto Stock Exchange and the TSX Venture Exchange. Even though more companies were listed, the market capitalization was down more than $700 billion, showing the severity of the market collapse during the Great Recession of 2008–2009. There were 359 new listings on these exchanges in 2008. 45 companies graduated from the TSX Venture Exchange to the more senior Toronto Stock Exchange. $153.3 billion of securities were traded in 2008. The Montreal Exchange traded 38.1 million contracts in 2008.

Source: TMX Group 2008 Annual Report.

Listing Requirements for the Toronto Stock Exchange and TSX Venture Exchanges

The Toronto Stock Exchange is the senior Canadian stock exchange where the shares of most large companies in Canada are listed and was founded in 1861. The TSX Venture Exchange grew out of a merger between the Vancouver and Alberta Stock Exchanges and handles more junior equities. Listing requirements for companies are less stringent on the TSX Venture Exchange, as shown in Table 9.1. Note that the ranges apply to various company categories, such as industrial company, technology company, research and development company, senior company, and profitable company, as designated by the Toronto Stock Exchange.

TABLE 9.1   Minimum Listing Requirements

	TSX	TSX Venture
Pre-tax income	$200,000–$300,000	$50,000–$100,000
Pre-tax cash flow	$500,000–$700,000	N/A
Net tangible assets	$2,000,000–$7,000,000	$500,000–$5,000,000
Public float (number of shares)	1,000,000	500,000–1,000,000 or 20% of outstanding shares
Market value of float	$4,000,000–$10,000,000	N/A

Sources: www.venturelawcorp.com/tsx_venture_exchange.htm, and www.venturelawcorp.com/listing_requirements _TSX.html, accessed March 2, 2007; www.tsx.com/en/listings/index.html, accessed March 3, 2007. © 2002 Venture Law Corporation. All rights reserved.

As a secondary market, the function of the stock exchange is to enable investors to sell their securities (that is, shares) with ease. The exchange provides a second-hand market where shares may be bought and sold. This role can greatly benefit a business, as investors are likely to be more prepared to invest if they know their investment can be easily turned into cash whenever required. As a result, businesses whose shares are traded on a stock exchange are likely to find it easier to raise long-term financing and to do so at lower cost.

Though investors are not obliged to use a stock exchange as the means of transferring shares, it is usually the most convenient way of buying or selling shares.

Ownership of Canadian Listed Shares

Shares in stock exchange–listed businesses are held principally by large financial institutions such as insurance companies, pension funds, mutual funds, and other investment funds. These institutions have strengthened their control over time, while the proportion of listed shares held directly by individuals has declined steadily.

We saw in Chapter 1 that the growing influence of financial institutions has contributed to the rise in shareholder activism in recent years.

The Size of Listed Businesses

Businesses listed on the stock exchange vary considerably in size. The top 500 companies in Canada have a **market capitalization** (colloquially known as *market cap*) ranging from $260 million to $61 billion. REAL WORLD 9.2 shows the number of companies and the market capitalization (number of shares outstanding multiplied by share price) ranges for large, medium, and small cap companies in Canada.

REAL WORLD 9.2   What Is Your Cap Size?

Figure 9.1 shows one way to classify Canadian companies by size. *Canadian Business* magazine prepares an annual list ranking the top 500 largest firms in Canada according to various different classifications, such as sales, profits, market capitalization, and total return to shareholders. In terms of market capitalization, the top 50 companies are classified as large cap companies. The threshold to make it into the large cap group in 2008 was a market capitalization of $6.5 billion. Medium cap stocks comprised the next 150 companies, covering a market cap range of $1 billion to $6.3 billion. Small cap stocks, the bottom 300 companies in the 500 largest Canadian firms, ranged in market capitalization from $221 million to $1 billion.

Size is relative, of course. The United States is home to much larger companies than we typically see in Canada. In the U.S., many would classify large cap companies as having a market capitalization over US$10 billion, medium cap between US$1 billion and US$10 billion, and small cap firms under US$1 billion.

In the 2008 rankings graphed in Figure 9.1, Research In Motion was the largest company, with market capitalization of over $68 billion. The largest medium cap company was Trans Alto Corp., an Alberta power generation company, at nearly $6.3 billion market capitalization. The Montreal Exchange Inc. is the largest company in the small cap sector.

▶

FIGURE 9.1   Canadian Firms by Market Capitalization for 2008

Source: Graph constructed from data provided by *Canadian Business* magazine: www.canadianbusiness.com/
rankings/investor500/list.jsp?showNum=50&pageID=list&i500=1&type=t50&listType=t50market&year=2006&
page=1&customView=&customCols=&content=, accessed September 20, 2009.

Stock Market Indices

Various indices are available to help monitor trends in overall share price movements
in the stock exchanges.

Canadian Indices

■ *S&P/TSX Composite.*   This index gives 95% coverage by market capitalization of the
Canadian equity market. It is probably the best-known stock market index in Canada.

■ *S&P/TSX 60.*   This index is based on the 60 largest Canadian companies by market capitalization and is regarded by analysts as the best measure of the Canadian
equity markets.

U.S. Indices

■ *Dow-Jones Industrial Average (DJIA).*   This is one of the oldest and most followed
of all indices. It follows only 30 companies, but these are among the largest and
most widely held firms in the U.S. The "industrial" part of the index's name is
retained for historical reasons, as most of the 30 companies comprising the DJIA
today are not involved with heavy industry.

■ *S&P 500 Index.*   This index is often used as the best proxy for the U.S. equity
markets. It comprises the 500 leading large cap companies, covering about 75% of
the entire market capitalization in the United States.

■ *S&P MidCap 400.*   This is often regarded as the best index for medium cap stocks.
It covers about 7% of the entire market capitalization in the United States.

■ *NASDAQ Composite.*   This index includes over 3,000 companies and is another of
the most widely followed indices. It is often used as a proxy (an indicator) of how
technology stocks are doing in the market, because such famous high-tech companies
as Microsoft and Apple are listed on the NASDAQ.

■ *NYSE Composite.*   Another widely quoted index. It covers all stocks listed on the
New York Stock Exchange.

Other Indices

■ *FTSE (Footsie) 100.*   This is the best known index of the London Stock Exchange (LSE) in England. It is based on the stock prices of the 100 largest businesses by market capitalization listed on the LSE.
■ *CAC 40.*   This index measures price movements of the 40 largest firms in France.
■ *Nikkei 225.*   This index consists of 225 companies listed on the Tokyo Stock Exchange (TSE) and is the most widely followed Asian index.

Each index is constructed using a base date and a base value, and is updated throughout each trading day. Inclusion in the index is frequently reviewed by the company that developed the index, and businesses within a particular index may be replaced as a result of changes in their relative size.

Advantages and Disadvantages of a Stock Exchange Listing

In addition to the advantages already mentioned, having a stock exchange listing can help a business by:

■ Raising its profile, which may be useful in dealings with customers and suppliers
■ Ensuring that its shares are valued in an efficient manner (a point to which we return later)
■ Broadening its investor base
■ Making it easier to acquire other businesses by using its own shares as payment rather than cash
■ Making it easier to attract and retain employees by offering incentives based on share ownership plans.

However, before a decision is made to float (that is, list on a stock exchange), these advantages must be weighed against the possible disadvantages of a listing.

Raising funds through a stock exchange can be a costly business. Shares issued from the initial listing of the business are known as an *initial public offering (IPO)*. To make such an offering, a business will rely on the help of various specialists such as lawyers, accountants, and bankers. However, their services are expensive. REAL WORLD 9.3 provides an example.

REAL WORLD 9.3

Heavy IPO Fees at Capital Power Corporation

Capital Power Corporation executed an initial public offering in June 2009 of just over $500 million. It was the first new IPO on the Toronto Stock Exchange in about a year, probably because of the market meltdown in 2008. The net proceeds were $468 million after deducting $32 million (6.4%) for underwriters' commissions and transaction costs.

Source: Capital Power Corporation website news release: www.capitalpowercorp.com/MediaRoom/Pages/070909b.aspx, accessed September 19, 2009.

In addition to these out-of-pocket expenses, a significant amount of management time is usually required to undertake an IPO, which can result in missed business opportunities.

Another important disadvantage to listing is the regulatory burden placed on listed businesses. Once a business is listed, there are continuing requirements that must be met, covering issues such as:

- Disclosure of financial information
- Informing shareholders of significant developments
- The rights of shareholders and lenders
- The obligations of directors.

These requirements can be onerous and can also involve substantial costs for the business.

Another potential disadvantage is that the activities of listed businesses are closely monitored by financial analysts, financial journalists, and other businesses. Such scrutiny may be unwelcome, particularly if the business is dealing with sensitive issues or is experiencing operational problems.

If investors become disenchanted with the business and the price of its shares falls, this may make it vulnerable to a takeover bid by another business or by private equity capital interests.

A potential disadvantage for smaller listed businesses is that they may be overlooked by investors and so may not reap the key benefit of a listing. REAL WORLD 9.4 explains why larger businesses tend to dominate the minds of investors.

REAL WORLD 9.4

Institutional Investing in Big Caps

The huge size of institutional investors such as pension funds, banks and insurance companies, mutual funds, and hedge funds means that they dominate the investing scene. Because of the amount of money they have to invest, they are mostly interested in investing in mid cap and large cap companies. The liquidity of a company's shares is a concern for these funds. When these institutions decide to invest in a company, it may take several months of discreet buying in bite-sized portions before they establish their full investment position. They do not want to drive up the share price with their extra demand for shares before their investment plan is executed. Share price sensitivity to small increases in demand is more likely to happen in small cap companies. Consequently, it makes it more difficult for small businesses to raise new equity because most institutional investment firms are not too interested. Thus for small firms the advantages of listing are outweighed by the disadvantages.

A final disadvantage claimed is that stock exchange investors suffer from a short-term investment perspective. It is argued that the investment myopia of investors puts pressure on listed businesses to produce good results in the short term, even though this may have adverse long-term effects. This claim is worthy of further investigation and so will be considered in a later section.

Raising Funds Through the Stock Exchange

A stock exchange can be a useful vehicle for a successful entrepreneur wishing to cash in on the value of the business that has been built up. By floating the shares on the stock exchange, and thereby making the shares available to the public, the entrepreneur will usually benefit from a gain in the value of the shares held and will be able to realize that gain easily, if required, by selling some shares. REAL WORLD 9.5 provides an example of a business IPO on the stock exchange making its owners a lot of money.

Google's IPO

Google's IPO on August 19, 2004, was the largest technology IPO in history. Google went public at US$85 per share, raising US$1.67 billion on 19.6 million shares sold to the public. Together with other shares held by insiders, this placed an initial market capitalization on Google of US$23.1 billion. The two Google founders—Sergey Brin and Larry Page—each held about 38.5 million shares, which were valued at US$3.3 billion. The stock first traded about two hours later at US$100.01, earning its new shareholders an immediate 17.65% return on investment. Try annualizing that return!

Subsequently, Google raised an additional US$4.18 billion from a second IPO, which sold approximately 14.2 million shares at US$295 on September 14, 2005. The shares for this IPO were priced 2.7% below the recent closing price of US$303. On February 27, 2007, Google shares were trading at US$456.23. On October 18, 2010, the shares were trading at US$617.71.

Sources: www.google-ipo.com/, accessed February 27, 2007; www.redherring.com/Article.aspx?a=13574&hed=Google+Offering+ Raises+%244.18B, accessed February 27, 2007.

Shares sold through an initial listing on a stock exchange may be new shares or already outstanding shares that the existing owners wish to sell.

It seems that we should be cautious when invited to buy shares arising from an initial listing. REAL WORLD 9.6 tells us why investing in new business share flotations may be bad for our wealth.

Recent IPO Investing Results

Many experts recommend that investors avoid IPOs until the stock has settled down a bit. They advise investors to look for an entry point for their investment when the stock makes its first correction—that is, when the stock has experienced a few weeks of falling prices and then starts to turn around again. This may not happen for several months. Therefore investors should wait a few weeks or months until the stock has had a chance to prove itself before committing money to such an investment.

Although studies have shown that many IPOs have a history of poor investment performance, it really depends on the type of stock market we have. IPO returns from 2000 to 2002 were not good because it was a poor stock market overall. The share prices of many internet companies crashed during this period. In 2009 IPOs were up an average of 27% as the market recovered from the Great Recession of 2008–2009. These IPOs included Changeyou.com Limited, Rosetta Stone Inc., Mead Johnson Nutrition Co., and DigitalGlobe Inc.

Source: http://247wallst.com/2009/05/18/2009-ipo-scorecard-up-almost-28-on-average-cyou-rst-mjn-dgi-bpi/, accessed September 20, 2009.

The Stock Exchange and the Problem of Short-Term Thinking

It seems to be the conventional wisdom that listed businesses are under pressure by stock exchange investors to perform well over the short term. Furthermore, as a result of this pressure, businesses are inhibited from undertaking projects that will yield benefits only in the longer term. Instead, they will opt for investments that perform well over the short term, even though the long-term prospects may be poor. Although this view of stock exchange investors seems to be widely held, it is not well supported by the evidence. Indeed, there is some compelling evidence to the contrary.

Evidence of share price behaviour suggests that investors take a long-term view when making investment decisions. For example, consider:

- *Share price reaction to investment plans.* If a short-term view is taken by investors, any announcement by a business that it plans to undertake long-term investment or research would be treated as bad news. It should lead investors to sell their shares and this, in turn, would result in a fall in the company's share price. Conversely, any announcement by a business that long-term investment plans are to be scrapped would be treated as good news and should result in a rise in share price. In fact, the opposite share price reaction will usually occur.
- *Dividend payments.* Investors demanding short-term returns would be expected to value businesses with a superior dividend yield more highly than businesses with a low dividend yield. This kind of behaviour would allow an astute investor to buy shares in low-yielding businesses at a lower price than their true value and so, over time, make higher returns. However, the evidence suggests that businesses with low dividend yields are more highly regarded by investors than businesses with high dividend yields.

If stock exchange investors are not to blame for the short-term perspective of managers, then who is to blame? Some believe that it is the managers themselves. It has been argued, for example, that managers have incorrect views about what stock exchange investors are really looking for. (There is certainly survey evidence to support the view that managers *believe* that investors have a short-term investment perspective.) It has also been suggested that managers adopt a short-term view because their rewards are linked to short-term results or because frequent job changes encourage the quest for short-term results. Finally, it has been suggested that the particular appraisal methods adopted by managers to evaluate investment opportunities encourage a short-term view. This is explored in Activity 9.1.

ACTIVITY 9.1

Can you think of an investment appraisal method, dealt with in Chapter 6, that may encourage a short-term view?

Solution

The payback method places emphasis on how quickly an investment repays its initial cost. This method is widely used and may encourage a short-term approach by managers. (An alternative explanation, however, is that the payback method is selected by managers because they adopt a short-term perspective.)

Some believe, however, that managers are not the real culprits and that it is high inflation and economic instability during the post-war years that have given managers a short-term perspective. Thus, to encourage long-term thinking we need a sustained period of stable monetary conditions.

THE EFFICIENCY OF THE STOCK MARKET

L.O. 2

It was mentioned earlier that the stock market helps share prices to be efficiently priced. *Efficiency* in this context does not relate to the way in which the stock market is administered, but rather to the way in which information is processed. An **efficient stock market** is one in which information is processed quickly and accurately and so share prices faithfully reflect all relevant information available. In other words, prices are determined in a rational manner and represent the best estimate of the true worth of the shares.

The term *efficiency* does not imply that investors have perfect knowledge concerning a business and its future prospects and that this knowledge is reflected in the share price. Information may come to light concerning the business that investors did not previously know about and which may indicate that the current share price is higher or lower than its true worth. However, in an efficient market, the new information will be quickly absorbed by investors and will lead to a quick share price adjustment.

Efficiency in relation to the stock market is not the same as the economists' concept of perfect markets, which you may have come across in your previous studies. The definition of an efficient capital market does not rest on a set of restrictive assumptions regarding the operation of the market (for example, that relevant information is freely available, or that all investors have access to all relevant information). In reality, such assumptions will not hold. The term *efficient market* is a narrower concept that has been developed by studying the behaviour of stock markets in the real world. It simply describes the situation where relevant information is *quickly* and *accurately* reflected in share prices. The speed at which new information is absorbed in share prices will mean that not even nimble-footed investors will have time to make superior gains by buying or selling shares when new information becomes available.

To understand why the stock market may be efficient, it is important to bear in mind that securities listed on a stock exchange are scrutinized by many individuals, including skilled analysts, who are constantly seeking to make gains from identifying securities that are inefficiently priced. They are alert to new information and will react quickly when new opportunities arise. If, for example, a share can be identified as being below its true worth, investors would immediately exploit this information by buying shares in that business. When this is done on a large scale, the effect will be to drive up the price of the share, thereby eliminating any inefficiency within the market. Thus, as a result of the efforts to make gains from inefficiently priced securities, investors will, paradoxically, promote the efficiency of the market.

Financial theorists have asserted that there are three levels of efficiency concerning the operation of stock markets. These are the weak form, the semi-strong form, and the strong form.

The Weak Form of Efficiency

The weak form reflects the situation where movements in share prices follow a random path. Current share price movements are independent of past share price movements, and any information contained in past share prices will already be reflected in current share prices. The random nature of share price movements means that any attempt to study past prices in order to detect a pattern of price movements will fail. It is not, therefore, possible to make gains from simply studying past price movements. Thus, investors and analysts who draw up charts of share price changes (which is known as technical analysis) in order to predict future price movements will be wasting their time.

The Semi-Strong Form of Efficiency

The semi-strong form takes the notion of efficiency a little further and describes the situation where all publicly available information, including past share prices, is reflected in the current share price. Other publicly available forms of information will include published accounts, business announcements, newspaper reports, and economic forecasts. These forms of information, which will become available at random intervals, are quickly absorbed by the market and so investors who study relevant reports and announcements (known as fundamental analysis), in an attempt to make above-average returns on a consistent basis, will be disappointed. The information will already be incorporated into share prices.

The Strong Form of Efficiency

The strong form of efficiency describes the situation where share prices fully reflect all available information, whether or not it is publicly available. This means that the share price will be a good approximation of the true value of the share. As all relevant information is absorbed in share prices, even those who have inside information concerning a business, such as unpublished reports or confidential management decisions, will not be able to make superior returns, on a consistent basis, from using this information.

The various forms of efficiency described above can be viewed as a progression where each higher form of efficiency incorporates the previous form(s). Thus, if a stock market is efficient in the semi-strong form it will also be efficient in the weak form. Similarly, if a stock market is efficient in the strong form, it will also be efficient in the semi-strong and weak forms (see Figure 9.2 and Activity 9.2).

FIGURE 9.2   The Three Levels of Market Efficiency

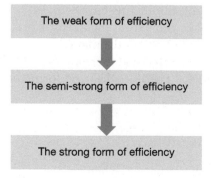

ACTIVITY 9.2

Can you explain why the relationship between the various forms of market efficiency explained above should be the case?

Solution

If a stock market is efficient in the semi-strong form, it will reflect all publicly available information. This will include past share prices. Thus, the semi-strong form will incorporate the weak form. If the stock market is efficient in the strong form, it will reflect all available information—which includes publicly available information. Thus, it will incorporate the semi-strong and weak forms.

It is worth noting that, within each of the three forms, there are varying degrees of efficiency. In other words, efficiency within each form should be viewed as a continuum ranging from total efficiency to total inefficiency. Activity 9.3 explores two efficiency scenarios.

ACTIVITY 9.3

Gilbert Ltd. is a large civil engineering business that is listed on the Toronto Stock Exchange. On May 1, it received a confidential letter stating that it had won a large building contract from an overseas government. The new contract is expected to increase the profits of the business by a substantial amount over the next five years. The news of the contract was announced publicly on May 4.

How would the shares of the business react to the formal announcement on May 4, assuming (a) a semi-strong form of market efficiency and (b) a strong form of market efficiency?

Solution

(a) Under the semi-strong form, the formal announcement would lead to an increase in the value of the shares.
(b) Under the strong form of efficiency, however, there would be no share reaction as the information would already be incorporated in the share price.

Evidence of Stock Market Efficiency

There is a very large body of evidence that spans many countries and many time periods supporting the idea of weak form efficiency. Much of this evidence has resulted from researchers checking whether security price movements follow a random pattern: that is, checking to find out whether successive price changes were independent of each other. The results point overwhelmingly to the existence of a random pattern of share prices. There has also been some research involving the examination of trading rules that are used by some investors. These rules are based on the identification of trend-like patterns to determine the point at which to buy or sell shares in order to achieve superior returns. Given the earlier findings on the random nature of share price movements, it is not surprising that the evidence suggests that the trading rules developed are useless. Activity 9.4 considers the implications of this.

ACTIVITY 9.4

If share prices follow a random pattern, does this not mean that the market is acting in an irrational (and inefficient) manner?

Solution

No. New information concerning a business is likely to arise at random intervals and so share price adjustments to the new information will arise at those random intervals. The randomness of share price movements is, therefore, to be expected if markets are efficient.

Despite the evidence concerning the random nature of price movements, some analysts (known as technical analysts) believe that price movements in financial markets do exhibit repetitive patterns of behaviour. REAL WORLD 9.7 illustrates some of the techniques used by these analysts to help predict future price movements.

REAL WORLD 9.7   Technical Analysis Signs

The charts in Figure 9.3 show the high, low, and closing weekly share prices for four companies. The share price is shown on the left-hand side of each chart. Although not depicted here, volume of shares traded is often shown at the bottom of a stock chart. A rising share price accompanied by rising volume is bullish (favourable). Conversely, a falling share price on rising volume is bearish (unfavourable). Moving average lines are often added to stock market charts. Some investors like to buy shares when the price crosses above the 50-day moving average line of share prices. The 50-day moving average is the average of the last 50 days' closing share prices. It is a moving average because each day the oldest share price drops out of the average and today's closing price is added into the average mix. (For these and other charting refinements, visit bigcharts.com.)

Technical analysts draw further trend lines on these graphs. Some well-known chart patterns include:

- *Line trends*—must go through at least three points on the graph.
- *Channel*—an upper resistance line at high price points and a lower support line at low price points. A breakout from a channel can indicate the end of the channel trend.
- *Triangle*—two converging lines. A breakout from a triangle (either above or below) can be a strong indicator of market direction.
- *Head and shoulders pattern*—a pattern with three tops or three bottoms. The share price reaches its first top and falls back. Then there is a push to a new high and a new higher top is made. The share then falls back again, only to try for another new high. However, this share price advance stops below the last high, so a lower high is made. The first high and the third high constitute the shoulders, with the second high, the actual real high, acting as the head. A head and shoulders top pattern is considered to be very negative. Investors should sell their shares before the price breaks down below the head and shoulders' neckline. A head and shoulders bottom is considered to be a positive sign.

▶

FIGURE 9.3   Technical Analysis Signs

The following weekly stock charts show some common chart patterns. The company name is followed by its ticker symbol on the Toronto Stock Exchange.

Uptrend

(A)

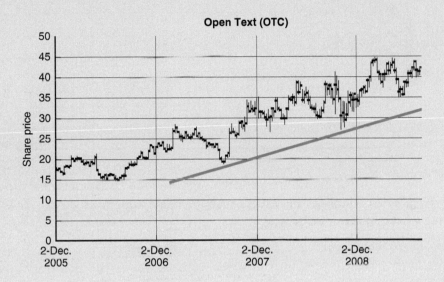

Open Text has been in an uptrend for a few years now.

Downtrend

(B)

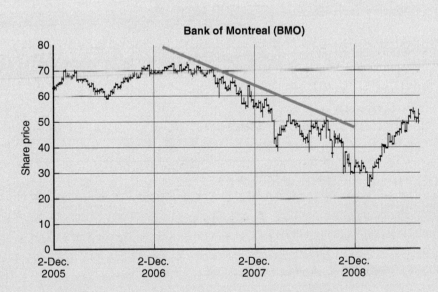

BMO had been in a two-year downtrend until the market bottomed in March 2009.

Sideways Channel

(C)

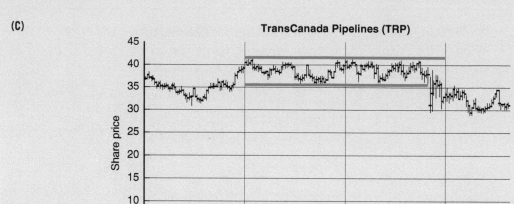

TRP shares were in about a two-year sideways channel from late 2006 to late 2008. In 2008 the entire market was falling because of the recession.

Head and Shoulders Bottom

(D)

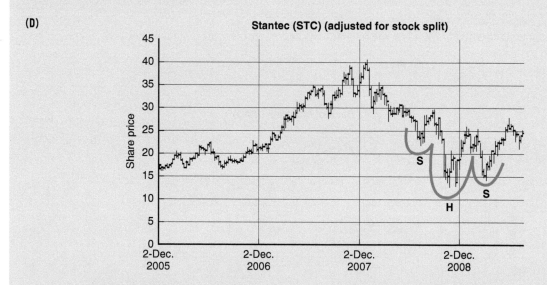

Stantec, a large Canadian engineering firm, formed a head and shoulders bottom in 2008–2009. The right-side shoulder bottomed with the market bottom in March 2009.

Source: Graphs constructed from data at Yahoo! Finance: http://ca.finance.yahoo.com/q/hp?s=BMO.TO&a=00&b=12&c=2005&d=08&e=20&f=2009&g=w&z=66&y=132, accessed September 20, 2009.

Research to test the semi-strong form of efficiency has usually involved monitoring the reaction of the share price to new information, such as profit announcements. This is done to see whether the market reacts to new information in an appropriate manner. The results usually show that share prices quickly and accurately readjust to any new information that affects the value of the business. This implies that investors cannot make superior returns by reacting quickly to new information. The results also show that investors are able to distinguish between new information that affects the value of the underlying business and new information that does not.

Research to test the strong form of efficiency has often involved an examination of the performance of investment fund managers. These managers are assumed to have access to a wide range of information, not all of which is in the public domain. The results show that despite this apparent advantage over private investors, fund managers are unable to generate consistently superior performance over time.

REAL WORLD 9.8 summarizes some of the evidence that actively managed investment funds are unable to consistently outperform the relevant stock market index.

REAL WORLD 9.8

Beating the Index Is Difficult

There is an ongoing debate about whether investors can beat the market. Academic studies tend to say no. But then how do we account for successful investors like Warren Buffett? Have they found a system that works?

The two schools of thought face off in an "active investment versus passive investment" duel. Active investing means the portfolio manager actively makes decisions to try to earn a better return than the average market return because she or he thinks the market is not perfectly efficient. Passive investing means the manager weights the portfolio according to the index weightings that are being mimicked. Exchange traded funds (ETFs) are generally forms of passive investing.

Recent evidence about which style is better is unclear. In 2006, active investing did worse than passive investing in all categories. In 2007, that situation reversed as active investing beat passive investing in 9 of 10 categories. The exception was investing in mid-size core holdings firms. It was much more of a mixed picture in 2008 and 2009. The sectors where active investing was outperforming passive investing as of June 2009, included large, mid-size, and small value sectors, and large and small mid-size core holdings sectors. All of the growth sectors performed worse for active investors than for passive investors.

Source: ICMA-RC website at: www.icmarc.org/xp/rc/marketview/chart/2009/20090619ActiveVsPassive.html, accessed September 22, 2009.

The Implications of Stock Market Efficiency for Managers

Having identified the various forms of market efficiency and the evidence in support of each form, we need to be clear what the implications are for the managers of a business. It seems that there are six important lessons that they should learn.

Lesson 1: Timing Doesn't Matter

If the managers of a business are considering a new issue of shares, they may feel that the timing of the issue is important. If the stock market is inefficient, there is always a risk that the price of a share will fall below its true worth, and issuing new shares at such a point could be very costly for the business. This would mean that the timing of new share issues is a critical management decision.

However, if the market is efficient, then, by definition, the price quoted for shares will accurately reflect the available information. This implies that the timing of new share issues will not be critical as there is no optimal point in time for making a new issue. Even if the market is very depressed and share prices are very low, it cannot be assumed that things will improve. The share prices prevailing at the low point will still reflect the market's estimate of the future returns from the shares. Activity 9.5 considers the issue of timing.

ACTIVITY 9.5

Why might a financial manager who accepts that the market is efficient in the semi-strong form nevertheless be justified in delaying the issue of new shares until what he or she believes will be a more appropriate time?

Solution

The justification for delaying a new share issue under the circumstance described would be that the manager believes the market has got it wrong. This situation could arise if the market has inadequate information with which to price securities correctly. The manager may have access to inside information, which, when made available to the market, will lead to an upward adjustment in share prices.

Lesson 2: Don't Search for Undervalued Businesses

If the stock market accurately absorbs information concerning businesses, the prices quoted for shares and other securities will represent the best estimates available of their true worth. This means that investors should not spend time trying to find undervalued shares in order to make gains. Unless they have access to information that the market does not have, they will not be able to beat the market on a consistent basis. To look for undervalued shares will only result in time being spent and transaction costs being incurred to no avail. Similarly, managers should not try to identify undervalued shares in other businesses with the intention of identifying possible takeover targets. While there may be a number of valid and compelling reasons for taking over another business, the argument that shares of the target business are undervalued by the stock market is not one of them.

Lesson 3: Take Note of Market Reaction

The investment plans and decisions of managers will be quickly and accurately reflected in the share price. Where these plans and decisions result in a fall in share price, managers may find it useful to review them. In effect, the market provides managers with a second opinion that is both objective and informed. This opinion should not go unheeded.

Lesson 4: You Can't Fool the Market

Some managers appear to believe that form is as important as substance when communicating new information to investors. This may induce them to window dress the financial statements in order to provide a better picture of financial health than is warranted by the facts. However, the evidence suggests that the market is able to see through any cosmetic attempts to improve the financial picture. The market quickly and accurately assesses the economic substance of the business and will price the shares accordingly. Thus, accounting policy changes (such as switching from one depreciation method to another in order to boost profits in the current year) will be a waste of time.

We saw earlier that businesses may issue mixed forms of securities. Convertible bonds, for example, have a debt element and a common share element. It is not possible, however, to fool an efficient stock market by the issue of such securities and, thereby, obtain an inexpensive form of financing. The hybrid nature of convertible bonds would be recognized and priced accordingly. Activity 9.6 considers convertible bonds in terms of market efficiency.

ACTIVITY 9.6

Convertible bonds will usually be issued with rates of interest that are lower than that of conventional bonds. Is this evidence that the market has been misled and is, therefore, inefficient?

Solution

If the market is prepared to accept a lower rate of interest for convertible bonds than for more conventional forms of debt, this need not imply that the market has been fooled. Indeed, it may well mean that the market is efficient and has taken account of all relevant information. Investors may be prepared to accept a lower rate of interest in return for the likely future benefits arising from the conversion rights.

Lesson 5: The Market Decides the Level of Risk, Not the Business

Investors will correctly assess the level of risk associated with an investment and will impose an appropriate rate of return. Moreover, this rate of return will apply to whichever business undertakes that investment. Managers will not be able to influence the required rate of return by adopting particular financing strategies. This means, for example, that the issue of certain types of securities, or combinations of securities, will not reduce the rate of return required by the market.

Lesson 6: Champion the Interests of Shareholders

It was mentioned in Chapter 1 that the primary objective of a business is the maximization of shareholder wealth. If managers make decisions and take actions that are consistent with this objective, it will be reflected in the share price. This is likely to benefit the managers of the business as well as the shareholders. REAL WORLD 9.9 describes how managers are now trying to maximize shareholder wealth by using indexing.

REAL WORLD 9.9   Canadian ETFs

In response to the lack of success that mutual funds have had in trying to beat the market, indexing has become more popular. A recent development on the index front has been the exchange traded fund (ETF). An ETF is a basket of assets, like an index fund, that trades like a stock on the stock exchange. Just as for a stock, prices fluctuate throughout the day whereas mutual fund prices are determined once a day at the end of stock trading for that day (the net asset value per unit). Investors can buy, buy on margin, sell, or sell short ETFs throughout the day, just as they can for any stock. Brokers charge commissions on ETFs just as for stocks. A big advantage in favour of ETFs is that the management expense ratio of an ETF is usually significantly lower than that on a mutual fund. As of September 2009, 103 ETFs were being

▶

traded on the Toronto Stock Exchange, covering a broad spectrum of investment categories. ETFs provide the individual investor with an easy way to lower risk through excellent diversification.

Here is a sample of Canadian ETFs available to the investor.

ETF	Ticker Symbol	Index Description
i-shares S&P/TSX 500 Index Fund	XSP	S&P 500 hedged to Canadian dollar
i-shares S&P/TSX 60 Index Fund	XIU	60 large cap Canadian stocks
i-shares S&P/TSX Capped Energy Index Fund	XEG	Canadian energy sector companies
Claymore Japan Fundamental Index EFT	CJP	FTSE RAFI Japan hedged to Canadian dollar
Claymore Oil Sands Sector EFT	CLO	Companies included in the sustainable oil sands sector index

Sources: www.fpanet.org/journal/articles/2007_Issues/jfp0107-art6.cfm and www.ishares.ca/product_info/fund_overview.do? ticker=XSP&search=true, accessed September 19, 2009.

Are the Stock Markets Really Efficient?

The view that capital markets are efficient (at least in the major industrialized countries) is now part of the conventional wisdom of finance. However, there is a growing body of evidence that casts doubt on the efficiency of capital markets and that has reopened the debate on this topic. Below we consider some of the evidence.

Stock Market Regularities

Researchers have unearthed regular share price patterns in some of the major stock markets. This suggests an element of inefficiency, as it would be possible to exploit these patterns in order to achieve superior returns over time. Some of the more important regularities that have been identified are as follows:

- *Business size.* There is now a substantial body of evidence indicating that, other things being equal, small businesses yield higher returns than large businesses. The evidence concerning this phenomenon also shows that the superior returns from small businesses will change over time. The size effect, as it is called, is more pronounced at the end of the calendar year, for example, than at any other point.
- *Price/earnings (P/E) ratio.* We saw in Chapter 4 that the P/E ratio is a measure of market confidence in a particular share: the higher the P/E ratio, the greater the expected future returns from that share. However, research has shown that a portfolio of shares held in businesses with a low P/E ratio will outperform a portfolio of shares held in businesses with a high P/E ratio. This suggests that investors can make superior returns from investing in businesses with low P/E ratios.
- *Investment timing.* There are various studies indicating that superior returns may be gained by timing investment decisions appropriately. For example, higher returns can sometimes be achieved by following the old adage, "Buy in the fall, sell in May, and go away for the summer." This was terrible advice for the summer of 2009, which produced some of the best investment gains in decades. Some studies have shown that there is an above-average fall in share price on Mondays. This may be because investors review their portfolio of shares on the weekend and then decide to sell unwanted shares when the market opens on Monday morning, thereby depressing prices. This suggests, of course, that it is better to buy rather than sell shares on a Monday. Other studies have revealed that the particular time of the day in which shares are traded can lead to superior returns.

Activity 9.7 explores an aspect of timing the Canadian market.

ACTIVITY 9.7

Can you suggest why the January–February period in Canada may provide better returns than other months of the year?

Solution

One reason may be that a new tax year begins in January. Investors may sell loss-making shares in December to offset any capital gains tax on shares sold at a profit during the tax year. As a result of these sales, share prices will become depressed. At the start of the new tax year, however, investors will start to buy shares again and so share prices will rise. In addition, registered retirement savings plan (RRSP) contribution season ends 60 days after December 31. As taxpayers make new RRSP contributions, new money flows into the market, driving up share prices.

The key question is whether these regularities seriously undermine the idea of market efficiency. Many believe that they are of only minor importance and that, on the whole, the markets are efficient most of the time. The view taken is that, in the real world, there are always likely to be inefficiencies. It can also be argued that if investors discover share price patterns, they will try to exploit these patterns in order to make higher profits. By so doing, they will eliminate the patterns and so make the markets even more efficient. However, others believe that these regularities reveal that previous research supporting the notion of market efficiency is seriously flawed and that we must seek alternative explanations for the way in which stock markets behave.

Bubbles, Bull Markets, and Behavioural Finance

In recent years, a new discipline called **behavioural finance** has emerged, which offers an alternative explanation for the way in which markets behave. This new discipline rejects the notion that investors behave in a rational manner, and there is a plethora of research evidence in psychology to support this view. Many studies have shown that individuals make systematic errors when processing information. It seems that individuals are prone to various biases and, when making investment decisions, these biases can result in the mispricing of shares. Where this occurs, there are profitable opportunities that can be exploited. A detailed study of these behavioural biases is beyond the scope of this book. However, it is worth providing one example to illustrate the challenge they pose to the notion of efficient markets.

One well-documented bias is the overconfidence that individuals have in their own information processing skills and judgment. In the context of investment decisions, overconfidence may lead to a number of errors including:

- An underreaction to new share price information, which arises from a tendency to place more emphasis on new information confirming an original share valuation than new information challenging this valuation
- A reluctance to sell shares that have incurred losses because it involves admitting to past mistakes
- An incorrect assessment of the riskiness of future returns
- A tendency to buy and sell shares more frequently than is prudent.

Such errors may help to explain share price bubbles and overextended bull markets, where investor demand keeps share prices high despite evidence suggesting they are overvalued.

Share price bubbles, which inflate and then burst, appear in stock markets from time to time. When they inflate, there is a period of high prices and high trading volumes, which is sustained by the enthusiasm of investors rather than by the fundamentals affecting the shares. During a bubble, investors appear to place too much faith in their optimistic views of future share price movements, and, for a while at least, ignore warning signals concerning future growth prospects. However, as the warning signals become stronger, the disparity between investors' views and reality eventually becomes too great and a correction occurs, bringing investors' views more into line with fundamental values. This realignment of investors' views leads to a large correction in share prices—in other words, the bubble bursts.

For similar reasons, overconfidence can result in overextended bull markets, where share prices in general become detached from fundamental values. REAL WORLD 9.10 describes two recent and well-known examples of overconfidence in the markets.

REAL WORLD 9.10

Investment Bubbles in the Markets

Dot.com Bubble, 1995–2001

A well-known speculative bubble was the run-up in internet and other high-tech stocks during the period of 1995 to 2001. Many investors thought the old bricks-and-mortar business model was dead and in the future the internet would dominate all business dealings. Market share became the focus instead of profits. A contributing factor may have been the Y2K switchover scare for computer programs, which prompted accelerated business capital spending. The NASDAQ stock market index, a key indicator of share prices for high-tech companies, rose from below 1,000 in 1995 to over 5,000 early in 2000. This means that on average share prices quintupled over that period, with many individual companies doing many times better than that. After the bubble collapsed, the NASDAQ bottomed out at 1,114 in October 2002, a loss of 78% from its peak valuation.

U.S. Housing Bubble, 2001–2007

The U.S. housing market experienced tremendous growth and price inflation during this period, which was made possible by very low interest rates and the expansion of floating-rate mortgages. So if interest rates increased, homeowners would be hit with higher mortgage payments. Also, the sub-prime mortgage market grew rapidly, as lenders made mortgage loans at higher interest rates to higher-risk buyers who did not qualify for regular-rate mortgages. When the economy slowed, the sub-prime mortgage market showed an increasing number of defaults. Repossessed houses came back onto the market, driving house prices down and bringing the house resale market almost to a halt.

Source: NASDAQ composite index figures from Yahoo! Finance at: http://finance.yahoo.com/q?s=%5EIXIC&d=t, accessed July 11, 2007.

How Should Managers Act?

At present, the debate concerning the efficiency of markets continues and further research is required before a clear picture emerges. Although this situation may be fine for researchers, we are left with the problem of how managers should respond to an increasingly mixed set of messages concerning the behaviour of the stock markets. Probably the best advice is for managers to assume that, as a general rule, the markets are efficient. The weight of evidence still supports this view, and failure to act in this way could be very costly indeed. Where it is clear that some market inefficiency exists, however, managers should be prepared to take advantage of the opportunities that it provides.

SHARE ISSUES

L.O. 3

The most common methods of issuing shares are as follows:

- Rights issues
- Stock dividend
- Bought deal
- Best efforts deal
- Private placement.

Rights Issues

Rights issues are made when businesses that have been established for some time seek to raise funds by issuing additional shares for cash. Corporate law gives existing shareholders the right of first refusal on these new shares, which are offered to them in proportion to their existing shareholding. Only where the existing shareholders waive their right would the shares be offered to the investing public generally.

Rights issues are a relatively cheap and straightforward way of issuing shares: issue expenses are quite low and issue procedures are simpler than for other forms of share issue. The fact that those offered new shares already have an investment in the business, which presumably suits their risk/return requirements, is likely to increase the chances of a successful issue. Right of first refusal is explored in Activity 9.8.

ACTIVITY 9.8

What is the advantage to shareholders of having the right of first refusal on new shares issued for cash?

Solution

The main advantage is that control of the business by existing shareholders will not be diluted, provided they acquire the new shares.

A rights offer usually allows existing shareholders to acquire shares in the business at a price below the current market price. This means that entitlement to participate in a rights offer has a cash value. Existing shareholders who do not wish to buy any more shares can sell their rights to other investors. Calculating the cash value of the rights entitlement is quite straightforward. Example 9.1 illustrates how this is done and Activity 9.9 considers the investors' options.

Example 9.1

Shaw Holdings Ltd. has 20 million common shares outstanding. These shares are currently valued on the stock exchange at $16.00 per share. The directors of Shaw Holdings believe the business requires additional long-term capital and have decided to make a one-for-four rights issue (that is, one new share for every four shares held) at $13.00 per share. What is the value of the rights per new share?

Solution

The first step in the valuation process is to calculate the price of a share following the rights issue. This is known as the *ex-rights price* and is simply a weighted average of the price of shares before the issue of rights and the price of the rights shares. In this example we have a one-for-four rights issue. The theoretical ex-rights price is calculated as follows:

	($)
Price of four shares before the rights issue (4 × $16.00):	64.00
Price of buying one rights share:	13.00
Total investment	77.00
Theoretical ex-rights price:	
Total investment	77.00
New number of shares outstanding (4 + 1)	5
Ex-rights price ($77.00 ÷ 5)	$15.40

As the price of each share, in theory, should be $15.40 following the rights issue and the price of a rights share is $13.00, the value of the rights offer will be the difference between the two:

$$\$15.40 - \$13.00 = \$2.40 \text{ per new share}$$

Market forces will usually ensure that the actual price of rights and the theoretical price will be fairly close.

ACTIVITY 9.9

An investor with 2,000 shares in Shaw Holdings Ltd. (see Example 9.1) has contacted you for investment advice. She is undecided whether to subscribe to the rights issue, sell the rights, or allow the rights offer to lapse.

Calculate the effect on the net wealth of the investor of each of the options being considered.

Solution

If the investor buys the rights shares, she will be in the following position:

Value of holding after rights issue [(2,000 + 500) × $15.40]	$38,500
Less: Cost of buying the rights shares (500 × $13.00)	6,500
Net investment	$32,000

▶

If the investor sells the rights, she will be in the following position:

Value of holding after rights issue (2,000 × $15.40)	$30,800
Sale of rights (500 × $2.40)	1,200
Net investment	$32,000

If the investor lets the rights offer lapse, she will be in the following position:

Value of holding after rights issue (2,000 × $15.40)	$30,800

As we can see, the first two options should leave her with the same net wealth as she had before the rights issue. Before the rights issue she had 2,000 shares worth $16.00 each, or $32,000. However, she will be worse off if she allows the rights offer to lapse than she would be under the other two options. In practice, the business may sell the rights offer on behalf of the investor and pass on the proceeds in order to ensure that she is not worse off as a result of the issue.

When considering a rights issue, the directors of a business must first consider the amount of funds that the business needs to raise. This will depend on the future plans and commitments of the business. The directors must then decide on the issue price of the rights shares. Generally speaking, this decision is not of critical importance. In Example 9.1, the business made a one-for-four issue with the price of the rights shares set at $13.00. However, it could have raised the same amount by making a one-for-two issue and setting the rights price at $6.50, or a one-for-one issue and setting the price at $3.25, and so on. The issue price that is finally decided upon will not affect the value of the underlying assets of the business or the proportion of the underlying assets and earnings of the business to which the shareholder is entitled. The directors must, however, ensure that the issue price is not *above* the current market price of the shares in order for the issue to be successful, as illustrated in Activity 9.10.

ACTIVITY 9.10

Why will a rights issue fail if the issue price of the shares is above the current market price of the shares?

Solution

If the issue price is above the current market price, it would be cheaper for the investor to purchase shares in the business in the open market (assuming transaction costs are not significant) than to acquire the shares by subscribing to the rights offer.

In practice, a rights issue will usually be priced at a significant discount to the market price of the shares at the date of the rights announcement. Time will elapse between the announcement date of the rights issue and the date at which the rights shares must be subscribed, and during this period there is always a risk that the market price of the shares will fall and the rights issue price will be higher than the market price at the subscription date. If this occurs, the rights issue will fail for the reasons mentioned in Activity 9.10. The higher the discount offered, therefore, the lower the risk of such failure.

Despite the attractions of rights issues, it can be argued that the rights given to existing shareholders will prevent greater competition for new shares in the business. This may, in turn, increase the costs of raising funds for the business because other forms of share issue may accomplish it more cheaply.

Stock Dividend

A **stock dividend** should not be confused with either the issuing of dividends to shareholders or a rights issue of shares. It involves the issue of new shares to existing shareholders in proportion to their existing shareholdings. However, shareholders do not have to pay for the new shares issued. In a stock dividend, a company transfers a sum from retained earnings to the common shares of the business and then issues shares, equivalent in value to the amount transferred, to existing shareholders. To understand this conversion process, and its effect on the financial position of the business, let us consider Example 9.2.

Example 9.2

Western Industries Ltd. has the following abbreviated balance sheet as at March 31:

	($ millions)
Net assets	20
Financed by	
Common shares	10
Retained earnings	10
Total equity	20

The directors decide to declare a two-for-one stock dividend totalling 500,000 shares. The market value of a share is $10, before the stock dividend. Following the stock dividend, the balance sheet of Western Industries Ltd. will be as follows:

	($ millions)
Net assets	20
Financed by	
Common shares	15
Retained earnings	5
Total equity	20

We can see in Example 9.2 that the common shares of the business have increased and there has been a corresponding decrease in the retained earnings of the business. The net assets of the business remain unchanged. Although each shareholder will own more shares following the stock dividend, the proportion held of the total number of shares in issue will remain unchanged and so the stake in the business and the net assets of the business will remain unchanged. Thus, stock dividends do not result in an increase in shareholder wealth, as illustrated in Activity 9.11. They will simply result in a bookkeeping entry from retained earnings to common shares.

ACTIVITY 9.11

Assume there were 250,000 shares outstanding in Western Industries Ltd. (see Example 9.2) before the stock dividend. What will be the market price per share following the share issue?

Solution

Recall from Example 9.2 that the share price before the stock dividend was $10.00. A holder of 100 shares would therefore be in the following position before the stock dividend issue:

100 shares held at $10.00 market price = $1,000.00

As the wealth of the shareholder has not increased as a result of the stock dividend, the total value of the shareholding will remain the same. This means that, as the shareholder holds 300 shares following the two-for-one stock dividend (i.e., 100 + 2 × 100), the market value per share will now be:

$$\frac{\$1,000.00}{300} = \$3.33$$

You may wonder from the calculations above why stock dividends are made by businesses, particularly as the effect of a stock dividend may be to reduce the retained earnings available for dividend payments. A number of reasons have been put forward to explain this type of share issue, including the following:

- *Share price.* The share price of a business may be very high and, as a result, its shares may become more difficult to trade on the stock exchange. By increasing the number of shares outstanding, the market price of each share will be reduced, which may make the shares more marketable, especially to individual investors.
- *Lender confidence.* The effect of making a transfer from distributable retained earnings to common shares will be to increase the permanent capital base of the business. This move may increase confidence among lenders. In effect, a stock dividend will lower the risk of the business reducing its common shareholders' equity investment through cash dividend distributions, which may leave lenders in an exposed position.
- *Market signals.* The directors may use a stock dividend as an opportunity to signal to investors their confidence in the future prospects of the business. The issue may be accompanied by the announcement of good news concerning the business (for example, having secured a large contract or achieved an increase in profits). Under these circumstances, the share price of the business may rise, with the expectation that earnings and dividends per share will be maintained. Shareholders would, therefore, be better off following the issue. However, it is the *information content* of the stock dividend, rather than the issue itself, that will create this increase in wealth.

A stock split is similar to a stock dividend except that no accounting entry is recorded to shift amounts from retained earnings to common shares. REAL WORLD 9.11 describes multiple stock splits at one company.

REAL WORLD 9.11

Percolating Stock Splits at GMCR

Green Mountain Coffee Roasters (GMCR) of Waterbury, Vermont, is one of the hottest stocks around. It specializes in high-end single brew coffee makers and recently signed a deal with Wal-Mart. In 2007 the company split its shares three-for-one. That took the share price from around $60 to $20 ($60 ÷ 3). In June of 2009, when most stocks were significantly below their year-ago price, GMCR again did a stock split—this time three-for-two. This split took the price per share from around $90 to $60 (($90 ÷ 3) × 2). On April 28, 2010 GMCR announced an additional three-for-one stock split. At the current price of one share on the NASDAQ of U.S. $37.00, GMCR's share price would have been $499.50 if no stock splits had been done since 2006.

Source: Yahoo! Finance, http://finance.yahoo.com/q/hp?s=GMCR&d=8&e=21&f=2009&g=d&a=8&b=27&c=1993&z=66,&y=66, accessed September 21, 2009, and www.tradingmarkets.com/news/stock-alert/gmcr_green-mountain-profit-up-announces-stock-split-945453.html, accessed September 22, 2010.

Bought Deal

A **bought deal** involves a listed business selling a new issue of shares, including IPOs, to a financial institution known as an investment dealer. The investment dealer will, in turn, sell the shares purchased from the business to the public. The investment dealer will publish a prospectus describing details of the business and the type of shares to be sold, and investors will be invited to apply for shares.

The advantage of this type of deal, from the business's viewpoint, is that the sale proceeds of the shares are certain. The investment dealer will take on the risk of selling the shares to investors. This type of deal is very common in Canada for a business that wishes to raise a large amount of funds.

Best Efforts Deal

A **best efforts deal** involves a direct invitation to the public to purchase shares in the business from an investment dealer. Typically, this is done through a newspaper advertisement, and the invitation to the public will be accompanied by the publication of a prospectus. An investment dealer will offer advice concerning an appropriate selling price. However, the business rather than the investment dealer will take on the risk of selling the shares. Both a bought deal and a best efforts deal will result in a widening of share ownership in the business.

Setting a Share Price

When issuing shares, the business or the investment dealer will usually set a price for the shares. However, establishing a share price is not an easy task, particularly where the market is volatile or where the business has unique characteristics. If the share price is set too high, the issue will not sell well and the business (or investment dealer) will not receive the amount expected. If the share price is set too low, the issue will sell out quickly and the business (or investment dealer) will receive less than could have been achieved.

One way of dealing with the pricing problem is to make a **tender issue** of shares. This involves the investors determining the price at which the shares are issued. Although the business (or underwriter) may publish a reserve price to help guide investors, it will be up to the individual investor to determine the number of shares to be purchased and the price he or she wishes to pay. Once the offers from investors have been received, a price at which all the shares can be sold will be established (this is known as the striking price). Investors that have made offers at, or above, the striking price will be issued shares at the striking price and offers received below the striking price will be rejected. Note that *all* of the shares will be issued at the same price, irrespective of the prices actually offered by individual investors.

Example 9.3 and Activity 9.12 illustrate the ways in which a striking price is achieved.

Example 9.3

Celibes Ltd. made a tender offer of shares through an investment dealer and the following offers were received by investors:

Share Price ($)	Number of Shares Tendered at this Particular Price (000s)	Cumulative Number of Shares Tendered (000s)
2.80	300	300
2.40	590	890
1.90	780	1,670
1.20	830	2,500

The directors of Celibes Ltd. wish to issue 2,000,000 shares, at a minimum price of $1.20.

The striking price would have to be $1.20 as, above this price, there would be insufficient interest to issue 2,000,000 shares. At the price of $1.20, the total number of shares tendered exceeds the number of shares available and so a partial allotment would be made. Normally, each investor would receive four shares for every five shares tendered (that is, 2,000/2,500).

ACTIVITY 9.12

Assume that, rather than issuing a fixed number of shares, the directors of Celibes Ltd. (see Example 9.3) wish to maximize the amount raised from the share issue. What would be the appropriate striking price?

Solution

The price at which the amount raised from the issue can be maximized is calculated as follows:

Share Price ($)	Cumulative Number of Shares (000s)	Share Sale Proceeds ($000)
2.80	300	840
2.40	890	2,136
1.90	1,670	3,173
1.20	2,500	3,000

The table shows that the striking price should be $1.90 to maximize the share sale proceeds.

Although tender issues are used occasionally, they are not popular with investors and are, therefore, not in widespread use.

Private Placement

A **private placement** does not involve an invitation to the public to subscribe to shares. Instead, the shares are sold to selected investors, such as large financial institutions. This can be a quick and relatively cheap method of raising funds because savings can be made in advertising and legal costs. However, it can result in the ownership of the business being concentrated in a few hands and may prevent small investors from participating in the new issue of shares. Usually, businesses seeking relatively small amounts of cash will employ this form of issuing shares.

REAL WORLD 9.12 shows the purchases of private placements made in 2008 by a renowned investor.

REAL WORLD 9.12

Warren Buffett Buys Private Placement Investments in 2008

In the bleakest period of the 2008 recession, when many companies were desperate to get enough cash to survive, famous investor Warren Buffett spent $14.5 billion to invest in private placements issued by three well-known companies. These fixed income securities from Wrigley (chewing gum), Goldman Sachs (investment bank), and General Electric yield at least 10% and all include warrants that could provide further investment gains.

Source: Berkshire Hathaway 2008 Annual Report, accessed September 19, 2009.

L.O. 4   PROVIDING LONG-TERM FINANCING FOR THE SMALLER BUSINESS

Although the stock exchange provides an important source of long-term financing for large businesses, it is not really suitable for smaller businesses. Thus, smaller businesses must look elsewhere for help in raising long-term financing, but they encounter problems in doing so. These problems, which can be a major obstacle to growth, include:

- A lack of financial management skills (leading to difficulties in developing credible business plans that will satisfy lenders)
- A lack of knowledge concerning the availability of sources of long-term financing
- An inability to provide sufficient security for loans and bonds
- An inability to meet rigorous assessment criteria (for example, a good financial track record over five years)
- An excessively bureaucratic screening process for loan applications.

In addition to the problems identified, it is worth pointing out that the cost of financing is often higher for smaller businesses than for larger businesses because of the higher risks involved.

Not all of the financing constraints are externally imposed; some arise from the attitude of owners. It seems that many owners of small businesses are unwilling to consider raising new funds through the issue of common shares to outsiders as it involves a dilution of control. As well, some owners do not take out loans because they do not believe in borrowing.

Although obtaining long-term financing is not always easy for smaller businesses (and one consequence may be excessive reliance on short-term sources of financing, such as bank overdrafts or lines of credit), things have improved in recent years.

VENTURE CAPITAL

L.O. 5

Venture capital is long-term capital provided to small and medium-sized businesses wishing to grow but which do not have ready access to stock markets. The supply of venture capital (or *private equity* capital, as it is sometimes called) has increased rapidly over recent years since both government and corporate financiers have shown greater commitment to entrepreneurial activity.

Types of Investment

Venture capitalists are interested in investing in small and medium-sized businesses. The businesses must have good growth potential and the owners and managers must have the ambition and ability to realize this potential. Businesses financed by venture capitalists have higher levels of risk than would be acceptable to other providers of financing, but will also have the potential for higher returns. Venture capitalists will usually invest for a period of five years or more, with the amount varying according to need.

Venture capitalists provide equity and debt financing for different types of business situations, including the following:

- *Start-up capital.* This is available to a range of businesses—from those that are still at the concept stage of development through to those that are ready to start selling their product. The financing provided is usually to help design, develop, or market new products and services.
- *Other early stage capital.* This is available to businesses that have undertaken their development work and are ready to begin operations.
- *Expansion (development) capital.* This aims to provide funding for growing businesses for additional working capital and new equipment. It may also include rescue financing, which is used to turn a business around after a period of poor performance.
- *Refinancing bank borrowings.* This is aimed at reducing the level of leverage.
- *Secondary purchases.* This refers to financing used to purchase shares in order to buy out part of the ownership of a business or to buy out another venture capitalist.
- *Buy-out capital.* This is capital available to acquire an existing business. A management buy-out (MBO) is where the funds are used to help the existing management team to acquire the business, and an institutional buy-out (IBO) is where the venture capitalist firm acquires the business and installs a management team of its choice.
- *Buy-in capital.* This is capital available to acquire an existing business by an external management team. This kind of acquisition is known as a management

buy-in (MBI). Buy-outs/buy-ins often occur when a large business wishes to divest itself of one of its operating units or when a family business wishes to sell out because of succession problems.

■ *Leveraged buy-outs (LBO).*   These are buy-outs that are almost entirely financed with borrowed money.

In practice, venture capitalists make much higher levels of investment in growth businesses and management acquisitions than in business start-ups. Although business start-ups may be important to the health of the economy, they are very high-risk: investing in existing businesses is a much safer bet. Furthermore, start-up businesses often require relatively small amounts of financing and so the high cost of investigating and monitoring the investment can make this type of investment unprofitable.

REAL WORLD 9.13 provides a graphical representation of venture capital investment in Canadian businesses.

REAL WORLD 9.13

Nothing Ventured, Nothing Gained

In 2008 almost all venture capitalist money in Canada went toward businesses in the expansion or start-up stages. Figures 9.4 and 9.5 show the investments by venture capitalists in Canada in 2008 according to financing stage.

FIGURE 9.4   Amount Invested in Canada by Venture Capitalists in 2008, by Financing Stage

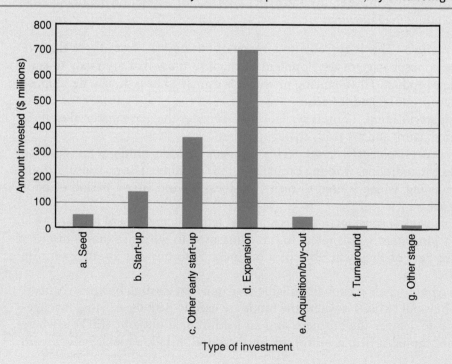

FIGURE 9.5   Number of Businesses in Canada Backed by Venture Capitalists in 2008, by Financing Stage

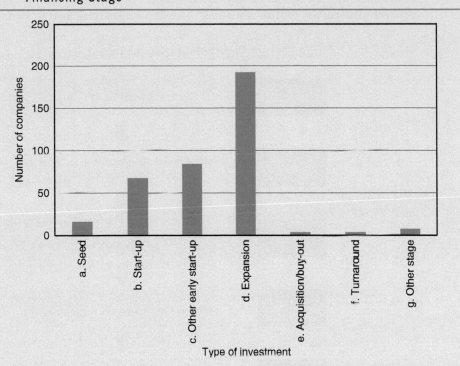

Figure 9.6 shows the industry sectors in Canada receiving venture capital money in 2008.

FIGURE 9.6   Canadian Venture Capital Amounts by Sector in 2008

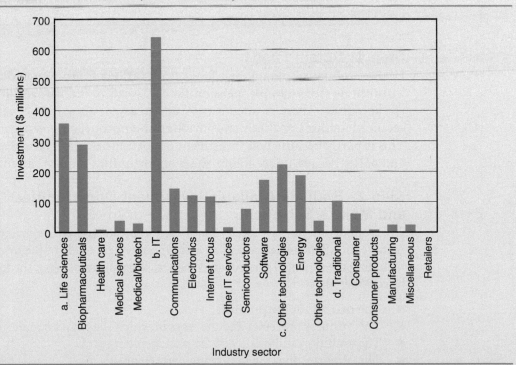

The three most popular areas in which venture capitalists invested in 2008 included the biopharmaceutical, in the Life sciences category; energy and environmental technologies, in the Other technologies sector; and software sectors, in the IT sector.

Source: Graphs constructed from data on Canada's Venture Capital and Private Equity Association website, www.cvca.ca/resources/statistics/, accessed September 21, 2009.

The Venture Capital Process

Venture capital investment involves a five-step process that is similar to the investment process undertaken within a business. The five steps are shown in Figure 9.7.

FIGURE 9.7   The Venture Capital Investment Process

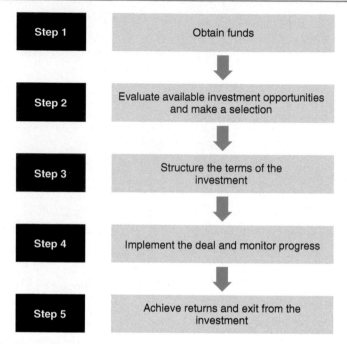

Source: M. Van der Wayer, "The Venture Capital Vacuum," *Management Today*, July 1995, pp. 60–64. Copyright © *Management Today* 2007.

Step 1: Obtain Funds

Venture capitalists obtain their funds from various sources, including large financial institutions (for example, pension funds), wealthy individuals, and direct appeals to the public. There is often a two- or three-year time lag between obtaining the required amount of funds and investing in appropriate investment opportunities. This is partly because new investment opportunities may take some time to identify and partly because, once found, these opportunities require careful investigation.

Step 2: Evaluate Available Investment Opportunities and Make a Selection

Once opportunities have been identified, the business plans prepared by the management team will be reviewed and an assessment will be made of the investment potential, including the potential for growth. When making an assessment, the following areas will be considered:

- The market for the products
- The business processes and the ways in which they can be managed
- The ambition and quality of the management team
- The opportunities for improving performance
- The types of risks involved and the ways in which they can be managed
- The track record and future prospects of the business.

The venture capitalists will also be interested in seeing whether the likely financial returns are commensurate with the risks that have to be taken. The internal rate of return (IRR) method is often used in helping to make this assessment, and an IRR in excess of 20% is normally required.

Step 3: Structure the Terms of the Investment

When structuring the financing agreement, venture capitalists will try to ensure that their own exposure to risk is properly managed. They will receive information on the progress of the business at regular intervals. The venture capitalists will often stage the injection of funds over time rather than providing all the required funds at the beginning of the venture. They will use the information provided by the business, as well as information collected from other sources, as a basis for agreeing to each payment stage. In this way, the progress of the business is reviewed on a regular basis and, where serious problems arise, the venture capitalists will retain the option of abandoning the project in order to contain any loss.

The financing provided may be in the form of common shares, debt, or preferred shares, and often a combination of these is employed. Convertible bonds can offer the venture capitalists a useful hedge against risk. If things do not go according to plan and the venture becomes unprofitable, the venture capitalists will have the bond agreement as a protection for the investment. If, however, the venture is profitable, the venture capitalists can exercise the option to convert the bond into common shares and thereby participate in the success of the business. Preferred shares are similar to bonds insofar as they confer priority over common shares in respect of annual returns and asset distributions and, like bonds, they can provide the option to convert into common shares at some future date. Preferred shares have the added advantage of not taking up the debt capacity of the business that may be useful to the future financing needs of the business.

Venture capitalists will usually expect the owner/managers to demonstrate their commitment by investing in the business. Although the amounts they invest may be small in relation to the total investment, they should be large in relation to their personal wealth.

Step 4: Implement the Deal and Monitor Progress

Venture capitalists usually have a close working relationship with client businesses throughout the period of the investment. It is quite common for the venture capitalists to have a representative on the board of directors in order to keep an eye on the investment. During the investment period it is usual for the venture capitalists to offer expert advice on technical and marketing matters. In this respect they provide a form of consultancy service to their clients. The venture capitalists will monitor whether the business plans prepared at the time of the initial investment are achieved. Monitoring by the venture capitalists is likely to be much closer at the early stages of the investment until certain problems, such as the quality of management and cost overruns, become less of a risk.

Step 5: Achieve Returns and Exit from the Investment

A major part of the total returns from the investment is usually achieved through the final sale of the investment. The particular method of divestment is, therefore, of great concern to the venture capitalist. The most common forms of divestment are through:

- A sale of the investment to another business
- An IPO of the business on a stock exchange
- A sale of the investment to the management team (buy-back)
- A sale of the investment to another venture capitalist or financial institution.

In some cases, there will be an involuntary exit when the business fails. The venture capitalist will then have to write off the investment.

REAL WORLD 9.14 shows the amounts divested in recent years by venture capitalists.

REAL WORLD 9.14

Getting Out of Dodge

Figure 9.8 shows venture capital–backed IPO and merger and acquisition (M&A) exit trends in Canada since 2003. The first graph shows the number of exits and the second graph shows the dollar size of the divestitures by venture capitalists.

FIGURE 9.8   Amounts Divested by Venture Capitalists for the Period 2003–2008

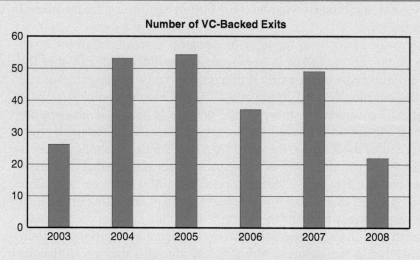

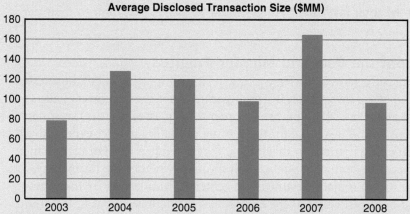

Source: Graphs constructed from data on Canada's Venture Capital and Private Equity Association website, www.cvca.ca/resources/statistics/, accessed September 21, 2009.

Venture Capital and Borrowing

A venture capitalist may require a business to borrow a significant proportion of its financing needs from a bank or other financial institution, thereby reducing the amount that the capitalist needs to invest in the business. In some cases, the cash flows generated by the business during the period in which the venture capitalist invests may then be used to reduce—or eliminate—the outstanding loan.

Example 9.4 provides a simple illustration of this process.

Example 9.4

Ippo Ltd. is a venture capitalist that has recently purchased Andante Ltd. for $80 million. The business requires an immediate injection of $60 million to meet its needs, and Ippo Ltd. has insisted that this be raised by a 10% bank loan. Ippo Ltd. intends to do an IPO for Andante Ltd. in four years' time to exit from the investment, and expects to receive $160 million on the sale of its shares. During the next four years, the cash flows generated by Andante Ltd. (after interest has been paid) will be used to eliminate the outstanding loan.

The business's operating cash flows (before interest) over the four years leading up to the IPO are predicted to be as follows:

	($ millions)			
Year	1	2	3	4
	20.0	20.0	20.1	15.0

Ippo Ltd. has a cost of capital of 18% and uses the internal rate of return (IRR) method to evaluate investment projects.

The following calculations reveal that the loan can be entirely repaid over the next four years.

	($ millions)			
Year	1	2	3	4
Cash flows:				
Operating cash flows	20.0	20.0	20.1	15.0
Loan interest (10%)	(6.0)	(4.6)	(3.1)	(1.4)
Cash available to repay loan	14.0	15.4	17.0	13.6
Loan repayments:				
Loan at start of year	60.0	46.0	30.6	13.6
Cash available to repay loan	14.0	15.4	17.0	13.6
Loan at end of year	46.0	30.6	13.6	–

There are no cash flows remaining after the loan is repaid, and so Ippo Ltd. will receive nothing until the end of the fourth year, when the shares are sold.

The IRR of the investment will be the discount rate, which, when applied to the net cash inflows, will provide an NPV of zero. Thus,

$$(\$160 \text{ million} \times \text{Discount factor}) - \$80 \text{ million} = 0$$

Solving this equation, we have:

$$\text{Discount factor} = 0.50$$

Using Table A2 in Appendix A for present value, a discount rate of approximately 19% will give a discount factor of 0.5 in four years' time. This result can be obtained by using interpolation as follows: [(0.5158 for 18% + 0.4823 for 20%) ÷ 2 = 0.4991 for 19%. 0.4991 is close enough to 0.50.]

Thus, the IRR of the investment is approximately 19%. This is higher than the cost of capital of Ippo Ltd. and so the investment will increase the wealth of its shareholders.

Taking on a large loan imposes tight financial discipline on the managers of a business as there must always be enough cash to make interest payments and capital repayments. This should encourage them to be aggressive in pursuing sales and containing costs. Taking on a loan may also boost the returns to the venture capitalist. Activity 9.13 explores the implications of not taking on a loan.

ACTIVITY 9.13

Building on Example 9.4, assume that:

(i) Ippo Ltd. provides additional common share equity at the beginning of the investment period of $60 million, thereby eliminating the need for Andante Ltd. to take on a bank loan;

(ii) Any cash flows generated by Andante Ltd. would be received by Ippo Ltd. in the form of annual dividends.

What would be the IRR of the total investment in Andante Ltd. for Ippo Ltd., assuming the investment is sold for $160 million at the end of four years, making the cash inflow for the fourth year equal to $175 (160 + 15) million?

Solution

The IRR can be calculated using the trial and error method as follows. At discount rates of 10% and 16%, the NPV of the investment proposal is:

| | | Trial 1 | | Trial 2 | |
Year	Cash Flows ($ millions)	Discount Rate* 10%	Present Value ($ millions)	Discount Rate* 16%	Present Value ($ millions)
0	(140.0)	1.00	(140.0)	1.00	(140.0)
1	20.0	0.91	18.2	0.86	17.2
2	20.0	0.83	16.6	0.74	14.8
3	20.1	0.75	15.1	0.64	12.9
4	175.0	0.68	119.0	0.55	96.3
		NPV	28.9	NPV	1.2

*Rounded to two decimal places.

The calculations reveal that, at a discount rate of 16%, the NPV is close to zero. Thus, the IRR of the investment is approximately 16%, which is lower than the cost of capital. This means that the investment will reduce the wealth of the shareholders of Ippo Ltd.

The calculations in Example 9.4 and Activity 9.13 show that, by Andante Ltd. taking on a bank loan, the returns to the venture capitalist are increased. This leverage effect is discussed in more detail in the next chapter.

REAL WORLD 9.15 describes some of the benefits and problems of using venture (private equity) financing.

REAL WORLD 9.15

Venture Capitalists—Saints or Sinners?

U.S. data shows that venture capital–backed employment represents 11% of private sector jobs and 21% of the U.S. gross domestic product. Most investments are in high-tech, high-growth industries such as information technology, biotechnology, semiconductors, and online retailing. Data from 2008 showed major increased investments

▶

in clean technology and social media. Figure 9.9 shows both revenue and job growth to be much faster at venture capital-backed firms.

Some critics argue that private equity from venture capitalists is an expensive source of capital. Debt levels are often high, adding to the risk.

FIGURE 9.9   Venture Capitalism and the Whole Economy

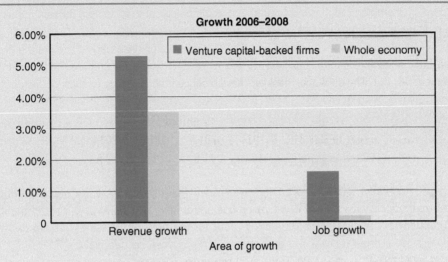

Source: Graph compiled from data included in Venture Impact 2008 report at www.nvca.org/, accessed September 22, 2009.

REAL WORLD 9.16 explains common terms used by venture capitalists, so that the everyday investor can understand their language.

Venturespeak

Highly specialized groups like venture capitalists often develop their own language. Some common terms used by venture capitalists are:

■ *MBO—Management buy-out.*   A team of managers employed at the business acquires controlling interest in the business.
■ *Angel investor.*   This is an individual with a high net worth who is active in venture financing, usually in a company's early stage of growth.
■ *Exit mechanism.*   This is the strategic means by which a private equity fund liquidates its stake in a business and achieves optimal returns.

Other definitions and acronyms used in the venture capital business can be found on the website for Canada's Venture Capital and Private Equity Association, www.cvca.ca.

Source: CVCA (Canada's Venture Capital and Private Equity Association), www.cvca.ca/resources/glossary.aspx, accessed March 2, 2007.

SELF-ASSESSMENT QUESTION   9.1

Champion Ltd. is a large conglomerate. Following a recent strategic review, management has decided to sell its agricultural foodstuffs division. The managers of this operating division believe that it could be run as a separate business and are considering a management buy-out. The division has made an operating profit of $10 million for the year to May 31, 2010, and the board of Champion Ltd. has indicated that it would be prepared to sell the division to the managers for a price based on a multiple of 12 times the operating profit for the most recent year.

The managers of the operating division have $5 million of the financing necessary to acquire the division and have approached Vesta Ltd., a venture capital business, to see whether it would be prepared to assist in financing the proposed management buy-out. The divisional managers have produced the following forecast of operating profits for the next four years:

	($ millions)			
Year to May 31	**2011**	**2012**	**2013**	**2014**
Operating profit	10.0	11.0	10.5	13.5

To achieve the profit forecasts shown above, the division will have to invest a further $1 million in working capital during the year to May 31, 2012. The division has buildings costing $40 million and plant and machinery costing $20 million. In calculating net operating profit for the division, these assets are depreciated, using the straight-line method, at the rate of 2.5% on cost and 15% on cost, respectively.

Vesta Ltd. has been asked to invest $45 million in return for 90% of the common shares in a new company specifically created to run the operating division. The divisional managers would receive the remaining 10% of the shares in return for their $5 million investment. The managers believe that a bank would be prepared to provide a 10% loan for any additional financing necessary to acquire the division. (The buildings of the division are currently valued at $80 million and so there would be adequate security for a loan up to this amount.) All net cash flows generated by the new company during each financial year will be applied to reducing the balance of the loan and no dividends will be paid to shareholders until the loan is repaid. (There are no other cash flows apart from those mentioned above.) The loan agreement will be for a period of eight years. However, if the company is sold during this period, the loan must be repaid in full by the shareholders.

Vesta Ltd. intends to realize its investment after four years when the fixed assets and working capital (excluding the bank loan) of the company are expected to be sold to a rival business at a price based on a multiple of 12 times the most recent annual operating profit. Out of these proceeds, the bank loan will have to be repaid by existing shareholders before they receive their returns. Vesta Ltd. has a cost of capital of 25% and employs the internal rate of return method to evaluate investment proposals.

Ignore taxes.

Calculations should be in millions of dollars and should be made to one decimal place.

Required:

(a) Calculate:
   (i)   The amount of the loan outstanding at May 31, 2014, immediately prior to the sale of the company
   (ii) The approximate internal rate of return for Vesta Ltd. of the investment proposal described above.

(b) State, with reasons, whether Vesta Ltd. should invest in this proposal.

Angel Investors

Angel investors are often wealthy individuals who have been successful in business. They are usually willing to invest somewhere between $10,000 and $600,000 in a start-up business or a business that is at an early stage of development through a shareholding. In some cases, larger amounts may be raised by a single angel or by a syndicate of angels. Angel investors fill an important gap in the market as the nature and size of investments that they find appealing will often be unappealing to venture capitalists. The investment is usually made for a period of three to five years and the exit strategies are basically the same as those used by venture capitalists. In addition to financing, angel investors can usually offer a wealth of business experience to budding tycoons.

Although angel investors are looking for financial returns, they may also be looking for an interesting involvement in a new venture. This may lead them to accept lower returns than would normally be expected for the risks involved. A further advantage of using angel investors is that they can often make investment decisions quickly, particularly where they have expertise in the relevant business sector. However, the amounts of financing available from individual angels are generally lower than what venture capitalists can provide.

Angel investors offer an informal source of share financing and it is not always easy for owners of small businesses to locate a suitable angel. However, a number of angel investor networks have now developed to help owners of small businesses find their perfect partner. These networks provide a variety of services, including informing angels concerning investment opportunities and advising businesses on developing business plans. Regular meetings may be organized where entrepreneurs can present their business plans to potential angels.

An appropriate exit strategy is the stock market. It can provide venture capitalists and angel investors with a useful means of liquidating an investment through the use of an IPO. **REAL WORLD 9.17** summarizes new financings by year on the Toronto Stock Exchange.

REAL WORLD 9.17

New Financing on the Toronto Stock Exchange and the TSX Venture Exchange

The TMX Group has a history of raising equity. In 2008, new financing declined. The recession crippled share prices and many companies thought it was not a good time to issue new shares because their shares were significantly undervalued.

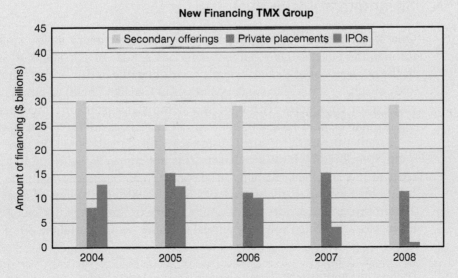

New Financing TMX Group

A secondary offering is the sale of new shares by a corporation that already has shares previously outstanding. The purpose is to raise funds like an IPO, except it is not the corporation's initial public offering but is instead a secondary public offering. Secondary offerings were the most important type of new share offerings across the board, usually followed by private placements.

Source: Graph constructed from data at the TMX Group website, http://search.tsx.com/query.html?col=tsxen&qt=IPOs% 2C+Secondary+by+sector&charset=iso-8859-1, accessed September 22, 2009.

Venture capital has figured into the history of Google, a well-known internet company. Google has grown considerably over its short life. In the beginning, the business relied heavily on family, friends, and an angel investor. Then it attracted venture capitalists before eventually going public. **REAL WORLD 9.18** charts this progress.

REAL WORLD 9.18

Google: A Financing Case History

Date	Financing Amount	Source
September 1998	$1 million	Family, friends, and an angel investor
June 1999	$25 million	Venture capital funds
August 2004	$1.673 billion	Google share IPO at $85.00 per share

Google Share	Price
August 2004, IPO price	$85.00
December 2004	$192.79
December 2005	$414.86
December 2006	$460.48

Source: www.google.com/corporate/history.html and www.venturelawcorp.com/tsx_venture_exchange.htm, accessed March 2, 2007.

Government Assistance

One of the most effective ways in which the government assists small businesses is through the Business Development Bank of Canada (BDC). The BDC is wholly owned by the government of Canada and plays a leading role in delivering financial, investment, and consulting services to small businesses in Canada. The BDC emphasizes technology and export companies. The BDC is a commercial bank offering long-term business financing to be paid back with interest. The BDC does not offer loan guarantees.[1]

Another program for small businesses is the Canada Small Business Financing Program, sponsored by Industry Canada. It is not connected with the BDC. This program seeks to increase the availability of loans for small businesses, with the federal government being willing to guarantee loans of up to 90% of the cost of asset acquisitions or asset improvement. Under this program, the maximum size of the loan is $500,000. Small businesses are defined as having annual revenues under $5 million. Since the interest rate

---

[1] Information from www.bdc.ca/en/home.htm, accessed May 1, 2007.

charged by the chartered bank cannot be higher than prime plus 3%, the Canada Small Business Financing Program is geared toward businesses with a reasonable amount of risk. For instance, if a chartered bank decided to take a chance by lending to a high-risk new business at prime plus 5%, this loan would not qualify for the loan guarantee reimbursement.[2]

THE LEASE VERSUS BUY DECISION

L.O. 6

Leasing

Leasing is a transaction in which the lessor owns the asset and leases it to the lessee. Leasing has become an important source of long-term financing, in addition to selling shares through an IPO or a secondary offering on the stock exchange, or issuing new bonds. By the mid-1970s, leasing was becoming such an important source of off-balance-sheet funding for companies that the accounting regulations had to be changed. Previously, all leases were treated as operating leases. This required a company to report only the lease payment as an expense in the income statement. So it became increasingly difficult for investors to compare, for example, the financial results of a company that owned its head office building with another company that had a long-term lease on its head office building. With the accounting rule change, a lease is now treated as a capital lease if:

■ The company retains title to the asset at the end of the lease, or
■ The company obtains the use of the asset for 75% of its useful life, or
■ The present value of the lease payments totals at least 90% of the fair value of the lease at the inception of the lease.

For example, a 20-year lease of a building with an estimated useful life of 25 years would be shown on the balance sheet as both a building asset and a long-term lease liability, because the lease life divided by the asset life is 80% (i.e., 20 ÷ 25), which exceeds the 75% cutoff. The accounting treatment for a long-term lease of an asset is now the same as for issuing debt to buy the asset outright.

Figure 9.10 presents the accounting decision-making rules in flow-chart form.

FIGURE 9.10   Capital Lease Flow Chart

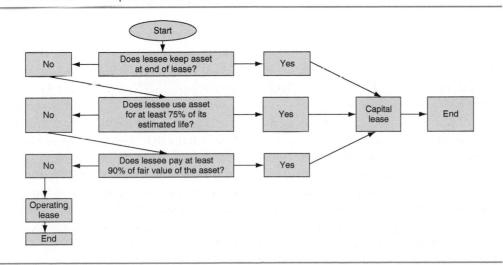

---

[2] Information at www.ic.gc.ca/epic/site/csbfp-pfpec.nsf/en/home.

Buy or Lease

Businesses often have a wide range of choices they can make in financing their purchases. One of the key decision areas is whether to buy or lease an asset. On the one hand, you might think that it is always better to buy, because then you own the asset and get to keep it. However, assets do not last forever. They break down, wear out, and become obsolete, so they must be replaced periodically. On the other hand, you might be biased toward leasing because you may have heard that it is more affordable. In reality, you must throw away your preconceptions and crunch the numbers in each case to determine whether it is better to buy or lease.

In a buy or lease decision analysis, we can usually disregard the revenue side of the equation and focus only on costs. For example, in the case where a company needs to replace an old machine in its factory, the principles for calculating the present value of revenues and costs for capital acquisitions, which we examined in Chapter 6, would have been used. Once the go-ahead is given with a positive net present value to acquire a specific new machine, the company must decide whether it is more cost-efficient to buy or lease it. We can ignore the revenues because they will be the same whether we lease or buy. Therefore, we need to determine the present value of the acquisition cash flows for buying and for leasing. Then we select the financing method that gives the lower cash flows. We are automatically maximizing the overall net present value of the acquisition and adding value to the company when we select the lower after-tax cash outflows between buying and leasing the new machine. Example 9.5 shows how this might be done.

Example 9.5

Assume that the purchasing manager for a major corporation is negotiating to buy a new machine that has an expected useful life of five years with no salvage value. It has a list price of $50,000 and a cash price of $46,640. An alternative is to lease the machine for five annual payments of $11,000 starting immediately. Is there a way to determine the implicit interest rate embedded in the lease payments of $11,000?

It turns out that we can apply the internal rate of return concepts from Chapter 6 to this problem. All we need to do is list the annual cash flows, as shown below.

Year	Cash Price Saved from Not Buying	Lease Cost	Net Cash Flow
0	$46,640	$(11,000)	$ 35,640
1		(11,000)	(11,000)
2		(11,000)	(11,000)
3		(11,000)	(11,000)
4		(11,000)	(11,000)

The cash price is shown as a positive cash inflow because that is the amount saved by choosing to lease instead of buying the machine. The present value annuity factor we need to look up is 3.24, given by the net cash flow at time equals zero, $35,640, divided by the annual lease cost, $11,000. Looking up the 3.24 factor in the present value of an annuity table, Table A4 in Appendix A, for $n = 4$, we get closest at 3.2397, which corresponds to an implicit interest rate of 9% for the lease.

Tax Issues

Taxes are a big influence on the decision to lease or buy. In addition, the government uses taxes as a policy tool to influence the economy in ways it deems important. For example, the federal government's budget in the spring of 2007 featured a tax rebate for purchasers of hybrid cars and increased taxes for purchasers of large SUVs. Sales of hybrid cars increased significantly in the wake of the budget. There is little doubt that tax policy influences economic behaviour.

Tax Deductions When Leasing

Lease payments are fully tax-deductible as long as the lessee will not own the asset at the termination of the lease. Upon buying an asset, there are two tax deductions: (1) capital cost allowance (CCA), and (2) interest on the loan to acquire the asset. For comparison purposes, we assume that a loan is used to buy the asset because leasing is equivalent to obtaining a loan to acquire an asset. This sets the two acquisition methods on an equal footing.

Tax Deductions When Buying

Capital cost allowance is the *Income Tax Act*'s equivalent to amortization expense. Unlike depreciation, which has no fixed rate, the maximum CCA rate allowed for various types of assets is prescribed in the *Income Tax Act*. The act divides asset categories into many different classes, each with its own CCA rate. For instance, the CCA rate for cars (Class 10) is 30%, for buildings (Class 1) it is 4%, and for machines (Class 39) it is 25%. You should recall from Chapter 2 that, in contrast to CCA, the accounting rules permit considerable leeway in setting the estimated useful life and consequently the amount of depreciation taken on an asset.

CCA is always calculated using the half-year rule and the declining balance method. The half-year rule means that in the year of the asset's acquisition, the CCA is half the normal maximum. In effect, the *Income Tax Act* is saying that, on average, purchases are made halfway through the year so the CCA deduction is equivalent to a half-year's deduction. The declining balance method computes the CCA deduction amount by multiplying the CCA rate by the opening balance of the undepreciated capital cost (UCC). The UCC at the end of the first year is the cost of the asset less the CCA amount claimed in the first year. This is demonstrated in Example 9.6.

Example 9.6

Jewellery Fashions Ltd. needs a new machine costing $50,000. This asset has a 25% capital cost allowance rate. The machine is expected to have a useful economic life of five years. The annual CCA claimed in the tax return and the closing UCC balance for each of the five years is shown in the following table.

Year	Opening UCC	CCA at 25%	Closing UCC
1	50,000.00	6,250.00	43,750.00
2	43,750.00	10,937.50	32,812.50
3	32,812.50	8,203.13	24,609.37
4	24,609.37	6,152.34	18,457.03
5	18,457.03	4,614.26	13,842.77

Notice the application of the half-year rule in Year 1. The CCA deduction is 25% × $50,000 × 0.5 = $6,250. This leaves a closing UCC balance of $50,000 − $6,250 = $43,750. In Year 2, the CCA deduction amount is 25% × $43,750 = $10,937.50. Notice that the half-year rule does not apply in Year 2 or any succeeding year.

Interest expense on money borrowed to buy an asset is also a tax-deductible expense. To determine the amount of interest each year, a loan amortization schedule is prepared, as shown in Example 9.7.

Example 9.7

Since almost all leases require the first payment to be made at the time that the lease agreement is signed, they are examples of an annuity due. To best compare the lease versus buy option, we will assume that the $50,000 asset acquired in Example 9.6 will be purchased with a loan at 7% interest, and that the first payment is made on the day the loan is taken out. There are five annual payments of $11,396.76. In effect, the machine is purchased with a down payment of $11,396.76 and a loan of $38,603.24.

Year	Opening Balance	Payment	Interest at 7%	Closing Balance
1	$50,000.00	$11,396.76	$2,702.23	$41,305.47
2	41,305.47	11,396.76	2,093.61	32,002.31
3	32,002.31	11,396.76	1,442.39	22,047.94
4	22,047.94	11,396.76	745.58	11,396.76
5	11,396.76	11,396.76		0.00

The interest calculation for Year 1 is 7% × ($50,000 − $11,396.76). For Year 2, the interest calculation is 7% × ($41,305.47 − $11,396.76). For Year 5, there is no interest, as the loan is fully paid off at the beginning of the year.

To summarize, the tax deductions permitted for leasing are the lease payments, and for buying an asset are the capital cost allowance and interest.

Tax Shields

A tax shield is the amount of cash saved by not having to pay taxes because of a tax deduction. The tax deduction shields the income from taxes. The tax shield in each year is given by Equation 9.1.

$$\text{Tax shield} = \text{Deduction amount} \times \text{Tax rate} \qquad 9.1$$

Example 9.8

Using the information from Examples 9.6 and 9.7, we will now additionally assume that the corporate income tax rate is 30%. The annual tax shield for the leasing option is obtained by multiplying the lease payment by the tax rate. Table 9.2 shows the annual tax shield for leasing the $50,000 machine.

TABLE 9.2   Tax Shield for Lease Option

Year	Payment	Tax Savings (30% tax rate)
1	$11,396.76	$3,419.03
2	11,396.76	3,419.03
3	11,396.76	3,419.03
4	11,396.76	3,419.03
5	11,396.76	3,419.03

In each year, the tax shield is 30% × $11,396.76.

The annual tax savings for the buy option is obtained by multiplying the tax rate times the sum of two deductions: interest expense plus capital cost allowance. Table 9.3 presents the annual tax shield for the buy option.

TABLE 9.3   Tax Shield for Buy Option

Year	Interest at 7%	CCA at 25%	Total Deductions	Tax Shield (30% tax rate)
1	$2,702.23	$ 6,250.00	$ 8,952.23	$2,685.67
2	2,093.61	10,937.50	13,031.11	3,909.33
3	1,442.39	8,203.13	9,645.52	2,893.65
4	745.58	6,152.34	6,897.92	2,069.38
5	0	4,614.26	4,614.26	1,384.28

Putting It All Together

We will select the purchase method that has the lowest net present value of the cash outflows. Table 9.4 shows the net present value of the lease option. Notice that although the lease payments are $11,396.76, Jewellery Fashions is only paying $7,977.73 on an after tax basis. The government is in effect paying the difference of $3,419.03 by allowing the company to deduct the lease payments. Also notice that a simplifying assumption has been made in that the annual payments and annual tax savings are assumed to have occurred at the same time. In reality, the payment occurs at the beginning of the year, assuming the asset is purchased then, and the tax deduction occurs at year-end when the tax return is completed. However, the simplifying assumption does not change the difference between the present value of leasing and the present value of buying, so it is a valid assumption.

TABLE 9.4   Net Present Value of Lease Option

Year	Payment	Tax Savings (30% tax rate)	Payment After Tax	Present Value Factor at 7%	Present Value at 7%
1	$11,396.76	$3,419.03	$7,977.73	0.9346	$ 7,455.99
2	11,396.76	3,419.03	7,977.73	0.8734	6,967.75
3	11,396.76	3,419.03	7,977.73	0.8163	6,512.22
4	11,396.76	3,419.03	7,977.73	0.7629	6,086.21
5	11,396.76	3,419.03	7,977.73	0.7130	5,688.12
				Net present value	**$32,710.29**

Table 9.4 shows that the present value of the leasing cash flows is $32,710.29. Table 9.5 shows the net present value for the buy option.

TABLE 9.5 Net Present Value of Buy Option

Year	Payment	Tax Shield (30% tax rate)	Net Cost of Buying	Present Value Factor at 7%	Present Value at 7%
1	$11,396.76	$2,685.67	$ 8,711.09	0.9346	$8,141.39
2	11,396.76	3,909.33	7,487.43	0.8734	6,539.52
3	11,396.76	2,893.65	8,503.11	0.8163	6,941.09
4	11,396.76	2,069.38	9,327.38	0.7629	7,115.86
5	11,396.76	1,384.28	10,012.48	0.7130	7,138.90
				Net present value	**$35,876.76**

Table 9.5 shows that the present value of the buying cash flows is $35,876.76. Furthermore, assuming the asset class is not depleted, the firm will continue to take CCA deductions in the future years. These amounts are ignored in the preceding example.

Conclusion

It is $3,166.47 (i.e., $35,876.76 – $32,710.29) *less expensive* for Jewellery Fashions *to lease* than to buy given a 7% discount rate, a 30% tax rate, and a CCA rate of 25%. In reality, the annual lease payments are usually less than the payments for buying an asset because with leasing there is often a residual asset value at the termination of the lease that the lessee is not paying for.

It should be noted that in the summer of 2008, just as the effects of the recession were starting to become fully apparent, both General Motors and Chrysler got out of the leasing business. The reason for this was that the estimated residual value of many cars was significantly higher than what the real value turned out to be. Consequently, the car companies were taking big losses on these cars at the end of the leases. Further, the car companies feared having many leased cars returned to them early before the leases were over because the customer had lost his/her job in the recession. In September, 2010, General Motors appeared to be ready to start vehicle leasing again.

Leasing makes sense when it is necessary to conserve cash flows or when an asset may become obsolete before it wears out. Leasing may be the better choice because the entire lease payment is deductible for tax purposes. Commercial leases sometimes impose restrictions on property use, such as competition restrictions, exclusivity protection, and non-compete restrictions. Car leases often impose mileage restrictions, excessive wear-and-tear restrictions, and early termination penalties.

SELF-ASSESSMENT QUESTION 9.2

Corn Products Ltd. is trying to determine whether to lease or buy a new machine. The CCA rate for the machine is 40%. The cost is estimated to be $100,000, with annual payments (whether leasing or buying) of $28,859.15. The machine will either be leased or purchased outright with a loan. In either case, payments will start at the end of the year. The machine has an economic life of four years. The appropriate discount rate is 6% and the tax rate is 30%.

Required:

Determine whether Corn Products should lease the machine or buy it. Ignore the remaining UCC at the end of four years. Show all relevant calculations.

SUMMARY

A Stock Exchange

- A stock exchange is an important primary and secondary market for capital for large businesses.
- Obtaining a stock exchange listing can help a business to raise financing and help to raise its profile, but obtaining a listing can be costly and the regulatory and other burdens can be onerous.
- Stock exchange investors are often accused of adopting a short-term perspective, although there is no real evidence to support this.
- The Toronto Stock Exchange is the main Canadian stock market.
- The TSX Venture Exchange is a second-tier stock market, which offers businesses the benefits of listing without as much burdensome regulation.
- The Montreal Exchange specializes in derivatives and options tracking.

The Efficiency of the Stock Market

- The stock market is efficient if information is processed by investors quickly and accurately so that prices faithfully reflect all relevant information.
- Three forms of efficiency have been suggested: the weak form, the semi-strong form, and the strong form.
- If the stock market is efficient, managers of a listed business should recognize six important lessons:
  - Timing doesn't matter
  - Don't search for undervalued businesses
  - Take note of market reaction
  - You can't fool the market
  - The market decides the level of risk, not the business
  - Champion the interests of shareholders.
- Stock market research into investor behaviour has cast doubt on the efficiency of stock markets.

Share Issues

- Share issues that involve the payment of cash by investors can take the form of a rights issue, a bought deal, a best efforts deal, or a private placement.
- A rights issue is made to existing shareholders. Most share issues are of this type, as the law requires that shares that are to be issued for cash must first be offered to existing shareholders.
- A best efforts deal involves a direct issue to the public and a bought deal involves an indirect issue to the public.
- A private placement is an issue of shares to selected investors.
- A stock dividend involves issuing shares to existing shareholders but the shareholders do not have to pay for them. The issue is achieved by transferring an amount from retained earnings to the common shares of the business.
- A tender issue allows the investors to determine the price at which the shares are issued.

Providing Long-Term Financing for the Smaller Business

- Smaller businesses do not have access to the stock exchange main market and so must look elsewhere for funds.

Venture Capital

- Venture capital (private equity) is long-term capital for small or medium-sized businesses that are not listed on the stock exchange. These businesses often have higher levels of risk but provide the venture capitalist with the prospect of higher levels of return.
- Venture capitalists are interested in businesses with good growth prospects and offer financing for start-ups, business expansions, and buy-outs.
- The investment period is five years or more and the venture capitalists may exit by a sale, an IPO, a buy-back, or a sale to another financial institution.
- Angel investors are wealthy individuals who are willing to invest in businesses at an early stage of development.

- A number of angel networks exist to help businesses find a suitable angel.
- The government assists small businesses through guaranteeing loans and by providing grants and tax incentives.

The Lease Versus Buy Decision

- The accounting treatment is the same whether an asset is acquired via a long-term lease or an outright purchase.
- The lease payments are tax-deductible and provide an annual tax shield equal to the tax rate times the lease payment.

- Buyers get two tax deductions:
  - Interest on the loan needed to buy the asset
  - Capital cost allowance (CCA), the *Income Tax Act*'s depreciation expense.
- The annual tax shield for buyers is the tax rate times the sum of the interest expense plus the CCA.
- The after-tax annual cash flow for costs is equal to the annual payment less the annual tax shield, for both leasing and buying.
- The decision rule is: Choose the lease or buy option according to which one has the lower net present value of after-tax cash flows.

KEY TERMS

Stock exchange	Rights issues	Tender issue
Market capitalization	Stock dividend	Private placement
Efficient stock market	Bought deal	Venture capital
Behavioural finance	Best efforts deal	Angel investors

LIST OF EQUATION

9.1   Tax shield = Deduction amount $\times$ Tax rate

REVIEW QUESTIONS

Answers to the Review Questions can be found on the Companion Website that accompanies this text at www.pearsoned.ca/atrill.

9.1 Canadian venture capitalists have been criticized for their low level of funding invested in business start-ups by comparison with the levels invested by their U.S. counterparts. Can you think of possible reasons why such a difference may exist?

9.2 Why might a public business that has a stock exchange listing revert to being an unlisted business?

9.3 Distinguish between a bought deal and a best efforts issue of shares.

9.4 What attributes should the owners and managers of a business possess in order to attract venture capital financing?

9.5 Warren Buffett is chairman of Berkshire Hathaway and is one of the most successful investors of all time. He has generally outperformed the market averages since the 1950s. Explain whether Mr. Buffett's success supports or contradicts the efficient market hypothesis.

PROBLEMS AND CASES

9.1 The following independent situations have occurred:

	Share price at beginning of the day	Situation	Share price at end of the day
1	Share price began the day at $20.30.	The founding CEO has publicly announced she has just been diagnosed with a heart ailment.	Share price closed at $18.75.
2	Share price began the day at $20.30.	The founding CEO has publicly announced she has just been diagnosed with a heart ailment.	Share price closed at $20.28.
3	Share price began the day at $25.00.	Quarterly EPS of $3.00 were publicly reported versus $2.00 a year ago.	Share price closed at $25.03.
4	Share price began the day at $25.00.	Quarterly EPS of $3.00 were publicly reported versus $2.00 a year ago. Analyst estimates for EPS were for $2.75.	Share price closed at $28.00.
5	Share price began the day at $25.00.	Quarterly EPS of $3.00 were publicly reported versus $2.00 a year ago. Analyst estimates for EPS were for $2.75.	Share price closed at $28.00 today, $25.00 one day later, $22.00 two days later, $30.00 three days later, $26.00 four days later.

Required:

For each of the independent situations described above, determine with reasons whether the shares were exhibiting a weak, semi-strong, or strong form of efficiency.

9.2 Go to http://bigcharts.marketwatch.com/. Enter the following ticker symbols, one at a time, at the top of the web page. Click on "Basic Chart," and then select a three-year timeframe.

Company	Ticker Symbol*
Loblaw	ca:l
Gildan	ca:gil
Microsoft	msft
Google	goog

*"ca" stands for Canada.

Required:

Print out the chart and draw some appropriate trend lines, as described in Real World 9.7 (page 330), which you feel best fit the pattern occurring for each company's stock chart. Based on these trend lines, make a prediction of where each company's stock price will be one month from now.

9.3 You have decided to split your $50,000 investable cash equally into exchange traded funds (ETFs) that mirror the two fastest growing stock sectors based on their one-year growth results.

ETF Sector	Now	1 Year Ago
Small Cap Index	7,500	5,600
Mid Cap Index	3,200	2,600
Large Cap Index	8,000	7,000
TSX 100	10,430	8,000

Required:

Which sectors would you invest in?

9.4 The J. Muserandathon portfolio and the S&P/TSX Composite Index closed the year at the following level, for each of the following years.

Year-End	J. Muserandathon Portfolio	S&P/TSX Composite Index*
2002	$ 90,000	6,615
2003	$ 89,000	8,221
2004	$ 93,000	9,247
2005	$ 99,000	11,272
2006	$125,000	12,908
2007	$143,000	13,833
2008	$ 96,000	8,988

*Source: http://finance.yahoo.com/q/hp?s=%5EGSPTSE, accessed September 20, 2009.

Required:
(a) Calculate the year-over-year percentage change in the J. Muserandathon portfolio and in the S&P/TSX Composite Index for each of the last four years.
(b) Evaluate J. Muserandathon's ability as an investor.

9.5 Your company has an opportunity to invest in four companies. You are trying to determine which of these investments make sense. Your company has a 9% cost of capital. It will invest in these companies and do an initial public offering (IPO) at the end of the term of investment.

	A Ltd.	B Ltd.	C Ltd.	D Ltd.
Term of investment (in years)	10	5	7	4
Amount invested	$ 100	$ 40	$ 77	$ 56
IPO value at end of term of investment	300	56	89	70

Required:
(a) Determine the internal rate of return for each investment. Round off to the nearest integer discount rate.
(b) Which investments would you recommend your company make?

9.6 Your company has an opportunity to invest in four companies. You are trying to determine which of these investments make sense. Your company has a 9% cost of capital. It will invest in these companies and receive an annual cash dividend each year starting one year after the investment. At the end of the term of investment, the investment will be scrapped with no salvage value.

	One Ltd.	Two Ltd.	Three Ltd.	Four Ltd.
Term of investment (in years)	15	10	6	5
Amount invested	$250	$ 110	$ 180	$ 450
Annual cash from dividend at end of each year	24.1	12.8	40	130

Required:

(a) Determine the internal rate of return for each investment. Round off to the nearest integer discount rate.
(b) Which investments would you recommend your company make?

9.7 Mahmood al-Fahdui Importers Limited (MFIL) of Vancouver has 30 million common shares outstanding at a market value of $7.80 per share on March 31, 2010. On April 1, 2010, MFIL issued one right for each outstanding share. To acquire a new share at $6.00 will require three rights. Your father currently owns 600 shares in MFIL.

Required:

(a) Calculate the market capitalization of MFIL on March 31, 2010, before the rights issue.
(b) Calculate the value of one right.
(c) Calculate the value of your father's holdings in MFIL on:
    (i)   March 31, 2010.
    (ii) April 1, 2010, assuming he uses the rights to buy new shares.
    (iii) April 1, 2010, assuming he sells his rights.
(d) Based on your results in part (c), what is your conclusion about the value of your father's holdings in MFIL?

9.8 Four companies are considering a rights offering. The data is as follows:

	A Ltd.	B Ltd.	C Ltd.	D Ltd.
Share price before rights issue	$ 40.00	$ 95.00	$ 36.50	$ 43.66
Rights issue: Number of existing				
shares needed for rights	5	2	4	4
Rights issue: New shares to be received	2	1	1	3
Rights exercise price	$ 34.00	$ 75.00	$ 30.25	$ 36.50

Required:

(a) Calculate the theoretical ex-rights share price for each company.
(b) Calculate the value of one right for each company.

9.9 Lots of Bend Curling Supplies Limited (LBCS) has 1 million shares outstanding as of November 30, 2010. The share price is $25.00.

Required:

Calculate the new share price on December 1, 2010, if:

(a) LBCS executes a four-for-one stock split.
(b) LBCS declares a stock dividend that will give each shareholder three shares for every one they currently own.

What is your conclusion about the post-event stock price for a four-for-one stock split and a three-share stock dividend per share?

9.10 These companies are considering a stock dividend as follows.

	A Ltd.	B Ltd.	C Ltd.	D Ltd.
Current share price	$ 40.00	$ 90.00	$ 33.00	$ 22.00
Number of shares outstanding	10,000,000	550,000	600,000	400,000
Proposed stock dividend				
Number of new shares issued				
under stock dividend	20,000,000	2,200,000	600,000	2,000,000

Required:

Calculate the new share price after the stock dividend.

9.11 EnviroCleaning Inc. (ECI) is considering issuing new shares and wants to maximize the investment funds it receives. However ECI has not yet determined a price at which the shares should be sold.

Share Price ($)	Number of Shares Tendered at This Particular Price	Cumulative Number of Shares Tendered
7.50	200,000	200,000
7.00	270,000	470,000
6.50	630,000	1,100,000
5.00	300,000	1,400,000

Required:
What striking price would you recommend that ECI adopt?

9.12 Venture capital is an important source of risk capital for smaller-businesses.

Required:
   (a) Explain the term *venture capital* and discuss the main types of business ventures that are likely to prove attractive to a venture capital business.
   (b) Identify the main issues that the board of directors of a business should take into account when deciding whether to use venture capital financing.
   (c) Identify and discuss the factors that a venture capitalist will take into account when assessing an investment proposal.

9.13 (a) Explain what is meant by the term *efficient market hypothesis* and discuss the three main forms of market efficiency.
   (b) Explain the implications of an efficient market for the managers of a business that is listed on the Toronto Stock Exchange.

9.14 Smaller businesses experience greater problems in raising financing than larger businesses.

Required:
   (a) Discuss the problems that smaller businesses may confront when trying to obtain long-term financing.
   (b) Describe how smaller businesses may gain access to long-term financing.

9.15 Pizza Shack Ltd. operates a chain of pizza restaurants in the Maritimes. The business started operations five years ago and has enjoyed rapid growth. The directors of the business believe, however, that future growth can only be achieved if the company seeks a listing on the Toronto Stock Exchange. If the directors go ahead with a listing, the financial advisers to the business have suggested that an issue of common shares by tender at a minimum price of $2.20 would be an appropriate method. The advisers have suggested that 3 million shares should be issued, although the directors of the business are keen to raise the maximum amount of funds possible.
   Initial research carried out by the financial advisers suggests that the following demand for shares at different market prices is likely:

Share Price ($)	Number of Shares Tendered at Each Share Price (000s)
3.60	850
3.20	1,190
2.80	1,380
2.40	1,490
2.00	1,540
1.60	1,560
	8,010

Required:

    (a) Discuss the advantages and disadvantages of making a tender issue of shares.

    (b) Calculate the expected proceeds from the tender issue, assuming the business:

        (i)   Issues 3 million shares

        (ii) Wishes to raise the maximum amount of funds possible.

9.16 Harbour Shipping Ltd. (HSL) is considering investing in a separate tug boat enterprise that would be held and managed for five years and then sold. The total cost at the end of 2009 would be $30 million. HSL would acquire 20% of the tugboat company for $5 million. Venture Capitalists Inc. (VCI) has been asked to invest $20 million to obtain the remaining 80% ownership of the tugboat business. VCI's cost of capital is 12%. The remaining purchase price would be obtained in the form of a long-term bank loan at 15% interest. The estimated annual operating profit, shown below, would be used each year to pay the interest on the bank loan and as much principal as possible. The remaining bank loan principal would be repaid at the end of five years when the tugboat company is re-sold. Additional working capital of $450,000 will be required at the end of 2012. New equipment, costing $2 million and having an economic life of 10 years with a salvage value of $100,000, is required at the end of 2011. HSL uses the straight-line depreciation method. At the end of five years, the tugboat company would be sold for $40 million.

	2010	2011	2012	2013	2014
Operating profit	$ 1,000,000	$ 1,400,000	$ 1,467,000	$ 1,678,000	$ 2,420,000

Required:

    (a) Calculate the loan outstanding at the end of 2014.

    (b) Calculate the approximate internal rate of return for VCI on this tugboat investment.

    (c) Should VCI invest in the tugboat operation?

9.17 Sunrise Foods Inc. has decided to add a fifth warehouse distribution centre, partly to take advantage of a new government incentive that has increased the CCA rate for such buildings to 10%. The cost is estimated to be $3 million, with annual payments (whether leasing or buying) of $394,421.33. The building will either be leased or be purchased outright with a loan. In either case, payments will start at the end of the year. The building has an economic life of 15 years. The appropriate discount rate is 10% and the tax rate is 45%.

Required:

Determine whether Sunrise should lease the building or buy it. Ignore remaining UCC at the end of 15 years. Show all relevant calculations.

9.18 Fanverse Athletic Shoes (FAS) wants to acquire a new leather-sewing machine. To buy it, FAS would have to borrow the entire cost, which would be $162,156.43. There are 10 equal annual payments starting immediately with an interest rate of 5%. On the other hand, FAS could lease the machine for the same payment per year, payable immediately for a 10 year period at 5% interest. Both interest rates and FAS's cost of capital are 5%. The machine will last 10 years and have no salvage value. The tax rate is 40%. The machine qualifies for a capital cost allowance of 30%.

Required:

    (a) Prepare the 10-year loan amortization schedule.

    (b) Prepare the 10-year capital cost allowance schedule under the purchase option.

    (c) Prepare the 10-year tax shield schedule for the purchase option.

    (d) Prepare the after-tax net present value of the purchase option.

    (e) Prepare the after-tax net present value of the lease option.

    (f) Is leasing or purchasing better for FAS?

CHAPTER 10

The Cost of Capital and the Capital Structure Decision

LEARNING OUTCOMES

When you have completed this chapter, you should be able to:

1 Calculate the cost of capital for a business and explain its relevance to investment decision making.

2 Calculate the degree of financial leverage for a business and explain its significance.

3 Evaluate different capital structure options available to a business.

4 Identify and discuss the main points in the debate concerning the optimal capital structure for a business.

INTRODUCTION

In appraising investment opportunities, the cost of capital has an important role to play. In this chapter, we shall see how the cost of capital may be computed. We then turn our attention to the factors that should be taken into account when making capital structure decisions and, in particular, the impact of leverage on the risks and returns to common shareholders. We touched on this area in Chapter 4 and will now consider it in more detail. We end the chapter by examining the debate concerning whether an optimal capital structure exists for a business.

L.O. 1   COST OF CAPITAL

We saw in Chapter 6 that the cost of capital is used as the appropriate discount rate in NPV calculations and as the appropriate hurdle rate when assessing IRR calculations. As investment projects are normally financed from long-term capital, the discount rate (or hurdle rate) that should be applied to new investment projects should reflect the expected returns required by the providers of these various forms of capital. From the viewpoint of the business, these expected returns by investors will represent the cost of capital that it employs. This cost is an *opportunity cost* as it represents the return that investors would expect to earn from investments with a similar level of risk.

Because the cost of capital is an essential element of investment appraisal, its calculation must be undertaken with care. Failure to do so could lead to adverse consequences for the business, as outlined in Activity 10.1.

ACTIVITY 10.1

What adverse consequences could result from failing to calculate the cost of capital for a business correctly?

Solution

If a business using the NPV approach to investment appraisal calculates its cost of capital incorrectly, it will apply the wrong discount rate to investment projects. On the one hand, if the cost of capital figure is understated, this may result in the acceptance of projects that will reduce shareholder wealth. This can arise when the understated cost of capital would produce a positive NPV, whereas the correct cost of capital would produce a negative NPV. This would result in the acceptance of unprofitable projects. If, on the other hand, the cost of capital figure is overstated, this may result in the rejection of profitable projects.

Similar problems can occur where a business adopts the IRR method and uses the incorrect cost of capital as the hurdle rate.

In Chapter 8, we saw that the main forms of *external* long-term capital for businesses include:

■ Common shares
■ Preferred shares
■ Debt (bonds and loans).

In addition, an important form of *internal* long-term capital is:

■ Retained earnings.

In the sections that follow, we will see how the cost of each element of long-term capital may be calculated. We will also see that there is a strong link between the cost of a particular element of capital and its value: both are determined by the level of return. As a result, our discussions concerning the cost of capital will also embrace the issue of value. We consider first how each element of capital is valued and then go on to calculate its cost to the business.

Common Shares

There are two major approaches to determining the cost of common shares to a business: the dividend-based approach and the risk/return-based approach.

Dividend-Based Approach

Investors hold assets (including shares) in the expectation of receiving future benefits. We can say that the value of a share can be defined as the future dividends that investors receive by holding the share. To be more precise, the value of a share will be the present value of the expected future dividends from the particular share.

In mathematical terms, the value of a common share (P_0) can be expressed as in Equation 10.1

$$P_0 = \frac{D_1}{(1 + K_0)^1} + \frac{D_2}{(1 + K_0)^2} + \frac{D_3}{(1 + K_0)^3} + \cdots + \frac{D_n}{(1 + K_0)^n} \qquad 10.1$$

where: P_0 = the current market value of the share
D = the expected future dividend in years 1 to n
n = the number of years over which the business expects to pay dividends
K_0 = the cost of common shares to the business (that is, the required return for investors)

Activity 10.2 explores the relevance of this valuation approach.

ACTIVITY 10.2

The valuation approach above takes into account the expected dividend stream over the whole life of the business. Is this really relevant for an investor who holds a share for a particular period of time (say five years) and then sells the share?

Solution

The valuation approach should still be relevant. The investor will receive dividends from the business, and so the market value of the share at the time of sale should reflect the present value of the future dividends. Thus, when determining an appropriate selling price, the expected dividend stream beyond the point at which the share is held should be highly relevant to the investor.

The valuation model above can also be used to determine the *cost* of common shares to the business (K_0). The cost of a share will be the discount rate that, when applied to the stream of expected future dividends, will produce a present value that is equal to the current market value of the share. Thus, the required rate of return for common share investors (that is, the cost of shares to the business) is similar to the internal rate of return (IRR) used to evaluate investment projects.

A simplifying assumption we can make is that dividends will remain constant over time. In that case, as shown in Equation 10.2, the fairly complicated equation to calculate the current market value of a share stated above can be reduced to:

$$P_0 = \frac{D_0}{K_0} \qquad 10.2$$

Equation 10.2 (which is the equation for capitalizing a perpetual annuity) can be rearranged to provide an equation for calculating the cost of capital of common shares to the business, as shown by Equation 10.3:

$$K_0 = \frac{D_0}{P_0} \qquad 10.3$$

So, a company with a constant dividend (with no expected growth in the dividend) has a cost of capital for common shares equal to the dividend yield of the stock—that is, equal to $D_0 \div P_0$.

Activity 10.3 applies the dividend-based approach.

ACTIVITY 10.3

Blackbird Investments Ltd. has common shares outstanding that have a current market value of $2.20. The annual dividend to be paid by the business in future years is expected to be $0.40. What is the cost of capital of shares to the business?

Solution

The cost of capital of shares will be:

$$K_0 = \frac{D_0}{P_0}$$

$$= \frac{\$0.40}{\$2.20}$$

$$= 0.182 \text{ or } 18.2\%$$

A different simplifying assumption is that dividends will grow at a constant rate over time. In that case, to calculate the current market value of a share, Equation 10.1 can be reduced to what's shown in Equation 10.4:

$$P_0 = \frac{D_1}{K_0 - g} \qquad\qquad 10.4$$

where g is the expected annual growth rate. (The model assumes that K_0 is greater than g.)

Equation 10.4 can also be rearranged to provide an equation for calculating the *cost* of capital of common shares, as shown in Equation 10.5:

$$K_0 = \frac{D_1}{P_0} + g \qquad\qquad 10.5$$

Determining the future growth rate in dividends (g) is often a problem in practice. One approach is to use the average past rate of growth in dividends (adjusted, perhaps, for any new information concerning future prospects). There are, however, several other approaches and a business must select whichever is likely to give the most accurate results. Activity 10.4 applies Equation 10.5.

ACTIVITY 10.4

Alberta Corp. has shares outstanding with a current market price of $1.50. The dividend expected for next year is $0.20 per share and future dividends are expected to grow at a constant rate of 3% a year. What is the cost of capital for common shares to the business?

Solution

The cost of capital for common shares is calculated as follows:

$$K_0 = \frac{D_1}{P_0} + g = \frac{\$0.20}{\$1.50} + 0.03 = 0.163 \text{ or } 16.3\%$$

Note the two differences here to the constant dividend example above. Here, we use next year's dividend (which is this year's dividend plus one year's growth) divided by today's price, P_0, and then we add on the growth factor to obtain the cost of capital for common shares.

We have now seen how the value of a share to an investor and the cost of capital for the business are linked and how valuation models can help in deriving the required returns from investors. This relationship between value and the cost of capital also applies to preferred shares and debt, as we shall see in a later section.

Risk/Return Approach

An alternative approach to calculating the returns required by common shareholders is to use the **capital asset pricing model (CAPM)**. This approach builds on the ideas that we discussed in Chapter 7.

We may recall that the higher the level of risk, the higher the risk premium that will be demanded, as depicted in Figure 10.1.

FIGURE 10.1   The Relationship between Risk and Return

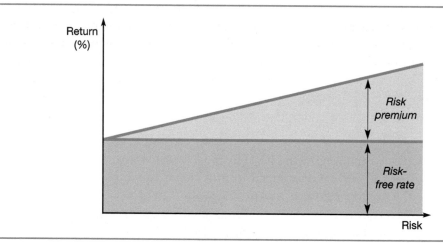

Although this idea was used in respect of investment projects undertaken by a business, it is equally valid when considering investments in common shares. CAPM (pronounced "cap-M") is based on the idea that the required rate of return to common share investors (and, therefore, the cost of capital of common shares to the business) is viewed as being made up of a risk-free rate of return *plus* a risk premium. This means that, to calculate the required return, we have to derive the risk-free rate of return and the risk premium associated with a particular share.

The returns from government bonds can be used as an approximation for the risk-free rate of return because the government guarantees payment. A more difficult problem, however, is deriving the risk premium for a particular share. CAPM does this by adopting a three-stage process:

1. Measure the risk premium for the common share market as a whole. This figure will be the difference between the returns from the common share market and the returns from an investment in risk-free investments.
2. Measure the returns from a particular share in relation to the returns from the common share market as a whole.
3. Apply this relative measure of returns to the common share market risk premium (calculated in Stage 1) to derive the risk premium for the particular share.

The second and third stages of the process require further explanation.

You may recall from Chapter 7 that total risk is made up of two elements: *diversifiable* and *non-diversifiable* risk. Diversifiable risk is specific to the investment project and can be eliminated by spreading available funds among investment projects. Non-diversifiable risk is common to all projects and therefore cannot be diversified away. This element of risk arises from general market conditions.

This distinction between the two types of risk is also relevant to investors. The total risk associated with holding shares is also made up of diversifiable and non-diversifiable risk. By holding a portfolio of shares, an investor can reduce and, perhaps, eliminate diversifiable risk, which is specific to the share, leaving only non-diversifiable risk, which is common to all shares.

We know that risk-averse investors will only be prepared to take on increased risk if there is the prospect of increased returns. However, because diversifiable risk can be eliminated through holding a diversified portfolio, there is no reason why investors should receive additional returns for taking on this form of risk. It is, therefore, only the non-diversifiable risk element of total risk for which investors should expect additional returns.

The non-diversifiable risk element for a particular share can be measured using **beta** (*b*). This is a measure of the degree to which a share fluctuates with movements in the market as a whole, or, to put it another way, it is the non-diversifiable risk of the share in relation to the market as a whole. A risky share is one that experiences greater fluctuations than those of the market as a whole and, therefore, has a high beta value. It follows that the expected returns for such a share should be greater than the average returns of the market.

Using the above ideas, the required rate of return for investors for a particular share can be calculated as in Equation 10.6

$$K_0 = K_{RF} + b(K_m - K_{RF}) \qquad \text{10.6}$$

where: K_0 = the required return for investors for a particular share
K_{RF} = the risk-free rate on government securities
b = beta of the particular share
K_m = the expected returns to the market for the next period
$(K_m - K_{RF})$ = the expected market average risk premium for the next period

This equation reflects the idea that the required return for a particular share is made up of two elements: the risk-free return plus a risk premium. We can see that the risk premium is equal to the expected risk premium for the market as a whole multiplied by the beta of the particular share. This adjustment to the market risk is undertaken to derive the relative risk associated with the particular share. (As stated earlier, beta measures the non-diversifiable risk of a particular share in relation to the market as a whole.)

The expected market average risk premium can be derived by reference to past periods, assuming that past periods provide a good predictor of future periods. A market average for a relatively long period is usually calculated, as share returns can fluctuate wildly over the short term. Then, the CAPM equation is used to calculate the risk premium by subtracting the returns from government securities (the risk-free rate) from the average returns to the market. **REAL WORLD 10.1** shows the average equity market returns, the average returns on long-term government of Canada bonds, and the equity market risk premium in Canada for a variety of time periods. The 2005–2008 period, with the negative 2.12% risk premium, is skewed by the 35.63% loss in 2008 for the S&P/TSX composite index. In the 2005–2007 period, the risk premium was 10.39% on average.

Common Share Risk Premiums

The following table shows the calculation of the equity market risk premium for the Canadian market for three decades starting from 1974 as well as the 2005 to 2008 period.

Decade	TSX Returns	Average Interest Rate Long-Term Canada Bonds	Canadian Equity Market Risk Premium
1974–1983	16.12%	10.00%	6.12%
1985–1994	9.25%	9.00%	0.25%
1995–2004	10.09%	7.00%	3.09%
2005–2008	2.14%	4.26%	(2.12%)

Source: www.bank-banque-canada.ca/en/rates/sel_hist.html and www.google.ca/ search?hl=en&q= tsx+historical+returns&meta=Canadian Equity Fund 21, accessed September 2, 2009.

A share with a return that moves in perfect step with the market will have a beta measure of 1.0. A share that is only half as volatile (risky) as the market will have a beta of 0.5, and a share that is twice as volatile (risky) as the market will have a beta of 2.0. The evidence suggests that many shares have a beta that is fairly close to the market measure of 1.0. Betas are normally measured using regression analysis on past data, again, on the assumption that past periods provide a good predictor of future periods. The monthly returns from a particular share (that is, dividends plus any increase in share value) for a period are regressed against the returns from the market as a whole (as represented by some stock exchange index such as the S&P/TSX Composite Index.).

To illustrate this approach, let us assume that the monthly returns from a particular share and the returns from the market are plotted on a graph, as shown in Figure 10.2.

FIGURE 10.2   Relationship between the Returns from an Individual Share and Returns from the Market

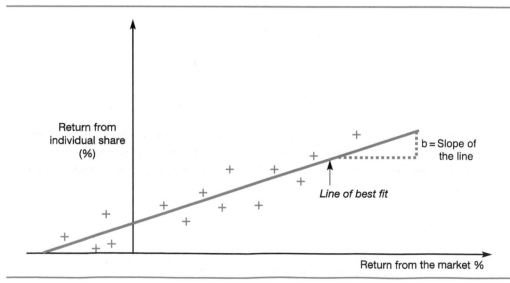

A line of best fit can then be drawn, using regression analysis. Note the slope of this line. We can see that, for this particular share, the returns do not change as much as the returns for the market as a whole. In other words, the beta is less than 1.

Measures of beta for the shares of listed businesses are available from various information agencies such as the investment and newspaper websites. Calculating beta, therefore, is not usually necessary. **REAL WORLD 10.2** provides examples of betas of some well-known Canadian listed businesses, and Activity 10.5 explores the use of such information.

REAL WORLD 10.2

Betas in Practice

Betas for some well-known Canadian companies are shown in Figure 10.3 below.

FIGURE 10.3   Beta for Some Canadian Companies

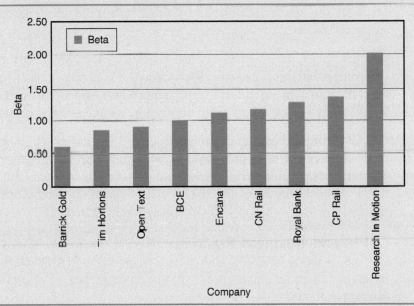

The figure shows that of these companies, Barrick Gold has the lowest beta of the sample and Research In Motion has the highest beta.

Source: Graph constructed from Standard and Poor's data provided at BMO InvestorLine: www1.bmoinvestorline.com/ILClientWeb/client/quickQuote.do?method=displayQuickQuoteResult&symbol=TD&market=C, accessed September 25, 2009.

ACTIVITY 10.5

Red Lake Ltd. has recently obtained a measure of its beta from a business information website. The beta obtained is 1.2. The expected returns to the market for the next period are 10% and the risk-free rate on government securities is 3%. What is the cost of capital of common shares to the business?

Solution

Using the CAPM equation we have:

$$K_0 = K_{RF} + b(K_m - K_{RF}) = 3\% + 1.2(10\% - 3\%) = 11.4\%$$

Figure 10.4 below illustrates the main elements in calculating the cost of capital of common shares using CAPM.

FIGURE 10.4   Calculating the Cost of Capital for Common Shares Using CAPM

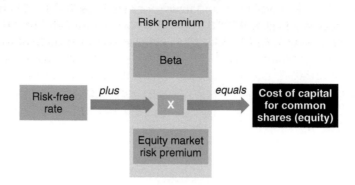

Criticisms of CAPM

Some of the key assumptions of CAPM have been challenged. These include the assumptions that:

- Investors hold a well-diversified portfolio of shares (and therefore need not be compensated for diversifiable risk)
- The return on a share will be influenced *only* by general market changes
- There is a linear relationship between beta and expected returns.

All theoretical models contain simplifying assumptions and these criticisms could be overlooked if CAPM provided a good explanation of the relationship between risk and return. Unfortunately, various studies have shown that it fails to do this. Until a more complete model of the risk/return relationship is developed, however, CAPM remains the best way to estimate common share returns.

CAPM and Business Practice

Despite its flaws, CAPM is widely used in practice. REAL WORLD 10.3 indicates that most chief financial officers use CAPM to estimate the cost of capital, even in the space tourism industry.

REAL WORLD 10.3

Beta Is Out of This World

A 2001 survey found that 75% of senior financial executives use CAPM to estimate their firm's cost of capital. This is not limited to earthbound ventures.

For example, a 1999 analysis estimated beta for the space tourism industry at 1.50, which, interestingly enough, is just slightly below the 1.55 beta of the luxury apparel and accessories fashion industry group. Applying this beta, CAPM estimated the cost of capital for the space tourism industry at 17.6%, assuming all equity financing. At the time of this study, a required rate of return of 6% was being used by the fledgling space tourism industry based on the assumption of receiving government-backed loan financing.

Sources: http://findarticles.com/p/articles/mi_m4130/is_4_31/ai_96904312, accessed April 28, 2007; F. Eilingsfeld and D. Schaetzler, "The Cost of Capital for Space Tourism Ventures," Proceedings of 2nd ISST, Daimler-Chrysler GmbH, 1999: www.spacefuture.com/archive/the_cost_of_capital_for_space_ventures.shtml, accessed April 28, 2007.

Retained Earnings

Retained earnings are an important source of financing from common shareholders and, as we saw in Chapter 8, cannot be regarded as cost-free. If profits are reinvested by the business, the shareholders will expect to receive returns on these funds that are equivalent to the returns expected from investments in opportunities with similar levels of risk. The common shareholders' interest in the business is made up of common share capital plus any retained earnings, and the expected returns from each should, in theory, be the same. Hence, when we calculate the cost of common share capital, we are also calculating the cost of any retained earnings. (In practice, however, we may require a slightly higher return from any new shares issued to compensate for transaction issue costs.)

Debt

We begin this section concerning debt as we began the sections relating to common shares. That is, we will consider the value of this element first and then go on to consider its cost. It cannot be emphasized enough that these two aspects are interrelated. Indeed, they may be seen as two sides of the same coin.

Even though each debt a company takes on must be repaid, overall debt can be viewed as perpetual because as each debt is repaid, the company can borrow again, maintaining a stable debt/equity ratio. As a result, interest will be paid indefinitely. When the rate of interest on the loan is fixed, the equation used to derive the value of debt is similar to the equation used to derive the value of common shares when the dividends remain constant over time. The value of debt is shown in Equation 10.7:

$$P_d = \frac{I}{K_d} \qquad \text{10.7}$$

where: P_d = the current market value of the bond or loan
K_d = the cost of debt to the business
I = the annual rate of interest on the bond or loan

Equation 10.7 can be rearranged to provide an equation for calculating the *cost* of capital for debt, as shown in Equation 10.8:

$$K_d = \frac{I}{P_d} \qquad \text{10.8}$$

Interest payments on debt are deductible for taxation purposes and so the numerator of Equation 10.8 is reduced by the tax charge. For investment appraisal purposes we take the after-tax net cash flows resulting from a project, and so, when calculating the appropriate discount rate, we should be consistent and use the after-tax rates for the cost of capital. Equation 10.9 shows the after-tax cost of debt as:

$$K_d = \frac{I(1 - t)}{P_d} \qquad \text{10.9}$$

where *t* is the tax rate.

Activity 10.6 applies Equation 10.9 to calculate the cost of capital a loan.

ACTIVITY 10.6

Tan Ltd. has a perpetual loan outstanding on which it pays an annual rate of interest of 10%. The current market value of the perpetual loan is $88 per $100 nominal value and the income tax rate is 20%. What is the cost of capital for the loan to the business?

Solution

Using Equation 10.9, the cost of capital for the loan is:

$$K_d = \frac{I(1-t)}{P_d}$$

$$= \frac{10(1-0.20)}{88}$$

$$= 9.1\%$$

In this case, the before-tax loan yield is $10 ÷ 88 = 11.4%. This makes the after-tax yield equal to (1 − 0.20) × 11.4% = 9.1%.

Note that the rate of interest payable on the nominal value of the debt (10%) does not represent the relevant cost for investment appraisal purposes. Rather, we are concerned with the *opportunity cost* of the debt. This represents the return that can be earned by investing in an opportunity that has the same level of risk. The *current market rate of interest* of the debt, (11.4%) as calculated above, will provide us with a measure of the relevant opportunity cost.

Where the debt is redeemable, deriving the cost of capital figure is a little more complex. However, the principles and calculations required to derive the relevant figure have already been covered in Chapter 5. An investor who purchases redeemable bond investments will pay an initial amount and then expect to receive annual interest payments plus a repayment of capital at the end of the loan period. The required rate of return for the investor will be the discount rate, which, when applied to the future cash flows, will produce a present value that is equal to the current market value of the investment. Thus, the rate of return can be computed in the same way as the IRR is computed for other forms of investment opportunity. Let us consider Example 10.1.

Example 10.1

Lim Associates Corp. issues $20 million in bonds on which it pays an annual rate of interest of 10% on the nominal value. The issue price of the bonds is $88 per $100 nominal value and the corporate tax rate is 20%. The bonds are due to be redeemed in four years' time at their nominal value.

What are the annual cash flows for this issue?

Solution

The cash flows for these bonds will be as follows:

		Cash Flows ($ millions)
Year 0	Current market value [$20 million × (88/100)]	17.6
Years 1–3	Interest payable $20 million × 10%	(2.0)
Year 4	Redemption value (−$20 million) + Interest (−$2 million)	(22.0)

To derive the cost of capital of the bonds to the business, the trial and error approach that is used in calculating the IRR can be used, as outlined in Activity 10.7.

ACTIVITY 10.7

Calculate the cost of capital for bonds for Lim Associates Corp. (*Hint*: Start with a discount rate of 10%.)

Solution

Using a discount rate of 10%, the NPV is calculated as follows:

	Cash Flows ($ millions)	Discount Rate* 10%	PV of Cash Flows ($ millions)
Year 0	17.6	1.00	17.6
Year 1	(2.0)	0.91	(1.8)
Year 2	(2.0)	0.83	(1.7)
Year 3	(2.0)	0.75	(1.5)
Year 4	(22.0)	0.68	(15.0)
		NPV	(2.4)

This discount rate is too low, as the discounted future cash outflows exceed the issue price of the bond—that is, the NPV is negative. Let us try 16%.

	Cash Flows ($ millions)	Discount Rate* 16%	PV of Cash Flows ($ millions)
Year 0	17.6	1.00	17.6
Year 1	(2.0)	0.86	(1.7)
Year 2	(2.0)	0.74	(1.5)
Year 3	(2.0)	0.64	(1.3)
Year 4	(22.0)	0.55	(12.1)
		NPV	1.0

*Rounded to two decimal places

This discount rate is a little too high, as the discounted cash outflows are less than the issue price of the bond. Thus, the appropriate rate lies somewhere between 10% and 16%.

We can see that the NPV changed by $3.4 million (that is, $2.4 million + $1.0 million) for a 6% (i.e., 16% − 10%) change in the discount rate, which is equivalent to $0.6 million for every 1% change. Thus, a discount rate of 14% would achieve an NPV of zero (10% + 2.4 ÷ 6). This represents the pre-tax cost for bonds. The tax is 20% and so the after-tax cost of capital for bonds is 14% × (1 − 0.2) = 11.2%.

Preferred Shares

Preferred shares may be either redeemable or nonredeemable. They are similar to bonds insofar as the holders receive an agreed rate of return each year (which is expressed in terms of the nominal value of the shares). However, preferred shares differ from bonds in that the annual dividends paid to preferred shareholders do not represent a tax-deductible expense. Thus, the full cost of the annual dividend payments must be borne by the business. Where the rate of dividend on the preferred shares is fixed (that is, there is no right to participate in additional profits), the equation used to derive the value of nonredeemable preferred shares is again similar to the equation used to derive the value of common shares where the dividends remain constant over time. Equation 10.10 shows nonredeemable preferred shares as:

$$P_p = \frac{D_p}{K_p}$$

10.10

where: P_p = the current market price of the preferred shares
K_p = the cost of preferred shares to the business
D_p = the annual dividend payments

Equation 10.11 can be rearranged to provide an equation for calculating the *cost* of capital for nonredeemable preferred shares, as shown in Equation 10.11:

$$K_p = \frac{D_p}{P_p}$$

10.11

Equation 10.11 is applied in Activity 10.8.

ACTIVITY 10.8

Nova Inc. has 12% preferred shares with a nominal (par) value of $100.00. The shares have a current market price of $90.00 (excluding dividends). What is the cost of capital for the preferred shares?

Solution

The cost of capital for the preferred shares is:

$$K_p = \frac{D_p}{P_p} = \frac{12\% \times 100}{90} = \frac{12}{90} = 13.3\%$$

As with common shares with a constant dividend, the yield on preferred shares—that is, the preferred share dividend divided by the market price of the preferred shares—is the cost of capital for preferred shares.

In the case of redeemable preferred shares, the cost of capital can be calculated using the IRR approach, which was used earlier to determine the cost of redeemable bonds, and is illustrated in Activity 10.9.

ACTIVITY 10.9

L. C. Conday Ltd. has $50 million worth of 10% $100 preferred shares outstanding. The current market price is $92 and the shares are due to be redeemed in three years' time at their nominal value. What is the cost of capital for the preferred shares? (*Hint:* Start with a discount rate of 10%.)

Solution

The annual cash flows are as follows:

		Cash Flows ($ millions)
Year 0	Current market value ($50 million × 92/100)	46.0
Years 1–2	Dividends ($50 million × 10%)	(5.0)
Year 3	Redemption value ($50 million) + Dividend ($5 million)	(55.0)

▶

Using a discount rate of 10%, the NPV is as follows:

	Cash Flows ($ millions)	Discount Rate 10%	PV of Cash Flows ($ millions)
Year 0	46.0	1.00*	46.0
Year 1	(5.0)	0.91	(4.6)
Year 2	(5.0)	0.83	(4.2)
Year 3	(55.0)	0.75	(41.3)
		NPV	(3.9)

This discount rate is too low, as the discounted future cash outflows exceed the issue price of the preferred share capital. Let us try 14%:

	Cash Flows ($ millions)	Discount Rate 14%	PV of Cash Flows ($ millions)
Year 0	46.0	1.00*	46.0
Year 1	(5.0)	0.88	(4.4)
Year 2	(5.0)	0.77	(3.9)
Year 3	(55.0)	0.68	(37.4)
		NPV	0.3

The discounted cash outflows are almost equal to the market value of the preferred share capital. Thus, the cost of capital for the preferred shares is approximately 14%.

*rounded to 2 decimals

WEIGHTED AVERAGE COST OF CAPITAL (WACC)

When making financing decisions, it is argued that managers of a business have a target capital structure in mind. Although the relative proportions of equity and debt may vary over the short term, these proportions, it is claimed, remain fairly stable when viewed over the medium to longer term. The existence of a fairly stable capital structure is consistent with the view that managers believe that a particular financing mix will minimize the cost of capital of the business, or, to put it another way, a particular financing mix provides an optimal capital structure for the business. (Whether or not there is such a thing as an optimal capital structure is discussed later in the chapter.) However, a target capital structure is unlikely to remain fixed. It may change from time to time in response to changes in factors such as the tax rates and interest rates, which affect the cost of particular elements of the capital structure.

The existence of a stable capital structure (presumably reflecting the target capital structure) has important implications for the evaluation of investment projects. It has already been argued that the required rates of return from investors (that is, the costs of capital to the business) should provide the basis for determining an appropriate discount rate for investment projects. If we accept that a business will maintain a fairly stable capital structure over the period of the project, then the average cost of capital can provide an appropriate discount rate. The average cost of capital can be calculated by taking the cost of the individual elements and then weighting each element in proportion to the target capital structure (by market value) of the business. Example 10.2 illustrates how the **weighted average cost of capital (WACC)** is calculated.

Example 10.2

Danton Ltd. has 10 million common shares outstanding with a current market value of $2.00 per share. The expected dividend for next year is $0.16 per share and this is expected to grow each year at a constant rate of 4%. The business also has:

- 10 million 9% $1 nonredeemable preferred shares in issue with a market price of $0.90 per share, and
- $20 million of perpetual loan with a nominal rate of interest of 6% and which is quoted at $80 per $100 nominal value.

Assume a tax rate of 20% and that the current capital structure reflects the target capital structure of the business.

What is the weighted average cost of capital of the business?

Solution

Step 1. Calculate the cost of the individual elements of capital. The cost of capital of common shares in Danton Ltd. is calculated as follows:

$$K_0 = \frac{D_1}{P_0} + g$$

$$= \frac{\$0.16}{2.00} + 0.04 = 12\%$$

Note: The dividend valuation model has been used to calculate the cost of capital for common shares; however, the CAPM model could have been used instead if the relevant information had been available.

The cost of capital for the preferred share capital is as follows:

$$K_p = \frac{D_p}{P_p}$$

$$= \frac{\$0.09}{0.90} = 10\%$$

The cost of capital of the loan is:

$$K_d = \frac{I(1 - t)}{P_d} = \frac{6(1 - 0.2)}{80} = 6.0\%$$

Step 2. Calculate the weighted average cost of capital:

	(a) Market Value ($ millions)	(b) Proportion of Total Market Value	(c) Cost %	(d) = (b × c) Contribution to WACC
Common shares (10 million × $2) (see note)	20	0.44	12	5.3
Preferred shares (10 million × $0.90)	9	0.20	10	2.0
Bonds ($20 million × 0.8)	16	0.36	6	2.2
	45	1.00		
			WACC	9.5%

Note: The market value of the capital rather than the nominal value has been used in the calculations. This is because we are concerned with the opportunity cost of capital invested, as explained earlier. Column (b), converted to percentages, gives the weights used in calculating WACC. Forty-four percent of the cost of capital is made up of the 12% cost of common shares, 20% is composed of the 10% cost of preferred shares, and the remaining 36% of the cost of capital is composed of the 6% cost of debt.

Figure 10.5 describes the approach used to calculate the WACC of a business. Most businesses maintain a target capital structure range.

FIGURE 10.5   Calculating WACC

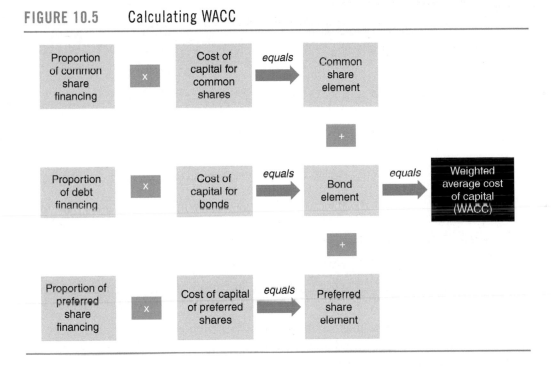

Specific or Average Cost of Capital?

An investment project may be financed by raising funds from a particular source. As a result, it is tempting to argue that the cost of capital for the project should be based on the particular type of financing that has been raised. However, this argument would be incorrect. When new funds are required for a particular project, it is not normally feasible to raise the funds in exactly the same proportions as in the existing capital structure. To minimize the cost of raising funds, it will usually make sense for a business to raise funds from one source and, later, to raise funds from another, even though this may lead to deviations from the required capital structure over the short term. The fact that a particular source of new funds is used for a project will be determined by the requirements for the long-term capital structure of the business rather than the requirements of the project.

Using the specific cost of funds raised for the project could lead to illogical decisions being made. Assume a business is considering an investment in two new machines that are identical in every respect and that each machine has an estimated IRR of 12%. Let us further assume that the first machine will be financed using long-term debt with an after-tax cost of 10%. However, as debt capacity of the business will then be used up, the second machine must be financed by common share capital at a cost of 14%. If the specific cost of capital is used to evaluate investment decisions, the business would be in the peculiar position of accepting the investment in the first machine, because the IRR exceeds the cost of capital, and rejecting the second (identical) machine because the IRR is lower than the cost of capital! By using the WACC, we avoid this kind of problem. Each machine will be evaluated according to the average cost of capital, which should then result in consistent decisions being made.

SELF-ASSESSMENT QUESTION   10.1

Montreal Controls Ltd. has gathered the following data:

Common share current annual dividend per share	$2.00
Interest rate on long-term permanent debt	10%
Preferred share dividend	$2.50
Common share dividend growth rate	15%
Common share market price	$40.50
Preferred share market price	$30.00
Tax rate, *t*	45%
Market value of capital structure:	
Long-term debt	$200,000
Preferred shares	$100,000
Common shares	$300,000

Required:
Calculate the weighted average cost of capital, WACC, for Montreal Controls Ltd.

REAL WORLD 10.4 describes some potential benefits, especially with respect to WACC for companies, that would accrue from achieving a free trade in securities.

REAL WORLD 10.4

WACC and Free Trade in Securities?

Canada is a partner in the free trade in goods and services within the North American Free Trade Agreement (NAFTA). However, this does not include free trade in securities. There are high costs involved with cross-border securities trading between Canada and the United States. In addition, U.S. restrictions make it difficult for Americans to buy Canadian shares listed only in Canada. It has been estimated that general free trade in securities could reduce costs by 60% and reduce the cost of capital by 9%.

Free trade in securities would also mean an increase in the more than 100 U.S. companies currently listed on the TSX. This would provide companies with more access to capital, especially in the oil and gas industry, where Canada is a world leader.

Source: Remarks by Richard Nesbitt, CEO, TSX Group, "Women in the Lead" Luncheon, November 30, 2006, from http://search.tsx.com/query.html?col=tsxen&qt=cost+of+capital&charset=iso-8859-1, accessed March 20, 2007.

Limitations of the WACC Approach

The WACC approach has been criticized for not taking proper account of risk in investment decisions. In practice, different investment opportunities are likely to have different levels of risk and so it can be argued that the cost of capital for each project should be adjusted accordingly. We may recall from Chapter 7 that investors who are normally risk-averse require higher returns to compensate for higher levels of risk. This means that the WACC is really only suitable where an investment project is expected to have the same level of risk as existing investments, or the proposed project is fairly small and is, therefore, not expected to have a significant effect on the overall risk level of the business.

It was mentioned earlier that the WACC approach assumes that the capital structure of the business remains stable over the period of the investment project. However, if this is not the case, the validity of the WACC approach is undermined. Changes in capital structure can result in changes in the proportions of the individual capital elements and, perhaps, changes in the costs of these elements.

Cost of Capital in Practice

REAL WORLD 10.5 below provides some evidence on the use of WACC as the appropriate discount rate in capital investment decisions.

Counting the Cost

Figure 10.6 shows that over 70% of 117 firms surveyed stated that they used WACC or WACC plus a premium as their discount rate to determine the economic viability of investment proposals. The cost of unleveraged equity as the discount rate is only appropriate if the firm has no debt outstanding and the project under consideration has a risk profile similar to the company's overall risk profile.

FIGURE 10.6   The Discount Rate Used for Investment Projects

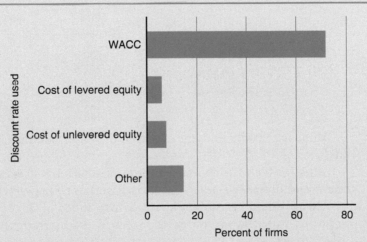

Source: Iwan Meier and Vefa Tarhan, abstract paper, "Corporate Investment Decision Practices and the Hurdle Rate Premium Puzzle," October 10, 2006, located at http:neumann.hec.ca/cref/sem/documents/060329.pdf, accessed April 28, 2007. © Neumann/ HEC Montreal.

L.O. 2   FINANCIAL LEVERAGE

We have already seen that the presence of capital with a fixed rate of return (such as debt and preferred shares) in the long-term capital structure of a business is referred to as leverage (or, to be more precise, financial leverage). The term *leverage* is used to convey the point that fixed return capital can accentuate the changes in earnings before interest and taxes (EBIT) and on the returns to common shareholders. Levers can be used to influence a large force at one end with a small force at the other. The same principle applies in finance. Figure 10.7 shows how the force of a small amount of capital, as represented by the 5 kg ball, is magnified through the debt lever, to obtain results equivalent to a large amount of capital (the 100 kg ball).

FIGURE 10.7   A Demonstration of Leverage

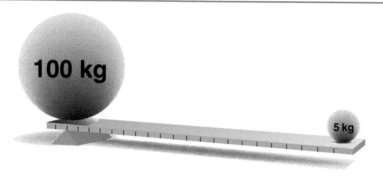

The effect of financial leverage on the returns to common shareholders is demonstrated in Example 10.3.

Example 10.3

Alpha Ltd. and Gamma Ltd. are similar businesses and have generated identical earnings before interest and taxes (EBIT) for Year 1 of $80 million. The long-term capital structure of each business is as follows:

	Alpha ($ millions)	Gamma ($ millions)
Common shares	200	340
12% preferred shares	100	50
10% loan	100	10
	400	400

Alpha has 200 million shares outstanding and Gamma has 340 million shares outstanding.

Although both businesses have the same total long-term capital, we can see that the amount of financial leverage differs significantly between the two businesses.

A widely used measure of leverage, mentioned in Chapter 4, is as follows:

$$\text{Leverage ratio} = \frac{\text{Long-term (non-current) debt}}{\text{Shareholders' equity} + \text{Long-term (non-current) debt}} \times 100\% \qquad 4.12$$

Since we are treating the preferred shares the same as long-term debt, the formula can be written as follows:

$$\text{Financial leverage ratio} = \frac{\text{Debt} + \text{Preferred shares (if any)}}{\text{Total long-term capital}} \times 100\%$$

For Alpha and Gamma, the leverage ratios are 50% [i.e., (100 + 100)/400 × 100%] and 15% [i.e., (50 + 10)/400 × 100%], respectively. These ratios indicate that Alpha has a high amount of financial leverage, that is, a high proportion of fixed return capital (debt plus preferred shares) in relation to its total long-term capital, and Gamma has a relatively low level of financial leverage.

Let us now consider the effect of financial leverage on the returns to common shareholders. The earnings per share (EPS) for the common share investors of each business for Year 1 can be calculated as follows:

	Alpha ($ millions)	Gamma ($ millions)
EBIT	80.0	80.0
Less: Loan interest	10.0	1.0
Earnings before taxes	70.0	79.0
Less: Income tax (30%)	21.0	23.7
Net income	49.0	55.3
Less: Preferred dividend paid	12.0	6.0
Earnings available to common shareholders	37.0	49.3
EPS	$0.185	$0.145

The EPS for common share investors of Alpha are $0.185 (that is, $37 million/200 million) and for Gamma they are $0.145 (that is, $49.3 million/340 million).

In this example, we can see that common share investors in Alpha earn higher returns in Year 1 than common share investors in Gamma. This arises from the use of a higher level of fixed return capital (debt and preferred share capital) in the capital structure. The advantage of financial leverage is that when additional profits generated from the use of fixed return capital exceed the additional fixed payments (interest and preferred dividends) incurred, the surplus will accrue to the common shareholders. The more leverage in the capital structure, the higher the potential benefits. So, in this case, the common share investors of Alpha achieve a higher return.

However, the financial leverage effect operates in both directions. To illustrate this point, let us assume that the earnings before interest and taxes for the following year are $40 million for each business. The earnings per share for common share investors for Year 2 would be as follows:

	Alpha ($ millions)	Gamma ($ millions)
EBIT	40.0	40.0
Less: Loan interest	10.0	1.0
Earnings before taxes	30.0	39.0
Less: Income tax (30%)	9.0	11.7
Net income	21.0	27.3
Less: Preferred dividend	12.0	6.0
Earnings available to common shareholders	9.0	21.3
EPS	$0.045	$0.063

In this case, we can see that the returns (as measured by EPS) to common shareholders of Alpha are lower than those of Gamma. The cost of servicing the debt and preferred share capital will remain the same as in Year 1 and so the fall in earnings before interest and taxes will be borne entirely by the common shareholders. We can also see from the example that the decrease in earnings per share is much greater for common shareholders in the higher-leveraged business than in the lower-leveraged business. This illustrates the point made earlier that the effect of financial leverage is to accentuate changes in returns to common share investors arising from changes in earnings before interest and taxes.

DEGREE OF FINANCIAL LEVERAGE

The higher the level of financial leverage, the more sensitive earnings per share become to changes in earnings before interest and taxes for any given level. The **degree of financial leverage** provides a measure of the financial leverage effect and can be calculated as in Equation 10.12:

$$\text{Degree of financial leverage} = \frac{\text{Percentage change in EPS}}{\text{Percentage change in EBIT}} \qquad 10.12$$

For Alpha, the degree of financial leverage, based on the changes between Year 1 and Year 2, will be:

$$\text{Degree of financial leverage} = \frac{(\$0.045 - \$0.185) \div \$0.185}{(\$40.0 - \$80.0) \div \$80.0} = \frac{-75.7\%}{-50\%} = 1.5$$

Activity 10.10 uses Equation 10.12 to calculate the degree of leverage for Gamma.

ACTIVITY 10.10

What is the degree of financial leverage for Gamma?

Solution

For Gamma, the degree of financial leverage will be:

$$\text{Degree of financial leverage} = \frac{\text{Percentage change is EPS}}{\text{Percentage change in EBIT}}$$

$$= \frac{(\$0.063 - \$0.145) \div \$0.145}{(\$40.0 - \$80.0) \div \$80.0}$$

$$= \frac{-56.6\%}{-50\%}$$

$$= 1.1$$

In both cases, the degree of financial leverage is greater than 1, which indicates the presence of financial leverage. The higher it is, the greater the sensitivity of earnings per share to changes in earnings before interest and taxes. This measure of financial leverage indicates that, in the case of Alpha, a 1.0% change in earnings before interest and taxes from the base level of $80 million will result in a 1.5% change in earnings per share, whereas for Gamma, a 1.0% change in earnings before interest and taxes from the base level of $80 million will only result in a 1.1% change in earnings per share.

Another way of arriving at the degree of financial leverage for a particular level of earnings before interest and taxes is as in Equation 10.13:

$$\text{Degree of financial leverage} = \frac{\text{EBIT}}{\text{EBIT} - I - \dfrac{P \times 100}{100 - t}} \qquad 10.13$$

where: I = interest charges
$\quad\quad\quad P$ = preferred dividend
$\quad\quad\quad t$ = tax rate

(Note that the preferred dividend is grossed up to a pre-tax amount by multiplying the dividend by $100/(100 - t)$. This is done to ensure consistency with the other variables in the equation.)

Equation 10.13 has the advantage that a single measure of EBIT is all that is required to derive the degree of financial leverage. For Alpha, the measure will be calculated as follows for Year 1:

$$\text{Degree of financial leverage} = \frac{80}{80 - 10 - \dfrac{12 \times 100}{100 - 30}}$$

$$= \frac{80}{52.9}$$

$$= 1.5$$

This equation yields the same results as the equation shown earlier. Activity 10.11 applies the equation to Gamma.

ACTIVITY 10.11

Calculate the degree of financial leverage for Gamma for Year 1 using Equation 10.13.

Solution

The calculation is:

$$\text{Degree of financial leverage} = \frac{\text{EBIT}}{\text{EBIT} - I - \dfrac{P \times 100}{100 - t}}$$

$$= \frac{80}{80 - 1 - \dfrac{6 \times 100}{100 - 30}}$$

$$= \frac{80}{70.4}$$

$$= 1.1$$

This is the same as previously calculated.

It is important to appreciate that the impact of financial leverage for a business will become less pronounced as the level of earnings before interest and taxes increases in relation to fixed capital payments (interest and preferred dividends). Where earnings before interest and taxes barely cover the fixed capital payments, even small changes in the former figure can have a significant impact on earnings per share. This high degree of sensitivity will be reflected in the degree of financial leverage measure. However, as earnings before interest and taxes increase in relation to fixed capital charges, earnings per share will become less sensitive to changes. As a result, the degree of financial leverage measure will be lower. Activity 10.12 considers the impact of financial leverage.

ACTIVITY 10.12

What is the degree of financial leverage for Alpha and Gamma for Year 2?
Hint: **Use the alternative calculation method.**

Solution

For Alpha the degree of financial leverage in Year 2 (when profit before interest and taxes are much lower) will be:

$$\text{Degree of financial leverage} = \frac{\text{EBIT}}{\text{EBIT} - I - \dfrac{P \times 100}{100 - t}}$$

$$= \frac{40}{40 - 10 - \dfrac{12 \times 100}{100 - 30}}$$

$$= 3.1$$

For Gamma, the degree of financial leverage in Year 2 will be:

$$\text{Degree of financial leverage} = \frac{\text{EBIT}}{\text{EBIT} - I - \dfrac{P \times 100}{100 - t}}$$

$$= \frac{40}{40 - 1 - \dfrac{6 \times 100}{100 - 30}}$$

$$= 1.3$$

EPS for both businesses is more sensitive to changes in the level of EBIT in Year 2 than in Year 1 when profits were higher. However, in Year 2, returns to common shareholders in Alpha, which has a higher level of financial leverage, have become much more sensitive to change than returns to common shareholders in Gamma.

L.O. 3 LEVERAGE AND THE EVALUATION OF CAPITAL STRUCTURE DECISIONS

When evaluating capital structure decisions, the likely impact of leverage on the expected risks and returns for common shareholders must be taken into account. The use of pro forma financial statements and leverage ratios, which were examined in earlier chapters, can help assess the likely effect of different capital structure options on the risks and returns for common shareholders. Example 10.4 and Activities 10.13 and 10.14 illustrate the ways in which capital structure options may be evaluated.

Example 10.4

Tawa Limited manufactures catering equipment for restaurants and hotels. The abridged financial statements for 2010 are as follows:

Tawa Limited
Abridged Income Statement
for the year ended May 31, 2010
(in $ millions)

Sales	137.4
Earnings before interest and taxes	23.2
Interest expense	2.4
Earnings before taxes	20.8
Income tax expense	5.2
Net income	15.6

Tawa Limited
Balance Sheet
as at May 31, 2010
(in $ millions)

Current assets		
Cash	1.3	
Accounts receivable	27.6	
Inventory	22.5	
Total current assets		51.4
Property, plant, and equipment		
Land	20.0	
Buildings	28.7	
Less: Accumulated depreciation	8.5	
Net buildings	20.2	
Machinery and equipment	24.6	
Less: Accumulated depreciation	7.2	
Net machinery and equipment	17.4	
Net property, plant, and equipment		57.6
Total assets		109.0
Current liabilities		
Accounts payable	25.2	
Income taxes payable	2.6	
Total current liabilities		27.8
Long-term liabilities		
Bank loan @ 12%		20.0
Total liabilities		47.8
Shareholders' equity		
Common shares (60 million outstanding)	15.0	
Retained earnings	46.2	
Total shareholders' equity		61.2
Total shareholders' equity and liabilities		109.0

Tawa Limited
Statement of Retained Earnings
for the year ended May 31, 2010
(in $ millions)

Opening retained earnings, June 1, 2009	36.6
Add: Net income	15.6
Less: Dividends paid	(6.0)
Closing retained earnings, May 31, 2010	46.2

The board of directors of Tawa Ltd. has decided to invest $20 million in new machinery and equipment to meet an expected increase in sales for the business's products. The expansion in production facilities is expected to result in an increase of $6 million in annual earnings before interest and taxes.

To finance the proposed investment, the board of directors is considering either:

1. The issue of 8 million common shares at $2.50 per share, resulting in 68 million (60 million + 8 million) shares outstanding, or
2. The issue of $20 million 10% bonds at par.

The directors wish to increase the dividend per share by 10% in the forthcoming year regardless of the financing method chosen. This will increase the dividend per share from $0.10 (i.e., $6 ÷ 60) per share to $0.11 per share (i.e., $0.10 × 1.10).

Assume a tax rate of 25%. Share issue costs can be ignored.

Required:

Which financing option should be chosen?

Solution

A useful starting point in tackling this problem is to prepare a pro forma income statement, including additions to retained earnings, for the year ended May 31, 2011, under each financing option.

Pro Forma Income Statement
with Additions to Retained Earnings
for the year ended May 31, 2011

	Shares ($ millions)	Bonds ($ millions)
Earnings before interest and taxes (23.2 + 6)	29.2	29.2
Interest expense	2.4	4.4 (2.4 + 10% × 20)
Earnings before taxes	26.8	24.8
Income tax (25% × 26.8)	6.7	6.2 (25% × 24.8)
Net income	20.1	18.6
Less: Dividend ($0.11 × 68)	(7.5)	(6.6) ($0.11 × 60)
Additions to retained earnings for the year	12.6	12.0

Having prepared the forecast, consider the impact of each financing option on the overall capital structure of the business. The projected capital structure under each option will be:

	Shares ($ millions)	Bonds ($ millions)
Equity		
Common shares ($15 + 8 × $2.50)	35.0	15.0[1]
Retained earnings	58.8[2]	58.2[3]
Total equity	93.8	73.2
Bonds	20.0	40.0

Notes
1. The common share amount did not change under the bonds option.
2. ($46.2 + $12.6)
3. ($46.2 + $12.0)

To help us further, leverage ratios and profitability ratios may be calculated under each option.

ACTIVITY 10.13

Using the forecast figures that have been calculated as at May 31, 2011, compute the return on common shareholders' equity ratio (ROE), earnings per share, times interest earned ratio, and leverage ratio, assuming:

(a) The business issues shares
(b) The business issues bonds.

Solution

These ratios are as follows:

	(a) Shares	(b) Bonds
Return on common shareholders' equity (ROE)		

ROE =

$$\frac{\text{Earnings (net income) available to common shareholders}}{\text{Common shares plus retained earnings}}$$

	(a) Shares	(b) Bonds
Share issue = $\dfrac{\$20.1}{\$93.8} \times 100\%$	21.43%	
Bond issue = $\dfrac{\$18.6}{\$73.2} \times 100\%$		25.41%

Earnings per share (EPS)

$$EPS = \frac{\text{Earnings available to common shareholders}}{\text{Number of common shares}}$$

	(a) Shares	(b) Bonds
Share issue = $\dfrac{\$20.1 \text{ million}}{68 \text{ million}}$	$0.296	

▶

$$\text{Bond issue} = \frac{\$18.6 \text{ million}}{60 \text{ million}} \qquad\qquad \$0.310$$

Times interest earned ratio

$$\text{Times interest earned ratio} = \frac{\text{Earnings before interest and taxes}}{\text{Interest expense}}$$

$$\text{Share issue} = \frac{\$29.2 \text{ million}}{\$2.4 \text{ million}} \qquad\qquad 12.2 \text{ times}$$

$$\text{Bond issue} = \frac{\$29.2 \text{ million}}{\$4.4 \text{ million}} \qquad\qquad 6.6 \text{ times}$$

Leverage ratio

$$\text{Leverage ratio} = \frac{\text{Debt}}{\text{Common shares} + \text{retained earnings}} \times 100\%$$

$$\text{Share issue} = \frac{\$20.0 \text{ million}}{(\$93.8 \text{ million} + \$20 \text{ million})} \times 100\% \qquad 17.6\%$$

$$\text{Bond issue} = \frac{(\$20.0 \text{ million} + \$20.0 \text{ million})}{(\$73.2 \text{ million} + \$40 \text{ million})} \times 100\% \qquad 35.3\%$$

The calculations we have undertaken in Activity 10.13 should help us assess the implications of each financing option.

ACTIVITY 10.14

Briefly evaluate each of the proposed financing options from the perspective of an existing shareholder.

Solution

The bond option provides the investor with better returns. We can see that EPS is slightly higher and the ROE is 4% higher than under the share option. However, the bond option also produces higher leverage and, therefore, a higher level of risk. Although the leverage ratio for the bond option does not seem excessive, it does represent a significant increase to the existing level of 24.6% (that is, $20 million/$81.2 million) and is twice as high as that for the share option. The times interest earned ratio for the bond option is almost half that for the share option. Nevertheless, the earnings before interest and taxes comfortably exceed the interest charges.

The investor must decide whether the fairly small increase in returns warrants the increase in leverage that must be undertaken to achieve those returns.

Leverage and Signalling

Managers must be aware that when a decision to change the existing level of leverage is announced, investors may interpret this as a signal concerning future prospects. Thus, an increase in leverage may be interpreted by investors as indicating management confidence in future profitability because they are willing to take on more risk. As a result, share prices may rise. Managers must therefore be sensitive to the possible signals that are being transmitted to the market by their actions and, where necessary, provide further explanation.

CONSTRUCTING AN EBIT–EPS INDIFFERENCE CHART

When making a financing decision, managers may wish to know the returns to common shareholders at different levels of earnings before interest and taxes under the different financing options available. It is often useful to present this information to managers in the form of a chart. To provide an illustration of such a chart, we can use the information contained in our answer to Example 10.4. The chart, which is referred to as an **EBIT–EPS indifference chart**, is set out in Figure 10.8. The vertical axis of the chart plots the earnings per share and the horizontal axis plots the earnings before interest and taxes.

FIGURE 10.8   EBIT–EPS Indifference Chart for Two Financing Options

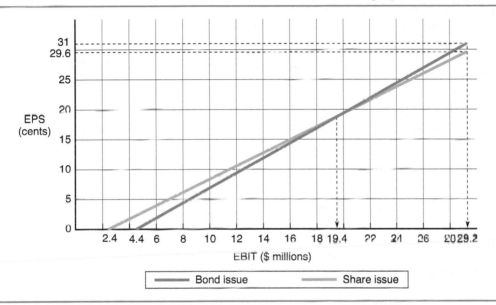

To show the returns to shareholders at different levels of profit, we need two coordinates for each financing option. The first will be the earnings before interest and taxes necessary to cover the fixed capital charges. For the bond issue, the relevant amount is $4.4 million interest expense, and for the common share issue, the amount is $2.4 million interest expense (see income statements above). This is because, at these amounts, there will be nothing available to the common shareholders and so earnings per share will be zero. These points will be plotted on the horizontal axis.

The second coordinate for each financing option will be the earnings per share at the expected earnings before interest and taxes. (However, an arbitrarily determined level of earnings before interest and taxes could also be used.) For the bond issue, the earnings per share at the expected earnings before interest and taxes is 31.0 cents, and for the common share issue it is 29.6 cents (see earlier calculations). By joining the two coordinates relevant to each financing option, we have a straight line that reveals the earnings per share at different levels of earnings before interest and taxes.

We can see from the chart that at lower levels of EBIT, the common share issue provides better returns to shareholders. We can see that beyond EBIT of $19.4 million, common shareholders begin to reap the benefits of leverage and their returns become higher under this alternative. The earnings before interest and taxes value of $19.4 million is referred to as the **indifference point** (that is, the point at which the two financing choices provide the same level of return to common shareholders).

The distance between the indifference point and the expected level of earnings before interest and taxes provides us with a margin of safety. The chart reveals that there is a reasonable margin of safety for the bond alternative: there would have to be a fall in earnings before interest and taxes of about 34% ($29.2 − 19.4)/29.2 before the common share alternative became more attractive. Thus, provided the managers were confident that the expected levels of profit could be maintained, the bond alternative would be more attractive.

A business may consider issuing preferred shares to finance a particular project. As preferred dividends are paid out of earnings *after taxes*, this means that, when calculating the first coordinate for the chart, the earnings *before* interest and taxes must be sufficient to cover both the dividends and the relevant corporate tax payments. In other words, we must gross up the preferred dividend by the relevant corporate tax rate to derive the earnings before interest and taxes figure.

The indifference point between any two financing options can also be derived by using a simple mathematical approach. Example 10.5 illustrates the process.

Example 10.5

The information for Tawa Ltd. in Example 10.4 can be used to illustrate how the indifference point is calculated.

Let x be the EBIT at which the two financing options provide the same EPS.

	Shares ($ millions)	Bonds ($ millions)
Earnings before interest and taxes	x	x
Interest expense	2.4	4.4
Earnings before taxes	$(x - 2.4)$	$(x - 4.4)$
Income tax (25%)	$0.25(x - 2.4)$	$0.25(x - 4.4)$
Net income	$0.75(x - 2.4)$	$0.75(x - 4.4)$
EPS	$\dfrac{0.75(x - \$2.4\text{ million})}{68\text{ million}}$	$\dfrac{0.75(x - \$4.4\text{ million})}{60\text{ million}}$

Thus, the EPS of the two financing options will be equal when:

$$\frac{0.75(x - \$2.4\text{ million})}{68\text{ million}} = \frac{0.75(x - \$4.4\text{ million})}{60\text{ million}}$$

We can solve this equation as follows:

$$\frac{(0.75x - \$1.8\text{ million})}{68\text{ million}} = \frac{(0.75x - \$3.3\text{ million})}{60\text{ million}}$$

$$45x - \$108\text{ million} = 51x - \$224.4\text{ million}$$

$$6x = \$116.4\text{ million}$$
$$\underline{x = \$19.4\text{ million}}$$

An indifference EBIT of $19.4 million matches the amount we obtained graphically in Figure 10.8.

SELF-ASSESSMENT QUESTION 10.2

Russell Ltd. installs and services heating and ventilation systems for commercial premises. The most recent balance sheet and income statement of the business are set out below:

Russell Ltd.
Balance Sheet
as at May 31, 2010
(in $ thousands)

Current assets		
Cash	18.4	
Accounts receivable	510.3	
Inventory	293.2	
Total current assets		821.9
Property, plant, and equipment		
Machinery and equipment	883.6	
Less: Accumulated depreciation	328.4	555.2
Vehicles	268.8	
Less: Accumulated depreciation	82.2	186.6
Total property, plant, and equipment		741.8
Total assets		1,563.7
Current liabilities		
Accounts payable	417.3	
Income taxes payable	64.0	
Total current liabilities		481.3
Long-term liabilities		
12% debentures (payable 2016/2017)		250.0
Total liabilities		731.3
Shareholders' equity		
Common shares (400,000 outstanding)		400.0
Retained earnings		432.4
Total shareholders' equity		832.4
Total shareholders' equity and liabilities		1,563.7

Russell Ltd.
Combined Income Statement and Addition to Retained Earnings
for the year ended May 31, 2010

	($000)
Sales revenue	5,207.8
Earnings before interest and taxes	542.0
Interest expense	30.0
Earnings before taxes	512.0
Income tax (25%)	128.0
Net income	384.0
Less: Dividend paid	153.6
Addition to retained earnings for the year	230.4

The business wishes to invest in more machinery and equipment in order to cope with increased demand for its services. Additional earnings before interest and taxes of $120,000 per year are expected if an investment of $600,000 is made in plant and machinery.

The directors of the business are considering an offer from a venture capital business to finance the expansion program. The financing will be made available immediately through either:

(i)   An issue of 150,000 common shares at $4 per share, or
(ii) An issue of $600,000 10% debentures at par.

The directors of the business wish to maintain the same dividend payout ratio in future years as in past years, whichever method of financing is chosen.

Required:

(a) For each of the financing options:
   (i)   Prepare a pro forma income statement for the year ended May 31, 2011
   (ii) Calculate the projected earnings per share for the year ended May 31, 2011
   (iii) Calculate the projected level of leverage as at May 31, 2011.

(b) Briefly assess both of the financing options under consideration from the viewpoint of the existing shareholders.

(c) Calculate the level of earnings before interest and taxes at which the earnings per share under each of the financing options will be the same.

WHAT DETERMINES THE LEVEL OF LEVERAGE?

In practice, the level of leverage adopted by a business is likely to be influenced by the attitudes of owners, managers, and lenders. The factors that these groups are likely to bear in mind when making leverage decisions are considered below.

The Attitude of the Owners

The attitude of owners is likely to be influenced by the following factors:

■ *Control.* Owners may be reluctant to issue new common shares where it results in a dilution of control. This may lead them to view debt as a better financing option.

■ *Flexibility.* Too high a level of leverage may eliminate the potential for future borrowing. As a result, financial flexibility may be lost. Debt can often be raised much more quickly than issuing new shares, which can be important when a business operates in a fast-changing environment.

■ *Risk.* Risk-averse investors will only be prepared to take on more risk if there is the opportunity for higher rates of return. Thus, the additional risks of higher leverage must be outweighed by the prospect of higher returns.

■ *Returns.* Where owners are receiving relatively poor returns, they may be reluctant to provide additional equity and may try to lift their returns through higher leverage.

REAL WORLD 10.6 describes the more aggressive role that large pension funds play in the investment world, both for equity and debt investments.

REAL WORLD 10.6

New Breed of Pension Funds

Pension funds are no longer the passive investors they once used to be. Two of the largest in Canada are the Canada Pension Plan ($116.6 billion as of June 2009) and the Ontario Teachers' Pension Plan, ($87.4 billion as of December 2008). It used to be that pension funds had little or no equity or real estate investments. But inflation in the 1970s changed all that when fixed income investments lost so much of their value.

Figure 10.9 shows the type of investments these two pension plans currently hold. In both pension plans, the majority of the assets are invested in equity and other inflation sensitive investments, including real estate. These are certainly not passive investment strategies.

FIGURE 10.9   Investments by Pension Plans

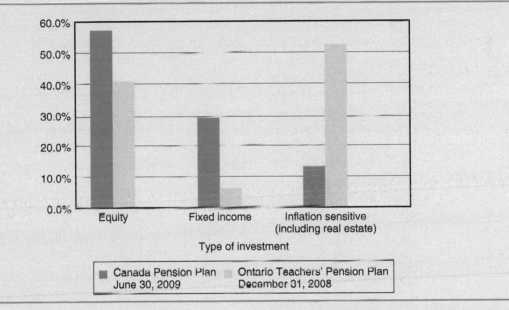

Source: Canada Pension Plan website at: www.cppib.ca/Investments/Equities/publicly_traded_securities.html and the Ontario Teachers' Pension Plan at: www.otpp.com/wps/wcm/connect/otpp_en/Home/Investments/Fast+Facts/, both accessed September 26, 2009.

The Attitude of Management

Although managers are employed to operate a business in the owners' best interests, they may not always do this. Managers may object to high levels of leverage if they feel that it places their income and job security at risk. Managers may also object to the tight financial discipline that debt imposes on them. They may feel under constant pressure to ensure that sufficient cash is available to cover interest payments and capital repayments.

These objections may lead them to avoid making investments that require debt funding.

The Attitude of Lenders

When deciding whether to provide debt financing, lenders will be concerned with the ability of the business to repay the amount borrowed and to pay interest at the due dates. Various factors will have a bearing on these issues.

Leverage can vary significantly between industries. Generally speaking, leverage will be higher in industries where profits are stable (which lenders are likely to prefer). Thus, higher levels of leverage are likely to occur in utilities such as electricity, gas, telephone, and cable television businesses, which are less affected by economic recession and changes in consumer tastes than most businesses. Activity 10.15 considers the factors that may limit the ability of a business to repay loans.

ACTIVITY 10.15

What factors are likely to influence the ability of a business to repay the amount borrowed and to pay interest at due dates?

Solution

The following factors are likely to be important:

- *Profitability.* Where a business has a stable level of profits, lenders may feel that there is less risk to their investment than where profits are volatile. Profit stability will depend on such factors as the nature of the products sold, and the competitive structure of the industry.
- *Cash-generating ability.* Where a business is able to generate strong, predictable cash flows, lenders may feel there is less risk to their investment.
- *Security for the loan.* The nature and quality of assets held by a business will determine whether there is adequate security for a loan. Generally speaking, lenders prefer assets that have a ready market value, can easily be sold, and will not deteriorate quickly (for example, land).
- *Fixed costs.* A business that operates with a high level of fixed costs has a high level of risk as fixed costs have to be paid no matter the level of sales and profits. Lenders may feel that a business with high fixed costs will only add to these by borrowing and this may increase the overall level of risk to unacceptable levels.

This is not an exhaustive list: you may have thought of other factors.

L.O. 4 # THE CAPITAL STRUCTURE DEBATE

It may come as a surprise that there is debate in the financial literature over whether the capital structure decision really is important. The value of a business can be defined as the net present value of its future cash flows. By lowering the cost of capital, which is used as the discount rate, the value of the business will be increased.

The Traditional View

According to the traditional view, the capital structure decision is very important. The traditionalists point out that the cost of debt is cheaper than the cost of common (equity) share capital (see Chapter 8). This difference in the relative cost of financing suggests that by increasing the level of borrowing (or leverage), the overall cost of capital of the business can be reduced. However, there are drawbacks to taking on additional borrowing. As the level of borrowing increases, shareholders will require higher levels of return on their investments to compensate for the higher levels of financial risk that they will have to bear. Existing lenders will also require higher levels of return.

The traditionalists argue, however, that at fairly low levels of borrowing, the benefits of raising funds through the use of debt will outweigh any costs that arise. This is because common shareholders and lenders will not view low levels of borrowing as having a significant effect on the level of risk that they have to bear and so will not require a higher level of return in compensation. As the level of borrowing increases, however, things will start to change. Common shareholders and existing lenders will become increasingly concerned with the higher interest charges that must be met and the risks this will pose to their own claims on the income and assets of the business. As a result, they will seek compensation for this higher level of risk in the form of higher expected returns.

The situation just described is shown in Figure 10.10. Note that the overall cost of capital (which is a weighted average of the cost of common shares and debt) declines when small increases in the level of borrowing occur. However, at significantly increased levels of borrowing, the increase in required returns from equity shareholders and lenders will result in a sharp rise in the overall cost of capital.

FIGURE 10.10   The Traditional View of the Relationship between Levels of Borrowing and Expected Returns

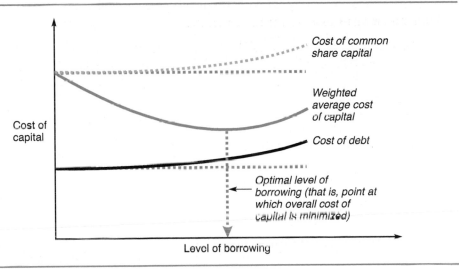

An important implication of the above analysis is that managers of the business should try to establish the mix of debt/equity financing that will minimize the overall cost of capital. At this point, the business will be said to have achieved an **optimal capital structure**. By minimizing the overall cost of capital in this way, the value of the business (that is, the net present value of future cash flows) will be maximized. This relationship between the level of borrowing, the cost of capital, and business value is illustrated in Figure 10.11.

FIGURE 10.11   Relationship between the Level of Borrowing, the Cost of Capital, and Business Value: The Traditional View

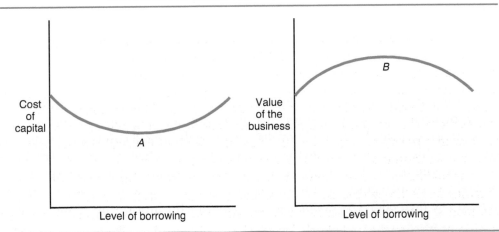

We can see that the graph of the value of the business displays an inverse pattern to the graph of the overall cost of capital. This is because a lower cost of capital will result in a higher net present value for the future cash flows of the business. When the cost of capital reaches a minimum at point *A*, the value of business reaches a maximum, at point *B*. This relationship suggests that the financing decision is critically important. Failure to identify and achieve the right financing mix could have serious adverse consequences for shareholder wealth.

The Modernist View

Franco Modigliani and Merton Miller (MM), who represent the modernist school, challenged the traditional view by arguing that the required returns to shareholders and to lenders would not follow the pattern as set out in Figure 10.11. They argued that shareholders in a business with financial leverage will expect a return that is equal to the returns expected from investing in a similar unleveraged business plus a premium, which rises in *direct proportion* to the level of leverage. Thus, the increase in returns required for common shareholders as compensation for increased financial risk will rise in constant proportion to the increase in the level of borrowing over the *whole range of borrowing*. This pattern contrasts with the traditional view, of course, which displays an uneven change in the required rate of return over the range of borrowing.

The MM position is shown in Figure 10.12. As you can see, the overall cost of capital remains constant at varying levels of borrowing. This is because the benefits obtained from raising funds through borrowing, which is cheaper than share capital, are exactly offset by the increase in required returns from common shareholders.

FIGURE 10.12   The MM View of the Relationship between Levels of Borrowing and Expected Returns

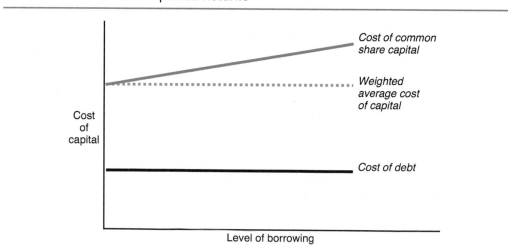

An important implication of the MM view is that the financing decision is not really important. Figure 10.12 shows that there is no optimal capital structure for a business, as suggested by the traditionalists, because the overall cost of capital remains constant—this is discussed in Activity 10.16. This means that one particular capital structure is no better or worse than any other and so managers should not spend time on evaluating different forms of financing mixes for the business. Instead, they should concentrate their efforts on evaluating and managing the investments of the business.

ACTIVITY 10.16

In Figure 10.11 we saw the traditional view of the relationships between the cost of capital and the level of borrowing and between the value of the business and the level of borrowing. How would the MM view of these two relationships be shown in graphical form?

Solution

The level of borrowing and the cost of capital have no effect on the value of the business.

MM argue that the value of a business is determined by the future income from its investments, and the risk associated with those investments, and not by the way in which this income is divided among the different providers of financing. In other words, it is not possible to increase the value of a business (that is, lower the overall cost of capital) simply by borrowing, as the traditionalists suggest. MM point out that borrowing is not something that only businesses are able to undertake. Borrowing can also be undertaken by individual investors. As business borrowing can be replicated by individual investors, there is no reason why it should create additional value for the investor. Example 10.6 explains the theory from a lighter perspective.

Example 10.6

The MM idea is that the method of financing a business—whether with high leverage or low leverage—does not affect the value of the business. It's a case of six of one, half a dozen of another. MM theory concludes that managers should not agonize over what capital structure to maintain, as it is irrelevant to the valuation of a company. For example, a 60:40 debt–equity ratio is just as efficient as a 40:60 debt–equity ratio.

Without breaking the speed limit, it takes about five hours to drive from Toronto to Montreal whether the distance is measured in kilometres (504) or miles (313). The measuring system does not affect the physical distance between the cities.

This is what MM theory is saying—various degrees of leverage, within reason, are just ways of measuring capital structure and have no effect on the valuation of the company.

Example 10.7 helps to illustrate the MM position that business borrowing should not create additional value for a business.

Example 10.7

Two businesses, Delta Industries Ltd. and Omega Foods Ltd., are identical except for the fact that Delta is financed entirely by common shares and Omega is 50% financed by loans. The earnings before interest for each business for the year are $2 million. The shareholders of Delta require a return of 12% and the common shareholders of Omega require a return of 14%. Omega pays 10% interest per year on the $10 million loans outstanding. (Tax is to be ignored for reasons that we shall discuss later.)

▶

	Delta ($ millions)	Omega ($ millions)
Earnings before interest	2.0	2.0
Interest expense	—	1.0 (10% × $10)
Available to common shareholders	2.0	1.0

The market value of the total shares of each business will be equivalent to the profits capitalized at the required rate of return. Thus, the market value of each business is as follows:

	Delta ($ millions)	Omega ($ millions)
Market value of shares:		
($2 million/0.12)	16.7	
($1 million/0.14)		7.1
Market value of debt	—	10.0
Market value of each business	16.7	17.1

MM argue that differences in the way in which each business is financed cannot result in a higher value for Omega, as shown above. This is because an investor who owns, say, 10% of the shares in Omega would be able to obtain the same level of income from investing in Delta, for the same level of risk as the investment in Omega and for a lower net investment. The investor, by borrowing an amount equivalent to 10% of the loans of Omega (that is, an amount proportional to the ownership interest in Omega), and selling the shares held in Omega in order to finance the purchase of a 10% equity stake in Delta, would be in the following position:

	($000)
Return from 10% equity investment in Delta	
(10% × $2 million EBIT)	200
Less: Interest on borrowing ($1,000 × 10%)	(100)
Net return	100
Purchase of shares (10% × $16.7 million)	1,670
Less: Amount borrowed	1,000
Net investment in Delta	670

The investor with a 10% stake in the common share capital of Omega is, currently, in the following position:

	($000)
Return from 10% investment in Omega	100
(10% × $1 million EBIT)	
Net investment in Omega existing shareholding	710
(10% × $7.1 million)	

As we can see, the investor would be better off taking on personal debt in order to acquire a 10% share of the shares of the unleveraged business, Delta, than continuing to invest in the leveraged business, Omega. The effect of a number of investors switching investments in this way would be to reduce the value of the shares in Omega (thereby increasing the returns to common shareholders in Omega), and to increase the value of shares in Delta (thereby reducing the returns to equity in Delta). This switching from Omega to Delta (which is referred to as an **arbitrage transaction**) would continue until the returns from each investment were the same, and so no further gains could be made from such transactions. At this point, the value of the two businesses would be identical.

The MM analysis, while extremely rigorous and logical, is based on a number of assumptions that do not hold in the real world. These include the following.

Perfect Capital Markets

The assumption of perfect capital markets means that there are no share transaction costs and investors and businesses can borrow unlimited amounts at the same rates of interest.

No Bankruptcy Costs

Assuming that there are no bankruptcy costs means that, if a business were liquidated, no legal and administrative fees would be incurred and the business assets could be sold at a price that would enable shareholders to receive cash equal to the market value of their shareholding prior to the liquidation. In the real world, bankruptcy costs can be very high.

Risk

It is assumed that businesses exist that have identical operating risks but different levels of borrowing. Although this is unlikely to be true, it does not affect the validity of MM's arguments.

No Taxes

A world without corporate or personal income taxes is clearly an unrealistic assumption. The real issue, however, is whether this undermines the validity of MM's arguments. We shall, therefore, consider next the effect of introducing taxes on the MM position.

MM and the Introduction of Taxes

When taxes are considered, MM found that the tax relief from interest payments on loans provides a real benefit to common shareholders. The more the level of borrowing increases, the more tax relief the business receives.

We should recall that the original MM position was that the benefits of inexpensive debt will be exactly offset by increases in the required rate of return by common share investors. Tax relief on loan interest should, therefore, represent an additional benefit to shareholders. As the amount of tax relief increases with the amount of borrowing, the overall cost of capital (after tax) will be lowered as the level of borrowing increases. The implication of this revised position is that there is an optimal degree of leverage and it is at 100% leverage. In Figure 10.13, we can see the MM position after taxes have been introduced—Activity 10.17 considers the implication of this.

Thus, the MM position moves closer to the traditional position in so far as it recognizes that there is a relationship between the value of the business and the way in which it is financed. It also recognizes that there is an optimal level of debt. Therefore, as the level of debt increases, the cost of capital falls, and the value of the business rises.

FIGURE 10.13 The MM View of the Relationship between Levels of Borrowing and Expected Returns (Including Tax Effects)

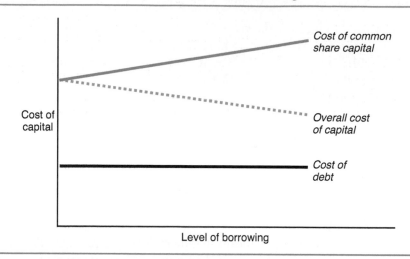

ACTIVITY 10.17

What do you think is the main implication of the above analysis for managers who are trying to decide on an appropriate capital structure?

Solution

This revised MM analysis implies that a business should borrow to capacity, as this will lower the after-tax cost of capital and thereby increase the value of the business.

In practice, however, few businesses follow the policy just described. When borrowing reaches very high levels, lenders are likely to feel that their security is threatened and common share investors will feel that bankruptcy risks have increased. Thus, both groups are likely to seek higher returns, which will, in turn, increase the overall cost of capital. (A business would have to attract *risk-seeking* investors in order to prevent a rise in its cost of capital.)

REAL WORLD 10.7 describes how hedge funds, which invest in other businesses, increase their level of leverage.

REAL WORLD 10.7

Hedge Funds Pump Up the Leverage with a 130:30 Asset Allocation

Hedge funds are funds that invest most of their money in long positions (that is, in owning stocks that they like) and some of their money in short positions (that is, in selling stocks that they do not own and do not like)—a perfectly legal strategy in the stock market. When a short sale is made, the investor hopes the stock price will decline and then they can buy it back at the lower price, thereby earning a profit. To execute a short sale, the broker must borrow stock from an owner.

One strategy employed by the hedge fund industry is known as 130:30. These numbers refer to the asset allocation of the hedge fund. For example, assume a hedge fund begins life with $100 million in cash to invest. This

▶

is 100% of its assets and it invests all of it in stocks it thinks will go up. The hedge fund then shorts $30 million of stocks it thinks will go down in price. These short sales result in a cash inflow to the hedge fund of $30 million, excluding transaction fees, which is then reinvested in the first group of stocks it thinks will increase in value. The result is an asset allocation of 130% of assets invested in long positions in companies it likes and 30% invested in short positions in companies it does not like.

Hedge funds are investment vehicles for sophisticated investors with at least $150,000 to invest or total personal assets of at least $1 million.

Source: Developed from information at www.growyourfunds.com/2006/10/the_transfer_coefficient_and_1.html, accessed March 20, 2007.

S U M M A R Y

Cost of Capital

- The cost of capital is an opportunity cost that reflects the returns that investors would expect to earn from investments with the same level of risk.
- There are two major approaches to determining the cost of common (equity) shares: the dividend-based approach, and the risk/return (CAPM) approach.
- The dividend-based approach reflects the fact that a share can be valued according to the future dividends received.
- Dividend valuation models often assume constant dividends over time, $K_0 = \dfrac{D_0}{P_0}$, or that dividends will grow at a constant rate, $K_0 = \dfrac{D_1}{P_0} + g$.
- The risk/return approach is based on the idea that the cost of a common share is made up of a risk-free rate of return plus a risk premium.
- The risk premium is calculated by measuring the risk premium for the market as a whole, then measuring the returns from a particular share in relation to the market, and applying this measure to the market risk premium: $[K_0 = K_{RF} + b(K_m - K_{RF})]$.
- The after-tax cost of perpetual debt can be derived in a similar way to that of common shares where the dividend stays constant: $K_d = \dfrac{I(1 - t)}{P_d}$.

- The cost of redeemable debt can be computed using an IRR approach.
- The cost of preferred shares can be derived in a similar way to that of common shares where the dividend stays constant: $K_p = \dfrac{D_p}{P_p}$.
- The weighted average cost of capital (WACC) is derived by taking the cost of each element of capital and weighting each element in proportion to the target capital structure.

Financial Leverage

- The effect of financial leverage is that changes in earnings before interest and taxes (EBIT) result in disproportionate changes in the returns to common shareholders.
- The degree of financial leverage measures the sensitivity of changes in returns to common shareholders to changes in EBIT.

Leverage and the Evaluation of Capital Structure Decisions

- An EBIT–EPS indifference chart can be constructed to reveal the returns to shareholders at different levels of EBIT for different financing options.
- In practice, leverage will be determined by the attitudes of owners, managers, and lenders.

The Capital Structure Debate

- There are two schools of thought: the traditional view is that the capital structure decision is important, and the modernist view is that it is not.

The Traditional View

- Traditionalists argue that at lower levels of leverage shareholders and lenders are unconcerned about risk; however, at higher levels they become concerned and demand higher returns.
- This leads to an increase in WACC.
- WACC decreases at lower levels of leverage (because investors do not demand increased returns) but then increases.
- This means that there is an optimal level of leverage.

The Modernist View

- Modernists (such as Modigliani and Miller) argue that shareholders are always concerned about the level of leverage.
- Cheaper loans are offset by the increasing cost of common shares and so the cost of capital remains constant.
- This means that there is no optimal level of leverage.
- If tax is introduced, the modernist view is changed.
- There are benefits arising from tax relief on debt that should be exploited by taking on debt up to the point where these benefits are offset by the potential costs of bankruptcy.

KEY TERMS

Cost of capital

Capital asset pricing model (CAPM)

Beta

Weighted average cost of capital (WACC)

Degree of financial leverage

EBIT–EPS indifference chart

Indifference point

Optimal capital structure

Arbitrage transaction

LIST OF EQUATIONS

10.1 $P_0 = \dfrac{D_1}{(1 + K_0)^1} + \dfrac{D_2}{(1 + K_0)^2} + \dfrac{D_3}{(1 + K_0)^3} + \cdots + \dfrac{D_n}{(1 + K_0)^n}$

10.2 $P_0 = \dfrac{D_0}{K_0}$

10.3 $K_0 = \dfrac{D_0}{P_0}$ for shares with a constant dividend

10.4 $P_0 = \dfrac{D_1}{K_0 - g}$ for shares with an annual dividend growth rate, g

10.5 $K_0 = \dfrac{D_1}{P_0} + g$

10.6 $K_0 = K_{RF} + b(K_m - K_{RF})$

10.7 $P_d = \dfrac{I}{K_d}$

10.8 $K_d = \dfrac{I}{P_d}$ for perpetual or permanent debt

10.9 $K_d = \dfrac{I(1 - t)}{P_d}$ for after-tax cost of perpetual debt

10.10 $P_p = \dfrac{D_p}{K_p}$

10.11 $K_p = \dfrac{D_p}{P_p}$ for preferred shares with a constant dividend

10.12 Degree of financial leverage
$$= \dfrac{\text{Percentage change in EPS}}{\text{Percentage change in EBIT}}$$

10.13 Degree of financial leverage
$$= \dfrac{\text{EBIT}}{\text{EBIT} - I - \dfrac{P \times 100}{100 - t}}$$

REVIEW QUESTIONS

Answers to the Review Questions can be found on the Companion Website that accompanies this text at www.pearsoned.ca/atrill.

10.1 How might a business find out whether a particular planned level of leverage would be acceptable to investors?

10.2 What factors might a prospective lender take into account when deciding whether to make a long-term loan to a particular business?

10.3 Should the specific cost of financing a particular project be used as the appropriate discount rate for investment appraisal purposes?

10.4 What are the main implications for the financial manager who accepts the arguments of:
(a) The traditional approach
(b) The MM (excluding tax effects) approach
(c) The MM (including tax effects) approach concerning capital structure?

10.5 Rank the following three forms of financing according to cost of capital to the corporation, from lowest to highest, and provide reasons for your ranking:
  Common shares
  Debt
  Preferred shares

PROBLEMS AND CASES

10.1 You have collected the following bond data from the annual reports of several of your global competitors.

Company	Coupon Rate	Market Value	Tax Rate
Jade Inc.	11%	$82.00	40%
Old Irish Ltd.	7	90.00	34
Tapestry Corp.	6	60.00	10

Required:
Determine the after-tax cost of debt for each company.

10.2 You have collected the following preferred share data from the annual reports of several of your global competitors.

Company	Current Dividend	Market Value	Par Value
Jade Inc.	$4.50	$43.00	$50.00
Old Irish Ltd.	4.00	48.00	50.00
Tapestry Corp.	3.60	35.00	50.00

Required:
Determine the cost of preferred shares for each company.

10.3 You have collected the following common share data from the annual reports of several of your global competitors.

Company	Current Dividend	Market Value	Dividend Growth Rate
Jade Inc.	$7.00	$93.00	10.00%
Old Irish Ltd.	6.10	98.00	7.20
Tapestry Corp.	4.50	75.00	8.70

Required:

Determine the cost of common shares for each company.

10.4 You have collected the following common share data from the annual reports of several of your global competitors.

Company	Risk-Free Interest Rate	Beta	Expected Return on the Market
Jade Inc.	6.50%	1.5	10.00%
Old Irish Ltd.	5.60	1.8	7.20
Tapestry Corp.	7.80	2.7	8.70

Required:

(a) Determine the cost of common shares for each company.
(b) Explain why Problem and Case 10.4 and Problem and Case 10.3 arrived at two different estimates for the cost of common shares for each company.

10.5 Richelieu Investments Limited has the following capital structure, which is considered ideal, taken from the annual report and market data as at December 31, 2010:

	Balance Sheet	Market Value	Price per Unit	Dividend per Share
10% bonds	$100,000,000	$90,000,000	$90.00	N/A
Preferred shares	20,000,000	15,000,000	30.00	$2.50
Common shares	200,000,000	*	30.00	1.50
Retained earnings	50,000,000		N/A	N/A

* There are 7 million shares outstanding at a market price of $30 per share.

The corporate income tax rate is 30%. The dividends on common shares are expected to grow at 5% per year.

Required:

(a) Determine the cost of capital as at December 31, 2010, for each of the following components:
   (i) Debt
   (ii) Preferred shares
   (iii) Common shares.
(b) Calculate the weighted average cost of capital for Richelieu Investments Limited.

10.6 You have gathered the following information on companies in your industry.

Company	D_0	P_0	g	K_{RF}	b	K_m
1	$1.30	$8.23				
2	5.60	24.00				
3	3.00	60.00	10%			
4	5.50	34.75	3%			
5				7%	1.50	15%
6				15%	0.80	19%
7				10%	2.00	17%

Required:

    (a) Calculate the cost of common shares for each of the companies.

    (b) Which company has the lowest cost of common shares?

10.7 With additional work, you have gathered more information on companies in your industry as shown below. These companies have both bonds and preferred shares outstanding. This table shows the amount of interest (I) and the price of the bonds (P_d) related to $100 face value bonds. The tax rate (t) varies for each company because of various provincial incentives.

Company	t	I	P_d	D_p	P_p
11	50%	$ 12	$ 120	$ 5.25	$ 100.00
12	45%	11	110	3.50	65.00
13	40%	10	100	1.96	36.50
14	30%	9	95	0.56	10.30
15	35%	7	90	1.75	22.50
16	25%	6	85	2.30	44.12
17	20%	5	80	3.64	56.32

Required:

Calculate the cost of debt and the cost of preferred shares for each of the companies.

10.8 Riphean and Silurian are two businesses operating in different industries. Both are financed by a mixture of common shares and debt and both are seeking to derive their cost of capital for investment decision making purposes. The following information is available concerning the two businesses for the year to November 30, 2010:

	Riphean	Silurian
Net income	$3.0 million	$4.0 million
Gross dividends	$1.5 million	$2.0 million
Market value per common share	$4.00	$1.60
Number of common shares	5 million	10 million
Gross interest yield on debt	8%	12%
Market value of debt	$10 million	$16 million

The annual growth rate in dividends is 5% for Riphean and 8% for Silurian. Assume a 30% rate of corporate tax.

Required:

    (a) Explain what is meant by the term *cost of capital* and state why it is important for a business to calculate its cost of capital correctly.

    (b) Calculate the weighted average cost of capital of Riphean and Silurian using the information provided.

    (c) Discuss two possible reasons why the cost of common share capital differs between the two businesses.

    (d) Discuss two limitations of using the weighted average cost of capital when making investment decisions.

10.9 With additional work, you have gathered more information on companies in your industry as shown below. This table shows the amount of interest and the price of the bonds related to $100 face value bonds.

Company	D_0	P_0	g	K_{RF}	b	K_m	t	I	P_d	D_p	P_P
101	$ 0.22	$10.00					40%	$ 6.50	$100	$ 5.25	$100.00
102	1.78	17.24					40%	13.25	120	3.50	65.00
103	2.40	35.50	5%				40%	7.50	95	1.96	36.50
104	0.84	28.60	8%				25%	8.75	70	0.56	10.30
105		30.00		2%	1.20	7%	25%	11.50	90	1.75	22.50
106		45.44		4%	2.50	9%	30%	9.40	85	2.30	44.12
107		56.00		6%	0.75	11%	30%	7.25	80	3.64	56.32

Company	Common Shares	Number of Preferred Shares	Bonds
101	2,000,000	500,000	100,000
102	15,000,000	1,000,000	2,000,000
103	70,000,000	2,500,000	456,000
104	2,500,000	560,000	452,300
105	2,000,000	–	1,250,000
106	13,000,000	2,000,000	3,458,900
107	250,000,000	35,000,000	12,000,000

Required:
(a) Calculate the cost of common shares, preferred shares, and debt for each of the companies.
(b) Calculate the market value of common shares, debt, and preferred shares for each of the companies.
(c) Calculate the weighted average cost of capital (WACC) for each company.

10.10 These companies in the same industry have the following capital structures:

Company	Common Shares	Preferred Shares	Long-term Debt
Flagpole Energy Ltd.	$100,000	$20,000	$80,000
Flagstaff Electric Ltd.	100,000	80,000	20,000
FlagMast Natural Gas Ltd.	100,000	10,000	200,000

Required:
Calculate the leverage ratio for each company.

10.11 You have gathered the following information on your competitors for 2010. The corporate income tax rate is 42%.

	Shuffle Shoes Ltd.	Cloudy Boots Ltd.	Rainy Day Wear Ltd.
EBIT	$890,500	$556,200	$1,490,540
Interest expense	85,000	200,000	600,000
Preferred dividends	160,000	25,000	300,000
Number of common shares outstanding	300,000	120,000	250,000

Required:

    (a) Calculate the earnings available to common shareholders for each company for 2010.

    (b) Calculate the earnings per share for each company for 2010.

10.12 The following data is for 2011. All other data remains the same as Problem and Case 10.11.

	Shuffle Shoes Ltd.	Cloudy Boots Ltd.	Rainy Day Wear Ltd.
EBIT	$ 500,000	$ 356,000	$ 1,200,000

Required:

Calculate the degree of financial leverage for each company.

10.13 You are examining various financing options that will yield the following results.

	Financing Options						
	1	2	3	4	5	6	7
EBIT	$ 150,000	$ 150,000	$ 150,000	$ 150,000	$ 150,000	$ 150,000	$ 150,000
I	20,000	25,000	30,000	35,000	40,000	45,000	50,000
P	40,000	43,000	46,000	49,000	52,000	55,000	58,000
t	35%	35%	35%	35%	35%	35%	35%

Required:

Calculate the degree of leverage associated with each financing option.

10.14 Celtor Ltd. is a property development business operating in London, Ontario. The business has the following capital structure as at November 30, 2011:

	($000)
Common shares (10 million outstanding)	10,000
Retained earnings	20,000
9% debentures	12,000
	42,000

The common shares have a current market value of $3.90 and the current level of dividend is $0.20 per share. The dividend has been growing at a compound rate of 4% a year in recent years. The debentures of the business are perpetual and have a current market value of $80 per $100 nominal. Interest due on the debentures at the year-end has recently been paid.

    The business has obtained planning permission to build a new office block in a redeveloping area. The business wishes to raise the whole of the financing necessary for the project by issuing more perpetual 9% debentures at $80 per $100 nominal. This is in line with a target capital structure set by the business where the amount of debt will increase to 70% of common share capital within the next two years. The corporate tax rate is 25%.

Required:

    (a) Explain what is meant by the term *cost of capital*. Why is it important for a business to calculate its cost of capital correctly?

    (b) Calculate the weighted average cost of capital of Celtor that should be used for future investment decisions.

10.15 Wireless Video Ltd. needs to expand operations for 2011 and is considering two financing options to raise $200 million—either issuing additional common shares or additional long-term bonds. The interest rate on the new bonds would be 10%. The new shares would require an additional annual dividend of $20 million. The most recent financial information is given below. EBIT is expected to grow by 10% in 2011.

	2010
EBIT	$ 92,000
Interest	$ 37,000
Dividends	$ 25,000
Corporate tax rate	30%
Number of shares outstanding	100,000
Share price	$ 1,000

	($000)
Current assets	75,000
Property, plant, and equipment	700,000
Total assets	775,000
Current liabilities	40,000
Long-term bonds	200,000
Total liabilities	240,000
Common shares	200,000
Retained earnings	335,000
Total shareholders' equity	535,000
Total shareholders' equity and liabilities	775,000

Required:

(a) Prepare a pro forma income statement including additions to retained earnings for 2011 for each financing option.

(b) Prepare the long-term financing (bonds and equity) portion of the pro forma balance sheet for 2011.

(c) Calculate the ROE, earnings per share, times interest earned ratio, and the leverage ratio for each financing option.

(d) Which financing option would you recommend?

10.16 Trexon Ltd. is a junior oil and gas exploration business that has most of its operations in Alberta. Recently, the business acquired rights to explore for oil and gas in the Gulf of Mexico. Trexon proposes to finance the new operations from the issue of common shares. At present, the business is financed by a combination of common share capital and debt. The common shares have a current market value of $2.60. The current level of dividend is $0.16 per share and this has been growing at a compound rate of 6% a year in recent years. The debt is perpetual and has a current market value of $94 per $100 nominal. Interest on the debt is at the rate of 12% and interest due at the year-end has recently been paid. At present, the business expects 60% of its financing to come from common shares and the rest from debt. In the future, however, the business will aim to finance 70% of its operations from common shares.

When the proposal to finance the new operations via a rights issue of shares was announced at the annual general meeting of the business, objections were raised by two shareholders present, as follows:

■ *Shareholder* A *argued*: "I fail to understand why the business has decided to issue shares to finance the new operation. Surely it would be better to reinvest profit, as this is, in effect, a free source of financing?"

■ *Shareholder* B *argued*: "I also fail to understand why the business has decided to issue shares to finance the new operation. However, I do not agree with the suggestion made by Shareholder *A*.

I do not believe that shareholder funds should be used at all to finance the new operation. Instead, the business should issue more debt, as it is inexpensive relative to common shares and would, therefore, reduce the overall cost of capital of the business."

The tax rate is 35%.

Required:

(a) Calculate the weighted average cost of capital of Trexon that should be used in future investment decisions.

(b) Comment on the remarks made by:
   (i) Shareholder *A*
   (ii) Shareholder *B*.

10.17 Ashcroft Corp., a family-controlled business, is considering raising additional funds to modernize its factory. The plan is expected to cost $2.34 million and will increase annual earnings before interest and taxes starting January 1, 2011, by $0.6 million. A summarized balance sheet and income statement are shown below. Currently, the share price is $2.00.

Ashcroft Corp.
Balance Sheet
as at December 31, 2010
(in $ thousands)

Current assets		
Accounts receivable	2.2	
Inventory	2.4	
Total current assets		4.6
Property, plant, and equipment (net)		1.4
Total assets		6.0
Current liabilities		
Accounts payable	3.2	
Income taxes payable	0.3	
Total current liabilities		3.5
Total liabilities		3.5
Shareholders' equity		
Common shares (4,000 outstanding)	1.0	
Retained earnings	1.5	
Total shareholders' equity		2.5
Total liabilities and shareholders' equity		6.0

Ashcroft Corp.
Income Statement and Addition to Retained Earnings
for the year ended December 31, 2010

	($ millions)
Sales revenue	11.2
Earnings before tax	1.2
Tax expense	0.6
Net income	0.6
Less: Dividends paid	0.3
Additions to retained earnings for the financial year	0.3

Two plans have been suggested. First, 1.3 million shares could be issued at $1.80 (net of issue costs). Second, a consortium of six local companies has offered to buy bonds from the business totalling $2.34 million. Interest would be at the rate of 13% per annum and capital repayments of equal annual installments of $234,000 starting on January 1, 2012, would be required. Assume a tax rate of 50%.

Required:

(a) Compute the earnings per share for 2011 under the bond and the common share alternatives.

(b) Compute the level of profits before bond interest and tax at which the earnings per share under the two plans will be equal.

(c) Discuss the considerations the directors should take into account before deciding upon bond financing or common share financing.

CHAPTER 11

Developing a Dividend Policy

INTRODUCTION

The issue of dividend policy has aroused much controversy over the years. At the centre of this controversy is whether the pattern of dividends adopted by a business has any effect on shareholders' wealth. In this chapter, we examine the arguments that have been raised. Although the importance of dividend policy to shareholders remains open to dispute, there is evidence to suggest that managers *perceive* the dividend decision to be important. We consider the attitudes of managers toward dividends and examine the factors that are likely to influence dividend policy in practice. We also consider the alternatives to a cash dividend that might be used.

THE PAYMENT OF DIVIDENDS

`L.O. 1`

A **dividend** represents a return by a business to its shareholders. This return is normally paid in cash, although it would be possible for it to be paid with assets other than cash. In your previous studies, you may have discovered that there are legal limits on the amount that can be distributed in the form of dividend payments to shareholders; Activity 11.1 explores the reasons for this.

ACTIVITY 11.1

Why does the law impose limits on the amount of cash that can be distributed as dividends?

Solution

If there were no legal limits, it would be possible for shareholders to approve massive dividend payments from the business and so leave the lenders and creditors in an exposed financial position. The law tries to protect lenders and creditors by preventing excessive withdrawals of shareholder capital. One way in which this can be done is through placing restrictions on dividend payments.

Companies normally consider retained earnings as the amount available for dividends. If a company pays out more than its retained earnings, it is returning some of the investors' initial capital to shareholders. This is permitted as long as there are sufficient assets available to meet all liabilities and the claims of any preferred shareholders. Activity 11.2 calculates the maximum dividend of a company.

ACTIVITY 11.2

Bio-tech Ltd. started trading three years ago. Net income (loss) was $200,000 for 2008, $(150,000) for 2009, and $30,000 for 2010. Bio-tech has never paid a dividend and wants to know the maximum dividend it can declare in early January 2011.

Solution

	($)
Net income, 2008	200,000
Net loss, 2009	(150,000)
Net income, 2010	30,000
Retained earnings, December 31, 2010	80,000

Under normal circumstances, the directors of Bio-tech would be able to declare a maximum dividend of $80,000.

It should be noted that businesses rarely distribute the maximum amount available for distribution. Indeed, the dividend paid is normally much lower than the net income. In other words, the net income usually exceeds the dividend payment by a comfortable margin.

Dividends can also take the form of common shares. Instead of receiving cash, the shareholders may receive additional shares in the business. We consider this particular form of dividend later in the chapter.

Listed businesses often pay dividends quarterly. The final dividend of the fiscal year will usually be paid after the annual financial reports have been published, and after the shareholders have agreed, at the annual general meeting, to the dividend payment proposed by the directors.

As shares are bought and sold continuously by investors, it is important to establish which investors have the right to receive the dividend declared. To do this, an investor must keep in mind several important dates.

Record date: A date set by the business. Investors whose names appear in the share register book on the date of record will receive the dividend.

Ex-dividend date:	Two business days before the record date. An investor who buys shares on or after the ex-dividend date *will not receive* the current dividend.
Cum dividend date:	One business day before the ex-dividend date (or three business days before the record date) is the last cum dividend date for the current dividend. An investor who buys before the ex-dividend date *will receive* the current dividend.
Transaction date:	The date an investor buys or sells shares.
Settlement date:	The date the investor's name is recorded in the share register book. Usually this is three business days after the transaction date, not counting the transaction date.

To receive the current dividend, the investor must buy before the ex-dividend date. For example, if the ex-dividend date is Wednesday, November 4, the investor must buy on November 3 at the latest to qualify for the dividend. This is because the record date is Friday, November 6, and the ex-dividend date is two business days before the record date. An investor who buys on Tuesday, November 3rd will have a settlement date of Friday, November 6, which is the record date, and the dividend will be received when it is paid. An easier way to look at it is that you receive the dividend if you buy on Tuesday because Wednesday is the ex-dividend date. This is explored more fully in Activity 11.3.

ACTIVITY 11.3

Which of the following investors are entitled to receive the current dividend?

Investor	Transaction Date	Record Date
A	Friday, November 15	Tuesday, November 19
B	Monday, December 30	Thursday, January 2
C	Monday, June 1	Thursday, June 4

Solution

Only investor C would receive the current dividend. Weekends and holidays are not counted. Investor A needed to buy on Thursday, November 14. Then, counting Friday, Monday, and Tuesday, the settlement date would fall on the record date and the investor would be entitled to the dividend. Investor B forgot that January 1 is a holiday. To qualify for the dividend, this investor needed to buy on Friday, December 27. Then counting Monday, Tuesday, and Thursday adds up to three days. Investor C qualifies for the dividend because the settlement date is Thursday, three days after the transaction date.

All things being equal, the share price will drop by the amount of the dividend per share on the ex-dividend date. This reflects that a new investor will not receive the upcoming dividend.

DIVIDEND POLICIES IN PRACTICE

It was just mentioned that businesses rarely distribute all of the profits available to shareholders in the form of dividends. The extent to which the profits generated during a particular period (and available for distribution) cover the dividend payment can be expressed in the **dividend cover ratio**. Recall Equation 4.15 for this ratio:

$$\text{Dividend cover ratio} = \frac{\text{Net income available to common shareholders}}{\text{Annual dividends to common shareholders}} \quad \text{4.15}$$

You may also recall that the higher the ratio, the lower the risk that dividends to shareholders will be affected by adverse business conditions. The inverse of this ratio is known as the *dividend payout ratio*, which was also discussed in Chapter 4. The lower this ratio, the lower the risk that dividends will be affected by adverse business conditions.

Many businesses express their dividend policy in terms of either a target dividend cover ratio or a target dividend payout ratio. REAL WORLD 11.1 sets out the targets established by several businesses.

REAL WORLD 11.1

Sample Target Dividend Payout Ratios at Canadian Businesses

Company	Target Payout Ratio (% of earnings)
BMO	45%–55%
CIBC	40%–50%
Royal Bank	40%–50%
TD Bank	35%–45%
Manulife*	25%–35%
Tim Hortons	20%–25%
Telus	45%–55%
BCE	65%–75%

*Subsequently, the dividend was cut in half in 2009.

Source: Various 2008 annual reports.

For various reasons, dividend payout ratios tend to vary among countries. Where there is access to capital markets, for example, profit retention becomes less important for businesses and so dividend distributions can be higher. Other factors can also be important, such as the different treatment of dividends for tax purposes and differences in the extent to which corporate governance procedures and shareholder activism exert pressure on managers to distribute dividends.

L.O. 2   DIVIDEND POLICY AND SHAREHOLDER WEALTH

Much of the interest surrounding dividend policy has been concerned with the relationship between dividend policy and shareholder wealth. Put simply, the key question to be answered is: can the pattern of dividends adopted by a business influence shareholder wealth? (Note that it is the *pattern* of dividends rather than dividends themselves that is the issue. Shareholders must receive cash at some point in order for their shares to have any value.) After more than three decades of research and debate, we have yet to solve this puzzle.

The notion that dividend policy is important may seem to be obvious. In Chapter 10, for example, we considered various dividend valuation models, which suggest that dividends are important in determining share price. One such model, you may recall, was the dividend growth model, expressed in Equation 10.4:

$$P_0 = \frac{D_1}{K_0 - g}$$

10.4

where: D_1 = Expected dividend next year
   g = A constant rate of dividend growth
   K_0 = The expected return on the share

Looking at this model, it may appear that by simply increasing the dividend (D_1) there will be an automatic increase in share price (P_0). If the relationship between dividends and share price was as just described, then, clearly, dividend policy would be important. However, the relationship between these two variables is not likely to be as straightforward as this, as explored in Activity 11.4.

ACTIVITY 11.4

Why might an increase in the dividend (D_1) not lead to an increase in share price (P_0)? (*Hint:* Think of the other variables in the equation.)

Solution

An increase in dividend payments will only result in an increase in share price if there is no consequential effect on the dividend growth rate. It is likely, however, that an increase in dividends will result in a fall in this growth rate, as there will be less cash to invest in the business. Thus, the beneficial effect on share price arising from an increase in next year's dividend may be cancelled out by a decrease in future years' dividends.

The Traditional View of Dividends

The dividend policy issue, like the capital structure issue discussed in the previous chapter, has two main schools of thought. The early financial literature accepted the view that dividend policy was important for shareholders. It was argued that a shareholder would prefer to receive $1 today rather than to have $1 reinvested in the business, even though this might yield future dividends. The reasoning for this was that future dividends (or capital gains) are less certain and so will be valued less highly. The saying that "a bird in the hand is worth two in the bush" is often used to describe this argument. Thus, if a business decides to replace an immediate and certain cash dividend with uncertain future dividends, shareholders will discount the future dividends at a higher rate in order to take account of this greater uncertainty. Referring back to the dividend growth model, the traditional view suggests that K_0 will rise if there is an increase in D_1, as dividends received later will not be valued so highly.

   If this line of reasoning is correct, the effect of applying a higher discount rate to future dividends will mean that the share value of businesses that adopt a high retention policy will be adversely affected. The implication for corporate managers is, therefore, quite clear. They should adopt as generous a dividend distribution policy as possible, given the investment and financing policies of the business, as this will represent the optimal dividend policy for the business. In view of the fact that the level of payout will affect shareholder wealth, the dividend payment decision will be an important policy decision for managers.

The Modernist (MM) View of Dividends

Franco Modigliani and Merton Miller (MM) have challenged this view of dividend policy. They argue that, given perfect and efficient markets, the pattern of dividend payments adopted by a business will have no effect on shareholder wealth. Where such markets exist, the wealth of shareholders will be affected solely by the investment projects that the business undertakes. To maximize shareholder wealth, therefore, the business should take on all investment projects that have a positive NPV. The way in which the returns from these investment projects are divided between dividends and retention is unimportant. Thus, a decision to pay a lower dividend will simply be compensated by an increase in share price.

Modigliani and Miller point out that it is possible for an individual investor to adjust the dividend policy of a business to conform to his or her particular requirements. On the one hand, if a business does not pay a dividend, the shareholder can create the equivalent of dividends by selling a portion of the shares held. If, on the other hand, a business provides a dividend that the shareholder does not wish to receive, the amount can be reinvested in additional shares in the business. In view of this fact, there is no reason for an investor to value the shares of one business more highly than another simply because it adopts a particular dividend policy.

The implications of the MM position for corporate managers are quite different from the implications of the traditional position. The MM view suggests that there is no such thing as an optimal dividend policy, and that one policy is as good as another (i.e., the dividend decision is irrelevant to shareholder wealth). Thus managers should not spend time considering the most appropriate policy to adopt, but should, instead, devote their energies to finding and managing profitable investment opportunities.

The MM Position Explained

Modigliani and Miller believe that dividends simply represent a movement of funds from inside the business to outside the business. This change in the location of funds should not have any effect on shareholder wealth. The MM position is explained in Example 11.1.

Example 11.1

Merton Ltd. has the following fair value balance sheet as at December 31, 2010:

Merton Ltd.
Fair Value Balance Sheet
as at December 31, 2010

	($000)
Assets at market value (excl. cash)	100
Cash	30
Gross assets	130
Less: Debt at fair value	40
Net assets	90
Common shares (30,000 shares) plus returned earnings	90

▶

Suppose that the business decides to distribute all the cash available (i.e., $30,000) to shareholders by making a $1.00 dividend per share. This will result in a fall in the value of net assets to $60,000 (i.e., $90,000 – $30,000) and a fall in the value of its shares from $3 (i.e., $90,000/30,000) to $2 (i.e., $60,000/30,000). The balance sheet following the dividend payment will therefore be as follows:

Merton Ltd.
Fair Value Balance Sheet
following the dividend payment

	($000)
Assets at market value (excl. cash)	100
Cash	—
Gross assets	100
Less: Debt at fair value	40
Net assets	60
Common shares (30,000 shares) plus retained earnings	60

Before the dividend distribution, an investor holding 10% of the shares in Merton Ltd. will have 3,000 shares worth $9,000 (i.e., 3,000 × $3). Following the distribution, the investor will have 3,000 shares worth $6,000 (i.e., 3,000 × $2.00) plus a cash dividend of $3,000 (i.e., 3,000 × $1.00), totalling $9,000. In other words, the total wealth of the investor remains the same.

If the investor did not want to receive the dividends, the cash received could be used to purchase more shares in the business. Although the number of shares held by the investor will change as a result of this decision, his or her *total wealth* will remain the same. If, on the other hand, Merton Ltd. did not issue a dividend, and the investor wished to receive one, he or she could create the desired dividend by simply selling a portion of the shares held. Once again, this will change the number of shares held by the investor, but will not change the total amount of wealth held.

What about the effect of a dividend payment on the amounts available for investment? We may feel that a high dividend payment will mean that less can be retained by the business, and this may, in turn, mean that the business will be unable to invest in projects that have a positive NPV. If this occurs, then shareholder wealth will be adversely affected. However, if we assume perfect and efficient capital markets exist, the business will be able to raise the financing required for investment purposes and will not have to rely on profit retention. In other words, dividend policy and investment policy can be regarded as quite separate issues.

The wealth of existing shareholders should not be affected by raising new funds rather than retaining of profits. Activity 11.5 reinforces this point.

ACTIVITY 11.5

Suppose that Merton Ltd. (see Example 11.1) replaces the $30,000 paid out as dividends by an issue of shares to new shareholders. Show the fair value balance sheet after the new issue and calculate the value of shares held by existing shareholders after the issue.

▶

Solution

The fair value balance sheet following the new issue will be almost the same as before the dividend payment was made. However, the number of shares outstanding will increase. If we assume that the new shares can be issued at fair value (i.e., current market value), the number of shares will increase by 15,000 shares ($30,000/$2.00 = 15,000).

Merton Ltd.
Fair Value Balance Sheet
following the issue of new shares

	($000)
Assets at market value (excl. cash)	100
Cash	30
Gross assets	130
Less: Debt at fair value	40
Net assets	90
Common shares (45,000 shares) plus retained earnings	90

The existing shareholders will own 30,000 of the 45,000 shares and will therefore own net assets worth $60,000 (i.e., 30,000/45,000 × $90,000). In other words, their wealth will not be affected by the financing decision.

What about the traditional argument in support of dividend policy (i.e., should investors prefer a bird in the hand)? The answer to this question is that the argument is probably not valid. It is based on a misconception of the nature of risk. The risks borne by a shareholder will be determined by the level of business borrowing and the nature of the business operations. These risks do not necessarily increase over time and are not affected by the dividend policy of the business. Dividends will only reduce risk if the amount received by the shareholder is then placed in a less risky form of investment (with a lower level of return). This could equally be achieved, however, through the sale of the shares in the business. Activity 11.6 discusses when a bird in hand may be preferrable.

ACTIVITY 11.6

There is one situation in which even Modigliani and Miller would accept that a bird in the hand is worth two in the bush (i.e., that immediate dividends are preferable). Can you think what it is? (*Hint*: Think of the way in which shareholder wealth is increased.)

Solution

Shareholder wealth is increased by the business accepting projects that have a positive NPV. If the business starts to accept projects with a negative NPV, this would decrease shareholder wealth. In such circumstances, a rational shareholder would prefer to receive a dividend rather than to allow the business to reinvest the profits of the business.

The MM Assumptions

The logic of the MM arguments has proven to be unassailable and it is now widely accepted that, in a world of perfect and efficient capital markets, dividend policy should have no effect on shareholder wealth. However, that world does not exist. The burning issue is whether or not the MM analysis can be applied to the real world of imperfect markets. There are three key assumptions, each unrealistic in the real world, on which the MM analysis rests.

1. The *no-share-issue-cost assumption* means that money paid out in dividends can be replaced by the business through a new share issue without incurring additional costs.
2. The *no-share-transaction-cost assumption* means that investors can make home-made dividends or reinvest in the business at no extra cost. In other words, there are no barriers to investors pursuing their own dividend and investment strategies.
3. The *no-taxation assumption* may be an important issue for investors. It is often argued that the taxation rules can have a significant influence on investor preferences. It may be more tax-efficient for an investor to receive benefits in the form of capital gains rather than dividends. In Canada, for example, only 50% of capital gains are included in taxable income and taxed at the investor's normal rate. However, dividends are grossed and included in taxable income. The investor then applies a dividend tax credit, which attempts to eliminate the double taxation of dividends—once at the corporation and again in the hands of the individual investor. In addition, it is possible for an investor to influence the timing of capital gains by choosing when to sell shares, whereas the timing of dividends is normally outside the investor's control. Activity 11.7 considers the influence of taxes on dividend policy and share price.

ACTIVITY 11.7

In a world where taxes are an important issue for investors, how will the particular dividend policy adopted by a business affect its share price?

Solution

If, as a result of the tax system, investors prefer capital gains rather than dividends, a business with a high dividend payout ratio would be valued less than a similar business with a low payout ratio.

Although differences between the tax treatments of dividend income and capital gains still exist, changes in tax policy have narrowed these differences in recent years. One important policy change has been the creation of tax deferral shelters (for example, registered retirement savings plans [RRSPs]), which allow investors to receive dividend income and capital gains free of immediate taxation. This has reduced the impact of taxation on dividend policy.

The three assumptions discussed undoubtedly weaken the MM analysis when applied to the real world. However, this does not necessarily mean that their analysis is destroyed. Indeed, the research evidence tends to support their position. One direct way to assess the validity of MM's arguments, in the real world, is to see whether there is a positive relationship between the dividends paid by businesses and their share price. If such a relationship exists, then MM's arguments would lose their force. The majority of studies, however, have failed to find any significant correlation between dividends and share prices.

Taxes and MM Dividend Theory

Corporate Tax Rate Versus the Personal Tax Rate

When the corporate tax rate is higher than the personal tax rate, the analysis below shows that investors would be better off if the company paid out dividends sooner rather than later. On the other hand, when corporate tax rates are lower than personal income tax rates, it is better for individuals not to receive a dividend immediately and instead let the company invest the money. Furthermore, there may be additional capital gains, which are taxed at an even lower rate than dividends, generated by allowing the company to invest its excess cash rather than pay a dividend. Consider the following situation.

Corporate tax rate higher than personal tax rate for individuals

Corporate tax rate	50%
Personal tax rate	40%
Dividend tax rate	37.215%
Interest rate	10.000%
Arc Ltd. has $1,000 excess cash.	

Choice 1: Arc pays a $1,000 dividend now.

Cash dividend to investors			$1,000.00
Taxes on dividends (37.215%)			372.15
After-tax cash dividend			$ 627.85
Investment for one year of the			
after-tax dividend	$627.85		
Interest rate	10%		
Interest earned		$62.79	
Personal tax rate		40%	
Taxes payable		$25.12	
After-tax interest earned			37.67
Total after-tax cash at the end of one year			$ 665.52

Choice 2: Arc invests $1,000 now and pays a dividend after one year.

Cash investment			$1,000.00
Interest earned (10% × $1,000)		$100.00	
Corporate taxes (50%)		50.00	
Extra after-tax cash available for dividends after one year			50.00
Cash dividend to investors			$1,050.00
Taxes on dividends (37.215%)			390.76
Total after-tax cash at the end of one year equals			
after-tax dividend			$ 659.24
Difference ($665.52 − $659.24)			$ 6.28

Conclusion

With a corporate tax rate higher than the personal tax rate, investors would be better off by $6.28 with Choice 1 (pay the dividend now) after one year.

THE IMPORTANCE OF DIVIDENDS

Whether or not we accept the MM analysis, there is little doubt that, in practice, the pattern of dividends is seen by investors and corporate managers to be important. It seems that there are three possible reasons to explain this phenomenon. These are:

- The clientele effect
- The information signalling effect
- The need to reduce agency costs.

The Clientele Effect

Investors may seek out businesses whose dividend policies closely match their particular cash flow needs and tax situation. Thus businesses with particular dividend policies will attract particular types of investors. This phenomenon is referred to as the **clientele effect**.

The existence of a clientele effect has important implications for managers. First, dividend policy should be clearly defined and consistently applied. Investors attracted to a particular business because of its dividend policy will not welcome unexpected changes. Second, managers need not concern themselves with trying to accommodate all the different needs of shareholders. The particular distribution policy adopted by the business will tend to attract a certain type of investor depending on his or her cash needs and tax position.

Investors should be wary, however, of making share investment decisions based primarily on dividend policy. Minimizing costs may not be an easy process for investors. For example, those requiring a regular cash income, who seek out businesses with high dividend payout ratios, may find that any savings in transaction costs are cancelled out by incurring other costs, as illustrated in Activity 11.8.

ACTIVITY 11.8

What kinds of costs may be borne by investors who invest in high dividend payout businesses?

Solution

Being committed to a high dividend payout may prevent a business from investing in profitable projects that would have increased shareholder wealth. Hence, there could be a loss of future benefits for the investor. If, however, a business decides to raise funds to replace the amount distributed in dividends, the cost of raising the required financing will be borne by existing shareholders.

Investors must therefore look beyond the dividend policy of a business in order to make a sensible investment decision.

The evidence concerning the clientele effect is fairly mixed. Although there are studies that support the existence of a clientele effect, other studies have cast doubt on these findings. More research—perhaps using different approaches to examining the issue—is required for a clearer picture to emerge.

The Information Signalling Effect

In an imperfect world, managers of a business will have greater access to information regarding the profits and performance of the business than investors will. This **information asymmetry**, as it is called, between managers and investors allows dividends to be used by managers as a means of passing on to investors information concerning the business. Thus, new information relating to future prospects may be signalled through changes in dividend policy. If, for example, managers are confident about the business's prospects, there may be **information signalling** to this effect through an increase in dividends. This approach is explored in Activity 11.9.

ACTIVITY 11.9

Why would managers wish to use dividends as a means of conveying information about the business's prospects? Why not simply issue a statement to shareholders?

Solution

At least three reasons have been put forward to explain why dividend signalling may be preferred. First, it may be that the managers do not want to disclose the precise nature of the events that improve the business's prospects. Suppose, for example, that a business has signed a large government defence contract, which will be formally announced by the government at some time in the future. In the intervening period, however, the price of the shares in the business may be depressed and the managers may be concerned that the business is vulnerable to a takeover. The managers might, under the circumstances, wish to boost the share price without specifying the nature of the good news.

Second, issuing a statement about, say, improved future prospects may not be convincing, particularly if earlier statements by managers have proven incorrect. Talk is cheap, whereas an increase in dividends would be more substantial evidence of the managers' confidence in the future.

Third, managers may feel that an explicit statement concerning future prospects will attract criticism from shareholders if things do not work out as expected. They may, therefore, prefer more coded messages to avoid being held to account at a later date.

Various studies have been carried out to establish the information content of dividends. Some of these studies have looked at the share price reaction to *unexpected* changes in dividends. If signalling exists, an unexpected dividend announcement should result in a significant share price reaction. The results from these studies provide convincing evidence that signalling does exist; that is, a surprise dividend increase (positive signal) results in an increase in share price, and a surprise dividend decrease (negative signal) results in a decrease in share price. One interesting feature of the evidence is that the market reaction to dividend reductions is much greater than the market reaction to dividend increases. It appears that investors regard dividend reductions much more seriously.

REAL WORLD 11.2 reveals how the market reacted to a dividend cut by one leading Canadian company.

Manulife Dividend Cut

On August 6, 2009, Manulife announced a surprise 50% cut in its dividend. Manulife said it wanted to use the annual savings of $800 million to build fortress levels of capital. The stock promptly lost about 15% of its value on the day of the announcement as it fell from around $26 to $22 a share. During the Great Recession of 2008–2009 Manulife shares had sunk from pre-recession levels of over $40 a share to below $9 a share at the bottom. The shares sit at $21.72 at the time of writing.

It turned out that Manulife was much more levered to the stock market than many investors had thought. The big problem was that commitments from variable-annuity sales and their invested premiums caused a shortfall of as much as $22 billion, according to some commentators.

This surprise cut led investors and financial commentators to speculate about what Manulife was signalling. Was it company-specific, or was Manulife now expecting years of slow growth as the economy tried to recover from the downturn?

Source: Manulife press release at their website, www.manulife.com/corporate/corporate2.nsf/Public/newsreleases.html, and www. bestwaytoinvest.com/stories/ is-manulife-dividend-cut-cause-larger-concern, both accessed September 27, 2009.

The Need to Reduce Agency Costs

In recent years, *agency theory* has become increasingly influential in the financial management literature. Agency theory views a business as a coalition of different interest groups (including managers, shareholders, lenders, employees, and suppliers) in which each group is seeking to maximize its own welfare. According to this theory, one group connected with the business may engage in behaviour that results in costs being borne by another group. However, the latter group may try to restrain the action of the former group, through contractual or other arrangements, so as to minimize these costs. Two examples of where a conflict of interest arises between groups, and the impact on dividend policy, are considered below.

The first example concerns a conflict of interest between shareholders and managers. If the managers (who are agents of the shareholders) decide to invest in lavish offices, expensive cars, and other perks, they will be pursuing their own interests at a cost to the shareholders. Shareholders, on the other hand, may insist that surplus cash be distributed to them in the form of a dividend. Managers may decide to support this policy to demonstrate their commitment to the shareholders' interests. Agency costs will be more of an issue where there is a clear separation between the shareholders and the managers of the business.

The second example concerns a conflict between shareholders and lenders. Shareholders may seek to reduce their stake in the business by withdrawing cash in the form of dividends. This may be done to reduce their exposure to the risks associated with the business. However, this is likely to be to the detriment of lenders, who will become more exposed to these risks. The lenders may, therefore, try to prevent this kind of behaviour by restricting the level of dividends to be paid to shareholders. Activity 11.10 considers how lenders might accomplish this.

Figure 11.1 summarizes the main reasons why dividends seem to be important in the real world.

FIGURE 11.1   Reasons for the Importance of Dividends

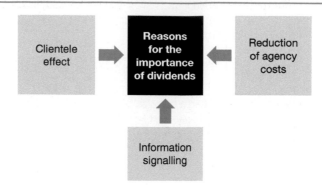

ACTIVITY 11.10

How can lenders go about restricting shareholders' rights to dividends? (*Hint*: Think back to Chapter 8.)

Solution

Lenders can insist that loan covenants, which restrict the level of dividends payable, be included in the loan agreement.

Factors Determining the Level of Dividends

Investment Opportunities

Businesses that have good investment opportunities may try to retain profits rather than distribute them. As we saw in Chapter 8, retained earnings come first in the pecking order when raising long-term financing, and are easily the most important source of long-term financing for businesses.

Investment opportunities may vary over the life cycle of a business and so its retention/dividend policies may also vary. In the early phase, when businesses are growing quickly, a policy of either low dividends or no dividends may be chosen in order to retain profits for reinvestment. At a more mature stage of the business cycle, when investment opportunities are restricted, a policy of higher dividends may be chosen.

REAL WORLD 11.3 provides an example of how one business varied its dividend policy over time.

REAL WORLD 11.3

Microsoft Reaches Middle Age

For years, Microsoft never paid a dividend. It was growing so fast that it needed all the cash it could get its hands on for business purposes. As Figure 11.2 shows, shareholders had no reason to complain about the lack of a dividend in the early years when Microsoft's share price rose from a split-adjusted share price of practically zero to around US$60 in 2000.

▶

FIGURE 11.2   Microsoft Monthly Chart (adjusted for stock splits)

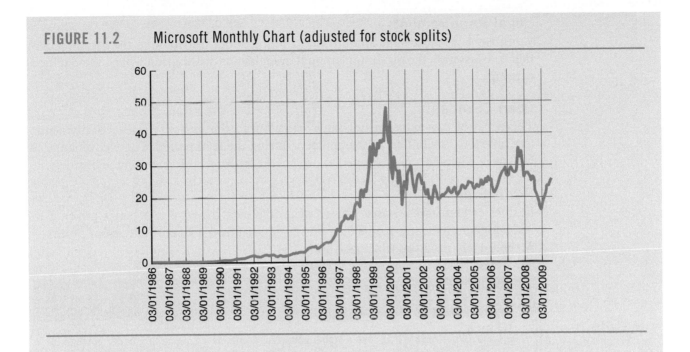

Then things started to slow down. Microsoft was sitting on US$56 billion in cash and as the share price stalled and started to retreat following the dot-com meltdown in 2000 and 2001, the company felt it had to do something. So, its first ever dividend was declared in 2003, paying out 12% of its earnings as dividends. Then in fiscal 2005 a special dividend of US$3.00 per share was declared, which, together with a share buy-back program, returned US$75 billion to shareholders. The following table shows Microsoft's dividend payout ratios in recent years.

	2001	2002	2003	2004	2005	2006	2007	2008
Dividend payout ratio	0%	0%	12%	21%	304%	29%	28%	24%

Sources: Microsoft annual report at their website: www.microsoft.com/msft/reports/ar08/index.html and Yahoo! Finance at http://finance. yahoo.com/q/hp?s=MSFT&a=02&b=13&c=1986&d=08&e=27&f=2009&g=m, both accessed September 27, 2009.

Residual Theory of Dividends

In some cases, raising external financing for new investment may be a problem, and so profit retention may be the only option available. It can be argued that where such a problem exists, and when investors are indifferent about dividends, it would make sense for managers to regard dividends as simply a residual. That is, the managers should make dividend distributions only where the expected return from investment opportunities is below the required return for investors. The implication of this policy is that dividends could fluctuate each year according to the investment opportunities available: the greater the investment needs of the business, the less that is available for distribution, and vice versa. This line of argument is consistent with the **residual theory of dividends**. Where, however, a business is able to finance easily and cheaply from external sources, there is less need to rely on retained profits, which can then be distributed in the form of dividends.

Legal Requirements

Company law restricts the amount that a business can distribute in the form of dividends. In essence, the maximum amount available for distribution will be the retained earnings.

Loan Covenants

There may be covenants included in a loan contract that restrict the level of dividends available for distribution to shareholders during the loan period. These covenants, as we saw in Chapter 8, are designed to protect the lenders' investment in the business.

Profit Stability

Businesses that have a stable pattern of profits over time are in a better position to make higher dividend payouts than businesses that have a volatile pattern of profits—Activity 11.11 discusses why this is so.

ACTIVITY 11.11

Why should businesses that have a stable pattern of profits over time be in a better position to make higher dividend payouts than businesses that have a volatile pattern of profits?

Solution

Businesses that have a stable pattern of profits are able to plan with greater certainty and are less likely to feel a need to retain profits for unexpected events.

Control

A high profit retention/low dividend policy can help avoid the need to issue new shares, and so existing shareholders' control will not be diluted.

Threat of Takeover

A further aspect of control concerns the relationship between dividend payments and the threat of takeover. It has been suggested, for example, that a high retention/low distribution policy can increase the vulnerability of a business to takeover—Activity 11.12 discusses why.

ACTIVITY 11.12

Why might it be suggested that a low payout policy increases the threat of takeover? Is this a very convincing point?

Solution

If a predator is seeking to acquire the business, it may be able to convince shareholders that the dividends paid are too low and that the existing management is not maximizing their wealth. Thus, a low dividend policy may make the task of acquisition much easier. Such arguments, however, are only likely to appeal to unsophisticated shareholders. More sophisticated shareholders will recognize that dividends represent only part of the total return from the shares held. (However, if profits are retained rather than distributed, they must be employed in a profitable manner. Failure to do this will make the threat of takeover greater.)

However, paying a large dividend may signal to the market the managers' confidence in the prospects of the business. This should, in turn, increase the value of the shares and so make a takeover more costly for the predator business. However, investors may regard a large dividend as a desperate attempt by the directors to gain their support and so will discount the dividend received.

Market Expectations
If dividend expectations are not met, there may be a loss of investor confidence in the business.

Inside Information
The managers of a business may have inside information concerning the prospects of a business, which cannot be published but which indicates that the shares are currently undervalued by investors. In such a situation, it may be sensible to rely on retained earnings rather than issuing more shares. Although this may lead to lower dividends, it could enhance the wealth of the existing shareholders.

Figure 11.3 summarizes the main influences on the level of dividends declared by a business.

FIGURE 11.3   Factors Influencing the Level of Dividends

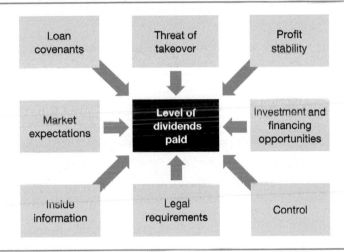

The Dividend Policy of Other Businesses

The dividend policy adopted by a business may be considered in relation to other, comparable businesses. Indeed, it has been suggested that investors make comparisons between businesses and when that a significant deviation in dividend policy from the sector norm will attract criticism. The implication seems to be that managers should shape the dividend policy of their business according to what comparable businesses are doing.

This, however, may be neither practical nor desirable. To begin with, there is the problem of identifying comparable businesses. In practice, there may be real differences between businesses concerning risk characteristics, rate of growth, and accounting policies adopted. There may also be real differences between businesses concerning the influences mentioned above, such as investment opportunities and loan covenants. Even if comparable businesses could be found, the use of such businesses as a benchmark assumes that they adopt dividend polices that are optimal, which may not be the case.

These problems suggest that dividend policy is best determined according to the particular requirements of the business. If the policy adopted differs from the norm, the managers should be able to provide reasons to investors.

Dividend Policy and Management Attitudes: Some Evidence

An interesting aspect of dividend policy concerns the attitudes and behaviour of managers. One of the earliest pieces of research on this topic was undertaken in the U.S. by J. Lintner,[1] who carried out interviews with managers in 28 businesses. Although this research is now quite old, it is still considered to be one of the most accurate descriptions of how managers set dividend policy in practice.

Lintner found that managers considered the dividend decision to be an important one and were committed to long-term target dividend payout ratios. He also found that managers were concerned more with variations in dividends than with the absolute amount of dividends paid. Managers held the view that investors preferred a smooth increase in dividend payments over time. Consequently the managers were reluctant to increase the level of dividends in response to a short-term increase in profits. They wished to avoid a situation where dividends would have to be cut in the future, and so dividends were increased only when it was felt that the higher level of dividends could be sustained through a permanent increase in earnings. As a result, there was a time lag between dividend growth and earnings growth. Activity 11.13 considers a different reason for these managers' approach to dividend policy.

ACTIVITY 11.13

Are the attitudes of managers described above consistent with another view of dividends discussed earlier?

Solution

The attitude of managers described by Lintner is consistent with more recent work concerning the use of dividends as a means of information signalling. The managers interviewed seem to be aware of the fact that a dividend cut would send negative signals to investors.

In a later study, Eugene Fama and Harvey Babiak[2] found that businesses distributed about half of their profits in the form of dividends. However, significant increases in earnings would only be followed by a *partial adjustment* to dividends in the first year. On average, the increase in dividends in the first year was only about one-third of the increase that would have been consistent with maintaining the target payout ratio. The smooth and gradual adjustment of dividends to changes in profits revealed by this study is consistent with the earlier study by Lintner and confirms that managers wish to ensure a sustainable level of dividends.

Where a business experiences adverse business conditions, Harry DeAngelo et al.[3] found that managers are often reluctant to reduce dividend payments immediately. Instead, they will try to maintain the existing level of dividends until it is clear that the former profit levels cannot be achieved. At this point, the managers will usually make a single large reduction, rather than a series of small reductions to a new level of dividends.

---

[1] J. Lintner, "Distribution of Incomes of Corporations Among Dividends, Retained Earnings and Taxes," *American Economic Review*, No. 46, May 1956, pp. 97–113.

[2] E.F. Fama and H. Babiak, "Dividend Policy: An Empirical Analysis," *Journal of the American Statistical Association*, December 1968.

[3] H. DeAngelo, L. DeAngelo, and D. Skinner, "Dividends and Losses," *Journal of Finance*, December 1992, pp. 281–289.

An important study by H. Kent Baker et al.[4] asked U.S. managers to express their views concerning dividend policy.

The study reveals that the majority of managers acknowledge the importance of a smooth, uninterrupted pattern of dividends. This is in line with the earlier findings of Lintner. The study also reveals that the majority of managers acknowledge the signalling effect and clientele effect but not the role of dividends in reducing agency costs. These views, therefore, do not precisely match the theories concerning why dividends are important. Finally, the study reveals that the majority of managers do not support the bird-in-the-hand argument, and they therefore reject the traditional view.

Dividend Smoothing in Practice

The attitude of managers toward dividend smoothing, as described by the Lintner study and by other studies, seems to be reflected in practice. For many businesses, the pattern of dividends is much smoother than the pattern of underlying earnings. REAL WORLD 11.4 provides an example.

REAL WORLD 11.4

Royal Bank: Smooth Dividends, Choppy Earnings

Canadian banks became famous in 2008 for their financial strength and solidity in the face of the worst recession since the 1930s. Figure 11.4 shows the Royal Bank raising its dividend even as its net income declined.

FIGURE 11.4   Earnings and Dividends at Royal Bank

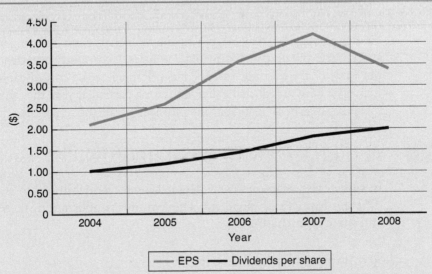

Source: Adapted from data in the Royal Bank's annual reports.

---

[4] H.K. Baker, G.E. Powell, and E.T. Veit, "Revisiting Managerial Perspectives on Dividend Policy," *Journal of Economics and Finance*, Fall 2002, pp. 267–283.

SELF-ASSESSMENT QUESTION   11.1

Sandarajan Ltd. is a business that has recently obtained a listing on the stock exchange. The business operates a chain of supermarkets in northern Nova Scotia and was the subject of a management buy-out in 2005. In the period since the buy-out, the business has grown rapidly. The managers and a venture capital organization owned 80% of the shares prior to the stock exchange listing. However, this has now been reduced to 20%. The record of the business over the past five years is as follows:

Year	Net Income ($000)	Dividend ($000)	Number of Shares Issued (000)
2006	420	220	1,000
2007	530	140	1,000
2008	650	260	1,500
2009	740	110	1,500
2010	880	460	1,500

Required:

(a) Comment on the dividend policy of the business prior to the stock exchange listing.
(b) What advice would you give to the managers of the business concerning future dividend policy?

What Should Managers Do?

Probably the best advice we can give is to make the dividend policy clear to investors and then make every effort to follow that policy. Investors are unlikely to welcome surprises in dividend policy and may react by selling their shares and investing in businesses that have more stable and predictable dividend policies. Uncertainty over dividend policy will lower the value of the business's shares and will increase the cost of capital. If, for any reason, managers have to reduce the dividends for a particular year, they should prepare investors for the change in dividend payout and clearly state the reasons for that change.

L.O. 4   ALTERNATIVES TO CASH DIVIDENDS

In some cases, a business may decide to make distributions to shareholders in a form different from a cash dividend. The two most important of these are stock dividends and share repurchases.

Stock Dividends

A business may make a **stock dividend** rather than making a cash distribution to shareholders. Thus, if a business announced a 20% stock dividend, this would mean that each shareholder would receive a 20% increase in the number of shares held. We saw in Chapter 8, however, that stock dividends do not result in an increase in shareholder wealth. Making a stock dividend is, in essence, a bookkeeping transaction that will not, of itself, create value. Nevertheless, the market may respond positively to a stock dividend if it is seen as a sign of the directors' confidence concerning the future.

The stock dividend may suggest that the directors will maintain the same dividend per share in the future, despite the increase in the number of shares in issue. Various research studies have shown a positive response to stock dividend announcements by the market. However, if a business does not maintain or increase its dividend per share in subsequent periods, the positive effect on share prices will evaporate.

Share Repurchase

In recent years, share repurchases have become a popular means of making distributions to shareholders. They are usually undertaken for one or more of the following reasons:

- To return cash to shareholders that is surplus to requirements
- To buy out unwelcome shareholders
- To adjust the capital structure to a more suitable degree of leverage
- To support the share price when it has temporarily fallen.

A repurchase can be achieved by acquiring shares through the stock market, through agreements with particular shareholders, or through a tender offer to all shareholders. In the case of a tender offer, the business will offer to purchase a particular number of shares for a specified price during the offer period. Shares that are repurchased by the business are cancelled. A share repurchase is a voluntary agreement between the business and its shareholders, which means that shareholders wishing to keep their shares can do so.

Businesses with surplus cash may prefer to repurchase shares rather than to pay higher dividends. It has the advantage that it is a one-time event, which does not oblige the business to make similar distributions in the future. Although the same effect may be achieved by a special cash dividend to shareholders, as we saw that Microsoft did in Real World 11.4, a repurchase focuses on those shareholders wishing to receive cash. There is also the advantage that payments to shareholders can be spread over a longer period.

REAL WORLD 11.5 provides an example of a business that decided to make a share repurchase.

 REAL WORLD 11.5

Buying High: Recent Share Buy-Back Programs

Many companies that used share buy-back programs in recent years have overpaid for their shares, in retrospect. Only Microsoft's share price is near the high of the buy-back price range, and even Microsoft could have bought back its stock at much lower prices if it had waited until the depths of the 2008–2009 recession (i.e., timed the market better).

Company	Buy-back Announcement	Buy-back Amount	Share Price During Buy-back Period	September 25, 2009 Share Price
General Electric	2007	$12–$14	$30–$40	$16.37
Intel	2005	500 million shares	$20–$28	$19.37
Microsoft	2008	$40 billion	$16–$28	$25.55
AIG	2007	$8 billion	$1,250–$1,400*	$44.60
CP Rail	2007	$1.1 billion	$60–$88	$50.15

*Adjusted for reverse split.

Source: Compiled from various websites.

When a business undertakes a repurchase, the shareholders can benefit from the adjustment to the capital structure. The leverage effect, which arises from changes in the relative proportions of equity and debt, can boost returns to shareholders, which can in turn boost the share price. However, a rise in share price will not automatically occur: the additional benefits of higher leverage must outweigh the additional risks for the share price to rise.

Managers must take care to ensure equity between shareholders during a share repurchase. In some cases, the market may undervalue the shares of a business, perhaps because it does not have access to information known to the managers of the business. If this situation exists, the shareholders who hold on to their shares will benefit at the expense of those who sell. In other cases, the market for shares in the business may be slow and the effect of repurchasing a large number of shares may be to create an artificially high price. This will benefit those who sell at the expense of those who continue to hold shares.

SUMMARY

The Payment of Dividends

- Dividends represent a return by a business to its shareholders.
- There are legal limits on dividend distributions to protect creditors and lenders.
- Dividends are usually paid quarterly by large businesses.
- Cum dividend share prices include the accrued dividend; ex-dividend prices exclude the dividend.
- Businesses often have a target dividend payout ratio.

Dividend Policy and Shareholder Wealth

- There are two major schools of thought concerning the effect of dividends on shareholder wealth.
- The traditional school argues that investors prefer dividends now because the amounts are more certain.
- The implication for managers is that they should adopt as generous a dividend policy as possible.
- The modernists (MM) argue that, given perfect and efficient markets, the pattern of dividends has no effect on shareholder wealth.
- The implication for managers is that one dividend policy is as good as another and so they should not spend time considering which policy should be adopted.

- The MM position assumes no share issue costs, no share transaction costs, and no taxes; these assumptions weaken (but do not necessarily destroy) their arguments.

The Importance of Dividends

- Dividends appear to be important to investors.
- The clientele effect, the signalling effect, and the need to reduce agency costs may explain this.
- The level of dividends distributed is dependent on various factors, including: investment and financing opportunities, legal requirements, loan covenants, profit stability, control issues (including takeover threats), market expectations, and inside information.
- Managers perceive dividends as being important for investors.
- Managers prefer a smooth increase in dividends and are reluctant to cut dividends.

Alternatives to Cash Dividends

- Stock dividends are a bookkeeping transaction, but the market may see them as a sign of managers' confidence in the future, and respond positively.
- Share repurchases involve repurchasing and then cancelling shares.

KEY TERMS

Dividend

Record date

Ex-dividend

Cum dividend

Dividend cover ratio

Clientele effect

Information asymmetry

Information signalling

Residual theory of dividends

Stock dividend

LIST OF EQUATIONS

Equations from previous chapters reused in Chapter 11:

4.15 Dividend cover ratio $= \dfrac{\text{Net income available to common shareholders}}{\text{Annual dividends to common shareholders}}$

10.4 $P_0 = \dfrac{D_1}{K_0 - g}$ for shares with a dividend growth rate, g

REVIEW QUESTIONS

Answers to the Review Questions can be found on the Companion Website that accompanies this text at www.pearsoned.ca/atrill.

11.1 List three reasons why a business should wish to repurchase some of its shares.

11.2 "The business's dividend decision is really a by-product of its capital investment decision." Discuss.

11.3 Is it really important for a business to try to meet the needs of different types of investors when formulating its dividend policy?

11.4 Describe how agency theory may help to explain the dividend policy of businesses.

11.5 In Chapter 10 we learned that the dividend growth model suggests that the fair value of a common share is based on next year's dividend. This is expressed in the formula $P_0 = \dfrac{D_1}{K_0 - g}$. With this in mind, how is it possible for a company like Google, which has never paid a dividend, to have a share price of around US$500?

PROBLEMS AND CASES

11.1 Which of the following investors are entitled to the current dividend?

Investor	Transaction Date	Record Date
A	Monday, May 1	Wednesday, May 3
B	Monday, February 28	Thursday, March 2
C	Wednesday, September 15	Monday, September 19
D	Thursday, June 28	Tuesday, July 2

11.2 Which of the following investors are entitled to the current dividend?

Investor	Transaction Date	Ex-Dividend Date
A	Monday, May 1	Wednesday, May 3
B	Monday, February 28	Thursday, March 2
C	Wednesday, September 15	Monday, September 19
D	Thursday, June 28	Tuesday, July 2

11.3 Northern Technology Inc. (NTI) closed the end of 2009 with a balance of $1,500,000 in retained earnings, as shown below. Because of a poor economy, NTI cut its total annual dividends to $30,000, after which it expects earnings and dividends to increase. For the next eight years, it expects the following results.

Year	Retained Earnings ($000)	Net income (loss) ($000)	Dividends ($000)
2009	1,500		
2010		(500)	30
2011		(200)	30
2012		400	45
2013		350	45
2014		700	125
2015		810	150
2016		950	225
2017		1,150	?

Required:

Calculate the maximum dividend NTI could pay at the end of 2017, assuming dividends are paid once annually at year-end.

11.4 Early Bird Bakeries Ltd. (EBB) is planning to pay a special dividend per share, over and above its regular quarterly dividend, at the end of the fourth quarter of 2012. EBB ended 2009 with retained earnings of $1,240,000.

Year	Quarterly Dividends Per Share ($)	Number of Shares Outstanding	Net Income ($000)
2010	$0.25	1,600,000	$3,000,000
2011	$0.30	1,610,000	$3,200,000
2012	$0.35	1,625,000	$3,350,000

Required:

Calculate the maximum special dividend per share EBB could pay at the end of the fourth quarter of 2012, assuming a bank covenant prevents retained earnings from falling below $500,000.

11.5 Community Electric Power Corporation (CEPC) is the one and only power supplier to Uranium City, located in the far north. The power rates are regulated by the government and consequently, CEPC has had a net income of $75 million for each of the last five years. Beginning January 1, 2011, CEPC will be the monopoly supplier of power to Zinc City, located in the southeast part of the far north. CEPC will earn an additional $45 million on this new deal. CEPC has 5 million common shares outstanding and maintains a dividend payout ratio of 40%.

Required:

(a) Calculate the annual dividend per share prior to the expansion to Zinc City.
(b) What would the information signalling theory of dividends indicate that CEPC should do in 2011? Quantify your answer.

11.6 You have collected the following data:

Company	Net Income ($)	Dividend ($)
DEF	40,000,000	5,000,000
GHI	100,000,000	40,000,000
JKL	75,000,000	nil
MNO	100,000	1,000,000

Required:
Use the concept of the life cycle of a business to rank these companies according to the following categories: pre-teenaged, teenaged, middle-aged, and old. Provide a reason for your choice.

11.7 You have $10,000 invested within your registered retirement savings plan (RRSP) in common shares of Canadian companies. All taxes on earnings within your RRSP are deferred until the time when you decide to withdraw money from your RRSP. Withdrawals are taxed fully as regular income in the year the withdrawal is made. Withdrawals do not have to start being made until the investor is aged 71.

You also have $10,000 outside of your RRSP that you have invested in Government of Canada bonds. Interest on bonds held outside your RRSP is fully taxed in the year it is earned.

You have recently been talking with your broker and she has suggested that your investment plan should be the opposite of what it currently is. That is, your RRSP should hold the bonds and your non-registered investments outside your RRSP should hold shares.

Required:
Explain in general terms the broker's thinking on this matter.

11.8 The dividend policies of businesses has been the subject of much debate in the financial management literature.

Required:
Discuss the view that dividends can increase the wealth of shareholders.

11.9 Identify and discuss the factors that may influence the dividend policies of businesses.

11.10 The following listed businesses have different policies concerning distributions to shareholders:

- North Ltd. pays all profits available for distribution to shareholders in the form of a cash dividend each year.
- South Ltd. has yet to pay any cash dividends to shareholders and has no plans to make dividend payments in the foreseeable future.
- West Ltd. repurchases shares from shareholders as an alternative to a dividend payment.
- East Ltd. offers shareholders the choice of either a small but stable cash dividend or a stock dividend each year.

Required:
Discuss the advantages and disadvantages of each of the above policies.

11.11 Fellingham Ltd. has 20 million common shares in issue. No shares have been issued during the past four years. The business's earnings and dividends as taken from the annual reports showed:

	2007	2008	2009	2010
Earnings per share	$0.11	$0.124	$0.109	$0.172
Dividend per share	$0.10	$0.109	$0.1188	$0.1295

At the annual general meeting for 2007, the chairman had indicated that it was the intention to consistently increase annual dividends by 9%, anticipating that, on average, this would maintain the spending power of shareholders and provide a modest growth in real income.

As it turns out, subsequent average annual inflation rates, measured by the general index of prices, have been:

2008	11%
2009	10%
2010	8%

The common shares are currently selling for $3.44, excluding the 2010 dividend.

Required:
Comment on the declared dividend policy of the business and its possible effects on both Fellingham Ltd. and its shareholders, illustrating your answer with the information provided.

11.12 Skywire Data Inc. has been in business for over thirty years and has never paid a dividend until this year, even though it has been one of the most successful tech companies ever. Skywire's share price has increased one hundred-fold since its IPO. However, as it matured, its growth slowed somewhat and this year the company decided to declare its first ever semi-annual dividend of $0.10 per share. The share price promptly declined for three days after the dividend announcement.

Required:
How would you explain this phenomenon of instituting a dividend only to see your share price decline to a manager in your company who is campaigning to raise the dividend at your firm?

11.13 Mondrian Ltd. is a new business that aims to maximize the wealth of its shareholders. The board of directors is currently trying to decide upon the most appropriate dividend policy to adopt for the business's shareholders. However, there is strong disagreement among three of the directors concerning the benefits of declaring cash dividends:

- Director A argues that cash dividends would be welcomed by investors and that as high a dividend payout ratio as possible would reflect positively on the market value of the business's shares.
- Director B argues that whether a cash dividend is paid or not is irrelevant in the context of shareholder wealth maximization.
- Director C takes an opposite view to Director A and argues that dividend payments should be avoided as they would lead to a decrease in shareholder wealth.

Required:
(a) Discuss the arguments for and against the position taken by each of the three directors.
(b) Assuming the board of directors decides to pay a dividend to shareholders, what factors should be taken into account when determining the level of dividend payment?

11.14 Your company is thinking of paying its first-ever dividend. You are interested in how dividend policy might affect your company's share price. Therefore, you gathered the following information from your closest competitors.

	Powerful Corp.			Winged IT Inc.		
	Average share price ($)	Net income (loss) ($000)	Dividend ($)	Average share ($000) ($)	Net income (loss) ($000)	Dividend ($)
2008	10.50	150,000	30,000	25.00	120,000	40,000
2009	11.20	200,000	30,000	20.00	(32,000)	–
2010	10.75	(45,000)	30,000	15.00	50,000	13,000
2011	13.50	140,000	35,000	30.00	120,000	50,000
2012	14.00	220,000	35,000	21.20	54,000	10,000
2013	18.20	350,000	45,000	32.50	200,000	85,000

Required:

Compare the dividend policy of these two firms and how each seems to affect its share price.

11.15 Arc Ltd. has $1,000 excess cash. It can declare a dividend now (choice 1) or invest the money and pay the dividend in one year (choice 2). The tax rates and interest rate are shown below.

Corporate tax rate	40%
Personal tax rate	50%
Dividend tax rate	37.215%
Interest rate	10.000%

Required:
  (a) Calculate the total after-tax cash flow to the investor under both choices.
  (b) Which choice leaves the investor better off?

11.16

Required:
Go to the DividendInvestors.ca website at www.dividendinvestors.ca/ and find the ex-dividend date and quarterly dividend payments for the following companies:

> Royal Bank (RY)
> Toronto-Dominion Bank (TD)
> Bank of Nova Scotia (BNS)
> Canadian Imperial Bank of Commerce (CM)
> Bank of Montreal (BMO)
> Tim Hortons (THI)
> Encana (ECA)

11.17 You are an analyst at Oil Patch Semiconductors Inc. (OPS), a small high-tech firm specializing in the design of proprietary chips used by oil companies to help find new sources of oil and natural gas. Your company has had a very successful quarter and currently has $1 million in excess cash to be invested. The president has come to you with an investment strategy that he thinks is conservative but guaranteed successful. He want to buy $1 million worth of common shares of one of the big five Canadian banks (listed in Problem and Case 11.16, among others) to ensure getting the dividend and then, once the ex-dividend date passes, sell all those shares and buy shares in another bank with the next closest ex-dividend date. In this manner he hopes to get dividends from all five Canadian banks each quarter.

Required:

(a) Is the president's strategy even feasible or do all the banks have the same ex-dividend date each quarter? Refer to your answer to 11.16.

(b) Will transaction costs outweigh any dividends received?

(c) Comment on the theoretical legitimacy of the president's investment strategy.

(d) Is there ever a time when the president's strategy would work?

Managing Working Capital

When you have completed this chapter, you should be able to:

1 Identify the main elements of working capital.

2 Discuss the purpose and the nature of the working capital cycle.

3 Explain the importance of establishing policies for the control and management of each element of working capital.

4 Explain the factors that small businesses must take into account to manage working capital.

INTRODUCTION

Working capital represents a significant investment for many businesses and so its proper management and control can be vital. In this chapter we consider the factors that must be taken into account when managing the working capital of a business. Each element of working capital is identified, and the major issues surrounding them are discussed. We saw in Chapter 6 that working capital may be an important aspect of new investment proposals. Some useful tools in the management of working capital are forecasts, which we explored in Chapter 3, and financial ratios, which were considered in Chapter 4.

THE MAIN ELEMENTS OF WORKING CAPITAL

L.O. 1

Working capital is usually defined as current assets less current liabilities. Equation 12.1 gives the formula for calculating working capital.

$$\text{Working capital} = \text{Current assets} - \text{Current liabilities} \qquad 12.1$$

The major elements of current assets are:

- Inventories
- Accounts receivable
- Cash.

The major elements of current liabilities are:

- Accounts payable
- Bank overdrafts and revolving lines of credit.

The amount and composition of working capital can vary between industries. For some types of businesses, the investment in working capital can be substantial. For example, a manufacturing business will typically invest heavily in raw materials, work in process, and finished goods, and will often sell its goods on credit, thereby generating accounts receivable. A retailer, on the other hand, will hold only one form of inventory (finished goods), and will usually sell goods for cash. Many service businesses hold no inventory. Most businesses buy goods and/or services on credit, giving rise to accounts payable. Few—if any—businesses operate without a cash balance, although in some cases it is a negative one (bank overdraft).

L.O. 2 THE NATURE AND PURPOSE OF THE WORKING CAPITAL CYCLE

Working capital represents a net investment in short-term assets. These assets are continually flowing into and out of the business, and are essential for day-to-day operations. The various elements of working capital are interrelated, and can be seen as part of a short-term cycle. For a manufacturing business, the working capital cycle can be depicted as shown in Figure 12.1.

FIGURE 12.1   The Working Capital Cycle

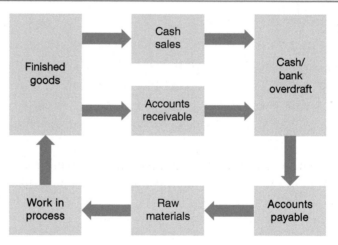

Cash is used to pay for raw materials, or raw materials are bought for immediate cash settlement; cash is spent on labour and other aspects that turn raw materials into work in process and, finally, into finished goods. The finished goods are sold to customers either for cash or on credit. In the case of credit customers, there will be a delay before the cash is received from the sales. Receipt of cash completes the cycle.

For a retailer, the situation would be as in Figure 12.1, except that there would be no work in process or raw materials. For a purely service business, the working capital cycle would also be similar to that depicted in Figure 12.1, except that there would be no inventory of raw materials and finished goods. There may well be work in process, however, since many services (for example, cases handled by a law firm) will take some time to complete and costs will build up before the client is billed for them.

Managing Working Capital

The management of working capital is an essential part of the business's short-term planning process. It is necessary for management to decide how much of each element should be held. As we shall see later in this chapter, costs are associated with holding either too much or too little of each element. Management must be aware of these costs, which include opportunity costs, in order to manage effectively. Hence, the potential benefits must be weighed against the likely costs in an attempt to achieve the optimal investment.

The working capital needs of a particular business are likely to change over time as a result of changes in the business environment. This means that working capital decisions are constantly being made. Managers must try to identify changes in an attempt to ensure that the level of investment in working capital is appropriate—Activity 12.1 considers what kinds of changes might be made.

ACTIVITY 12.1

What kinds of changes in the business environment might lead to a decision to change the level of investment in working capital?

Solution

Working capital needs might be affected by changes in:

- Interest rates
- Market demand
- The seasons
- The state of the economy.

In addition to changes in the external environment, changes arising within the business could alter the required level of investment in working capital. Examples of such internal changes include the use of different production methods (resulting, perhaps, in a need to hold less inventory) and changes in the level of risk that managers are prepared to take.

The Scale of Working Capital

We might imagine that, compared with the scale of investment in capital (non-current) assets by the typical business, the amounts involved with working capital are pretty trivial. This would be a false assessment of reality—the scale of the working capital elements for most large businesses is vast.

REAL WORLD 12.1 gives some impression of the working capital investments for five Canadian businesses. For each business, the major balance sheet items are expressed as a percentage of the total investment by the providers of long-term financing.

These types of variation in the amounts and types of working capital elements are typical of other businesses. In the sections that follow, we consider each element of working capital separately and how it might be properly managed.

REAL WORLD 12.1

Working Capital for Five Canadian Companies

	Tim Hortons %	Shoppers Drug Mart %	Gildan %	CN Rail %	Research In Motion %
Non-current assets	94%	88%	60%	101%	54%
Current assets (C.A.)					
Cash	10%	1%	2%	2%	26%
Accounts receivable	11%	10%	25%	3%	38%
Inventory	4%	38%	35%	1%	11%
Other	3%	3%	1%	1%	6%
Total current assets	28%	52%	63%	7%	81%
Current liabilities (C.L.)					
Cash overdraft (bank indebtedness)	0%	5%	0%	0%	0%
Accounts payable	10%	34%	17%	8%	7%
Taxes payable	2%	0%	5%	0%	6%
Other	10%	1%	0%	0%	22%
Total current liabilities	22%	40%	23%	8%	35%
Working capital (C.A. − C.L.)	6%	12%	40%	−1%	46%
Total investment (non-current assets + working capital)	100%	100%	100%	100%	100%

The non-current assets, current assets, and current liabilities are expressed as a percentage of the total net investment (equity plus non-current liabilities, which is the same as non-current assets plus working capital). Notice that CN Rail has a negative working capital. Companies may operate for a short while with negative working capital, but sooner or later they must get their finances in order.

Total current assets range from 7% to 81% of total investment. Nearly two-thirds (63%) of Research In Motion's (RIM) total investment is represented by cash and accounts receivable. Assuming the latter will be collected, the company is indeed cash rich. Notice that inventory is insignificant at Tim Hortons (who wants stale donuts or coffee?) and CN Rail, a shipping company. At RIM, inventory is only 11%. This is good for assets that may quickly become technologically out of date.

Source: Compiled from the 2008 annual report of each company, except Research In Motion, for which the 2009 annual report was used.

L.O. 3   POLICIES FOR CONTROLLING THE WORKING CAPITAL CYCLE

In the following sections, we shall consider policies for managing and controlling:

1. Inventories
2. Accounts receivable
3. Cash
4. Accounts payable.

Managing Inventories

A business may hold inventory for various reasons, the most common of which is to meet the immediate day-to-day requirements of customers and production. However, a business may hold more than is necessary for this purpose if it is believed that future supplies may be interrupted or scarce. Similarly, if the business believes that the cost of inventory will rise in the future, it may decide to stockpile.

For some types of businesses, the inventory held may represent a substantial proportion of the total assets held. For example, a car dealership that rents its premises may have nearly all of its total assets in the form of inventory. In the case of manufacturing businesses, inventory levels tend to be higher than in many other types of businesses because it is necessary to hold three kinds of inventory: raw materials, work in process, and finished goods. Each form of inventory represents a particular stage in the production cycle. For some types of businesses, the level of inventory held may vary substantially over the year owing to the seasonal nature of the industry. An example of such a business is a greeting card manufacturer. For other businesses, inventory levels may remain fairly stable throughout the year.

Where a business holds inventory simply to meet the day-to-day requirements of its customers and for production, it will normally seek to minimize the amount of inventory held. There are significant costs associated with holding inventory, including storage and handling costs, financing costs, the risks of pilferage and obsolescence, and the opportunities forgone by tying up funds in this form of asset. However, a business must also recognize that if the level of inventory held is too low, there will also be associated costs, as illustrated in Activity 12.2.

ACTIVITY 12.2

What costs might a business incur as a result of holding too low a level of inventory?

Solution

Too low an inventory level might lead to the following costs:

- Loss of sales, from being unable to provide the goods required immediately
- Loss of satisfaction from customers, for being unable to satisfy customer demand
- High transportation costs incurred to ensure that inventory is replenished quickly
- Lost production due to shortage of raw materials
- Inefficient production scheduling due to shortages of raw materials
- Purchasing inventory at a higher price than might otherwise have been possible in order to replenish the inventory quickly.

One problem faced by management is that many of the costs of holding inventory just mentioned will not be separately identified by conventional accounting systems. Cost classification methods used in practice are likely to include some of these costs within a broad cost category, or as part of an overall total for the business. For example, storage costs may be included under the broad heading of security and maintenance, and financing costs may be included as part of the total financing charges incurred by the business. Furthermore, other costs—such as the opportunity cost of not holding sufficient inventory resulting in lost sales or the opportunity cost of tying up funds—will not be directly recorded by the accounting system. This lack of information concerning the costs of holding particular levels of inventory makes the management of inventory more difficult.

Before we go on to deal with the various approaches that can be taken in managing inventory, REAL WORLD 12.2 provides an example of two recent inventory writedowns in Canada.

REAL WORLD 12.2 Two Canadian Inventory Writedowns

Potash Corp., based in Saskatchewan, wrote down nitrogen and phosphate inventory values to the tune of $88.9 million at the end of 2008. This represented an 11% writedown of its inventory and it chopped $0.22 (2%) off its earnings per share.

Russel Metals, based in Mississauga, Ontario, is one of the largest metals distribution and processing companies in North America. In June 2009, the company wrote down its inventory by $55 million (almost 8%).

Source: Potash Corp. 2008 Annual Report and Russel Metals June 2009 Quarterly Report.

To ensure that the inventory is properly managed, a number of procedures and techniques may be used.

Forecasting Future Demand

These forecasts should deal with each product that the business makes and/or sells, and should be accurate, as they will determine future ordering and production levels. The forecasts may be derived in various ways. We saw in Chapter 3 that they may be developed using statistical techniques such as time series analysis, or they may be based on the judgment of the sales and marketing staff.

REAL WORLD 12.3 discusses inventory management issues in the Canadian automotive sector.

REAL WORLD 12.3 JIT in Canada

An Industry Canada paper on the automotive sector suggests that Canadian firms must become better at managing their inventory. Supply chain management uses a just-in-time (JIT) philosophy for inventory. Key performance measures of inventory management are on-time delivery and inventory turns. In the automotive industry, wholesalers and retailers lag behind the manufacturers in inventory turnover. Also, the motor vehicle manufacturers, such as General Motors, are far ahead of the automotive parts manufacturers in reducing total logistics distribution costs.

Source: Industry Canada, http://strategis.ic.gc.ca/epic/site/dsib-logi.nsf/en/h_pj00312e.html, accessed September 29, 2009.

Financial Ratios

One ratio that can be used to help monitor inventory levels is the average inventory turnover period, which we examined in Chapter 4. As we should recall, this ratio is calculated by Equation 4.5:

$$\text{Average inventory turnover period} = \frac{\text{Average inventory held}}{\text{Cost of goods sold}} \times 365 \qquad 4.5$$

This will provide a picture of the average period for which inventory is held, and can be useful as a basis for comparison. It is possible to calculate the average inventory turnover period for individual product lines as well as for inventory as a whole.

Recording and Reordering Systems

The management of inventory in a business of any size requires a sound method of recording inventory movements. There must be proper procedures for recording inventory purchases and sales. Periodic inventory checks may be required to ensure that the amount of physical inventory held is consistent with what is indicated by the inventory records.

There should also be clear procedures for reordering inventory. Authorization for both the purchase and the issue of inventory should be confined to a few senior staff. This should avoid problems of duplication and lack of coordination. To determine the point at which inventory should be reordered, information will be required concerning the **lead time** (i.e., the time between the placing of an order and the receipt of the goods) and the likely level of demand. Activity 12.3 calculates the inventory level at which a business should reorder.

ACTIVITY 12.3

An electrical retailer keeps a particular type of light switch in stock. The annual demand for the light switch is 10,400 units, and the lead time for orders is four weeks. Demand is steady throughout the year. At what level of inventory should the business reorder?

Solution

The average weekly demand for the inventory item is 10,400/52 = 200 units. During the time between ordering and receiving the goods, the inventory sold will be 4 × 200 units = 800 units. So the business should reorder no later than when the inventory level reaches 800 units, in order to avoid a stockout.

In most businesses, there will be some uncertainty surrounding the above factors and so a buffer or safety inventory level may be maintained in case problems occur. The amount of buffer inventory to be held is really a matter of judgment, which will depend on:

- The degree of uncertainty concerning the demand, the lead time, and the consistency of the demand
- The likely costs of running out of inventory
- The cost of holding the buffer inventory.

The effect of holding buffer inventory will be to raise the reorder point for goods, as illustrated in Activity 12.4.

ACTIVITY 12.4

Assume the same facts as in Activity 12.3. However, we are also told that the business maintains a buffer inventory of 300 units. At what level of inventory should the business reorder?

Solution

Reorder point = Expected level of demand during the lead time + Level of buffer inventory
= 800 + 300
= 1,100 units

Carrying buffer inventory will increase the cost of holding inventory; however, this must be weighed against the cost of stockouts in terms of lost sales and production problems.

REAL WORLD 12.4 provides an example of how small businesses can use technology in inventory reordering to help them compete against their larger rivals.

REAL WORLD 12.4

Taking on the Big Boys

Technology can help small companies to compete with large companies through better inventory management. Retail management technology, including automated point of sale and data analysis technology, can help small bookstores stay on top of their inventory. One company advertises that its systems can help bookstores "control inventory, track sales profitability, capture sales data and accelerate customer checkout and manage your bookstore more efficiently."[1]

Many affordable inventory software and tracking solutions incorporating barcode technology are aimed at small and medium-sized companies. These systems can provide up-to-the-minute inventory control along with information on where inventory is located, onsite or offsite.

Source: [1]www.fheg.follett.com/wholesale/mgntSoftware.cfm, accessed April 25, 2007, with permission of Follett Higher Education Group; www.waspbarcode.com/inventory_control/, accessed April 25, 2007.

Levels of Control

Senior managers must make a commitment to the management of inventory. However, the costs of controlling inventory must be weighed against the potential benefits. It may be possible to have different levels of control according to the nature of the inventory held. The **ABC system of inventory control** is based on the idea of selective levels of control.

A business may find that it is possible to divide its inventory into three broad categories: A, B, and C. Each category will be based on the value of inventory held, as is illustrated in Example 12.1.

Example 12.1

Alascan Products Ltd. makes door handles and door fittings in brass, steel, and plastic. The business finds that brass fittings account for 10% of the physical volume of the finished inventory that it holds, but represent 65% of its total value. This is treated as Category A inventory. There are sophisticated recording procedures, tight control is exerted over inventory movements, and there is a high level of security at the inventory's location. This is economic because the inventory represents a relatively small proportion of the total volume.

The business finds that steel fittings account for 30% of the total volume of finished inventory and represent 25% of its total value. This is treated as Category B inventory, with a lower level of recording and management control being applied.

The remaining 60% of the volume of inventory is plastic fittings, which represent the least valuable items and account for only 10% of the total value of finished inventory held. This is treated as Category C inventory, so the level of recording and management control would be lower still. It would be uneconomic to apply to this inventory the level of control that is applied to Category A or even Category B inventory.

Categorizing inventory in this way seeks to direct management effort to the most important areas, and tries to ensure that the costs of controlling inventory are proportional to the inventory's importance.

Inventory Management Models

It is possible to use decision models to help manage inventory. The **economic order quantity (EOQ)** model is concerned with answering a question: how much inventory should be ordered? In its simplest form, the EOQ model assumes that demand is constant, so that inventory will be depleted evenly over time and replenished just at the point that the inventory runs out.

The EOQ model recognizes that the key costs associated with inventory management are the costs of holding it and ordering it. The model can be used to calculate the optimal size of a purchase order by taking account of both of these costs. The cost of holding inventory can be substantial, and so management may try to minimize the average amount of inventory held. However, by reducing the level of inventory held, and therefore the holding costs, there will be a need to increase the number of orders during the period, and so ordering costs will rise.

Figure 12.2 shows how, as the level of inventory and the size of inventory orders increase, the annual cost of placing orders will decrease because fewer orders will be placed. However, the cost of holding inventory will increase, as there will be higher average inventory levels. The total costs curve, which is based on the sum of holding costs and ordering costs, will fall until point E is reached, which represents the minimum total cost.

Thereafter, total costs begin to rise. The EOQ model seeks to identify point E, at which total costs are minimized. This will represent half of the optimal amount that should be ordered on each occasion. Assuming, as we are doing, that inventory is used evenly over time and that inventory falls to zero before being replaced, the average inventory level equals half of the order size.

FIGURE 12.2   Inventory Holding and Inventory Order Costs

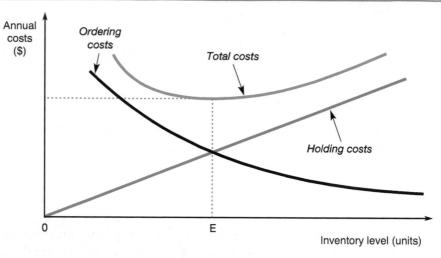

Source: After McLaney and Atrill (2004), Fig. 16.3.

The EOQ model (Equation 12.2), which can be used to derive the most economic order quantity, is:

$$EOQ = \sqrt{\frac{2DC}{H}}$$

12.2

where: D = the annual demand for the item (expressed in units)
C = the cost of placing an order
H = the cost of holding one unit for one year

Activity 12.5 demonstrates the EOQ model.

ACTIVITY 12.5

HLA Ltd. sells 2,000 bags of cement each year. It has been estimated that the cost of holding one bag of cement for a year is $4. The cost of placing an order for inventory is estimated at $250. Calculate the EOQ for bags of cement.

Solution

$$EOQ = \sqrt{\frac{2 \times 2,000 \times 250}{4}} = 500 \text{ units}$$

This will mean that the business will have to order bags of cement four times each year so that sales demand of 2,000 units can be met.

Note that the cost of the inventory—that is, the price paid to the supplier—does not directly affect the EOQ model. The EOQ model is only concerned with the administrative costs of placing each order and the costs of looking after the inventory. Where the business operates an ABC system of inventory control, however, more expensive inventory items will have greater holding costs. So the cost of the inventory may have an indirect effect on the economic order quantity that the model recommends.

The basic EOQ model has a number of limiting assumptions. In particular, it assumes that:

- Demand for the product can be predicted with accuracy
- Demand is constant over the period and does not fluctuate through seasonality or other reasons
- No buffer inventory is required
- There are no discounts for bulk purchasing.

However, the model can be developed further to accommodate the problems of each of these limiting assumptions. Many businesses use this model (or a development of it) to help in the management of inventory.

SELF-ASSESSMENT QUESTION   12.1

You have gathered the following information about laptop computers for your company:

Quantity sold each year	75,000
Annual unit holding cost	$250.00
Cost of placing an order	$750.00

Required:

(a) Calculate the EOQ for laptop computers for your company.
(b) Calculate the number of orders per year. Round up to the nearest unit.

Materials Requirement Planning Systems

A **materials requirement planning (MRP) system** takes planned sales demand as its starting point. It then uses a software program to help schedule the timing of deliveries of parts and materials to coincide with production requirements. It is a coordinated approach that links materials and parts deliveries to the scheduled time of their input to the production process. By ordering only those items that are necessary to ensure the flow of production, inventory levels are likely to be reduced. MRP is really a top-down approach to inventory management, which recognizes that inventory ordering decisions cannot be viewed as being independent from production decisions. In recent years, this approach has been extended to provide a fully integrated approach to production planning. The approach also takes account of other manufacturing resources such as labour and machine capacity.

Just-in-Time Inventory Management

In recent years, many businesses have tried to eliminate the need to hold inventory by adopting **just-in-time (JIT) inventory management**, which was introduced in Real World 12.3. This approach was invented in the U.S. defence industry during the Second World War. It was first used on a wide scale by Japanese manufacturing businesses and has spread from there to almost all facets of manufacturing and retail. The essence of JIT is, as the name suggests, to have supplies delivered to a business just in time for them to be used in the production process or in a sale. Under this approach, the inventory holding costs rest with suppliers rather than with the business itself. On the other hand, a failure by a particular supplier to deliver on time could cause enormous problems and costs to the business. Thus JIT can reduce costs, but it tends to increase risk.

For JIT to be successful, it is important that the business inform suppliers of its inventory requirements in advance. Thus a close relationship is required between the business and its suppliers.

Although a business that applies JIT will not have to hold inventory, other costs may be associated with this approach. As the suppliers will be required to hold inventory for the business, they may try to recover this additional cost through increased prices. The close relationship necessary between the business and its suppliers may also prevent the business from taking advantage of cheaper sources of supply if they become available.

REAL WORLD 12.5 shows that companies cut inventory levels significantly during the most recent recession.

REAL WORLD 12.5

Managing Inventory in the 2008–2009 Recession

Managers were quick to cut or lay off workers, cut production, and decrease inventories during the most recent recession. As shown below, inventory size as measured by the number of days of sales in inventory declined during the recession. Companies were carrying about 14% less inventory by mid-year 2009 compared to the same period in 2008. This helped firms conserve cash.

Number of Days of Sales in Inventory

June 2009	March 2009	June 2008
20.8 days	22.0 days	24.2 days

Source: CFO website at: www.cfo.com/article.cfm/14362098, accessed September 30, 2009.

REAL WORLD 12.6 shows a well-known company focusing on inventory management to generate higher profits.

REAL WORLD 12.6

Sony Canada Implements JIT Inventory System

Sony is replacing inventory with knowledge. Instead of carrying sufficient inventory just in case it might be sold, a more efficient just-in-time inventory system was adopted in 2006. This system helps Sony use information and statistics to more accurately forecast which products are going to sell well at which retail locations. This means the company can carry a smaller inventory and generate a higher inventory turnover, resulting in more profits.

Source: Deloitte website at: www.deloitte.com/view/en_CA/ca/industries/manufacturing/case-study/c7c83b0be12fb110VgnVCM 100000 ba42f00aRCRD.htm, accessed September 30, 2009.

Managing Receivables

Selling goods or services on credit will result in costs being incurred by a business. These include credit administration costs, bad debts, and opportunities forgone in using the funds for more profitable purposes. However, these costs must be weighed against the benefits of increased sales resulting from the opportunity for customers to delay payment.

Selling on credit is widespread, and appears to be the norm. When a business offers to sell its goods or services on credit, it must have clear policies concerning:

- Which customers should receive credit
- How much credit should be offered
- What length of credit it is prepared to offer
- Whether discounts will be offered for prompt payment
- What collection policies should be adopted
- How the risk of non-payment can be reduced.

Which Customers Should Receive Credit?

A business offering credit runs the risk of not receiving payment for goods or services supplied. Thus, care must be taken over the type of customer to whom credit is offered. When considering a proposal from a customer for the supply of goods or services on credit, the business must take a number of factors into account. The following **five Cs of credit** provide a useful checklist that all businesses should adopt, although, in practice, small and medium-sized firms may not have the resources to do this except for their largest, most significant customers.

- *Capital.*   The customer must appear to be financially sound before any credit is extended. Where the customer is a business, its financial statements should be examined. Particular regard should be given to the customer's likely future profitability and liquidity. In addition, any major financial commitments (for example, capital expenditures, contracts with suppliers) must be taken into account.
- *Capacity.*   The customer must appear to have the capacity to pay amounts owing. Where possible, the payment record of the customer should be examined. If the customer is a business, the type of business operated and the physical resources of the business will be relevant. The value of goods that the customer wishes to buy on credit must be related to the customer's total financial resources.
- *Collateral.*   On occasion, it may be necessary to ask for some kind of security for goods supplied on credit.
- *Conditions.*   The state of the industry in which the customer operates, and the general economic conditions of the particular region or country, may have an important influence on the ability of a customer to pay the amounts outstanding on the due date.
- *Character.*   It is important for a business to make some assessment of the customer's character. The willingness to pay will depend on the honesty and integrity of the individual with whom the business is dealing.

It is clear that a business will need to gather information concerning the ability and willingness of the customer to pay the amounts owing at the due dates. Many companies have new customers complete a credit application form that managers review before credit is approved. Activity 12.6 examines the information used to make decisions about customer credit.

ACTIVITY 12.6

Assume that you are the credit manager of a business and that a corporation approaches you about buying goods on credit. What sources of information might you use to assess the financial health of the potential customer?

Solution

There are various possibilities. You may have thought of some of the following:

■ *Supplier references.* Some businesses ask potential customers for references from other suppliers who have made sales on credit to them. This may be extremely useful, provided that the references are truly representative of the opinions of a customer's suppliers. A potential customer may well be selective when giving details about other suppliers, to cultivate a more favourable impression than is deserved.

■ *Bank references.* It is possible to ask the potential customer for a bank reference. Although banks are usually prepared to supply references, the contents of such references are not always very informative. If customers are in financial difficulties, the bank may be unwilling to add to their problems by supplying poor references. It is worth remembering that the bank's loyalty is likely to be to the customer rather than the enquirer. In addition, the bank will usually charge a fee for providing a reference.

■ *Published financial statements.* A listed company is obliged by law to file quarterly reports and annual financial statements. These financial statements are available for public inspection and provide a useful source of information. The annual reports of many companies are available on their websites or on computer-based information systems (for example, www.sedar.com).

■ *The customer.* Interviews with the management of the customer business and visits to its premises may be carried out to gain some impression of how the customer conducts its business. Where a significant amount of credit is required, the business may ask the customer for access to internal budgets and other unpublished financial information to help assess the level of risk involved.

■ *Credit agencies.* Specialist agencies exist to provide information that can be used to assess the creditworthiness of a potential customer. The information may be gleaned from various sources, including the financial statements of the customer and news items relating to the customer from both published and unpublished sources. The credit agencies may also provide a credit rating for the business.

■ *Court judgments.* Any money judgments against the business or an individual in a court will be maintained in a court registry. This registry is available for inspection by any member of the public.

■ *Other suppliers.* Similar businesses will often be prepared to exchange information concerning slow payers or defaulting customers through an industry credit circle. This can be a reliable and relatively cheap means of obtaining information.

How Much Credit Should Be Offered?

Once a customer is considered creditworthy, credit limits for the customer should be established and procedures should be laid down to ensure that these limits are adhered to. Unfortunately, there are no theories or models to help a business decide on the appropriate credit limit to adopt; it is really a matter of judgment. Some businesses adopt simple rule-of-thumb methods based on either the amount of sales made to the customer (say, twice the monthly sales figure for that customer) or a maximum the business is prepared to be owed (say, a maximum of 20% of the working capital).

Length of Credit Period

A business must determine what credit terms it is prepared to offer its customers. The length of credit offered to customers can vary significantly between businesses, and may be influenced by such factors as:

- The typical credit terms operating within the industry
- The degree of competition within the industry
- The bargaining power of particular customers
- The risk of non-payment
- The capacity of the business to offer credit
- The marketing strategy of the business.

The marketing strategy of a business may have an important influence on the length of credit allowed. For example, if a business wishes to increase its market share, it may decide to be more generous in its credit policy in an attempt to stimulate sales. Potential customers may be attracted by the offer of a longer credit period. However, any such change in policy must consider the likely costs and benefits. To illustrate this point, look at Example 12.2.

Example 12.2

Torrance Ltd. produces a new type of golf putter. The business sells the putter to wholesalers and retailers and has annual sales of $600,000. The following data relate to each putter produced:

	($)	($)
Selling price		40
Variable costs	20	
Fixed cost apportionment	6	26
Net profit		14

The business's cost of capital is estimated at 10% a year.

Torrance Ltd. wishes to expand the sales volume of the new putter. It believes that offering a longer credit period can achieve this. The business's average collection period is currently 30 days. It is considering three options in an attempt to increase sales revenue. These are as follows:

	Option		
	1	2	3
Increase in average collection period (days)	10	20	30
Increase in sales revenue ($)	30,000	45,000	50,000

For the business to decide on the best option to adopt, it must weigh the benefits of the options against their respective costs. The benefits will be represented by the increase in profit from the sale of additional putters. From the cost data supplied, we can see that the contribution (i.e., selling price of $40 less variable costs of $20) is $20 a putter, that is, 50% of the selling price. So, whatever increase there may be in sales revenue, the additional contributions will be half of that figure. The fixed costs can be ignored in our calculations, as they will remain the same whichever option is chosen.

The increase in contribution under each option will therefore be:

	Option		
	1	2	3
50% of the increase in sales revenue ($)	15,000	22,500	25,000

The increase in receivables under each option will be as follows:

	Option		
	1	2	3
Projected level of accounts receivable	($)	($)	($)
40 × $630,000/365 (Note 1)	69,041		
50 × $645,000/365		88,356	
60 × $650,000/365			106,849
Less: Current level of accounts receivable			
30 × $600,000/365	49,315	49,315	49,315
Increase in accounts receivable	19,726	39,041	57,534

The increase in accounts receivable that results from each option will mean an additional financing cost to the business.

The net increase in the business's profit arising from the projected change is:

	Option		
	1	2	3
Increase in contribution (from above)	15,000	22,500	25,000
Less: Increase in financing cost (Note 2)	1,973	3,904	5,753
Net increase in profits	13,027	18,596	19,247

The calculations show that Option 3 will be the most profitable one.

Notes

1. If the annual sales revenue totals $630,000 and 40 days' credit are allowed (both of which will apply under Option 1), the average amount that will be owed to the business by its customers, at any point during the year, will be the daily sales revenue (i.e., $630,000/365) multiplied by the number of days that the customers take to pay (i.e., 40).
   Exactly the same logic applies to Options 2 and 3 and to the current level of debtors.
2. The increase in the financing cost for Option 1 will be the increase in accounts receivable ($19,726) × 10%. The equivalent figures for the other options are derived in a similar way.

Example 12.2 illustrates the way in which a business should assess changes in credit terms. However, if there is a risk that extending the duration of credit will cause the business to experience an increase in bad debts, this should also be taken into account in the calculations, as should any additional collection costs that will be incurred.

REAL WORLD 12.7 provides some insight into the typical periods of credit taken by Canadian businesses to collect receivables and pay payables.

REAL WORLD 12.7

Estimated Number of Days Taken to Collect the Receivables and Pay the Payables

Using Equations 4.6 and 4.7 from Chapter 4

$$\text{Average collection period for receivables} = \frac{\text{Accounts receivable}}{\text{Credit sales revenue}} \times 365 \qquad 4.6$$

$$\text{Average payment period for payables} = \frac{\text{Accounts payable}}{\text{Credit purchases}} \times 365 \qquad 4.7$$

and assuming all sales and purchases were on credit, we arrive at the following estimates of the average number of days taken for these companies to collect their receivables and pay their payables.

	Canadian Tire	Tim Hortons	Shoppers Drug Mart	Goldcorp	Research In Motion
Average collection period (days)	33	43	17	27	70
Average payment period (days)	63	48	43	49	26

Research in Motion (RIM) can afford to pay its payables before it collects its receivables because it generates strong cash flows. Consider also that RIM does significant business with governments, which are often slow to pay.

Source: 2008 annual reports of Canadian Tire, Tim Hortons, Shoppers Drug Mart, and Goldcorp, and Research In Motion 2009 Annual Report.

An Alternative Approach to Evaluating the Credit Decision   It is possible to view the credit decision as a capital investment decision. The granting of credit involves an outlay of resources in the form of cash (which has been temporarily forgone) in the expectation that future cash flows will be increased (through higher sales) as a result. A business will usually have choices concerning the level of investment to be made in credit sales and the period over which credit is granted. These choices will result in different returns and different levels of risk. There is no reason in principle why the NPV investment appraisal method, which we considered in Chapter 6, should not be used to evaluate these choices. We have seen that the NPV method takes into account both the time value of money and the level of risk involved.

Cash Discounts

A business may decide to offer a **cash discount** in an attempt to encourage prompt payment from its credit customers. The size of any discount will be an important influence on whether a customer decides to pay promptly.

From the business's viewpoint, the cost of offering discounts must be weighed against the likely benefits: reductions in the cost of financing receivables and in the amount of bad debts.

In practice, there is always the danger that a customer may be slow to pay and yet may still take the discount offered. Where the customer is important to the business, it may be difficult to insist on full payment. An alternative to allowing the customer to take discounts by reducing payment is agreeing in advance to provide discounts for prompt payment through quarterly credit notes. As credit notes will only be given for those amounts paid on time, the customer will often make an effort to qualify for the discount.

SELF-ASSESSMENT QUESTION   12.2

Williams Wholesalers Ltd. currently requires payment from its customers by the end of the month after the month of delivery. On average, customers take 70 days to pay. Sales revenue amounts to $4 million a year and bad debts to $20,000 a year.

The company plans to offer customers a cash discount of 2% for payment within 30 days. Williams estimates that 50% of customers will accept this offer but that the remaining customers, who tend to be slow payers, will not pay until 80 days after the sale. At present, Williams has an overdraft facility at an interest rate of 13% a year. If the plan goes ahead, bad debts will be reduced to $10,000 a year and there will be savings in credit administration expenses of $6,000 a year.

Required:

Should Williams Wholesalers offer the new credit terms to customers? You should support your answer with any calculations and explanations that you consider necessary.

Debt Factoring and Invoice Discounting   We saw in Chapter 8 that accounts receivable can, in effect, be turned into cash by either factoring them or having sales invoices discounted. These both seem to be fairly popular approaches to managing receivables.

Collection Policies

A business offering credit must ensure that amounts owing are collected as quickly as possible. Various steps can be taken to achieve this, as outlined below.

Develop Customer Relationships   For major customers, it is often useful to cultivate a relationship with the key staff responsible for paying sales invoices. By so doing, a business may increase its chances of prompt payment. For less important customers, the business should at least identify key staff who can be contacted in the event of a payment problem.

Publicize Credit Terms   The credit terms of the business should be made clear in all relevant correspondence, such as order acknowledgments, invoices, and statements. In early negotiations with the prospective customer, credit terms should be discussed openly and an agreement should be reached.

Issue Invoices Promptly   An efficient collection policy requires an efficient accounting system. Invoices (bills) must be sent out promptly to customers, as must regular monthly statements. Reminders must also be dispatched promptly to customers who are late in paying. If a customer fails to respond to a reminder, the accounting system should alert managers so that a stop can be placed on further deliveries.

Monitor Outstanding Debts   Management can monitor the effectiveness of collection policies in a number of ways. One method is to calculate the **average collection period for receivables** ratio, which we dealt with in Chapter 4. This ratio is calculated as in Equation 4.6.

$$\text{Average collection period for receivables} = \frac{\text{Accounts receivable}}{\text{Credit sales revenue}} \times 365 \quad \text{\small 4.6}$$

Although this ratio can be useful, it is important to remember that it produces an *average* figure for the number of days for which debts are outstanding. This average may be distorted by a few large customers who are very slow or very fast payers.

Produce an Aging Schedule of Receivables A more detailed and informative approach to monitoring debtors may be to produce an **aging schedule of receivables**. Receivables are divided into categories according to the length of time the debt has been outstanding. An aging schedule can be produced, on a regular basis, to help managers see the pattern of outstanding debts. An example of an aging schedule is set out in Example 12.3.

Example 12.3

Aging Schedule of Receivables at December 31

Customer	Days Outstanding				Total
	1–30 ($)	31–60 ($)	61–90 ($)	90+ ($)	($)
A Ltd	20,000	10,000	–	–	30,000
B Ltd	–	24,000	–	–	24,000
C Ltd	12,000	13,000	14,000	18,000	57,000
Total	32,000	47,000	14,000	18,000	111,000

This shows a business's accounts receivable figure at December 31, which totals $111,000. Each customer's balance is analyzed according to how long the receivable has been outstanding.

Thus we can see from the schedule that A Ltd. has $20,000 outstanding for 30 days or fewer (i.e., arising from sales during December), and $10,000 outstanding for between 31 and 60 days (arising from November sales). This information can be very useful for credit control purposes.

Many accounting software packages now include this aging schedule as one of the routine reports available to managers. Such packages often have the ability to put customers on hold when they reach their credit limits. Putting a customer on hold means that no further credit sales will be made to that customer until receivables arising from past sales have been settled.

Identify the Pattern of Cash Receipts A slightly different approach to exercising control over receivables is to identify the pattern of cash receipts from credit sales on a monthly basis. This involves monitoring the percentage of accounts receivable that are paid (and the percentage of debts that remain unpaid) in the month of sale and the percentage that are paid in subsequent months. To do this, credit sales for each month must be examined separately. To illustrate how a pattern of credit sale cash receipts is produced, consider a business that made credit sales of $250,000 in June and received 30% of the amount owing in the same month, 40% in July, 20% in August, and 10% in September. The pattern of credit sale receipts and amounts owing is shown in Example 12.4.

Example 12.4

	Cash Receipts from June Credit Sales ($)	Pattern of Credit Sale Cash Receipts		
		Received (%)	Amount Outstanding from June Sales at Month-End ($)	Outstanding (%)
June	75,000	30	175,000	70
July	100,000	40	75,000	30
August	50,000	20	25,000	10
September	25,000	10	–	–
Total	$250,000	100	0	0

Example 12.4 shows how sales made in June were received over time. This information can be used as a basis for control. The actual pattern of cash receipts can be compared with the expected (budgeted) pattern of cash receipts in order to see if there was any significant deviation (see Figure 12.3). If this comparison shows that customers are paying more slowly than expected, management may decide to take corrective action.

FIGURE 12.3   Comparison of Actual and Budgeted Cash Receipts over Time for Example 12.4

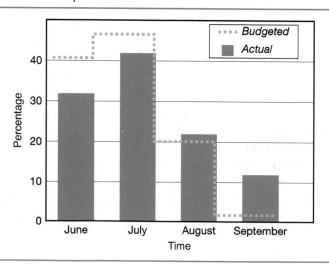

Answer Questions Quickly   It is important for relevant staff to deal with customer questions quickly and efficiently. Payment is unlikely to be made by customers until their questions have been dealt with.

Deal with Slow Payers   It is almost inevitable that a business making significant sales on credit will sometimes be faced with customers who do not pay. When this occurs, there should be agreed procedures for dealing with the situation. However, the cost of any action to be taken against delinquent customers must be weighed against the likely returns. For example, there is little point in taking legal action against a customer and incurring large legal expenses if there is evidence that the customer does not have the necessary resources to pay. Where possible, an estimate of the cost of bad debts should be taken into account when setting prices for products or services.

As a footnote to our consideration of managing debtors, REAL WORLD 12.8 outlines some of the excuses that long-suffering credit managers must listen to when chasing payment for outstanding debt.

REAL WORLD 12.8

Can't/Won't Pay Excuses

Excuses given by accounts payable departments or higher management for delaying payment are many and varied:

- "Your product doesn't work."
- "We can't pay until our paperwork is correct."
- "You didn't send enough copies of the invoice."
- "You just missed our last computer run; we'll pay again in two weeks."
- "We lost your invoice."
- "Our computer is down."
- "Cash is tight this time of the year."

Source: www.smartbiz.com/article/articleprint/562/-1/5, accessed April 25, 2007.

Reducing the Risk of Non-Payment

Efficient collection policies are important in reducing the risk of non-payment. However, there are other ways in which a business can reduce this type of risk. Possibilities include:

- Requiring customers to pay part of the sales value in advance of the goods being sent
- Agreeing to offset amounts owed for the purchase of goods against amounts due for goods supplied to the same business
- Requiring a third-party guarantee from a financially sound business such as a bank or parent company
- Making it a condition of sale that the legal title of the goods is not passed to the customer until the goods are paid for
- Taking out insurance to cover the costs of any legal expenses incurred in recovering the debt (some customers may refuse to pay if they feel that the business does not have the resources to pursue the debt through the courts)
- Taking out insurance against risk of non-payment. Accounts receivable insurance can cover the whole of the credit sales of the business up to an agreed limit or can cover a number of specified customers.

The practical circumstances will determine which of the above methods is appropriate to use. For example, it would not be feasible to try to retain the legal title of raw materials or components that are intended to become part of a finished product. Remember also that, in a highly competitive environment, customers may be unwilling to accept stringent conditions. The risk of non-payment must always be weighed against the risk of lost sales.

Managing Cash

Why Hold Cash?

Most businesses hold a certain amount of cash. The amount of cash held tends to vary considerably between businesses. Activity 12.7 considers the reasons that businesses hold cash.

ACTIVITY 12.7

Why do you think a business may decide to hold at least some of its assets in the form of cash? (*Hint:* There are three general reasons.)

Solution

A business may decide to hold at least some of its assets in the form of cash:

1. *To meet day-to-day commitments.* Payments for wages, overhead expenses, and goods purchased must be made at the due dates. Cash has been described as the lifeblood of a business. Unless it circulates through the business and is available to make payments as bills come due, the survival of the business will be at risk. Profitability is not enough: a business must have sufficient cash to pay its debts when they fall due.
2. *To hedge against uncertain future cash flows.* For example, a major customer that owes a large sum to the business may be in financial difficulties. Given this situation, the business can retain its capacity to meet its obligations by holding a cash balance. Similarly, if there is some uncertainty concerning future outlays, a cash balance will be required.
3. *To put itself in a position to exploit profitable opportunities.* For example, by holding cash, a business may be able to acquire a competitor business that suddenly becomes available at an attractive price.

How Much Cash Should Be Held?

Although cash can be held for each of the reasons identified in Activity 12.7, this may not always be necessary. If a business is able to borrow quickly, the amount of cash it needs to hold can be reduced. Similarly, if the business holds assets that can easily be converted to cash (for example, marketable securities such as shares in stock exchange listed businesses or government bonds), the amount of cash held can be reduced.

The decision as to how much cash a particular business should hold is a difficult one—the major factors influencing this decision are outlined in Activity 12.8. Different businesses will have different views on the subject.

ACTIVITY 12.8

What do you think are the major factors that influence how much cash a business will hold?

Solution

Among the major factors that influence how much cash a business will hold are:

- *The nature of the business.* Some businesses such as utilities (for example, water, electricity, and gas suppliers) may have cash flows that are both predictable and reasonably certain. This will enable them to hold lower cash balances. A seasonal business may accumulate cash during the high sales season to enable it to meet commitments during the low sales season.
- *The opportunity cost of holding cash.* Where there are profitable opportunities, it might not be wise to hold a large cash balance.
- *The level of inflation.* Holding cash during a period of rising prices will lead to a loss of purchasing power. The higher the level of inflation, the greater will be this loss.
- *The availability of near-liquid assets.* If a business has marketable securities or inventory that may easily be liquidated, the amount of cash held may be reduced.

▶

- **The availability of borrowing.**   If a business can borrow easily (and quickly), there is less need to hold cash.
- **The cost of borrowing.**   When interest rates are high, the option of borrowing becomes less attractive.
- **Economic conditions.**   When the economy is in recession, businesses may prefer to hold cash so that they can be well placed to invest when the economy improves. In addition, during a recession, businesses may experience difficulties in collecting debts. They may therefore hold higher cash balances than usual in order to meet commitments.
- **Relationships with suppliers.**   Too little cash may hinder the ability of the business to pay suppliers promptly. This can lead to a loss of goodwill. It may also lead to discounts being forgone.

Controlling the Cash Balance

Several models have been developed to help control the cash balance of the business. One such model proposes the use of upper and lower control limits for cash balances and the use of a target cash balance. The model assumes that the business will invest in marketable investments that can easily be liquidated. These investments will be purchased or sold, as necessary, in order to keep the cash balance within the control limits.

The model proposes two upper and two lower control limits (see Figure 12.4). If the business exceeds an *outer* limit, the managers must decide whether or not the cash balance is likely to return to a point within the *inner* control limits over the next few days. If this seems likely, then no action is required. If it does not seem likely, management must change the cash position of the business by either lending or borrowing (or possibly by buying or selling marketable securities).

In Figure 12.4 we can see that the lower outer control limit has been breached for four days. If a four-day period is unacceptable, managers must sell marketable securities to replenish the cash balance.

FIGURE 12.4   Controlling the Cash Balance

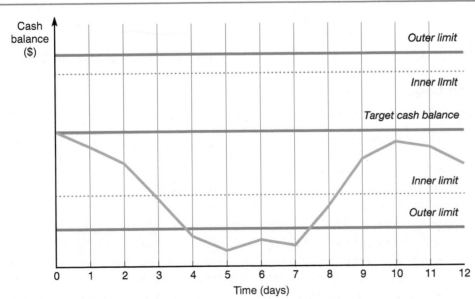

Source: After McLaney and Atrill (2004), Fig. 16.5.

The model relies heavily on management judgment to determine where the control limits are set and the period within which breaches of the control limits are acceptable. Experience may be useful in helping managers decide on these issues. There are other models, however, that do not rely on management judgment. Instead, these use quantitative techniques to determine an optimal cash policy. One model proposed is the cash equivalent of the inventory economic order quantity model, discussed earlier in the chapter.

Pro Forma Cash Flow Budgets and the Management of Cash

To manage cash effectively, it is useful for a business to prepare a pro forma cash flow budget. This is a very important tool for both planning and control purposes. Pro forma cash flow budgets were considered in Chapter 3, and so we shall not consider them again in detail here. However, it is worth repeating the point that these statements enable managers to see the expected impact of planned events on the cash balance. The pro forma cash flow budgets will identify periods when cash surpluses and cash deficits are expected.

In the event of a cash surplus, managers must decide on the best use of the surplus funds. When a cash deficit is expected, managers must make adequate provision by borrowing, liquidating assets, or rescheduling cash payments or receipts to deal with this. Pro forma cash flow budgets are useful in helping to control the cash held. The actual cash flows can be compared with the projected, or forecast, cash flows for the period. If there is a significant divergence between the forecast cash flows and the actual cash flows, explanations must be sought and corrective action taken where necessary.

To refresh your memory, an example of a cash flow budget is given in Example 12.5. Remember there is no set format for this budget. Managers can determine how the information should be presented. However, the format set out in the example appears to be in widespread use.

Example 12.5

Pro Forma Cash Flow Budget for the Six Months to November 30

	June ($)	July ($)	August ($)	September ($)	October ($)	November ($)
Cash inflows						
Credit sales	–	–	4,000	5,500	7,000	8,500
Cash sales	4,000	5,500	7,000	8,500	11,000	11,000
	4,000	5,500	11,000	14,000	18,000	19,500
Cash outflows						
Motor vehicles	6,000					
Equipment	10,000					7,200
Buildings	40,000					
Purchases	–	29,000	9,250	11,500	13,750	17,500
Wages/salaries	900	900	900	900	900	900
Commission	–	320	440	560	680	680
Overheads	500	500	500	500	650	650
	57,400	30,720	11,090	13,460	15,980	26,930
Net cash flow	(53,400)	(25,220)	(90)	540	2,020	(7,430)
Opening balance	60,000	6,600	(18,620)	(18,710)	(18,170)	(16,150)
Closing balance	6,600	(18,620)	(18,710)	(18,170)	(16,150)	(23,580)

Although cash budgets are prepared primarily for internal management purposes, prospective lenders sometimes require them when a loan to a business is being considered.

Operating Cash Cycle

When managing cash, it is important to be aware of the **operating cash cycle (OCC)** of the business. For a retailer, for example, this may be defined as the time period between the payment of cash necessary for the purchase of inventory and the ultimate receipt of cash from the sale of the goods. In the case of a business—for example, a wholesaler that purchases goods on credit for subsequent resale on credit—the OCC is as shown in Figure 12.5.

FIGURE 12.5   The Operating Cash Cycle

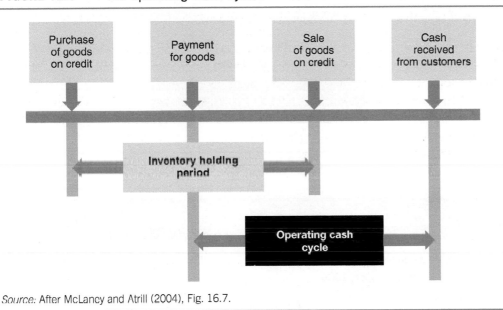

Source: After McLancy and Atrill (2004), Fig. 16.7.

Figure 12.5 shows that payment for goods acquired on credit occurs sometime after the goods have been purchased, and therefore no immediate cash outflow arises from the purchase. Similarly, cash receipts from customers will occur sometime after the sale is made, and so there will be no immediate cash inflow as a result of the sale. The operating cash cycle is the period between making the payment to the creditor for goods supplied and receiving the cash from the customer. Although Figure 12.5 depicts the position for a retailing or wholesaling business, the precise definition of the OCC can easily be adapted for both service and manufacturing businesses.

The operating cash cycle is important because it has a significant influence on the financing requirements of the business: the longer the cycle, the greater the financing requirements of the business and the greater the financial risks. For this reason, a business is likely to want to reduce the OCC to the minimum possible period.

For the type of business mentioned above, which buys and sells on credit, the OCC can be calculated from the financial statements by the use of certain ratios. It is calculated using equations from Chapter 4, as shown in Figure 12.6. Activity 12.9 demonstrates how to calculate the operating cash cycle for a business.

FIGURE 12.6   Calculating the Operating Cash Cycle

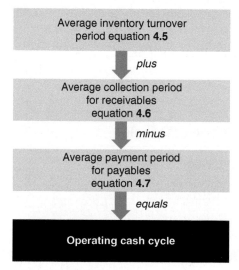

Source: After McLaney and Atrill (2004), Fig. 16.7.

ACTIVITY 12.9

The financial statements of Freezeqwik Ltd., a distributor of frozen foods, are shown below for the year ended December 31, 2009.

Freezeqwik Ltd.
Income Statement
for the year ended December 31, 2009

	($000)	($000)
Sales revenue		820
Less: Cost of goods sold		
Opening inventory	142	
Purchases	568	
Goods available for sale	710	
Less: Closing inventory	166	544
Gross profit		276
Administration expenses	(120)	
Selling and distribution expenses	(95)	
Financial expenses	(32)	(247)
Earnings before taxes		29
Income tax		(7)
Net income		22

Freezequik Ltd.
Balance Sheet
as at December 31, 2009
(in $ thousands)

Current assets		
Cash	24	
Accounts receivable	264	
Inventory	166	
Total current assets		454
Property, plant, and equipment		
Land	100	
Buildings, net	80	
Furniture and fixtures, net	82	
Motor vehicles, net	102	364
Total assets		818
Current liabilities		
Accounts payable	159	
Income taxes payable	7	
Total current liabilities		166
Shareholders' equity		
Preferred shares	200	
Common shares	300	
Retained earnings	152	
Total shareholders' equity		652
Total liabilities and shareholders' equity		818

All purchases and sales are on credit. There has been no change in the levels of accounts receivable and accounts payable over the period.

Required:

Calculate the length of the operating cash cycle for the business and suggest ways the business might reduce this period.

Solution

The OCC may be calculated as follows:

Equation		Number of Days
4.5	Average inventory turnover period	

$$= \frac{\text{Average inventory held}}{\text{Cost of goods sold}} \times 365$$

$$= \frac{\dfrac{(\text{Opening inventory} + \text{Closing inventory})}{2}}{\text{Cost of goods sold}} \times 365$$

$$= \frac{\dfrac{(\$142,000 + \$166,000)}{2}}{\$544,000} \times 365 \qquad = \qquad 103$$

4.6   Average collection period for receivables:

$$= \frac{\text{Accounts receivable}}{\text{Credit sales revenue}} \times 365$$

$$= \frac{\$264,000}{\$820,000} \times 365 \qquad\qquad = \qquad \underline{118}$$

$$221$$

▶

4.7   Less: Average payment period for payables:

$$= \frac{\text{Accounts payable}}{\text{Credit purchases}} \times 365$$

$$= \frac{\$159,000}{\$568,000} \times 365 \qquad\qquad\qquad = \qquad \underline{102}$$

Operating cash cycle $\underline{\underline{119}}$

The business can reduce the length of the operating cash cycle in a number of ways. The average inventory turnover period seems quite long. At present, average inventory held represents more than three months' sales revenue. Lowering the level of inventory held will reduce this. Similarly, the average collection period for receivables seems long, at nearly four months' sales revenue. Imposing tighter credit control, offering discounts, and charging interest on overdue accounts may reduce this. However, any policy decisions concerning inventory and receivables must take account of current business conditions.

Extending the period of credit taken to pay suppliers could also reduce the OCC. However, for reasons that will be explained later, this option must be given careful consideration.

Cash Transmission

A business will normally wish to benefit from receipts from customers at the earliest opportunity. The benefit is immediate where payment is made in cash. However, when payment is made by cheque, there is normally a 24-hour delay before the cheque can be cleared through the banking system. The business must therefore wait for this period before it can benefit from the amount paid. In the case of a business that receives large amounts in the form of cheques, the opportunity cost of this delay can be significant.

To avoid this delay, the business could require payments to be made in cash. This is impractical, however, mainly because of the risk of theft and the expense of conveying cash securely. Another option is to ask for payment to be made by standing order or by direct debit from the customer's bank account. This should ensure that the amount owing is always transferred from the bank account of the customer to the bank account of the business on the day that has been agreed.

It is also possible for funds to be transferred directly to the business's bank account. As a result of developments in computer technology, software programs such as PayPal and EZ PayManager allow customers to make electronic payments (e-payments), which result in the appropriate account being instantly debited and the seller's bank account being instantly credited with the required amount. This method of payment is widely used by large retail businesses, and may well extend to other types of business.

Bank Overdrafts and Lines of Credit

Bank overdrafts are bank current accounts that contain a negative amount of cash. They are a type of bank loan. We looked at these in Chapter 8 in the context of short-term bank lending. They can be a useful tool in managing the business's cash flow requirements. Bank overdrafts are a flexible form of borrowing and are inexpensive relative to other sources of financing. For this reason, some Canadian businesses use bank overdrafts to finance their operations. Although in theory bank overdrafts are a short-term source of financing, in practice they can extend over a long period of time, as some businesses continually renew their overdraft facility with the bank. Although renewal may not usually be a problem, there is always a danger that the bank will demand repayment at short notice, as it has the right to do. If the business is highly dependent on borrowing, and alternative sources of borrowing are difficult to find, this could raise severe problems.

When deciding whether or not to have a bank overdraft, the business should first consider the purpose of the borrowing. Overdrafts are most suitable for overcoming short-term funding problems (for example, increases in inventory holding requirements owing to seasonal fluctuations), and should be self-liquidating, as explained in Chapter 8. For longer-term funding problems or for borrowings that are not self-liquidating, other sources of financing may be more suitable.

It is important to make the appropriate overdraft arrangements with the bank, as borrowings in excess of the overdraft limit may incur high charges. To determine the amount of the overdraft allowed, the business should produce pro forma cash flow statements. There should also be regular reporting of cash flows to ensure that the overdraft limit is not exceeded.

Managing Accounts Payable

Most businesses buy their goods and service requirements on credit. In effect, suppliers are lending the business money, interest-free, on a short-term basis. Accounts payable are the other side of the coin from accounts receivable; one business's payable is another one's receivable. Payables are an important source of financing for most businesses. They have been described as an automatic source of financing, as they tend to increase in line with the increase in the level of activity of a business. Accounts payable are widely regarded as a free source of financing and, therefore, a good thing for a business to use.

There may, however, be real costs associated with having accounts payable. For example, customers who use credit may not be treated as well as those who pay immediately. For example, when goods are in short supply, credit customers may receive lower priority when the business allocates the inventory available. In addition, credit customers may be less favoured in terms of delivery dates or the provision of technical support services. Sometimes, the goods or services provided may be more costly if credit is required. Nevertheless, in most industries, credit is the norm. As a result, the above costs will not apply except, perhaps, to customers that abuse the credit facilities. A business purchasing supplies on credit may also have to incur additional administration and accounting costs in dealing with the scrutiny and payment of invoices, and maintaining and updating creditors' accounts.

REAL WORLD 12.9 examines the effect of a company's accounts payable timing on its working capital needs.

REAL WORLD 12.9 Conserving Cash

When a company pays its accounts payable it can have a dramatic effect on its working capital needs. The following model calculates a firm's cash cycle.

Cash cycle = Average inventory turnover period + Average collection period for receivables − Average payment period for payables

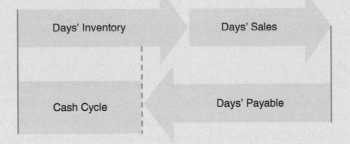

The lower the cash cycle metric, the better, as it means a company requires fewer funds to be tied up in working capital. Here are the results for the same companies as shown in Real World 12.7.

	Companies				
	Canadian Tire	Tim Hortons	Shoppers Drug Mart	Goldcorp	Research In Motion
1 Average inventory turnover (days)	38	20	70	46	33
2 Average collection period (days)	33	43	17	27	70
3 Average payment period (days)	63	48	43	49	26
4 Cash cycle (1 + 2 − 3)	8	15	44	24	77

It seems that Research In Motion could improve its cash cycle. In particular, accounts receivable collection strategies could be developed to enable companies to collect their money sooner.

Source: Adapted and compiled from www.investoralternatives.net/ia/blog/ccc.htm, accessed April 25, 2007, and the 2008 and 2009 annual reports of the companies. Image used with permission of Investopedio.com, www.investopedia.com.

When a supplier offers a discount for prompt payment, the business should give careful consideration to the possibility of paying within the discount period. Example 12.6 illustrates the cost of forgoing possible discounts.

Example 12.6

Haskell Ltd. takes 70 days to pay for goods from its supplier. To encourage prompt payment, the supplier has offered the business a 2% discount if payment for goods is made within 30 days.

Haskell Ltd. is not sure whether it is worth taking the discount offered.

If the discount is taken, payment could be made on the last day of the discount period (i.e., the thirtieth day). However, if the discount is not taken, payment will be made after 70 days. This means that, by not taking the discount, the business will receive an extra 40 days' credit (i.e., 70 days − 30 days). The cost of this extra credit to the business will be the 2% discount forgone. If we annualize the cost of this discount forgone, we have:

$$\frac{365}{40} \times 2\% = 18.3\%^*$$

* This is an approximate annual rate. For the more mathematically minded, the precise rate is: $\{[(1 + 2/98)^{9.125}] − 1\} \times 100\% = 20.2\%$, where the 2/98 is the ratio of the discount to the actual cash to be collected (income price less discount) and 9.125 is 365 days divided by the 40 extra days' credit.

We can see that the annual cost of forgoing the discount is very high, and it may be profitable for the business to pay the supplier within the discount period, even if it means that it will have to borrow to enable it to do so.

The points we have outlined are not meant to imply that using credit is a burden to a business. There are, of course, real benefits that can accrue. Provided that credit is not abused, it can represent a form of interest-free loan. It can be a much more convenient method of paying for goods and services than paying by cash, and during a period of inflation there will be an economic gain by paying later rather than sooner for goods and services purchased. For most businesses, these benefits will exceed the costs involved.

Controlling Payables

To help monitor the level of trade credit taken, management can calculate the **average payment period for payables**. As we saw in Equation 4.7 in Chapter 4, this ratio is:

$$\text{Average payment period for payables} = \frac{\text{Accounts payable}}{\text{Credit purchases}} \times 365 \qquad \text{4.7}$$

Once again, this provides an average figure, which could be misleading. A more informative approach would be to produce an aging schedule for accounts payable. This would look much the same as the aging schedule for accounts receivable described earlier.

Since, as was pointed out earlier in this section, one business's payable is another's receivable, the information contained in Real World 12.7 (page 465) provides some indication of typical lengths of time taken to pay accounts payable by businesses.

WORKING CAPITAL AND THE SMALL BUSINESS

L.O. 4

We saw earlier (in Real World 12.1) that the amounts invested by businesses in working capital are often high in proportion to the total assets employed. It is, therefore, important that these amounts be properly managed. Although this point applies to businesses of all sizes, it may be of particular importance to small businesses. It is often claimed that many small businesses suffer from a lack of capital and, where this is the case, tight control over working capital investment becomes critical. There is evidence, however, that small businesses are not very good at managing their working capital, and this has been cited as a major cause of their high failure rate compared with that of large businesses.

Credit Management

Small businesses often lack the resources to manage their receivables effectively. It is not unusual for a small business to operate without a separate credit department. This tends to mean that both the expertise and the information required to make sound judgments concerning terms of sale may not be available. A small business may also lack proper collection procedures, such as prompt invoicing and sending out regular statements. This will increase the risks of late payment and defaulting customers.

These risks probably tend to increase where there is an excessive concern for growth. In an attempt to increase sales, small businesses may be too willing to extend credit to customers that are poor credit risks. While this kind of problem can occur in businesses of all sizes, small businesses seem particularly susceptible.

Another problem faced by small businesses is their lack of market power. They will often find themselves in a weak position when negotiating credit terms with larger businesses. Moreover, when a large customer exceeds the terms of credit, the small supplier may feel inhibited from pressing the customer for payment in case future sales are lost.

It seems that small businesses have a much greater proportion of overdue receivables than large businesses. **REAL WORLD 12.10** refers to evidence of this.

Surprise—Big Companies Are Slow Payers

The reason for the delay suffered by small businesses probably relates to one of the factors mentioned earlier, namely the bargaining power of customers. The customers of small businesses may well be larger businesses, which can use a threat (perhaps implied) of cutting business ties in order to force the small businesses to accept a later accounts receivable collection date. Although small businesses may be able to charge interest on overdue accounts, they will often avoid doing so because they fear that large customers will view this as a provocative act. What is really needed to help small businesses is a change in the payment culture.

We saw in Chapter 8 that one way of dealing with the credit management problem is to factor the outstanding receivables. Under this kind of arrangement, the factor will take over the sales ledger of the business and will take responsibility for the prompt collection of debts. However, some businesses are too small to take advantage of this. The set-up costs of a factoring arrangement often make businesses with a small annual sales figure (up to, say, $250,000 a year) an uneconomic proposition for the factor.

Managing Inventory

A lack of financial management skills within a small business often creates problems in managing inventory in an efficient and effective way. The owners of small businesses are not always aware that there are costs involved in holding either too much inventory or too little. These costs, which were discussed earlier, may be very high in certain industries such as manufacturing and wholesaling, where inventory accounts for a significant proportion of the total assets held.

It was mentioned earlier in the chapter that the starting point for an effective inventory management system is good planning and budgeting systems. In particular, there should be reliable sales forecasts, or budgets, available for inventory ordering purposes. Inventory management can also benefit from good reporting systems and the application of quantitative techniques (for example, the economic order quantity model) to try to optimize inventory levels.

Managing Cash

Cash management raises issues similar to those of inventory management. There are costs involved in holding too much or too little cash. Thus, there is a need for careful planning and monitoring of cash flows over time. A survey by Chittenden et al. found, however, that only 63% of those replying prepared a cash forecast. It was also found that cash balances are generally proportionately higher for smaller businesses than for larger ones. More than half of those in the survey held surplus cash balances on a regular basis. Although this may reflect a more conservative approach to liquidity among the owners of smaller businesses, it may also suggest a failure to recognize the opportunity costs of cash balances.

Managing Accounts Payable

In practice, small businesses often try to cope with the late payment of credit customers by delaying payments to their credit suppliers. We saw earlier in the chapter, however, that this can be an expensive option. Where discounts are forgone, the annual cost of this financing option compares unfavourably with most other forms of short-term financing. Nevertheless, the vast majority of small and medium-sized businesses are unaware of the very high cost of delaying payment, according to the Chittenden survey.

Managing and Using Information Technology (IT) Resources

A 2006 survey found that U.S. small and medium-sized enterprise (SME) manufacturers make better use of IT resources than their Canadian counterparts. A significant difference is that U.S. SMEs made more of an effort to understand their information needs and this affected what information was collected, stored, processed, and disseminated to managers. Another big difference is the higher levels of formal educational attainment by the U.S. managers and users of IT data. The survey concluded that Canadian SMEs should better manage the implementation and use of IT for improved profitability.[1]

---

[1] Ali Reza Montazemi, "How They Manage IT: SMEs in Canada and the U.S.," *Communications of the ACM*, December 2006, Vol. 49, No. 12.

SUMMARY

The Main Elements of Working Capital

- Working capital is the difference between current assets and current liabilities
- That is, Working capital = Cash + Accounts receivable + Inventory − Accounts payable − Bank overdrafts
- An investment in working capital cannot be avoided in practice. Typically, large amounts are involved.

The Nature and Purpose of the Working Capital Cycle

- Working capital represents a net investment in short-term assets
- For a manufacturing business, the working capital cycle is as follows:
  - Cash is used to pay for raw materials

- Cash is spent on labour and other inputs that turn raw materials into work in process
- Work in process is turned into finished goods
- Finished goods are sold
- Receipt of cash completes the cycle.
- The scale of the working capital elements for most large businesses is vast.

Policies for Controlling the Working Capital Cycle

Managing Inventories

- There are costs of holding inventory, which include:
  - Lost interest
  - Storage cost
  - Insurance cost
  - Obsolescence.

- There are also costs of not holding sufficient inventory, which include:
  - Loss of sales and customer satisfaction
  - Production disruption
  - Loss of flexibility—cannot take advantage of opportunities
  - Reorder costs—low inventory implies more frequent ordering.
- Practical points on inventory management include:
  - Identify optimal order size—models can help with this
  - Set inventory reorder levels
  - Use forecasts
  - Keep reliable records
  - Use accounting ratios (for example, average inventory turnover period ratio)
  - Establish systems for security of inventory and authorization
  - Consider just-in-time (JIT) inventory management.

Managing Receivables

- When assessing which customers should receive credit, the five Cs of credit can be used:
  - Capital
  - Capacity
  - Collateral
  - Conditions
  - Character.
- The costs of allowing credit include:
  - Lost interest
  - Lost purchasing power
  - Costs of assessing customer creditworthiness
  - Administration cost
  - Bad debts
  - Cash discounts (for prompt payment).
- The costs of denying credit include:
  - Loss of customer satisfaction.
- Practical points on accounts receivable management:
  - Establish a policy
  - Assess and monitor customer creditworthiness
  - Establish effective administration of receivables
  - Establish a policy on bad debts
  - Consider cash discounts
  - Use financial ratios (for example, average collection period for receivables ratio)
  - Use aging summaries.

Managing Cash

- The costs of holding cash include:
  - Lost interest
  - Lost purchasing power.
- The costs of holding insufficient cash include:
  - Loss of supplier goodwill if unable to meet commitments on time
  - Loss of opportunities
  - Inability to claim cash discounts
  - Costs of borrowing (should an obligation need to be met at short notice).
- Practical points on cash management:
  - Establish a policy
  - Plan cash flows
  - Make judicious use of bank overdraft financing—it can be cheap and flexible
  - Use short-term cash surpluses profitably
  - Make frequent bank deposits
  - Operating cash cycle (for a retailer) is the length of time from buying inventory to receiving cash from customers less suppliers' payment period (in days)
  - Transmit cash promptly.
- An objective of working capital management is to limit the length of the operating cash cycle, subject to any risks that this may cause.

Managing Accounts Payable

- The costs of taking credit include:
  - Higher price than for purchases for immediate cash settlement
  - Administrative costs
  - Restrictions imposed by seller.
- The costs of not taking credit include:
  - Lost interest-free borrowing
  - Lost purchasing power
  - Inconvenience—paying at the time of purchase can be inconvenient.
- Practical points on creditor management:
  - Establish a policy
  - Exploit free credit as far as possible
  - Use accounting ratios (for example, average payment period for payables ratio).

Working Capital and the Small Business

- Small businesses often lack the skills and resources to manage working capital effectively.
- Small businesses often suffer from large businesses' delaying payments for goods supplied.

KEY TERMS

Working capital
Lead time
ABC system of inventory
   control
Economic order quantity
   (EOQ)

Materials requirement
   planning (MRP) system
Just-in-time (JIT) inventory
   management
Five Cs of credit
Cash discount

Average collection period
   for receivables
Aging schedule of receivables
Operating cash cycle (OCC)
Average payment period
   for payables

LIST OF EQUATIONS

12.1 Working capital = Current assets − Current liabilities

12.2 $EOQ = \sqrt{\dfrac{2DC}{H}}$

Equations from Chapter 4, reused in Chapter 12

4.5 Average inventory turnover period $= \dfrac{\text{Average inventory held}}{\text{Cost of goods sold}} \times 365$

4.6 Average collection period for receivables $= \dfrac{\text{Accounts receivable}}{\text{Credit sales revenue}} \times 365$

4.7 Average payment period for payables $= \dfrac{\text{Accounts payable}}{\text{Credit purchases}} \times 365$

REVIEW QUESTIONS

Answers to the Review Questions can be found on the Companion Website that accompanies this text at www.pearsoned.ca/atrill.

12.1 Terry is the credit manager of Heltex Ltd. He is concerned that the pattern of monthly sales receipts shows that accounts receivable collection is poor compared with budget. Heltex's sales manager believes that Terry is to blame for this situation, but Terry insists that he is not. Why might Terry not be to blame for the deterioration in the receivable collection period?

12.2 How might each of the following affect the level of inventory held by a business?
   (a) An increase in the number of production bottlenecks experienced by the business

   (b) A rise in the level of interest rates
   (c) A decision to offer customers a narrower range of products in the future
   (d) A change of suppliers from an overseas business to a local business
   (e) A deterioration in the quality and reliability of purchased components.

12.3 What are the reasons for holding inventory? Are these reasons different from the reasons for holding cash?

12.4 Identify the costs of holding:
   (a) Too little cash
   (b) Too much cash.

12.5 Define working capital and describe the working capital cycle for a retailing company.

PROBLEMS AND CASES

12.1 Your company is planning to cut inventory levels to reduce working capital to $250,000 for next year. You are developing a sensitivity analysis for next year's budget and have arrived at the following scenarios.

	1	2	3	4	5	6
Cash	$125,000	$349,000	$421,000	$300,000	$250,000	$725,000
Accounts receivable	245,000	211,000	153,000	200,000	146,000	600,000
Inventory	310,000	222,000	245,000	130,000	300,000	300,000
Accounts payable	350,000	320,000	343,000	289,000	280,000	1,200,000

Required:

(a) Calculate the inventory reduction required to reduce working capital to $250,000 for each scenario.
(b) For which scenarios does it not seem feasible to cut inventory by the amounts suggested in part (a)?

12.2 Your company has six product lines as shown below.

	1	2	3	4	5	6
Annual unit inventory sales	500,000	1,300,000	110,000	240,000	644,000	377,000
Lead time in weeks for inventory orders	3	2	6	3	7	4
Inventory buffer in units	3,000	10,000	50	4,000	25,000	15,000

Required:
Calculate the reorder point for inventory for each product.

12.3 You have recently been hired to work in the accounts receivable department of Canadian Moonlighting Film Inc. (CMF). As part of your introduction and familiarization with the company, you are comparing the aging listings for accounts receivable and accounts payable as shown below:

Accounts Receivable
Aging Listing
as at December 31, 2010
($ thousands)

Number of Days Outstanding				
0–30	31–60	61–90	Over 90	Total
4,500	3,200	1,200	600	9,500

as at December 31, 2009

1,200	4,500	1,800	1,000	8,500

Accounts Payable
Aging Listing
as at December 31, 2010
($ thousands)

Number of Days Outstanding				
0–30	31–60	61–90	Over 90	Total
1,500	2,000	200	1,800	5,500

as at December 31, 2009

600	900	300	700	2,500

Required:
    (a) Analyze and comment on the accounts receivable and accounts payable aging listings for CMF.
    (b) What can you conclude about your new employer's working capital management program based on these two aging listings?

12.4 For the six product lines from Problem and Case 12.2, you have collected the following additional information.

	1	2	3	4	5	6
Annual unit inventory sales	500,000	1,300,000	110,000	240,000	644,000	377,000
Cost of placing an order	$400	$150	$900	$350	$500	$430
Cost of holding one unit for one year	$5.50	$10.00	$32.00	$63.00	$9.50	$15.70

Required:
Calculate the economic order quantity (EOQ) for each inventory product.

12.5 You have been attending a small and medium-sized companies' trade conference where one of the topics was inventory management. You have gathered and shared the following information on cutting tools:

	Alton Ltd.	West Industries Ltd.	Niagara Supplies Ltd.
Quantity of tools sold each year	5,000	12,000	7,500
Annual unit holding cost	$7.50	$4.50	$6.75
Cost of placing an order	$500.00	$375.00	$425.00

Required:
    (a) Calculate the EOQ for cutting tools for each company.
    (b) Calculate the number of orders per year. Round up to the nearest unit.

12.6 You are looking at changing the credit policy on credit sales from n60 to either n30 or n45. If the collection period is decreased, you can expect decreases in average accounts receivable, the opportunity cost financing charge on accounts receivable, bad debts expenses, and sales. You have gathered the following data.

		Option	
	Current	1	2
Annual Sales	$3,000,000		
Unit selling price	$200		
Contribution margin per unit	$80		
Terms	n60	n30	n45
Cost of capital	16%		
Accounts receivable	$493,151		
Annual sales decrease		$280,000	$230,000
Bad debts	$300,000	$200,000	$240,000

Required:
Prepare calculations to determine which option is more profitable.

12.7 You manage your firm's accounts receivable and are dissatisfied with the current credit policy. You are analyzing two alternative plans, shown below.

	Current	Proposed Plan	
		1	2
	n60	3/30/n60	5/20/n50
Annual sales	$10,000,000	$10,000,000	$10,000,000
% cash sales	5%	10%	25%
% of credit sales to have discount taken		50%	60%
Average collection period*	90	80	70
Interest rate on line of credit	8%	8%	8%
Bad debts	$300,000	$270,000	$250,000
Credit administration savings		$5,000	$7,000

* for those not taking the discount

Required:
Recommend, with supporting calculations, which proposed plan is better.

12.8 Castlefield Furniture Ltd. wants to change its credit policy to stimulate the sales of its new line of leather sofas. The credit manager has asked you to analyze the situation. You have gathered the following data from your company's records and forecasts:

Annual sofa sales	$1,300,000.00
Average selling price per sofa	$1,500.00
Average variable costs	$900.00
Weighted average cost of capital (WACC)	12%
Average collection period (current)	25 days

Credit Options

	1	2	3
	---	---	---
Increase in collection period (days)	5	10	15
Increase in sales revenue per year	$150,000	$175,000	$200,000

Required:
Determine which length of credit period option will result in the greatest increase in profits. Show all calculations.

12.9 Your company has been offered a choice of two discounts because of a new policy change at a major supplier. Your company normally takes 60 days to pay for purchased goods. The discount choices are as follows:

Option 1:   3% discount if paid within 10 days
Option 2:   2% discount if paid within 20 days

Required:
(a) Calculate the approximate annualized interest rate if the discount is not taken.
(b) Calculate the exact compound annualized interest rate if the discount is not taken.
(c) Should your company take the discount? If so, which one should it take?

12.10 Nanaimo Candy Company (NCC) expects sales for the first six months of 2010 to show the following pattern. Previously, NCC made sales on the basis of a cash-only policy. For 2010, NCC will institute a net 30 (n30) payment policy for its customers. NCC expects that, on average, 40% of credit sales will be collected in the month following the sale, 30% in the next month, and 25% in the third month after the sale. The remainder are written off as bad debts.

	Jan	Feb	Mar	Apr	May	Jun
Total monthly sales	$ 125,000	$135,000	$145,000	$155,000	$165,000	$175,000
% cash sales	10%	11%	12%	13%	14%	15%

Required:
Prepare the cash flow pattern for sales for the January to June period in 2010.

12.11 Your firm is considering several options concerning its inventory, receivables, and payables. Data is shown below.

	Options						
	1	2	3	4	5	6	7
	Number of Days						
Average inventory turnover period	72	86	30	30	60	30	40
Average collection period for receivables	45	57	30	30	60	60	75
Average payment period for payables	55	90	60	30	60	45	110

Required:
  (a) Which option has the longest operating cash cycle?
  (b) Which option has the shortest operating cash cycle?

12.12 Selected information from the income statement and balance sheet of Fraser River Adventures Ltd. (FRA) is as follows:

Sales	$5,300,000
Percentage of credit sales	80%
Cost of goods sold as a percentage of sales	60%
Inventory, December 31, 2009	$500,000
Inventory, December 31, 2010	$800,000
Accounts receivable, December 31, 2010	$1,200,000
Accounts payable, December 31, 2010	$600,000
Credit purchases as a percentage of purchases	90%

Required:
Calculate the length of the operating cash cycle for FRA.

12.13 International Electric Ltd. at present offers its customers 30 days' credit. Half the customers, by value, pay on time. The other half take an average of 70 days to pay. The business is considering offering a cash discount of 2% to its customers for payment within 30 days.

    The credit manager anticipates that half of the customers who now take an average of 70 days to pay (i.e., one-quarter of all customers) will pay in 30 days. The other half (the final quarter) will still take an average of 70 days to pay. The plan will also reduce bad debts by $300,000 a year.

    Annual sales revenue of $365 million is made evenly throughout the year. At present, the business has a large overdraft ($60 million) with its bank at 12% a year.

Required:
  (a) Calculate the approximate equivalent annual percentage cost of a discount of 2%, which reduces the time taken by customers to pay from 70 days to 30 days. (*Hint:* This part can be answered without reference to the narrative above.)

(b) Calculate accounts receivable outstanding under both the old and new plans.

(c) How much will the plan cost the business in discounts?

(d) Should the business go ahead with the plan? State what other factors, if any, should be taken into account.

(e) Outline the controls and procedures that a business should adopt to manage the level of its receivables.

12.14 Mayo Computers Ltd. has annual sales of $20 million before taking into account bad debts of $0.1 million. All sales made by the business are on credit and, at present, credit terms are negotiable by the customer. On average, the collection period for accounts receivable is 60 days. Receivables are financed by an overdraft bearing a 14% rate of interest per year. The business is currently reviewing its credit policies to see whether more efficient and profitable methods could be employed. Only one proposal has so far been put forward concerning the management of receivables.

The credit control department has proposed that customers should be given a 2.5% discount if they pay within 30 days. For those who do not pay within this period, a maximum of 50 days' credit should be given. The credit department believes that 60% of customers will take advantage of the discount by paying at the end of the discount period, and the remainder will pay at the end of 50 days. The credit department believes that bad debts can be effectively eliminated by adopting the above policies and by employing stricter credit investigation procedures, which will cost an additional $20,000 a year. The credit department is confident that these new policies will not result in any reduction in sales revenue.

Required:

Calculate the net annual cost (or savings) to the business of abandoning its existing credit policies and adopting the proposal of the credit control department. (*Hint*: To answer this question, you must weigh the costs of administration and cash discounts against the savings in bad debts and interest charges.)

12.15 Boswell Enterprises Ltd. is reviewing its credit policy. The business, which sells all of its goods on credit, has estimated that sales revenue for the forthcoming year will be $3 million under the existing policy; 30% of accounts receivable are expected to be collected one month after being invoiced and 70% are expected to be collected two months after being invoiced. These estimates are in line with previous years' figures.

At present, no cash discounts are offered to customers. However, to encourage prompt payment, the business is considering giving a 2.5% cash discount to customers who pay in one month or less. Given this incentive, the business expects 60% of receivables to be collected one month after being invoiced and the remaining amounts two months after being invoiced. The business believes that the introduction of a cash discount policy will prove attractive to some customers and will lead to a 5% increase in total sales revenue.

The gross profit margin of the business will remain at 20% for the forthcoming year and three months' inventory will be held. Fixed monthly expenses of $15,000 and variable expenses (excluding discounts) equivalent to 10% of sales revenue will be incurred and will be paid one month in arrears. Accounts payable will be paid in arrears and will be equal to two months' cost of sales. The business will hold a fixed cash balance of $140,000 throughout the year, whichever trade credit policy is adopted. No dividends will be proposed or paid during the year.

Ignore taxes.

Required:

(a) Calculate the investment in working capital at the end of the forthcoming year under:
   (i) The existing policy
   (ii) The proposed policy.
   (*Hint:* The investment in working capital will be made up of inventory, receivables, and cash, less accounts payable and any unpaid expenses at the year-end.)

(b) Calculate the expected net income for the forthcoming year under:
   (i) The existing policy
   (ii) The proposed policy.

(c) Advise the business as to whether it should implement the proposed policy.

12.16 Delphi Ltd. has recently decided to enter the expanding market for minidisc players. The business will manufacture the players and sell them to small TV and hi-fi specialists, medium-sized music stores, and large retail chain stores. The new product will be launched next February and predicted sales revenue for the product from each customer group for February and the expected rate of growth for subsequent months are as follows:

Customer Type	February Sales Revenue ($000)	Monthly Compound Sales Revenue Growth (%)	Credit Sales (months to payment)
TV and hi-fi specialists	20	4	1
Music stores	30	6	2
Retail chain stores	40	8	3

The business is concerned about the financing implications of launching the new product, as it is already experiencing liquidity problems. In addition, it is concerned that the credit control department will find it difficult to cope. This is a new market for the business and there are likely to be many new customers who will have to be investigated for creditworthiness.

Calculations should be in thousands of dollars and to one decimal place only.

Required:

(a) Prepare an aging schedule of the monthly accounts receivable balance relating to the new product for each of the first four months of the new product's life, and comment on the results. The schedule should analyze the outstanding receivables according to customer type. It should also indicate, for each customer type, the relevant percentage outstanding in relation to the total amount outstanding for each month.

(b) Identify and discuss the factors that should be taken into account when evaluating the creditworthiness of the new business customers.

12.17 You are employed as an analyst at the Candy Company of Canada Ltd. (CCC). CCC manufactures candy and sells it to various retailers across the country. You have gathered the following information.

Annual sales	$18,000,000
Gross margin	30%
Weighted average cost of capital (WACC)	7%
Average collection period	60 days

CCC is trying to increase its profits and one of the strategies being considered is a change in the credit terms offered to its customers. Here are four options the company is considering.

	Credit Options			
	1	2	3	4
Increase (decrease) in collection period, days	10	20	(10)	(20)
Increase (decrease) in sales revenue per year	$100,000	$80,000	$(90,000)	$(400,000)

Required:

Determine which option will result in the greatest increase in profits. Show all calculations.

CHAPTER 13

Measuring and Managing for Shareholder Value

INTRODUCTION

For some years, shareholder value has been a hot issue among managers. Many leading businesses now claim that the quest for shareholder value is the driving force behind their strategic and operational decisions. In this chapter we begin by asking what is meant by the term shareholder value and, in the sections that follow, we look at some of the main approaches to measuring shareholder value.

L.0. 1 THE QUEST FOR SHAREHOLDER VALUE

Let us start by considering what **shareholder value** means. In simple terms, it is about putting the needs of shareholders at the heart of management decisions. It is argued that shareholders invest in a business with a view to maximizing their financial returns in relation to the risks that they are prepared to take. As managers are appointed by the shareholders to act on their behalf, management decisions and actions should reflect a concern for maximizing shareholder returns. Although the business may have other stakeholder groups—such as employees, customers, suppliers, and bankers—it is the shareholders that should be seen as the most important group.

This, of course, is not a new idea. Take a look at most books on finance or economics, including this one, and you will see that maximizing shareholder returns is assumed to be the key objective of a business. However, not everyone accepts this idea. Some believe that a balance must be struck between the competing claims of the various stakeholders. A debate about whether shareholders should be regarded as the most important group is beyond the scope of this chapter. What we can say, however, is that changes in the economic environment over recent years have often forced managers to focus their attention on the needs of shareholders.

In the past, shareholders have been accused of being too passive and of accepting too readily whatever profits and dividends the managers have delivered. However, this has changed. Nowadays, shareholders are much more assertive and, as owners of the business, are in a position to insist that their needs be given priority. Since the 1980s we have witnessed the deregulation and globalization of business as well as enormous changes in technology. The effect has been to create a much more competitive world. This has meant competition not only for products and services but also for funds. Businesses must now contend more strongly for shareholder funds and so must offer competitive rates of return.

Thus, self-interest may be the most powerful reason for managers to commit themselves to maximizing shareholder returns. If they do not do this, there is a real risk of shareholders either replacing them with managers who will, or allowing the business to be taken over by another business with managers who are dedicated to maximizing shareholder returns.

Creating Shareholder Value

Creating shareholder value involves a four-stage process. The first stage is to formulate objectives for the business that recognize the central importance of the shareholder. This will set a clear direction for the business. The second stage is to establish an appropriate means of measuring the returns that have been generated for shareholders. For reasons that we shall discuss later, the traditional methods of measuring returns to shareholders are inadequate for this purpose. The third stage is to manage the business in order to ensure that shareholder returns are maximized. This means setting demanding targets and then achieving them through the best possible use of resources, the use of incentive systems, and the embedding of a shareholder value culture throughout the business. The final stage is to measure the shareholder returns over a period of time to see whether the objectives have actually been achieved. These stages are depicted in Figure 13.1.

FIGURE 13.1   Creating Shareholder Value

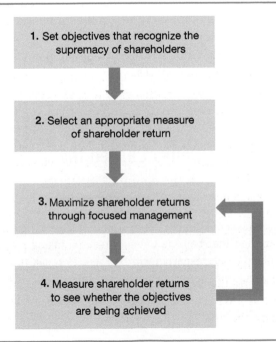

L.O. 2 THE NEED FOR NEW FORMS OF MEASUREMENT

Given a commitment to maximize shareholder returns, an appropriate measure must be selected that will help in assessing the returns to shareholders over time. It has been argued that the conventional methods for measuring shareholder returns are seriously flawed and so should not be used for this purpose. These methods are identified in Activity 13.1.

ACTIVITY 13.1

What are the conventional methods of measuring shareholder returns?

Solution

Managers normally use accounting profit or some ratio that is based on accounting profit, such as return on equity (ROE) or earnings per share.

One problem with using accounting profit, or a ratio based on profit, is that profit is measured over a relatively short period of time (usually one year). However, when we talk about maximizing shareholder returns, we are concerned with maximizing returns over the long term. It has been suggested that using profit as the key measure may encourage managers to make decisions that improve performance in the short term but may adversely affect it in the long term. For example, profits may be increased in the short term by cutting back on staff training and product research, even though these types of expenditures may be vital to long-term survival.

A second problem that arises with conventional methods of measuring shareholder returns is that risk is ignored. We saw in Chapter 7 that there is a relationship between the level of returns achieved and the level of risk that must be taken to produce those returns. The higher the level of returns required, the higher the level of risk that must be taken to realize the returns. A management strategy that produces an increase in profits can reduce shareholder value if the profit increase is not commensurate with the increase in the level of risk. Thus, profit alone is not enough.

REAL WORLD 13.1 describes the excessive risk-taking many banks undertook in the pursuit of profits and management bonuses.

REAL WORLD 13.1

Excessive Risk-Taking at Banks Caused the 2008–2009 Recession

On September 15, 2009, the one-year anniversary of the collapse of Wall Street giant investment bank Lehman Brothers, U.S. President Barack Obama warned that bankers cannot "resume taking risks without regard for consequences, and expect that next time, American taxpayers will be there to break their fall." The Lehman bankruptcy caused systemic panic throughout the world's banking systems. Credit markets froze virtually overnight. Since September 2008, the U.S. government and other governments in many countries have been forced to backstop the banks by pouring billions of dollars into rescuing them from bankruptcy.

▶

Many blamed the banking troubles on excessive risk-taking by bankers in the pursuit of bonuses. Bonuses are tied to profits. Governments cried foul when bankers took government bailout money and used it to continue to pay high bonuses to retain key employees.

Throughout this period the Canadian banking system was a pillar of strength. Not only did no Canadian banks need a government bailout, they all continued to pay their quarterly dividends at a time when many companies completely eliminated their dividends. The share prices of Canadian banks had fallen so low that the dividend yields were very high—in the 5%–7% range.

The Canadian banking system is more conservative than many in the world, and Canadian financial institutions did not get into risky sub-prime mortgage lending like many of their U.S. counterparts.

Source: CBC website at: www.cbc.ca/world/story/2009/09/14/obama-wall-street-speech.html, accessed October 2, 2009.

A third problem with the use of profit, or a ratio based on profit, is that it does not take account of all of the costs of the capital invested by the business. The conventional approach to measuring profit will deduct the cost of debt (i.e., interest charges) in arriving at net profit, but there is no similar deduction for the cost of shareholder funds. (Remember that dividends are paid *after* arriving at the net income figure and represent only part of the total return to shareholders.) Critics of the conventional approach point out that a business will not make a profit—in an economic sense—unless it covers the cost of all capital invested, including shareholder funds. Unless the opportunity cost of shareholders' equity is considered, the business may operate at a loss and so shareholder value will be reduced.

A final problem is that the accounting profit reported by a business can vary according to the particular policies that have been adopted. Some businesses adopt a very conservative approach, which would be reflected in particular accounting policies such as depreciating assets over relatively short lives or using the declining balance method of depreciation (which favours high charges in the early years). Businesses that do not adopt conservative accounting policies would report profits more quickly. Depreciating assets over a longer period or using the straight-line method of depreciation will mean that profits are reported more quickly.

In addition, there are some businesses that may adopt particular accounting policies or structure transactions in a particular way to create a misleading appearance for their financial performance. This practice, which we discussed in Chapter 4, is referred to as creative accounting and has been a major problem for accounting standard setters.

As noted in Chapter 6, an alternative form of measuring performance that is gaining ground is the triple bottom line, which attempts to measure financial, social, and environmental costs and returns on investments. The triple bottom line method became the standard for urban and community accounting in 2007.

Net Present Value (NPV) Analysis

To summarize the points just made, we can say that, in order to measure changes in shareholder value, what we really need is a measure that will consider the long term, take account of risk and the cost of shareholders' equity, and not be affected by accounting policy choices. Fortunately, we have a measure that can, in theory, do just this.

Net present value analysis was discussed in Chapter 6. We saw that if we want to know the net present value (NPV) of an asset (whether this is a physical asset such as a machine or a financial asset such as a share), we must discount the future cash flows generated by the asset over its life.

Shareholders have a required rate of return and managers must strive to generate long-term cash flows for shares (in the form of dividends or proceeds that investors receive from the sale of the shares) that meet this rate of return. A negative net present value will indicate that the cash flows generated do not meet the minimum required rate of return. If a business is to create value for its shareholders, it must generate cash flows that exceed the required returns of shareholders. In other words, the cash flows generated must produce a positive present value.

The NPV method fulfills the criteria that we mentioned earlier for the following reasons:

- *It considers the long term.* The returns from an investment, such as shares, are considered over the whole of the investment's life.
- *It takes account of the cost of capital and risk.* The higher the level of risk, the higher the required level of return and the higher the risk-adjusted cost of capital.
- *It is not sensitive to the choice of accounting policies.* Cash rather than profit is used in the calculations and is a more objective measure of return.

L.O. 3 EXTENDING NPV ANALYSIS: SHAREHOLDER VALUE ANALYSIS AND ECONOMIC VALUE ADDED

We know from our earlier study of NPV that, when evaluating an investment project, shareholder wealth will be maximized when the net present value of cash flows generated by the project are maximized. In essence, the business is simply a portfolio of investment projects and so the same principles should apply when considering the business as a whole. Shareholder value analysis is founded on this basic idea.

Shareholder Value Analysis (SVA)

The **shareholder value analysis (SVA)** approach involves evaluating strategic decisions according to their ability to maximize value, or wealth, for shareholders. To undertake this evaluation, conventional measures are discarded and replaced by discounted cash flows. We have seen that the net present value of a project represents the value of that particular project. Given that the business can be viewed as a portfolio of projects, the value of the business as a whole can therefore be viewed as the net present value of the cash flows that it generates. SVA seeks to measure the discounted cash flows of the business as a whole and then seeks to identify the part that is available to the shareholders — this is illustrated in Activity 13.2.

ACTIVITY 13.2

If the net present value of future cash flows generated by the business represents the value of the business as a whole, how can we derive the part of the value of the business that is available to shareholders?

Solution

A business will normally be financed by a combination of debt and equity. Thus, bondholders will also have a claim on the total value of the business. The part of the total business value that is available to common shareholders can therefore be derived by deducting from the total value of the business (i.e., total NPV) the market value of any loans outstanding. Hence:

Shareholder value = Total business value − Market value of outstanding debt

Measuring Free Cash Flows

The cash flows used to measure total business value are the **free cash flows**. These are the cash flows generated by the business that are available to common shareholders and long-term lenders—the net cash flows from operations after deducting tax paid and cash for additional investment. These free cash flows can be derived from information contained in the income statement and balance sheet of a business.

Example 13.1 demonstrates important ideas in using free cash flow concepts.

Example 13.1

Saginaw Ltd. generated sales of $220 million during the year and has an operating profit margin of 25% of sales. Depreciation charges for the year were $8.0 million and the tax rate for the year was 20% of operating profit. During the year, $11.3 million was invested in additional working capital and $15.2 million was invested in additional long-term capital assets. A further $8.0 million was invested in the replacement of existing capital assets.

The free cash flows are calculated as follows:

	($ millions)	($ millions)
Sales		220.0
Operating profit (25% × $220 million)		55.0
Add: Depreciation charge		8.0
Operating cash flows		63.0
Less: Taxes (20% × $55 million)		11.0
Operating cash flows after tax		52.0
Less: Additional working capital	11.3	
Additional capital assets	15.2	
Replacement capital assets	8.0	34.5
Free cash flows		17.5

We can see from Example 13.1 that, to derive the operating cash flows, the depreciation expense is added back to the operating profit figure. We can also see that the cost of replacement of existing capital assets is deducted from the operating cash flows in order to arrive at the free cash flows. When we are trying to predict future free cash flows, one way of obtaining an approximate figure for the cost of replacing existing assets is to assume that the depreciation charge for the year is equivalent to the replacement charge for capital assets. This would mean that the two adjustments mentioned cancel each other out and the calculation in Example 13.1 could be shortened to:

	($ millions)	($ millions)
Sales		220.0
Operating profit (25% × $220 million)		55.0
Less: Taxes (20% × $55 million)		11.0
Operating cash flows (ignoring depreciation)		44.0
Less: Additional working capital	11.3	
Additional capital assets	15.2	26.5
Free cash flows		17.5

This shortened approach enables us to identify the key variables in determining free cash flows as being:

- Sales
- Operating profit margin
- Tax rate
- Additional investment in working capital
- Additional investment in capital assets.

Figure 13.2 shows the process in the form of a flow chart.

Figure 13.2   Measuring Free Cash Flows

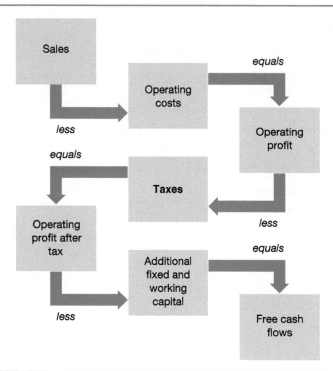

The five variables identified are **value drivers** of the business that reflect key business decisions. These decisions convert into free cash flows and finally into shareholder value.

Ideally, the free cash flows that should be measured are all those that will occur in the life of a business from the present moment into the future. This is a difficult (if not impossible) task. To overcome the problem, it is helpful to divide the future cash flows into two elements:

- Cash flows within the planning horizon and which may be forecast with a reasonable level of reliability; and
- Cash flows occurring beyond the planning horizon, which will be represented by a terminal value.

It is a good idea to try to make the planning horizon as long as possible. This is because the discounting process ensures that values beyond the planning horizon are given little weight. As can be imagined, cash flows in the distant future can be extremely difficult to forecast with accuracy and so the less weight given to them, the better. Activity 13.3 illustrates this concept.

ACTIVITY 13.3

Little Ltd. has an estimated terminal value (representing cash flows beyond the planning horizon) of $100 million. What is the present value of this figure assuming a discount rate of 12% and a planning horizon of:

(a) 5 years
(b) 10 years
(c) 15 years?

(You may find it helpful to refer to the discount tables in Appendix A at the end of the text.)

Solution

The present values are:
(a) $100 million × 0.5674 = $56.74 million
(b) $100 million × 0.3220 = $32.20 million
(c) $100 million × 0.1827 = $18.27 million

We can see that there is a dramatic difference in the present values of the terminal calculation among the three time horizons, given a 12% discount rate.

To calculate the terminal value of a business, it is usually necessary to make simplifying assumptions. It is beyond the scope of this book to discuss this topic in detail. However, one common assumption is that returns beyond the planning horizon will remain constant (perhaps at the level achieved in the last year of the planning period). Using the formula for a perpetuity, the calculation (Equation 13.1) for determining the terminal value will be:

$$\text{Terminal value} = \frac{C_1}{r} \qquad \text{13.1}$$

where: C_1 = the free cash flows in the following year
r = the required rate of return from investors (i.e., the weighted average cost of capital)

This formula provides a capitalized value for future cash flows. Thus, if an investor receives a constant cash flow of $100 per year and has a required rate of return of 10%, the capitalized value of these cash flows will be $100/0.1 = $1,000. In other words, the future cash flows are worth $1,000 (when invested at the required rate of return) to the investor. This formula is similar to the dividend formula, Equation 10.2, where dividends are assumed to be constant, which we covered in Chapter 10.

Example 13.2 and Activity 13.4 illustrate the way in which shareholder value can be calculated. Figure 13.3 on page 500 shows the key steps in calculating shareholder value.

Example 13.2

The directors of United Grainaries Ltd. are considering the purchase of all the shares in Health Inc., which produces vitamins and health foods. Health Inc. has a strong presence in western Canada and it is expected that the directors of the business will reject any bids that value the shares of the business at less than $11.00 per share.

Health Inc. generated sales for the most recent year-end of $3,000 million. Extracts from the balance sheet of the business at the end of 2010 are as follows:

Long-term liabilities	($ millions)
Bank loans	120.0
Equity	
Common shares (400 million outstanding)	400.0
Retained earnings	380.0
Total shareholders' equity	780.0

Forecasts that have been prepared by the business planning department of Health Inc. are as follows:

- Sales will grow at 10% a year for the next five years
- The operating profit margin is currently 15% and is likely to be maintained at this rate in the future
- The tax rate is 25%
- Replacement capital asset investment (RCAI) will be in line with the annual depreciation charge each year
- Additional capital asset investment (ACAI) over the next five years will be 10% of sales growth
- Additional working capital investment (AWCI) over the next five years will be 5% of sales growth.

After five years, the sales of the business will stabilize at their 2015 level.

The business has a cost of capital of 10% and the bank loans amount in the balance sheet reflects their current market value.

The free cash flow calculation will be as follows:

	2011 ($ millions)	2012 ($ millions)	2013 ($ millions)	2014 ($ millions)	2015 ($ millions)	After 2015 ($ millions)
Sales	3,300.0	3,630.0	3,993.0	4,392.3	4,831.5	4,831.5
Operating profit (15%)	495.0	544.5	599.0	658.8	724.7	724.7
Less: Taxes (25%)	(123.8)	(136.1)	(149.8)	(164.7)	(181.2)	(181.2)
Operating profit after taxes	371.2	408.4	449.2	494.1	543.5	543.5
Less:						
ACAI (Note 1)	(30.0)	(33.0)	(36.3)	(39.9)	(43.9)	—
AWCI (Note 2)	(15.0)	(16.5)	(18.2)	(20.0)	(22.0)	—
Free cash flows	326.2	358.9	394.7	434.2	477.6	543.5

Notes
1. The additional capital asset investment is 10% of sales growth. In the first year, sales growth is $300 million (i.e., $3,300 million − $3,000 million). Thus, the investment will be 10% × $300 million = $30 million. Similar calculations are carried out for the following years.
2. The additional working capital investment is 5% of sales growth. In the first year the investment will be 5% × $300 million = $15 million. Similar calculations are carried out in following years.
3. The RCAI is excluded because it is offset by the annual depreciation charge.

Having derived the free cash flows (FCF), we can calculate the total business value as follows:

Year	FCF ($ millions)	Discount Rate* 10.0%	Present Value ($ millions)
2011	326.2	0.91	296.8
2012	358.9	0.83	297.9
2013	394.7	0.75	296.0
2014	434.2	0.68	295.3
2015	477.6	0.62	296.1
Terminal value 543.5/0.10	5,435.0	0.62	3,369.7
Total business value			4,851.8

*rounded to two decimal places

ACTIVITY 13.4

What is the shareholder value figure for the business in Example 13.2? Would the sale of the shares at $11 per share really add value for the shareholders of Health Inc.?

Solution

Shareholder value will be the total business value less the market value of the bank loans. Hence, shareholder value is:

	($ millions)
$4,851.8 million − $120 million =	4,731.8
The proceeds from the sale of the shares to	
United Grainearies Ltd. would yield 400 million × $11 =	4,400.0

Thus, from the point of view of the shareholders of Health Inc., the sale of the business at the share price mentioned would not increase shareholder value.

Managing the Business with Shareholder Value Analysis

We saw earlier that the adoption of SVA indicates a commitment to managing the business in a way that maximizes shareholder returns. Those who support this approach argue that SVA can be a powerful tool for strategic planning. For example, SVA can be extremely useful when considering major shifts of direction such as:

- Acquiring new businesses
- Selling existing businesses
- Developing new products or markets
- Reorganizing or restructuring the business.

FIGURE 13.3 Deriving Shareholder Value

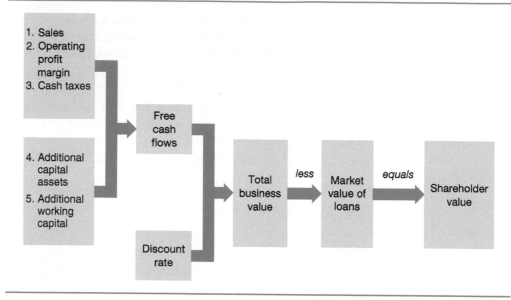

This is because SVA takes account of all the elements that determine shareholder value.

To illustrate this point, let us suppose that a business develops a new product that is quite different from those within its existing range of products and appeals to a quite different market. Profit forecasts may indicate that the product is likely to be profitable, and so a decision to launch the product may be made. However, this decision may increase the level of risk for the business and, if so, investors will demand higher levels of return. In addition, there may have to be a significant investment in additional capital assets and working capital in order to undertake the venture. When these factors are taken into account, using the type of analysis shown above, it may be found that the present value of the venture is negative. In other words, shareholder value will be destroyed.

SVA is also useful in focusing attention on the value drivers that create shareholder wealth. In order to improve free cash flows and, in turn, shareholder value, management targets can be set for improving performance in relation to each value driver and responsibility can be assigned for achieving these targets. Activity 13.5 considers the practical problems of adopting this approach.

ACTIVITY 13.5

What do you think are the practical problems of adopting an SVA approach?

Solution

Two practical problems spring to mind:

- Forecasting future cash flows lies at the heart of this approach. In practice, forecasting can be difficult and simplifying assumptions will usually have to be made.
- SVA requires more comprehensive information (for example, information concerning the value drivers) than the traditional measures discussed earlier.

You may have thought of other problems.

Implication of SVA

Supporters of SVA believe that this measure should replace the traditional accounting measures of value creation such as profit, earnings per share, and return on shareholders' equity. To see whether shareholder value has increased or decreased, we must compare shareholder value at the beginning and the end of a period.

We can see that SVA is a radical departure from the conventional approach to managing a business. It will require different performance indicators, different financial reporting systems, and different management incentive methods. It may also require a change of culture within the business to accommodate the shareholder value philosophy, as not all employees may be focused on the need to maximize shareholder wealth.

Economic Value Added (EVA)

Economic value added (EVA) was developed in the U.S. by the management consulting firm Stern Stewart, which trademarked the technique. However, EVA is based on the idea of economic profit, which has been around for many years. The measure reflects the point made earlier that, in order for a business to be profitable in an economic sense, it must generate returns that exceed the required returns from investors. It is not enough simply to make an accounting profit because this measure does not take full account of the returns required from investors.

EVA indicates whether the returns generated exceed the required returns from investors. The formula, shown in Equation 13.2, is:

$$\text{Economic value added (or EVA)} = \text{EBIT less taxes} - (R \times C) \qquad 13.2$$

where: EBIT = earnings before interest and taxes, also known as operating profit or income from operations

R = required returns from investors (i.e., the weighted average cost of capital)

C = capital invested (i.e., the net assets of the business)

$R \times C$ = the total minimum economic profit required by investors

Only when EVA is positive can we say that the business is increasing shareholder wealth. To maximize shareholder wealth, managers must increase EVA by as much as possible.

EVA relies on conventional financial statements to measure the wealth created for shareholders. However, the EBIT and capital figures shown on these statements are used only as a starting point. They have to be adjusted because of the problems and limitations of conventional measures. A major problem is that EBIT (Step 1) and capital (Step 2) are understated because of the conservative bias in accounting measurement. EBIT is understated as a result of arbitrary write-offs such as research and development expenditure and also as a result of excessive allowances being created (such as allowance for doubtful debts). Capital is also understated because assets are reported at their original cost (less amounts written off), which can produce figures considerably below current market values. In addition, certain assets such as internally generated goodwill and brand names are omitted from the financial statements because no external transactions have occurred. Also, accounting places no value on the balance sheet for the human resource factor; wage and salary expense appears on the income statement.

Activity 13.6 considers the actions that managers can take to increase EVA.

ACTIVITY 13.6

What can managers do in order to increase EVA? (*Hint*: Use Equation 13.2 as your starting point.)

Solution

The equation suggests that in order to increase EVA, managers may try the following tactics:

- Increase EBIT. This may be done by either reducing expenses or increasing sales.
- Use capital invested more efficiently. This means selling off assets that are not generating returns that exceed their cost, and investing in assets that do.
- Reduce the required rates of return for investors. This may be achieved by changing the capital structure in favour of debt (which is cheaper than share capital). This strategy can create problems, however, as discussed in Chapter 10.

Figure 13.4 summarizes the steps necessary to calculate a firm's EVA.

FIGURE 13.4   Steps for Calculating EVA

Step 1
Calculate EBIT after taxes.

Make after-tax EBIT adjustments

Step 2
Calculate *C*.

Make long-term capital invested adjustments
(or long-term debt and shareholders' equity adjustment)

Step 3
Calculate $R \times C$.

Multiply investors' required rate of return by the result of Step 2

Step 4
Calculate EVA.

EVA = Step 1 – Step 3

There are more than 100 adjustments that could be made to the conventional financial statements to eliminate the conservative bias. However, Stern Stewart believes that, in practice, probably only a handful of adjustments need to be made to the accounting figures of any particular business. Unless an adjustment is going to have a significant effect on the calculation of EVA, it is really not worth making. The adjustments made should reflect the nature of the particular business. Each business is unique and so must customize the calculation of EVA to its particular circumstances. (This aspect of EVA can be seen either as indicating flexibility or as being open to manipulation, depending on whether you support or do not support this measure.)

The most common adjustments that have to be made are as follows:

- *Research and development (R&D) costs and marketing costs.* These costs should be written off over the period that they benefit. In practice, however, they are often written off in the period in which they are incurred. This means that any amounts written off immediately should be added back to the assets on the balance sheet, thereby increasing invested capital, and then written off over time.
- *Goodwill.* Leave goodwill, which includes intangible items such as brand names and reputation, on the balance sheet. Goodwill impairment write-offs, if any, should be added back to assets.
- *Restructuring costs.* This item can be viewed as an investment in the future rather than an expense to be written off. Supporters of EVA argue that by restructuring, the business is better placed to meet future challenges and so any amounts incurred should be added back to assets.
- *Marketable investments.* Investment in assets such as shares and bonds are not included as part of the capital invested in the business. This is because the income from marketable investments is not included in the calculation of operating profit (EBIT). (Income from this source will be added in the income statement *after* operating profit has been calculated.)

Once Steps 1 and 2 are complete, we calculate the minimum economic profit required by the shareholders as $R \times C$ (Step 3). Finally EVA (Step 4) is calculated as Step 1–Step 3.

Let us now consider in Example 13.3 and Activity 13.7 how EVA may be calculated.

Example 13.3

St. John's Software Inc. was established in 2008 and has produced the following balance sheet and income statement at the end of 2010, the second year of business.

St. John's Software Inc.
Balance Sheet
as at the end of 2010
($ millions)

Current assets		
Cash	2.1	
Accounts receivable	29.3	
Inventory	34.5	
Total current assets		65.9
Property, plant, and equipment		
Land	34.0	
Plant and equipment, net	46.0	
Motor vehicles, net	12.4	
Total property, plant, and equipment, net		92.4
Marketable investments		6.6
Total assets		164.9

▶

Current liabilities

Accounts payable	30.3	
Income tax payable	0.9	
Total current liabilities		31.2
Long-term liabilities		
Loans		50.0
Total liabilities		81.2
Shareholders' equity		
Common shares	60.0	
Retained earnings	23.7	
Total shareholders' equity		83.7
Total liabilities and shareholders' equity		164.9

St. John's Software Inc.
Income Statement
For 2010
($ millions)

Sales revenue		148.6
Cost of goods sold		76.2
Gross profit		72.4
Wages	24.5	
Depreciation of plant and equipment	8.8	
Marketing costs	22.5	
Allowance for doubtful accounts expense	4.5	60.3
Operating profit (EBIT)		12.1
Income from investments		0.4
		12.5
Interest expense	0.5	
Restructuring costs	2.0	2.5
Earnings before taxes		10.0
Tax expense		1.8
Net income		8.2

Discussions with the vice-president of finance reveal the following:

1. Marketing costs relate to the launch of a new product. The benefits of the marketing campaign are expected to last for three years (including this most recent year).
2. The allowance for doubtful accounts was created this year and the amount of the provision is very high. A more realistic figure for the allowance would be $2.0 million.
3. Restructuring costs were incurred as a result of a collapse in a particular product market. If the business is restructured, benefits are expected to flow for an infinite period.
4. The business has a 10% required rate of return for investors.

Step 1. Adjust the net operating profit (EBIT) after tax to take account of the various points revealed from the discussion with the vice-president of finance. The revised figure is calculated as follows:

EBIT Adjustment

	($ millions)	($ millions)
Operating profit (EBIT)		12.1
Less: Income tax		1.8
Operating profit (EBIT) after tax		10.3

EVA Adjustments (To Be Added Back to Profit)

	($ millions)	($ millions)
Marketing costs (2/3 × $22.5 million)	15.0	
Excess allowance for doubtful accounts		
($4.5 million − $2.0 million)	2.5	17.5
Adjusted after-tax EBIT		27.8

Step 2. Adjust the net assets (as represented by equity and long-term liabilities) to take account of the points revealed.

Adjusted Long-Term Capital Invested (Or Total Assets Less Current Liabilities)

	($ millions)	($ millions)
Long-term liabilities and shareholders' equity per balance sheet		
($50.0 million + $83.7 million)		133.7
Marketing costs (Note 1)	15.0	
Allowance for doubtful accounts	2.5	
Restructuring costs (Note 2)	2.0	19.5
		153.2
Less: Marketable investments (Note 3)		(6.6)
Adjusted long-term capital invested (C)		146.6

Notes

1. The marketing costs represent two years' benefits added back (2/3 × $22.5 million).
2. The restructuring costs are added back to the long-term capital invested as they provide benefits over an infinite period. (Note that they were not added back to the operating profit as these costs were deducted *after* arriving at operating profit in the income statement.)
3. The marketable investments do not form part of the operating assets of the business and the income from these investments is not part of the operating income.

ACTIVITY 13.7

What is the EVA for 2010 in Example 13.3?

Solution

Step 3. Calculate $R \times C$.

$$R \times C = 10\% \times \$146.6 \text{ million} = \$14.7 \text{ million}$$

Step 4. Calculate EVA.

$$\text{EVA} = \text{Step 1} - \text{Step 3} = \$27.8 \text{ million} - \$14.7 \text{ million} = \$13.1 \text{ million}$$

We can see that EVA is positive $13.1 million and so the business has increased shareholder wealth during the year.

The main advantage of this measure is the discipline to which managers are subjected as a result of the charge for capital that has been invested. Before any increase in shareholder wealth can be recognized, an appropriate deduction is made for the use of business resources. Thus, EVA encourages managers to use these resources efficiently. Where managers are focused simply on increasing profits, there is a danger that the resources used to achieve any increase in profits will not be taken into proper account. REAL WORLD 13.2 provides an example of how business is using EVA to determine executive pay.

REAL WORLD 13.2

George Weston Limited Uses EVA Salary and Bonus Plan

George Weston Limited, based in Toronto and parent company of Loblaw, granted two senior managers an employment contract whereby an annual bonus could double their annual salary, providing certain EVA and other objectives were met. The EVA bonus earned in any year is paid out equally over a three-year period. Subsequent years' EVA results affect the amount of the EVA bonuses paid and therefore ensure that long-term performance is not sacrificed by decisions to enhance profitability for the short term.

Source: www.weston.ca/en/pdf_en/02gwl_ar_en_mpc.pdf, accessed October 2, 2009.

SELF-ASSESSMENT QUESTION   13.1

The financial statements for Moose Jaw Beer Ltd. after its first year of operations are as follows:

Moose Jaw Beer Ltd.
Income Statement
for the year ended December 31, 2010
(in $ thousands)

Sales		5,000
Cost of goods sold		3,800
Gross profit		1,200
Operating expenses:		
Selling expenses	380	
Marketing expenses	50	
Lease expenses	100	
Depreciation	30	
Other expenses	175	
Total operating expenses		735
Earnings before interest and taxes		465
Interest expense	123	
Less: Dividend income from the investment		
in Truro Travel	(75)	48
Earnings before taxes		417
Less: Income tax expense [40% × ($465,000 − $123,000)]		(137)
Net income		280

▶

Moose Jaw Beer Ltd.
Statement of Retained Earnings
for the year ended December 31, 2010
(in $ thousands)

Opening retained earnings, January 1	0
Add: Net income	280
Less: Dividends paid	(180)
Closing retained earnings, December 31	100

Moose Jaw Beer Ltd.
Balance Sheet
as at December 31, 2010
(in $ thousands)

Current assets			
Cash		5	
Accounts receivable		70	
Inventory		15	
Total current assets			90
Property, plant, and equipment			
Land		10	
Buildings	190		
Less: Accumulated depreciation	20	170	
Furniture and fixtures	40		
Less: Accumulated depreciation	10	30	
Total property, plant, and equipment			210
Investment in Truro Travel Ltd. common shares			750
Total assets			1,050
Current liabilities			
Accounts payable		60	
Income taxes payable		5	
Loans payable		5	
Total current liabilities			70
Long-term debt			
Bonds, 6%			60
Total liabilities			130
Shareholders' equity			
Common shares		820	
Retained earnings		100	
Total shareholders' equity			920
Total liabilities and shareholders' equity			1,050

Notes

1. The marketing costs, although expensed to meet the accounting standards, are expected to last for five years.
2. Other expenses include allowance for doubtful accounts receivable expenses of $90,000, which is considered excessively high due to it being Moose Jaw's first year of operations. Normal losses on receivables in the beer industry for a similar-sized business would be $20,000.

▶

3. Investors in the beer industry generally demand a 15% return on investment while investors in the travel industry require a 20% return.

Required:

(a) Calculate EVA for Moose Jaw Beer for its first year of operations. Show all steps.
(b) Is the investment in Truro Travel a wise use of company funds, given that there was no price appreciation for the Truro shares?

EVA and SVA Compared

Although at first glance it may appear that EVA and SVA are worlds apart, this is not the case. In fact, the opposite is true. EVA and SVA are closely related and, in theory at least, should produce the same figure for shareholder value. The way in which shareholder value is calculated using SVA has already been described. The EVA approach to calculating shareholder value adds the capital invested to the present value of future EVA flows and then deducts the market value of any debt. Figure 13.5 illustrates the two approaches to determining shareholder value.

FIGURE 13.5   Two Approaches to Determining Shareholder Value

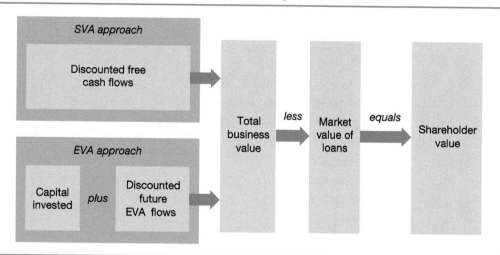

Example 13.4

Lighthouse Ltd. has just been formed and has been financed by a $20 million issue of shares and a $10 million issue of bonds. The proceeds have been invested in capital assets with a life of three years and during this period these assets will depreciate by $10 million per year. The operating profit (EBIT) after tax is expected to be $15 million each year. There will be no replacement of capital assets during the three-year period and no investment in working capital. At the end of the three years, the business will be wound up and the capital assets will have no residual value.

The required rate of return by investors is 10%.
The SVA approach to determining shareholder value will be as follows:

Year	FCF ($ millions)	Discount Rate** 10%	Present Value ($ millions)
1	25.0*	0.91	22.8
2	25.0	0.83	20.7
3	25.0	0.75	18.7
		Total business value	62.2
		Less: Bonds	(10.0)
		Shareholder value	52.2

*The free cash flows will be the operating profit after tax *plus* the depreciation charge (i.e., $15 million + $10 million). In this case, there are no replacement capital assets against which the depreciation expense can be netted off. It must therefore be added back.

The EVA approach to determining shareholder value will be as follows:

Year	Opening Capital Invested (C) ($ millions)	Capital Charge (10% × C) ($ millions)	Operating Profit (EBIT) After Tax ($ millions)	EVA ($ millions)	Discount Rate** 10%	Present Value of EVA ($ millions)
1	30.0***	3.0	15.0	12.0	0.91	10.9
2	20.0	2.0	15.0	13.0	0.83	10.8
3	10.0	1.0	15.0	14.0	0.75	10.5
						32.2
				Opening capital		30.0
						62.2
				Less: Bonds		(10.0)
				Shareholder value		52.2

**rounded to two decimal places
***The capital invested decreases each year by the depreciation expense (i.e., $10 million).

EVA or SVA?

Although both EVA and SVA are consistent with the objective of maximizing shareholder wealth and, in theory, should produce the same decisions and results, the supporters of EVA claim that this measure has a number of practical advantages over SVA. One such advantage is that EVA sits more comfortably with the conventional financial reporting systems and financial reports. There is no need to develop entirely new systems to implement EVA as it can be calculated by making a few adjustments to the conventional income statements and balance sheets.

It is also claimed that EVA is more useful as a basis for rewarding managers. Both EVA and SVA support the idea that management rewards be linked to increases in shareholder value. This should ensure that the interests of managers are closely aligned with the interests of shareholders. Under the SVA approach, management rewards will be determined on the basis of the contribution made to the generation of long-term cash flows. However, there are practical problems in using SVA for this purpose, as discussed in Activity 13.8

ACTIVITY 13.8

What are the practical problems that may arise when using SVA calculations to reward managers? (*Hint*: Think about how SVA is calculated.)

Solution

The SVA approach measures changes in shareholder value by reference to predicted changes in future cash flows and it is unwise to pay managers on the basis of predicted rather than actual achievements. If the predictions are optimistic, the effect will be that the business rewards optimism rather than real achievement. There is also a risk that unscrupulous managers will manipulate predicted future cash flows in order to increase their rewards.

Under EVA, managers can receive bonuses based on actual achievement during a particular period. If management rewards are linked to a single period, however, there is a danger that managers will place undue attention on increasing EVA during this period rather than over the long term. The objective should be to maximize EVA over the longer term. Where a business has stable levels of sales, operating assets, and borrowing, a current-period focus is likely to be less of a problem than where these elements are unstable over time. A stable pattern of operations minimizes the risk that improvements in EVA during the current period are achieved at the expense of future periods. Nevertheless, any reward system for managers must encourage a long-term perspective and so rewards should be based on the ability of managers to improve EVA over a number of years rather than a single year.

It is worth noting that some experts believe that bonuses, calculated as a percentage of EVA, should form a very large part of the total compensation package for managers. Thus, the higher the EVA figure, the higher the rewards to managers—with no upper limits. The philosophy is that EVA should make managers wealthy, provided it makes shareholders extremely wealthy. A bonus system should encompass as many managers as possible in order to encourage a widespread commitment to implementing EVA.

EVA in Practice

REAL WORLD 13.3 provides an example of an EVA-based bonus.

REAL WORLD 13.3

$30 Million Bonus from 2006 to 2008

CEO Liew Mun Leong of CapitaLand, based in Singapore and one of Asia's largest real estate firms, was paid a $3 million bonus in 2008, bringing the total of the bonus over the three years to $430 million. The bonuses were based on EVA calculations. During this period, net income totalled more than $5 billion. However, Mr. Liew did not get to take home all that cash in 2008. The yearly bonus is added to an account and he receives one-third of the account balance every year. If the company had performed poorly, the account would have been reduced and the bonus lowered.

Source: http://lushhomemedia.com/2009/03/25/2986m-accrued-bonus-over-3-yrs-for-capland-ceo/, accessed October 2, 2009.

REAL WORLD 13.4 gives some indication of the extent of the usage of value-based management (of which SVA and EVA are examples) in Canada and the U.S.

REAL WORLD 13.4   The Extent of Value-Based Management in Practice

Respondents to a 2002 survey of Canadian businesses employed the following value-based management techniques: discounted cash flow (DCF), return on invested capital, cash flow return on investment, and economic value added (EVA), in that order. Surveys of U.S. businesses have shown a higher frequency use (around 50%) of EVA than Canadian businesses (around 35%).

Source: George Athanassakos, "The Utilisation, Efficiency and Determinants of Usage of Value-Based Management in Canada," 2002.

MARKET VALUE ADDED (MVA) AND TOTAL SHAREHOLDER RETURN (TSR)

L.O. 4

EVA was developed to provide a means of motivating managers and other employees to increase shareholder value. It is really designed for internal management purposes. However, a further measure has been developed to complement EVA and to provide shareholders with a way of tracking changes in shareholder value over time.

Market Value Added (MVA)

Market value added (MVA) attempts to measure the gains or losses in shareholder value by measuring the difference between the market value of the business and the total investment that has been made in it over the years. The market value of the business is usually taken to be the market value of shares and debt. The total investment is the long-term capital invested, which is made up of long-term debt plus shareholders' equity. Figure 13.6 and Equation 13.3 illustrate the derivation of market value added.

FIGURE 13.6   Market Value Added (MVA)

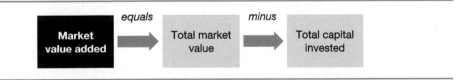

Market value added (or MVA) = Total market value − Total capital invested   13.3

It is worth going through a simple example to show how market value can be calculated.

Example 13.5

Kitchener Ceramics Ltd. began business 10 years ago. It has 2 million common shares outstanding that have a current market value of $5 per share, although they were issued at $1 per share when the business was founded. The business also has $6 million in 10% long-term debt. The book value of the debt is the same as its current market value. In addition, the business has retained earnings of $3 million.

The market value added can be calculated as follows:

	($ millions)	($ millions)
Market value of shares and debt		
Common shares (2 million × $5)		10
Long-term debt		6
Total current market value		16
Less: Total amount invested		
Common shares (2 million × $1)	2	
Retained earnings	3	
Long-term debt	6	(11)
Market value added		5

Market valued added is, in essence, a very simple idea. The cash value of the investment is compared with the cash invested. If the cash value of the investment is more than the cash invested, there has been an increase in shareholder value. If the cash value of the investment is less than the cash invested, there has been a decrease in shareholder value. There are, however, complications in measuring the figure for cash invested, which arises because of the conservative bias in accounting measurement. Thus, the adjustments to the balance sheet that are necessary for the proper calculation of EVA are also required when measuring MVA.

The measurement of the cash value of capital invested is straightforward. The market value of each share is simply multiplied by the number of shares in issue in order to derive the total market value of the shares. If shares are not listed on a stock exchange, it is not really possible to measure MVA, unless perhaps a bid for the business has been received from a possible buyer.

In Example 13.5, it was assumed that the market value and book value of the long-term debt are the same. This is a common assumption used in practice, and where this assumption is made, the calculation of MVA reduces to the difference between the market value of shares and the shareholders' equity (common shares plus retained earnings). Thus, in the example, MVA is simply the difference between $10 million and $5 million (i.e., $2 million + $3 million) = $5 million.

In the example, we calculated MVA over the whole life of the business. The problem with doing this, in the case of an established business, is that it would not be clear when the value was actually created. The pattern of value creation over time may be useful in the assessment of past and likely future performance. It is perfectly feasible, however, to measure the change in MVA over any period by comparing the opening and closing positions for that period.

The Link Between MVA and EVA

There is a strong relationship between MVA and EVA. We saw earlier that the value of a business is equal to the present value of future expected EVA plus the capital invested. Thus:

$$\text{Business value} = \text{Capital invested} + \text{PV of future EVA}$$

This equation could be rearranged as in Equation 13.4 so that:

$$\text{PV of future EVA} = \text{Business value} - \text{Capital invested} \qquad 13.4$$

We have also seen that market value added is the difference between the value of the business and the capital invested. Thus, as in Equation 13.5:

$$\text{MVA} = \text{Business value} - \text{Capital invested} \qquad 13.5$$

By comparing Equation 13.4 and Equation 13.5 we can see that as in Equation 13.6:

$$\text{PV of future EVA} = \text{MVA} \qquad 13.6$$

The relationship described holds in practice as well as in theory. The correlation between MVA and EVA is much stronger than the correlation between MVA and other measures of performance such as earnings per share, return on equity, or cash flows.

Given that MVA reflects the expected future EVA of a business, it follows that an investor using this measure will be able to see whether a business generates returns above the cost of capital invested. If a business only manages to provide returns in line with the cost of capital, the EVA will be zero and so there will be no MVA. Thus, MVA can be used to impose a capital discipline on managers in the same way that EVA does.

Limitations of MVA

MVA has a number of limitations as a tool for investors. To begin with, it has a fairly narrow scope. As mentioned earlier, MVA relies on market share prices and so it can only really be calculated for those businesses that are listed on a stock exchange. Similarly, MVA can only be used to assess the business as a whole as there are no separate market share prices available for strategic business units or divisions of a company.

The interpretation of MVA can also be a problem. It is a measure of the absolute change occurring over time and so its significance is difficult to assess when deciding among competing investment opportunities involving businesses of different sizes or trading over different periods. Consider the following financial information relating to three separate businesses:

Business	Total Market Value (a) ($ millions)	Total Capital Invested (b) ($ millions)	Market Value Added (a) – (b) ($ millions)	Number of Years in Business
Alpha	250	120	130	18
Beta	480	350	130	16
Gamma	800	670	130	15

The table shows that each business has an identical MVA, but does this mean that each business has performed equally well? We can see that they operate with different amounts of capital invested and have operated over different periods.

The problems identified are not insurmountable but they reveal the difficulties of relying on an absolute measure when making investment decisions , as illustrated in Activity 13.9.

ACTIVITY 13.9

How could the problems of interpretation mentioned above be overcome?

Solution

The problem of the different time periods is probably best dealt with by comparing the businesses over the same time period. The problem of scale is probably best dealt with by comparing the MVA for each business with the capital invested in the business. (The ratio of MVA to capital provides a relative measure of wealth creation for investors.)

Research shows that the most successful businesses at generating MVA are also the largest. Because MVA is an absolute measure of performance, large businesses have a greater potential to generate MVA. However, they also have a greater potential to destroy MVA.

SELF-ASSESSMENT QUESTION   13.2

Canadian Spirits Ltd. has the following balance sheet at the end of 2010, its third year in business:

Canadian Spirits Ltd.
Balance Sheet
as at the end of 2010
(in $ millions)

Current assets		
Cash	12.0	
Accounts receivable	53.0	
Inventory	39.0	
Total current assets		104.0
Property, plant, and equipment		
Land	60.0	
Computer equipment, net	90.0	
Vehicles, net	22.0	
Total property, plant, and equipment		172.0
Total assets		276.0

▶

Current liabilities		
Accounts payable		45.0
Long-term liabilities		
Loan		90.0
Total liabilities		135.0
Shareholders' equity		
Common shares	60.0	
Retained earnings	81.0	
Total shareholders' equity		141.0
Total liabilities and shareholders' equity		276.0

An analysis of the underlying records reveals the following:

1. R&D costs relating to the development of a new product in 2010 had been written off at a cost of $10 million. However, the benefits are expected to last for 10 years.
2. Land has a current value of $200 million.
3. The current market value of a common share is $8.50.
4. The book value of the loan reflects its current market value.
5. There are 60 million common shares outstanding.

Required:

Calculate the MVA for the business over its first three years.

Total Shareholder Return (TSR)

Total shareholder return (TSR) has been used for many years by investors as a means of assessing value created and is often used as a basis for management reward systems. The total return from a share is made up of two elements: the increase (or decrease) in share value over a period plus any dividends paid during the period as shown in Equation 13.7.

$$\text{Total shareholder return} = \frac{D_1 + (P_1 - P_0)}{P_0} \times 100\% \qquad \text{13.7}$$

To illustrate how total shareholder return is calculated, let us assume that a business commenced operations by issuing shares for $50 each ($P_0$), and by the end of the first year the shares had increased in value to $55 ($P_1$). Furthermore, the business paid a dividend of $6 ($D_1$) per share during the period. We can calculate the total shareholder return as follows:

$$\text{Total shareholder return} = \frac{D_1 + (P_1 - P_0)}{P_0} \times 100\%$$

$$= \frac{\$6 + (55 - 50)}{\$50} \times 100\%$$

$$= 22\%$$

The figure calculated has little information value when taken alone. It can only really be used to assess performance when compared with some benchmark. Activity 13.10 considers the most suitable benchmark.

ACTIVITY 13.10

What benchmark would be most suitable?

Solution

Perhaps the best benchmark to use would be the returns made by similar businesses operating in the same industry over the same period of time. At the lowest risk level for returns, another benchmark is the risk-free interest rate on long-term Government of Canada bonds.

A benchmark using the returns of similar businesses is usually suitable because it will compare the returns generated by the business with those generated from other investment opportunities that have the same level of risk. We have seen in earlier chapters that the level of return from an investment should always be related to the level of risk that has to be taken.

TSR in Practice

REAL WORLD 13.5 provides an example of a business that sets a target total shareholder return in relation to other broadly similar businesses.

REAL WORLD 13.5

TSR at Royal Bank of Canada (RBC)

The goal at RBC is to achieve a total shareholder return that is in the top quartile of TSRs compared to the Canadian banking and life insurance group and 13 other U.S. financial institutions. RBC's three-years TSR was 8% versus (9%) for its peer group. Its five-year TSR was 12% versus (2%). The negative TSRs for the peer group are a testament to the severity of the 2008–2009 recession, with its plummeting share prices and dividend cuts. Dividends increased at an average annual compound rate of 19% over the 2006–2008 period.

Source: RBC 2008 Annual Report.

Many large businesses now publish total shareholder returns in their annual reports. REAL WORLD 13.6 provides data for the Canadian banking industry.

2008 Was a Very Bad Year for TSRs

REAL WORLD 13.6

As bad as the economy was in 2008, only CIBC fared worse than the most popular benchmarks for total shareholder return. On a relative basis, the strongest of Canada's banks put forth a stellar performance in 2008. Even so, cash was a better investment than owning bank shares in 2008.

FIGURE 13.7   2008 TSRs for the Canadian Banking Industry

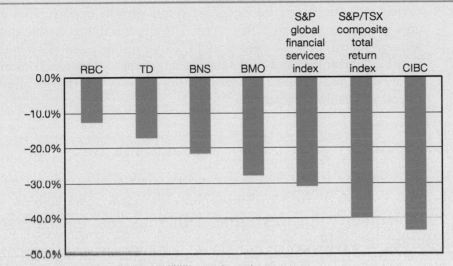

Source: Graph constructed from data in the banks' 2008 annual reports.

TSR and Managers' Rewards

When total shareholder return is to be used as a basis for management reward, the issue of risk is very important. Higher returns can be achieved by taking on higher risk projects. Managers should not be given rewards for increasing returns through this means.

Figure 13.8 shows the main value measures that we have discussed in this chapter.

FIGURE 13.8   The Main Value Measures

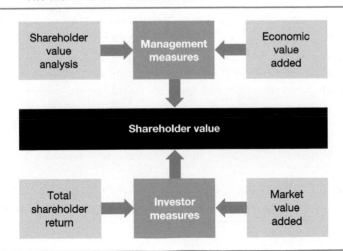

CRITICISMS OF THE SHAREHOLDER VALUE APPROACH

In recent years, there has been growing criticism of the shareholder value approach. It is claimed that the pursuit of shareholder value has resulted in conflicts between shareholders and other stakeholders and has created a crisis for the world of business. However, there is no reason, in theory, why such problems should occur. We have seen that shareholder value reflects a concern for long-term value creation, and to achieve this, the interests of other stakeholders cannot be trampled over. Nevertheless, it is easy to see how, in practice, the notion of shareholder value may be corrupted.

The quest for shareholder value implies a concern for improving the efficiency of current operations and for exploiting future growth opportunities. Driving future growth is by far the more difficult task. The future is unpredictable and risks abound. Managers must therefore tread carefully. They must be painstaking in their analysis of future opportunities and in developing appropriate strategies. However, this is not always done. REAL WORLD 13.7 shows the size of losses incurred by investors in 2008 at several well-known companies.

REAL WORLD 13.7

Shareholder Value Destroyed: $ Billions Lost on the Stock Market in 2008

The year 2008 produced the worst stock market since the Great Depression of the 1930s. The graph below shows the size of shareholder value wiped out as share prices plummeted. The total decline in market capitalization from peak to trough is calculated as: (high price for the year − low price for the year) × average number of shares outstanding during the year. Share prices have since recovered somewhat.

FIGURE 13.9   2008 Peak to Trough Lost Market Cap

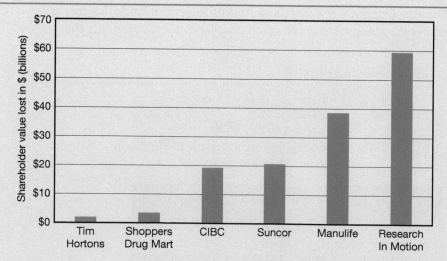

Source: Graph constructed from data in the companies' 2008 annual reports and at Yahoo! Canada Finance at: http://ca.finance. yahoo.com/q/hp?s=RIM.TO&a=11&b=15&c=1997&d=9&e=3&f=2009&g=d&z=66&y=396, accessed October 3, 2009.

Given the problems of exploiting future growth opportunities, managers may prefer to focus on improving efficiency. This is usually achieved by cutting costs through working assets harder, laying staff off, and putting pressure on suppliers to lower prices. If, however, these cost reduction measures are taken too far, the result will be a business that is unable to take advantage of future growth opportunities and that has its major stakeholder groups locked in conflict.

To be successful, the shareholder value approach must strike the right balance between a concern for efficiency and a concern for future growth. In order to achieve this balance, the way in which managers are assessed and rewarded must reflect the importance of both.

MEASURING THE VALUE OF FUTURE GROWTH

If managers are to be assessed and rewarded—at least in part—on the basis of developing future growth potential, a suitable measure of this potential is required. The EVA approach can provide such a measure.

We saw earlier that the value of a business can be described as:

$$\text{Business value} = \text{Capital invested} + \text{PV of future EVA}$$

If a business has no growth potential and EVA remains constant, we can use the formula for a perpetuity, so that the present value of future EVA is as in Equation 13.8:

$$\text{PV of future EVA} = \frac{\text{EVA}}{r} \qquad \text{13.8}$$

where: r = required returns from investors (i.e., the weighted average cost of capital)

Thus, the value of a business with no growth potential is as in Equation 13.9:

$$\text{Business value} = \text{Capital invested} + \frac{\text{EVA}}{r} \qquad \text{13.9}$$

Where the business has growth potential (as measured by growth in EVA), business value (as measured by the market value of shares and long-term debt) will be greater than this. The value placed on future growth potential by investors is, therefore, as in Equation 13.10:

$$\text{Future growth value (or FGV)} = \text{Business value} - \left(\text{Capital invested} + \frac{\text{EVA}}{r} \right) \qquad \text{13.10}$$

This is called the **future growth value (FGV)**, and by using this measure periodically we can see whether managers are creating or destroying future value.

The percentage contribution to the value of the business arising from investor expectations concerning future growth in EVA is as in Equation 13.11:

$$\text{Percentage contribution to business value} = \left(\frac{\text{FGV}}{\text{Business value}} \right) \times 100\% \qquad \text{13.11}$$

This measure can be used to see whether managers are striking the right balance between efficiency and future growth. Future growth is explored in Activity 13.11.

ACTIVITY 13.11

The Medicine Hat Shoe Company has 5 million shares outstanding with a market value of $8.40 per share. The company has $14.2 million capital invested and for the most recent year, EVA was $1.8 million. The required return from investors is 10% a year.

What is the percentage contribution to the market value of the business arising from future growth?

Solution

Assuming no growth,

$$\text{PV of future EVA} = \frac{\text{EVA}}{r}$$

$$= \frac{\$1.8 \text{ million}}{0.10}$$

$$= \$18.0 \text{ million}$$

$$\text{Future growth value (FGV)} = \text{Business value} - \left(\text{Capital invested} + \frac{\text{EVA}}{r}\right)$$

$$= (5 \text{ million} \times \$8.40) - (\$14.2 \text{ million} + \$18.0 \text{ million})$$

$$= \$9.8 \text{ million}$$

$$\text{Percentage contribution to business value} = \left(\frac{\text{FGV}}{\text{Business value}}\right) \times 100\%$$

$$= \frac{\$9.8 \text{ million}}{5 \text{ million} \times \$8.40} \times 100\%$$

$$= 23.3\%$$

IMPLEMENTING THE SHAREHOLDER VALUE APPROACH

We have seen that shareholder value may not always be implemented properly within a business. REAL WORLD 13.8 describes four different levels of implementation of shareholder value that may be found in practice, using an analogy of mobility to describe each level.

REAL WORLD 13.8

Walking the Talk

The extent to which businesses implement a fully developed shareholder value approach can be described in terms of four distinct levels.

Level 1: Sitting

At the lowest level, shareholder value is embraced only as a slogan. Shareholder value appears in the company's mission statement, its investor communications, or its managerial lexicon. Existing cost-cutting programs may be relabelled as shareholder value initiatives. Nothing concrete is done to promote actual value gain.

Level 2: Hopping

Shareholder value is adopted with an exclusive emphasis on efficiency. The program is formally communicated within the firm, organizational structures such as shareholder value committees and champions are created, and shareholder

▶

value metrics such as EVA are introduced and used to measure the performance of divisions, departments, and projects. The rewards of at least the senior management are tied in some way to the achievement of shareholder value targets.

Level 3: Shuffling

The two legs of shareholder value are recognized in principle by the statement of a growth vision or mission alongside the focus on efficiency. However, the use of the growth strategy is limited to communicating to investors that the firm is adopting fashionable strategies—"we will focus on our core business and grow it organically and through overseas acquisitions." It is not lived inside the company—if a value-creating opportunity is spotted that is at odds with the stated strategy, it will nevertheless be pursued.

Managers are judged by today's value created and not by how they prepare the stage for tomorrow's growth. The growth vision is not deeply rooted and is likely to be abandoned under external pressure, such as investor desire to see a move into internet-related business.

Level 4: Marching

Both legs of shareholder value are adopted and implemented. A clear growth strategy is developed and used as the template for future investments. The growth strategy is communicated and sold to investors. The strategy is followed, even under pressure. Metrics and rewards are instituted around both the attainment of efficiency improvements and the attainment of growth strategy goals. The growth strategy is owned and lived throughout the organization.

Source: "Companies Must Achieve the Right Balance for a Successful Strategy," *Financial News*, February 22, 2004.

SUMMARY

The Quest for Shareholder Value

- *Shareholder value* means putting shareholders' interests at the heart of management decisions.
- To create shareholder value, the objectives of the business must reflect a concern for shareholder value, there must be appropriate methods of measurement, the business must be managed to create shareholder value, and there must be periodic assessment of whether shareholder value has been achieved.

The Need for New Forms of Measurement

- Conventional forms of accounting measurement are inadequate—they focus on the short term, ignore risk, fail to take proper account of the cost of capital invested, and are influenced by accounting methods employed.

Extending NPV Analysis: Shareholder Value Analysis and Economic Value Added

- Two main approaches are used to measure shareholder value using internal (management) measures: shareholder value analysis (SVA) and economic value added (EVA).

- SVA is based on the concept of net present value analysis.
- It identifies key value drivers for generating shareholder value.
- EVA provides a means of measuring whether the returns generated by the business exceed the required returns from investors.
- EVA = EBIT after taxes $- (R \times C)$
- EVA relies on conventional financial statements, which are adjusted because of their limitations.
- In theory, EVA and SVA should produce the same decisions and results.

Market Value Added (MVA) and Total Shareholder Return (TSR)

- Two main approaches to measuring shareholder value using external (investor) measures are market value added (MVA) and total shareholder return (TSR).
- MVA measures the difference between the market value of the business and the investment made in the business.
- MVA = Present value of future EVA

- MVA is really only suitable for listed businesses.
- Interpreting MVA can be a problem.
- TSR measures the total return to shareholders over a period.
- TSR is made up of the increase (decrease) in share value plus the dividends paid.
- TSR can be sensitive to the time period chosen.

Criticisms of the Shareholder Value Approach

- There are two elements of shareholder value: efficiency of current operations and future growth.

- Undue emphasis on efficiency can undermine the prospects for future growth.

Measuring the Value of Future Growth

- One approach is to use the EVA methodology.
- Future growth value

$$= \text{Business value} - \left(\text{Capital invested} + \frac{\text{EVA}}{r} \right)$$

- To check whether managers strike the right balance between efficiency and future growth, the future growth potential can be compared with the market value of the business.

KEY TERMS

Shareholder value	Free cash flows	Market value added (MVA)
Shareholder value analysis (SVA)	Value drivers	Total shareholder return (TSR)
	Economic value added (EVA)	Future growth value (FGV)

LIST OF EQUATIONS

13.1 Terminal value $= \dfrac{C_1}{r}$

13.2 Economic value added (or EVA) = EBIT less taxes $- (R \times C)$

13.3 Market value added (or MVA) = Total market value $-$ Total capital invested

13.4 PV of future EVA = Business value $-$ Capital invested

13.5 MVA = Business value $-$ Capital invested

13.6 PV of future EVA = MVA

13.7 Total shareholder return $= \dfrac{D_1 + (P_1 - P_0)}{P_0} \times 100\%$

13.8 PV of future EVA $= \dfrac{\text{EVA}}{r}$, for a business with no growth potential

13.9 Business value $=$ Capital invested $+ \dfrac{\text{EVA}}{r}$, for a business with no growth potential

13.10 Future growth value (or FGV) = Business value $- \left(\text{Capital invested} + \dfrac{\text{EVA}}{r} \right)$

13.11 Percentage contribution to business value $= \left(\dfrac{\text{FGV}}{\text{Business value}} \right) \times 100\%$

REVIEW QUESTIONS

Answers to the Review Questions can be found on the Companion Website that accompanies this text at www.pearsoned.ca/atrill.

13.1 The shareholder value approach to managing businesses is different from the stakeholder approach to managing businesses. In the latter case, the different stakeholders of the business (employees, customers, and suppliers) are considered of equal importance and so the interests of shareholders will not dominate.

Is it possible for these two approaches to managing businesses to coexist in harmony within a particular economy?

13.2 Why is MVA not really suitable as a tool for internal management purposes?

13.3 Should managers interpret changes in the total market value of the shares (i.e., share price multiplied by the number of shares outstanding) over time as an indicator of shareholder value created (or lost)?

13.4 It has been argued that many businesses are overcapitalized. If this is true, what may be the reasons for businesses having too much capital, and how can EVA help avoid this problem?

13.5 Comment on these facts taken from the most recent annual report of Island Conglomerates. "Island posted a 21% total shareholder return last year. This was 50% higher than the average for the past five years. Halfway through last year, Island, which is mainly a communications company, acquired 80% ownership of Diamond Gold Inc., a junior resource company. The CEO of Island was awarded a total compensation increase of 120% last year."

PROBLEMS AND CASES

13.1 You are analyzing seven competitors.

	1 (millions)	2 (millions)	3 (millions)	4 (millions)	5 (millions)	6 (millions)	7 (millions)
NPV of the firm	$125	$224	$789	$56	$418	$150	$390
Bank loans payable	$30	$76	$45	$34	$239	$37	$110
Fair value of bonds payable	$60	$10	$23	$30	$79	$43	$50
Number of shares outstanding	100	250	45	83	10	5	49

Required:
(a) Calculate the shareholder value for each firm.
(b) Calculate the fair value per share for each firm.

13.2 You are analyzing three competitors, shown below.

	1 ($000)	2 ($000)	3 ($000)
Net income	153,000	95,000	291,000
Depreciation expense	15,000	17,000	23,000
Increase (decrease) in working capital	23,000	(15,000)	(29,000)
Capital expenditures	30,000	12,000	30,000

Required:
Calculate the free cash flows for the three firms.

13.3 Wood Industries has the following data for 2010:

Sales	$25,000,000
Depreciation expense	$4,000,000
Reduction in working capital in 2010	$1,200,000
New capital assets acquired	$500,000
Cost of capital assets acquired as replacements	$2,300,000
Gross profit margin	40%
Income tax rate	25%

Required:

Calculate the free cash flows for 2010 for Wood Industries.

13.4 Sandy River Oil Sands Ltd. (SROS) has a terminal value of $200 million. SROS used a cost of capital of 20%.

Required:

  (a) Calculate the present value of the terminal value of SROS with a planning horizon of:
      1. 8 years
      2. 15 years
      3. 20 years.
  (b) Define present value of the terminal value.
  (c) What do you conclude about the terminal value of the business using a planning horizon of 20 years?

13.5 It is now the end of 2009 and Astrid Sportswear Inc. (ASI) is considering acquiring Halloween Attire Ltd. (HAL). ASI uses a 12% discount rate. ASI has gathered the following data on HAL.

	2010 ($ millions)	2011 ($ millions)	2012 ($ millions)	2013 ($ millions)	2014 ($ millions)	2015 ($ millions)	2016 ($ millions)	After 2016 ($ millions)
EBIT	1,265	1,388	1,499	1,530	1,550	1,560	1,568	1,570
Interest expense	100	100	100	100	100	100	100	100
Depreciation expense	200	250	290	333	301	200	140	75
Tax rate	25%	25%	30%	30%	30%	35%	35%	35%
Capital expenditures	150	175	190	210	245	265	201	125
Working capital increases/ (decreases)	25	45	76	90	150	(50)	(100)	(200)

Required:

Calculate HAL's total business value at the end of 2009.

13.6 Refer to the data in Problem and Case 13.5. HAL has 100 million shares outstanding and $1 billion in debt.

Required:

What is the minimum per share offer for HAL shares that HAL's board of directors would consider accepting?

13.7 You have gathered the following information on your competitors.

	1 ($ millions)	2 ($ millions)	3 ($ millions)	4 ($ millions)
EVA	?	75	425	100
EBIT	100	300	?	400
Tax expense	20	80	125	250
R	15%	20%	10%	?
C	200	?	150	900

Required:

Calculate the missing information.

13.8   You have gathered data from the annual reports of the following companies:

	Moose Ltd.	Gateau Inc.	Ski Corp.
Total assets	$10,000,000	$70,000,000	$120,000,000
Current liabilities	$1,100,000	$5,000,000	$10,000,000
EBIT	$1,400,000	$7,200,000	$22,400,000
Advertising expense	$500,000	$1,000,000	$3,000,000
Restructuring costs	$2,000,000	$400,000	$700,000
Tax expense (paid)	$200,000	$1,000,000	$5,000,000
Advertising benefit period	1 year	2 years	3 years
Restructuring costs benefit period	5 years	10 years	2 years
Investors' required return	15%	22%	17%

Required:

(a) Calculate EVA for each company.

(b) In which company would you buy shares? Why?

13.9   Prairie WindPower Ltd. is a venture that will operate for five years, at which time it will be wound up. $50 million in shares have been sold to the public, and $20 million in five-year bonds have been purchased by the Manitoba Heritage Fund. Capital assets totalling $70 million are being depreciated on a straight-line basis over five years. Capital assets will not be replaced. Working capital will increase by $1 million by the end of the first year, after which it will not change until the venture is wound up. The operating profit before taxes is expected to be $10 million in the first two years and $20 million in the last three years. There is no tax for the first three years and then a 10% tax on operating profit is imposed and paid in the fourth and fifth years. Investors require a return of 8%

Required:
Use the SVA approach to calculate shareholder value.

13.10   Refer to the same data as Problem and Case 13.9.

Required:
Use the EVA approach to calculate shareholder value.

13.11   The Bluenose Ship Company executed an initial public offering five years ago by selling 10 million shares at $10 each after brokerage costs. At the same time, $50 million of 10% bonds maturing in 20 years were issued at par ($100). The shares now sell at $25 and the bonds trade at $102. Retained earnings stand at $44,500,000.

Required:
Calculate the market value added by Bluenose since its initial public offering (IPO) five years ago.

13.12   Cole Harbour Silver Ltd. (CHS) was formed by a hockey player to sell engraved silver teacups. CHS is capitalized by $4 million in shares and $1 million in bonds. It will use all that money to buy assets with a five-year economic life and use straight-line depreciation. EBIT is expected to be $500,000 per year. Taxes are $100,000 per year. After five years the firm will be wound up and the capital assets will have no residual value. Investors require a 16% return on investment.

Required:

(a) Use the shareholder value analysis (SVA) approach to calculate shareholder value.

(b) Use the economic value added (EVA) approach to calculate shareholder value.

(c) How do the final results of the two approaches compare?

13.13 You are using market value added to examine your closest competitors.

	1	2	3	4
Number of shares outstanding	80,000,000	6,500,000	4,000,000	15,000,000
Current share price	$7.42	$25.32	?	$40.00
Market value of long-term debt	$26,543,987	$10,789,000	$4,000,000	?
Book value of long-term debt at date of issue	$30,000,000	$9,000,000	$3,500,000	$6,000,000
Retained earnings	$ 20,500,000	?	$12,000,000	$43,500,000
IPO share price	$5.00	$15.00	$23.00	$25.00
Market value added	?	$65,354,000	$17,000,000	$355,000,000

Required:

Calculate the missing data for each company.

13.14 Drinks Inc. has estimated the following free cash flows for its five-year planning period:

Year	Free Cash Flows ($ millions)
1	35.0
2	38.0
3	45.0
4	49.0
5	53.0

Required:

How might it be possible to check the accuracy of these figures? What internal and external sources of information might be used to see whether the figures are realistic?

13.15 Ahmed Trucking Ltd. was recently formed and issued 80 million shares at $0.50 each and obtained loans of $24 million. The business used the proceeds to purchase the remaining leases on some commercial properties that are rented out to small businesses. The leases will expire in four years' time and during that period the annual operating profits are expected to be $12 million each year. At the end of the four years, the business will be wound up and the leases will have no residual value.

The rate of return required by investors is 12%. Round present value factors to two decimals.

Required:

Calculate the expected shareholder value generated by the business over the four years, using:
(a) The SVA approach
(b) The EVA approach
Round present value factors to two decimals.

13.16 Valley Forms Ltd. is considering introducing a system of EVA and wants its managers to focus on the longer term rather than simply on the year-to-year EVA results. The business is seeking your advice as to how a management bonus system could be arranged so as to ensure that the longer term is taken into account. The business is also unclear as to how much of the managers' pay should be paid in the form of a bonus and when such bonuses should be paid. Finally, the business is unclear as to where the balance between individual performance and corporate performance should be struck within any bonus system.

The vice-president of finance has recently produced figures showing that if Valley Forms had used EVA over the past three years, the EVA results would have been as follows:

	($ millions)
2003	25
2004	(20)
2005	10

Required:

Describe your recommendations for a suitable bonus system for the divisional managers of the business.

13.17 You are a financial analyst employed at Clarington Quarry Works (CQW). CQW has a December 31 year-end. CQW's board of directors is considering a change to the company's executive compensation plan so that in the future it will be based on economic value added. Your manager, who reports to the vice-president of finance, has asked you to determine what the company's EVA was for its most recent fiscal year. You have gathered the following data.

	($ millions)
Common shares	1,289
WACC	15%
Retained earnings	734
Long-term debt	500
R&D costs expensed in past years but expected to benefit the future	14
Bad debt expense per income statement	10
Additional bad debt write-offs after year-end due to bankruptcy of a customer on January 2	3
R&D costs expensed this year but expected to have benefits in the future	56
Restructuring costs expensed two years ago but expected to have benefits for 10 years starting at the beginning of last year	80
Operating income	320

Required:

Calculate EVA for the most recent year for CQW.

13.18 Peterborough Outboard Motors (POM), a profitable maker of outboard motors for pleasure boats, would like to enter the snow blower market. POM's weighted average cost of capital is 7% and its accounting department notes depreciation expense will approximate capital cost allowances in the company's tax return. POM has gathered the following information concerning the snow blower project.

	Yr 1 $m	Yr 2 $m	Yr 3 $m	Yr 4 $m	After Yr 4 $m
Sales	92	84	140	180	180
Cost of goods sold	65	46	69	78	78
Operating expenses (including depreciation)	45	42	55	65	74
Depreciation expense	10	10	10	10	10
Replacement capital assets investments	7	3	11	12	15
Additional capital assets investments	5	4	11	5	5
Additional working capital investments	40	2	3	6	8
Income Tax Rate	20%	20%	20%	20%	20%

Required:

(a) Use the SVA approach to determine whether POM should proceed with producing the new snow blower.

(b) In addition to the financials, and possibly bad weather, why do you think POM is considering making and selling a snow blower?

CHAPTER 14

Mergers, Acquisitions, and the Valuation of Shares

LEARNING OUTCOMES

When you have completed this chapter, you should be able to:

1 Identify and discuss the main reasons for mergers and acquisitions.

2 Discuss the advantages and disadvantages of each of the main forms of purchase consideration used in an acquisition.

3 Identify the likely winners and losers from merger and acquisition activity.

4 Outline the tactics that may be used to defend against a hostile bid.

5 Identify and discuss the main methods of valuing the shares of a business.

INTRODUCTION

In this chapter, we consider various aspects of mergers and acquisitions (M&A). We begin by examining the reasons for mergers and acquisitions and then go on to consider the ways in which they can be financed. We also identify the likely winners and losers in a takeover and the defences available to a business seeking to fend off a hostile bid. In the final part of this chapter, we consider how the shares of a business can be valued. This is relevant to a range of financial decisions, including M&A activity.

MERGERS AND ACQUISITIONS

When two (or possibly more) businesses combine, it can take the form of either a *merger* or an *acquisition* (which is sometimes called a *takeover*). The term **merger** is normally used to describe a situation where the two businesses are of roughly equal size and there is agreement among the managers and owners of each business on the desirability of combining them. A merger is usually achieved by creating an entirely new business from the assets of the two existing businesses, with both shareholder groups receiving a substantial ownership stake in the new business. However, even in this situation, the recently changed accounting rules for reporting the consolidated financial results of mergers require that one company be identified as the purchaser and the other be identified as the acquired company. So the distinction between mergers and acquisitions has become less important.

The term **acquisition** or *takeover* is normally used to describe a situation where a larger business acquires control of a smaller business, which is then absorbed by the larger business. When a takeover occurs, the shareholders of the target business may cease to have any financial interest in the business and the resources of the business may come under entirely new ownership. For example, the shareholders of the target corporation could sell their shares to the buying company and then simply walk away from both companies. However, if they are paid with shares in the buying company, they become part owners in the combined company. Although the vast majority of takeovers are not contested, there are occasions when the management of the target business will fight to retain its separate identity.

Mergers and acquisitions can be classified according to the relationship between the businesses being merged; Activity 14.1 discusses examples of each type of merger.

■ A **horizontal merger** occurs when two businesses in the same industry, and at the same point in the production/distribution process, decide to combine.
■ A **vertical merger** occurs when two businesses in the same industry, but at different points in the same production/distribution process, decide to combine.
■ A **conglomerate merger** occurs when two businesses in unrelated industries decide to combine.

ACTIVITY 14.1

Can you think of an example of each type of merger for a tire retailer?

Solution

An example of a horizontal merger would be where a tire retailer merges with another tire retailer to form a larger retail business. An example of a vertical merger would be where a tire retailer merges with a manufacturer of tires. This would mean that the combined business operates at different points in the production/distribution chain. An example of a conglomerate merger would be where a tire retailer merges with an ice cream manufacturer.

Merger and Takeover Activity

Although mergers and acquisitions are a normal part of the business landscape, there are surges in M&A activity from time to time. REAL WORLD 14.1 shows recent M&A activity in Canada. Important economic factors are usually rising share prices and low interest rates, which make financing mergers and takeovers much easier.

REAL WORLD 14:1   Canadian Mergers

FIGURE 14.1   M&A Activity in Canada by Dollar Amount

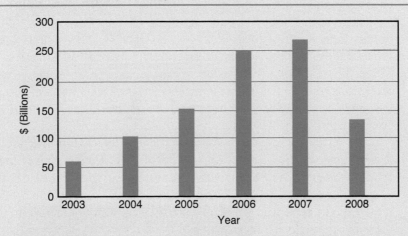

Figure 14.1 depicts merger and acquisition activity in Canada in recent years. The data shows that M&A activity rose dramatically from 2002 through 2007 and then fell off to pre-2005 levels in the wake of the severe recession that started in 2008. After Lehman Brothers failed, credit tightened almost overnight. Banks stopped almost all lending, even to other banks, so there was less money available to help fund merger activity.

Source: graph constructed from data at: www.2ontario.com/welcome/bcfs_604.asp, accessed April 18, 2007 and http://bx.businessweek.com/corporate-finance/view?url=http%3A%2F%2Fc.moreover.com%2Fclick%2Fhere.pl%3Fr1768144872%26f%3D9791, accessed October 8, 2009.

L.O. 1

THE RATIONALE FOR MERGERS AND ACQUISITIONS

In economic terms, a merger will be worthwhile only if combining the two businesses will lead to gains that would not arise if the two businesses had stayed apart. We saw in the previous chapter that the value of a business can be defined in terms of the *present value of its future cash flows*. Thus, if a merger is to make economic sense, the present value of the combined business should be equal to the present value of future cash flows of the bidding and target businesses *plus* a gain from the merger. The term **synergy** is often used for the extra gain that companies hope exists upon merger. You can think of synergy as the combined company being bigger than the sum of the parts. Or, 2 + 2 = 5. Figure 14.2 illustrates this point.

Gaining Economies of Scale

A merger or acquisition will result in a larger business being created that may enable certain economies of scale to be achieved. For example, a larger business may be able to negotiate lower prices with suppliers in exchange for larger orders. A merger or acquisition may also provide the potential for savings, as some operating costs may be duplicated (for example, administrative costs, IT costs, marketing costs, or research and development costs). That is why layoffs frequently occur after a merger. These benefits are more likely to be gained from horizontal and vertical mergers than from conglomerate mergers; it is more difficult to achieve economies where the businesses are unrelated. The benefits outlined, however, must be weighed against the increased costs of organizing and controlling a larger business.

FIGURE 14.2   The Rationale for Mergers

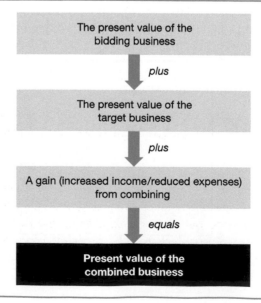

REAL WORLD 14.2 describes the anticipated cost savings arising from a merger between two well-known oil companies.

Eliminating Competition

REAL WORLD 14.2

Suncor–Petro-Canada merger Savings

Suncor Energy and Petro-Canada merged early in 2009. By September of the same year, Suncor had announced layoffs of 1,000 employees as a result of the merger. Most of the job losses were contract positions and in the human resources and IT areas of its head office. At the time of the merger, Suncor said it expected to save $300 million annually in operating expenses and $1 billion annually in capital expenditures.

Source: CBCNews.ca at www.cbc.ca/money/story/2009/09/03/calgary-suncor-jobs.html, accessed October 8, 2009.

Activity 14.2 considers whether obtaining economies of scale are possible without mergers.

ACTIVITY 14.2

Is it necessary for a business to merge with—or take over—another business in order to reap the benefits of scale? Can these benefits be obtained by other means?

Solution

A business may be able to obtain lower prices from suppliers, or reduced research and development costs, by joining a consortium of businesses or by entering into joint ventures with other businesses. This form of cooperation can result in benefits of scale and yet avoid the costs of a merger. However, there will be costs in negotiating a detailed joint venture agreement.

A business may combine with or take over another business in order to eliminate competition and to increase the market share of its goods. This, in turn, can lead to increased profits. Activity 14.3 discusses this motive for mergers.

ACTIVITY 14.3

What type of merger will achieve the objective of eliminating competition? What are the potential problems with this kind of merger from the consumer's point of view?

Solution

A horizontal merger will normally increase market share. The potential problems of such mergers are that consumers will have less choice following the merger and that the market power of the merged business will lead to an increase in consumer prices. For these reasons, governments often try to ensure that the interests of the consumer are protected when mergers resulting in a significant market share are proposed. (This point is considered in more detail later in the chapter.)

Exploiting Underutilized Resources

The full potential of a business may not be achieved because of a weak management team. In such a situation, there is an opportunity to install a management team that could do better. This argument is linked to what is sometimes referred to as the market for corporate control. The term is used to describe the idea that mergers and takeovers are motivated by teams of managers that compete for the right to control business resources. The market for corporate control ensures that weak management teams will not survive and that, sooner or later, they will be succeeded by stronger management teams. The threat of takeover, however, may motivate managers to improve their performance. This suggests that M&A activity is good for the economy as it helps to ensure that resources are fully utilized and that shareholder wealth maximization remains the top priority.

REAL WORLD 14.3 summarizes some thoughts on savings concerning proposed bank mergers that occasionally make it onto the national agenda in Canada. The banks appear to think that their collective investment in the bricks and mortar of their branches is underutilized and that real savings could be achieved by merging.

REAL WORLD 14.3

Canadian Bank Merger Synergies and the "Too Big to Fail" Concept

The proposed mergers of the Royal Bank of Canada and the Bank of Montreal, and the Canadian Imperial Bank of Commerce and the Toronto Dominion Bank sparked considerable debate in political and policy circles in Canada. These mergers have been consistently denied by the government.

One very important result of bank mergers would be the consolidation of bank branches, which would downsize or eliminate redundant and underutilized branches. Total annual savings have been estimated to range from $3 billion to $9 billion for the above mergers along with other banking consolidations. Over a 10-year period, it is estimated the two mergers noted would amount to cumulative savings of $1,000 to $3,000 per person in Canada. It has been argued that automated teller machines (ATMs) are a direct substitute for traditional face-to-face banking in branches, so not as many full-service branches are needed. Internet banking is gaining ground as well. However, very large banks began to be looked at in a different light during the 2008–2009 recession. When Lehman Brothers, a giant U.S. investment bank, went bankrupt in September 2008, a ripple effect was felt throughout the world. Credit channels dried up virtually overnight. Many argued that Lehman was too big to fail and that the government should have bailed it out.

There are currently some who argue that systemically important banks should have special regulations restricting their activities. However, Canada disagrees, because designating some banks as too big to fail and subjecting them to special international regulations would give those banks too much of a competitive advantage. Investors would see this as an implicit government guarantee. These banks could obtain funds at a lower cost (lower cost of capital) because the "too big to fail" label would take some risk off the table.

Source: Globe and Mail at www.theglobeandmail.com/report-on-business/too-big-to-fail-status-seen-distorting-markets/article1313290/, accessed October 9, 2009, and Jason Clemens and Fazil Mihlar, "Bank Mergers: The Rational Consolidation of Banking in Canada," September 1, 1998. Copyright © 2007 The Fraser Institute.

Combining Complementary Resources

Two businesses may have complementary resources that, when combined, will allow higher profits to be made than if the businesses remain separate. By combining the two businesses, the relative strengths of each business will be brought together and this may lead to additional profits being generated. It may be possible, of course, for each business to overcome its particular deficiency and continue as a separate entity. Even so, it may still make sense to combine, as described in Activity 14.4.

ACTIVITY 14.4

Why might there still be an argument in favour of a merger, even though a business could overcome any deficiency on its own?

Solution

Combining the resources of two businesses may lead to a quicker exploitation of the strengths of each business than if the businesses remained separate.

Using Surplus Funds

A business may operate within an industry that offers few investment opportunities. In such a situation, management may find that it has surplus cash that is not earning a reasonable return. The solution to this problem may be to invest in a new industry where there is no shortage of profitable investment opportunities. By acquiring an existing business within the new industry, a business can easily access necessary specialist managerial and technical know-how.

The M&A motives just considered are consistent with the objective of enhancing the wealth of shareholders. However, other motives, which are more difficult to justify, may provide the driving force for business combinations. Activity 14.5 considers the argument against the use of surplus funds for M&A.

ACTIVITY 14.5

Could management deal with the problem of surplus funds in some other way? Why might this other way not be acceptable to shareholders and managers?

Solution

The surplus funds could be distributed to shareholders through a special dividend or a share repurchase arrangement. However, shareholders might not like this idea because a tax liability might arise from the distribution. Managers might not like this idea as it would result in reduced resources for them to manage. (It is also worth mentioning that lenders might not like the idea of funds being returned to shareholders, because this increases the lenders' exposure to risk.)

Diversifying

A business may invest in another business that operates in a different industry in order to reduce risk. You may recall the discussion in Chapter 7 of the benefits of diversification in dealing with the problem of risk. At first sight, such a policy may seem appealing. However, it must be asked whether diversification by *management* will provide any benefits to shareholders that the *shareholders themselves* cannot provide more cheaply. It is often easier and cheaper for a shareholder to deal with the problem of risk by holding a diversified portfolio of shares than for the business to acquire another company. It is quite likely that the latter approach will be expensive, as a premium will usually have to be paid to acquire the shares, and external investment advisers and consultants may have to be hired at substantial cost.

REAL WORLD 14.4 summarizes the diversification strategies employed by a Canadian conglomerate that invests in many businesses, and Activity 14.6 considers who might benefit from diversification.

REAL WORLD 14.4

Diversification Strategies at Onex

Onex Corporation describes itself as a diversified holding company with autonomous subsidiaries in several industries. Onex deliberately diversifies by industry and by geography in order to reduce the risk inherent in business cycles. It has 4% of its assets in electronics (Celestica), 5% in cinema (Cineplex Galaxy), 24% in health care, 9% in aerospace, and 7% in commercial vehicles (Allison Transmission).

Source: Onex Corporation 2008 Management Discussion and Analysis and Financial Statements.

ACTIVITY 14.6

Who within a company might benefit from diversification?

Solution

Diversification may well benefit the managers of the bidding business. Managers cannot diversify their investment of time and effort in the business easily. By overseeing a more diversified business, managers reduce their risks of unemployment and lost income.

There may be circumstances, however, where shareholders are in a similar position to managers. For example, owner–managers may find it difficult to diversify their time and wealth because they are committed to the business. In these particular circumstances, there is a stronger case for diversifying the business.

Fulfilling Managers' Interests and Goals

A merger or acquisition may be undertaken to fulfill the personal goals or interests of managers. They may acquire another business simply to reduce the risks that they face or to increase the amount of resources that they control. REAL WORLD 14.5 also points out that managers may enjoy the excitement of M&A activity.

REAL WORLD 14.5

Mergers Can Be Fun

Mergers and acquisitions can be very exciting and managers often enjoy the thrill of the chase. Warren Buffett, one of the world's most successful investors and chief executive officer of Berkshire Hathaway, has stated:

> Leaders, business or otherwise, seldom are deficient in animal spirits and often relish increased activity and challenge. At Berkshire, the corporate pulse never beats faster than when an acquisition is in prospect.

Source: Warren Buffett's letter to Berkshire Hathaway Inc. shareholders, 1981, retrieved from www.berkshirehathaway.com.

The personal goals and interests of managers may also explain why some proposed takeovers are fiercely contested by them.

Management Interests and the Agency Problem

Although shareholders have the final say concerning whether a business should be acquired, they will rely heavily on information supplied to them by the managers. If the managers are determined to pursue their own goals, shareholders may not receive all the information required in order to make the correct decision. This is linked to the agency problem that was first discussed in Chapter 1. As you may recall, there is a risk that managers, who are employed to act on behalf of shareholders, will operate in a way that is designed to maximize their own benefits.

A merger, however, can sometimes be the solution to the agency problem. Where managers are not acting in the interests of the shareholders and are busy pursuing their own interests and goals, the effect is likely to be a decline in business performance and share price. The market for corporate control, mentioned earlier, should ensure that the business is taken over by another whose managers are committed to serving the interests of shareholders.

FORMS OF PURCHASE CONSIDERATION

L.O. 2

When a business takes over another business, payment for the shares acquired may be made in different ways, as outlined in Activity 14.7.

ACTIVITY 14.7

What different methods of payment may be used?

Solution

The main methods of payment are:

- Cash
- Shares in the bidding business
- Long-term debt incurred by the bidding business
- A combination of the above.

Cash

Payment by cash means that the amount of the purchase consideration will be both certain and clearly understood by the target business's shareholders. This may improve the chances of a successful bid. It will also mean that shareholder control of the bidding business will not be diluted as no additional shares will be issued.

It may only be possible to raise the amount required for the acquisition by obtaining a loan or issuing shares or by selling off assets, which the bidding business's shareholders may not like. On occasion, it may be possible to spread the cash payments over a period of time.

The receipt of cash will allow the target business's shareholders to adjust their share portfolios without incurring transaction costs on disposal. However, transaction costs will be incurred when new shares or bonds are acquired to replace the shares sold. Moreover, the receipt of cash may result in a liability for capital gains tax (which arises on gains from the disposal of certain assets, including shares).

Shares

The issue of shares by the acquirer will avoid any strain on its cash position. However, some dilution of existing shareholder control will occur and there may also be a risk of dilution in earnings per share. (Dilution will occur if the additional earnings from the merger divided by the number of new shares issued are lower than the existing earnings per share.) However, a substantial fall in share price would reduce the value of the bid and could undermine the chances of acceptance. The cost of this form of financing must also be taken into account. We saw in Chapter 10 that the cost of capital for share capital is relatively expensive.

The target business's shareholders may find a share-for-share exchange attractive. As they currently hold shares, they may wish to continue with this form of investment rather than receive cash or other forms of security. A share-for-share exchange does not result in a liability for capital gains tax. (For tax purposes, no disposal is deemed to have occurred when this type of transaction takes place.) The target shareholders will also have a continuing ownership link with the original business, although it will now be part of a larger business. However, the precise value of the offer may be difficult to calculate, owing to movements in the share prices of the two businesses. In rare circumstances, the bidding company may have to issue more of its shares to the shareholders of the target company than are currently outstanding. In this situation, a **reverse takeover** has occurred because the shareholders of the target company are in control and hold more shares than the bidder's original shareholder group.

Long-Term Debt

Like the issue of shares, the issue of long-term debt is simply an exchange of paper and so it avoids any strain on the cash resources of the bidding business. It has certain advantages over shares, however, in that the issue of debt involves no dilution of shareholder control and the service costs will be lower. A disadvantage of a debt-for-share exchange is that it will increase the leverage of the bidding business and, therefore, the level of financial risk.

Debt may be acceptable to shareholders in the target business if they have doubts over the future performance of the combined business. Debt provides investors with both a fixed level of return and security for their investment. When a takeover bid is being made, convertible bonds may be offered as purchase consideration. Activity 14.8 discusses the attraction of convertible bonds.

ACTIVITY 14.8

What is the attraction of convertible bonds from the point of view of the target business's shareholders?

Solution

The issue of convertible bonds would give target business shareholders a useful hedge against uncertainty. This type of hybrid debt will provide relative security in the early years with an option to convert to common shares at a later date. Investors will, of course, only exercise this option if things go well for the combined business.

There may be various factors influencing the form of consideration used by bidding businesses. Market conditions may be a critical factor. Research evidence suggests that common shares are more likely to be used following a period of strong stock market performance. Recent high returns are seen as making shares more attractive to investors.

Businesses with good growth opportunities are more likely to use common shares when financing acquisitions. It seems that growth businesses prefer to use common shares because this form of financing is less constraining than the issue of debt or the payment of cash. Businesses with poor growth opportunities may not be able to offer shares in payment, however.

REAL WORLD 14.6 reveals the ways in which cross-border mergers involving Canadian companies have been financed in recent years.

Research suggests that businesses using common shares as a means of acquisition achieve significantly poorer returns following the acquisition than those using cash.[1] The reasons for this are not entirely clear. Perhaps the relatively poor performance of share-for-share deals indicates that the bidding businesses' shares were too highly valued to begin with.

When purchasing another business, the debts of that business may be taken over. This can, of course, be regarded as partial payment for the assets acquired.

REAL WORLD 14.6   Who Says You Can't Print Money?

A study by Statistics Canada revealed that the most popular means of financing cross-border mergers and acquisitions involving Canadian companies was to issue shares. In most years, 70–80% of the value of all deals was financed by share exchanges, as shown in Figure 14.3. In other words, companies paid for these acquisitions by issuing their own shares in exchange for the shares of the target corporation.

▶

---

[1] A. Gregory, "The Long-Run Performance of U.K. Acquirers: Motives Underlying the Method of Payment and Their Influence On Subsequent Performance," University of Exeter Discussion Paper, 1998.

FIGURE 14.3   Percentage of Financing Value Attributed to Shares

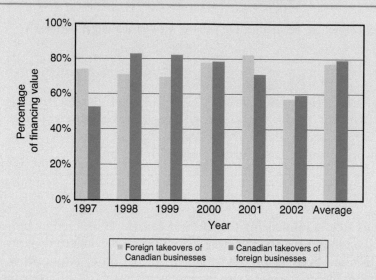

The data in the study do not include mergers of Canadian companies with other Canadian companies.

Source: Adapted from the Statisics Canada publication "Cross-Border Acquisitions: A Canadian Perspective," Analysis in Brief, catalogue 11-621, no. 13, Released May 25, 2004, www.statcan.ca/english/research/11-621-MIE/11-621-MIE2004013.htm.

REAL WORLD 14.7 shows how the acquisition of Fording Coal by Teck Resources was financed.

REAL WORLD 14.7   How Teck Paid for Fording Coal

Teck Resources is Canada's largest diversified mining company. Its head office is located in Vancouver. In 2008, Teck acquired Fording Coal. The acquisition was paid for as follows:

Cash paid to Fording unit holders	US$14.64 billion
Issuance of Class B shares	1.50 billion
Sale of Fording units	(2.88) billion
Cash for transaction costs (taxes, legal and brokerage fees)	0.38 billion
Total	US$13.64 billion

Source: Teck Resources 2008 Annual Report.

WHO BENEFITS FROM MERGERS AND ACQUISITIONS? L.O. 3

In this section, we shall try to identify the likely winners and losers in a merger. Everything depends on whether the bidding shareholders or the target shareholders are being discussed. Overall, mergers do create value, but it is unevenly allocated.[2]

Shareholders of the Target Business

Studies show that shareholders of the target business are usually the main beneficiaries. They are likely to receive substantial benefits from a takeover through a premium on the share price. Activity 14.9 discusses the reasons a bidding business might pay a premium.

ACTIVITY 14.9

Why might a bidding business be prepared to pay a premium above the market value for the shares of a business?

Solution

Various reasons have been put forward to explain why a business might pay more than the market value.

- The managers of the bidding business have access to information that is not available to the market and not, therefore, reflected in the share price.
- The managers of the bidding business may misjudge the value of the target business.
- The managers may feel that there will be significant gains arising from combining the two businesses that are worth paying for
- Where there is more than one bidder or where the takeover is being resisted, the managers of a bidding business may fail to act rationally and may raise the bid price above an economically justifiable level. This may be done in order to salvage the managers' pride, as they may feel humiliated by defeat.

Share prices in the target business will usually reflect the bid premium for as long as the bid is in progress. Where a takeover bid is unsuccessful and the bid is withdrawn, the share price of the target business will usually return to its pre-offer level. However, shares may fall below their pre-bid prices if investors believe that the managers have failed to exploit a profitable opportunity. The same fate may be experienced by shares in the bidding business.

REAL WORLD 14.8 outlines details of several merger and takeover bids and Activity 14.10 calculates their bid premiums.

---

[2] F. Weston, J. Siu, and B. Johnson, *Takeovers, Restructuring and Corporate Governance*, Third Edition, Prentice Hall, 2001, Chapter 8.

REAL WORLD 14.8

Takeover Bid Premiums

When a company wants to acquire another company, it must make a public announcement, through the stock exchange, of the takeover bid and the price it is willing to pay. Usually, the bid price constitutes a significant premium over the previously quoted stock price. Some recent Canadian examples are:

Bid Company	Target Company	Bid Price per Share ($)	Pre-Bid Price per Share ($)
		(a)	(b)
Xstrata	Falconbridge	52.50	47.21
Teck	Fording Coal	92.00	77.97
Suncor	Petro-Canada	37.95	29.65
Rio Tinto	Alcan	101.00	61.03
First Reserve Corp.	CHC Helicopter	32.68	21.88
Shell Canada	Duvernay Oil	82.59	58.44
Phillip Morris	Rothmans	30.00	26.09

Source: Obtained from various corporate websites, accessed October 12, 2009.

ACTIVITY 14.10

Calculate the percentage bid premium for each of the target businesses in Real World 14.8 and comment on the findings.

Solution

The bid premiums are calculated as follows:

Bid Company	Target Company	Bid Price per Share ($)	Pre-Bid Price per Share ($)	Percentage Bid Premium
		(a)	(b)	(a − b) ÷ (b)
Xstrata	Falconbridge	52.50	47.21	11%
Phillip Morris	Rothmans	30.00	26.09	15%
Teck	Fording Coal	92.00	77.97	18%
Suncor	Petro-Canada	37.95	29.65	28%
Shell Canada	Duvernay Oil	82.59	58.44	41%
First Reserve Corp.	CHC Helicopter	32.68	21.88	49%
Rio Tinto	Alcan	101.00	61.03	65%

We can see that takeover bid premiums ranged from 11% to 65%.

Shareholders of the Bidding Business

Shareholders of the bidding business usually have little to celebrate. Although early studies offered some evidence that a merger provided them with either a small increase or no increase in the value of their investment, more recent studies suggest that, over the long run, takeovers produce a significant decrease in shareholder value.[3] Some studies also suggest that conglomerate takeovers provide the worst performance, as indicated by both lower profitability and higher subsequent sell-offs of the acquired business.[4] Activity 14.11 explores why this might be the case.

ACTIVITY 14.11

Why might shares in the bidding business lose value as a result of a takeover of a target business? Try to think of two reasons why this may be so.

Solution

Various reasons have been suggested. These include:

- *Overpayment.*   The bidding business may pay too much to acquire the target business. We saw earlier that large premiums are often paid to acquire another business and this may result in a transfer of wealth from the bidding business's shareholders to the target business's shareholders.
- *Integration problems.*   Following a successful bid, it may be difficult to integrate the target business's operations. Problems relating to organizational structure, key personnel, management style, and management rivalries may work against successful integration. These problems are most likely to arise in horizontal mergers where an attempt is made to fuse the systems and operations of the two separate businesses into a seamless whole. There are likely to be fewer problems where a conglomerate merger is undertaken and where there is no real attempt to adopt common systems or operations.
- *Management neglect.*   There is a risk that, following the takeover, managers may relax and expect the combined business to operate smoothly. If the takeover has been bitterly contested, the temptation for management to ease back after the struggle may be very strong.
- *Hidden problems.*   Problems relating to the target business may be unearthed following the takeover. This is most likely to happen where a thorough investigation was not carried out prior to the takeover.

Managers

Any discussion concerning winners and losers in a merger should include the senior managers of the bidding business and the target business. They are important stakeholders in their respective businesses and play an important role in takeover negotiations. This does not always mean, however, that they will benefit from a merger, as discussed in Activity 14.12.

---

[3] A. Gregory, "An Examination of the Long Run Performance of UK Acquiring Firms," *Working Papers in Accounting and Finance,* The University of Wales, Aberystwyth, 1997.

[4] D. Ravenscroft, "Gains and Losses From Mergers: The Evidence," *Managerial Finance,* Vol. 17, No. 1, 1991.

ACTIVITY 14.12

Following a successful bid, what is the likelihood that the senior managers will benefit from the merger if they are in (a) the bidding business, and (b) the target business?

Solution

(a) The managers of the bidding business are usually beneficiaries as they will manage an enlarged business, which will, in turn, result in greater status, income, and security for them.

(b) The position of senior managers in the acquired business is less certain. In some cases, they may be retained and may even become directors of the enlarged business. In other cases, however, the managers may lose their jobs. A study by Julian Franks and Colin Mayer found that nearly 80% of senior executives in a target business either resign or lose their job within two years of a successful takeover.[5]

Where managers in the target business lose their job, compensation may be payable. **REAL WORLD 14.9** outlines recent executive compensation packages paid to retiring executives.

Recent Golden Parachutes

When the top executive of a company retires or loses his or her job due to a takeover, the company often has a way of taking care of these former bosses, as shown below.

Company	Executive	Lump-Sum Payment ($ million)	Year
Bombardier	Paul Tellier	5.84	2009
BCE	Michael Sabia	21.00	2008
Manulife	Dominic D'Allesandro	12.60	2009
Torstar	Robert Pritchard	9.58	2009
GM	Rick Wagoner	23.00	2009

Sources: CBC.ca www.cbc.ca/canada/story/2009/04/03/f-newsweek.html and www.cbc.ca/money/story/2005/05/02/ tellier-050502.html, accessed October 12, 2009.

Advisers

Mergers and acquisitions can be very rewarding for investment advisers and lawyers employed by each business during the bid period. It seems that, whatever the outcome of the bid, the advisers are winners. **REAL WORLD 14.10** describes some recent rewarding mergers for advisers.

---

[5] J. Franks and C. Mayer, "Corporate Ownership and Corporate Control: A Study of France, Germany and the UK," *Economic Policy*, No. 10, 1994.

High Acquisition Costs: Nice Work (If You Can Get It)

The M&A investment banking firms and M&A legal departments of large law firms are big winners when a merger or acquisition occurs. The following table sets out some recent acquisition costs for takeovers:

Year	Buyer	Target	Deal Size ($ billion)	Acquisition Costs ($ million)
2008	Teck	Fording Coal	13.64	375
2008	Rio Tinto	Alcan	38.65	132
2006	Vale (CVRD)	Inco	15.01	38

Sources: 2008 Annual Reports for Teck and Rio Tinto; 2006 Vale Annual Report.

WHY DO MERGERS OCCUR?

A substantial body of evidence now exists, covering different time periods and across several different countries, that demonstrates the dubious value of takeovers for bidding business shareholders. This evidence raises the question of why businesses persist in acquiring other businesses. The answer is still unclear. Perhaps it is because takeovers satisfy the interests of managers, or perhaps it reflects Samuel Johnson's view of remarriage—the triumph of hope over experience.

REAL WORLD 14.11 sets out the thoughts of Warren Buffett on why mergers occur.

A Modern Fairy Tale

"Many managements apparently were overexposed in impressionable childhood years to the story in which the imprisoned handsome prince is released from a toad's body by a kiss from a beautiful princess. Consequently, they are certain their managerial kiss will do wonders for the profitability of Company T[arget] . . . Investors can always buy toads at the going price for toads. If investors instead bankroll princesses who wish to pay double for the right to kiss the toad, those kisses had better pack some real dynamite. We've observed many kisses but very few miracles. Nevertheless, many managerial princesses remain serenely confident about the future potency of their kisses—even after their corporate backyards are knee-deep in unresponsive toads. . . .

"We have tried occasionally to buy toads at bargain prices with results that have been chronicled in past reports. Clearly our kisses fell flat. We have done well with a couple of princes—but they were princes when purchased. At least our kisses didn't turn them into toads. And, finally, we have occasionally been quite successful in purchasing fractional interests in easily identifiable princes at toadlike prices."

Source: Warren Buffett's letter to Berkshire Hathaway Inc. shareholders, 1981, www.berkshirehathaway.com.

Ingredients for Successful Mergers

Although many mergers and takeovers do not add value for shareholders, not all are unsuccessful. Why do some succeed? What are the magic ingredients of success?

Consistent success in acquiring businesses can only be achieved if the following three factors are present:

■ *Commitment.*   This involves maintaining a clear focus on creating long-term value and committing the required resources to the merger process. It also involves reviewing performance in managing a merger in order to learn lessons for next time.

■ *Competencies.*   To assess the risks and opportunities of a merger, a business must be able to assess its own strengths and weaknesses. It must be able to assess whether the areas of competence that it possesses will create value from the merger. Business platforms (such as IT and manufacturing processes) that support core competencies should be designed in such a way that they can easily and quickly be expanded to accommodate newly acquired businesses.

■ *Control.*   There must be strategic analysis of acquisitions to help determine when, where, and what to buy. There must also be a careful assessment of risks, including financial and operating risks. Systematic and rigorous planning must be applied throughout the whole transaction—starting with the bid and continuing through-out the subsequent integration process.[6]

These key elements are summarized in Figure 14.4.

FIGURE 14.4   **Key Factors Required to Ensure Long-Term Merger and Acquisition (M&A) Capability**

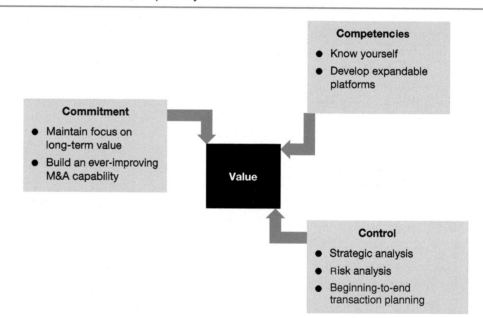

Source: PA Consulting Group, *Creating Long-Term Value Through Mergers and Acquisitions,* PA Knowledge Ltd., 2003.

L.O. 4   ## REJECTING A TAKEOVER BID

A takeover bid may, of course, be rejected. This need not imply that the bid is unwelcome and that shareholders are committed to maintaining the business as an independent entity. It may simply be a tactic to increase the bid premium and thereby increase shareholder wealth. If, however, it is not a negotiating tactic but a genuine attempt to remain independent, there is no certainty that rejection will be the end of the story. The spurned business may decide to press ahead with a hostile bid.

---

[6] PA Consulting Group, *Creating Long-Term Value Through Mergers and Acquisitions,* PA Knowledge Ltd., 2003.

Defensive Tactics

Various tactics may be used to fend off a hostile bid. Some of these must be put in place before receiving a hostile bid, whereas others can be deployed when the bid has been made. Defensive tactics include the following:

- *Converting to private company status.* By converting to private limited company status, a company makes its shares more difficult to acquire. This conversion must be undertaken before a bid has been received, however.

- *Promoting employee share option plans.* If employees are encouraged to acquire shares in the business, the proportion of shareholders that are likely to resist a bid is increased. This is a further example of a defence that must be in place before a bid is received.

- *Communicating with shareholders.* When an offer has been received, the managers (directors) of the target business will normally notify the shareholders. The case for rejection may be set out in this communication. It might be argued, for example, that it is not in the long-term interests of the shareholders to accept the offer, or that the price offered is too low. In support of such arguments, the managers may disclose previously confidential information such as profit forecasts, future dividend payments, asset valuations, and details of new contracts. This may have the effect of boosting the share price, thereby making the takeover more expensive.

- *Making the business unattractive.* The managers may take steps to make the business unattractive to a bidder. In the colourful language of mergers, this may involve taking a **poison pill** through the sale of prized assets of the business (the **crown jewels**). Other tactics include agreements to pay large sums to senior management for loss of their jobs resulting from a takeover (**golden parachutes**) and the purchase of certain assets that the bidding business does not want. Some businesses have tried to fend off unwelcome takeover bids by making large dividend distributions to shareholders. These distributions resulted in both a reduction in cash balances and an increase in the leverage of the businesses.

- *Using the Pac-man defence.* The **Pac-man defence** involves the target business launching a counterbid for the bidding business. However, this tactic is difficult to carry out where the target business is much smaller than the predator business. There was some speculation that Alcan might use the rare Pac-man defence by launching a counterbid for Alcoa in July 2007.

- *Looking for a white knight.* A target business may avoid a takeover by an unwelcome bidder by seeking out another business (a **white knight**) with which to combine. This tactic will normally be used only as a last resort, however, as it will result in the loss of independence. There is also a risk that the white knight will be less gallant after the merger than was hoped. Rio Tinto became Alcan's white knight in July 2007 by rescuing it from Alcoa's takeover bid.

- *Looking for a white squire.* This is a variation of the white knight tactic. In this case, a **white squire**—another business that is regarded as supportive—will purchase a block of shares in the target business that is big enough to prevent any real prospect of a takeover but not big enough to provide a controlling interest. The white squire will usually be given some incentive to ride to the rescue of the target business. This might take the form of a seat on the board or a discount on the price of the shares purchased.

    REAL WORLD 14.12 describes some recent tactics employed against or by Canadian firms.

REAL WORLD 14.12

Two Defensive Tactics—Against Agrium and by Inco

In 2009, Agrium Inc., based in Calgary, fought a long-drawn-out battle to acquire CF Industries, which itself was try-ing to acquire Terra Industries. CF is based in Delaware, and under Delaware law, CF can rebuff takeover attempts by just saying no. By September 2009, only 11.2 million shares out of 55 million shares had been tendered, so Agrium extended the deadline one more time to October 22, 2009. Agrium eventually gave up on this merger attempt.

In 2006, Inco tried to defend itself from being taken over by Teck by raising its offer to acquire Falconbridge. Eventually Inco was acquired by Vale (CVRD) for $19 billion. Xstrata ended up with Falconbridge.

Sources: Agrium website www.agrium.com/investor_information/news/5784_9390.jsp, accessed October 12, 2009, and www.cbc.ca/money/story/2006/09/25/inco-cvrd.html, accessed September 25, 2006.

Overcoming Resistance to a Bid

Managers of the bidding business may try to overcome resistance to the bid by communicating directly to shareholders of the target business information that coun-ters any claims made against the commercial logic of the bid or the offer price. They may also increase the offer price for the shares in the target business. In some cases, the original offer price may be pitched at a fairly low level as a negotiating ploy. The offer price will then be increased at a later date, thereby allowing the target business's man-agers and shareholders to feel that they have won some sort of victory.

PROTECTING THE INTERESTS OF SHAREHOLDERS AND THE PUBLIC

Any merger that could affect competition in Canada is subject to the *Competition Act*, which could block all or part of the merger. In the case where some of the merger is blocked, the ruling would allow the merger to proceed upon divesting certain specified assets. Areas considered in determining the effect a merger would have on competition include the degree of concentration within an industry, barriers to entry in the industry, and the remaining effective competition in the industry. Pre-merger notification to the Commissioner of Competition must be made if the combined assets in Canada or rev-enues of the new entity (both parent and subsidiary together) would exceed $400 million.

RESTRUCTURING A BUSINESS: DIVESTMENTS AND SPIN-OFFS

A business may wish to decrease, rather than increase, its scale of operations. Restruc-turing a business in this way can be achieved through either a divestment or a spin-off.

Divestment

A **divestment** or *sell-off* of business operations may be undertaken for various reasons including:

■ *Financial problems.* A business that is short of cash or too highly leveraged may sell off certain operations to improve its financial position.

- *Defensive tactics.*   A business that is vulnerable to a takeover may take pre-emptive action by selling its crown jewels.
- *Strategic focus.*   A business may wish to focus exclusively on core operations that are in line with its strategic objectives. As a result, non-core operations will be sold off.
- *Poor performance.*   Where the performance of a particular business operation is disappointing, it may be sold off to enable more profitable use of resources.

Divestment and the Agency Problem

When a divestment is undertaken, the managers of the particular business operations may bid to become the new owners. This, however, may give rise to an agency problem for the shareholders, as discussed in Activity 14.13.

ACTIVITY 14.13

What kind of agency problem may arise for shareholders?

Solution

The managers have a duty to act in the interests of the shareholders. However, when a management buy-out is being considered, the managers have a conflict of interest. On the one hand, they have a duty to ensure that the sale of the business will maximize the wealth of the owners and, on the other, they will be keen to acquire the business for as low a price as possible. There is a risk, therefore, that unscrupulous managers will suppress important information or will fail to exploit profitable opportunities in the period leading up to a buy-out in order to acquire the business operations at a cheap price. Shareholders must be aware of this risk and must seek independent advice concerning the value and potential of the business operations for which the managers are bidding.

If the bid by managers is successful, the purchase arrangement is referred to as a *management buy-out.* We saw in Chapter 9 that management buy-outs are often financed by venture capitalists, who usually acquire a shareholding in the business.

Spin-Offs

Rather than business operations being sold to a third party, they may be transferred to a new business. This kind of restructuring is referred to as a **spin-off**. In this case, ownership of the business operations remains unchanged, as the current owners will be given shares in the newly created business. The allocation of shares to the owners is usually made in proportion to their shareholdings in the existing business. A spin-off can be undertaken for various reasons, including:

- *Market appeal.*   Where part of the business operations is unattractive to investors (for example, very high risk), sentiment toward the business as a whole may be adversely affected. By spinning off the unattractive operations, the business may increase its market appeal.
- *Defensive tactics.*   A business may have certain operations that are prized by another business. By spinning off particular operations, the business may successfully avoid the risk of takeover. (As mentioned earlier, a divestment can also be used for this purpose.)
- *Unlocking potential.*   It is usually extremely difficult for a conglomerate to manage a diverse range of businesses effectively. A decision to spin off part of its operations

should make the business easier to manage and more focused. It will also give the managers of the operations that have been spun off greater autonomy, which may in turn lead to improved performance.

■ *Investors' needs.* Investors in a conglomerate are unlikely to find the different corporate businesses equally attractive. By having separate independent companies for different kinds of business operations, investors should benefit, as they will be able to adjust their portfolios to more accurately reflect the required level of investment for each business operation.

REAL WORLD 14.13 provides an example of a business spin-off resulting in two pure-play companies—one for natural gas and one for oil.

REAL WORLD 14.13 Encana Spins Off Assets to Create Cenovus

In 2009 Encana Corp. decided to proceed with a spin-off it had cancelled in 2008 due to terrible stock market conditions. Encana became a pure-play on natural gas and the spin-off, Cenovus Energy Inc., became an integrated oil company with major oil sands assets. The spin-off was accomplished by Encana shareholders retaining their Encana shares and receiving one Cenovus share for each Encana share held, similar to a stock dividend. Encana felt the spin off would unlock value for shareholders because the stock market finds it easier to value pure-play companies than conglomerates.

Source: Encana website www.encana.com/media/newsreleases/, accessed October 12, 2009.

As a footnote to the topics of divestment and spin-offs, it is worth pointing out that both forms of restructuring result in a smaller business. Thus, some of the benefits of size, such as the economies of scale, will be lost.

L.O. 5 THE VALUATION OF SHARES

An important aspect of any merger or takeover negotiation is the value to be placed on the shares of the businesses to be merged or acquired. In this section, we explore the various methods that can be used to derive an appropriate share value for a business.

In theory, the value of a share can be defined in terms of either the current value of the assets held or the future cash flows generated from those assets. In a world of perfect information and perfect certainty, share valuation would pose few problems. However, in the real world, measurement and forecasting problems make the valuation process difficult. Various valuation methods have been developed to deal with these problems, but they often produce quite different results.

The main methods used to value a share can be divided into three broad categories:

■ Methods based on the value of the business's assets
■ Methods based on stock market information
■ Methods based on future cash flows.

Let us now examine some of the more important methods falling within each of these categories using Example 14.1.

Example 14.1

CDC Ltd. owns a chain of muffler shops in central Canada. The business has been approached by ATD Corp., which owns a large chain of gas stations, with a view to a takeover of CDC. ATD is prepared to make an offer in cash or a share-for-share exchange. The most recent financial statements of CDC are summarized below.

CDC Ltd.
Income Statement
for the year ended November 30, 2010
($ millions)

Sales revenue	18.7
Earnings before interest and taxes	6.4
Interest	1.6
Earnings before taxes	4.8
Tax expense	1.2
Net income	3.6

CDC Ltd.
Statement of Retained Earnings
for the year ended November 30, 2010
(in $ millions)

Opening retained earnings, December 1, 2009	1.0
Add: Net income for 2010	3.6
Less: Dividends paid	(1.0)
Closing retained earnings, November 30, 2010	3.6

CDC Ltd.
Balance Sheet
as at November 30, 2010
(in $ millions)

Current assets

Cash	2.6	
Accounts receivable	0.4	
Inventory	2.8	
Total current assets		5.8

Property, plant, and equipment

Land		2.0
Buildings	2.6	
Less: Accumulated depreciation	0.6	2.0
Plant and machinery	9.5	
Less: Accumulated depreciation	3.6	5.9
Total property, plant, and equipment		9.9
Total assets		15.7

▶

Current liabilities

Accounts payable	5.9	
Income taxes payable	0.6	
Total current liabilities		6.5

Long-term liabilities

Bank loans		3.6
Total liabilities		10.1

Shareholders' equity

Common shares	2.0	
Retained earnings	3.6	
Total shareholders' equity		5.6
Total liabilities and shareholders' equity		15.7

Note: There are 2 million shares of CDC outstanding.

The accountant for CDC has estimated the future free cash flows of the business to be as follows:

	($ millions)
2011	4.4
2012	4.6
2013	4.9
2014	5.0
2015	5.4

Note: After 2015, the free cash flows remain constant at $5.4 million for the following 12 years.

The business has a cost of capital of 10%.

CDC has recently had a professional appraiser establish the current resale value of its assets. The current resale value of each asset was as follows:

	($ millions)
Land and buildings	18.2
Plant and machinery	4.2
Inventory	3.4

The current resale values of the remaining assets are considered to be in line with their book values.

A company that is listed on the stock exchange and is in the same business as CDC has a dividend yield of 5% and a P/E ratio of 11 times.

The vice-president of finance believes that replacement costs are $1 million higher than the resale values for both land and buildings together, and plant and machinery, and $0.5 million higher than the resale value of the inventory. The replacement costs of the remaining assets are considered to be in line with their balance sheet values. In addition, she believes the brand recognition of the business has a replacement value of $10 million. The balance sheet values of the liabilities of the company also reflect their current market values.

Asset-Based Methods

Asset-based methods attempt to value a share by reference to the value of the assets held by the business. Shareholders own the business and, therefore, own the underlying net assets (total assets less liabilities) of the business. This means that a single share can be valued by dividing the value of the net assets of the business by the number of shares outstanding.

Balance Sheet Method

The simplest method is to use the balance sheet values of the assets held. The **balance sheet method** (or **net book value method**) will determine the value of a common share (P_0) as in Equation 14.1:

$$P_0 = \frac{\text{Total assets at balance sheet values} - \text{Total liabilities}}{\text{Number of common shares outstanding}} \qquad 14.1$$

Where the business has preferred shares outstanding, these must also be deducted (at their book value) from the total assets in order to obtain the net book value of a common share, as demonstrated in Activity 14.14.

ACTIVITY 14.14

Calculate the net book value of a common share in CDC Ltd. from Example 14.1

Solution

The net book value of a common share will be:

$$P_0 = \frac{\$15.7 \text{ million} - \$10.1 \text{ million}}{2.0 \text{ million}} = \$2.80$$

The balance sheet method has the advantage that the valuation process is straightforward and the data are easy to obtain. However, the balance sheet value—or net book value—of a share is likely to represent a conservative value. This is because certain intangible assets, such as internally generated brand names, may not be recorded on the balance sheet and will, therefore, be ignored for the purposes of valuation. In addition, those assets that are shown on the balance sheet are recorded at their historical cost (less any depreciation to date, where relevant), and these figures may be below their current market values. It should be noted that, because Canada switched to international (IFRS) accounting in 2011, companies are now permitted to revalue their assets to fair value.

Often, a share value based on balance sheet values is calculated to obtain a minimum value for a share. A bidder, for example, may compare the bid price with the net book value to measure the downside risk associated with acquiring a business. Where the bid price is close to the balance sheet value, the level of investment risk is likely to be small. It is fairly rare for the shares of a business to have a current market value that is below the net book value, although this happened during the Great Depression of the 1930s.

Current Market Value Methods

Another approach to share valuation is to use the current market value—rather than the balance sheet value—of assets held. In economic theory, the value of any asset (including a share in a business) should reflect the present value of the future benefits that it will generate. The current market value of an asset should reflect the market's view of the present value of these future benefits as investors will be prepared to pay up to the present value of the future benefits to acquire the asset. Current market value can be expressed in terms of either **net realizable value** or **replacement cost**. In practice, both valuation approaches are used.

Liquidation method.   The **liquidation method** values the assets held according to the net realizable values (i.e., selling price less any costs of selling) that could be obtained in an orderly liquidation of the business. This method adopts the same basic equation as before, but uses net realizable values instead of balance sheet values for assets and liabilities. Thus, the liquidation value for a common share is calculated in Equation 14.2 as:

$$P_0 = \frac{\text{Total assets at net realizable values} - \text{Total liabilities at current market values}}{\text{Number of common shares outstanding}} \qquad \text{14.2}$$

Activity 14.15 applies the liquidation method using Equation 14.2.

ACTIVITY 14.15

Calculate the value of a common share in CDC Ltd. in Example 14.1 (p. 549) using the liquidation method.

Solution

The liquidation value for a common share will be:

$$P_0 = \frac{[(\$18.2 \text{ million} + \$4.2 \text{ million} + \$3.4 \text{ million} + \$0.4 \text{ million} + \$2.6 \text{ million}) - \$10.1 \text{ million}^*]}{2.0 \text{ million}}$$

$$= \$9.35$$

*Recall from Example 14.1 that the balance sheet values of liabilities reflect their current market values.

Although it is an improvement on the balance sheet method, the liquidation method is also likely to reflect a conservative value. This is because it fails to take account of the value of the business as a going concern. Usually, the going concern value of a business will be higher than the sum of the individual values of the assets when sold piecemeal, because of the benefits of combining the assets. Net realizable values represent a lower limit for the current market value of assets held. The value of an asset *in use* is likely to be greater than the net realizable value of that asset. If this were not the case, a business would, presumably, sell the asset rather than keep it.

Using net realizable values can pose a number of practical problems. Where, for example, the asset is unique, such as a custom-built piece of equipment, it may be particularly hard to obtain a reliable value. Realizable values can vary according to the circumstances of the sale. The amount obtained in a hurried sale may be considerably below that which could be obtained in an orderly, managed sale.

Replacement cost method.   Replacement cost can also be used as an indicator of the market value of the assets held by a business. Replacement will represent the cost of replacing a particular asset with an identical asset. The value of a common share, based on replacement cost, is calculated in Equation 14.3 as follows:

$$P_0 = \frac{\text{Total assets at replacement cost} - \text{Total liabilities at current market values}}{\text{Number of common shares outstanding}} \qquad \text{14.3}$$

The replacement cost approach will take account of assets that can be sold on an individual basis as well as off-balance-sheet assets such as brand recognition, which will exist only where the business is a going concern. When this is done, the amount derived will represent an upper limit for the market value of assets held. Activity 14.16 applies the replacement cost method using Equation 14.3.

ACTIVITY 14.16

Calculate the value of a common share in CDC in Example 14.1 (p. 549) using the replacement cost method.

Solution

The replacement cost method will yield the following value for a common share:

$$P_0 = \frac{[(\$19.2 \text{ million} + \$5.2 \text{ million} + \$3.9 \text{ million} + \$0.4 \text{ million} + \$2.6 \text{ million} + \$10.0 \text{ million}) - \$10.1 \text{ million}]}{2.0 \text{ million}}$$

$$= \$15.6$$

Adopting the replacement cost method can lead to practical difficulties. Factors such as technological change may make it difficult to calculate an accurate replacement cost as the asset may no longer be in production.

Stock Market Methods

Where a business is listed on a stock exchange, the quoted share price provides an indication of value. We saw in Chapter 8 that there is evidence to suggest that share prices react quickly and in an unbiased manner to new information that becomes publicly available, and so, in that sense, the stock market can be described as efficient. As information is fully absorbed in share prices it can be argued that, until new information becomes available, shares are correctly valued. The efficiency of the stock market is largely due to the efforts of investors who closely monitor listed businesses in an attempt to identify undervalued shares. The activities of these investors ensure that undervalued shares do not stay undervalued for very long because they will buy the shares and so drive up the price.

It is possible to use stock market information and ratios to help value the shares of an unlisted business. The first step in this process is to find a listed business within the same industry that has similar risk and growth characteristics. Stock market ratios relating to the listed business can then be applied to the unlisted business in order to derive a share value. Two ratios that can be used in this way are the price/earnings (P/E) ratio and the dividend yield ratio.

Price/Earnings (P/E) Ratio Method

The **price/earnings (P/E) ratio** relates the current share price to the current earnings of the business. We may recall from Equation 4.18 in Chapter 4 that the ratio is as follows:

$$\text{Price/earnings ratio} = \frac{\text{Market value per share}}{\text{Earnings per share}} \qquad 4.18$$

The P/E ratio reflects the market's view of the likely future growth in earnings. The higher the P/E ratio, the more highly regarded are the future growth prospects.

This equation can be rearranged in Equation 14.4 so that:

$$P_0 = \text{P/E ratio} \times \text{Earnings per share} = \frac{\text{P/E ratio} \times \text{Net income}}{\text{Number of common shares outstanding}} \quad \text{14.4}$$

Thus, we can see that the market value is a multiple of the benefits (earnings) that the share will provide.

The P/E ratio of a listed business can be applied to the earnings of a similar unlisted business to derive a share value. Using the rearranged equation above, the value of a common share of an unlisted business is calculated as follows:

$P_0 = $ P/E ratio of similar listed business $\times$ Earnings per share of unlisted business

Activity 14.17 applies the P/E ratio method.

ACTIVITY 14.17

Calculate the value of a common share in CDC from Example 14.1 (p. 549), using the P/E ratio method.

Solution

The value of a common share using the P/E ratio method will be:

$$P_0 = 11 \times \frac{\$3.6 \text{ million}}{2.0 \text{ million}}$$

$$= \$19.80$$

Although the calculations are fairly simple, this valuation approach should not be viewed as a mechanical exercise. Care must be taken to ensure that differences between the two businesses do not affect the valuation process. As can be imagined, a potential problem with this method is finding a listed business with similar risk and growth characteristics. Other differences, such as differences in accounting policies and accounting year-ends between the two businesses, can lead to problems when applying the P/E ratio to the earnings of the unlisted business. An unlisted business may adopt different policies on such matters as depreciation periods, which will require adjustment before applying the P/E ratio.

Keep in mind that shares in unlisted businesses are less marketable than those of similar listed businesses. To take account of this difference, a discount is usually applied to the share value derived by using the above equation. A discount of 30% is not uncommon, although determining an appropriate discount figure is difficult.

Dividend Yield Ratio Method

The **dividend yield ratio** offers another approach to valuing the shares of an unlisted business. This ratio relates the cash return from dividends to the current market value per share and we saw in Equation 4.16 in Chapter 4 that it is calculated as follows:

$$\text{Dividend yield} = \frac{\text{Dividend per share}}{\text{Market value per share}} \times 100\% \quad \text{4.16}$$

The dividend yield can be calculated for shares listed on a stock exchange as both the market value per share and dividend per share will normally be known. However, for unlisted businesses, the market value per share is not usually known and, therefore, this ratio cannot normally be applied.

The equation can be expressed in terms of the market value per share by rearranging, as in Equation 14.5:

$$\text{Market value per share, } P_0 = \frac{\text{Dividend per share}}{\text{Dividend yield}} \times 100\% \qquad 14.5$$

Equation 14.5 can be used to value the shares of an unlisted business. For this purpose, the equation uses the dividend per share of the unlisted business, whose shares are to be valued, and the dividend yield of a similar listed business. Activity 14.18 uses the dividend yield method to calculate the value of shares.

ACTIVITY 14.18

Calculate the value of a common share in CDC in Example 14.1 using the dividend yield ratio method.

Solution

The value of a common share using the dividend yield ratio method will be:

$$P_0 = \frac{(\$1 \text{ million} \div 2 \text{ million})}{5\%}$$

$$= \$10.0$$

This approach to share valuation has a number of weaknesses. Once again, we are faced with the problem of finding a similar listed business as a basis for the valuation. We must also recognize that dividend policies may vary considerably between businesses in the same industry, and may also vary between listed and unlisted businesses. Unlisted businesses, for example, are likely to be under less pressure to distribute profits in the form of dividends than listed businesses.

Dividends represent only part of the earnings stream of a business, and to value shares on this basis may be misleading. The valuation obtained will be largely a function of the dividend policy adopted (which is at the discretion of management) rather than the earnings generated. Where a business does not make dividend distributions, this method cannot be applied.

Cash Flow Methods

We have already seen that the value of an asset is equivalent to the present value of the future cash flows that it generates. The most direct—and theoretically appealing— approach is therefore to value a share on this basis. The **dividend valuation method** and **free cash flow method** adopt this approach and both are discussed here.

Template for
Share Valuation

Dividend Valuation Method

The cash returns from holding a share take the form of dividends received. It is possible, therefore, to view the value of a share in terms of the stream of future dividends that are received. We have already seen in Chapter 10 that the value of a share will be the *discounted value of the future dividends*.

SELF-ASSESSMENT QUESTION   14.1

You have collected the following information about two companies you are considering investing in:

	Pastel Dreams Ltd.	Hard Core Reality Ltd.
Assets per balance sheet	$ 34,000,000	$129,000,000
Liabilities per balance sheet	$ 20,000,000	$ 65,000,000
Number of common shares outstanding	30,000,000	60,000,000
Assets—Market value	$160,000,000	$210,000,000
Liabilities—Market value	$ 18,500,000	$ 70,000,000
Net income	$ 62,000,000	$195,000,000
P/E ratio	20	40
Dividends	$ 22,000,000	$ 95,000,000

Required:

Determine the value of a common share using the:

(a) Balance sheet method
(b) Liquidation method
(c) P/E ratio method

Although this model is theoretically appealing, there are practical problems in forecasting future dividend payments and in calculating the required rate of return on the share. The first problem arises because dividends tend to fluctuate over time. If, however, dividends can be assumed to remain constant over time, we have already seen in Equation 10.2 that the discounted dividend model amounts to:

$$P_0 = \frac{D_0}{K_0} \qquad \text{10.2}$$

$$P_0 = \frac{D_1}{K_0} \qquad \text{10.2(a)}$$

where $D_0 = D_1 =$ the dividend received at the end of period 1, because we are assuming the dividend remains constant over time in this case.

Activity 14.19 applies the discounted dividend approach to calculating common share value.

ACTIVITY 14.19

Assume that CDC, in Example 14.1 (p. 549), has a constant dividend payout and the cost of capital for its common shares is estimated at 12%. Calculate the value of a common share in the business using the discounted dividend approach.

The value of a common share using the discounted dividend approach will be:

$$P_0 = \frac{\$1.0 \text{ million/2.0 million}}{0.12}$$

$$= \$4.17$$

The assumption of constant dividends may not be very realistic, however, as many businesses attempt to increase their dividends to shareholders over time.

We saw in Equation 10.4 in Chapter 10 that, where businesses increase their dividends at a constant rate of growth, the discounted dividend model can be revised to:

$$P_0 = \frac{D_1}{K_0 - g} \qquad\qquad 10.4$$

where: g = the constant growth rate in dividends (the model assumes K_0 is greater than g)

In practice, an attempt may be made to forecast dividend payments for a manageable period (say, five years). After this period, accurate forecasting may become too difficult, and so a constant growth rate may be assumed for dividends received beyond the forecast horizon. Thus, the future dividend stream is divided into two separate elements: the first element based on dividend estimates over a particular forecast horizon, and the second representing dividends beyond the forecast horizon (and involving the use of a simplifying assumption). Although it avoids one problem, this approach creates another of deciding on an appropriate growth rate to use.

Figure 14.5 illustrates the process just described.

FIGURE 14.5   The Dividend Valuation Method

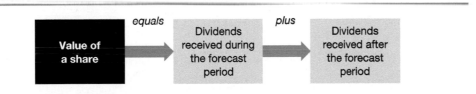

The use of dividends as a basis for valuation can create difficulties because of their discretionary nature. Different businesses will adopt different dividend payout policies and this can affect the calculation of share values. In some cases, no dividends may be declared by a business for a considerable period. There are, for example, high-growth businesses that prefer to plough profits back into the business rather than make dividend payments.

Free Cash Flow Method

Another approach to share valuation is to value the free cash flows that are generated by a business over time. Free cash flows were considered in Chapter 13. They represent the cash flows available to lenders and shareholders after any new investments in assets. In other words, they are equivalent to the net cash flows from operations after deducting tax paid and cash for investment.

The valuation process is the same as the process that we looked at in the preceding chapter. To value shares using free cash flows, we have to discount the future free cash flows over time, using the cost of capital. The present value of the free cash flows, after deducting amounts owing to long-term lenders at current market values, will represent the portion of the free cash flows that accrue to the common shareholders. If this amount is divided by the number of common shares in issue, we have a figure for the value of a common share:

$$P_0 = \frac{\text{Present value of future free cash flows} - \text{Long-term loans at current market values}}{\text{Number of common shares outstanding}} \qquad 14.6$$

Activity 14.20 applies the free cash flow method to calculate the value of a common share.

ACTIVITY 14.20

Calculate the value of a common share in CDC from Example 14.1 (p. 549), using the free cash flow method.

Solution

The value of a common share will be:

Year	Cash Flows ($ millions)	Discount Rate 10%	Present Value ($ millions)
2011	4.4	0.9091	4.00
2012	4.6	0.8264	3.80
2013	4.9	0.7513	3.68
2014	5.0	0.6830	3.42
Next 13 years	5.4	4.8516*	26.20
			41.10

$$P_0 = \frac{\text{Present value of future free cash flows} - \text{Long-term loans at current market values}}{\text{Number of common shares outstanding}}$$

$$= \frac{\$41.10 \text{ million} - \$3.6 \text{ million**}}{2.0 \text{ million}}$$

$$= \$18.75$$

*This is the total of the individual discount rates for the 13-year period. This shortcut can be adopted where cash flows are constant. For the sake of simplicity, it is assumed that there are no cash flows after the 13-year period.

**This method, unlike the balance sheet methods discussed earlier, does not deduct short-term liabilities in arriving at a value per share. This is because they are dealt with in the calculation of free cash flows. We are told in the example that the balance sheet values of liabilities reflect their current market values.

We saw in Chapter 13 that a major problem with free cash flows is accurate forecasting. However, this can be tackled in the same way as described above. Free cash flows may be forecast over a manageable time horizon (say, five years) and then a terminal value can be substituted for free cash flows arising beyond that period. Determining the terminal value is, of course, a problem—and an important one—as it may be a significant proportion of the total cash flows.

In the previous chapter we used an example to illustrate the valuation of a business where it was assumed that returns remained constant after the planning period, and we used the following formula for a perpetuity in order to determine the terminal value (TV):

$$\text{Terminal value (or TV)} = \frac{C_1}{r} \qquad \text{13.1}$$

where: C_1 = the free cash flows in the following year
r = the required rate of return from investors

However, another approach would be to assume a constant growth rate over time, just as we did with dividends earlier. The terminal value of the business as a whole (TVB) would then be:

$$\text{TVB} = \frac{C_1}{r - g} \qquad \text{14.7}$$

where: C_1 = free cash flows in the following year
r = the cost of capital
g = the constant rate of growth in free cash flows

Although free cash flows may appear to be clearly defined, in practice there may be problems. The discretionary policies of management concerning new investments will have a significant influence on the free cash flow figure calculated. Free cash flows are likely to fluctuate considerably between periods. Unlike earnings, management has no incentive to smooth out cash flows over time. However, for valuation purposes, it may be useful to smooth out cash flow fluctuations between periods in order to establish trends over time.

OTHER METHODS OF SHARE VALUATION

We have now discussed the main methods of valuing shares; however, other methods can be found in practice. One such method is to use the ratio between a key financial measure such as sales and share value, using information from a similar business. Example 14.2 illustrates how this method works in practice.

Example 14.2

Arts Ltd. has sales of $12 million and has 500,000 shares outstanding. A similar business, Inch Inc., has sales of $30 million and a market capitalization (i.e., total value of common shares outstanding) of $10 million.
What is the value of a common share in Arts Ltd?

Solution

Inch has $3 of sales for every $1 of market capitalization. Using this ratio of 3:1, the total value of the common shares in Arts Ltd. will be $4 million (i.e., $12 million/3).
Dividing $4 million (the total value of shares) by 500,000 (the number of shares outstanding) will provide a value of $8 for each share.

Although the calculations required are straightforward, it is assumed that the relationship between sales and market capitalization will hold from one business to another. This may be an unwarranted assumption, however. The fact that two businesses sell the same kind of product or service does not mean that they will have the same profitability, asset structure, risk, and growth prospects. Ultimately, it is these factors that determine value.

The relationship between market capitalization and other key financial measures (such as net income or the net book value of assets) may also be used as a basis for valuation. The approach used in each case is basically the same—and so are the problems.

A further method of valuing shares is the economic value added (EVA) method that we discussed in Chapter 13. We may recall from Equation 13.4 that the value of a business could be derived as follows:

$$\text{PV of future EVA} = \text{Business value} - \text{Capital invested} \qquad \text{13.4}$$

$$\text{Business value} = \text{Capital invested} + \text{PV of future EVA} \qquad \text{13.4, rearranged}$$

To derive the total value of the common shares, the value of any debt must be deducted. By dividing the total value of shares by the number of shares outstanding, we can derive a value for a common share. (We saw in Chapter 13 that this method should arrive at the same business value as the free cash flow approach discussed earlier.)

Accounting Change Affects Valuations

As we have seen, the starting point for analyst valuation models is the financial statements reported by the company. These financial statements are prepared according to generally accepted accounting principles. REAL WORLD 14.14 shows what happens when the standards change.

REAL WORLD 14.14

The iPhone—Valuing Apple Inc.

In September 2009, the U.S. Financial Accounting Standards Board (FASB) changed the way firms could account for certain high-tech gadgets. This affected how Apple could account for its hugely successful iPhone. Apple can now report 100% of the revenue at the time of the sale. Previously, Apple had to spread the revenue over two years because the high software content of the iPhone required it to be accounted for like a software sale. Analysts were quick to note the change and upgraded the target price for Apple's shares from US$160 to US$260, mostly on the back of the accounting change. Apple shares quickly moved to US$190.

Source: www.macobserver.com/tmo/article/new_rule_lets_apple_dump_iphone_subscription_accounting/, accessed October 12, 2009.

River Holdings Ltd. is a large conglomerate company that is listed on the Toronto Stock Exchange. The board of directors of River Holdings has decided to restructure the business. As part of the restructuring plan, it has agreed to spin off one of its largest subsidiaries, Lake Effects Corp., as a separate business. Lake Effects will not seek an immediate stock exchange listing.

The most recent financial statements of Lake Effects are set out below.

Lake Effects Corp.
Statement of Retained Earnings
for the year ended November 30, 2010
(in $ millions)

Opening retained earnings, December 1, 2009	41.1
Add: Net income for 2010	17.2
Less: Dividends paid	(8.2)
Closing retained earnings, November 30, 2010	50.1

Lake Effects Corp.
Balance Sheet
as at November 30, 2010
(in $ millions)

Current assets			
Accounts receivable			29.6
Inventory			34.8
Total current assets			64.4
Property, plant, and equipment			
Land		10.0	
Buildings	38.4		
Less: Accumulated depreciation	15.2	23.2	
Plant and machinery	36.7		
Less: Accumulated depreciation	12.4	24.3	
Furniture and fixtures	18.9		
Less: Accumulated depreciation	8.5	10.4	
Total property, plant, and equipment			67.9
Total assets			132.3
Current liabilities			
Bank overdraft		11.4	
Accounts payable		35.9	
Income taxes payable		3.9	
Total current liabilities			51.2
Long-term liabilities			
Bank loans, 10%			21.0
Total liabilities			72.2

▶

Shareholders' equity

Common shares	10.0	
Retained earnings	50.1	
Total shareholders' equity		60.1
Total liabilities and shareholders' equity		132.3

Note

1. There are 40 million shares of Lake Effects outstanding.

Lake Effects Corp.
Income Statement
for the year ended November 30, 2010
($ millions)

Sales revenue		153.6
Less: Cost of goods sold		102.4
Gross profit		51.2
Less: Selling and distribution expenses	12.3	
Administrative expenses	10.2	
Interest expenses	3.6	26.1
Net earnings before taxes		25.1
Income tax expense		7.9
Net income		17.2

The following additional information has been gathered concerning Lake Effects:

1. A firm of independent assessors has recently established the current realizable value of the business's assets as:

	($ millions)
Land and buildings	65.4
Plant and equipment	18.8
Furniture and fixtures	4.6
Inventory	38.9

The balance sheet value of accounts receivable reflects their current realizable values.

2. A similar business to Lake Effects is listed on the TSX and has a price/earnings (P/E) ratio of 11.
3. The net income for Lake Effects for the forthcoming year is expected to be the same as for 2010. The dividend payout ratio is expected to be 40% and dividends are expected to grow at 4% per annum for the foreseeable future.
4. The business has an estimated cost of capital for common shares of 10%.

Required:

(a) Calculate the value of a share in Lake Effects using the following valuation methods:
   (i)   Balance sheet method
   (ii) Liquidation method
   (iii) P/E ratio method
   (iv) Dividend growth method.

(b) Explain what is meant by *spin-off* in the context of restructuring and suggest reasons why River Holdings might undertake this form of restructuring.

Choosing a Valuation Model

When deciding on the appropriate valuation model to use, it is essential to consider the purpose for which the shares are being valued. Different valuation models may be appropriate for different circumstances. For example, an asset stripper (i.e., someone who wishes to acquire a business with a view to selling off its individual assets) would probably be most interested in the liquidation basis of valuation. A financial adviser to a new business's initial public offering on the stock market, on the other hand, may rely more heavily on the P/E ratio method or the free cash flow method. We saw earlier that the former approach takes account of share values of similar businesses already listed on the stock exchange.

In cases such as mergers and acquisitions, share valuations derived from the models can be used as a basis for negotiation. In such circumstances, they can be used to help set boundaries within which a final share value will be determined. The final figure will, however, be influenced by various factors, including the negotiating skills and the relative bargaining positions of the parties.

SUMMARY

Mergers and Acquisitions

- A merger occurs when two businesses of equal size combine; an acquisition occurs when a larger business absorbs a smaller business.
- These terms have lost their significance for accounting purposes, because all business combinations are now treated as if one business has acquired another business.
- Mergers can be achieved through horizontal or vertical integration or by combining with unrelated businesses.
- There are surges in merger activity from time to time, usually as a result of a combination of political, economic, and technological factors.
- To make economic sense, the merged businesses should generate greater cash flows than if the two businesses remained apart.

The Rationale for Mergers

- There are various reasons for a merger, which include:
  - Gaining economies of scale
  - Eliminating competition
  - Exploiting underutilized resources
  - Combining complementary resources
  - Using surplus funds
  - Diversifying
  - Fulfilling managers' interests and goals.
- The last two of these may not be consistent with the objective of maximizing shareholder wealth.

Forms of Purchase Consideration

- Payment for the shares in an acquired business may take the form of:
  - Cash
  - Shares in the bidding business
  - Long-term debt incurred by the bidding business
  - A combination of the above.

Who Benefits from Mergers and Acquisitions?

- Shareholders in the target business see an increase in the value of their investment.
- Shareholders in the bidding business often see a decrease in the value of their investment.
- Managers of the bidding business may gain through an increase in status, income, and security.
- Managers of the target business often leave within a few years of the takeover.
- Financial advisers and lawyers usually benefit from a merger.

Rejecting a Takeover Bid

- Various tactics may be employed to resist a bid, including:
  - Converting to private company status
  - Promoting employee share option plans
  - Making the business unattractive
  - Using the Pac-man defence

- • Looking for a white knight
- • Looking for a white squire.
- Managers of the bidding business may try to overcome resistance by communicating directly with shareholders to explain the logic of the case, or by increasing the bid price.

Protecting the Interests of Shareholders and the Public

- The *Competition Act* gives the government the power to block any merger that could diminish competition.

Restructuring a Business: Divestments and Spin-Offs

- A divestment involves selling off part of the business's operations.

- A spin-off involves transferring business operations to a new business that is owned by the current shareholders.

The Valuation of Shares

- Shares may be valued using methods based on:
  - • The value of the business's assets (balance sheet method, liquidation method, replacement cost method)
  - • Stock market information (price/earnings ratio method and dividend yield ratio method)
  - • Future cash flows (dividend valuation method and free cash flow method).
- The choice of valuation methods will depend on the reasons for the valuation.

KEY TERMS

Merger
Acquisition
Horizontal merger
Vertical merger
Conglomerate merger
Synergy
Reverse takeover
Poison pill
Crown jewels

Golden parachutes
Pac-man defence
White knight
White squire
Competition Act
Divestment
Spin-off
Balance sheet (net book value) method

Net realizable value
Replacement cost
Liquidation method
Price/earnings (P/E) ratio method
Dividend yield ratio
Dividend valuation method
Free cash flow method

LIST OF EQUATIONS

14.1 Balance sheet method: $P_0 = \dfrac{\text{Total assets at balance sheet values} - \text{Total liabilities}}{\text{Number of common shares outstanding}}$

14.2 Liquidation method:

$$P_0 = \frac{\text{Total assets at net realizable values} - \text{Total liabilities at current market values}}{\text{Number of common shares outstanding}}$$

14.3 Replacement cost method:

$$P_0 = \frac{\text{Total assets at replacement cost} - \text{Total liabilities at current market values}}{\text{Number of common shares outstanding}}$$

14.4 P/E ratio method:

$$P_0 = \text{P/E ratio} \times \text{Earnings per share} = \frac{\text{P/E ratio} \times \text{Net income}}{\text{Number of common shares outstanding}}$$

14.5 Dividend yield ratio method:

$$P_0 = \frac{\text{Dividend per share}}{\text{Dividend yield}} \times 100\%$$

14.6 Free cash flow method:

$$P_0 = \frac{\text{Present value of future free cash flows} - \text{Long-term loans at current market values}}{\text{Number of common shares outstanding}}$$

14.7 $\text{TVB} = \dfrac{C_1}{r - g}$

Equations from other chapters, reused in Chapter 14:

4.18 $\text{Price/earnings ratio} = \dfrac{\text{Market value per share}}{\text{Earnings per share}}$

4.16 $\text{Dividend yield} = \dfrac{\text{Dividend per share}}{\text{Market value per share}} \times 100\%$

10.2 $P_0 = \dfrac{D_0}{K_0}$, for shares with a constant dividend

10.2(a) $P_0 = \dfrac{D_1}{K_0}$, for shares with a constant dividend

10.4 $P_0 = \dfrac{D_1}{K_0 - g}$, for shares with a dividend growth rate, g

13.1 Terminal value (or TV) $= \dfrac{C_1}{r}$

13.4 PV of future EVA $=$ Business value $-$ Capital invested

REVIEW QUESTIONS

Answers to the Review Questions can be found on the Companion Website that accompanies this text at www.pearsoned.ca/atrill.

14.1 Distinguish between a merger and an acquisition. What is the significance of this distinction?

14.2 Identify and discuss four reasons why a business may divest part of its operations.

14.3 Identify four reasons why a business seeking to maximize the wealth of its shareholders may wish to take over another business.

14.4 Identify four tactics the directors of a target company might use to resist an unwelcome bid.

14.5 Bonaventure Cabinets Ltd. is a small publicly traded company that prides itself on being one of the few independent Canadian furniture makers listed on the TSX. It has an enviable record of profitability growth over the past 10 years. Bonaventure is known for its very conservative accounting policies and management style. Its shares trade at $40 per share and its earnings per share in the most recent fiscal year amounted to $3.40 per share. The annual dividend is $0.20 per share and has not changed in five years. The cash balance on the balance sheet has quadrupled over the past five years and represents 20% of total assets. The TSX 100 Index has a price/earnings ratio of 17. Comment on the management strategy described above.

PROBLEMS AND CASES

14.1 A Company is interested in a merger with B Company. B Company is growing very fast and the price of its shares has risen rapidly. The two firms will continue as separate companies after the merger, with one being a subsidiary of the other. However, the two parties are having difficulty agreeing to a price. They have agreed that A Company will issue shares to B Company shareholders and then both A's original shareholders and B's former shareholders will own A company. Three scenarios are under review as shown below.

	Scenario		
	1	**2**	**3**
Number of shares outstanding of A Company	1,000,000	1,000,000	1,000,000
Price of one A Company share	$25	$25	$25
Number of shares outstanding of B Company	250,000	250,000	250,000
Price of one B company share	$50	$50	$50
Consideration given	3 shares of A for 1 share of B	4 shares of A for 1 share of B	5 shares of A for 1 share of B

Required:

    (a) For each scenario, determine who owns the shares of A Company and B Company after the merger.

    (b) For each scenario, determine which shareholder group is in control of A Company after the merger.

    (c) For each scenario, determine which company is the parent company and which is the subsidiary after the merger.

14.2 The following takeovers have been in the news recently:

Takeover Candidate	Takeover Bid Price per Share ($)	Pre-Bid Price per Share ($)
NewPort Ltd.	55.40	42.20
Electric City Corp.	21.90	19.75
Green Controls Ltd.	10.50	8.40
Vick Sounds Ltd.	34.00	30.60

Required:

Calculate the bid premium for each takeover.

14.3 Your friend has read an article in the business press and is confused. The article reads in part as follows:

> *Fashion Accessories Ltd. today took a poison pill by putting its three-year-old factory in East Harbour up for sale. In addition, golden parachutes have been arranged for the chief executive officer and the chair of the board of directors that require the firm to continue paying them for two years after dismissal in the event of a corporate takeover of Fashion Accessories. They will also each receive a $2 million bonus in the event of a takeover. The board is considering a Pac-man defence in addition to searching for a white knight.*

Required:

Explain to your friend the meaning of this business story by translating all of the jargon used in the newspaper.

14.4 Air Porters Inc. has common shares of $100 million and retained earnings of $23 million according to its latest balance sheet. There are 5 million shares outstanding. Inventory has a net realizable value $1 million less than book value (balance sheet values) and a replacement cost of $2 million less than book value. The land has been appraised at $3 million less than book value and the building has an appraisal value of $5 million less than book. The latter's replacement cost is considered to be $10 less than book value.

Required:

Estimate the share price for Air Porters Inc. shares using the following three methods:
- (a) Net book value method
- (b) Liquidation method
- (c) Replacement cost method.

14.5 The balance sheet for Yaphuto Research Inc. is as follows:

Yaphuto Research Inc.
Balance Sheet
as at December 31, 2010
(in $ thousands)

Current assets		33
Property, plant, and equipment		250
Total assets		283
Current liabilities	35	
Long-term liabilities (loans)	50	
Total liabilities		85
Shareholders' equity		
Common shares	150	
Retained earnings	48	
Total shareholders' equity		198
Total liabilities and shareholders' equity		283

Notes

1. Yaphuto has 10,000 shares outstanding.
2. Current assets include inventory at cost of $20,000. This inventory could be sold for $25,000 less a sales commission of 10% of the selling price. Replacement cost is $26,000.
3. The building and land owned by Yaphuto is listed on the balance sheet at $160,000 but has been appraised at $320,000. Because of the building's architectural design, its replacement cost is considered to be $50,000 above its appraisal value.

Required:

Estimate the price for Yaphuto shares using the following three methods:

- (a) Net book value method
- (b) Liquidation method
- (c) Replacement cost method.

14.6 You have gathered the following information about your competitors.

Company	P/E Ratio	EPS ($)	Dividend per share ($)	Dividend Yield
Flight Ltd.	10	4	4	10.00%
Light Ltd.	15	5	1.5	2.00%
Ite Ltd.	20	6	1	0.83%

Required:

Estimate the market price of the common shares for each company using the:
- (a) P/E ratio method
- (b) Dividend yield ratio method.

14.7 You have collected the following information on a number of firms:

Company Ticker Symbol	P/E Ratio	Net Income ($)	Dividends Paid to Preferred Shareholders ($)	Number of Common Shares Outstanding	Common Share Dividend Yield	Dividend per Common Share ($)
TRE	32	32,000,000	–	10,000,000	1.46%	1.50
BAC	7	120,000,000	20,000,000	5,000,000	3.00%	4.20
PULP	22	45,000,000	3,000,000	15,000,000	3.57%	2.20
KEEN	15	425,000,000	60,000,000	100,000,000	2.83%	1.55

Required:

Estimate the market price of a common share using the:
   (a) P/E ratio method
   (b) Dividend yield ratio method

14.8 Grande Hotel Limited (GHL) is expected to generate free cash flows of $500,000 next year. Free cash flow will increase at an annual rate of $250,000 for Years 2 to 4 after which it will stabilize at $1.2 million per year from Years 5 to 10. GHL's cost of capital is 5%. Long-term debt is $3 million. There are 1.5 million shares outstanding. The annual dividend per share is $0.30.

Required:

Estimate the market price of the common shares for GHL using the:
   (a) Dividend valuation method
   (b) The free cash flow method.

14.9 Atlantick Corp. has gathered the following data on four companies in which it might make an investment or an outright purchase.

	At Ltd.	Sat Inc.	Assat Corp.	Fassat Ltd.
Dividend per share	$0.48	$0.72	$1.32	$2.40
Cost of capital	14%	8%	15%	12%
Market value of loans outstanding	$750,000	$1,000,000	$1,500,000	$2,500,000
Next year's free cash flows	$1,200,000	$1,400,000	$180,000	$2,400,000
Annual growth rate for free cash flows	0%	3%	6%	8%
Number of shares outstanding	3,000,000	4,000,000	5,000,000	6,000,000

Required:

   (a) Estimate the share price of each company using the dividend valuation method
   (b) Estimate the share price of each company using the free cash flow method.

14.10 For TRE, you have collected the following information:

Company Ticker Symbol	Year	Free Cash Flow per Year ($)	Dividend per Common Share ($)	Number of Common Shares Outstanding	Market Value of Long-Term Loans ($)	Cost of Capital
TRE			1.50	10,000,000	5,000,000	9%
	1	12,000,000				
	2	22,000,000				
	3	30,000,000				
	4	40,000,000				
	5–15	50,000,000				

Required:

Estimate the market price of a common share using the:
- (a) Dividend valuation method
- (b) Free cash flow method.

14.11 When a business wishes to acquire another, it may make a bid in the form of cash, a share-for-share exchange, or cash obtained from a debt-for-share exchange.

Required:

Discuss the advantages and disadvantages of each form of consideration from the viewpoint of:
- (a) The bidding business's shareholders
- (b) The target business's shareholders.

14.12 Pea Inc. is considering the acquisition of Shooter Ltd. The most recent data is presented below. Pea will offer one of its shares for two shares of Shooter if they decide to go ahead with the deal. Net income for 2011 is expected to grow by 10% at Pea and by 20% at Shooter, excluding any synergistic merger savings. The most recent data is presented below.

	2010 Pea Inc.	2010 Shooter Ltd.
Net assets	$50,000,000	$15,000,000
Number of shares outstanding	3,000,000	750,000
Share price	$40	$16
Net income	5,000,000	600,000
Merger savings in 2011	1,000,000	

Required:
- (a) Calculate the 2010 EPS and P/E ratio for both Pea and Shooter.
- (b) Calculate the percentage premium contained in the acquisition price.
- (c) Calculate the number of new shares outstanding for Pea if the acquisition goes ahead.
- (d) Calculate the estimated new share price for Pea Inc. using 2011 data as if the deal proceeds.

14.13 Dawn Raider Ltd. has just offered one of its shares for two shares in Sleepy Giant Corp., a business in the same industry as itself. Extracts from the financial statements of each business for the year ended May 31, 2010, appear below:

	Dawn Raider ($ millions)	Sleepy Giant ($ millions)
Income statements		
Sales revenue	150	360
Net income	18	16
Dividends	4	14
Balance sheet data		
Net current assets (Note 1)	48	182
Property, plant, and equipment, net	150	304
Total assets	198	486
Loans	80	40
Common shares (Note 2)	50	100
Retained earnings	68	346
Total liabilities and shareholders' equity	198	486

Notes	Dawn Raider	Sleepy Giant
1. Includes cash/(overdrafts):	$(60 million)	$90 million
2. Number of common shares outstanding:	200 million	200 million

Stock market data for each business is as follows:

	May 31, 2008	May 31, 2009	May 30, 2010
Dawn Raider			
Share price ($)	1.20	1.44	1.98
Earnings per share ($)	0.053	0.069	0.090
Dividends per share ($)	0.02	0.02	0.02
Sleepy Giant			
Share price ($)	0.45	0.43	0.72
Earnings per share ($)	0.084	0.074	0.080
Dividends per share ($)	0.08	0.07	0.07

If the takeover succeeds, Dawn Raider plans to combine Sleepy Giant's marketing and distribution channels with its own, with after-tax savings of $1 million a year. In addition, it expects to be able to increase Sleepy Giant's net income by at least $5 million a year by better management. Dawn Raider's own net income is expected to be $23 million (excluding the $1 million savings already mentioned), in the year ended May 31, 2011.

One of the shareholders of Sleepy Giant has written to its chairman arguing that the bid should not be accepted. The following is an extract from his letter: "The bid considerably undervalues Sleepy Giant since it is below Sleepy Giant's net assets per share. Furthermore, if Dawn Raider continues its existing policy of paying only $0.02 a share as a dividend, Sleepy Giant's shareholders will be considerably worse off."

Required:
   (a) Calculate:
      (i)   The total value of the bid and the bid premium
      (ii)   Sleepy Giant's net assets per share at May 31, 2010
      (iii) The dividends the holder of 100 shares in Sleepy Giant would receive in the year before and the year after the takeover
      (iv)   The earnings per share for Dawn Raider in the year after the takeover
      (v)   The share price of Dawn Raider after the takeover, assuming that it maintains its existing price/earnings ratio.
   (b) Comment on:
      (i)   The points that the shareholder in Sleepy Giant raises in his letter
      (ii)   The amount of the bid consideration.

14.14 An investment business is considering taking a minority stake in two businesses, Montreal Foods Ltd. and Snacks Corp. Both are in the same line of business and both are listed on the stock exchange.

Montreal Foods Ltd. has had a stable dividend policy over the years. In the financial reports for the current year, the chair stated that a dividend of $0.30 a share would be paid in one year's time and financial analysts employed by the investment business expect dividends to grow at an annual compound rate of 10% for the indefinite future.

Snacks Corp. has had an erratic dividend pattern over the years and future dividends have been difficult to predict. However, to defend itself successfully against an unwelcome takeover, the business recently announced that dividends for the next three years were expected to be as follows:

Year	Dividend per Share
1	$0.20
2	$0.32
3	$0.36

Financial analysts working for the investment business believe that, after Year 3, Snacks should enjoy a smooth pattern of growth, and dividends should grow at a compound rate of 8% for the indefinite future.

The investment business believes that a return of 14% is required to compensate for the risks associated with the industry in which the two businesses are engaged. Ignore taxes.

Required:
(a) State the arguments for and against valuing a share on the basis of its future dividends.
(b) Based on the expected future dividends of each business, calculate the value of a share in:
  (i) Montreal Foods Ltd.
  (ii) Snacks Corp.
Round present value factors to two decimals.

14.15 You are trying to estimate the proper share price for each of the following companies using data at the end of 2010.

	Air Ltd.	Fair Inc.	Share Corp.
Net assets	$1,250,000	$3,000,000	$7,000,000
2010 net income	$211,000	$659,000	$1,211,000
Liquidation basis fair value adjustments	$450,000	$(950,000)	$600,000
Number of shares outstanding	300,000	400,000	500,000
2010 annual dividend	$95,000	$356,000	$792,000
Dividend yield = dividends per share /share price	3.04%	6.07%	8.25%
P/E ratio	10	15	20

Required:
(a) Calculate the net book value per share, ignoring the liquidation adjustments, for each company.
(b) Calculate the net book value per share on a liquidation basis for each company
(c) Calculate the estimated share price using the dividend yield method
(d) Calculate the estimated share price using the P/E ratio method.

14.16 The directors of TNT Industries have adopted a policy of expansion based on the acquisition of other businesses. The special projects division of TNT has been given the task of identifying suitable businesses for acquisition.

Sulu Ltd. has been identified as a suitable business, and negotiations between the boards of directors of both businesses have begun. Information relating to Sulu is shown below:

Sulu Ltd.
Statement of Retained Earnings
for the year ended May 31, 2010

	($)
Opening retained earnings, June 1, 2009	83,500
Add: Net income for 2010	48,500
Less: Dividends paid	(18,000)
Closing retained earnings, May 31, 2010	114,000

Sulu Ltd.
Balance Sheet
as at May 31, 2010
($)

Current assets

Cash	24,000	
Accounts receivable	49,000	
Inventory	84,000	
Total current assets		157,000

Property, plant, and equipment

Land		180,000	
Plant and machinery	120,000		
Less: Accumulated depreciation	30,000	90,000	
Vehicles	35,000		
Less: Accumulated depreciation	16,000	19,000	
Total property, plant, and equipment			289,000
Total assets			446,000

Current liabilities

Accounts payable	42,000	
Long-term liabilities		
Bond, 10%	140,000	
Total liabilities		182,000

Shareholders' equity

Common shares	150,000	
Retained earnings	114,000	
Total shareholders' equity		264,000
Total liabilities and shareholders' equity		446,000

Notes

1. There are 300,000 shares of Sulu outstanding.
2. Profits and dividends of the business have shown little change over the past five years.
3. The realizable values of the assets of Sulu, at the balance sheet date, were estimated to be as follows:

	($)
Land	285,000
Plant and machinery	72,000
Vehicles	15,000

For the remaining assets, the balance sheet values were considered to reflect current realizable values.

4. The special projects division of TNT has also identified another business, Armour Ltd., which is listed on the stock exchange and which is broadly similar to Sulu Ltd. The following details were taken from a recent financial newspaper:

2009–2010		Share	Price	Yield	P/E
High	Low			(%)	(times)
$5.60	$4.80	Armour Ltd.	$5.00	2.76	11

Required:

(a) Calculate the value of a common share of Sulu Ltd. using each of the following valuation methods:

    (i) Net assets (liquidation) basis

    (ii) Dividend yield

    (iii) Price/earnings ratio.

(b) Critically evaluate each of the valuation methods identified in part (a) above.

14.17 You are employed by Eel Company and are trying to decide which company to acquire—Feel Ltd. or Feelings Corp. The relevant data are shown below.

	Eel Ltd.	Feel Inc.	Feelings Corp.
Number of shares outstanding	1,130,000	1,567,000	1,945,000
Share price	$30.00	$40.00	$50.00
Number of Eel shares offered for each target share		2	2
Post-acquisition savings		$1,800,000	$6,320,000
2010 net income	$3,000,000	$4,000,000	$5,000,000

Required:

(a) Calculate the market value of each of the three companies involved.

(b) Calculate the market value of Eel's potential bid for Feel and for Feelings.

(c) Calculate the bid premium for both potential acquisitions.

(d) Calculate the pre-acquisition EPS of the three companies involved.

(e) Calculate the pre-acquisition P/E ratio of the three companies involved.

(f) Calculate the estimated post-acquisition EPS for each of the potential acquisitions.

(g) Calculate the estimated post-acquisition share price for Eel for each of the potential acquisitions, assuming the pre-acquisition P/E ratio for Eel applies after the deal goes forward.

(h) Which acquisition do you recommend for Eel?

APPENDIX A

Financial Tables

TABLE A1 Future Value Interest Factors (FVIF) for One Dollar Compounded at r Percent for n Periods:

$$\text{FVIF}_{r,n} = (1 + r)^n$$

TABLE A2 Present Value Interest Factors (PVIF) for One Dollar Discounted at r Percent for n Periods:

$$\text{PVIF}_{r,n} = \frac{1}{(1 + r)^n}$$

TABLE A3 Future Value Interest Factors for an Annuity (FVIFA) of One Dollar Compounded at r Percent for n Periods:

$$\text{FVIFA}_{r,n} = \sum_{t=1}^{n}(1 + r)^{n-t} = \frac{(1 + r)^n - 1}{r} \text{ (for non-zero } r\text{)}$$

TABLE A4 Present Value Interest Factors for an Annuity (PVIFA) of One Dollar Discounted at r Percent for n Periods:

$$\text{PVIFA}_{r,n} = \sum_{t=1}^{n}\frac{1}{(1 + r)^t} = \frac{1 - \dfrac{1}{(1 + r)^n}}{r} = \frac{1}{r} - \frac{1}{r(1 + r)^n} \text{ (for non-zero } r\text{)}$$

TABLE A5 Annual Equivalent Factor Table

$$\frac{r}{1 - \dfrac{1}{(1 + r)^n}}$$

Note: Using the factors in these tables rather than Excel software to solve problems may produce slightly different answers because of rounding differences.

TABLE A1 Future Value Interest Factors (FVIF) for One Dollar Compounded at *r* Percent for *n* Periods:

$$FVIF_{r,n} = (1 + r)^n$$

Interest Rate, *r*

Number of Periods, *n*	0%	1%	2%	3%	4%	5%	6%	7%	8%	9%	10%
0	1.0000	1.0000	1.0000	1.0000	1.0000	1.0000	1.0000	1.0000	1.0000	1.0000	1.0000
1	1.0000	1.0100	1.0200	1.0300	1.0400	1.0500	1.0600	1.0700	1.0800	1.0900	1.1000
2	1.0000	1.0201	1.0404	1.0609	1.0816	1.1025	1.1236	1.1449	1.1664	1.1881	1.2100
3	1.0000	1.0303	1.0612	1.0927	1.1249	1.1576	1.1910	1.2250	1.2597	1.2950	1.3310
4	1.0000	1.0406	1.0824	1.1255	1.1699	1.2155	1.2625	1.3108	1.3605	1.4116	1.4641
5	1.0000	1.0510	1.1041	1.1593	1.2167	1.2763	1.3382	1.4026	1.4693	1.5386	1.6105
6	1.0000	1.0615	1.1262	1.1941	1.2653	1.3401	1.4185	1.5007	1.5869	1.6771	1.7716
7	1.0000	1.0721	1.1487	1.2299	1.3159	1.4071	1.5036	1.6058	1.7138	1.8280	1.9487
8	1.0000	1.0829	1.1717	1.2668	1.3686	1.4775	1.5938	1.7182	1.8509	1.9926	2.1436
9	1.0000	1.0937	1.1951	1.3048	1.4233	1.5513	1.6895	1.8385	1.9990	2.1719	2.3579
10	1.0000	1.1046	1.2190	1.3439	1.4802	1.6289	1.7908	1.9672	2.1589	2.3674	2.5937
11	1.0000	1.1157	1.1234	1.3842	1.5395	1.7103	1.8983	2.1049	2.3316	2.5804	2.8531
12	1.0000	1.1268	1.2682	1.4258	1.6010	1.7959	2.0122	2.2522	2.5182	2.8127	3.1384
13	1.0000	1.1381	1.2936	1.4685	1.6651	1.8856	2.1329	2.4098	2.7196	3.0658	3.4523
14	1.0000	1.1495	1.3195	1.5126	1.7317	1.9799	2.2609	2.5785	2.9372	3.3417	3.7975
15	1.0000	1.1610	1.3459	1.5580	1.8009	2.0789	2.3966	2.7590	3.1722	3.6425	4.1772
16	1.0000	1.1726	1.3728	1.6047	1.8730	2.1829	2.5404	2.9522	3.4259	3.9703	4.5950
17	1.0000	1.1843	1.4002	1.6528	1.9479	2.2920	2.6928	3.1588	3.7000	4.3276	5.0545
18	1.0000	1.1961	1.4282	1.7024	2.0258	2.4066	2.8543	3.3799	3.9960	4.7171	5.5599
19	1.0000	1.2081	1.4568	1.7535	2.1068	2.5270	3.0256	3.6165	4.3157	5.1417	6.1159
20	1.0000	1.2202	1.4859	1.8061	2.1911	2.6533	3.2071	3.8697	4.6610	5.6044	6.7275
25	1.0000	1.2824	1.6406	2.0938	2.6658	3.3864	4.2919	5.4274	6.8485	8.6231	10.8347
30	1.0000	1.3478	1.8114	2.4273	3.2434	4.3219	5.7435	7.6123	10.0627	13.2677	17.4494
35	1.0000	1.4166	1.9999	2.8139	3.9461	5.5160	7.6861	10.6766	14.7853	20.4140	28.1024
40	1.0000	1.4889	2.2080	3.2620	4.8010	7.0400	10.2857	14.9745	21.7245	31.4094	45.2593
45	1.0000	1.5648	2.4379	3.7816	5.8412	8.9850	13.7646	21.0025	31.9204	48.3273	72.8905
50	1.0000	1.6446	2.6916	4.3839	7.1067	11.4674	18.4202	29.4570	46.9016	74.3575	117.391

Number of Periods, *n*	12%	14%	16%	18%	20%	25%	30%	35%	40%	45%	50%
0	1.0000	1.0000	1.0000	1.0000	1.0000	1.0000	1.0000	1.0000	1.0000	1.0000	1.0000
1	1.1200	1.1400	1.1600	1.1800	1.2000	1.2500	1.3000	1.3500	1.4000	1.4500	1.5000
2	1.2544	1.2996	1.3456	1.3924	1.4400	1.5625	1.6900	1.8225	1.9600	2.1025	2.2500
3	1.4049	1.4815	1.5609	1.6430	1.7280	1.9531	2.1970	2.4604	2.7440	3.0486	3.3750
4	1.5735	1.6890	1.8106	1.9388	2.0736	2.4414	2.8561	3.3215	3.8416	4.4205	5.0625
5	1.7623	1.9254	2.1003	2.2878	2.4883	3.0518	3.7129	4.4840	5.3782	6.4097	7.5938
6	1.9738	2.1950	2.4364	2.6996	2.9860	3.8147	4.8268	6.0534	7.5295	9.2941	11.3906
7	2.2107	2.5023	2.8262	3.1855	3.5832	4.7684	6.2749	8.1722	10.5414	13.4765	17.0859
8	2.4760	2.8526	3.2784	3.7589	4.2998	5.9605	8.1573	11.0324	14.7579	19.5409	25.6289
9	2.7731	3.2519	3.8030	4.4355	5.1598	7.4506	10.6045	14.8937	20.6610	28.3343	38.4434
10	3.1058	3.7072	4.4114	5.2338	6.1917	9.3132	13.7858	20.1066	28.9255	41.0847	57.6650
11	3.4785	4.2262	5.1173	6.1759	7.4301	11.6415	17.9216	27.1439	40.4957	59.5728	86.4976
12	3.8960	4.8179	5.9360	7.2876	8.9161	14.5519	23.2981	36.6442	56.6939	86.3806	129.7463
13	4.3635	5.4924	6.8858	8.5994	10.6993	18.1899	30.2875	49.4697	79.3715	125.2518	194.6195
14	4.8871	6.2613	7.9875	10.1472	12.8392	22.7374	39.3738	66.7841	111.1201	181.6151	291.9293
15	5.4736	7.1379	9.2655	11.9737	15.4070	28.4217	51.1859	90.1585	155.5681	263.3419	437.8939
16	6.1304	8.1372	10.7480	14.1290	18.4884	35.5271	66.5417	121.7139	217.7953	381.8458	656.8408
17	6.8660	9.2765	12.4677	16.6722	22.1861	44.4089	86.5042	164.3138	304.9135	553.6764	985.2613
18	7.6900	10.5752	14.4625	19.6733	26.6233	55.5112	112.4554	221.8236	426.8789	802.8308	1477.8919
19	8.6128	12.0557	16.7765	23.2144	31.9480	69.3889	146.1920	299.4619	597.6304	1164.1047	2216.8378
20	9.6463	13.7435	19.4608	27.3930	38.3376	86.7362	190.0496	404.2736	836.6826	1687.9518	2325.2567
25	17.0001	26.4619	40.8742	62.6686	95.3962	264.698	705.641	1812.78	4499.88	10819.3	25251.2
30	29.9599	50.9502	85.8499	143.371	237.376	807.794	2620.00	8128.55	24201.4	69349.0	191751
35	52.7996	98.1002	180.314	327.997	590.668	2465.19	9727.86	36448.7	130161	444509	1456110
40	93.0510	188.884	378.721	750.378	1469.77	7523.16	36118.9	163437	700038	2849181	11057332
45	163.988	363.679	795.444	1716.68	3657.26	22958.9	134107	732858	3764971	18262495	83966617
50	289.002	700.233	1670.70	3927.36	9100.44	70064.9	497929	3286158	20248916	117057734	637621500

TABLE A2 Present Value Interest Factors (PVIF) for One Dollar Discounted at r Percent for n Periods:

$$PVIF_{r,n} = \frac{1}{(1+r)^n}$$

Discount Rate, r

Number of Periods, n	0%	1%	2%	3%	4%	5%	6%	7%	8%	9%	10%
0	1.0000	1.0000	1.0000	1.0000	1.0000	1.0000	1.0000	1.0000	1.0000	1.0000	1.0000
1	1.0000	0.9901	0.9804	0.9709	0.9615	0.9524	0.9434	0.9346	0.9259	0.9174	0.9091
2	1.0000	0.9803	0.9612	0.9426	0.9246	0.9070	0.8900	0.8734	0.8573	0.8417	0.8264
3	1.0000	0.9706	0.9423	0.9151	0.8890	0.8638	0.8396	0.8163	0.7938	0.7722	0.7513
4	1.0000	0.9610	0.9238	0.8885	0.8548	0.8227	0.7921	0.7629	0.7350	0.7084	0.6830
5	1.0000	0.9515	0.9057	0.8626	0.8219	0.7835	0.7473	0.7130	0.6806	0.6499	0.6209
6	1.0000	0.9420	0.8880	0.8375	0.7903	0.7462	0.7050	0.6663	0.6302	0.5963	0.5645
7	1.0000	0.9327	0.8706	0.8131	0.7599	0.7107	0.6651	0.6227	0.5835	0.5470	0.5132
8	1.0000	0.9235	0.8535	0.7894	0.7307	0.6768	0.6274	0.5820	0.5403	0.5019	0.4665
9	1.0000	0.9143	0.8368	0.7664	0.7026	0.6446	0.5919	0.5439	0.5002	0.4604	0.4241
10	1.0000	0.9053	0.8203	0.7441	0.6756	0.6139	0.5584	0.5083	0.4632	0.4224	0.3855
11	1.0000	0.8963	0.8043	0.7224	0.6496	0.5847	0.5268	0.4751	0.4289	0.3875	0.3505
12	1.0000	0.8874	0.7885	0.7014	0.6246	0.5568	0.4970	0.4440	0.3971	0.3555	0.3186
13	1.0000	0.8787	0.7730	0.6810	0.6006	0.5303	0.4688	0.4150	0.3677	0.3262	0.2897
14	1.0000	0.8700	0.7579	0.6611	0.5775	0.5051	0.4423	0.3878	0.3405	0.2992	0.2633
15	1.0000	0.8613	0.7430	0.6419	0.5553	0.4810	0.4173	0.3624	0.3152	0.2745	0.2394
16	1.0000	0.8528	0.7284	0.6232	0.5339	0.4581	0.3936	0.3387	0.2919	0.2519	0.2176
17	1.0000	0.8444	0.7142	0.6050	0.5134	0.4363	0.3714	0.3166	0.2703	0.2311	0.1978
18	1.0000	0.8360	0.7002	0.5874	0.4936	0.4155	0.3503	0.2959	0.2502	0.2120	0.1799
19	1.0000	0.8277	0.6864	0.5703	0.4746	0.3957	0.3305	0.2765	0.2317	0.1945	0.1635
20	1.0000	0.8195	0.6730	0.5537	0.4564	0.3769	0.3118	0.2584	0.2145	0.1784	0.1486
25	1.0000	0.7798	0.6095	0.4776	0.3751	0.2953	0.2330	0.1842	0.1460	0.1160	0.0923
30	1.0000	0.7419	0.5521	0.4120	0.3083	0.2314	0.1741	0.1314	0.0994	0.0754	0.0573
35	1.0000	0.7059	0.5000	0.3554	0.2534	0.1813	0.1301	0.0937	0.0676	0.0490	0.0356
40	1.0000	0.6717	0.4529	0.3066	0.2083	0.1420	0.0972	0.0668	0.0460	0.0318	0.0221
45	1.0000	0.6391	0.4102	0.2644	0.1712	0.1113	0.0727	0.0476	0.0313	0.0207	0.0137
50	1.0000	0.6080	0.3715	0.2281	0.1407	0.0872	0.0543	0.0339	0.0213	0.0134	0.0085

Discount Rate, r

Number of Periods, n	12%	14%	16%	18%	20%	25%	30%	35%	40%	45%	50%
0	1.0000	1.0000	1.0000	1.0000	1.0000	1.0000	1.0000	1.0000	1.0000	1.0000	1.0000
1	0.8929	0.8772	0.8621	0.8475	0.8333	0.8000	0.7692	0.7407	0.7143	0.6897	0.6667
2	0.7972	0.7695	0.7432	0.7182	0.6944	0.6400	0.5917	0.5487	0.5102	0.4756	0.4444
3	0.7118	0.6750	0.6407	0.6086	0.5787	0.5120	0.4552	0.4064	0.3644	0.3280	0.2963
4	0.6355	0.5921	0.5523	0.5158	0.4823	0.4096	0.3501	0.3011	0.2603	0.2262	0.1975
5	0.5674	0.5194	0.4761	0.4371	0.4019	0.3277	0.2693	0.2230	0.1859	0.1560	0.1317
6	0.5066	0.4556	0.4104	0.3704	0.3349	0.2621	0.2072	0.1652	0.1328	0.1076	0.0878
7	0.4523	0.3996	0.3538	0.3139	0.2791	0.2097	0.1594	0.1224	0.0949	0.0742	0.0585
8	0.4039	0.3506	0.3050	0.2660	0.2326	0.1678	0.1226	0.0906	0.0678	0.0512	0.0390
9	0.3606	0.3075	0.2630	0.2255	0.1938	0.1342	0.0943	0.0671	0.0484	0.0353	0.0260
10	0.3220	0.2697	0.2267	0.1911	0.1615	0.1074	0.0725	0.0497	0.0346	0.0243	0.0173
11	0.2875	0.2366	0.1954	0.1619	0.1346	0.0859	0.0558	0.0368	0.0247	0.0168	0.0116
12	0.2567	0.2076	0.1685	0.1372	0.1122	0.0687	0.0429	0.0273	0.0176	0.0116	0.0077
13	0.2292	0.1821	0.1452	0.1163	0.0935	0.0550	0.0330	0.0202	0.0126	0.0080	0.0051
14	0.2046	0.1597	0.1252	0.0985	0.0779	0.0440	0.0254	0.0150	0.0090	0.0055	0.0034
15	0.1827	0.1401	0.1079	0.0835	0.0649	0.0352	0.0195	0.0111	0.0064	0.0038	0.0023
16	0.1631	0.1229	0.0930	0.0708	0.0541	0.0281	0.0150	0.0082	0.0046	0.0026	0.0015
17	0.1456	0.1078	0.0802	0.0600	0.0451	0.0225	0.0116	0.0061	0.0033	0.0018	0.0010
18	0.1300	0.0946	0.0691	0.0508	0.0376	0.0180	0.0089	0.0045	0.0023	0.0012	0.0007
19	0.1161	0.0829	0.0596	0.0431	0.0313	0.0144	0.0068	0.0033	0.0017	0.0009	0.0005
20	0.1037	0.0728	0.0514	0.0365	0.0261	0.0115	0.0053	0.0025	0.0012	0.0006	0.0003
25	0.0588	0.0378	0.0245	0.0160	0.0105	0.0038	0.0014	0.0006	0.0002	0.0001	0.0000
30	0.0334	0.0196	0.0116	0.0070	0.0042	0.0012	0.0004	0.0001	0.0000	0.0000	0.0000
35	0.0189	0.0102	0.0055	0.0030	0.0017	0.0004	0.0001	0.0000	0.0000	0.0000	0.0000
40	0.0107	0.0053	0.0026	0.0013	0.0007	0.0001	0.0000	0.0000	0.0000	0.0000	0.0000
45	0.0061	0.0027	0.0013	0.0006	0.0003	0.0000	0.0000	0.0000	0.0000	0.0000	0.0000
50	0.0035	0.0014	0.0006	0.0003	0.0001	0.0000	0.0000	0.0000	0.0000	0.0000	0.0000

TABLE A3 Future Value Interest Factors for an Annuity (FVIFA) of One Dollar Compounded at r Percent for n Periods:

$$FVIFA_{r,n} = \sum_{t=1}^{n} (1 + r)^{n-t} = \frac{(1 + r)^n - 1}{r} \text{ (for non-zero } r)$$

Interest Rate, r

Number of Annuity Payments, n	0%	1%	2%	3%	4%	5%	6%	7%	8%	9%	10%
1	1.0000	1.0000	1.0000	1.0000	1.0000	1.0000	1.0000	1.0000	1.0000	1.0000	1.0000
2	2.0000	2.0100	2.0200	2.0300	2.0400	2.0500	2.0600	2.0700	2.0800	2.0900	2.1000
3	3.0000	3.0301	3.0604	3.0909	3.1216	3.1525	3.1836	3.2149	3.2464	3.2781	3.3100
4	4.0000	4.0604	4.1216	4.1836	4.2465	4.3101	4.3746	4.4399	4.5061	4.5731	4.6410
5	5.0000	5.1010	5.2040	5.3091	5.4163	5.5256	5.6371	5.7507	5.8666	5.9847	6.1051
6	6.0000	6.1520	6.3081	6.4684	6.6330	6.8019	6.9753	7.1533	7.3359	7.5233	7.7156
7	7.0000	7.2135	7.4343	7.6625	7.8983	8.1420	8.3938	8.6540	8.9228	9.2004	9.4872
8	8.0000	8.2857	8.5830	8.8923	9.2142	9.5491	9.8975	10.2598	10.6366	11.0285	11.4359
9	9.0000	9.3685	9.7546	10.1591	10.5828	11.0266	11.4913	11.9780	12.4876	13.0210	13.5795
10	10.0000	10.4622	10.9497	11.4639	12.0061	12.5779	13.1808	13.8164	14.4866	15.1929	15.9374
11	11.0000	11.5668	12.1687	12.8078	13.4864	14.2068	14.9716	15.7836	16.6455	17.5603	18.5312
12	12.0000	12.6825	13.4121	14.1920	15.0258	15.9171	16.8699	17.8885	18.9771	20.1407	21.3843
13	13.0000	13.8093	14.6803	15.6178	16.6268	17.7130	18.8821	20.1406	21.4953	22.9534	24.5227
14	14.0000	14.9474	15.9739	17.0863	18.2919	19.5986	21.0151	22.5505	24.2149	26.0192	27.9750
15	15.0000	16.0969	17.2934	18.5989	20.0236	21.5786	23.2760	25.1290	27.1521	29.3609	31.7725
16	16.0000	17.2579	18.6393	20.1569	21.8245	23.6575	25.6725	27.8881	30.3243	33.0034	35.9497
17	17.0000	18.4304	20.0121	21.7616	23.6975	25.8404	28.2129	30.8402	33.7502	36.9737	40.5447
18	18.0000	19.6147	21.4123	23.4144	25.6454	28.1324	30.9057	33.9990	37.4502	41.3013	45.5992
19	19.0000	20.8109	22.8406	25.1169	27.6712	30.5390	33.7600	37.3790	41.4463	46.0185	51.1591
20	20.0000	22.0190	24.2974	26.8704	29.7781	33.0660	36.7856	40.9955	45.7620	51.1601	57.2750
25	25.0000	28.2432	32.0303	36.4593	41.6459	47.7271	54.8645	63.2490	73.1059	84.7009	98.3471
30	30.0000	34.7849	40.5681	47.5754	56.0849	66.4388	79.0582	94.4608	113.283	136.308	164.494
35	35.0000	41.6603	49.9945	60.4621	73.6522	90.3203	111.435	138.237	172.317	215.711	271.024
40	40.0000	48.8864	60.4020	75.4013	95.0255	120.800	154.762	199.635	259.057	337.882	442.593
45	45.0000	56.4811	71.8927	92.7199	121.029	159.700	212.744	285.749	386.506	525.859	718.905
50	50.0000	64.4632	84.5794	112.797	152.667	209.348	290.336	406.529	573.770	815.084	1163.91

Number of Annuity Payments, n	12%	14%	16%	18%	20%	25%	30%	35%	40%	45%	50%
1	1.0000	1.0000	1.0000	1.0000	1.0000	1.0000	1.0000	1.0000	1.0000	1.0000	1.0000
2	2.1200	2.1400	2.1600	2.1800	2.2000	2.2500	2.3000	2.3500	2.4000	2.4500	2.5000
3	3.3744	3.4396	3.5056	3.5724	3.6400	3.8125	3.9900	4.1725	4.3600	4.5525	4.7500
4	4.7793	4.9211	5.0665	5.2154	5.3680	5.7656	6.1870	6.6329	7.1040	7.6011	8.1250
5	6.3528	6.6101	6.8771	7.1542	7.4416	8.2070	9.0431	9.9544	10.9456	12.0216	13.1875
6	8.1152	8.5355	8.9775	9.4420	9.9299	11.2588	12.7560	14.4384	16.3238	18.4314	20.7813
7	10.0890	10.7305	11.4139	12.1415	12.9159	15.0735	17.5828	20.4919	23.8534	27.7255	32.1719
8	12.2997	13.2328	14.2401	15.3270	16.4991	19.8419	23.8577	28.6640	34.3947	41.2019	49.2578
9	14.7757	16.0853	17.5185	19.0859	20.7989	25.8023	32.0150	39.6964	49.1526	60.7428	74.8867
10	17.5487	19.3373	21.3215	23.5213	25.9587	33.2529	42.6195	54.5902	69.8137	89.0771	113.330
11	20.6546	23.0445	25.7329	28.7551	32.1504	42.5661	56.4053	74.6967	98.7391	130.162	170.995
12	24.1331	27.2707	30.8502	34.9311	39.5805	54.2077	74.3270	101.841	139.235	189.735	257.493
13	28.0291	32.0887	36.7862	42.2187	48.4966	68.7596	97.6250	138.485	195.929	276.115	387.239
14	32.3926	37.5811	43.6720	50.8180	59.1959	86.9495	127.913	187.954	275.300	401.367	581.859
15	37.2797	43.8424	51.6595	60.9653	72.0351	109.687	167.286	254.738	386.420	582.982	873.788
16	42.7533	50.9804	60.9250	72.9390	87.4421	138.109	218.472	344.897	541.988	846.324	1311.68
17	48.8837	59.1176	71.6730	87.0680	105.931	173.636	285.014	466.611	759.784	1228.17	1968.52
18	55.7497	68.3941	84.1407	103.740	128.117	218.045	371.518	630.925	1064.70	1781.85	2953.78
19	63.4397	78.9692	98.6032	123.414	154.740	273.556	483.973	852.748	1491.58	2584.68	4431.68
20	72.0524	91.0249	115.380	146.628	186.688	342.945	630.165	1152.21	2089.21	3748.78	6648.51
25	133.334	181.871	249.214	342.603	471.981	1054.79	2348.80	5176.50	11247.2	24040.7	50500.3
30	241.333	356.787	530.312	790.948	1181.88	3227.17	8729.99	23221.6	60501.1	154107	383500
35	431.663	693.573	1120.71	1816.65	2948.34	9856.76	32422.9	104136	325400	987794	2912217
40	767.091	1342.03	2360.76	4163.21	7343.86	30088.7	120393	466960	1750092	6331512	22114663
45	1358.23	2590.56	4965.27	9531.58	18281.3	91831.5	447019	2093876	9412424	40583319	167933233
50	2400.02	4994.52	10435.6	21813.1	45497.2	280256	1659761	9389020	50622288	260128295	1275242998

TABLE A4 Present Value Interest Factors for an Annuity (PVIFA) of One Dollar Discounted at r Percent for n Periods:

$$PVIFA_{r,n} = \sum_{t=1}^{n} \frac{1}{(1+r)^t} = \frac{1 - \dfrac{1}{(1+r)^n}}{r} = \frac{1}{r} - \frac{1}{r(1+r)^n} \text{ (for non-zero } r)$$

Discount Rate, r

Number of Annuity Payments, n	0%	1%	2%	3%	4%	5%	6%	7%	8%	9%	10%
1	1.0000	0.9901	0.9804	0.9709	0.9615	0.9524	0.9434	0.9346	0.9259	0.9174	0.9091
2	2.0000	1.9704	1.9416	1.9135	1.8861	1.8594	1.8334	1.8080	1.7833	1.7591	1.7355
3	3.0000	2.9410	2.8839	2.8286	2.7751	2.7232	2.6730	2.6243	2.5771	2.5313	2.4869
4	4.0000	3.9020	3.8077	3.7171	3.6299	3.5460	3.4651	3.3872	3.3121	3.2397	3.1699
5	5.0000	4.8534	4.7135	4.5797	4.4518	4.3295	4.2124	4.1002	3.9927	3.8897	3.7908
6	6.0000	5.7955	5.6014	5.4172	5.2421	5.0757	4.9173	4.7665	4.6229	4.4859	4.3553
7	7.0000	6.7282	6.4720	6.2303	6.0021	5.7864	5.5824	5.3893	5.2064	5.0330	4.8684
8	8.0000	7.6517	7.3255	7.0197	6.7327	6.4632	6.2098	5.9713	5.7466	5.5348	5.3349
9	9.0000	8.5660	8.1622	7.7861	7.4353	7.1078	6.8017	6.5152	6.2469	5.9952	5.7590
10	10.0000	9.4713	8.9826	8.5302	8.1109	7.7217	7.3601	7.0236	6.7101	6.4177	6.1446
11	11.0000	10.3676	9.7868	9.2526	8.7605	8.3064	7.8869	7.4987	7.1390	6.8052	6.4951
12	12.0000	11.2551	10.5753	9.9540	9.3851	8.8633	8.3838	7.9427	7.5361	7.1607	6.8137
13	13.0000	12.1337	11.3484	10.6350	9.9856	9.3936	8.8527	8.3577	7.9038	7.4869	7.1034
14	14.0000	13.0037	12.1062	11.2961	10.5631	9.8986	9.2950	8.7455	8.2442	7.7862	7.3667
15	15.0000	13.8651	12.8493	11.9379	11.1184	10.3797	9.7122	9.1079	8.5595	8.0607	7.6061
16	16.0000	14.7179	13.5777	12.5611	11.6523	10.8378	10.1059	9.4466	8.8514	8.3126	7.8237
17	17.0000	15.5623	14.2919	13.1661	12.1657	11.2741	10.4773	9.7632	9.1216	8.5436	8.0216
18	18.0000	16.3983	14.9920	13.7535	12.6583	11.6896	10.8276	10.0591	9.3719	8.7556	8.2014
19	19.0000	17.2260	15.6785	14.3238	13.1339	12.0853	11.1581	10.3356	9.6036	8.9501	8.3649
20	20.0000	18.0456	16.3514	14.8775	13.5903	12.4622	11.4699	10.5940	9.8181	9.1285	8.5136
25	25.0000	22.0232	19.5235	17.4131	15.6221	14.0939	12.7834	11.6536	10.6748	9.8226	9.0770
30	30.0000	25.8077	22.3965	19.6004	17.2920	15.3725	13.7648	12.4090	11.2578	10.2737	9.4269
35	35.0000	29.4086	24.9986	21.4872	18.6646	16.3742	14.4982	12.9477	11.6546	10.5668	9.5442
40	40.0000	32.8347	27.3555	23.1148	19.7928	17.1591	15.0463	13.3317	11.9246	10.7574	9.7791
45	45.0000	36.0945	29.4902	24.5187	20.7200	17.7741	15.4558	13.6055	12.1084	10.8812	9.8628
50	50.0000	39.1961	31.4236	25.7298	21.4822	18.2559	15.7619	13.8007	12.2335	10.9617	9.9148

Discount Rate, *r*

Number of Annuity Payments, *n*	12%	14%	16%	18%	20%	25%	30%	35%	40%	45%	50%
1	0.8929	0.8772	0.8621	0.8475	0.8333	0.8000	0.7692	0.7407	0.7413	0.6897	0.6667
2	1.6901	1.6467	1.6052	1.5656	1.5278	1.4400	1.3609	1.2894	1.2245	1.1653	1.1111
3	2.4018	2.3216	2.2459	2.1743	2.1065	1.9520	1.8161	1.6959	1.5889	1.4933	1.4074
4	3.0373	2.9137	2.7982	2.6901	2.5887	2.5616	2.1662	1.9969	1.8492	1.7195	1.6049
5	3.6048	3.4331	3.2743	3.1272	2.9906	2.6893	2.4356	2.2200	2.0352	1.8755	1.7366
6	4.1114	3.8887	3.6847	3.4976	3.3255	2.9514	2.6427	2.3852	2.1680	1.9831	1.8244
7	4.5638	4.2883	4.0386	3.8115	3.6046	3.1611	2.8021	2.5075	2.2628	2.0573	1.8829
8	4.9676	4.6389	4.3436	4.0776	3.8372	3.3289	2.9247	2.5982	2.3306	2.1085	1.9220
9	5.3282	4.9464	4.6065	4.3030	4.0310	3.4631	3.0190	2.6653	2.3790	2.1438	1.9480
10	5.6502	5.2161	4.8332	4.4941	4.1925	3.5704	3.0915	2.7150	2.4136	2.1681	1.9653
11	5.9377	5.4527	5.0286	4.6560	4.3271	3.6564	3.1473	2.7519	2.4383	2.1849	1.9769
12	6.1944	5.6603	5.1971	4.7932	4.4392	3.7251	3.1903	2.7792	2.4559	2.1965	1.9846
13	6.4235	5.8424	5.3423	4.9095	4.5327	3.7801	3.2233	2.7994	2.4685	2.2045	1.9897
14	6.6282	6.0021	5.4675	5.0081	4.6106	3.8241	3.2487	2.8144	2.4775	2.2100	1.9931
15	6.8109	6.1422	5.5755	5.0916	4.6755	3.8593	3.2682	2.8255	2.4839	2.2138	1.9954
16	6.9740	6.2651	5.6685	5.1624	4.7296	3.8874	3.2832	2.8337	2.4885	2.2164	1.9970
17	7.1196	6.3729	5.7487	5.2223	4.7746	3.9099	3.2948	2.8398	2.4918	2.2182	1.9980
18	7.2497	6.4674	5.8178	5.2732	4.8122	3.9279	3.3037	2.8443	2.4941	2.2195	1.9986
19	7.3658	6.5504	5.8775	5.3162	4.8435	3.9424	3.3105	2.8476	2.4958	2.2203	1.9991
20	7.4694	6.6231	5.9288	5.3527	4.8696	3.9539	3.3158	2.8501	2.4970	2.2209	1.9994
25	7.8431	6.8729	6.0971	5.4669	4.9476	3.9849	3.3286	2.8556	2.4994	2.2220	1.9999
30	8.0552	7.0027	6.1772	5.5168	4.9789	3.9950	3.3321	2.8568	2.4999	2.2222	2.0000
35	8.1755	7.0700	6.2153	5.5386	4.9915	3.9984	3.3330	2.8571	2.5000	2.2222	2.0000
40	8.2438	7.1050	6.2335	5.5482	4.9966	3.9995	3.3332	2.8571	2.5000	2.2222	2.0000
45	8.2825	7.1232	6.2421	5.5523	4.9986	3.9998	3.3333	2.8571	2.5000	2.2222	2.0000
50	8.3045	7.1327	6.2463	5.5541	4.9995	3.9999	3.3333	2.8571	2.5000	2.2222	2.0000

TABLE A5 Annual Equivalent Factor Table

$$\frac{r}{1 - \dfrac{1}{(1 + r)^n}}$$

Annual equivalent factor $A_{N,r}^{-1}$

	r	0.04	0.06	0.08	0.10	0.12	0.14	0.16	0.18	0.20
N	1	1.0400	1.0600	1.0800	1.1000	1.1200	1.1400	1.1600	1.1800	1.2000
	2	0.5302	0.5454	0.5608	0.5762	0.5917	0.6073	0.6230	0.6387	0.6545
	3	0.3603	0.3741	0.3880	0.4021	0.4163	0.4307	0.4453	0.4599	0.4747
	4	0.2755	0.2886	0.3019	0.3155	0.3292	0.3432	0.3574	0.3717	0.3863
	5	0.2246	0.2374	0.2505	0.2638	0.2774	0.2913	0.3054	0.3198	0.3344
	6	0.1908	0.2034	0.2163	0.2296	0.2432	0.2572	0.2714	0.2859	0.3007
	7	0.1666	0.1791	0.1921	0.2054	0.2191	0.2332	0.2476	0.2624	0.2774
	8	0.1485	0.1610	0.1740	0.1874	0.2013	0.2156	0.2302	0.2452	0.2606
	9	0.1345	0.1470	0.1601	0.1736	0.1877	0.2022	0.2171	0.2324	0.2481
	10	0.1233	0.1359	0.1490	0.1627	0.1770	0.1917	0.2069	0.2225	0.2385
	11	0.1141	0.1268	0.1401	0.1540	0.1684	0.1834	0.1989	0.2148	0.2311
	12	0.1066	0.1193	0.1327	0.1468	0.1614	0.1767	0.1924	0.2086	0.2253
	13	0.1001	0.1130	0.1265	0.1408	0.1557	0.1712	0.1872	0.2037	0.2206
	14	0.0947	0.1076	0.1213	0.1357	0.1509	0.1666	0.1829	0.1997	0.2169
	15	0.0899	0.1030	0.1168	0.1315	0.1468	0.1628	0.1794	0.1964	0.2139

Solutions
to Self-Assessment Questions

CHAPTER 2

2.1 Prince George Airport Authority

(a)

Prince George Airport Authority
Income Statement
for the year ended December 31, 2010

Revenues		$1,200,000
Expenses		
Gas expense	$670,000	
Salaries expense	300,000	
Depreciation expense	60,000	
Total expenses		1,030,000
Net income		$ 170,000

(b)

Prince George Airport Authority
Statement of Retained Earnings
for the year ended December 31, 2010

Retained earnings, January 1, 2010	$203,000
Add: Net income	170,000
Less: Dividends	(100,000)
Retained earnings, December 31, 2010	$273,000

Note: Using the factors in the tables in Appendix A rather than Excel software to solve problems may produce slightly different answers because of rounding differences.

(c)

Prince George Airport Authority
Balance Sheet
as at December 31, 2010

Current assets			
Cash		$ 25,000	
Accounts receivable		70,000	
Total current assets			$ 95,000
Property, plant, and equipment			
Land		100,000	
Hangars	$275,000		
Less: Accumulated depreciation—Hangars	100,000	175,000	
Airplanes	450,000		
Less: Accumulated depreciation—Airplanes	100,000	350,000	
Total property, plant, and equipment, net			625,000
Total assets			$720,000
Current liabilities			
Accounts payable		$ 47,000	
Long-term liabilities			
Bonds payable, due 2020		200,000	
Total liabilities			247,000
Shareholders' equity			
Common shares		200,000	
Retained earnings, December 31, 2010		273,000	
Total shareholders' equity			473,000
Total liabilities and shareholders' equity			$720,000

2.2   North Battleford Gypsum Ltd.

(a)

Purchase of new furniture and equipment		
2010 balance		$276,000
2009 balance	$296,000	
Less: Cost of furniture and equipment sold	50,000	
Adjusted 2009 furniture and equipment		246,000
Purchase of new furniture and equipment		$ 30,000

(b)

North Battleford Gypsum Ltd.
Balance Sheet
as at December 31

	2010	2009	Difference
Cash	$ 350,000	$ 267,000	$ 83,000
Accounts receivable	221,000	180,000	41,000
Inventory	362,000	300,000	62,000
Land	428,000	300,000	128,000
Buildings	728,000	728,000	—
Accumulated depreciation—Buildings	(354,000)	(320,000)	(34,000)
Furniture and equipment	276,000	296,000	(20,000)
Accumulated depreciation—F. & E.	(150,000)	(175,000)	25,000
Trucks	163,000	140,000	23,000
Accumulated depreciation—Trucks	(50,000)	(35,000)	(15,000)
Total assets	$1,974,000	$1,681,000	
Accounts payable	$ 300,000	$ 420,000	(120,000)
Bonds payable, 2020	450,000	350,000	100,000
Common shares	500,000	350,000	150,000
Retained earnings	724,000	561,000	163,000
Total liabilities and shareholders' equity	$1,974,000	$1,681,000	

North Battleford Gypsum Ltd.
Cash Flow Statement
for the year ended December 31, 2010

Cash flows from operating activities

Net income	$ 806,000	
Add back: Depreciation	64,000	
Less: Gain on sale of furniture	(30,000)	
	840,000	
Less: Increase in accounts receivable	(41,000)	
Less: Increase in inventory	(62,000)	
Less: Decrease in accounts payable	(120,000)	
Decrease in cash from operating activities		$ 617,000

Cash flows from investing activities

Proceeds from sale of furniture	40,000	
Purchase of new land	(128,000)	
Purchase of new furniture and equipment	(30,000)	
Purchase of new truck	(23,000)	
Decrease in cash from investing activities		(141,000)

Cash flows from financing activities

Issue of new bonds	100,000	
Issue of new shares	150,000	
Dividends paid	(643,000)	
Increase in cash from financing activities		(393,000)
Total increase in cash		83,000
Cash at January 1, 2010		267,000
Cash at December 31, 2010		$ 350,000

CHAPTER 3

3.1   Lizard Gameware Inc.

(a) The breakeven point is 5,200 units.

Contribution margin (CM) = $46−21   = $25
B/E in units   = $130,000/25 = 5,200 units

(b) First, you must generate data for graphing. At zero sales, there is still the fixed cost. At 1,000 games sold, sales are 1,000 × $46 = $46,000. Total costs are fixed costs of $130,000 plus variable costs of 1,000 units × $21 = $151,000. Net income is $46,000 revenue less $151,000 total costs = ($105,000) loss. Continue this process until you reach a positive net income.

Unit Sales	Sales	Total Costs	Net Income (Loss)
0	$ −	$130,000	$(130,000)
1,000	$ 46,000	$151,000	$(105,000)
2,000	$ 92,000	$172,000	$ (80,000)
3,000	$138,000	$193,000	$ (55,000)
4,000	$184,000	$214,000	$ (30,000)
5,000	$230,000	$235,000	$ (5,000)
6,000	$276,000	$256,000	$ 20,000

Then, graph the data.

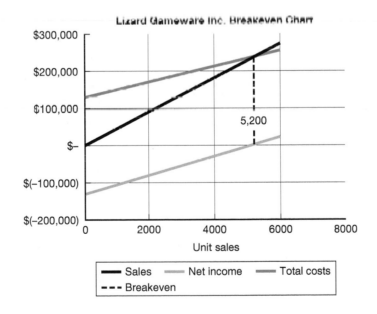

3.2   LillyPad Home Furniture Ltd.

(a)

Cash Budget for 2011
($ thousands)

	Jan.	Feb.	Mar.	Apr.	May	Jun.	Jul.	Aug.	Sep.	Oct.	Nov.	Dec.
Opening cash	2.00	(1.45)	(1.40)	2.15	5.70	9.25	12.80	16.35	19.90	23.45	27.00	30.55

Cash Receipts   **Cash Inflows from Sales**

Sales	Total Sales	Jan.	Feb.	Mar.	Apr.	May	Jun.	Jul.	Aug.	Sep.	Oct.	Nov.	Dec.	Total Cash Collections
Jan.	20.00	2.00	8.50	8.50										19.00
Feb.	20.00		2.00	8.50	8.50									19.00
Mar.	20.00			2.00	8.50	8.50								19.00
Apr.	20.00				2.00	8.50	8.50							19.00
May	20.00					2.00	8.50	8.50						19.00
Jun.	20.00						2.00	8.50	8.50					19.00
Jul.	20.00							2.00	8.50	8.50				19.00
Aug.	20.00								2.00	8.50	8.50			19.00
Sep.	20.00									2.00	8.50	8.50		19.00
Oct.	20.00										2.00	8.50	8.50	19.00
Nov.	20.00											2.00	8.50	10.50
Dec.	20.00												2.00	2.00
Total receipts per month		2.00	10.50	19.00	19.00	19.00	19.00	19.00	19.00	19.00	19.00	19.00	19.00	202.50

Cash Payments   **Cash Outflows from Purchases**

Purchases	Total Purchases	Jan.	Feb.	Mar.	Apr.	May	Jun.	Jul.	Aug.	Sep.	Oct.	Nov.	Dec.	Total Cash Payments
Jan.	10.00	5.00	5.00											10.00
Feb.	10.00		5.00	5.00										10.00
Mar.	10.00			5.00	5.00									10.00
Apr.	10.00				5.00	5.00								10.00
May	10.00					5.00	5.00							10.00
Jun.	10.00						5.00	5.00						10.00
Jul.	10.00							5.00	5.00					10.00
Aug.	10.00								5.00	5.00				10.00
Sep.	10.00									5.00	5.00			10.00
Oct.	10.00										5.00	5.00		10.00
Nov.	10.00											5.00		5.00
Dec.	10.00													0.00
Total inventory payments per month		0.00	5.00	10.00	10.00	10.00	10.00	10.00	10.00	10.00	10.00	10.00	10.00	105.00

Rent	1.00	1.00	1.00	1.00	1.00	1.00	1.00	1.00	1.00	1.00	1.00	1.00	12.00
Salaries	3.50	3.50	3.50	3.50	3.50	3.50	3.50	3.50	3.50	3.50	3.50	3.50	42.00
Commissions	0.95	0.95	0.95	0.95	0.95	0.95	0.95	0.95	0.95	0.95	0.95	0.95	11.40
Total cash outflows	5.45	10.45	15.45	15.45	15.45	15.45	15.45	15.45	15.45	15.45	15.45	15.45	170.40
Net cash flows per month	(3.45)	0.05	3.55	3.55	3.55	3.55	3.55	3.55	3.55	3.55	3.55	3.55	32.10
Closing cash balance	(1.45)	(1.40)	2.15	5.70	9.25	12.80	16.35	19.90	23.45	27.00	30.55	34.10	

(b) The cash budget shows that LillyPad will need either overdraft protection or a loan to cover the cash shortfall in January and February 2011. After that, the company's cash balance turns positive, growing throughout the year to $34,100 by year-end.

3.3   Quardis Ltd.

(a) The pro forma income statement for the year ended May 31, 2011, is:

Quardis Ltd.
Pro Forma Income Statement
for the year ended May 31, 2011
(in $ thousands)

Sales revenue		$280
Less: Cost of goods sold		
Opening inventory	$ 24	
Purchases	186	
	210	
Closing inventory	(30)	
Cost of goods sold		180
Gross profit		100
Wages	34	
Other overhead expenses	21	
Interest expense [13% × (125−30)]	12	
Depreciation—Buildings (2%× 240)	5	
Depreciation Furniture and fixtures [10% × (35 + 25)]	6	78
Net profit before tax		22
Income tax (35%)		8
Net income		14

(b)

Quardis Ltd.
Pro Forma Statement of Retained Earnings
for the year ended May 31, 2011
(in $ thousands)

Opening retained earnings, June 1	$144
Add: Net income	14
Less: Dividends paid $0.05 × 200,000	(10)
Closing retained earnings, May 31	148

(c)

Quardis Ltd.
Pro Forma Balance Sheet
as at May 31, 2011
(in $ thousands)

Current assets			
Accounts receivable (60% × $280 × 3/12)		42	
Inventory ($24 × 125%)		30	
Total current assets			72
Property, plant, and equipment			
Land		220	
Buildings	240		
Less: Accumulated depreciation (30 + 5)	35	205	
Furniture and fixtures (35 + 25)	60		
Less: Accumulated depreciation (10 + 6)	16	44	
Total property, plant, and equipment			469
Total assets			541
Current liabilities			
Bank overdraft (balancing figure)		56	
Accounts payable ($186 × 2/12)		31	
Accrued expenses (4 + 3)		7	
Income tax payable (50% × 8)		4	
Total current liabilities			98
Long-term liabilities			
Bank loan payable—First Nations' Bank (125 − 30)			95
Total liabilities			193
Shareholders' equity			
Common shares		200	
Retained earnings		148	
Total shareholders' equity			348
Total liabilities and shareholders' equity			541

(d) The pro forma statements reveal a poor profitability and liquidity position for the business. The liquidity position at May 31, 2011, reveals a serious deterioration when compared with the previous year. The management of Quardis Ltd. may wish to make certain changes to their plans. For example, the repayment of part of the loan may be deferred or the dividend may be reduced in order to improve liquidity. Similarly, the pricing policy of the business and the level of expenses proposed may be reviewed in order to improve profitability.

CHAPTER 4

4.1   Robert Paddle Inc.

(a) The horizontal and vertical analysis is:

Robert Paddle Inc.
Balance Sheets
as at December 31,

	2010	Vertical Analysis %	2009	Vertical Analysis %	Horizontal Analysis % change
Current assets					
Cash	$100,000	5.87%	$ 71,000	5.94%	40.84%
Accounts receivable	254,000	14.90%	340,000	28.43%	−25.29%
Inventory	300,000	17.60%	210,000	17.55%	42.86%
Total current assets	654,000	38.37%	621,000	51.92%	5.31%
Property, plant, and equipment					
Land	235,000	13.79%	100,000	8.36%	135.00%
Buildings (net)	652,000	38.25%	342,000	28.60%	90.64%
Equipment (net)	137,500	8.07%	122,000	10.20%	12.70%
Total property, plant, and equipment	1,024,500	60.11%	564,000	47.16%	81.65%
Intangible assets					
Patents	26,000	1.52%	11,000	0.92%	136.36%
Total assets	$1,704,500	100.00%	$1,196,000	100.00%	42.52%
Current liabilities					
Accounts payable	$85,000	4.99%	$95,000	7.94%	−10.53%
Income taxes payable	12,433	0.73%	22,467	1.88%	−44.66%
Total current liabilities	97,433	5.72%	117,467	9.82%	−17.06%
Long-term liabilities					
Bonds payable, (9%)	142,000	8.33%	264,000	22.07%	−46.21%
Total liabilities	239,433	14.05%	381,467	31.89%	−37.23%
Shareholders' equity					
Common shares (Note 1)	1,000,000	58.67%	650,000	54.35%	53.85%
Retained earnings	465,067	27.28%	164,533	13.76%	182.66%
Total shareholders' equity	1,465,067	85.95%	814,533	68.11%	79.87%
Total liabilities and shareholders' equity	$1,704,500	100.00%	$1,196,000	100.00%	42.52%

Robert Paddle Inc.
Income Statements
for the year ended December 31,

	2010	Vertical Analysis %	2009	Vertical Analysis %	Horizontal Analysis % change
Sales (Note 2)	$724,300	100.00%	$ 610,000	100.00%	18.74%
Less: Cost of goods sold (Note 3)	500,000	69.03%	356,000	58.36%	40.45%
Gross profit	224,300	30.97%	254,000	41.64%	−11.69%
Less: Operating costs	134,600	18.59%	110,690	18.15%	21.60%
Earnings before interest and taxes (EBIT)	89,700	12.38%	143,310	23.49%	−37.41%
Less: Interest expense	15,000	2.07%	25,000	4.09%	−40.00%
Earnings before taxes	74,700	10.31%	118,310	19.40%	−36.86%
Less: Income tax expense	30,000	4.14%	42,500	6.97%	−29.41%
Net income	$ 44,700	6.17%	$75,810	12.43%	−41.04%

(b) It seems that the Bobby Oar may have had a negative impact on the company in 2010. Although sales increased nearly 19%, gross profit was greatly reduced, from about 42% to 31%. Perhaps the company had some extra expenses in manufacturing the new oar, or perhaps it was offered at a discount price in order to gain market share in its first year. Either or both would hurt profits.

On the balance sheet, the company seems safe, as cash grew by 41% and liabilities fell nicely. Inventory grew by 43%. This may be planned as demand for the new oar is expected to increase next year. The company seems to be gearing up to meet this increased demand because its land and buildings also were significantly increased in 2010. It looks like another oar factory was added.

So the jury is still out on the expansion. It looks like growth due to the new Bobby Oar is likely in the future, perhaps as early as 2011.

4.2   Ali Limited and Bhaskar Corp. (I)

Profitability ratios	Ali Limited	Bhaskar Corp.
ROE	$\dfrac{99.9 \times 100}{687.6} = 14.53\%$	$\dfrac{104.6 \times 100}{1,417.7} = 7.38\%$
ROCE	$\dfrac{151.3 \times 100}{687.6 + 190.0} = 17.24\%$	$\dfrac{166.9 \times 100}{874.6 + 250.0} = 14.84\%$
Operating profit margin	$\dfrac{151.3 \times 100}{1,478.1} = 10.24\%$	$\dfrac{166.9 \times 100}{1,790.9} = 9.32\%$
Gross profit margin	$\dfrac{459.8 \times 100}{1,478.1} = 31.11\%$	$\dfrac{575.5 \times 100}{1,790.4} = 32.14\%$

Efficiency ratios		
Average inventory turnover period	$\dfrac{(480.8 + 592.0)/2 \times 365}{1,018.3} = 192.3 \text{ days}$	$\dfrac{(372.6 + 403.0)/2 \times 365}{1,214.9} = 116.5 \text{ days}$
Average collection period for receivables	$\dfrac{176.4 \times 365}{1,478.1} = 43.6 \text{ days}$	$\dfrac{321.9 \times 365}{1,790.4} = 65.6 \text{ days}$
Average payment period for payables	$\dfrac{271.4 \times 365}{1,129.5} = 87.7 \text{ days}$	$\dfrac{180.7 \times 365}{1,245.3} = 53.0 \text{ days}$
Sales to capital employed	$\dfrac{1,478.1}{687.6 + 190.0} = 1.68 \text{ times}$	$\dfrac{1,790.4}{874.6 + 250.0} = 1.59 \text{ times}$

Ali has mostly higher profitability ratios but is less efficient than Bhaskar because it takes longer to turn over its inventory and pay its payables. By taking so long to pay its bills, Ali may engender bad feelings from its suppliers, thereby affecting its ability to obtain good service in the future. The slower inventory turnover is a concern, but if it is improved to match Bhaskar, it could increase Ali's profitability significantly.

4.3   Ali Limited and Bhaskar Corp. (II)

In order to answer this question you may have used the following ratios:

	Ali Limited	Bhaskar Corp.
Current ratio	$= \dfrac{853.0}{422.4}$ $= 2.0$	$= \dfrac{816.5}{293.1}$ $= 2.8$
Acid test ratio	$= \dfrac{(853.0 - 592.0)}{422.4}$ $= 0.6$	$= \dfrac{(816.5 - 403.0)}{293.1}$ $= 1.4$
Leverage ratio	$= \dfrac{190}{(687.6 + 190)} \times 100$ $= 21.6\%$	$= \dfrac{250}{(874.6 + 250)} \times 100$ $= 22.2\%$
Times interest earned ratio	$= \dfrac{151.3}{19.4}$ $= 7.8$ times	$= \dfrac{166.9}{27.5}$ $= 6.1$ times
Dividend payout ratio	$= \dfrac{135.0}{99.9} \times 100$ $= 135\%$	$= \dfrac{95.0}{104.6} \times 100$ $= 91\%$
P/E ratio	$= \dfrac{6.50}{(99.9/320)}$ $= 20.8$ times	$= \dfrac{8.20}{(104.6/250)}$ $= 19.6$ times

Ali Limited has a much lower current ratio and acid test ratio than Bhaskar Corp. This may be partly due to Ali Limited having a lower average collection period for receivables. The acid test ratio of Ali is substantially below 1.0, suggesting a liquidity problem.

The leverage ratios of the businesses are quite similar. Neither business has excessive borrowing. The times interest earned ratio for each business is also similar. The respective ratios indicate that both businesses have good profit coverage for their interest charges.

The dividend payout ratio for each business seems very high. In the case of Ali the dividends announced for the year are considerably higher than the earnings generated during the year available for dividend. As a result, part of the dividend was paid out of retained earnings from previous years. This is an unusual occurrence and is not sustainable over the long term.

The P/E ratio for both businesses is high, which indicates that the market has confidence in both their future prospects or that their share prices are expensive.

CHAPTER 5

5.1   Several situations

	a	b	c	d	e	f
Deposit	$1,000	$2,000	$4,000	$10,000	$25,000	$100,000
Interest rate	5%	6%	7%	8%	10%	12%
Years	5	6	10	20	25	30
Future value factor	1.2763	1.4185	1.9672	4.661	10.8347	29.9599
Future value balance	1,276.30	2,837.00	7,868.80	46,610.00	270,867.50	2,995,990.00

5.2   World Lottery

You should choose option (b) and receive $1.5 million after five years.

	a	b	c	d	e	f
Prize ($)	1,000,000	1,500,000	2,000,000	3,000,000	5,000,000	10,000,000
Interest rate	3%	6%	9%	12%	16%	20%
Years	2	5	9	15	20	40
Present value factor	0.9426	0.7473	0.4604	0.1827	0.0514	0.0007
Present value ($)	942,600.00	1,120,950.00	920,800.00	548,100.00	257,000.00	7,000.00

5.3   Several situations

	a	b	c	d	e	f
Savings ($)	500	1,000	1,500	2,000	2,500	3,000
Interest rate	3%	6%	9%	12%	16%	20%
Years	2	5	9	15	20	40
Future value annuity factor	2.03	5.6371	13.021	37.2797	115.38	7343.86
Annuity due factor	1.03	1.06	1.09	1.12	1.16	1.20
(a) Future value —ordinary annuity	1,015.00	5,637.10	19,531.50	74,559.40	288,450.00	22,031,580.00
(b) Future Value —Annuity due	1,045.45	5,975.33	21,289.34	83,506.53	334,602.00	26,437,896.00

5.4   Several situations

	a	b	c	d	e	f
Payment ($)	500	1,000	1,500	2,000	2,500	3,000
Interest rate	3%	6%	9%	12%	16%	20%
Years	2	5	9	15	20	40
Present value annuity factor	1.9135	4.2124	5.9952	6.8109	5.9288	4.9966
Annuity due factor	1.03	1.06	1.09	1.12	1.16	1.20
(a) Present value—Ordinary annuity ($)	956.75	4,212.40	8,992.80	13,621.80	14,822.00	14,989.80
(b) Present value—Annuity due ($)	985.45	4,465.14	9,802.15	15,256.42	17,193.52	17,987.76

5.5   LawnCare Ltd

		A		B		C

	A	B	C
Down payment	–	$ 10,000	$ 20,000
Annual payments	$75,000	70,000	65,000
PV annuity factor @ 7% interest	7.0236	7.0236	7.0236
PV annual payments	526,770	491,652	456,534
Total PV payments	$526,770	$501,652	$476,534

Payment option C is the best choice because it is the least expensive way to pay for the new machine.

5.6   Karena Oberne

Machine B should be the least expensive machine.

Interest rate 5%

Cash Flows

Year	Machine A			Machine B			Machine C		
1	2,000	0.9524	$ 1,904.80	1,500	0.9524	$1,428.60	1,000	0.9524	$ 952.40
2	500	0.9070	453.50	2,000	0.9070	1,814.00	1,300	0.9070	1,179.10
3	0	0.8638	0.00	1,000	0.8638	863.80	1,600	0.8638	1,382.08
4	0	0.8227	0.00	4,000	0.8227	3,290.80	1,900	0.8227	1,563.13
5	7,000	0.7835	5,484.50	500	0.7835	391.75	2,200	0.7835	1,723.70
6	2,000	0.7462	1,492.40	1,000	0.7462	746.20	2,500	0.7462	1,865.50
7	1,000	0.7107	710.70	500	0.7107	355.35	2,800	0.7107	1,989.96
8	500	0.6768	338.40	300	0.6768	203.04	3,100	0.6768	2,098.08
9	0	0.6446	0.00	0	0.6446	0.00	3,400	0.6446	2,191.64
10	0	0.6139	0.00	0	0.6139	0.00	3,700	0.6139	2,271.43
NPV			$10,384.30			$9,093.54			$17,217.02

CHAPTER 6

6.1   Confederation Printing Press Ltd.

(a) and (b)

Year	Cost	Salvage	Net Income After Deducting Depreciation	Add Back: Depreciation	Forgone Lease Revenue	Increased Inventory Investment	Increased Receivable Investment	Net Cash Flows	Present Value Factor 16%	Present Value
0	(250,000)					(23,000)	(15,000)	(288,000)	1.0000	(288,000)
1			50,000	22,500	(12,000)			60,500	0.8621	52,157
2			50,000	22,500	(12,000)			60,500	0.7432	44,964
3			50,000	22,500	(12,000)			60,500	0.6407	38,762
4			50,000	22,500	(12,000)			60,500	0.5523	33,414
5			50,000	22,500	(12,000)			60,500	0.4761	28,804
6			50,000	22,500	(12,000)			60,500	0.4104	24,829
7			50,000	22,500	(12,000)			60,500	0.3538	21,405
8			50,000	22,500	(12,000)			60,500	0.3050	18,453
9			50,000	22,500	(12,000)			60,500	0.2630	15,912
10		25,000	50,000	22,500	(12,000)	23,000	15,000	123,500	0.2267	27,997
									NPV	18,697

The net present value of this project is positive $18,697, so Confederation should proceed with the acquisition of the second printing press.

Cash flows mentioned in the question that are not relevant to the analysis:

- The $10,000 already spent modernizing the unused second floor is a sunk cost and should not be included in the decision making process
- The $20,000 interest charge per annum should not be included because the discounting process already takes interest into account.

6.2   Beacon Chemicals Limited

(a) The relevant cash flows are:

	Year					
	0 ($000)	1 ($000)	2 ($000)	3 ($000)	4 ($000)	5 ($000)
Sales revenue	–	80	120	144	100	64
Less: Cash profit	–	(15)	(15)	(15)	(15)	(15)
Variable costs	–	(40)	(50)	(48)	(30)	(32)
Fixed costs	–	(8)	(8)	(8)	(8)	(8)
Operating cash flows		17	47	73	47	9
Working capital	(30)					30
Capital cost	(100)					
Net relevant cash flows	(130)	17	47	73	47	39

Notes

1. Only the fixed costs that are incremental to the project (only existing because of the project) are relevant. Depreciation is irrelevant because it is not a cash flow.
2. The research and development cost is irrelevant because it is a sunk cost.

(b) The payback period is calculated as follows:

	Year 0 ($000)	Year 1 ($000)	Year 2 ($000)	Year 3 ($000)
Cumulative cash flows	(130)	(113)	(66)	7

Thus the equipment will have repaid the initial investment by the end of the third year of operations.

(c) The calculation for the net present value is:

	Year 0 ($000)	Year 1 ($000)	Year 2 ($000)	Year 3 ($000)	Year 4 ($000)	Year 5 ($000)
Discount factor*	1.000	0.926	0.857	0.794	0.735	0.681
Present value	(130.00)	15.74	40.28	57.96	34.55	26.56

Net present value   45.09 (that is, the sum of the present values for years 0 to 5)

*Rounded to three decimal places

CHAPTER 7

7.1   Choi Ltd.

(a) In evaluating the two machines, the first step is to calculate the NPVs of both projects over their respective time periods:

Lo-tek	Cash Flows ($)	Discount Rate 12%	Present Value ($)
Initial cost	(10,000)	1.0000	(10,000)
1 year's time	4,000	0.8929	3,572
2 years' time	5,000	0.7972	3,986
3 years' time	5,000	0.7118	3,559
		NPV	1,117

Hi-tek	Cash Flows ($)	Discount Rate 12%	Present Value ($)
Initial cost	(15,000)	1.0000	(15,000)
1 year's time	5,000	0.8929	4,465
2 years' time	6,000	0.7972	4,783
3 years' time	6,000	0.7118	4,271
4 years' time	5,000	0.6355	3,178
		NPV	1,697

The shortest common period of time over which the machines can be compared is 12 years (that is, 3 × 4). This means that Lo-tek will be repeated four times and Hi-tek will be repeated three times during the 12-year period.

The NPV for Lo-tek will be, using Table A2 in Appendix A (calculated):

Total NPV = $1,117 + $1,117 × 0.5066 + $1,117 × 0.3606 + $1,117 × 0.2567
    = $2,372.4

The NPV for Hi-tek will be:

Total NPV = $1,697 + $1,697 × 0.4039 + $1,697 × 0.2567
    = $2,818.0

The equivalent-annual-annuity approach (calculated using Table A5 in Appendix A) will provide the following results for Lo-tek over three years at 12%:

$$\$1,117 \times 0.4163 = \$465.01$$

and the following results for Hi-tek over four years:

$$\$1,697 \times 0.3292 = \$558.65$$

(b) Hi-tek is the better buy because calculations show that it has the higher NPV over the shortest common period of time and provides the higher equivalent-annual-annuity value.

7.2   Dynamic Capital Inc.

Step 1	NPV	Project 1 Probability	ENPV	NPV	Project 2 Probability	ENPV
	100	0.4	40.0	69	0.6	41.4
	60	0.3	18.0	55	0.3	16.5
	13	0.3	3.9	40	0.1	4.0
			61.9			61.9

		Project 1			Project 2	
Step 2	NPV	ENPV	Deviations	NPV	ENPV	Deviations
	100	61.9	38.1	69	61.9	7.1
	60	61.9	(1.9)	55	61.9	(6.9)
	13	61.9	(48.9)	40	61.9	(21.9)

	Project 1		Project 2	
	Deviations	Deviations Squared	Deviations	Deviations Squared
	38.1	1,451.61	7.1	50.41
	(1.9)	3.61	(6.9)	47.61
	(48.9)	2,391.21	(21.9)	479.61
Variance		3,846.43		577.63
Standard deviation		62.02		24.03

Project 2 is a better investment because, although it has the same expected net present value (ENPV) as Project 1 ($61.90), it has a much lower risk level with a standard deviation of $24.03.

CHAPTER 8

8.1   Oak Ltd., Elm Ltd., and Birch Ltd.

Some relevant ratios are shown below:

	Oak Ltd.	Elm Ltd.	Birch Ltd.
Current ratio = CA ÷ CL	4	2	1
Current ratio judgment	Too high	Good	Too low
Long-term debt to equity ratio	4.5	1	0.25
LTD ÷ Equity judgment	Too high	Okay	Perhaps too low

Oak Ltd.

Recall from Chapter 4 that an excessively high current ratio is not beneficial for a company. Perhaps Oak could reduce accounts receivable and inventory levels and use excess cash to pay off some of its long-term debt, which is too high. Oak's debt–equity ratio is much too high, making it a very risky company. Oak should consider issuing new shares and using the proceeds to pay down some long-term debt so that creditors and shareholders have about the same amount of money invested in the firm.

Elm Ltd.

It appears that Elm's capital structure is fine. No action needs to be taken.

Birch Ltd.

The current ratio for Birch is probably too low. A financial accident or surprise may result in panic borrowing at the last minute at excessive interest rates. It is a little more difficult to state that Birch's long-term debt is too low because the amount of corporate debt often reflects the personal preferences of the board of directors and the company's culture. Some companies choose to have no debt. However, because of the current ratio problem Birch is experiencing, it is evident that some new long-term debt could be issued and used to pay down some current liabilities. This would improve the current ratio.

8.2   Sudbury Shoes Limited (SSL)

Data:

Annual credit sales	$2,000,000
Average collection period	30 days
Industry average collection period	15 days
Average annual bad debt write-offs	$20,000
Revolving line of credit financing charge	8%

Factor data:

Advance on accounts receivable	90%
Collection fee on credit sales	3.00%

Collection period assumption:

Industry average collection period	15 days
Interest rate	6%
Annual bad debt write-offs	$2,000
Administrative savings	$20,000

(a) Cost of SSL collecting its own receivables:

Revolving line of credit charge (30/365 × $2 million × 8%)	$13,150.68
Bad debts	20,000.00
Total cost of SSL collecting its own receivables:	$33,150.68

(b) Cost of SSL factoring its receivables:

Factor collection fee (3.0% × $2 million)	$60,000.00
Finance charges (15/365 × (90% × $2 million) × 6%)	4,438.36
Revolving line of credit charge (15/365 × ((1 − 90%) × $2 million) × 8%)	657.53
Bad debts	2,000.00
Less: Administrative savings	(20,000.00)
Total cost of SSL factoring its receivables:	$47,095.89

(c) SSL should not factor its receivables due to extra costs of $13,945.21.

8.3   Helsim Limited

(a) The liquidity position may be assessed by using the liquidity ratios discussed in Chapter 4.

$$\text{Current ratio} = \frac{\text{Current assets}}{\text{Current liabilities}}$$

$$= \frac{\$7.5 \text{ million}}{\$5.4 \text{ million}}$$

$$= 1.4$$

$$\text{Acid test ratio} = \frac{\text{Current assets (less inventory)}}{\text{Current liabilities}}$$

$$= \frac{\$3.7 \text{ million}}{\$5.4 \text{ million}}$$

$$= 0.7$$

The ratios calculated above reveal a fairly weak liquidity position. The current ratio seems quite low and the acid test ratio seems very low. This latter ratio suggests that the business does not have sufficient liquid assets to meet its obligations. It would, however, be useful to have details of the liquidity ratios of similar businesses in the same industry in order to make a more informed judgment. The bank overdraft represents 67% of the short-term liabilities and 40% of the total liabilities of the business. The continuing support of the bank is therefore important to the ability of the business to meet its commitments.

(b) The financing required to reduce accounts payable to an average of 40 days outstanding is calculated as follows:

	($ millions)
Accounts payable at balance sheet date	1.80
Accounts payable outstanding based on 40 days' credit	
(40/365 × $8.4 million) (that is, credit purchases)	(0.92)
Financing required	0.88 (say $0.9 million)

(c) The bank may not wish to provide further financing to the business. The increase in overdraft will reduce the level of accounts payable but will increase the exposure of the bank. The additional financing invested by the bank will not generate further funds and will therefore not be self-liquidating. The question does not make it clear whether the business has sufficient security to offer the bank for the increase in overdraft facility. The profits of the business will be reduced and the times interest earned ratio, based on the profits generated for the year ended May 31, would decrease to 1.4 times if the additional overdraft were granted (based on interest charged at 12% a year). This is very low and implies that a relatively small decline in profits would mean that interest charges would not be covered.

(d) A number of possible sources of financing might be considered. Four possible sources are as follows:

- *Issue common shares.* This option may be unattractive to investors. The return on shareholders' funds is fairly low at 7.9% and there is no evidence that the profitability of the business will improve. If profits remain at their current level the effect of issuing more shares will be to further reduce the returns to common shareholders.
- *Obtain loans.* This option may also prove unattractive to investors. The effect of obtaining further loans will be similar to that of increasing the overdraft. The profits of the business will be reduced and the times interest earned ratio will decrease to a low level. The leverage ratio of the business is already quite high at 48% and it is not clear what security would be available for the loan.
- *Collect receivables.* It may be possible to improve cash flows by reducing the level of credit outstanding from customers. At present the average collection period is 93 days, which seems quite high. A reduction in the average collection period by approximately one-quarter would generate the funds required. However, it is not clear what effect this would have on sales.
- *Reduce inventory.* This appears to be the most attractive of the four options discussed. At present the average inventory turnover period is 178 days, which seems to be very high. A reduction in this inventory turnover period by less than one-quarter would generate the funds required. However, if the business holds a large amount of slow-moving and obsolete inventory it may be difficult to reduce inventory levels easily.

CHAPTER 9

9.1   Champion Ltd.

(a) (i) *Preliminary calculations*

Annual depreciation is $4 million (that is, buildings [$40 million × 2.5%] and plant and machinery [$20 million × 15%]).

Cost of acquiring the business is $120 million (that is, $10 million $\times$ 12).

Loan financing required is $70 million (that is, $120 million – $50 million).

Loan outstanding at May 31, 2014

($ millions)

Year to May 31	2011	2012	2013	2014
Operating profit	10.0	11.0	10.5	13.5
Add: Annual amortization	4.0	4.0	4.0	4.0
Operating cash flow	14.0	15.0	14.5	17.5
Less: Working capital	–	(1.0)	–	–
Loan interest	(7.0)	(6.3)	(5.5)	(4.6)
Cash available to repay loan	7.0	7.7	9.0	12.9
Loan at start of year	70.0	63.0	55.3	46.3
Cash to repay loan	7.0	7.7	9.0	12.9
Loan at end of year	63.0	55.3	46.3	33.4

(ii) *Internal rate of return (IRR)*

The net amount to be received in 2014 by the venture capitalist is calculated as follows:

	$ millions
Sale proceeds (12 $\times$ $13.5 million)	162.0
Less: Loan repayment	(33.4)
Proceeds to shareholders	128.6
Less:	
Amount to shareholders/managers (10%)	(12.9)
Available for venture capitalist	115.7

Trial 1—Discount rate 25%
NPV is:

$$($115.7 \text{ million} \times 0.4096) - $45 \text{ million} = $2.4 \text{ million}$$

As NPV is positive, the IRR is higher.

Trial 2—Discount rate 30%
NPV is:

$$($115.7 \text{ million} \times 0.3501) - $45 \text{ million} = ($4.5 \text{ million})$$

As NPV is negative, the IRR is lower.

A 5% change in the discount rate leads to a $6.9 million (i.e., $2.4 million + $4.5 million) change in the NPV. Thus, a 1% change in the discount rate results in a $1.38 million change in NPV. The IRR is:

$$25\% + \left(\frac{$2.4 \text{ million}}{$1.38 \text{ million}}\right)\% = 26.7\%$$

(b) The IRR exceeds the cost of capital—but only just. It is likely to be sensitive to forecast inaccuracies. The forecast inputs should be re-examined, particularly the forecast profit in the year of sale. It is much higher than in previous years and forms the basis for calculating the sale price.

9.2   Corn Products Ltd.

Buying Loan Schedule

Year	Opening Balance	Payment	Interest @ 6%	Closing Balance
1	$100,000.00	$28,859.15	$6,000.00	$77,140.85
2	77,140.85	28,859.15	4,628.45	52,910.15
3	52,910.15	28,859.15	3,174.61	27,225.61
4	27,225.61	28,859.15	1,633.54	0.00

Leasing

Year	Payment	Tax savings (30% tax rate)	Payment After Tax	Present Value Factor @ 6%	Present Value @ 6%
1	$28,859.15	$8,657.75	$20,201.40	0.9434	$19,058.00
2	28,859.15	8,657.75	20,201.40	0.8900	17,979.25
3	28,859.15	8,657.75	20,201.40	0.8396	16,961.10
4	28,859.15	8,657.75	20,201.40	0.7921	16,001.53
				Net present value	$69,999.88

CCA amounts are:

Buying

Year	Opening UCC	CCA @ 40%	40% Closing UCC
1	100,000	20,000	80,000
2	80,000	32,000	48,000
3	48,000	19,200	28,800
4	28,800	11,520	17,280

The annual tax shields are:

Buying

Year	Interest @ 6%	CCA @ 40%	Total Deductions	30% Tax Shield (30% tax rate)
1	6,000.00	20,000.00	26,000.00	7,800.00
2	4,628.45	32,000.00	36,628.45	10,988.54
3	3,174.61	19,200.00	22,374.61	6,712.38
4	1,633.54	11,520.00	13,153.54	3,946.06

Buying

Year	Payment	Tax Shield (30% tax rate)	Net Cost of Buying	Present Value Factor @ 6%	Present Value @ 6%
1	$28,859.15	$ 7,800.00	$21,059.15	0.9434	$19,867.20
2	28,859.15	10,988.54	17,870.61	0.8900	15,904.84
3	28,859.15	6,712.38	22,146.77	0.8396	18,594.43
4	28,859.15	3,946.06	24,913.09	0.7921	19,733.66
				Net present value	$74,100.13
				Cheaper to lease by:	$ 4,100.25

Leasing will save Corn Products $4,100.25 (i.e., $74,100.13 – $69,999,88).

CHAPTER 10

10.1   Montreal Controls Ltd.

The weighted average cost of capital for Montreal Controls Ltd. is 13.56%, as shown below.

Step 1. Calculate the cost of capital for the various components.

After-tax cost of debt:

Interest rate on LTD	10%	
Tax rate	45%	

After-tax cost of debt:

$(100\% - 45\%) \times 10\% =$ ___5.50%___

Cost of preferred shares:

D_p	$ 2.50	
P_p	30.00	
$K_p = 2.50 \div 30$		8.33%

Cost of common shares:

D_0	$ 2.00	
g	15%	
D_1 (1.15 × $2.00)	$ 2.30	
P_0	$40.50	
$K_0 = 2.30 \div 40.50 + 15\% =$		20.68%

Step 2. Calculate the weighted average cost of capital (WACC).

Market value of capital structure:

	Market Value	Market %	After-Tax Costs	WACC
Long-term debt	$200,000	33.33%	5.50%	1.83%
Preferred shares	100,000	16.67%	8.33%	1.39%
Common shares	300,000	50.00%	20.68%	10.34%
	$600,000	100.00%		13.56%

10.2   Russell Ltd.

(a) (i)

Russell Ltd.
Pro Forma Income Statements
and Additions to Retained Earnings
for the year ended May 31, 2011

	Shares ($000)	Debentures ($000)
Earnings before interest and taxes	662.0	662.0
Interest	30.0	90.0
Earnings before taxes	632.0	572.0
Income tax (25%)	158.0	143.0
Net income	474.0	429.0
Less: Dividend	(189.6)	(171.6)
Addition to retained earnings	284.4	257.4

(ii) Earnings per share (EPS)

$$\text{EPS} = \frac{\text{Profit available to shareholders}}{\text{Number of shares}}$$

	Shares	Debentures
	$\dfrac{474}{(400 + 150)}$	$\dfrac{429}{400}$
	$0.86	$1.07

(iii) Leverage ratio

$$\frac{\text{Debt}}{\text{Common shares} + \text{Retained earnings} + \text{Debt}} \times 100\%$$

$$\text{Shares:} \quad \frac{250}{(832.4 + 284.4 + 600.0 + 250)} \times 100\% = 12.7\%$$

$$\text{Debentures:} \quad \frac{850}{(832.4 + 257.4 + 850)} \times 100\% = 43.8\%$$

(b) The debenture option provides a significantly higher EPS figure than the share option. The EPS for the most recent year is $0.96 (i.e., $384/400) and this lies between the two options being considered. On the basis of the EPS figures, it seems that the debenture option is more attractive. Pursuing the share option will lower EPS compared with the current year, and will result in a single shareholder obtaining over 27% of the voting shares. As a result, this option is unlikely to be attractive. However, the leverage ratio under the debenture option is significantly higher than that for the share option. This ratio is also much higher than the current leverage ratio of the business of 23.1% (i.e., 250/1,082.4). The existing shareholders must balance the significant increase in financial risk with the additional returns that are generated.

(c) The level of earnings before interest and taxes at which EPS is the same under each option will be:

Common shares	Common shares plus debentures
$\dfrac{(x - 30.0)(1 - 0.25)}{(400.0 + 150.0)}$	$= \dfrac{(x - 90.0)(1 - 0.25)}{(400.0)}$
$400(0.75x - 22.5)$	$= 550(0.75x - 67.5)$
$300x - 9,000$	$= 412.5x - 37,125$
$112.5x$	$= 28,125$
x	$= 250$ ($000)

The above figure could also have been calculated using an EBIT–EPS indifference chart as shown in the chapter.

CHAPTER 11

11.1   Sandarajan Ltd.

(a) The dividend per share and dividend payout ratio over the five-year period is as follows:

Year	Dividend Per Share ($)	Dividend Payout (%)
2006	0.220	52.4
2007	0.140	26.4
2008	0.173	40.0
2009	0.073	14.9
2010	0.307	52.3

The figures above show an erratic pattern of dividends over the five years. Such a pattern is unlikely to be welcomed by investors. In an imperfect world, dividends may be important to investors because of taxation policy and information signalling.

(b) Managers should, therefore, decide on a payout policy and then make every effort to stick with that policy. This will ensure that dividends are predictable and contain no surprises for investors. Any reduction in the dividend is likely to be seen as a sign of financial weakness and the share price is likely to fall. If a reduction in dividends cannot be avoided, the managers should make clear the change in policy and the reasons for the change.

CHAPTER 12

12.1   Your Company

Quantity sold each year	75,000
Annual unit holding cost	$250.00
Cost of placing an order	$750.00

(a) $\text{EOQ} = \sqrt{\dfrac{2 \times 75{,}000 \times 750}{250}} = 671$

(b) Number of orders per year $= 75{,}000 \div 671 = 112$

12.2   Williams Wholesalers Ltd.

	($)	($)
Existing level of receivables ($4 million × 70/365)		767,123
New level of receivables: ($2 million × 80/365)	438,356	
($2 million × 30/365)	164,384	602,740
Reduction in receivables		164,383

Costs and benefits of policy

Cost of discount ($2 million × 2%)		40,000
Less: Savings:		
Interest payable ($164,383 × 13%)	21,370	
Administration costs	6,000	
Bad debts ($20,000 − $10,000)	10,000	37,370
Net cost of policy		2,630

No, Williams should not offer the new credit terms to customers; it will cost the company an extra $2,630.

CHAPTER 13

13.1   Moose Jaw Beer Ltd.

(a) EVA

Step 1   After-tax EBIT adjustments

EBIT	$465
Less: Taxes	(137)
	328
Adjustments:	
Add back:	
Marketing expenses that will	
benefit the future 4/5 × $50	40
Excess allowance for doubtful	
accounts expense $90 − $20	70
Adjusted after-tax EBIT	$438

Note: Dividend income from Truro Travel is not included in after-tax EBIT as it is not operating income.

Step 2   Calculate C

Long-term capital invested adjustment	
(or long-term debt and shareholders' equity adjustment)	
Long-term debt	$ 60
Shareholders' equity	920
Adjustments:	
Add back:	
Marketing expenses that will	
benefit the future 4/5 × $50	40
Excess allowance for doubtful	
accounts expense $90 − $20	70
Less:	
Investment in Truro Travel Ltd.	(750)
Adjusted long-term capital	$340

Note: The investment in Truro Travel is excluded because the dividend income is also excluded from after-tax EBIT.

Step 3   Calculate $R \times C$

Multiply investors' required rate of return by Step 2

Step 2, invested capital, C	$ 340
R, required rate of return in the beer industry	15%
$R \times C$	$ 51

Step 4   Calculate EVA

EVA = Step 1 – Step 3

Step 1	$438
Step 2	51
EVA	$387

(b) The investment in Truro Travel is not a good one since the return on investment was 10% (i.e., $75,000 dividend income ÷ $750,000 investment) compared to the industry-required return on investment of 20% for the travel industry.

13.2   Canadian Spirits Ltd.

Canadian Spirits Ltd.
Adjusted Capital Invested (or Total Assets Less Current Liabilities)

	($ millions)	($ millions)
Total assets less current liabilities ($276.0 million – $45.0 million)		231.0
Add: Fair value increase in land ($200 million – $60 million)	140.0	
R&D future value (9/10 × $10 million)	9.0	149.0
Adjusted total assets less current liabilities		380.0*

*This figure represents the adjusted figure for capital invested.

Market Value Added Calculation

	($ millions)
Market value of shares (60 million × $8.50)	510.0
Less: Capital invested (see above)	380.0
MVA	130.0

CHAPTER 14

14.1   Pastel Dreams Ltd. and Hard Core Reality Ltd.

	Pastel Dreams Ltd.	Hard Core Reality Ltd.
Assets per balance sheet	$ 34,000,000	$129,000,000
Liabilities per balance sheet	$ 20,000,000	$ 65,000,000
Number of common shares outstanding	30,000,000	60,000,000
Assets—Market value	$160,000,000	$210,000,000

Liabilities—Market value	$18,500,000	$ 70,000,000
Net income	$62,000,000	$195,000,000
P/E ratio	20	40
Dividends	$22,000,000	$ 95,000,000

(a) Balance sheet method

$P_0 = (\$34 \text{ million} - \$20 \text{ million})/ 30 \text{ million}$

$P_0 = \$0.47$

$P_0 = (\$129 \text{ million} - \$65 \text{ million})/ 60 \text{ million}$

$P_0 = \$1.07$

(b) Liquidation method

$P_0 = (\$160 \text{ million} - \$18.5 \text{ million})/ 30 \text{ million}$

$P_0 = \$4.72$

$P_0 = (\$210 \text{ million} - \$70 \text{ million})/ 60 \text{ million}$

$P_0 = \$2.33$

(c) P/E ratio method

EPS	$2.07	$3.25
Share value ($P_0 =$ P/E ratio × EPS)	20 × $2.07 = $41.40	40 × $3.25 = $130.00

14.2   River Holdings Ltd. and Lake Effects Corp.

(a) (i) Balance sheet method

$$\text{Price of a common share } (P_0) = \frac{\text{Net assets at balance sheet values}}{\text{Number of common shares}}$$

$$= \frac{\$132.3 \text{ million} - \$72.2 \text{ million}}{40 \text{ million}}$$

$$= \frac{\$60.1 \text{ million}}{40 \text{ million}}$$

$$= \$1.50$$

(ii) Liquidation method

$$P_0 = \frac{\text{Net assets* at current realizable values}}{\text{Number of common shares}}$$

$$= \frac{\$85.1 \text{ million}}{40 \text{ million}}$$

$$= \$2.13$$

*The net assets figure is derived as follows:

	($ millions)	($ millions)
Land and buildings		65.4
Plant and equipment		18.8
Furniture and fixtures		4.6
Inventory		38.9
Accounts receivable		29.6
		157.3
Less: Liabilities		
Current	51.2	
Non-current	21.0	72.2
Net assets		85.1

(iii) Price/earnings ratio method

$$P_0 = \frac{\text{Price/earnings ratio} \times \text{Net income}}{\text{Number of common shares}}$$

$$= \frac{11 \times \$17.2 \text{ million}}{40 \text{ million}}$$

$$= \frac{\$189.2 \text{ million}}{40 \text{ million}}$$

$$= \$4.73$$

(iv) Dividend growth method

$$P_0 = \frac{D_1}{K_0 - g}$$

$$= \frac{(\$17.2 \text{ million} \times 40\%)/40 \text{ million}}{(0.10 - 0.04)}$$

$$= \$2.87$$

(b) This topic is covered in the chapter. Refer as necessary.

Glossary

ABC system of inventory control A method of applying different levels of inventory control based on the value of each category of inventory. *(p. 456)*

Accounting rate of return (ARR) The average profit from an investment, expressed as a percentage of the average investment made. *(p. 201)*

Accounts receivable factoring A service offered by a financial institution known as a factor. The factor takes over the accounts receivable collection for a business and may offer to undertake credit investigations and advise on the creditworthiness of customers. It may also offer protection for approved credit sales. *(p. 301)*

Acid test ratio A liquidity ratio that relates the current assets (minus inventory) to the current liabilities. *(p. 128)*

Acquisition A term normally used to describe a situation where a larger business acquires control of a smaller business, which is then absorbed by the larger business. *(p. 528)*

Agency problem The conflict of interest between the shareholders (the principals) and the managers (agents) of a business, which arises when the managers seek to maximize their own welfare. *(p. 12)*

Aging schedule of receivables A report dividing receivables into categories, depending on the length of time outstanding. *(p. 467)*

Amortization The apportionment of cost of a long-lived intangible asset to the income statement as an expense. *(p. 39)* (See also **Depreciation**)

Angel investors Wealthy individuals willing to invest in businesses at an early stage in their development. *(p. 356)*

Annuity A series of equal payments or receipts at a constant interest rate at equal time intervals over a specified time period. *(pp. 173, 241)*

Annuity due A stream of equal cash flow amounts with the first payment or receipt starting immediately. *(p. 173)*

Arbitrage transaction A transaction that exploits differences in price between similar shares (or other assets) and that involves selling the overpriced shares and purchasing the underpriced shares. *(p. 409)*

Asset Anything the company owns that is expected to provide future benefits. *(p. 20)*

Asset-based financing A form of financing where assets are used as security for cash advances to a business. Factoring and invoice discounting, where the security is accounts receivable, are examples of asset-based financing. *(p. 304)*

Average collection period for receivables The average time taken by a business to collect its receivables. *(pp. 120, 466)*

Average inventory turnover period An efficiency ratio that measures the average period during which inventory is held by a business. *(p. 119)*

Average payment period for payables The average time taken by a business to pay the amounts owing to its creditors. *(pp. 121, 479)*

Balance sheet Shows the financial position (assets, liabilities, and shareholders' equity) of the company at one point in time. *(p. 26)*

Balance sheet (net book value) method A method of valuing the shares of a business by reference to the value of the net assets as shown in the balance sheet. *(p. 551)*

Bank overdraft An amount owing to a bank that is repayable on demand. The amount borrowed and the rate of interest may fluctuate over time. *(p. 300)*

Behavioural finance An approach to finance that rejects the notion that investors behave in a rational manner and, instead, make systematic errors when processing information. *(p. 337)*

Best efforts deal A method of selling shares to the public through the use of an issuing house, which acts as an intermediary, but which does not, itself, purchase the shares. *(p. 344)*

Beta A measure of the extent to which the returns on a particular share vary compared to the market as a whole. *(p. 377)*

Bond discount The difference between the bond's face value and its fair value when the market interest rate is greater than the bond's coupon rate. *(p. 179)*

Bond premium The difference between the bond's fair value and its face value when the market interest rate is lower than the bond's coupon rate. *(p. 179)*

Bought deal When a listed business sells a new issue of shares to a financial institution known as an investment dealer, which, in turn, sells the shares to the public. The investment dealer will publish a prospectus describing details of the business and the type of shares to be sold, and investors will be invited to apply to purchase shares. *(p. 344)*

Capital asset pricing model (CAPM) A method of establishing the cost of share capital that identifies two forms of risk: diversifiable risk and non-diversifiable risk. *(p. 376)*

Capital cost allowance (CCA) The tax return's equivalent to depreciation expense. *(p. 39)*

Capital markets Financial markets for long-term loans, bonds and debentures, and shares. *(p. 4)*

Capital rationing Limiting the long-term funds available for investment during a period. Soft capital rationing is imposed by managers; hard capital rationing is imposed by investors. *(p. 194)*

Cash discount A reduction in the amount due for goods or services sold on credit in return for prompt payment. *(p. 465)*

Cash flow statement Measures the sources (cash inflows) and uses (cash outflows) of cash for the company throughout a period. *(p. 30)*

Clientele effect The phenomenon where investors seek out businesses whose dividend policies match their particular needs. *(p. 431)*

Coefficient of correlation A statistical measure of association that can be used to measure the degree to which the returns from two separate projects are related. The measure ranges from +1 to −1. A measure of +1 indicates a perfect positive correlation and a measure of −1 indicates a perfect negative correlation. *(p. 266)*

Competition Act Canadian legislation governing mergers that could affect competition in Canada, which could block all or part of the merger. In the case where some of the merger is blocked, the ruling would allow the merger to proceed if the parties sell certain specified assets. Areas considered in determining the effect a merger would have on competition include the degree of concentration within an industry, barriers to entry in the industry, and the remaining effective competition in the industry. *(p. 546)*

Competitor profiling Building a profile of the strengths and weaknesses of each major competitor in order to understand the threats posed. *(p. 64)*

Compounding Computing interest on the principal and accrued interest, usually to arrive at a future value amount. *(p. 169)*

Compound interest A situation where the interest an investment earned last year also earns interest this year, resulting in interest on interest. *(p. 169)*

Conglomerate merger A merger between two businesses engaged in unrelated activities. *(p. 529)*

Convertible bond A bond that can be converted into common shares at the option of the bond holders. *(p. 291)*

Corporate governance Systems for directing and controlling a business. *(p. 13)*

Cost of capital The rate of return required by investors in the business. The cost of capital is used as the criterion rate of return when evaluating investment proposals using the NPV and IRR methods of appraisal. *(pp. 209, 372)*

Coupon rate The rate of interest that a bond pays is its coupon rate *(p. 177)*

Creative accounting Adopting accounting policies to achieve a particular view of performance and position that preparers would like users to see rather than what is a true and fair view. *(p. 148)*

Credit note A written agreement requiring one party to the agreement to pay (Notes payable) a particular amount at some future date to the other party to the agreement (Notes receivable). *(p. 301)*

Crown jewels The most valued part of a business (which may be sold to fend off a hostile takeover bid). *(p. 545)*

Cum dividend A term used to describe the price of a share that includes the right to receive a forthcoming dividend. *(p. 423)*

Current ratio A liquidity ratio that relates the current assets of the business to the current liabilities. *(p. 127)*

Debenture A bond that does not pledge specific assets as security for the loan is called a debenture *(pp. 177, 287)*

Degree of financial leverage A measure of the sensitivity of earnings per share to changes in earnings before interest and taxes (EBIT). *(p. 392)*

Depreciation The apportionment of cost of a long-lived tangible asset to the income statement as an expense. *(p. 39)* (See also **Amortization**)

Discounting The act of computing the present value of amounts to be received in the future. *(p. 171)*

Discount rate The interest rate used to discount future cash flows back to the present to determine their present value. *(p. 171)*

Diversifiable risk The part of the total risk that is specific to an investment or project and which can be diversified away through combining the investment or project with other ones. *(p. 268)*

Diversification The process of reducing risk by investing in a variety of different projects or assets. *(p. 265)*

Divestment A selling-off of business operations undertaken for various reasons including financial problems, defensive tactics, strategic focus, and poor performance. *(p. 546)*

Dividend A transfer of assets (usually cash) made by a business to its owners, the shareholders. *(pp. 21, 421)*

Dividend cover ratio An investment ratio that divides the net income available to common shareholders by the annual dividends to common shareholders; the reciprocal of the dividend payout ratio. *(pp. 133, 423)*

Dividend payout ratio An investment ratio that divides the dividends announced for the period by the net income generated during the period and available for dividends. *(p. 132)*

Dividend per share An investment ratio that divides the dividends announced for a period by the number of shares outstanding. *(p. 133)*

Dividend valuation method Uses the company's dividend, dividend growth rate, and return required by its investors to calculate the market value of one of the company's shares. *(p. 555)*

Dividend yield ratio An investment ratio that relates the cash return from a share to its current market value. *(pp. 133, 554)*

Earnings per share (EPS) An investment ratio that divides the earnings (profits) generated by a business, and available to common shareholders, by the number of shares outstanding. *(p. 134)*

EBIT–EPS indifference chart A chart that plots the returns to shareholders at different levels of earnings before interest and taxes for different financing options. *(p. 399)*

Economic order quantity (EOQ) The quantity of inventory that should be purchased in order to minimize total inventory costs. *(p. 457)*

Economic value added (EVA) The difference between the net operating profit after tax and the required returns from investors. *(p. 501)*

Efficient stock market A stock market where new information is quickly and accurately absorbed by investors, resulting in an appropriate share price adjustment. *(p. 327)*

Equivalent-annual-annuity approach An approach to deciding among competing investment projects with unequal lives that involves converting the NPV of each project into an annual annuity stream over the project's expected life. *(p. 242)*

Eurobonds Bearer bonds that are issued by listed businesses and other organizations in various countries with the funds being raised on an international basis. *(p. 289)*

Event tree diagram A diagram that portrays the various events or outcomes associated with a particular course of action and the probabilities associated with each event or outcome. *(p. 257)*

Ex-dividend A term used to describe the price of a share that excludes any right to a forthcoming dividend. *(p. 423)*

Expected net present value (ENPV) A method of dealing with risk that involves assigning a probability of occurrence to each possible outcome. The expected net present value of the project represents a weighted average of the possible net present values where the probabilities are used as weights. *(p. 255)*

Expected value A weighted average of a range of possible outcomes where the probabilities are used as weights. *(p. 254)*

Expected value–standard deviation rules Decision rules that can be employed to discriminate among competing investments where the possible outcomes are known and are normally distributed. *(p. 264)*

Expenses May be viewed as assets that were used up during the accounting period. *(p. 21)*

Financial derivative Any form of financial instrument, based on shares or bonds, that can be used by investors either to increase their returns or to decrease their exposure to risk. *(p. 283)*

Financial leverage The existence of fixed-payment-bearing securities (for example, loans) in the capital structure of a business. *(p. 129)*

Five Cs of credit A checklist of factors to be taken into account when assessing the creditworthiness of a customer. *(p. 461)*

Fixed charge Where a specific asset is offered as security for a loan or debenture. *(p. 286)*

Fixed costs Costs that stay the same even though the level of output changes. *(p. 65)*

Fixed interest rate A rate of return payable to lenders that will remain unchanged despite rises and falls in market interest rates. *(p. 296)*

Floating charge Where the whole of the assets of the business is offered as security for a loan or debenture. The charge will become fixed on specific assets in the event of a default in loan obligations. *(p. 286)*

Floating interest rate A rate of return payable to lenders that will rise and fall with market rates of interest. *(p. 296)*

Free cash flow method Uses the present value of a company's free cash flows less market value of its outstanding debt divided by the number of its outstanding shares to calculate the market value of one share in the company. *(p. 555)*

Free cash flows Cash flows available to long-term lenders and shareholders after any new investment in assets. *(p. 495)*

Future growth value (FGV) Value placed on the future growth potential of a business by investors. *(p. 519)*

Future value (FV) The value of an amount of money invested today at some time in the future. *(p. 169)*

Golden parachute Substantial fee payable to a manager of a business in the event of the loss of his or her job the business is taken over. *(p. 545)*

Gross profit margin ratio A profitability ratio relating the gross profit for the period to the sales for that period. *(p. 116)*

Hedging arrangement An attempt to reduce or eliminate the risk associated with a particular action by taking some form of counteraction. *(p. 296)*

High-yield bonds See **Junk bonds**. *(p. 293)*

Horizontal analysis Analyzing and comparing accounts between two or more years. *(p. 110)*

Horizontal merger A merger between two businesses in the same industry and at the same point in the production/distribution chain. *(p. 529)*

Income statement Measures revenues minus expenses, which equals the amount of earnings (profit or loss) the company has incurred during a period. *(p. 24)*

Indifference point The level of earnings before interest and taxes at which two, or more, financing plans provide the same level of return to common shareholders. *(p. 399)*

Inflation A general rise in the price for goods and services. *(p. 168)*

Information asymmetry Where the availability of information about a business differs between groups (such as managers and shareholders). *(p. 432)*

Information signalling Conveying information to shareholders through management actions (for example, increasing dividends to convey management optimism concerning the future). *(p. 432)*

Interest rate swap An arrangement between two businesses whereby each business assumes responsibility for the other's interest payments. *(p. 296)*

Internal rate of return (IRR) The discount rate for a project that has the effect of producing zero NPV. *(p. 209)*

Interpolation A technique involving the prorating of present value or future value factors or results. *(p. 212)*

Junk bonds Bonds with a relatively high level of investment risk for which investors are compensated by relatively high levels of return. Also called *high yield bonds*. *(p. 293)*

Just-in-time (JIT) inventory management A system of inventory management that aims to have supplies delivered to production just in time for their required use. *(p. 459)*

Lead time The time lag between placing an order for goods or services and their delivery. *(p. 455)*

Lease An arrangement in which a business does not buy an asset directly from a supplier but instead has another business (usually a financial institution) buy it and then allow the business exclusive use of the asset for a specific time in return for payment. *(p. 297)*

Leverage ratio A ratio that relates the contribution of long-term lenders to the total long-term capital of the business. *(p. 130)*

Liability An amount that the business owes. *(p. 20)*

Linear programming A mathematical technique for rationing limited resources in such a way as to optimize the benefits. *(p. 238)*

Liquidation method A method of valuing the shares of a business by reference to the net realizable values of its net assets. *(p. 552)*

Loan covenants Obligations, or restrictions, on the business that form part of a loan contract. *(p. 286)*

Market capitalization The total market value of the shares of a business. *(p. 321)*

Market value added (MVA) The difference between the market value of the business and the total investment that has been made in it. *(p. 511)*

Matching principle Expenses incurred to generate revenues must be reported in the period in which the related revenues were generated. *(p. 22)*

Materials requirement planning (MRP) system A computer-based system of inventory control that schedules the timing of deliveries of brought-in parts and materials to coincide with production requirements to meet demand. *(p. 459)*

Merger When two or more businesses of roughly the same size combine in order to form a single business. *(p. 528)*

Mission statement A statement setting out the purpose for which a business exists. *(p. 8)*

Mixed costs Costs that have an element of both fixed and variable costs. *(p. 65)*

Mortgage A loan secured on property. *(p. 288)*

Net present value (NPV) The net cash flows from a project that have been adjusted to take account of the time value of money. The NPV measure is used to evaluate investment projects. *(p. 207)*

Net realizable value The selling price of an asset, minus any costs incurred in selling the asset. *(p. 552)*

Non-diversifiable risk The part of the total risk that is common to all investments or projects and that cannot be diversified away by combining investments or projects. *(p. 269)*

Normal distribution The description applied to the distribution of a set of data that, when displayed graphically, forms a symmetrical bell-shaped curve. *(p. 263)*

Objective probabilities Probabilities based on information gathered from past experience. *(p. 264)*

Operating cash cycle (OCC) The time period between the outlay of cash to purchase inventory and the ultimate receipt of cash from the sale of those goods. *(p. 473)*

Operating lease A short-term lease where the rewards and risks of ownership stay with the owner. *(p. 298)*

Operating profit margin ratio A profitability ratio relating the earnings before interest and taxes (EBIT) for the period to the sales for that period. *(p. 115)*

Opportunity cost The monetary value of being deprived of the next best opportunity in order to pursue the particular objective. *(p. 216)*

Optimal capital structure The particular mix of long-term funds employed by a business that minimizes the cost of capital. *(p. 405)*

Ordinary annuity A stream of equal cash flows with the first payment or receipt starting one period from now. *(p. 173)*

Overtrading The situation arising when a business is operating at a level of activity that cannot be supported by the amount of financing that has been committed. *(p. 140)*

Pac-man defence A means of defending against a hostile takeover bid that involves launching a bid for the bidding company. *(p. 545)*

Payback period (PP) The time taken for the initial investment in a project to be repaid from the net cash inflows of the project. *(p. 205)*

Percent-of-sales method A method of financial planning that first estimates the sales for the planning period and then estimates other financial variables as a percentage of the sales figure. *(p. 85)*

Poison pill A defensive measure taken by a business that is designed to make it unattractive to potential acquirers. *(p. 545)*

Post-completion audit A review of the performance of an investment project to see whether actual performance matched planned performance and whether any lessons can be drawn from the way in which the investment was carried out. *(p. 198)*

Present value (PV) The value today of an amount of money to be received at some time in the future. *(p. 171)*

Price/earnings (P/E) ratio An investment ratio that divides the market value of a share by the earnings per share. *(pp. 135, 553)*

Price/earnings (P/E) ratio method A company's value under the **price/earnings** business valuation **method** is equal to the P/E ratio multiplied by the company's earnings per share. If the company is not publicly traded, you can use the P/E ratio of a similar listed company can be used. If the company has no net income, this method cannot be used to estimate a company's value. *(p. 553)*

Private placement A share issue that does not involve an invitation to the public to subscribe to shares; instead, the shares are placed with selected investors, such as large financial institutions. *(p. 346)*

Pro forma financial statements Financial statements such as the cash flow statement, income statement, statement of retained earnings, and balance sheet that have been prepared on the basis of estimates and that predict the financial outcome of a future course of action. *(p. 60)*

Profitability index The present value of the future cash flows from a project divided by the cost of the project. *(p. 237)*

Receivables discounting When a business approaches a factor or other financial institution for a loan based on a proportion (usually 75–80%) of the face value of accounts receivable outstanding. The business must agree to repay the advance within a relatively short period—perhaps 60 or 90 days. The responsibility for collecting the accounts receivable outstanding remains with the business and repayment of the advance is not dependent on the receivables being collected. *(p. 304)*

Record date A date that is set by the directors of a business to establish who is eligible to receive dividends. Those shareholders registered with the company on this date will receive any dividends announced for the period. *(p. 422)*

Relevant costs Costs that are relevant to a particular decision. *(p. 216)*

Replacement cost The cost of replacing an asset with an identical asset. *(p. 552)*

Residual theory of dividends Dividends should only be paid when the firm has financed all its positive NPV projects. *(p. 435)*

Return on capital employed (ROCE) A profitability ratio expressing the relationship between the earnings (before interest and taxes) for the period and average the long-term capital invested in the business. *(p. 114)*

Return on equity (ROE) A profitability ratio expressing the relationship between the profit available for common shareholders for the period and the average common shareholders' funds invested in the business for the same period. *(p. 112)*

Revenues Include sales of the company's goods and fees charged for services performed. *(p. 21)*

Reverse takeover Acquisition where the bidding company has to issue more of its shares to the shareholders of the target company than are currently outstanding. *(p. 536)*

Rights issue An offer to existing shareholders allowing them to buy shares at a price usually below market value.   *(p. 339)*

Risk The likelihood that what is estimated to occur will not actually occur.   *(pp. 89, 167, 245)*

Risk-adjusted discount rate A method of dealing with risk that involves adjusting the discount rate for projects according to the level of risk involved. The risk-adjusted discount rate will be the risk-free rate plus an appropriate risk premium.   *(p. 253)*

Risk-averse investors Investors who select the investment with the lowest risk where the returns from different investments are equal.   *(p. 252)*

Risk-neutral investors Investors who are indifferent to the level of risk associated with different investments whose returns are equal.   *(p. 252)*

Risk premium An extra amount of return from an investment, owing to a perceived level of risk: the greater the perceived level of risk, the larger the risk premium.   *(p. 168)*

Risk-seeking investors Investors who select the investment with the highest risk where the returns from different investments are equal.   *(p. 252)*

Sale-and-leaseback arrangement An agreement to sell an asset (usually property) to another party and simultaneously lease the asset back in order to continue using the asset.   *(p. 299)*

Sales revenue per employee An efficiency ratio that relates the sales generated during a period to the number of employees of the business.   *(p. 123)*

Sales revenue to capital employed An efficiency ratio that relates the sales generated during a period to the long-term capital employed.   *(p. 122)*

Satisficing The idea that managers should try to provide each stakeholder group of the business with a satisfactory level of return.   *(p. 8)*

Scenario analysis A method of dealing with risk that involves changing a number of variables simultaneously so as to provide a particular scenario for managers to consider.   *(pp. 89, 250)*

Securitization Bundling together illiquid financial or physical assets of the same type in order to provide backing for issuing interest-bearing securities, such as bonds.   *(p. 299)*

Security An asset pledged or a guarantee provided against a loan.   *(p. 286)*

Sensitivity analysis A method of dealing with risk which examines the key variables affecting a project to see how changes in each variable might influence the outcome.   *(pp. 89, 245)*

Shareholders' equity The residual amount belonging to the shareholders, which includes contributed capital and retained earnings.   *(p. 20)*

Shareholder value Putting the needs of shareholders at the heart of management decisions.   *(p. 490)*

Shareholder value analysis (SVA) A method of measuring and managing business value based on the long-term cash flows generated, and identifying those available to the shareholders.   *(p. 494)*

Shareholder wealth maximization The idea that the main purpose of a business is to maximize the wealth of its owners (shareholders). This idea underpins modern financial management.   *(p. 5)*

Share options Financial instruments that allow managers and employees to acquire shares in the business at some future date on favourable terms.   *(p. 13)*

Shortest-common-period-of-time approach A method of comparing the profitability of projects with unequal lives that establishes the shortest common period of time over which the projects can be compared.   *(p. 240)*

Simple interest A simple interest investment earns interest only on the initial investment.   *(p. 169)*

Simulation A method of dealing with risk that involves calculating probability distributions for a range of key variables in order to obtain a range of possible outcomes.   *(pp. 90, 251)*

Spin-off The transfer of part of the assets in an existing business to a new business. Shareholders in the existing business will be given shares, usually on a pro rata basis, in the new business.   *(p. 547)*

Standard deviation A measure of spread that is based on deviations from the mean or expected value and measures the variability of possible future outcomes associated with a project.   *(p. 261)*

Statement of retained earnings Measures the changes in retained earnings from one period to the next.   *(p. 25)*

Stock dividend A dividend to shareholders consisting of additional shares rather than cash; transfer of retained earnings to common share capital requiring the issue of new shares to shareholders in proportion to existing shareholdings.   *(pp. 342, 440)*

Stock exchange A primary and secondary market for business capital.   *(p. 319)*

Strip bonds Redeemable bonds that are issued at a zero rate of interest and at a large discount to their redeemable value. Also called *zero-coupon bonds*, as the interest coupons have been stripped away.   *(p. 290)*

Subjective probabilities Probabilities based on opinion rather than past data.   *(p. 265)*

Subordinated loan A loan that is ranked below other loan capital in order of interest payment and capital repayment.   *(p. 288)*

Synergy Gain obtained from combining two businesses: the whole is bigger than the sum of the parts; 2 + 2 = 5.   *(p. 530)*

Tender issue An issue of shares to investors that requires the investors to state the amount that they are prepared to pay for the shares.   *(p. 344)*

Term loan A loan, usually from a bank, that is tailored specifically to the needs of the borrower. The loan contract usually specifies the repayment date, interest rate, and so on.   *(p. 287)*

Times interest earned ratio A leverage ratio that divides the operating profit before interest and taxes by the interest expense for a period.   *(p. 130)*

Total shareholder return (TSR) The change in share value over a period plus any dividends paid during the period.   *(p. 515)*

Utility function A chart that portrays the level of satisfaction or pleasure obtained from receiving additional wealth at different levels of existing wealth.   *(p. i)*

Value drivers Key variables that determine business performance.   *(p. 496)*

Variable costs Costs that vary according to the volume of activity.   *(p. 65)*

Venture capital Long-term capital provided by certain institutions to small and medium-sized businesses to exploit relatively high-risk opportunities.   *(p. 347)*

Vertical analysis Analyzing account relationships within one year such as, for example, comparing various expenses to sales.   *(p. 111)*

Vertical merger A merger between a supplier of goods or services and its customer.   *(p. 529)*

Warrants and stock options Documents that give holders the right, but not the obligation, to buy common shares at a given price, and are often used as a sweetener to accompany a loan issue. *(p. 283)*

Weighted average cost of capital (WACC) A weighted average of the post-tax costs of the forms of long-term financing employed within a business where the market values of the particular forms of financing are used as weights.   *(p. 385)*

White knight A potential bidder for a business that is approached by the managers of that business to make a bid. The approach is made to defend the business against a hostile bid from another business.   *(p. 545)*

White squire A company (or individual investor) that is approached by the managers of another business to purchase a large block of shares in the business with the object of rescuing it from a hostile takeover.   *(p. 545)*

Working capital Current assets less current liabilities.   *(pp. 21, 449)*

Zero coupon bonds Bonds that carry a zero rate of interest.   *(p. 290)*

Index